Treating Adult and Juvenile Offenders With Special Needs

The LAW AND PUBLIC POLICY: PSYCHOLOGY AND THE SOCIAL SCIENCES series includes books in three domains:

Legal Studies—writings by legal scholars about issues of relevance to psychology and the other social sciences, or that employ social science information to advance the legal analysis;

Social Science Studies—writings by scientists from psychology and the other social sciences about issues of relevance to law and public policy; and

Forensic Studies—writings by psychologists and other mental health scientists and professionals about issues relevant to forensic mental health science and practice.

The series is guided by its editor, Bruce D. Sales, PhD, JD, University of Arizona; and coeditors, Stephen J. Ceci, PhD, Cornell University; Norman J. Finkel, PhD, Georgetown University; and Bruce J. Winick, JD, University of Miami.

***

Treating Adult and Juvenile Offenders With Special Needs

EDITED BY

José B. Ashford
Bruce D. Sales
William H. Reid

AMERICAN PSYCHOLOGICAL ASSOCIATION

WASHINGTON, DC

Published by
American Psychological Association
750 First Street, NE
Washington, DC 20002

Copies may be ordered from
APA Order Department
P.O. Box 92984
Washington, DC 20090-2984

In the UK and Europe, copies may be ordered from
American Psychological Association
3 Henrietta Street
Covent Garden, London
WC2E 8LU England

Typeset in Times Roman by EPS Group Inc., Easton, MD

Printer: United Book Press, Baltimore, MD
Cover Designer: Berg Design, Albany, NY
Editor/Project Manager: Debbie K. Hardin, Charlottesville, VA

The opinions and statements published are the responsibility of the authors, and such opinions and statements do not necessarily represent the policies of the APA.

Library of Congress Cataloging-in-Publication Data
Introduction to treating adult and juvenile offenders with special needs / [edited by] José B. Ashford, Bruce D. Sales, William H. Reid.
    p. cm.
    Includes bibliographical references.
    ISBN 1-55798-667-3 (cb : alk. paper)
    1. Criminals—Mental health.   2. Criminals—Mental health services.   3. Juvenile delinquents—Mental health.   4. Juvenile delinquents—Mental health services.
    I. Ashford, José B.   II. Sales, Bruce Dennis.   III. Reid, William H., 1945–

    RC451.4.P68 I67 2000
    616.89′0086′927—dc21

                                                            00-041635

British Library Cataloguing-in-Publication Data
A CIP record is available from the British Library.

Printed in the United States of America
First Edition

CONTENTS

PREFACE

It is not typical to have multidisciplinary collaboration in mental health services research and scholarship. We believe that this is a major omission in the correctional field. The relevant literature exists in criminology (including penology), program planning and administration, psychiatry, psychology, social work, and sociology, with correctional services typically involving psychiatrists, psychologists, and social workers. We individually recognized this fact and sought out each other to provide the editorial balance and perspective that should characterize future scholarship in this area. In addition, we drew our contributing authors from these diverse disciplines. We hope that this multidisciplinary effort, emphasizing biological, psychological, and social contributions to the treatment of special needs offenders, will promote scientific development of treatment and rehabilitative models for offenders with varying needs, and that these models will result in effective outcomes that are sufficiently comprehensive and empirically validated to ensure that state and federal governments view them as necessary components of all corrections systems.

Acknowledgments

We thank our colleague, Stanley Brodsky, PhD, and our APA development editor, Adrian Forman, for their insightful comments on, and advice for revision of, an earlier version of this book. We also thank our contributing authors for providing valuable information for our introductory chapter. They provided us with a review of the data on the prevalence rates for their topics. Marnie Rice, Grant Harris, and Vernon Quinsey deserve special mention because they also provided material about methodological problems in treatment outcome research. Although in some instances we used their textual descriptions verbatim, any errors in the introduction should be attributed to us and not to the contributing authors.

CONTRIBUTORS

Cindy Wheeler Anderson, Arizona State University, Tempe

B. Jaye Anno, Commission on Correctional Health Care, Santa Fe, NM

Elizabeth M. Arnold, University of North Carolina at Chapel Hill

José B. Ashford, Arizona State University, Tempe

Judith V. Becker, University of Arizona, Tucson

Thomas Berney, Northumberland Mental Health NHS, Morpeth, England

Robert Bodholdt, Bastrop, TX

Charles M. Borduin, University of Missouri, Columbia

Tamara L. Brown, University of Kentucky, Lexington

Kenneth Day, Tynemouth, England

Joel A. Dvoskin, Tucson, AZ

John F. Edens, Sam Houston State University, Huntsville, TX

Carl B. Gacono, Austin, TX

Heather M. Griller-Clark, Arizona Department of Juvenile Corrections, Phoenix

Thomas L. Hafemeister, Illinois Institute of Technology, Chicago

Susan R. Hall, Yale University

Craig Haney, University of California at Santa Cruz

Grant T. Harris, Mental Health Centre, Penetanguishene, Ontario, Canada

Lindsay M. Hayes, National Center on Institutions and Alternatives, Mansfield, MA

Scott W. Henggeler, Medical University of South Carolina, Columbia

André Ivanoff, Columbia University

Bradley R. Johnson, University of Arizona, Tucson

H. Richard Lamb, University of Southern California

Craig Winston LeCroy, Arizona State University, Tucson

Gordon MacNeil, University of Alabama, Tuscaloosa

C. Aaron McNeece, Institute for Health and Human Services Research, Tallahassee, FL

Ron J. Nieberding, Austin, TX

Randy K. Otto, University of South Florida, Tampa

Amy Owen, Austin, TX

Denise L. Preston, Correctional Service of Canada, Kingston, Ontario

Vernon L. Quinsey, Queen's University, Kingston, Ontario

William H. Reid, Horseshoe Bay, TX

Marnie E. Rice, Mental Health Centre, Penetanguishene, Ontario, Canada

Richard Rogers, University of North Texas, Denton

John Rubel, Integrated Mental Health Systems, Austin, TX

Robert B. Rutherford Jr., Arizona State University, Tempe

Randall T. Salekin, Florida International University, Miami

Bruce D. Sales, The University of Arizona, Tucson

Ralph C. Serin, Correctional Service of Canada, Kingston, Ontario

Donald Specter, Prison Law Office, San Quentin, CA

David W. Springer, University of Texas at Austin

Phillip Stevenson, Illinois Criminal Justice Information Authority, Chicago

Linda E. Weinberger, University of Southern California

Treating Adult and Juvenile Offenders With Special Needs

INTRODUCTION

José B. Ashford, Bruce D. Sales, and William H. Reid

Since the 1950s, there has been significant controversy in criminology regarding the utility of matching treatments to distinct offender typologies. On the one hand, exponents of general theories of crime have contended that the behavior of offenders is sufficiently homogeneous to be explained by a single or common set of causal factors (Cressey, 1969). A contemporary example of this viewpoint is Gottfredson and Hirschi's (1990) *A General Theory of Crime*. Their theory focuses on assessing the extent to which offenders can exercise self-restraint, with poor self-control considered the key factor associated with all forms of crime. The aim of treatment, then, is to modify the factors contributing to the development of propensities toward poor self-control.

On the other hand, many other criminologists (e.g., Clinard & Quinney, 1967; Gibbons, 1979) argue that offenders are too heterogeneous to be explained by a common set of causes. According to this view, offenders should be categorized into distinct classes or types for the purposes of identifying distinct etiologies. The specification of appropriate interventions for controlling crime cannot occur without understanding the differing causes of crime, which can involve biological, psychological, and social factors.

Although construction of offender typologies witnessed a marked decline during the 1970s (Paternoster & Brame, 1997), the career criminal framework (Blumstein, Cohen, Roth, & Visher, 1986) and developmental theories of crime (Loeber & LeBlanc, 1990; Moffit, 1993; Patterson & Yoerger, 1993) have reintroduced interest in taking into account offender types in understanding causes of crime. For example, Moffit (1993) and Patterson, DeBaryshe, and Ramsey (1989) have contended that early entrants into crime constitute a different type of offender from late starters. As a consequence, these authors have advanced the proposition that the onset of crime for early starters and late starters is explained by a different set of causal factors (Tremblay & Craig, 1995), which should logically lead to differing treatment strategies.

A more sophisticated version of the typological approach in criminology is being propelled by developments in offender classification (Andrews & Bonta, 1998; Clements, 1986; Hoge & Andrews, 1996). For example, the General Personality and Social Psychological Model of Criminal Conduct developed by Andrews and Bonta (1994, 1998) builds on the notion that treatments should be matched to information derived from the underlying concerns or foci of offender classification: offender risk, offender needs, and offender responsivity. The concept of offender risk is not new. Before the 1920s assessment of an offender's risk for criminality was based on purely clinical or subjective judgments. In 1928, Burgess published a manuscript identifying 21 factors that statistically differentiated parole successes from parole failures. This statistical approach to risk assessment has been termed "second-generation-assessments" (Bonta, 1996). The major problem with second-generation instruments for predicting risk is that they offer limited direction for the actual treatment of offenders (Andrews & Bonta, 1994; Krauss, Sales, Becker, & Figueredo, in press). Accurately predicting that someone will offend does not reveal *why* the person is going to reoffend, and without knowing the "why" clinicians cannot design treatments to effectively disrupt the causal pathway leading to criminality. To this end, Andrews and Bonta (1994) have identified a special category of needs known as criminogenic needs. These needs are defined as changeable (dynamic) factors that are empirically linked to criminal behavior. Finally, offender responsivity refers to partially selecting treatments based on the individual's learning style and abilities.

From a public safety standpoint, criminogenic needs should be considered primary in deciding how to treat any population of offenders. Thus the selection of the appropriate treatment should be based on meeting offender criminogenic needs, taking into account offender responsivity and thereby reducing the risk of the offender to society. For this reason, research on the identification of criminogenic needs has witnessed a marked increase in the past two decades.

Two of the most intriguing issues for mental health professionals arising from this literature is whether there is a relationship between types of mental disorder and criminality (e.g., Bonta, Law, & Hanson, 1998; Hodgins, 1993; Link, Cullen, & Andrews, 1992; Monahan & Steadman, 1994; Swanson, 1994; Swanson, Holzer, Ganju, & Jono, 1990), and if there is, whether the type of disorder or disability or other special causal (hereafter *special*) need should influence the selection of treatment to reduce or prevent risk of criminal involvement (Hodgins, 1993; Monahan & Steadman, 1994; Rice, Harris, & Quinsey, 1996).

Before the 1990s, a generation of criminologists assumed that crime and serious mental disorders were unrelated (Beck & Wencel, 1998). Studies of the arrest rates for persons with major mental disorders indicated that they were no higher than the rates for the general population of Americans from a comparable social class (Monahan & Steadman, 1984). However, more recent research indicates that persons with major mental disorders are at increased risk for criminal offending (Link, Cullen, & Andrews, 1992; Link & Stueve, 1994, 1995) and for violence (Ashford, 1989; Steury & Choinski, 1995; Swanson, 1994) when these persons are in an actively psychotic state (Bonta et al., 1998). These and other results have prompted increased research into the relationships between specific pathologies and risk of criminality (Beck & Wencel, 1998; Malmquist, 1996; Raine, 1993).

Empirical and scholarly concern with developing approaches to the clinical treatment of offenders with mental disorders and other special needs is far less prevalent in the literature. The correctional mental health field continues to adopt generic approaches to treating offenders, as if the needs of offenders were homogeneous. "Most offenders are assumed to be rational beings with sufficient capacity to respond to social sanctions or to survive the ordeal of trial and punishment" (Halleck, 1986, p. 2). In addition, in many jurisdictions psychological and social services are not recognized as required interventions for rehabilitating offenders with special needs because of narrow conceptions of offender treatment that focus strictly on severe symptom reduction through psychopharmacological intervention in hospital settings (Blackburn, 1993, 1996).

In the following sections of this introduction, we will provide an overview of issues relevant to examining the clinical science of treating offenders with special needs. We begin with a brief review of research on prevalence to aid readers in understanding the criminogenic needs that require mental health services in our justice system. We then describe in some detail the book's purpose and organization, and conclude with an overview of the methodological challenges confronting clinical scientists involved in evaluating the effectiveness of treatment for offenders with special needs and confronting practitioners when they try to use existing research.

Prevalence of Special Needs Within the Offender Population

"Although psychologists, psychiatrists, social workers, and other social service providers have long noted the need to identify and attend to offender needs, wide-scale application of needs assessment in criminal justice is only a recent phenomenon" (Bonta, 1996, p. 22). In fact, there is less research on the specific needs of offenders than there is on the effectiveness of parole and other correctional interventions (Clements, 1996; Duffee & Duffee, 1981; Palmer, 1996; Waller, 1974). In other words, substantial lip service is given to meeting offender needs, but actual knowledge of the prevalence of ordinary and special needs in offender populations has been subjected to minimal empirical scrutiny (Duffee & Duffee, 1981; Glaser, 1969; Palmer, 1996).

For the purposes of this book, special needs are defined as *any changeable factors associated with disorders of cognition, thought, mood, personality, development, or behavior that are linked to desired outcomes for offenders at any phase of the justice process.* The philosophical foundations underlying this definition are provided in chapter 1. A brief review of the evidence for these special needs follows.

Conduct Disorder, Antisocial, and Psychopathic Personalities

For at least two centuries, mental health professionals have assumed that they can identify individuals who habitually fail to conform their behavior to the rules of society (Halleck, 1986). In the evolution of these various diagnostic categories, some of the noteworthy examples include *manie sans délier*; defects of passion or affect (e.g., lacking feelings of shame or hesitation over the consequences of one's behavior); born delinquency; defective delinquency; moral insanity; insanity as a result of defects in natural affections; criminality by impulse, sociopathy, antisocial personality, conduct disorder, and psychopathy (Millon, Simonsen, & Birket-Smith, 1998). Each of these categories assumes that the person is either constitutionally, psychologically, or socially "damaged" (Blackburn, 1998).

Accurate estimates of the prevalence of these disorders are compromised by the debates surrounding the appropriate conceptualizations of these disorders as either deviations of constitution, personality, or socialization. Estimates also vary depending on the methods of research and populations sampled. Keeping these limitations in mind, let us consider the known prevalence rates.

Conduct disorder is a condition that pertains directly to behavior and traits observed in children and adolescents. For all males under 18, rates for conduct disorder range from 6% to 16%. For juvenile offenders prevalence rates have been estimated to be between 50% and 90%, making it the most common diagnosis among this population (Otto, Greenstein, Johnson, & Friedman, 1992). For example, Halikas, Meller, Morse, and Lyttle (1990) found that 81% of their sample of 114 juvenile offenders qualified for a diagnosis of conduct disorder, and 61% were diagnosed with conduct disorder–aggressive type. Similarly, Cairns, Peterson, and Neckerman (1988), in a sample of 520 children (primarily juvenile offenders) who were certified for the Willie M. Program (i.e., a program for violent and aggressive youth with emotional, mental, or neurological handicaps; Behar, 1985; *Willie M. v. Hunt*, 1979), found 66% of the females and 57% of the males met diagnostic criteria for conduct disorder. Hollander and Turner (1985), in a sample of 200 12- to 18-year-old incarcerated male youths admitted to correctional facilities for index offenses, found that 85% had a diagnosis of conduct disorder. It is important to note that 70% met criteria for undersocialized-conduct disorder, a label assigned to youths who, in addition to engaging in antisocial behavior over an extended period of time, have a history of poor relations with others (e.g., lack of sustained interpersonal relationships with peers, lack of responsible concern for others).

Subtyping of conduct disorder may help distinguish which juvenile offenders with conduct disorder are more likely to commit serious crimes and thereby influence intervention strategy. For example, Hollander and Turner (1985) found that a higher percentage of violent crimes (e.g., aggravated assault, rape, murder) are committed by youths classified as having undersocialized-conduct disorder. Although 40% of all youths in their sample were violent offenders, 50% of those with undersocialized-conduct disorder had committed violent crimes.

The prevalence rates for antisocial personality disorder (ASPD) vary from 3% to 30% in clinical settings and 2% to 3% in community samples in the United States, Canada, and New Zealand (Coid, 1998b). The prevalence of this disorder in correctional institutions appears much higher. For example, Hare (1993) contended that, on average, about 20% of prison populations consist of individuals diagnosed with psychopathy, in both male and female institutions. However, rates vary across studies. One comparison of lifetime rates of psychopathy per 100 inmates found a range from 61.7% in a prison in Quebec (Hodgins & Cote, 1990) to 86 percent in a special prison unit in the United Kingdom (Coid, 1996). Although rates of ASPD range from 28.9% to 50.1% in three correctional institutions in the United States (Hodgins & Cote, 1990), rates in jails[1] appear somewhat lower. For instance, Teplin (1996) found 13.8% per 100 inmates with a diagnosis of antisocial personality disorder in a sample of the Cook County Jail.

Given the prevalence of conduct disorder, antisocial, and psychopathic personality disorder, does the mental health need relate to a criminogenic need? Unfortunately, there is a lack of research on the associations between personality disorder and violence (Widiger & Trull, 1994). However, what epidemiological and clinical research exists suggests "that antisocial personality disorder and psychopathy increased the risk that an individual will engage in violent behavior" (Coid, 1998a, p. 57). Recent research also continues to support the conclusion that there is an association between antisocial personality disorder and crime. For instance, Coid (1998a) found an association between antisocial personality disorder and the index offenses of robbery, firearm violations, and theft in Britain. He also found an association between antisocial personality disorder and offenses involving "hyper-irritability, offenses carried out for financial gain, and offenses carried out in a gang or as a

---

[1] Jails are primarily used as detention facilities for persons awaiting trial or convicted of misdemeanor offenses. Prisons are typically used as detention facilities for persons convicted of felonies.

group activity" (Coid, 1998a, p. 79). In addition, Geberth and Turco (1997) found a correlation between ASPD and homicide in a study of serial sexual murders. Their sample consisted of 248 murders, of which 27% of the convicted offenders were diagnosed with an antisocial personality disorder.

Substance Abuse Disorders

In 1996, about 36% of convicted offenders under the jurisdiction of correctional agencies were estimated to have been drinking at the time of the offense for which they were convicted. "Among violent offenders, 41% of probationers, 41% of those in local jails, 38% of those in State prisons, and 20% of those in Federal prisons were estimated to have been drinking when they committed the crime" (Bureau of Justice Statistics, 2000). In the 1997 survey of inmates, 51% of the prisoners in state and federal correctional facilities reported use of alcohol or drugs while committing their offenses (Mumola, 1999).

The association between delinquency and substance abuse–dependence is important because delinquent youths who also abuse substances tend to have more psychiatric distress than delinquent youths without concomitant substance abuse problems. In fact, the co-occurrence of substance abuse and other psychiatric disorders in delinquent populations is well-established. For example, Neighbors, Kempton, and Forehand (1992) reported that 96% of the alcohol–marijuana abusers and 97% of the polysubstance abusers in their sample had at least one other psychiatric disorder, most often depression or conduct disorder. In other words, delinquent youths who had substance abuse problems were also more likely to be depressed and display conduct disorder problems than were delinquent youths who did not abuse substances. Similarly, Riggs, Baker, Mikulich, Young, and Crowley (1995), in a sample of 99 delinquent, substance-involved adolescent boys, found depression to be associated with substance use and suggested that delinquent youths who are depressed have more serious drug and alcohol problems than nondepressed counterparts. In general, substance-abusing delinquent youths usually meet criteria for at least one other psychiatric diagnosis (Neighbors et al., 1992).

Numerous studies have reported a link between juvenile delinquency and substance abuse (Halikas et al., 1990; Milin, Halikas, Meller, & Morse, 1991; Neighbors, Kempton, & Forehand, 1992). McManus, Alessi, Grapentine, and Brickman (1984) found that 63% of the 71 juvenile offenders in their sample met diagnostic criteria for substance abuse. Similarly, Neighbors et al. (1992) reported a strong association between substance abuse–dependence and antisocial behavior in their sample of 111 juvenile offenders. Indeed, the prevalence of substance abuse among juvenile offenders may be as high as 67% (Otto et al., 1992). Although substance abuse and delinquent behavior are correlated, no evidence demonstrates that one causes the other. Rather, the two behaviors often co-occur during adolescence (Donovan, Jessor, & Costa, 1988; Farrell, Danish, & Howard, 1992). The co-occurrence of substance abuse and other antisocial behavior is not surprising in light of findings from multivariate research (e.g., Elliott, Huizinga, & Ageton, 1985; Hawkins, Catalano, & Miller, 1992; Rhodes & Jason, 1990) indicating that the causes and correlates of adolescent substance abuse are quite similar to those reported for adolescent antisocial behavior in general (see reviews by Henggeler, 1989, 1993; Kazdin, 1995).

Developmental–Learning Disabilities Among the Offender Population

Accurate estimates of the rates of offenders with mental retardation in our prison systems are hard to come by because most systems do not routinely screen for mental retardation (Petersilia, 1997). Although estimates for the general population range from 2% to 3% (Gardner, Graeber, & Machkovitz, 1998), estimates of the U.S. prison population suggest that 4.2% have an IQ of below 70 and can be diagnosed as mentally retarded (Petersilia, 1997). Earlier research by MacEachron (1979) found prevalence rates for offenders ranged from 2.6% to 39.6%, depending on the definition of mental retardation. "Of those offenders who do have a mental retardation diagnosis, it is estimated that 88% of the total group is mildly impaired, with most of the remaining 12% demonstrating moderate retardation" (Gardner et al., 1998, p. 331). Although the estimate of 4.2% of offenders with low IQ is larger than the estimate for offenders infected with HIV (2.4% in 1995) (Petersilia, 1997), the population of mentally retarded offenders receives minimal attention from scholars and policy analysts compared with the attention given to HIV-positive offenders. Specific rates for offenders with learning disabilities in the justice system range from 2% to 10%, depending on the study (Cullen, 1993). For information on comorbidity in this group of offenders, see chapter 8.

Although there are serious gaps in the recent literature on the relationship between mental retardation and learning disability and crime, the association is visible. Therefore, it would be imprudent not to treat these offenders while waiting for clear causal data to emerge.

Violent Offenders

Serious violent youthful offenders have been a focal concern in youth-offender policy debates in recent years (Ashford, 1997). The results of the National Youth Survey (Elliott, 1994) showed that about 5 percent of all juveniles (aged 12 to 17) were classified at each of these ages as serious violent offenders (those who have engaged in three or more of the following offenses: aggravated assault, sexual assault, gang fights, and strong-arm robbery). Other research from New York and Colorado (Huizinga, Loeber, & Thornberry, 1994) indicates that although more than 50% of youth who were surveyed reported having committed at least one act of violence, those deemed to be chronic offenders accounted for the vast proportion of the violent crime in these studies. In New York, those designated as nonchronic violent offenders had an incidence of 3.9 offenses per person, whereas those designated as chronic violent offenders had an average of 33.6 violent offenses per person (Huizinga et al., 1994). For Colorado the rates were 4.5 for nonchronic and 51.7 per chronic violent offenders. Further, chronic violent offenders constituted 15% of the New York sample and 14% of the Colorado sample, yet they accounted for 75% and 82%, respectively, of the violence. It appears that the high incidence of violence by specific youths may be a more serious issue than trends regarding violent crime per se.

A review of a large adult correctional population database is instructive in determining the incidence of violence committed by adult offenders. The federal Canadian correctional jurisdiction, the Correctional Service of Canada (CSC), receives all adult offenders serving sentences of two years or more, regardless of offense type. Based solely on admitting offense, the population in 1995 for the CSC was made up of 78% (N = 10,983) violent offenders (offenses include robbery, murder, assault, sexual assault). In 1994 the CSC implemented a systematic, automated assessment strategy for all new admissions. The purpose of this initiative was to assist in the risk assessment of offenders, their treatment planning, and policy development. The database now contains more than 16,000 completed intake protocols for consecutive admissions. These data allow violence to be defined in terms of history, not just index offense. Restricting the definition to persistently violent offenders, that is, those with three or more victims in their criminal history, the prevalence drops from 78% to 35.4%. Further, considering variables from eight domains of treatment needs that have been identified in the literature as related to risk of violence (i.e., impulsivity, poor empathy, age of onset, lifestyle stability, weapon use, use of threats, escape risk), a persistently violent offender index was calculated (Motiuk, Nafekh, & Serin, 1998). A cutoff for the index of one standard deviation above the mean was used. Preliminary analyses with a sample of 764 offenders indicate this index accurately predicts violent recidivism (serious assaults, armed robbery, manslaughter, murder), with high scorers on the index (persistently violent) having recidivism rates of 50.5% versus 15.4% for the low scorers. In addition, relative to other offenders, persistently violent offenders show significantly greater needs in the areas of employment, family, associations, substance abuse, community functioning, personal–emotional skills, and criminal attitudes.

Sex Offenders

The idea that sex offenders, or many of them at least, suffer from a mental disorder and should receive treatment has been debated at length. In the United States, the diversion of sex offenders from the criminal justice system to the mental health system began with the enactment of the first "sex psychopath" statute in Michigan in 1937 (La Fond, 1992). Between then and the early 1970s, an increasing number of states passed such laws. Then, over a span of several years, many such laws were repealed, only to be reintroduced in the 1990s and ruled constitutional by the U.S. Supreme Court (*Kansas v. Hendricks*, 1997).

Data from the Bureau of Justice Statistics (2000) indicates that on any given day in 1994 there were approximately 234,000 offenders convicted of rape or sexual assault that were under the care and control of some correctional agency. In North America, sex offenders make up an increasing proportion of persons held in custody. In some states, there are more persons in prison convicted of sex offenses than of any other category of offense (Morris & Tonry, 1990). In Canada, a sex offense was the admission offense of 10.7% of the offenders admitted to its Correctional Service in 1990–1991, compared to 8.9% in 1986–1987 (Porporino & Motiuk, 1991). Among incarcerated sex offenders, the largest group (40%) were rapists (i.e., men who had sexually assaulted adult women). A smaller percentage were child molesters (i.e., men who had committed "hands-on" offenses against pre-pubertal or pubescent children). Of these, 21% were extrafamilial offenders and 6% were incest offenders. Most of the remainder (28%) had offended against both children and adults. Only a tiny fraction of incarcerated sex offenders have solely committed less serious sexual offenses such as exhibitionism, indecent exposure, voyeurism, or frottage, although these offenses account for a large percentage of officially recorded offenses, and offenders apprehended for these offenses form a sizable proportion of those in many outpatient treatment programs (Abel & Rouleau, 1990; Berlin et al., 1991; Maletzky, 1991a; Marshall, Eccles, & Barbaree, 1991; Miner & Dwyer, 1995). Because sex offenders are mentally abnormal, there is the assumption that treatment can reduce or eliminate recidivism with some of these individuals, and that effective treatments can eventually be developed for others.

Offenders at Risk for Suicide

There is only one national study of suicides by juveniles in custody (Flaherty, 1980), which unfortunately contained several flaws in the calculation of suicide rates. A recalculation of suicide rates in that study found that youth suicide in juvenile detention centers was estimated as more than four times greater than the general population (Memory, 1989). There remains a serious lack of accurate data on the total scope and rate of suicide among juveniles in custody.

Suicide is the leading cause of death in jails across the country (Bureau of Justice Statistics, 1995), although in some urban jail facilities, AIDS-related deaths outnumber suicide (Camp & Camp, 1993). The jail suicide rate is estimated to be nine times greater than the general population (Hayes, 1989). Suicide is the third leading cause of death in prisons, behind natural causes and AIDS (Bureau of Justice Statistics, 1997), and the rate of suicide in prisons is estimated to be 1.5 times greater than the general population (Hayes, 1995). Suicide is the ninth leading cause of death in the general population (Centers for Disease Control and Prevention, 1995).

The causes of suicides in jails are well-established, including both personal crises and the extreme and provoking environment of the jail (Bonner, 1992; Hayes, 1989). Many jail suicide victims are young, White, and were arrested for nonviolent, alcohol-related offenses. During the first 24 hours of incarceration, the period of highest risk for suicide, an individual may be suffering the effects of drugs or alcohol and shame or guilt over the alleged offense.

The causes of suicides in prisons are not yet established. The three jurisdictions with the largest prison populations—California, New York, and the Federal Bureau of Prisons—provide interesting data on inmate suicides within their respective systems. In California, 60% of suicide victims were diagnosed with serious mental disorders and 53% had histories of substance abuse. All but one of the victims were housed in a single cell, and 40% were confined in administrative segregation units (California Department of Corrections, 1991). In New York, White inmates represented 18% of the prison population but 42% of the suicides, and Black inmates represented 50% of the prison population but only 20% of suicides. Further, although inmates convicted of a violent felony represented 56% of the prison population, they accounted for 80% of the suicides. Regarding length of incarceration, 64% of all victims committed suicide within two years of entering the prison system, and 66% had mandatory minimum sentences of at least four years, with 23% serving life sentences (New York State Department of Correctional Services, 1994). Within the Federal Bureau of Prisons, 53% of victims of suicide had a documented mental health problem, and 63% of all suicides occurred in segregation, administrative detention, or a psychiatric seclusion unit (White & Schimmel, 1995). In addition, new legal problems, marital or relationship difficulties, and inmate-related conflicts were possible precipitating factors in federal prison suicides. The problem for correctional administrators is concern for the inmate and criticism from their superiors, not a crimogenic need related to the "crime" of suicide.

Offenders With Serious Mental Disorders

Pallone (1991) concluded that a minimum of 19% of the U.S. correctional population suffered from serious mental disorder. "The level of mental disorder observed in a variety of investigations among prisoners exceeds that in the general population in every category surveyed in the NIMH Epidemiological Catchment Area studies" (Pallone, 1991, p. 120). Hodgins (1993) also arrived at similar conclusions from her review of the U.S. (Collins & Schlenger, 1983; Daniel, Robins, Reid, & Wilfley, 1988; Hyde & Seiter, 1987; Neighbors et al., 1987) and Canadian studies (Hodgins & Cote, 1990; Motiuk & Porporino, 1991). As of June 30 1998, it is estimated by the U.S. Department of Justice's Bureau of Justice Statistics that 283,800 of the inmates in jails and prisons were mentally ill (Ditton, 1999).

Estimates for the prevalence of serious mental disorders in jails range from 8% to 16% (Ditton, 1999). For these estimates, persons were considered mentally disordered if they met one of the following criteria: "They reported a current mental or emotional condition, or they reported an overnight stay in a mental hospital or treatment program" (Ditton, 1999, p. 3). Estimates for the prevalence of mental disorders in prisons is not uniform. For schizophrenia, the range is from 1.5% to 4.4%, which is either the same as the general population or up to three times higher (Jemelka, Rahman, & Trupin, 1993). For depression, estimates ranges from 3.5% to 11.4%, which is more than three times the rate in the general population. And for mania, the range is from .7% to 3.9%, which is 2.3 to 13 times the rate in the general population (Jemelka et al., 1993). However, the absolute number of mentally disordered offenders is probably on the rise given the overall increases in prison populations (Blackburn, 1996) and the reported inadequacies of existing resources for treating offenders in these facilities (Bosoni, 1995).

Considerable evidence shows that juvenile offenders are at high risk for mental health problems. Indeed, in a study of incarcerated juvenile offenders, McManus et al. (1984) reported that all of the youths had at least two psychiatric diagnoses and that 38% also had a history of psychiatric hospitalization. Other reviewers (e.g., Melton & Pagliocca, 1992; Otto et al., 1992) have also reported high rates of mental health problems in samples of juvenile offenders. These findings suggest that juvenile offenders have mental health needs that do not differ appreciably from those of emotionally disturbed youth in other child service systems (e.g., mental health, child welfare; see Melton & Pagliocca, 1992).

So is serious mental disorder a legitimate criminogenic need? As Rice et al. (1996, p. 143) argued, "There is now sufficient data to support the view that when mental disorder and criminal behavior occur in the same individual, it is imperative for treatment providers to attend to both the mental disorder and the criminal behavior."

Purpose and Organization of this Volume

Given the magnitude of special needs observed in correctional populations, we undertook this project to help provide a foundation, or baseline, for practitioners concerned with the treatment of adult and juvenile offenders (clinical criminologists; clinical, counseling, and educational psychologists; psychiatrists; social workers; and other mental health and mental retardation professionals), program planners–administrators, and clinical scientists to start rethinking what we do and how we can improve our methods for intervening systematically with adult and juvenile offenders with special needs. As the chair of the American Correctional Association Task Force on Offenders With Special Needs wrote, "More and more of today's offenders have at least one of the following conditions: developmental disability, emotional disturbance, mental health disability, terminal illness, physical disability, and advanced age" (Briscoe, 1994, p. 1). These conditions require special programming from medical, psychological, and social service professionals.

This volume contains carefully crafted reviews of what works in treating recognized categories of adult and juvenile offenders with special mental and behavioral health needs,[2] including those with

- Conduct disorder and antisocial and psychopathic personalities;
- Axis I mental disorders;
- Substance abuse disorders;
- Violent syndromes;
- Sexual syndromes;
- Mental retardation;
- Educational disabilities;
- Suicide risk; and
- Persons acquitted because of insanity.

The book is divided into six parts. The first part reviews the evolution of law, rights, and standards governing the definition and treatment of offenders with special needs. This section provides an overview of societal responses to special statuses and of how the law and professional standards respond to the special needs of offenders. The second part then links current knowledge of specific mental health disorders commonly found in offender populations to empirically proven treatment technology. The three chapters in Part II critically review the science and art of treating specific diagnostic categories encountered by mental health professionals in working with offender populations. In Part III, the chapters review literature on the treatment and habilitation of developmental disabilities and other learning–cognitive impairments in offender populations. Part IV focuses on the treatment of high-risk offenders with needs requiring special programming from mental and behavioral health professionals. The authors in this section examine approaches to treating offenders at risk to themselves and the community because of clinically relevant conditions. In Part V the authors examine literature on the clinical management of cases in the pre- and the postrelease phases of the treatment and the rehabilitation pro-

---

[2]Three special needs are not covered in this volume: advanced age, physical disability, and physical health issues, including terminal illness.

cesses for offenders with special needs. Part VI consists of four chapters on administrative, fiscal, organizational, and other service system considerations in providing treatment in community and institutional settings.

Part I: History, Rights and Standards

In chapter 1, Ashford, Sales, and Reid review the history of Anglo-American society's attempts at establishing boundaries between ordinary and special offender needs. In this review, the authors illustrate how the terms *special*, *needs*, and *treatment* are without clear meanings or referents in the history of special offender legislation and policy. This chapter also considers the perennial division in correctional and forensic treatment between issues of offender–patient health and issues of community safety. Specifically, what offender, justice system, and societal needs should drive development of particular types of correctional mental health interventions and treatment-outcome research? Without clear articulation of the reasons and goals for our interventions, it is not surprising that we still know very little about what works well for various types of special status offenders.

Beginning this book with a historical perspective on the field provides a needed foundation for understanding (a) current interactions between mental health professionals and various categories of offender needs and (b) why specific chapters were selected for this book. Chapter 1 limits its historical coverage to the 18th, 19th, and 20th centuries, but the most modern legal history is presented in chapter 2 and in other chapters in the book. Readers are introduced to current special need categories in Parts II and III of the book, as well as in the chapters in Part VI that examine the affects of extra-therapeutic variables on clinical services and outcomes.

In chapter 2, Haney and Specter introduce readers to current uncertainties about the law's role in protecting offenders from deliberate indifference to their mental health needs, focusing on the legal status of two groups of special need offenders —mentally ill and developmentally disabled individuals. Their analysis of the law uncovers a reluctance on the part of some courts to consider legal protections for mental conditions as equivalent to providing protections for physical conditions because of doubts about treatment efficacy for offenders with special needs. They also point out the limits of minimum standards of care required by the U.S. Constitution and state constitutions and call for state legislators to pay increased attention to the needs of offenders. Finally, in their review of the law, the authors examine various applicable federal statutes that can help in securing treatment for this population.

There are drastic differences in the practice of mental health in correctional facilities and in the community at large. In correctional settings, mental health takes second place to goals of security and punishment (Prout & Ross, 1988). In chapter 3, Jaye Anno presents a case for promulgating standards for correctional institutions and correctional services in community settings. Anno not only provides a thorough accounting of current standards but also examines questions about how to ensure that their implementation is being properly monitored by public authorities. It is one thing to establish standards and another thing to translate abstract rights and standards into concrete action (Prout & Ross, 1988). This chapter was included to introduce practitioners to current guidelines for treating offenders in correctional and forensic settings.

Part II: Treating Disordered Offenders

Most writing on the treatment of mentally disordered offenders (Blackburn, 1993, 1996) has approached the subject as if mentally disordered offenders were a homogenous class or type of offender. In this section of the book, we challenge this long-standing tradition of providing nondifferential treatment services to mentally disordered offenders by relating treatment to specific disorders, forensic types (e.g., persons found not guilty by reason of insanity), and forensic outcomes. This approach is predicated on the assumption that there are differential relationships between specific pathologies and crime and between specific pathologies and forensic outcomes that cannot be ignored in designing treatment strategies (Beck & Wencel, 1998; Hodgins, 1993; Malmquist, 1996). These differential relationships are in part explained by the variability between and within disorders. Hodgins (1993) pointed out that if various mental disorders differ in their course, response to treatment, and etiology, then these mental disorders should also vary in terms of their relationships with criminality.

The contributors to this section on disordered offenders were asked to provide (a) an overview of the target population, (b) clarification of relevant treatment outcomes, (c) a critical review of the most appropriate treatment modalities, (d) a critical review of relevant treatment outcome research, and (e) future directions for research and practice for the special need category.

In chapter 4, Gacano and his colleagues review the treatment literature for conduct disorder, antisocial, and psychopathic personalities. Their chapter begins with a critical assessment of the social deviancy model that guides current classifications of psychopathy in the present DSM (American Psychiatric Association, 1994) system of classifying mental disorders. They contrast the clinical characteristics of this diagnostic category with other psychometric classifications of psychopathy and introduce a number of conceptual dilemmas affecting the identification of appropriate treatments and treatment outcomes. Because psychopathy is one of the personality disorders with long-standing links to criminality (Millon et al., 1998), this chapter provides readers with a clear and organized overview on treating a population of offenders that has fascinated clinical professionals for more than 200 years.

In chapter 5, McNeece and his colleagues examine the treatment of substance abuse disorders in offender populations. Substance abuse and alcohol abuse in particular "makes a far larger contribution to American violence than all other mental disorders combined" (Beck & Wencel, 1998, p. 4). For this reason, it is one of the more significant criminogenic needs of interest to public authorities. Their chapter begins with an overview of instruments for assessing substance abuse problems and provides a description of how this data should be linked to the treatment process. Their review covers a diverse array of methods of intervention used in inpatient and outpatient treatment contexts. They also explore the relevance of self-help and other informal support-service traditions to treating substance abusing offender populations.

Although forensic patients should have treatment that directly relates to specific forensic outcomes, the field has not previously clarified what clinical outcomes should differentiate treatment for persons found not guilty by reason of insanity from other populations of offenders with serious mental disorders.

In chapter 6, Salekin and Rogers clarify appropriate clinical outcomes for persons found not guilty by reason of insanity and discuss the differences and similarities between this population and other populations of persons with serious mental disorders.

Part III: Treating Developmentally and Learning Disabled Offenders

Part III moves from mental disorder to developmentally and learning disabled offenders. These individuals pose unique problems for the criminal and correctional systems and were traditionally the first group of special need offenders to be ignored by correctional administrators. As Haney and Specter point out in chapter 2 and Rutherford, Griller-Clark, and Anderson discuss in chapter 8, federal law is beginning to target this oversight.

In chapter 7, Day and Berney clarify the relationships between mental retardation and crime and the ways that this condition mediates the characteristics and patterns of various kinds of crime (e.g., arson, sex offenses). This chapter reviews the limited empirical work on the subject and confronts the effects of comorbidity on treating offenders with mental retardation in various settings. The interventions described in this chapter range from behavioral approaches to psychopharmacological interventions.

In chapter 8, Rutherford and his colleagues review policy and other issues relevant to treating learning disabilities in offender populations and identify best educational practices including presenting specific types of curriculum used in correctional settings. Although this area, like mental retardation, is rarely championed by reformers or program administrators, the authors discuss key pieces of legislation that should guide special education programming in correctional settings.

Part IV: Treating High-Risk Offenders

Harm reduction is an emerging model for dealing with many categories of offenders in our justice system. This model is replacing traditional cure models that had their roots in distinctly medical orientations to mental and behavioral health problems. In this section of the book, we include categories of offenders who pose serious safety issues to the community or themselves and require specialized programming from mental and behavioral health professionals.

We begin this section with chapter 9 by Serin and Preston on using clinical technology in treating violent offenders. The authors open the chapter with an operational definition of violence and a critical assessment of current misconceptions about violent offenders. They then connect specific types of interventions with specific targets for change in various types of violent offenders, thereby demonstrating how to implement an evidence-based approach to the treatment of violence in adult and juvenile populations.

In chapter 10, Becker and Johnson clarify the involvement of juvenile offenders in sexual crimes in the United States. Following this introduction to the problem, they consider the relationship between assessment and the treatment process. This discussion includes a detailed description of the kinds of information practitioners need to include in their assessments of juvenile offenders and of how to gather sensitive sexual history information in this process. Next, the authors offer an overview of what is required in formulating a comprehensive treatment plan, and review the current literature on various interventions used in treating juvenile offenders.

In chapter 11, Rice, Harris, and Quinsey confront the lack of quality, controlled research on the subject of treating adult sex offenders. Their chapter examines research on the effectiveness of various types of treatment, including nonbehavioral approaches, surgical and pharmacological treatments, and cognitive–behavioral interventions. The chapter concludes with a valuable critique of Hall's (1995) meta-analysis of sexual offender treatments. In particular, they show how Hall's (1995) review introduces some questionable conclusions about the relative effectiveness of hormonal treatments that warrants further scrutiny.

Ivanoff and Hayes, in chapter 12, look at a range of issues surrounding the prevention, management, and treatment of suicidal behavior in prisons, jails, and juvenile detention facilities. After identifying the characteristics that place inmates at risk for suicide, they discuss treatment and other intervention strategies (e.g., staffing, training, housing considerations, and monitoring individuals on suicide watch) to respond to this serious correctional problem.

Part V: Release Planning and Aftercare

Part V of the book deals with an area of the treatment process that is often overlooked in corrections: discharge planning and aftercare. The effectiveness of treatments can be significantly compromised or treatment rendered useless by inadequate attention to these two topics.

In chapter 13, Edens and Otto confront many of the issues mental health professionals face in making discharge decisions. They begin the chapter by reviewing the factors that practitioners should take into account in making release decisions about key categories of offenders with special needs. This discussion includes consideration of current data on known base rates, and links this to release decision-making processes. This linkage of risk assessment processes to actual release procedures bridges a number of important gaps in the current literature on risk assessment and discharge planning.

In chapter 14, Ashford, Sales, and LeCroy examine factors relevant to formulating strategies for maintaining changes achieved in the treatment process and in achieving specific rehabilitative objectives for preventing relapse. The authors begin with a description of similarities and differences in the historical development of aftercare in the fields of corrections and mental health. This introductory information is followed by an examination of the outcome literature on case management, intensive supervision, psychosocial rehabilitation, and relapse prevention. In reviewing these approaches, the authors identify unexamined areas (e.g., supported employment and housing for offenders with serious mental disorders) and issues affecting the integration of correctional and mental health technology in caring for offenders in the community, which, if unattended to, are associated with relapse and recidivism.

Part VI: Systems and Settings

The concluding section of the book first takes into account the role of context (i.e., policy, administration, and finances) on the treatment of offenders with special needs.

It then explores the role of setting on the treatment process, contrasting the effects of community with institutional approaches to treatment.

In chapter 15, LeCroy, Stevenson, and MacNeil examine key variables affecting how systems of care respond to juvenile offenders with special needs. The authors begin the chapter with an analysis of the distinct theoretical and philosophical approaches to, and concerns underlying, the present design of the juvenile justice system. They also consider such fundamental questions as who gets treatment in the system, who is responsible for the treatment, and who pays for the treatment. Their chapter demonstrates the important role played by social policy in determining the quality of care received by juvenile offenders.

In chapter 16, Hafemeister, Hall, and Dvoskin overview the administrative considerations in managing and treating offenders in prisons and jails. The authors identify common issues and strategies for running efficient units within correctional facilities that are responsible for the mental health care of all inmates, clarify the key decision points and factors to take into account when managing these units, and consider the continuum of care concerns, staffing, and other requirements for the proper implementation of treatment programming in correctional facilities.

In chapter 17, the focus shifts to the community treatment of juvenile offenders. Brown, Borduin, and Henggeler offer readers a comprehensive overview of an evidence-based approach to treating juvenile offenders in the community. Their chapter illustrates the importance of integrating services when treating this population of special need offenders, and reviews the literature and outcomes for various community-based interventions, including adventure-based programs, behavioral parent training, teaching family models, individualized wraparound care, family ties, intensive supervision programs, and multisystem therapy.

Finally, in chapter 18, Lamb and Weinberger share their extensive experience in treating offenders with serious mental illness in the community. This chapter uses actual cases to illustrate the issues and principles for treating the biological, psychological, and social needs of offenders with serious mental disorders in community based settings.

Evaluating the Treatment of Offenders With Special Needs

It is important to keep in mind that the treatment recommendations contained in this volume should of necessity be considered "best practices at this point in time" for two reasons. First, in most cases there is insufficient outcome research to prove the value of the treatments being used today. Second, the research that is available is often methodologically flawed.

Lack of an Adequate Control Group

Most of the early research on correctional (Andrews & Bonta, 1998) and psychotherapeutic (Acierno, Hersen & Ammerman, 1994) interventions rarely adopted any form of experimental controls. Yet to evaluate the effects of treatment, it is necessary to compare the outcomes of treated offenders with that of untreated offenders or offenders given a different treatment. Otherwise, there is no way of demonstrating that any changes in identified outcomes are a result of the treatment per se rather than of other factors. With proper selection of control groups, research on treatment can offer better assessments of the enduring nature of therapeutic effects or lack thereof. Frequently, the outcome of treated offenders is compared to that of untreated offenders reported elsewhere in the literature or of unselected offenders in the same jurisdiction. Comparisons with general offender populations assume a degree of homogeneity that does not take into account important differences between the composition of the groups. For example, comparing the treatment of rapists with a general sexual offender population ignores significant variability in recidivism outcomes among other types of sexual offenders such as child molesters (Furby, Weinrott, & Blackshaw, 1989; Quinsey, 1986). Comparisons with research on nonequivalent groups is often further limited by variations in lengths of follow-up that can bias conclusions about treatment efficacy.

Appropriate Outcome Measures

Determining appropriate outcome measures is one of the most challenging policy issues facing practitioners in correctional and forensic mental health. The foundational issues underlying many of these challenges are discussed by Ashford, Sales, and Reid in the first chapter of this book. As they note, mixing criminal justice and correctional and mental health goals creates significant complexity in the design for treatment outcome studies.

For example, to evaluate the effectiveness of various treatments, we need agreement on appropriate yardsticks for guiding evaluations of treatment effectiveness research. Do we want to measure general recidivism, violent recidivism, sexual recidivism, or specific modes of recidivism reflecting specific psychopathological or criminogenic processes? In addition, specified treatment outcomes for one population may not be appropriate for other populations of special need offenders (e.g., sex offenders versus learning disabled offenders versus severely mentally ill offenders). And composition of the release sample studied (e.g., combining offenders who are psychotic at the time of release with offenders not showing psychotic symptoms at the time of release) will affect rates of recidivism (Rice et al., 1996).

There is also the issue of whether we should use self-reports of recidivism, informal reports from parole or police officials, official arrest, or conviction data to prove recidivism. Unfortunately, although it is possible to obtain valid self-reports of delinquency under certain conditions (Elliott, 1994), the validity of self-reports has rarely been evaluated in treatment outcome studies. But relying on self-report also can be dangerous. Distortion, minimization, and denial are extremely common among substance abusing offenders, sexual offenders, and other categories of special need offenders (Abel, Mittelman, Becker, Rathner, & Rouleau, 1988; Pollack & Hahmall, 1991). If special steps are not taken to ensure and evaluate the validity of self reported crime, then the results of these measures are not worthy of much trust. Another measure sometimes used is informal reports by police or supervising authorities involved in monitoring the behavior of offenders in the community. The rationale behind using this measure is that police and parole authorities will often know whether an offender has reoffended even though they lack sufficient evidence to file charges. Although this measure has the advantage of including more offenses than would be included in official police records, these results are also of unknown validity. Moreover, police or parole officers can overestimate the offending behaviors among untreated versus treated offenders. Finally, arrest or conviction data are also frequently used as outcome measures. Both—especially conviction data—have the advantage of being "hard" in the sense that it is unlikely that an arrest or especially a conviction will be recorded if nothing happened. On the other hand, both measures are conservative in that there are many offenses that do not result in an arrest or conviction because of official (e.g., police) unawareness, lack of official investigation, police discretion, plea bargaining, or diversion. Indeed, the data can be seriously comprised when plea bargaining leads to convicting a lesser offense or inappropriate offense type for the actual criminal behavior engaged in.

Many issues that challenge measurement of recidivism as an outcome also apply to measuring relevant clinical outcomes such as symptom elimination, skill development, harm reduction, or quality of life considerations. Each of these outcomes cannot be properly captured using unidimensional assessments of the offender and their situation. In addition, no one model of treatment is capable of addressing each of these outcomes. Each of these outcomes has multidimensional components requiring the skills of professionals from many different disciplines. Indeed issues of outcome multidimensionality are fundamental to why this book includes contributions from professionals from criminal justice, psychology, psychiatry, social work, and sociology.

Capturing Treatment Refusers and Drop Outs

There is good evidence that if persons who refuse, or drop out of, treatment are ignored then treatment effectiveness can be grossly overestimated (e.g., Foa & Emmelkamp, 1983). This dilemma is exacerbated if persons who refuse treatment are excluded from the treatment group but persons who would have accepted treatment if it were offered to them are included in the comparison group. Similarly, counting as treated only those individuals who remained in the treatment group until treatment was completed and ignoring the outcome of persons who dropped out (or even worse, putting those who dropped out or refused into a control group), permits the possibility that estimates of treatment effectiveness will be extremely inflated. Attrition problems are best handled by analyses in which all individuals initially assigned to each group are examined (Chambless & Hollon, 1998; Flick, 1988).

Subtypes Among Special Need Offenders

Most published evaluations of treatments of special need offenders have examined the effects of treatment on groups of legally defined categories (e.g., insanity acquittees, mentally disordered sex offenders) without regard to specific diagnostic variations within the group. This lack of diagnostic specificity is particularly problematic because most conclusions reached about specific treatments "are meaningless when one is not fully aware of the nature of the disorder (or disorders) treated" (Acierno et al., 1994, p. 5).

Similarly, research on treatment of specific disorders recognizes that assessments for targeting areas of change must address multiple factors. For instance, treatments targeted to eliminate symptoms cannot ignore (a) the maintaining factors of symptoms, (b) etiological factors, and (c) offender characteristics and the history of their problems (Acierno et al., 1994). Each of these variables can differentially influence an offender's responsivity. "Indeed, several investigators have reported that patients who manifest similar symptoms often differ in etiology or maintaining factors—and will respond differently to treatment" (Acierno et al., 1994, p. 22). Unfortunately, many studies on treatment effectiveness do not include the kinds of data that allow for the identification of these clinical subtypes.

Meta-Analysis of Treatment Effectiveness

Some scholars are increasingly interested in the use of meta-analysis to reveal the effectiveness of correctional treatments. Meta-analysis is a procedure that treats each study as one observation, and that allows data from many studies to be combined to determine the average treatment effects. Since Martinson's (1974) narrative review and conclusion that correctional interventions have no appreciable effect on reducing criminal recidivism, there has been an increase in meta-analytical reviews of correctional effectiveness research (Andrews et al., 1990; Lab & Whitehead, 1988; Lipsey, 1992, 1995; Losel, 1995; Simon, 1998). Many of these reviews reported positive effects from correctional interventions. For example, Lipsey's (1992) seminal meta-analysis of nearly 400 control or comparison group studies of delinquents indicated that there is an overall 10% reduction in delinquency for juveniles in treatment groups compared to control groups.

Yet combining studies that suffer from the problems noted earlier in this section will produce results that are arguably meaningless. For example, what does a meta-analysis that combines all types of special need offenders reveal about the success of matching a specific treatment type with a specific special need? Although meta-analysis is efficient, unless there are sufficient primary outcome studies assessing each matched treatment to each special need and subtype, meta-analysis offers few opportunities for improving correctional and forensic mental health. The problem is that with an inadequate number of such studies to review, meta-analysis will be unable to reveal the effect of intervening or moderating variables (e.g., personal characteristics, situation and environmental characteristics, treatment approach and setting) on desired outcomes.

To exemplify part of this flaw in the existing meta-analytic studies, consider an evaluation of medical practices that lumped together outcomes, without regard to matching patients' needs with treatments and without evaluating each pairing independently. By combining all types of diseases (cancers, cardiovascular diseases, liver diseases, kidney diseases, etc.) with all types of treatments in one omnibus evaluation, we learn nothing about what treatments work with what medical problems. The dilemma is no different in criminal justice. If we intend to promote the development of a clinical science of correctional and forensic mental health, then these flaws in treatment outcome research must be confronted and eliminated. For this reason, needs and outcomes should not only be considered essential variables in selecting appropriate treatments but also key variables in guiding the evaluation of correctional clinical procedures and programs (Beutler & Clarkin, 1990; Frances, Clarkin, & Perry, 1984).

Final Reflection: It All Comes Down to Money

Perhaps the biggest reason that correctional treatment has not yet achieved prominence in the United States is because federal funds have not been provided systematically to develop treatment protocols for use in correctional services and to validate the effectiveness of these interventions for specific special needs. Engaging in such service development and treatment outcome research requires the same level of effort and skill that is applied in the development of any treatment protocol used outside of the correctional process. It cannot occur without the commitment of sufficient clinical resources and research dollars. Perhaps social, political, and philosophical problems hamper governmental officials from diverting resources from programs that are more popular with constituents to developing effective treatments for people who have preyed on society (see, e.g., Poythress & Miller, 1991). We hope that this book will stimulate clinicians, clinical scientists, correctional administrators, and policy makers, to commit to treating offenders with special needs and to develop the scientific knowledge to make that effort effective. In the long run, society will reap the most benefits from this effort.

References

Abel, G. G., Mittelman, M., Becker, J. V., Rathner, J., & Rouleau, J. L. (1988). Predicting child molesters' response to treatment. In R. Prentky & V. L. Quinsey (Eds.), *Human sexual aggression: Current perspectives* (pp. 223–243). New York: Annals of the New York Academy of Sciences.

Abel, G. G., & Rouleau, J. L. (1990). Male sex offenders. In M. E. Thase, B. A. Edelstein, & M. Hersen (Eds.), *Handbook of outpatient treatment of adults* (pp. 271–290). New York: Plenum Press.

Acierno, R., Hersen, M., & Ammerman, R. T. (1994). Overview of the issues in prescriptive treatments. In M. Hersen & R. T. Ammerman (Eds.), *Handbook of prescriptive treatments for adults* (pp. 3–27). New York: Plenum Press.

American Psychiatric Association. (1994). *Diagnostic and statistical manual of mental disorders* (4th ed.). Washington, DC: Author.

Andrews, D. A., & Bonta, J. (1994). *The psychology of criminal conduct*. Cincinnati, Ohio: Anderson.

Andrews, D. A., & Bonta, J. (1998). *The psychology of criminal conduct* (2nd ed). Cincinnati, OH: Anderson.

Andrews, D. A., Zinger, I., Hoge, R. D., Bonta, J., Gendreau, P., & Cullen, F. T. (1990). Does correctional treatment work? A clinically relevant and psychologically informed meta-analysis. *Criminology, 28*, 369–404.

Ashford, J. B. (1989). Offense comparisons between mentally disordered and non-mentally disordered inmates. *Canadian Journal of Criminology, 31*, 35–48.

Ashford, J. B. (1997). Aftercare: The neglected phase of the juvenile justice process. In C. A. Mcneece & A. R. Roberts (Eds.), *Policy & practice in the justice system* (pp. 29–47). Chicago: Nelson Hall.

Beck, J. C., & Wencel, H. (1998). Violent crime and Axis I psychopathology. In A. E. Skodol (Ed.), *Psychopathology and violent crime* (pp. 1–27). Washington, DC: American Psychiatric Press.

Behar, L. (1985). Changing patterns of state responsibility: A case study of North Carolina. *Journal of Clinical Child Psychology, 14*, 188–195.

Berlin, F. S., Hunt, W. P., Malin, H. M., Dyer, A., Lehne, G. K., & Dean, S. (1991). A five-year plus follow-up survey of criminal recidivism within a treated cohort of 406 pedo-philes, 111 exhibitionists and 109 sexual aggressives: Issues and outcome. *American Journal of Forensic Psychiatry, 12,* 5–27.

Beutler, L. E., & Clarkin, J. F. (1990). *Systematic treatment selection: Toward targeted ther-apeutic interventions.* New York: Brunner/Mazel.

Blackburn, R. (1993). *The psychology of criminal conduct: Theory, research and practice.* Chichester, England: John Wiley & Sons.

Blackburn, R. (1996). Mentally disordered offenders. In C. Hollin (Ed.), *Working with of-fenders: Psychological practice in offender rehabilitation* (pp. 119–149). Chichester, England: John Wiley & Sons.

Blackburn, R. (1998). Psychopathy and the contribution of personality to violence. In T. Millon, E. Simonsen, M. Birtket-Smith, & R. D. Davis (Eds.), *Psychopathy: Antisocial, criminal, and violent behavior* (pp. 50–68). New York: Guilford Press.

Blumstein, A., Cohen, J., Roth, J. A., & Visher, C. A. (Eds.). (1986). *Criminal Careers and "Career criminals."* (Vol. 1). Washington, DC: National Academy Press.

Bonner, R. L. (1992). Isolation, seclusion, and psychosocial vulnerability as risk factors for suicides behind bars. In R. W. Maris, A. L. Berman, J. T. Maltsberger, & R. I. Yufit (Eds.), *Assessment and prediction of suicide* (pp. 398–419). New York: Guilford Press.

Bonta, J. (1996). Risk-needs assessment and treatment. In A. T. Harland (Ed.), *Choosing correctional options that work: Defining demand and evaluating the supply* (pp. 18–32). Thousand Oaks, CA: Sage.

Bonta, J., Law, M., & Hanson, R. K. (1998). The prediction of criminal and violent recidivism among mentally disordered offenders: A meta-analysis. *Psychological Bulletin, 123,* 123–142.

Bosoni, A. J. (1995). *Post-release assistance programs for prisoners: A national directory* 2nd ed. Jefferson, MO: McFarland.

Briscoe, J. (1994). A centralized approach to managing special needs offenders. *Forum of Correctional Service of Canada, 6,* 1–5. http://www.csc.scc.gc.ca/text/publct/forum/e062/h.shtml.

Bureau of Justice Statistics. (1995). *Jail and jail inmates 1993–1994.* Washington, DC: U.S. Department of Justice.

Bureau of Justice Statistics. (1997). *HIV in prisons and jails, 1995* (August): NCJ-164260. http://www.ojp.usdoj.gov/bjs/pubalp.htm#hiv.

Bureau of Justice Statistics. (2000). *Criminal offenders statistics: Summary findings* (May). http://www.ojp.usdo.gov/bjs.

Burgess, E. (1928). Factors determining success or failure on parole. In A. Bruce, A. Harno, E. Burgess, & J. Landesco (Eds.), *The working of the indeterminate-sentence law and the parole system in Illinois.* Springfield, IL: State Board of Parole.

Cairns, R. B., Peterson, G., & Neckerman, H. J. (1988). Suicidal behavior in aggressive adolescents. *Journal of Clinical Child Psychology, 17,* 289–309.

California Department of Corrections. (1991). *Suicide prevention in the California Department of Corrections: Annual report—1990.* Sacramento, CA: Author.

Camp, G. M., & Camp, C. G. (1993). *The corrections yearbook.* South Salem, NY: Criminal Justice Institute.

Centers for Disease Control and Prevention. (1995). *Suicide in the United States: 1980–1992.* Atlanta, GA: U.S. Department of Health and Human Services.

Chambless, D. L., & Hollon, S. D. (1998). Defining empirically supported therapies. *Journal of Consulting and Clinical Psychology, 66,* 7–18.

Clements, C. B. (1986, August). *Offender need assessment: Trends and barriers.* Paper pre-sented for the 116th Congress of Corrections, Las Vegas, NV.

Clements, C. B. (1996). Offender classification: Two decades of progress. *Criminal Justice and Behavior. 23,* 121–143.

Clinard, M. B., & Quinney, R. (1967). *Criminal behavior systems: A typology*. New York: Holt, Rinehart & Winston.

Coid, J. W. (1996). *Psychopathology in psychopaths: A study of diagnostic comorbidity and aetiology*. Unpublished doctoral dissertation, University of London.

Coid, J. W. (1998a). Axis II disorders and motivation for serious criminal behavior. In A. E. Skodol (Ed.), *Psychopathology and violent crime* (pp. 53–97). Washington, DC: American Psychiatric Press.

Coid, J. W. (1998b). The management of dangerous psychopaths in prison. In T. Millon, E. Simonsen, M. Birtket-Smith, & R. D. Davis (Eds.), *Psychopathy: Antisocial, criminal, and violent behavior* (pp. 431–457). New York: Guilford Press.

Collins, J. J., & Schlenger, W. E. (1983, November). *The prevalence of psychiatric disorder among admissions to prison*. Paper presented at the annual meeting of the American Society of Criminology, Denver, CO.

Cressey, D. R. (1969). Role theory, differential association and compulsive crimes. In D. R. Cressey & D. Ward (Eds.), *Delinquency, crime, and social process* (pp. 1114–1128). New York: Harper & Row.

Cullen, C. (1993). The treatment of people with learning disabilities who offend. In K. Howells & C. R. Hollin (Eds.), *Clinical approaches to the mentally disordered offender* (pp. 145–163). Chichester, England: John Wiley & Sons.

Daniel, A. E., Robins, A. J., Reid, J. C., & Wilfley, D. E. (1988). Lifetime and six-month prevalence of psychiatric disorders among sentenced female offenders. *Bulletin of the American Academy of Psychiatry and the Law, 16*, 333–342.

Ditton, P. M. (1999). Mental health and treatment of inmates and probationers. Washington, DC: U.S. Department of Justice Bureau of Justice Statistics. (NCJ 174463).

Donovan, J. E., Jessor, R., & Costa, F. M. (1988). Syndrome of problem behavior in adolescence: A replication. *Journal of Consulting and Clinical Psychology, 56*, 762–765.

Duffee, D. E., & Clark, D. (1985). The frequency and classification of the needs of offenders in community settings. *Journal of Criminal Justice, 13*, 243–253.

Duffee, D. E., & Duffee, B. W. (1981). Studying the needs of offenders in prerelease centers. *Journal of Research in Crime and Delinquency, 18*, 251–253.

Elliott, D. S. (1994). Serious violent offenders: Onset, developmental course, and termination—The American Society of Criminology 1993 Presidential Address. *Criminology, 32*, 1–21.

Elliott, D. S., Huizinga, D., & Ageton, S. S. (1985). *Explaining delinquency and drug use*. Beverly Hills, CA: Sage.

Farrell, A. D., Danish, S. J., & Howard, C. W. (1992). Relationship between drug use and other problem behaviors in urban adolescents. *Journal of Consulting and Clinical Psychology, 60*, 705–712.

Flaherty, M. G. (1980). *An assessment of the national incidence of juvenile suicide in adult jails, lockups and juvenile detention centers*. Urbana: University of Illinois.

Flick, S. N. (1988). Managing attrition in clinical research. *Clinical Psychology Review, 8*, 499–515.

Foa, E. B., & Emmelkamp, P. M. G. (1983). *Failures in behavior therapy*. New York: Wiley.

Frances, A., Clarkin, J., & Perry, S. (1984). *Differential therapeutics in psychiatry: The art and science of treatment selection*. New York: Bruner/Mazel.

Furby, L., Weinrott, M. R., & Blackshaw, L. (1989). Sex offender recidivism: A review. *Psychological Bulletin, 105*, 3–30.

Gardner, W. I., Graeber, J. L., & Machkovitz, S. J. (1998). Treatment of offenders with mental retardation. In R. M. Wettstein (Ed.), *Treatment of offenders with mental disorders* (pp. 329–364). New York: Guilford Press.

Geberth, V. J., & Turco, R. N. (1997). Antisocial personality disorder, sexual sadism, malignant narcissism, and serial murder. *Journal of Forensic Science, 42*, 49–60.

24 ASHFORD, SALES, AND REID

Gibbons, D. C. (1979). *The criminological enterprise.* Englewood Cliffs, NJ: Prentice Hall.

Glaser, D. (1969). *The effectiveness of a prison and parole system.* Indianapolis, IN: Bobbs-Merrill.

Gottfredson, M. R., & Hirschi, T. (1990). *A general theory of crime.* Stanford, CA: Stanford University Press.

Halikas, J. A., Meller, J., Morse, C., & Lyttle, M. D. (1990). Predicting substance abuse in juvenile offenders: Attention deficit disorder vs. aggressivity. *Child Psychiatry and Human Development, 21,* 49–55.

Hall, G. C. N. (1995). Sexual offender recidivism revisited: A meta-analysis of recent treatment studies. *Journal of Consulting and Clinical Psychology, 63,* 802–809.

Halleck, S. L. (1986). *The mentally disordered offender.* Rockville, MD: U.S. Department of Health and Human Services.

Hare, R. D. (1993). *Without conscience: The disturbing world of the psychopaths among us.* New York: Guilford Press.

Hawkins, J. D., Catalano, R. F., & Miller, J. Y. (1992). Risk and protective factors for alcohol and other drug problems in adolescence and early adulthood: Implications for substance abuse prevention. *Psychological Bulletin, 112,* 64–105.

Hayes, L. M. (1989). National study of jail suicides: Seven years later. *Psychiatric Quarterly, 60*(1), 7–29.

Hayes, L. M. (1995). Prison suicide: An overview and a guide to prevention. *The Prison Journal, 75*(4), 431–456.

Henggeler, S. W. (1989). *Delinquency in adolescence.* Newbury Park, CA: Sage.

Henggeler, S. W. (1993). Multisystemic treatment of serious juvenile offenders: Implications for treatment of substance-abusing youths. In L. S. Onken, J. D. Blaine, & J. J. Boren (Eds.), *Behavioral treatments for drug abuse and dependence. NIDA Research Monograph 137* (pp. 181–199). Rockville, MD: U.S. Department of Health and Human Services.

Hodgins, S. (1993). The criminality of mentally disordered persons. In S. Hodgins (Ed.), *Mental disorder and crime* (pp. 3–21). Newbury Park, CA: Sage.

Hodgins, S., & Cote, G. (1990). The prevalence of mental disorder among penitentiary inmates. *Canada's Mental Health, 38,* 1–5.

Hoge, R. D., & Andrews, D. A. (1996). *Assessing the youthful offender: Issues and techniques.* New York: Plenum Press.

Hollander, H. E., & Turner, F. D. (1985). Characteristics of incarcerated delinquents: Relationship between development disorders, environmental and family factors, and patterns of offense and recidivism. *Journal of the American Academy of Child and Adolescent Psychiatry, 24,* 221–226.

Huizinga, D., Loeber, R. & Thornberry, T. P. (1994). *Urban delinquency and substance abuse.* Washington, DC: Office of Juvenile Justice and Delinquency Prevention, U.S. Department of Justice.

Hyde, P. S., & Seiter, R. P. (1987). *The prevalence of mental illness among inmates in the Ohio prison system.* Columbus: Ohio Department of Mental Health and Ohio Department of Rehabilitation and Correction Interdepartmental Planning and Oversight Committee for Psychiatric Services to Corrections.

Jemelka, R. P., Rahman, S., & Trupin, E. W. (1993). Prison mental health: An overview. In H. J. Steadman & J. J. Cocozza (Eds.), *Mental illness in prisons.* Seattle, WA: National Coalition for the Mentally Ill in the Criminal Justice System.

Kansas v. Hendricks. (1997). 521 U.S. 346.

Kazdin, A. E. (1995). *Conduct disorders in childhood and adolescence.* (2nd ed.). Thousand Oaks, CA: Sage.

Krauss, D. A., Sales, B. D., Becker, J. V., & Figueredo, A. J. (in press). Beyond prediction to explanation in risk assessment research: A comparison of two explanatory theories of criminality & recidivism. *International Journal of Law and Psychiatry.*

Lab, S., & Whitehead, J. (1988). An analysis of juvenile correctional treatment. *Crime & Delinquency, 34*, 60–85.

La Fond, J. Q. (1992). Washington's sexually violent predator law: A deliberate misuse of the therapeutic state for social control. *University of Puget Sound Law Review, 15.* 655–703.

Link, B. G., Cullen, F., & Andrews, H. (1992). Violent and illegal behavior of current and former mental patients compared to community controls. *American Sociological Review, 57*, 272–292.

Link, B. G., & Stueve, A. (1994). Psychotic symptoms and the violent/illegal behavior of mental patients comparted to community controls. In J. Monahan & H. J. Steadman (Eds.), *Violence and mental disorder: developments in risk assessment* (pp. 137–159). Chicago: University of Chicago Press.

Link, B. G., & Stueve, A. (1995). Evidence bearing on mental illness as a possible cause of violent behavior. *Epidemiological Review, 17*, 172–181.

Lipsey, M. W. (1992). Juvenile delinquency treatment: A meta-analytic inquiry into the variability of effects. In T. D. Cook, H. Cooper, D. S. Cordray, H. Hartmann, L. V. Hedges, R. J. Light, T. A. Lousis, & F. Mosteller (Eds.), *Meta-analysis for explanation: A casebook* (pp. 83–127). New York: Russell Sage.

Lipsey, M. W. (1995). What do we learn from 400 research studies on the effectiveness of treatment with juvenile delinquents. In J. McQuire (Ed.), *What works: Reducing reoffending* (pp. 63–78). Chichester, England: John Wiley & Sons.

Loeber, R., & LeBlanc, M. (1990). Toward a developmental criminology. In M. Tonry & N. Morris (Eds.), *Crime and Justice: An Annual Review of Research* (Vol. 12). Chicago: University of Chicago Press.

Losel, F. (1995). The efficacy of correctional treatment: A review and synthesis of meta-evaluations. In J. McQuire (Ed.), *What works: Reducing reoffending* (pp. 79–111). Chichester, England: John Wiley & Sons.

MacEachron, A. E. (1979). Mentally retarded offenders: Prevalence and characteristics. *American Journal of Mental Deficiency, 84*, 165–176.

Maletzky, B. M. (1991a). *Treating the sexual offender.* Newbury Park, CA: Sage.

Malmquist, C. P. (1996). *Homicide: A psychiatric perspective.* Washington, DC: American Psychiatric Press.

Marshall, W. L., Eccles, A., & Barbaree, H. E. (1991). The treatment of exhibitionists: A focus on sexual deviance versus cognitive and relationship features. *Behaviour Research and Therapy, 29*, 129–135.

Martinson, R. (1974). What works? Questions and answers about prison reform. *Public Interest, 35*, 22–54.

McManus, M., Alessi, N. E., Grapentine, W. L., & Brickman, A. (1984). Psychiatric disturbance in serious delinquents. *Journal of the American Academy of Child Psychiatry, 23*, 602–615.

Melton, G. B., & Pagliocca, P. M. (1992). Treatment in the juvenile justice system: Directions for policy and practice. In J. J. Cocozza (Ed.), *Responding to the mental health needs of youth in the juvenile justice system* (pp. 107–139). Seattle, WA: National Coalition for the Mentally Ill in the Criminal Justice System.

Memory, J. M. (1989). Juvenile suicides in secure detention facilities: Correction of published rates. *Death Studies, 13*, 455–463.

Milin, R., Halikas, J. A., Meller, J. E., & Morse, C. (1991). Psychopathology among substance abusing juvenile offenders. *Journal of the American Academy of Child and Adolescent Psychiatry, 30*, 569–574.

Millon, T., Simonsen, E., & Birtket-Smith, M. (1998). Historical conceptions of psychopathy in the United States and Europe. In T. Millon, E. Simonsen, M. Birtket-Smith, & R. D. Davis (Eds.), *Psychopathy: Antisocial, criminal, and violent behavior* (pp. 3–31). New York: Guilford Press.

Miner, M. H., & Dwyer, S. M. (1995). Analysis of dropouts from outpatient sex offender treatment. *Journal of Psychology and Human Sexuality, 7,* 77–93.

Moffit, T. E. (1993). Adolescence-limited and life course persistent antisocial behavior: A developmental taxonomy. *Psychological Review, 100,* 674–701.

Monahan, J., & Steadman, H. J. (1984, September). Crime and mental disorder. Washington, DC: National Institute of Justice.

Monahan, J., & Steadman, H. J. (1994). Toward a rejuvenation of risk assessment research. In J. Monahan & H. J. Steadman (Eds.), *Violence and mental disorder: Developments in risk assessment* (pp. 1–17). Chicago: University of Chicago Press.

Morris, N., & Tonry, M. (1990). *Between prison and probation.* New York: Oxford University Press.

Motiuk, L. L., Nafekh, M., & Serin, R. C. (1998). *Systematic assessment of treatment needs of persistently violent offenders.* Unpublished manuscript.

Motiuk, L. L., & Porporino, F. J. (1991). *The prevalence, nature and severity of mental health problems among federal male inmates in Canadian penitentiaries: Report No. 24.* Ottawa: Research and Statistical Branch, Correctional Service of Canada.

Mumola, C. J. (1999). Substance abuse and treatment, state and federal prisoner, 1997. *Bureau of Justice Statistics: Special Report.* Washington, DC: U.S. Department of Justice.

Neighbors, B., Kempton, T., & Forehand, R. (1992). Co-occurrence of substance abuse with conduct, anxiety, and depression disorders in juvenile delinquents. *Addictive Behaviors, 17,* 379–386.

Neighbors, H. W., Williams, D. H., Gunnings, T. S., Lipscomb, W. D., Browman, C., & Lepkowski, J. (1987). *The prevalence of mental disorder in Michigan prisons.* Final report submitted to the Michigan Department of Corrections.

New York State Department of Correctional Services. (1994). *Characteristics of suicide victims in NYSDOCS between 1986–1994.* Albany, NY: Author.

Otto, R. K., Greenstein, J. J., Johnson, M. K., & Friedman, R. M. (1992). Prevalence of mental disorders among youth in the juvenile justice system. In J. J. Cocozza (Ed.), *Responding to the mental health needs of youth in the juvenile justice system* (pp. 7–48). Seattle, WA: National Coalition for the Mentally Ill in the Criminal Justice System.

Pallone, N. J. (1991). *Mental disorder among prisoners: Toward an epidemiological inventory.* New Brunswick, NJ: Transaction.

Palmer, T. (1996). Programmatic and nonprogrammatic aspects of successful intervention. In A. T. Harland (Ed.), *Choosing correctional options that work: Defining the demand and evaluating the supply* (pp. 131–182). Thousand Oaks, CA: Sage.

Paternoster, R., & Brame, R. (1997). Multiple routes to delinquency? A test of developmental and general theories of crime. *Criminology, 35,* 49–80.

Patterson, G. R., DeBaryshe, B. D., & Ramsey, E. (1989). A developmental perspective on antisocial behavior. *American Psychologist, 44,* 329–335.

Patterson, G. R., & Yoerger, K. (1993). Orderly change in a stable world: The antisocial trait as a chimera. *Journal of Consulting and Clinical Psychology. 61,* 911–919.

Petersilia, J. (1997). Justice for all? Offenders with mental retardation and the California corrections system. *The Prison Journal, 77,* 358–380.

Porporino, F. J., & Motiuk, L. L. (1991). *Preliminary results of national sex offender census: Report No. 29.* Ottawa: Correctional Service of Canada.

Poythress, N. G., & Miller, R. D. (1991). The treatment of forensic patients: Major issues. In S. A. Shah & B. D. Sales (Eds.), *Law and mental health: Major developments and research needs.* Washington, DC: U.S. Government Printing Office (National Institute of Mental Health Monograph).

Prout, C., & Ross, R. N. (1988). *Care and punishment: The dilemmas of prison medicine* Pittsburgh, PA: University of Pittsburgh Press.

Quinsey, V. L. (1986). Men who have sex with children. In D. Weisstub (Ed.), *Law and Mental Health: International Perspectives* (Vol. 2, pp. 140–172). New York: Pergamon Press.

Raine, A. (1993). *The psychopathology of crime: Criminal behavior as a clinical disorder.* San Diego, CA: Academic Press.

Rhodes, J. E., & Jason, L. A. (1990). A social stress model of substance abuse. *Journal of Consulting and Clinical Psychology, 58,* 395–401.

Rice, M. E., Harris, G. T., & Quinsey, V. L. (1996). Treatment for forensic patients. In B. D. Sales & S. A. Shah (Eds.), *Mental health and law: Research, policy and services* (pp. 141–189). Durham, NC: Carolina Academic Press.

Riggs, P. D., Baker, S., Mikulich, S. K., Young, S. E., & Crowley, T. J. (1995). Depression in substance dependent delinquents. *Journal of the American Academy of Child and Adolescent Psychiatry, 34,* 764–771.

Simon, L. M. J. (1998). Does criminal offender treatment work? *Applied & Preventive Psychology, 7,* 137–159.

Steury, E. H., & Choinski, M. (1995). "Normal" crimes and mental disorder: A two group comparison of deadly and dangerous felonies. *International Journal of Law and Psychiatry, 18,* 183–207.

Swanson, J. W. (1994). Mental disorder, substance abuse, and community violence: An epidemiological approach. In J. Monahan & H. J. Steadman (Eds.), *Violence and mental disorder: developments in risk assessment* (pp. 101–136). Chicago: University of Chicago Press.

Swanson, J. W., Holzer, C. E., Ganju, V. K., & Jono, R. T. (1990). Violence and psychiatric disorder in the community: Evidence from the epidemiological catchment area surveys. *Hospital and Community Psychiatry, 41,* 761–770.

Teplin, L. A. (1996). Prevalence of psychiatric disorders among incarcerated women. I: pretrial detainees. *Archives of General Psychiatry, 43,* 505–511.

Tremblay, R. E., & Craig, W. M. (1995). Developmental crime prevention. In M. Tonry & D. P. Farrington (Eds.), *Building a safer society: Strategic approaches to crime prevention,* 151–236. Chicago: University of Chicago Press.

Waller, I. (1974). *Men released from prison.* Toronto: University of Toronto Press.

White, T. W., & Schimmel, D. J. (1995). Suicide prevention in federal prisons: A successful five-step program. In L. M. Hayes (Ed.), *Prison Suicide: An Overview and Guide to Prevention.* Washington, DC: National Institute of Corrections, U.S. Department of Justice.

Widiger, T. A., & Trull, T. J. (1994). Personality disorders and violence. In J. Monahan & H. J. Steadman (Eds.), *Violence and mental disorder: developments in risk assessment* (pp. 203–226). Chicago: University of Chicago Press.

Willie M. v. Hunt. (1979). 657 F.2d 55.

Part I

History, Rights, and Standards

Chapter 1
POLITICAL, LEGAL, AND PROFESSIONAL CHALLENGES TO TREATING OFFENDERS WITH SPECIAL NEEDS

José B. Ashford, Bruce D. Sales, and William H. Reid

Mental health professionals (MHPs) have experienced a paradoxical relationship with the criminal law in at least two ways. First, MHPs face the conundrum of working within criminal justice and correctional systems in which law clearly favors the needs of society and the legal system that employs them over the needs of offenders. Because MHPs are trained to put the interests of their clients first, responding to the needs and interests of the former entities, rather than the interests of offenders–patients, places MHPs in an unusual situation. Second, MHPs have been seen by some as holding the key to crime control and prevention (Halleck & White, 1977; Menninger, 1968; Raine, 1993). Yet the therapeutic ideal is viewed by others (American Friends Services Committee, 1971; La Fond, 1992; Wilson, 1997) as posing a fundamental threat to moral order. According to this latter view, prison should be a place of punishment for people who run afoul of the law (Logan & Gaes, 1993).

The paradoxical relationship of MHPs to the criminal law was made salient following the antipsychiatry movements[1] of the early 1960s (Conrad & Schneider, 1980; Mower, 1960; Sedgwick; 1982; Szasz, 1960; Zola, 1981) and the early research literature on the ineffectiveness of correctional treatments (Martinson, 1974; Sechrest, White, & Brown, 1979; Whitehead & Lab, 1989). Assuming the accuracy of the findings, were MHPs to abandon their traditional role and avoid work in the correctional system, or should they stay and use their skills for order maintenance within jail and prison settings? Despite calls for ending rehabilitative efforts, the public's confidence in rehabilitation never completely eroded (Applegate, Cullen, & Fisher, 1997; Cullen, Cullen, & Woznizk, 1988; Van Voorhis, 1994).

Even today, the relationship between MHPs and the correctional process remains unsettled. There is a movement that supports policies designed to humiliate, punish, and control offenders (Clear, 1994; Cullen, 1995), rather than habilitate or rehabilitate them. Many jurisdictions have reintroduced determinate sentences and mandatory periods of incarceration, chain gangs, striped uniforms for inmates, boot camps, and decreased access for prisoners to many desired amenities (Applegate et al., 1997; Clear, 1994). Some scholars suggest, however, that these "get-tough policies" are futile; "Not a single review of the controlled outcome research in criminal justice

---

[1] The authors who contributed to the antipsychiatry movements all attacked the legitimacy of psychiatry as an agent of social control. They questioned whether it was appropriate to conceptualize deviations in behavior, ideas, and beliefs in the same way that you would characterize a physical defect. Many of their writings supported Thomas Szasz's contention of a myth of mental illness and challenged the medicalization of behaviors previously considered bad or socially deviant. In general, the antipsychiatry movements of the 1960s and 1970s in the social and behavioral sciences challenged the legitimacy of using psychiatric models to control moral and political modes of behavioral deviance.

31

and corrections has found large or consistent effects on recidivism through variations in the type or severity of the criminal penalty or judicial disposition" (Andrews, 1995, p. 38). Given this finding, rehabilitation efforts continue (George & Marlatt, 1989; Inciardi, 1993; Palmer, 1992).

The debate over the value of treatment as a response, or as part of a response, to offenders is also prominent in the juvenile justice system. For example, the legitimacy of considering an offender's youth a "special" status necessitating treatment in place of punishment, and the utility of having a special court for the treatment and rehabilitation of juvenile offenders (Feld, 1993, 1997; Hirschi & Gottfredson, 1993; Morse, 1997; Scott & Grisso, 1997), are still contested topics. These issues are part of a broader debate about the legitimacy of diverting "special" groups of offenders for treatment in place of punishment and of maintaining parallel systems for responding to these offenders (e.g., mental health system, juvenile justice system, criminal justice system, and correctional system). Even among those who support treatment, some argue for the coordination of treatment between systems, or the placement of treatment and punishment within one system (Peay, 1990).

Thus the public policy pendulum continues to swing because of uncertainties about the value of treating adult and juvenile offenders, and, if value is determined, the most appropriate place for such services to occur. These uncertainties include (a) whether the vulnerabilities of certain offenders threaten their safety in correctional institutions and, ultimately, the fundamental fairness and humaneness of the correctional process (Blackburn, 1996; Halleck, 1986); (b) whether all or some subset of offenders are treatable (Quinsey, 1988; Rogers, 1988); (c) whether treatment can change behavior deemed relevant to protecting the public from dangerous behaviors; (d) whether we can specify a priori where treatments should take place to be effective (Blackburn, 1996; Freeman & Roesch, 1989; Halleck, 1986), and (e) whether treatable offenders make up a homogenous group.

The way correctional administrators have answered this last question has perhaps created the largest problem for improving treatment technologies for offenders. Treating offenders as a homogeneous group has controlled the way correctional mental health services have been offered to these individuals, has influenced treatment outcome studies in this area, and has fundamentally affected past and current debates about the value of treatment in corrections. This chapter explores this issue because, as we will show, a critical oversight in corrections has been to provide generic services and then evaluate their effectiveness without regard to offender need (see the introduction to this volume). This has led to biased outcome information, which in turn has clouded the debate over the appropriate role of treatment in corrections.

To understand this concern, we start by outlining the history of treatment in criminal law and demonstrate how it was tied to the special legal status of the offender, examine the terms offender "needs" and "special needs," consider the fallacious assumption of homogeneity of special needs across offenders, and emphasize the importance of linking the special needs of offenders with the selection of treatments.

History of Special Statuses for Offenders Who Need Treatment

The idea of responding differently to certain groups of offenders was, at least in comparatively recent jurisprudence, tied to those offenders who exhibited a severe mental disorder. The attempt to differentiate this group from nonmentally disordered offenders was initially denounced in 18th-century criminal law reforms (Pound, 1911/1968; Saleilles, 1968). During this period, legal theory focused on criminal acts and ignored offender personality or mental status to achieve increased uniformity in the administration of justice (Barnes, 1972; Reckless, 1973; Saleilles, 1968).[2] By the turn of the 19th-century, however, there occurred a noticeable shift in philosophy. Most of the dangerous and nondangerous "insane" were housed in family homes, almshouses, workhouses, or in general hospitals (Quen, 1989; Shorter, 1997). Although these facilities were more noticeable for the custodial care they provided, rather than for the treatment offered,[3] during the second half of the 19th century, when reformist social philosophers focused on the problems of crime and mental illness (Barnes, 1972), the seeds were sowed for eventually establishing what some historians have termed the "psychiatric turn" in handling social problems (Boorse, 1975). This change reflected a shift in societal preferences for clinical intervention over moral judgment in handling such problems (Ashford & Littrell, 1998; Conrad, 1992).

Treatment of Insanity Acquittees

As just noted, the first special legal status in Anglo-American law was for mentally disordered offenders. This status was established in England around 1800 after James Hadfield attempted to shoot King George III. Hadfield was acquitted of this offense because of insanity, although the courts were perplexed about what to do with him (Partridge, 1975). Noncriminal "lunatics" were typically sent to Bethlem Hospital and were not under strict supervision. The court feared that "if Hadfield were to escape he probably would take another shot at the King" (Partridge, 1975, p. 1). The alternative of placing Hadfield in jail was not considered appropriate by Lord Arnold (the attorney general in the Hadfield case) because the criminally insane in the eyes of the English law were to be treated as if they were innocent (Partridge, 1975; Walker, 1968).

Within a month of Hadfield's acquittal, Parliament passed the Criminal Lunatics Act of 1800 (Partridge, 1975), which authorized the imprisonment of Hadfield and other persons acquitted because of insanity until they were released by the King (Walker, 1968). It also provided for detaining individuals who were unfit to be tried for a crime (Walker, 1968). This provision introduced an implicit policy of "a lifetime confinement as the penalty for being incompetent to stand trial" (Stone, 1982, p. 13), or for being found to be insane at the time of the crime; Hadfield remained in detention for the remainder of his life (Walker & McCabe, 1973). This special-status law did not call for interventions to restore the criminally insane to sufficient

---

[2] This approach continues to influence Anglo American law. Special laws involving mental status are still being challenged by advocates who fear individualization of punishment based on offender needs (Blackburn, 1993; Peay, 1990; Raine, 1993; Saleilles, 1968; Wilson, 1997).

[3] Some European cities developed special hospitals for the treatment of insane individuals, but the United States lagged behind England, France, Germany, Italy, and other countries on the continent in building such special institutions (Dershowitz, 1974). The first hospital built in the United States specifically for the noncriminally insane individuals was in Williamsburg, Virginia, in 1773, although hospitalized persons were there for support and maintenance rather than therapy (Shorter, 1997).

capacity to be able to stand trial or to be released, but instead focused on the confinement of individuals for an indeterminate period. "The special verdict of insanity
..., therefore, [was] special only to the extent that it ... result[ed] in mandatory
confinement in cases where, under ordinary legal principles, the accused would simply be acquitted" (Gostin, 1984, p. 228).

By 1807, a Select Committee of the House of Commons recommended constructing a separate facility for the confinement of persons detained under the Criminal Lunatics Act (Quen, 1989). This special ward, which was attached to the Bethlem Hospital in 1814, became overcrowded in a few years and the development
of special hospitals for criminal "lunatics" ensued (Partridge, 1975). Moreover, The
Criminal Lunatics Act introduced what is often referred to in the literature as a
"quasi-criminal-justice system" for restraining potentially violent individuals (Stone,
1982).

Despite the creation of these special hospitals, the primary legal justification for
incarcerating mentally disordered offenders was for preventive and custodial purposes (Dershowitz, 1974). This changed in the first half of the 19th century when
the "cult of curability" began to dominate the thinking of psychiatry (Deutsch, 1949;
Robinson, 1996; Shorter, 1997). According to this view, the "environmental chaos"
(e.g., poverty, rapid social change as a result of the industrial revolution) of the times
contributed to the development of many kinds of mental illnesses (Robinson, 1996),
and placement of patients in asylums was necessary to remove individuals from their
chaotic living conditions and to substitute a healthy dose of morality and discipline.
This emphasis on environmental interventions led to the policies for involuntary
confinement of nondangerous mentally ill persons for treatment (Dershowitz, 1974).

The focus on curability, however, did not stop the continuing debates about the
appropriate response to mentally disordered offenders (Curran, 1977; Dershowitz,
1974). Many physicians, including some asylum directors, believed that people who
committed criminal acts were "[un]worthy of medical-psychological treatment" and
needed to be confined in jails (Curran, 1977, p. 4; Dershowitz, 1974). Despite this
view, some policy makers in the United States wanted to differentially respond to
the "criminally insane," and started constructing separate facilities for them. The
Utica State Hospital in New York, for example, was the first U.S. facility used for
this purpose. In 1848 the New York legislature authorized the transfer of any insane
prisoner to the newly designated ward at that hospital, which was known as the New
York Lunatic Asylum at Utica (Quen, 1989). When the population at this ward
exceeded its capacity, a special facility was built adjacent to New York's Auburn
Prison in 1859, which some historians consider the first hospital for the criminally
insane in the United States (Quen, 1989).

Early hospitals for the criminally insane held insanity acquittees, persons found
incompetent to stand trial, and persons who became insane while incarcerated
(Deutsch, 1949; Swisher, 1978). Some also accepted dangerous, civilly committed
patients (Blackburn, 1993; Dershowitz, 1974; Gostin, 1984). However, hospitals designed to treat these special categories of offenders did not become commonplace
until the beginning of the 20th century. Once again, special treatment (i.e., hospital
confinement) has not been without controversy (Halleck, 1986). Although the commitment to the special facility is purportedly for purposes of treatment, many believed—and still believe today—that this obscures its true justification, which is
preventive confinement. In fact, this was the only justification for commitment before

the passage of New York's comprehensive insanity legislation of 1842. Although this legislation authorized confinement of nondangerous insane persons for purposes of treatment, the statute also authorized the confinement of dangerous insane persons for an indefinite period (Dershowitz, 1974).

Whether it be because of the belief in the value of treatment or because of the opportunity to impose long-term confinement, legislators became so enamored with these special facilities that they expanded their services to focus on other groups of criminally deviant persons. Many jurisdictions created special sentencing and commitment legislation for psychopathic offenders and sexual psychopaths (Halleck, 1986).

From Insanity to Psychopathic Commitment Legislation

The intellectual antecedent for this development in the United States can be traced to Isaac Ray (1838). Ray argued that the simple test of insanity, which developed in England for mentally disordered offenders, was inadequate to deal with all people deserving of treatment for insanity. The English test focused on whether the mentally disordered offender could distinguish right from wrong (*M'Naghten's Case*, 1843). In Ray's opinion, the law of insanity ignored the special category of individuals who understood the wrongfulness of their acts but were powerless to stop themselves from engaging in criminal behavior (Colaizzi, 1989; Hughes, 1986; Ray, 1838). In his view, this latter group of persons, who suffered from partial insanity (also referred to as moral insanity), were likely to engage in repetitive, motiveless, and compulsive forms of behavior that he considered beyond their control. *Partial–moral insanity*, and its more modern equivalent *psychopathy,* is a controversial diagnostic category but has contributed to the formation of a number of special statuses in the law (Halleck, 1986).

Gostin (1984) observed that one of the great dilemmas for modern mental health practice has been whether to use compulsory mental health powers to treat offenders suffering with psychopathic disorders. His argument is made poignant by the fact that the psychopathic disorder is not a category that is currently included in the *Diagnostic and Statistical Manual of Mental Disorders* (American Psychiatric Association, 1994) or in the *International Classification of Diseases, 9th Revision, Clinical Modification International Classification of Diseases* (World Health Organization, 1998). Despite this fact, there are a number of statutes in the United States that still call for treating psychopathic offenders. Many of these laws operate on assumptions about psychopathy that have roots in earlier historical conceptualizations of the disorder that focused primarily on a person's defects or diseases that involved compulsions of a sexual nature (Walker, 1968). This subtype of psychopathy was described by Kraeplin (1896) in one of his early textbooks and by Krafft-Ebing (1886) in his popular book *Psychopáthia Sexualis.*

For some reason, this subtype has captured the imagination of many policy makers in the United States (Walker, 1968). In fact, a number of states passed sexual psychopath laws during the 1930s when Freudian psychology was gaining control over psychiatric thinking (Blackburn, 1993; Sutherland, 1950) and the medical model was beginning to dominate most correctional reforms (Carney, 1980). In 1938, Illinois was one of the first states to enact legislation for sexual psychopaths (Blackburn,

1993). In 1939, Minnesota also passed a law dealing with the civil commitment of individuals with psychopathic personalities, which was challenged in the case of *State ex rel. Pearson v. Probate Court* (1939). The legislation was designed to reach "those people who, by habitual course of misconduct in sexual matters, have evidenced an utter lack of power to control their sexual impulses and who, as a result, are likely to attack or otherwise inflict injury, loss, pain or other evil on the objects of their uncontrolled and uncontrollable desire" (*Minnesota ex rel. Pearson v. Probate Court*, 1939, p. 302). The court "upheld the legislation as a legitimate state exercise of [both its *police power*] to protect the public from future harm and of its *parens patriae* authority to treat those in need of treatment" (La Fond, 1992, p. 660; italics added).

Besides legislation that relied on a civil commitment model, a number of states also enacted other forms of special sentencing legislation for treating other categories of psychopathic and dangerous offenders (Halleck, 1986). For instance, the Ohio legislature passed the Asherman Act (1939), which gave sentencing authorities options for three classes of disordered offenders: mentally ill, mentally deficient, and psychopathic individuals (Swisher, 1978). Offenders with any other mental health classification were not eligible for these special sentencing provisions. This legislation authorized the criminal commitment of psychopathic offenders for an indeterminate period following their conviction for any kind of crime. Commitment was to a special hospital for purposes of treatment, thereby granting judges the authority to divert offenders to treatment in place of traditional penal sanctions.

During the 1970s, civil and criminal statutes for the special handling of psychopathic offenders came under heavy criticism. The Group for the Advancement of Psychiatry (1977) and the American Bar Association (1989) called for the repeal of this kind of legislation. For example, many of the critics of laws involving sexual psychopaths questioned the assumptions underlying the presumed justification for the adjudication and confinement of these persons. These assumptions include

> (1) sexual psychopaths can be reliably distinguished from other sex offenders; (2) sex offenders offend because of mental disorder or disease; (3) such mental disorders and diseases are curable; and (4) mental health clinicians can accurately predict which sex offenders will or will not offend over the long-term-future. (Wettstein, 1992; p. 599)

In spite of mounting criticism against the legitimacy of legislation for treating and controlling sexual psychopaths, a new wave of legislation was initiated for individuals with psychopathic disorders after a rash of violent sex crimes during the 1990s (Gleb, 1991). For instance, the state of Washington enacted its Sexually Violent Predator Law (WASH. REV. CODE ANN., 1990) after a highly visible crime was committed by a mentally retarded person. After serving a 10-year sentence for a sexual crime, Earl Shriner was released. Two years after his release, he raped a seven-year-old boy, cut off his penis, and left him near death. The state of Washington responded by enacting its Sexually Violent Predator Law (see, e.g., Winick & La Fond, 1998). Under this legislation, the state is authorized to civilly commit a person who has completed a criminal sentence for a sexually violent crime if it is proved at the commitment hearing that this individual remains a sexually violent predator. Although the terminology changed from *sexual psychopath* to *sexually violent predator*, the targeted offenders remained the same. To be adjudicated a sexually violent predator, the offender had to be suffering from "a mental abnormality or personality disorder which makes the person likely to engage in predatory acts of violence" (La Fond, 1992, p. 656).

Unlike previous sexual psychopath laws, these newer laws do not rely on a merging of *police power*, which justifies preventive detention, with *parens patriae*, which justifies treatment. Indeed, the U.S. Supreme Court, in reviewing a similar Kansas statute, held that incapacitation (i.e., a *police power* exercise) is a legitimate end in and of itself for a sexually violent predator law (*Kansas v. Hendricks*, 1997).

Drug Dependent Persons Legislation

Drug dependent persons (substance abusers) are another major example of a special status being provided within the criminal law. Although before the 1960s drug dependent offenders were treated as criminals in need of strict penal sanctions (Lindesmith, 1965), this position was altered in 1966 by the enactment of the Narcotic Addict Rehabilitation Act (NARA). The NARA, which legitimized medical approaches to intervening with drug dependent offenders, ended the mandatory minimum sentences for these persons (Ashford, 1986, 1987; Himmelstein, 1978). The NARA granted the judiciary the discretion either to divert offenders into treatment programs or to impose traditional penal sanctions. However, the act was not widely used because most drug addicted offenders did not commit crimes that fell under federal jurisdiction (Comptroller General of the United States, 1971).

For this reason, most states enacted legislation by the 1970s that allowed for the diversion of drug offenders to treatment in lieu of the traditional criminal process (Aronowitz, 1983; Ashford, 1986, 1987; Uelmen & Haddox, 1983). Of these diversionary schemas, the drug dependent persons (DDP) statutes were the most controversial because they made offenders involved in non–drug-related offenses eligible for treatment in lieu of punishment solely based on their status of being addicted. Because policy makers feared that offenders would use addiction status to avoid the traditional penal consequences (Ashford, 1986), many schemas also required that offenders be likely to benefit from treatment (Perlman & Jaszi, 1976; Robertson, 1972). Although there is some question of whether an offender's treatability can be reliably assessed (Ashford, 1988a, 1988b; Perlman & Jaszi, 1976; Robertson, 1972), offenders continue to be diverted to drug treatment programs under the authority of specialty courts for adult and juvenile offenders with substance abuse problems (see chapter 5, this volume).

Delinquency and Youthful Offender Legislation

A third special legal status was created for juvenile offenders. Toward the end of the 19th century, prison reformers began separating juveniles from adult offenders. This is also the period that gave birth to the establishment of a specialty court for the treatment and rehabilitation of juvenile offenders (Lempert & Sanders, 1986). In part, the focus on rehabilitation grew out of positivistic principles of criminology that viewed criminal conduct as a symptom of an underlying condition requiring treatment. In the case of delinquency, most reformers assumed that adolescents possessed different capacities and needs from adults that were a direct reflection of their immaturity (Morse, 1997; Scott & Grisso, 1997) and that "the condition that required treatment was caused by poor parental guidance, care, and supervision as well as social harms associated with poverty" (Scott & Grisso, 1997). This belief not only limited the responsibility of youths but also influenced how they should be treated by the justice system.

The early approach to the rehabilitation of delinquent youths has many similarities with how the rehabilitation ideal was implemented in other areas of justice administration. Persons were typically classified as being in need of treatment based on a single need, or specific legal status, without regard to variations in their needs and in their amenability to treatment. All persons who were classified as youthful offenders were presumably homogenous in their treatment needs and in their amenability to treatment. In addition, all youthful offenders were considered more amenable to treatment than older offenders. However, there were some minor variations across legislative schemas in drawing the lines between youthful and older offenders. For instance, Ohio mandated that youths between 16 and 21 years of age had to be sent to a reformatory. However, the courts in this state had the discretion to sentence young adults between 22 and 30 years of age to the same reformatory, but any offender older than 30 had to be sentenced to a penitentiary (Swisher, 1978). The conceptualization of youth in this Ohio legislation differed in some respects from the federal Youth Correction Act (YCA) of 1950. A youthful offender was defined in this act as any individual under the age of 22 at the time of their conviction. These age thresholds are an excellent example of the kind of simplistic classification used in our early systems of juvenile justice.

These special statutes for youthful offenders were repealed in the 1980s because of the growing dissatisfaction with the rehabilitation ideal and mounting policy support for principles of just desserts in adult and juvenile offender dispositions. Whether this change is desirable depends on how we define needs in the justice and correctional processes.

Defining Needs and Special Needs in the Legal System

The rehabilitation ideal in corrections relies heavily on the ability of the system to reliably and validly classify needs (Clements, 1996; Van Voorhis, 1994), with these needs being viewed as the justification for special legal statuses and their treatment. But which needs should be responded to, particularly with rehabilitative treatments? We now consider how needs have been defined in the juvenile justice, criminal justice, and correctional literatures.

The concept of need has played a major role in social policy (Baldwin, 1998; Braybrooke, 1987; Doyal & Gough, 1991; Meeker, 1998; Moroney, 1977; Ohlsson, 1995). It has been used, for example, to justify different responses to different kinds of offenders (e.g., youthful offenders need more educational services than adult offenders) and to prioritize policy responses. "The reason for the central position of needs . . . is that needs are related to human suffering. Needs normally indicate urgency. They indicate that something vital is missing. They therefore exercise a certain kind of force" (Liss, 1998, p. 9). Moreover, need can be used to differentiate something essential that should be fulfilled from simple wants, desires, or preferences (Doyal & Gough, 1991). If a person does not have a need satisfied, then they will incur some form of serious social, physical, or emotional harm.

There are three types of need discussed in the juvenile justice, criminal justice, and correctional processes: offender, societal, and justice system needs. In short, need is a multilevel concept that will vary with the contexts in which it is used and the goals of the labeler (e.g., society, policy maker, criminal justice personnel, forensic MHP, offender). Thus it is not surprising that there is no widely accepted theory or definition of need guiding justice and correctional policy (Berwin, Wing, Mangen, Brugha, & MacCarthy, 1987; Duffee & Clark, 1985; Wing, 1990).

Offender Needs

In the literature on philosophy of needs (Black, 1998; Bradshaw, 1972; Braybooke, 1987), an important distinction is made between subjectively and objectively defined needs. We begin our examination of need as a multilevel concept by likening this philosophical distinction to the varying definitions of offender needs. These distinctions in conceptualizing need raise important dilemmas of choice for policy makers and practitioners involved in identifying appropriate treatment outcomes for criminal offenders.

Subjective Needs

Considering the subjective needs of offenders is generally justified for therapeutic reasons, not for the social control functions of the criminal law (Schopp, 1995). A subjective, felt need refers to what an offender perceives his needs to be (Moroney, 1977). A subjective, expressed need refers both to what the offender perceives as his needs and what he communicates to others (Berwin et al., 1987). Although an offender can experience a sense of need, it does not mean that he will seek satisfaction for it. It also does not mean that he knows how to communicate these needs to criminal justice personnel (Black, 1998; Bradshaw, 1972; Moroney, 1977).

Expressed needs are part of the demand theories of need (Baldwin, Godfrey, & Popper, 1990; Wing, 1990; Wolf, 1997).[4] Whether these expressed needs (demands) get addressed is a function of the public's view of its obligation as a society (Loewry, 1987) and whether the demands are perceived by criminal justice personnel as coming under some right or entitlement the law guarantees to offenders. Traditionally, offender demands for services (expressed needs) are not viewed as important because of resource scarcity and the public attitude that the only obligation government should have to its citizens is to sustain or restore minimal functioning—not optimize human abilities (Carney, 1980; DeJong & Rutten, 1983; Loewry, 1987; Pitch, 1995). Nonetheless, offender-expressed needs are included in many rehabilitation frameworks to enable offenders to optimize their potential to lead law-abiding productive lives (Ohlsson, 1995) and to achieve their personal goals (Wolf, 1997).

---

[4]Not all demand theories focus on expressed needs however (Schopp, 1995; Stone, 1982). Harland's (1996) book on correctional interventions ignores the expressed needs or demands of offenders and focuses instead on the demands of justice professionals and other key societal stakeholders.

Objective Needs

When correctional policy rejects offender-expressed needs and focuses on helping the offender achieve a socially selected and acceptable, albeit minimum, level of health and social functioning, it requires a determination of society's or the legal system's standard (Berwin et al., 1987; Bradshaw, 1972; Wing, 1990). This standard, referred to as a standard of objective need, can be either normatively or comparatively (empirically) derived (Berwin et al., 1987; Black, 1998).[5] Some scholars point out that any notion of objective need is groundless and subject to abuse by authoritarian and paternalistically driven decision makers (Braybrooke, 1987; Doyal & Gough, 1991). Such critics believe that the preferences and demands of "consumers" are better guides to policy. However, policy in the justice and correctional systems rarely rely on the preferences of offenders, because offenders are not true consumers who can assert their preferences in a manner that is consistent with the requirements of a market-oriented economy. That is, offenders do not operate in a free market and lack the necessary capital to purchase services that can meet their subjective, expressed needs.

Overlap Potential Between Subjective and Objective Needs

Despite the often assumed independence of subjective and objective needs, the two types of need can overlap. Offenders' subjective preferences might be identical with the external, objective classification of needs (e.g., where a prisoner seeks treatment to curtail his or her desire to commit sexual offenses). This identity does not always occur, however, because external definitions vary based on who is doing the classifying (e.g., legislators, judges, correctional administrators, or mental health professionals) and what orientation the classifier takes (e.g., libertarian, antilibertarian, communitarian). In addition, subjective definitions are more likely to support individualized treatment interventions for therapeutic goals than for social control goals, whereas objective definitions are likely to do the reverse.

In conclusion, an important issue for the justice and correctional systems is whether its policies ought to respond to offender survival or enhancement needs that are not directly related to their likelihood of recidivism. This is partially a normative issue. For example, should society provide treatment benefits to people who commit crimes solely to benefit the individual and not society? Values alone can be used to answer this type of question. But empirical data can and should be valuable in shaping one's views. For example, if it can be empirically demonstrated that treating offenders' needs reduces recidivism and saves the state more than the treatment costs (e.g., because of the savings in the law enforcement, adjudication, and detention costs that are associated with recidivism), then policy makers should be much more interested in providing treatment to respond to offender needs.

---

[5] For obvious reasons, subjective needs are also referred to as *internally derived needs*, and objective needs are referred to as *externally derived needs*.

Societal Needs

Society assumes that the most important offender needs are the ones that influence their probability of recidivism (Andrews & Bonta, 1994). For this reason, it is important to distinguish criminogenic from noncriminogenic needs (Andrews & Bonta, 1994, 1998). Criminogenic needs are "dynamic attributes of the offender that, when changed, are associated with changes in the probability of recidivism" (Andrews & Bonta, 1998, p. 243). This implies that there are many attributes of the offender and his environment that when changed may influence his potential for recidivism. An example of a criminogenic need is eliminating antisocial attitudes and feelings (Andrews, 1995; Andrews & Bonta, 1998; Bonta, 1996). When offenders have needs that even if satisfied will not reduce recidivism, they are referred to as noncriminogenic needs. According to the "societal" notions of need, responding to noncriminogenic needs is not a useful response.

The Needs of the Justice and Correctional Systems

According to many justice and correctional personnel, offender treatment should be provided to reduce crime, comport with fundamental principles of justice, and facilitate the day to day functioning of the legal systems. It is this last need that is unique to legal systems' perspective. Thus intrainstitutional expectations and other management problems dictate how needs are defined in many justice and correctional systems' conceptualizations of need. For example, the day to day management of violent and out of control offenders is of primary interest to correctional authorities.

This approach to defining need covers more than just the interests of corrections. There can be preinstitutional problems (e.g., ability to engage in the adversarial process), intrainstitutional problems (e.g., problems in moving offenders between jails and prisons), and postinstitutional problems (e.g., problems in managing offenders on probation or parole) (Hippchen, 1977; Van Voorhis, 1994). Justice and correctional systems' needs, therefore, must address problems encountered by legal authorities in effectively managing offenders in the courts, and in the correctional, probation, and parole systems. Because of this management need, most psychologically based systems of classification are used to classify offenders in a way that directly helps reduce dysfunctional behaviors and rectify other problems an offender might have being involved in a legal system. These classification systems are not designed to address crime control following release or personal enhancement for the offender (Van Voorhis, 1994).

Conclusions Regarding Need

In summary, American legal policy has experienced a swinging pendulum with regard to response to offenders. This is not surprising because selecting which needs to respond to involves substantial factual and value dilemmas. "It not only includes who? what? and where? issues, but also an analysis of the political environment and assessment of the community's readiness to deal with the problem and a measure of the resources it is willing to commit to its solution" (Moroney, 1977, pp. 132–133). In other words, defining which needs to address will never be a purely technical process that can be removed from its social, political, and legal environments. A partial solution to this decisional complexity is to differentiate ordinary from "special" needs.

Offenders With Special Needs

"Special" is a term that is used to set apart an object or a person from others in the same category. In other words, the label special denotes that something is in some sense extraordinary or unusual. Because the term special can be applied to many categories of offenders, the criteria used in making such designations are as relative as the criteria used in defining ordinary offender needs. For instance, special legal remedies have been established for responding to persons found incompetent to stand trial, not guilty by reason of insanity, or guilty but insane; mentally retarded offenders; sex offenders; drug-dependent offenders; psychopathic offenders; and dangerous offenders. However, the justifications for labeling these categories "special" is not without controversy. Why should drug and violent sexual offenders be handled differently from other nondisordered violent offenders, for example? The answer to questions like these depend on what policy makers see as the purposes of the correctional process (e.g., restoration, retribution, incapacitation, deterrence, rehabilitation) and on the system's capabilities to achieve these goals.

Today special handling in the justice and correctional systems is based on three purposes: to provide for the care and safety of prisoners (see e.g., *Deshaney v. Winnebago County Department of Social Services*, 1989; *Doe v. Sullivan County*, 1992; *Farmer v. Brennan*, 1994); to ensure that offenders are treated fairly (Halleck, 1986); and to protect society from the offenders. For example, offenders at risk of harming themselves (see chapter 12, this volume) or of being abused by other offenders (Halleck, 1986) must be given special care, protection, and treatment under current constitutional requirements (Belbot & del Carmen, 1993; see also chapter 2, this volume). Other purposes of the system (e.g., reducing recidivism) could justify special need classification as well. Given these multiple goals of the justice and correctional systems, we define special needs as *"any changeable factors associated with disorders of cognition, thought, mood, personality, development or behavior that are linked to desired outcomes for offenders at any phase of the justice process"* (see the introduction to this book). The value of this definition is twofold. First, it requires that justice system and correctional administrators specify the needs that they wish to address. This process is valuable because it will allow for a clearer more focused discussion among all interested parties in society about the appropriate needs for the law to address. Second, it anticipates that treatments will be developed to match each special need to achieve particular outcomes.

Treatment Interventions in Light of Special Needs

As already noted, in traditional correctional mental health planning, offenders are matched to existing services rather than services being matched to the special needs of offenders. Treating special needs with available services presumes that available services can address all of the problems—special needs (Maser, Cassano, & Michelini,

1997). This assumption has proven unhelpful in treating special need offenders because their special needs are not homogeneous. To treat them as such dooms hopes of reducing recidivism and achieving rehabilitation (Bonta, 1996; Clements, 1996; Van Voorhis, 1994).

So how should offender classification and needs be related to offender treatment? Generic solutions should be replaced by differentiated services; "clinical wisdom has always held that patient and problem variables [should] dictate the use of specific treatment approaches" (Beutler & Clarkin, 1990, p. 14). This approach is consistent with the social planners of the 1970s, who stressed individualized needs assessment and the matching of those assessments to specific services (i.e., "need-based services") (Baldwin, 1998; Moroney, 1977).

To make the individual treatment approach work will require scientific knowledge of what kinds of interventions are effective in achieving desired outcomes with each type of special need. No longer should we impose a diagnosis and then match the treatment to the diagnosis (see, e.g., Matthew, 1971). Current diagnostic categories do not capture important variables that lead to good treatment outcomes (e.g., because these categories ignore atypical and subclinical symptoms that affect the success of treatments). Rather, interventions should be tailored to influence person and situation variables that are critical to outcome but may not be included in the diagnostic categories (Acierno, Hersen, & Ammerman, 1994; Beutler & Clarkin, 1990; Francis, Clarkin, & Perry, 1984; Maser et al., 1997; Sperry, Brill, Howard, & Grisson, 1996). The differential therapeutics movement in psychiatry (Francis et al., 1984) and the technical eclecticism movement in psychotherapy research (Beutler & Consoli, 1992) emerged in part in response to many of these observed limitations in selecting treatments based on diagnostic categories of *DSM* systems of classification. For example, we know that violence perpetuated by persons with schizophrenia generally occurs during the acute phase of their disorder (Hodgins, 1993; Link, Cullen, & Andrews, 1990), but criminal history and victim selection variables are also critical to deal with in treatment because they help shape the elicitation and focus of the offender's violent outburst (see chapter 9, this volume).

Despite the mounting scientific support for using an individualized treatment approach and for rejecting a simple diagnosis-treatment match, most correctional decisions continue to be determined by the presence of a legally sanctioned diagnosis (Blackburn, 1993, 1996). This practice would not be problematic if actual treatment plans were based on other information besides the offender's legal diagnosis (e.g., insanity acquittee). For example, Sperry et al. (1996) recommend that prescriptive treatments in mental health require the focused assessment of "(a) symptoms and level of functioning (psychopathology), (b) predisposing factors (vulnerabilities), (c) perpetuating factors, and (d) readiness for treatment" (Sperry et al., 1996, p. 50). To this list we would add (e) targets for psychological and behavioral change that focus on criminogenic and forensic needs–goals because offenders represent a unique clinical population with distinct needs that should be treated in conjunction with clinical signs and symptoms to achieve desired criminal justice outcomes.

Our suggested approach to selecting treatments in correctional and forensic mental health is consistent with many of the principles of Beutler and Clarkin's (1990) model for the systematic selection of treatment in psychotherapy. Their model "eschews treatment decisions that are derived from narrow theoretical frameworks in favor of basing treatment prescriptions on empirically observed relationships between client needs and the efficacies of specific treatment procedures" (Beutler & Hodgson, 1993, p. 152). What is needed therefore is a prescriptive approach to treating offenders with special needs—"the prescription of a highly specified, thoroughly evaluated treatment regimen in order to ameliorate a highly specified, thoroughly assessed complaint" (Sperry et al., 1996, p. 50). This requires developing research programs in which interactions between person (including offender responsivity), target outcomes, and treatment (including treatment setting) are systematically controlled and studied. In addition, research also is needed to identify other factors that can affect treatment outcome. With this kind of focus, we are much more likely to develop the highly differentiated systems of classification and treatment that can lead to empirically justified clinical interventions with offenders. Parts II through VI of this book present the state of the science on the treatments of offenders with special needs.

Finally, we also require research on the kinds of diagnostic categories and need profiles that are resistant to available treatments. If a group is treatment resistant (e.g., psychopathic offenders) using current technology, society should not waste scarce treatment resources on them (see chapter 4, this volume; Reid, 1998). If they are untreatable, to include them with offenders who have a chance of profiting from treatment can only increase the chance of failure for the entire group. Treatment resistant and untreatable offenders should be separated from the treatable offender population so that members of the former group do not become the role models or coaches for those who have a chance of working out of the recidivistic cycle. Once separation occurs, and if funding is available, research can help determine how currently untreatable and treatment resistant offenders will fare under newly developed therapies tailored to their special needs.

References

Acierno, R., Hersen, M., & Ammerman, R. T. (1994). Overview of the issues in prescriptive treatments. In M. Hersen & R. T. Ammerman (Eds.), *Handbook of prescriptive treatments for adults* (pp. 3–27). New York: Plenum Press.

American Bar Association. (1989). *ABA criminal justice mental health standards.* Washington, DC: Author.

American Friends Services Committee. (1971). *A Struggle for justice: A report on crime and punishment in America.* New York: Hill & Wang.

American Psychiatric Association. (1994). *Diagnostic and statistical manual of mental disorders* (4th ed). Washington, DC: Author.

Andrews, D. (1995). The psychology of criminal conduct and effective treatment. In J. Mcquire (Ed.), *What works: Reducing reoffending* (pp. 35–62). New York: John Wiley & Sons.

Andrews, D. A., & Bonta, J. (1994). *The psychology of criminal conduct.* Cincinnati, OH: Anderson.

Andrews, D. A., & Bonta, J. (1998). *The psychology of criminal conduct* (2nd ed.). Cincinnati, OH: Anderson.

Applegate, B. K., Cullen, F. T., & Fisher, B. S. (1997). Public support for correctional treatment: The continuing appeal of the rehabilitation ideal. *Prison Journal, 77,* 237–258.

Aronowitz, D. (1983). Civil commitment of narcotic addicts. In G. Uelmen & V. G. Haddox (Ed.), *Drug abuse and the law* (pp. 10.20–10.29). New York: Clark Boardman.

Asherman Act. (1939). GD §§ 13451 to 13451-23, 118 Ohio Laws 686.

Ashford, J. B. (1986). A survey of clinical standards in selected drug dependent persons statutes. *Contemporary Drug Problems, 8,* 607–709.

Ashford, J. B. (1987). Legal criteria and clinical predictions in drug legislation. *Social Casework, 68,* 364–373.

Ashford, J. B. (1988a). Assessing treatability in drug offenders. *Behavioral Sciences and the Law, 6,* 139–149.

Ashford, J. B. (1988b). Clinical or nonclinical judgments: The prognostic labeling of drug offenders. *American Journal of Forensic Psychology, 6,* 43–55.

Ashford, J. B., & Littrell, J. (1998). Psychopathology. In J. Figueira-McDonough, F. E. Netting, & A. Nichols-Casebolt (Eds.), *The role of gender in practice knowledge: Claiming half the human experience* (pp. 127–167). New York: Garland.

Baldwin, S. (1998). Problem with needs: Where theory meets practice in mental health services. In S. Baldwin (Ed.), *Needs assessment & community care: Clinical practice & policy making* (pp. 1–7). Oxford: Butterworth/Heinemann.

Baldwin, S., Godfrey, C., & Popper, C. (1990). Introduction. In S. Baldwin, C. Godfrey, & C. Popper (Eds.), *Quality of life: Perspectives and policies* (pp. 1–6). London: Routledge.

Barnes, H. E. (1972). *The story of punishment.* Montclair, NJ: Patterson Smith.

Belbot, B., & del Carmen, R. V. (1993). Legal issues in classification. In American Correctional Association (Ed.), *Classification: A tool for managing today's offenders* (pp. 17–31). Lanham, MD: American Correctional Association.

Berwin, C. R., Wing, J. K., Mangen, S., Brugha, T. S., & MacCarthy, B. (1987). Principles and practice of measuring needs in the long-term mentally ill: The MRC needs for care assessment. *Psychological Medicine, 17,* 971–981.

Beutler, L. E., & Clarkin, J. F. (1990). *Systematic treatment selection: Toward targeted therapeutic interventions.* New York: Brunner/Mazel.

Beutler, L. E., & Consoli, A. J. (1992). Systematic eclectic psychotherapy. In J. C. Norcross & M. R. Goldfried (Eds.), *Handbook of psychotherapy integration* (pp. 264–299). New York: Basic Books.

Beutler, L. E., & Hodgson, A. B. (1993). Prescriptive psychotherapy. In G. Stricker & J. R. Gold (Eds.), *Comprehensive handbook of psychotherapy integration* (pp. 151–163). New York: Plenum Press.

Black, K. (1998). Needs assessment in rehabilitation. In S. Baldwin (Ed.), *Needs assessment & community care: Clinical practice & policy making* (pp. 43–54). Oxford: Butterworth-Heinemann.

Blackburn, R. (1993). *The psychology of criminal conduct: Theory, research and practice.* Chichester, England: John Wiley & Sons.

Blackburn, R. (1996). Mentally disordered offenders. In C. R. Hollin (Ed.), *Working with offenders: Psychological practice in offender rehabilitation* (pp. 119–149). Chichester, England: John Wiley & Sons.

Bonta, J. (1996). Risk-needs assessment and treatment. In A. T. Harland (Ed.), *Choosing correctional options that work* (pp. 18–32). Thousand Oaks, CA: Sage.

Boorse, C. (1975). On the distinction between disease and illness. *Philosophy and Public Affairs, 5,* 49–68.

Bradshaw, J. (1972). The concept of need. *New Society, 19,* 640–643.

Braybrooke, D. (1987). *Meeting needs.* Princeton, NJ: Princeton University Press.

Carney, L. P. (1980). *Corrections: Treatment and philosophy.* Englewood Cliffs, NJ: Prentice-Hall.

Clear, T. R. (1994). *Harm in American penology: Offenders, victims, and their communities.* Albany: State University of New York Press.

Clements, C. B. (1996). Offender classification two decades of progress. *Criminal Justice and Behavior, 23,* 121–143.

Colaizzi, J. (1989). *Homicidal insanity, 1800–1985.* Tuscaloosa: University of Alabama Press.

Comptroller General of the United States. (1971). *Limited use of federal programs to commit narcotic addicts for treatment and rehabilitation.* Washington: DC: Comptroller General of the United States.

Conrad, P. (1992). Medicalization and social control. *Annual Review of Sociology, 18,* 209–232.

Conrad, P., & Schneider, J. W. (1980). *Deviance and medicalization: From badness to sickness.* St. Louis, MO: C.V. Mosby.

Cullen, F. T. (1995). Assessing the penal harm movement. *Journal of Research in Crime and Delinquency, 32,* 338–358.

Cullen, F. T., Cullen, J. B., & Wozniak, J. F. (1988). Is rehabilitation dead? The myth of the punitive public. *Journal of Criminal Justice, 16,* 303–317.

Curran, W. J. (1977). Legal psychiatry in the 19th century. In R. J. Bonnie (Ed.), *Psychiatrists and the legal process: Diagnosis and debate* (pp. 3–9). New York: Insight Communications.

DeJong, G. A., & Rutten, F. F. H. (1983). Justice and health for all. *Social Science in Medicine, 17,* 1085–1095.

Dershowitz, A. (1974). The origins of preventive confinement in Anglo-American law. Part II: The American experience. *Cincinnati Law Review, 1974,* 781–846.

Deshaney v. Winnebago County Department of Social Services. (1989). 489 U.S. 189.

Deutsch, A. (1949). *The mentally ill in America.* New York: Columbia University Press.

Doe v. Sullivan County. (1992). 956 F. 2d 545 (6th Cir.).

Doyal, L., & Gough, I. (1991). *A theory of human need.* Houndmills: Macmillan Education.

Duffee, D. E., & Clark, D. (1985). The frequency and classification of the needs of offenders in community settings. *Journal of Criminal Justice, 13,* 243–268.

Farmer v. Brennan. (1994). 511 U.S. 825.

Feld, B. C. (1993). Juvenile (in) justice and the criminal court. *Crime and Delinquency, 39,* 403–424.

Feld, B. C. (1997). Abolish the juvenile court: Youthfulness, criminal responsibility, and sentencing policy. *Journal of Criminal Law and Criminology, 88,* 68–136.

Francis, A., Clarkin, J. F., & Perry, S. (1984). *Differential therapeutics in psychiatry: The art and science of treatment selection.* New York: Brunner/Mazel.

Freeman, R. J., & Roesch, R. (1989). Mental disorder and the criminal justice system: A review. *International Journal of Law and Psychiatry, 12,* 105–115.

George, W. H., & Marlatt, G. A. (1989). Introduction. In D. R. Laws (Ed.), *Relapse prevention with sex offenders* (pp. 1–31). New York: Guilford Press.

Gleb, G. (1991). Washington's sexually violent predator law: The need to bar unreliable psychiatric predictions of dangerousness from civil commitment proceedings. *UCLA Law Review, 39,* 213–250.

Gostin, L. (1984). Towards the development of principles for sentencing and detaining mentally abnormal offenders. In M. Craft & A. Craft (Eds.), *Mentally abnormal offenders* (pp. 224–241). London: Bailliere Tindall.

Group for the Advancement of Psychiatry. (1977). *Psychiatry and sex psychopath legislation: The 30s to the 80s.* Washington, DC: Author.

Halleck, S. L. (1986). *The mentally disordered offender.* Rockville, MD: National Institute of Mental Health.

Halleck, S. L., & White, A. D. (1977). Is rehabilitation dead? *Crime and Delinquency, 23,* 372–382.

Harland, A. T. (Ed.). (1996). *Choosing correctional options that work: Defining the demand and evaluating the supply.* Thousand Oaks, CA: Sage.

Himmelstein, J. L. (1978). Drug politics theory: Analysis and critique. *Journal of Drug Issues, 8,* 37–52.

Hippchen, L. J. (1977). Trends in classification philosophy and practice. In L. J. Hippchen (Ed.), *Handbook on correctional classification: Programming for treatment and reintegration* (pp. 1–11). Cincinnati, OH: Anderson.

Hirschi, T., & Gottfredson, M. (1993). Rethinking the juvenile justice system. *Crime and Delinquency, 39*, 262–271.

Hodgins, S. (1993). Introduction: Mental disorder and crime. In S. Hodgins (Ed.), *Mental disorder and crime* (pp. ix–xvii). Newbury Park, CA: Sage.

Hughes, J. S. (1986). *In the law's darkness: Isaac Ray and the medical jurisprudence of insanity in nineteenth-century America.* New York: Oceana.

Inciardi, J. A. (Ed.). (1993). *Drug treatment and criminal justice.* Newbury Park, CA: Sage.

Kansas v. Hendricks. (1997). 117 S. Ct. 2106.

Kraepelin, E. (1896). *Psychiatire: Ein Lehrbuch für Stuidierende und Aerzte* [Psychiatry: A guidebook for students and practitioners] (8th ed.). Leipzig, Germany.

Krafft-Ebing, R. (1886). *Psychopathia sexualis.* Stuttgart, Germany. (Trans. G. C. Chaddock).

La Fond, J. Q. (1992). Washington's sexually violent predator law: A deliberate misuse of the therapeutic state for social control. *University of Puget Sound Law Review, 15*, 655–703.

Lempert, R., & Sanders, J. (1986). *An invitation to law and social science: Desert, disputes and distribution.* New York: Longman.

Lindesmith, A. R. (1965). *The addict and the law.* New York: Vintage.

Link, B., Cullen, F., & Andrews, H. (1990). *Violent and illegal behavior of current and former mental patients compared to community controls.* Paper presented at the meeting of the Society for the Study of Social Problems, San Francisco.

Liss, P. E. (1998). Assessing health care need: The conceptual foundation. In S. Baldwin (Ed.), *Needs assessment & community care: Clinical practice & policy making* (pp. 8–24). Oxford: Butterworth-Heinemann.

Loewry, E. H. (1987). Communities, obligations, and health care. *Social Science in Medicine, 25*, 783–791.

Logan, C. H., & Gaes, G. G. (1993). Meta-analysis and the rehabilitation of punishment. *Justice Quarterly, 10*, 245–263.

Martinson, R. (1974). What works? Questions and answers about prison reform. *Public Interest, 35*, 22–54.

Maser, J. D., Cassano, G., & Michelini, S. (1997). Treatment implications of comorbid mental disorders. In S. Wetzler & W. C. Sanderson (Eds.), *Treatment strategies for patients with psychiatric comorbidity.* New York: John Wiley & Sons.

Matthew, G. K. (1971). Measuring need and evaluating services. In G. McLachlan (Ed.), *Portfolio for health: Problems and progress in medical care* (Sixth series). London: Oxford University Press.

Meeker, B. F. (1998). Need as a basis of reward allocation. *Advances in Group Processes, 15*, 81–102.

Menninger, K. (1968). *The crime of punishment.* New York: Viking.

Minnesota ex rel. Pearson v. Probate Court. (1939). 309 U.S. 270, 277 (1940), *aff'g* 287 N.W. 297 (Minn.).

M'Naghten's Case. (1843). 8 Eng. Rep. 718.

Moroney, R. (1977). Needs assessment for human services. In W. F. Anderson, B. J. Frieden, & M. J. Murphy (Eds.), *Managing Human Services* (pp. 128–154). Washington, DC: International City Management Association.

Morse, S. J. (1997). Immaturity and irresponsibility. *Journal of Criminal Law and Criminology, 88*, 15–67.

Mower, O. H. (1960). Sin, the lesser of two evils. *American Psychologist, 15*, 301–304.

Narcotic Addict Rehabilitation Act. (1966). 28 U.S.C. § 2901.

Ohlsson, R. (1995). *Morals based on needs.* Lanham, MD: University Press of America.

Palmer, T. (1992). *The re-emergence of correctional intervention.* Newbury Park, CA: Sage.

Partridge, R. (1975). *Broadmoor: A history of criminal lunacy and its problems*. Westport, CT: Greenwood.

Peay, J. (1990). A criminological perspective—The influence of fashion and theory on practice and disposal: Life chances in the criminological tombola. In W. Watson & A. Grounds (Eds.), *The mentally disordered offender in an era of community care: New directions in provision* (pp. 41–58). Cambridge: Cambridge University Press.

Perlman, H., & Jaszi, P. (1976). *Legal issues in addict diversion*. Lexington, MA: Lexington.

Pitch, T. (1995). *Limited responsibilities: Social movements and criminal justice*. London: Routeledge.

Pound, R. (1968). Introduction to English version. In R. Saleilles (Ed.), *The individualization of punishment*. Montclair, NJ: Patterson Smith. (Original work published 1911).

Quen, J. M. (1989). Insane criminals and the criminally insane: A persistent problem for psychiatry, law and society. In R. Rosner & R. Harmon (Eds.), *Correctional Psychiatry* (pp. 3–16). New York: Plenum Press.

Ouinsey, V. L. (1988). Assessment of the treatability of forensic patients. *Behavioral Sciences & the Law, 6*, 443–452.

Raine, A. (1993). *The psychopathology of crime: Criminal behavior as a clinical disorder*. San Diego, CA: Academic Press.

Ray, I. (1838). *Treatise on the medical jurisprudence of insanity*. Boston: Charles C. Little and James Brown.

Reckless, W. C. (1973). *The crime problem* (5th ed.). New York: Appleton-Century-Crofts.

Reid, W. H. (1998). Antisocial character and behavior: Threats and solutions. In T. Millon, E. Simonsen, M. Birket-Smith, & R. D. Davis (Eds.), *Psychopathy: Antisocial, criminal, and violent behavior* (pp. 110–121). New York: Guilford Press.

Robertson, J. A. (1972). Pretrial diversion of drug offenders: A statutory approach. *Boston University Law Review, 52*, 335–371.

Robinson, D. N. (1996). *Wild beasts & idle humours: The insanity defense from antiquity to the present*. Cambridge, MA: Harvard University Press.

Rogers, R. (1988). Treatability and treatment outcome. *Behavioral Sciences & the Law, 6*, 441–442.

Saleilles, R. (1968). *The individualization of punishment*. Montclair, NJ: Patterson Smith.

Schopp, R. F. (1995). Sexual predators and the structure of the mental health system: Expanding the normative focus of therapeutic jurisprudence. *Psychology, Public Policy, and Law, 1*, 161–192.

Scott, E. S., & Grisso, T. (1997). The evolution of adolescence: A developmental perspective on juvenile justice reform. *Journal of Criminal Law and Criminology, 88*, 137–189.

Sechrest, L., White, S. O., & Brown, E. D. (1979). *The rehabilitation of criminal offenders: Problems and prospects*. Washington, D.C: National Academy of Sciences.

Sedgwick, P. (1982). Antipsychiatry from the sixties to the eighties. In W. R. Grove (Ed.), *Deviance and mental illness* (pp. 199–233). Beverly Hill, CA: Sage.

Shorter, E. (1997). *A history of psychiatry: From the era of the asylum to the age of Prozac*. New York: John Wiley & Sons.

Sperry, L., Brill, P. L., Howard, K. I., & Grisson, G. R. (1996). *Treatment outcomes in psychotherapy and psychiatric interventions*. New York: Brunner/Mazel.

Swisher, T. R. (1978). *Sentencing in Ohio*. Columbus: Ohio State Bar Foundation.

State ex rel. Pearson v. Probate Court. (1939). 287 N.W. 297, 302–303 (Minn.).

Stone, A. A. (1982). Psychiatric abuse and legal reform: Two ways to make a bad situation worse. *International Journal of Law and Psychiatry, 5*, 9–28.

Sutherland, E. H. (1950). The diffusion of sexual psychopath laws. *American Journal of Sociology, 56*, 142–148.

Swisher, T. R. (1978). *Sentencing in Ohio*. Columbus: Ohio State Bar Foundation.

Szasz, T. (1960). The myth of mental illness. *American Psychologists, 15*, 113–118.

Uelmen, G. F., & V. G. Haddox. (1983). *Drug abuse and the law*. New York: Clark Boardman.

Van Voorhis, P. (1994). *Psychological classification of the adult male prison inmate*. Albany: State University of New York Press.

Walker, N. (1968). *Crime and insanity in England* (Vol. 1). Edinburgh: Edinburgh University Press.

Walker, N., & McCabe, S. (1973). *Crime and insanity in England: New solutions new problems* (Vol. 2). Edinburgh: Edinburgh University Press.

WASH. REV. CODE ANN. (1990). § 71,09.010 (West).

Wettstein, R. M. (1992). A psychiatric perspective on Washington's sexually violent predators statute. *University of Puget Sound Law Review*, *15*, 597–653.

Whitehead, J. T., & Lab, S. P. (1989). A meta-analysis of juvenile correctional treatment. *Journal of Research in Crime and Delinquency*, *26*, 276–295.

Wilson, J. Q. (1997). *Moral judgment*. New York: Basic Books.

Wing, J. K. (1990). Defining need and evaluating services. In W. Watson & A. Grounds (Eds.), *The mentally u。。 :.'.ᵣed offender in an era of community care: New directions in provisions* (pp. 90–101). Cambridge: Cambridge University Press.

Winick, B. J., & La Fond, J. Q. (Eds.). (1998). Sex offenders: Scientific, legal and policy perspectives. A special issue of *Psychology, Public Policy, and Law*, *4*(1–2).

Wolf, J. R. L. M. (1997). Client needs and quality of life. *Psychiatric Rehabilitation Journal*, *20*, 16–24.

World Health Organization. (1998). *International Classification of Diseases, 9th Revision, Clinical Modification International Classification of Diseases*. Geneva: Author.

Youth Correction Act. (1950). 18 U.S.C. §§ 5005–5026.

Zola, I. K. (1981). Medicine as an institution of social control. In P. Conrad & R. Kern (Eds.), *The sociology of health and illness* (pp. 509–527). New York: St. Martin's.

Chapter 2
TREATMENT RIGHTS IN UNCERTAIN LEGAL TIMES

Craig Haney and Donald Specter

In this chapter we address what has become a challenging area of law—the standards that govern the treatment of "special needs" of vulnerable criminal offenders. The challenging nature of the topic stems largely from the fact that applicable legal doctrines are often contradictory and operate at cross-purposes with one another. These core contradictions are simple to articulate but difficult to resolve. On the one hand, the special needs of offenders ostensibly entitle them to enhanced services and treatment while incarcerated. These same needs also make the prisoners uniquely vulnerable to the potential pains of incarceration that, in turn, theoretically afford them greater claim to special protections. On the other hand, in a political climate in which correctional agencies focus more on delivering punishment than providing services, these claims can take on problematic significance. Special needs and heightened vulnerability may mean that offenders are less able to conform their conduct to the requirements of the institution, resulting in their exclusion from already limited programs and subjecting them to increased punishment. Rather than more treatment, they may get less than other offenders and little of what they need.

Another contradiction affecting offenders with special needs is that contemporary criminal justice thinking still emphasizes punishment over rehabilitation, and there are now reduced overall levels of services and programs available for offenders in general (e.g., Haney, 1997a; Haney & Zimbardo, 1998). In times like these, mandates for more specialized treatment and heightened levels of protection may come at the expense of other things, like procedural fairness and overall conditions of confinement. Similarly, the tension between the presumed autonomy of offenders—who are autonomous enough to be punished for their criminal law transgressions—and the vulnerability of some offenders that derives from their "special needs" is difficult to resolve. Moreover, whenever the vulnerabilities of offenders not only create special needs but also seemingly undermine their capacity to make important life decisions, a different set of legal issues comes into play. The legal mandate to protect persons from certain kinds of unwanted, intrusive state intervention is severely tested in the case of vulnerable offenders. Constitutional requirements to follow proper procedures before persons can be compelled to submit to certain kinds of treatment —even when they are administered allegedly "for their own good," or for the protection of others—apply in varying degrees for special needs offenders. Properly balancing respect for personal autonomy against the state's responsibility to make informed decisions for those who appear unable to do so for themselves has proven an elusive endeavor (e.g., Bersoff, 1992).

The special needs of offenders must also be understood in terms of the context of their confinement. That is, the unique characteristics of penal institutions help to shape the nature and extent of inmate vulnerability. For one, many correctional environments are dangerous places. Prisoners regularly confront the risk of attack from other prisoners and, in some instances, mistreatment at the hands of correctional staff. Those who are perceived as weak or break the inmate code generally are more at risk of assault from other prisoners. In addition, prisoners must depend on the correctional staff for their well-being and, indeed, their survival. If the prison does not provide food, prisoners will starve; if it does not afford them the means with which to clean their cells and maintain personal hygiene, they will live in filth; if medical care is delayed too long, they may die. In some cases, danger and dependency interact, as when prisoners depend on correctional officers to protect them from harm by other prisoners or other staff.

Indeed, this combination of dependency and vulnerability appears to resonate with some courts having oversight responsibilities for the institutions in which special needs offenders are housed. For example, as we will note in more detail later in this chapter, although the current U.S. Supreme Court has been generally unsympathetic to the rights of prisoners in general (Haney, 1997a), it has been somewhat more responsive to the plight of those with special needs. Thus, in *Farmer v. Brennan* (1994) a transsexual complained that prison officials failed to take any action to protect him from a sexual assault, even though he had notified prison officials that he was at risk. The Court agreed that the failure of prison officials to protect this person from assault was cruel and unusual punishment and, therefore, unconstitutional: "Having stripped them of virtually every means of self-protection and foreclosed their access to outside aid, the government and its officials are not free to let the state of nature take its course" (p. 833).

In *Farmer*, protection from physical assault was at issue. But dependency and vulnerability may coalesce even more clearly when an inmate's right to medical or mental health care is at issue. Anyone with a serious medical condition is, by definition, vulnerable. However, unlike most others in society, inmates have no independent ability to obtain medical care—making them uniquely at risk.[1] This combination of dependency and vulnerability is present to the same degree when a mental condition causes the impairment. A prisoner who is suicidal, for example, is vulnerable to a form of potentially lethal harm and, in many cases, is dependent on guards and mental health workers to provide the treatment and support necessary for him to stay alive.

Courts and legislatures have addressed these and related concerns by developing legal standards of care and treatment that must be adhered to in a variety of correctional settings. Persons like mental health professionals charged with the responsibility of administering to the needs of vulnerable offenders should be knowledgeable about these standards and the contexts in which they have been applied—both because legal standards represent one set of statements about minimally adequate, humane treatment and also because prison personnel are legally responsible for upholding them. In this chapter, we will concentrate primarily on the legal status of two groups of "special needs" offenders—the mentally ill and developmentally disabled—because they are the largest such groups (cf. Veneziano, Veneziano, & Tribolet, 1987; Veneziano & Veneziano, 1996). We will, however, review legal doctrines that provide protection to other groups of special needs offenders.

---

[1] Indeed, in some prison systems a prisoner who has the resources to obtain access to his own physician does not have the right to the treatment ordered by that physician. (For example, see 15 CAL. CODE REG. § 3354.) The California Department of Corrections justified this position by noting that it has the sole legal responsibility to provide adequate care.

Legal Protections for "Special Needs" Offenders

One of the major sources of legal protection for special needs offenders is the United States Constitution. Primarily through the Eighth Amendment, which bans "cruel and unusual punishment," the Constitution serves indirectly to set minimum standards of care by prohibiting treatment and conditions of confinement that offend "evolving standards of decency." Such protection typically is initiated through the process of litigation. That is, someone sues on behalf of special needs offenders alleging that the lack of care they have been afforded in the prison has violated their constitutional rights. Because many provisions of the Constitution are broadly written to convey abstract principles that are difficult to apply in specific cases, the exact meaning of the provisions themselves must come from the courts and, ultimately, from the United States Supreme Court. Courts are also called upon to render decisions about whether the provisions themselves have been violated in a specific case. In this section we will review a number of constitutional provisions that have been applied to special needs offenders, and pay particular attention to the interpretation they have been given by the Supreme Court.

Historical Context

For a brief period in the recent history of constitutional law—primarily the 1960s and 1970s—the Constitution was used on an increasingly widespread basis as a powerful tool to promote decent prison conditions and humane treatment. However, when the Supreme Court declared in a 1981 case that "the Constitution does not mandate comfortable prisons" (*Rhodes v. Chapman*, 1981, p. 349), it seemed to signal the beginning of the end of that era. The case focused on the decision of prison officials to put two prisoners in cells built for one—a practice known as "double-celling." In retrospect, the fact that the Court approved this practice seems neither extraordinary nor unexpected. However, by characterizing constitutional challenges like this as disputes over "comfortable prisons," the Court sent a broader message that would become clearer in subsequent cases: the Justices were relatively unsympathetic to these kinds of claims and would take a narrow view of "evolving standards of decency" in prison litigation.

Indeed, eventually the Court would make clear its view that *any* prison condition was tolerable as long as it did not, by itself or in combination with other conditions, create a significant risk of serious harm to prisoners (*Helling v. McKinney*, 1993). And even some actions by guards that directly caused serious injury to prisoners (such as the use of excessive force) would be deemed acceptable as long as they could be justified in the name of prison security (*Hudson v. McMillian*, 1992; *Whitley v. Albers*, 1986). Under the narrowest reading of the Court's current view of these issues, prison officials are responsible only for providing the basic necessities of life (food, shelter, medical care, personal safety). Indeed, even the deprivation of these things will not be found to violate the Constitution unless it can be proven that prison officials actually knew that the conditions they created or maintained were substandard and recklessly disregarded the risks to prisoners (e.g., *Farmer v. Brennan*, 1994).

By narrowing the set of valid constitutional claims to those that create a significant risk or actually cause serious harm, the Supreme Court indirectly—and likely inadvertently—shifted some of the focus away from the "typical" to the "vulnerable" prisoner (i.e. to those groups that are most at risk for serious harm). Vulnerable prisoners, by definition, are more likely to be harmed, the harm to them is more likely to be serious, and their injury generally will be easier to prove. Below we discuss some of the most important constitutional principles that are applied to this population of special needs offenders and some of the cases in which they have been articulated.[2]

"Deliberate Indifference" and the Applicable Standard of Care

One of the landmark Supreme Court decisions establishing the legal rights of vulnerable prisoners—*Estelle v. Gamble* (1976)—provides a useful starting point for our discussion. Prisoner J. W. Gamble suffered a back injury while engaged in a prison work assignment. He also had high blood pressure and a heart problem. Gamble complained that his constitutional rights had been violated in part because prison medical staff failed to perform adequate diagnostic tests to determine the extent of his condition. In deciding his claim, the Supreme Court acknowledged that the government has an "obligation to provide medical care for those whom it is punishing by incarceration," and that an inmate "must rely on prison authorities to treat his medical needs; if the authorities fail to do so, those needs will not be met" (p. 103). Thus when prison officials fail to act reasonably in response to a serious medical problem that is brought to their attention they may be liable under the law.

However, the Court also reasoned that although the Eighth Amendment required authorities to provide necessary medical care, there needed to be limits to the nature and level of the care that was mandated. For example, claims of malpractice or "merely" inadequate medical care should not be elevated to the level of a constitutional violation just because the victim was a prisoner. Thus the Court concluded in *Gamble* that inadvertence, oversight, or other forms of mere malpractice did not represent constitutional violations *unless* the actions of prison personnel manifested "*deliberate indifference* to serious medical needs" (p. 104) of prisoners that resulted in the infliction of unnecessary suffering.

In addition to its significance as legal doctrine, the *Gamble* opinion is useful for another reason—its illustration of how different views of the factual record can significantly shape the legal outcome of a case. On the face of it, the Supreme Court's view—that the prison had not been "indifferent" to Gamble's medical needs—seemed amply supported. Gamble had been seen 17 times by prison doctors or other prison medical personnel over a three-month period and the majority opinion concluded that it was "apparent" from Gamble's complaint "that he received extensive medical care and that the doctors were not indifferent to his needs" (p. 108, n. 16). However, Justice Stevens disagreed with this view of the matter and filed a separate, dissenting opinion in which he surfaced several other facts that the majority had omitted, including the following:

---

[2]In this chapter we will concentrate primarily on U.S. Supreme Court cases establishing constitutional minimum standards of care and federal legislation affecting the greatest number of special needs cases. Additional state laws and specific administrative procedures that apply to special needs offenders may vary somewhat from jurisdiction to jurisdiction across the country, making any chapter-length encapsulation impossible.

Gamble was placed in solitary confinement for prolonged periods as punishment for refusing to perform assigned work which he was physically unable to perform. . . . The only medical evidence presented to the disciplinary committee was the statement of a medical assistant that he was in first-class condition, when in fact he was suffering not only from the back sprain but also from high blood pressure. . . . Prison guards refused to permit him to sleep in the bunk that a doctor had assigned. . . . [And] when he suffered chest pains and blackouts while in solitary, he was forced to wait 12 hours to see a doctor because clearance had to be obtained from the warden. (pp. 109–110)

Justice Stevens also wondered whether "an overworked, undermanned medical staff in a crowded prison is following the expedient course of routinely prescribing nothing more than pain killers when a thorough diagnosis would disclose an obvious need for remedial treatment" (p. 110, footnote omitted). He worried that "by its repeated references to 'deliberate indifference' and the 'intentional' denial of adequate medical care, I believe the Court improperly attaches significance to the subjective motivation of the [prison official] as a criterion for determining whether cruel and unusual punishment has been inflicted" (p. 116, footnote omitted). Indeed, he argued that "whether the constitutional standard has been violated should turn on the character of the punishment rather than the motivation of the individual who inflicted it" (p. 116).

Even though the Supreme Court in *Gamble* had recognized that prisoners retained the right to adequate medical care, it still afforded prison health care providers a degree of legal protection unparalleled in any other context. By ruling that prison officials are liable only if they are "deliberately indifferent" to serious medical needs, the majority found that negligence—the standard commonly used to judge medical malpractice—was too generous in this context.[3] In other words, a mere mistake in diagnosis or treatment (negligence) was not enough for a prisoner–patient to prevail. The prisoner must prove that prison guards or doctors knew about a serious problem and failed to take any reasonable action in response. A reasonable response, even if ultimately incorrect, may protect prison officials from being held liable for constitutional violations.

One final note on *Gamble*'s applicability to mental health care. Although in theory legal protections for mental conditions are the equivalent of those for physical conditions, in practice the courts have been somewhat more reluctant to rule that the failure to provide treatment for a prisoner's mental health represents a constitutional violation. In part this reluctance may stem from a perceived difficulty in proving that the absence of treatment caused the injury (e.g., *Farmer v. Brennan*, 1994). Alternatively, some courts may be skeptical of psychological science and frankly doubt whether uniform standards of care can be articulated. For example, one federal district court made such skepticism explicit in ruling on a claim that two Oregon correctional institutions lacked appropriate psychiatric care (*Capps v. Atiyeh*, 1982). Here the judge suggested that because so much was unknown about mental illness, the courts should be especially deferential to the judgments of mental health professionals. That is, the judge concluded that the Constitution required only that courts "make certain that professional judgment in fact was exercised" but it did not require

---

[3]However, in many states prisoners can sue for medical malpractice under state law and avoid the deliberate indifference standard. In California, for example, the state waives its immunity from suit for medical malpractice claims brought by prisoners, but not for most other torts.

them to "specify which of several professionally acceptable choices should have been made" (p. 917). This court articulated a high standard of proof that would need to be met to demonstrate that the appropriate professional judgment had been lacking:

> The inmates must, therefore, show a pattern of cases, each of which discloses, with little or no room for reasonable mental medical opinions to differ, (1) serious mental illness (2) for which the inmate wants treatment (3) which he does not receive (4) thereby causing the inmate to suffer mental pain. (pp. 917–918)

Not surprisingly, given this high legal threshold, the judge found that the mental health care at the correctional institutions in question met the constitutionally required standard even though it was "grievously minimal," afforded prisoners only infrequent contact with treatment staff, and lacked any articulated treatment plans.

Raising the Deliberate Indifference Threshold

Over the past decade, the Supreme Court has issued a series of rulings that have constricted the constitutional rights of prisoners including, in some instances, those with special needs (Haney, 1997a). Several of these decisions involved applying the "deliberate indifference" standard that had been developed in *Gamble* and other cases involving a failure to provide medical treatment. In 1991, the Court used this standard to resolve what is called a "conditions of confinement" claim (*Wilson v. Seiter*, 1991), one focusing on the totality of the prison conditions under which prisoners are forced to live. In this case, Ohio prisoners challenged the overcrowding, high levels of noise, and unsanitary living conditions at the penitentiary where they were confined, as well as the fact that they were housed with mentally and physically ill prisoners. To decide this case the Court ruled that Eighth Amendment claims concerning conduct that did not purport to be punishment required an inquiry into prison officials' *state of mind*—in this case, their "deliberate indifference."

However, in the course of applying this standard the Court also cautioned lower courts to focus less on the effects of the treatment on the prisoner and more on "the constraints facing the official" involved (p. 303). This part of the opinion raised concerns among prisoners' rights advocates that otherwise inhumane living conditions might be defended on the grounds that prison officials simply lacked the resources with which to remedy the problems of which they were aware. It raised a parallel set of concerns that instances of deliberate indifference might be dismissed in the same way—on the basis of limited resources or other constraints faced by caregivers rather than the negative consequences for special needs offenders.

A few years later, the Court again clarified and narrowed the definition of "deliberate indifference" (*Farmer v. Brennan*, 1994). The Court restated its previous position that an Eighth Amendment violation must be based on an objectively serious deprivation that results in denying "the minimal civilized measure of life's necessities" (p. 834, citing to *Rhodes*). In the case of failure to prevent harm, there must be a substantial risk of *serious* harm to the prisoner. But the Court also restated the second, subjective prong of the Eighth Amendment test that requires an inquiry into the state of mind of prison officials. It did so in a way that defined deliberate indifference more precisely but also more narrowly. The Court said specifically that a prison official "must both be aware of facts from which an inference could be drawn that substantial risk of serious harm exists, and he must also draw that inference" (p. 837). Thus the mere fact that officials *should have* perceived the risk but did not, "while no cause for commendation" (p. 838), would not mean that the officials were liable under the Eighth Amendment.

In response to this decision, many commentators complained that the Supreme Court had gone too far and could be perceived as having embraced the criminal law concept of "subjective recklessness"—namely, that one would first have to find that "prison officials acted like criminals" before finding them liable for their deliberate indifference. The Court seemed to have anticipated this criticism and simply dismissed it as "misplaced." Indeed, the *Farmer* opinion asserted that "subjective recklessness as used in the criminal law is a familiar and workable standard" to serve as the measure of an Eighth Amendment violation (*Farmer v. Brennan*, 1994, p. 839). In practice, however, most lower courts have used *Farmer* simply to support the view that actual knowledge of a risk is required and that, if prison officials acted "reasonably" in response to that actually known risk, then there is no liability.

"Professional Judgments" Affecting Vulnerable Offenders

Another line of Supreme Court cases speaks to the legal standards that are applied when medical and mental health professionals—rather than correctional officials—make judgments that directly affect the well-being of special needs offenders. In *Youngberg v. Romeo* (1982), the Supreme Court decided a case brought by the mother of a profoundly mentally retarded young man, Nicholas Romeo, who had been involuntarily admitted into a state institution. At issue were the nature and scope of the rights to be afforded persons over whom the state assumed such institutional control. When Romeo's mother learned of injuries her son had suffered at the institution, she became concerned about the quality of his treatment and the level of safety provided during his confinement. She sued to improve them. The Supreme Court ruled that persons in Romeo's position had constitutionally protected interests to be housed in reasonably safe conditions of confinement, to be free from unreasonable bodily restraints, and to receive minimally adequate training. The rights were said to be "liberty interests" in this case—ones designed to further a patient's constitutional right to a degree of freedom that was compatible with his treatment. The Court required that right to be balanced against "relevant state interests" through an inquiry primarily into whether "professional judgment" had been exercised in constricting Romeo's freedom.

Indeed, the Court made it very clear that it was not eager to second guess such judgments:

> The decision, if made by a professional, is presumptively valid; liability may be imposed only when the decision by the professional is such a substantial departure from accepted professional judgment, practice, or standards as to demonstrate that the person responsible actually did not base the decision on such a judgment. (p. 323, footnotes omitted)[4]

---

[4]By "professional" the Court meant "a person competent, whether by education, training or experience, to make the particular decision at issue" (p. 323, footnote 30).

In part, this "presumption of correctness" was extended apparently to allow such state institutions—ones that the Court noted are "unfortunately, overcrowded and understaffed" (p. 324)—to continue to function. That is, because "a single professional may have to make decisions with respect to a number of residents with widely varying needs and problems in the course of a normal day" inside a state institution, he or she "should not be required to make each decision in the shadow of an action for damages" (p. 324).

In addition to establishing such a strong presumption of correctness for professional decision makers, the Court in *Youngberg* made another distinction that had potentially ominous implications for special needs offenders confined in correctional institutions. The Justices noted that persons such as Romeo who had been involuntarily committed under civil law provisions were "entitled to more considerate treatment and conditions of confinement than criminals whose conditions of confinement are designed to punish" (p. 322). Affording even broader deference to correctional decision makers creates the potential for conflict between the kind of "appropriate professional" whose judgment was endorsed in *Youngberg* and the decisions of custody-oriented correctional staff who may lack any professional training and experience with special needs offenders. This is especially problematic in light of the marginalization of mental health professionals that has taken place in many correctional settings over the past several decades (Haney, 1997a). In too many instances, their professional judgment has not only been discounted by custodial staff but also simply ignored or considered irrelevant.

On the other hand, one aspect of the *Youngberg* opinion had potentially beneficial implications for right-to-treatment arguments in correctional contexts. The Supreme Court had found the right to training or "habilitation" the most difficult to grant. But it linked this right to the others in a thoughtful and important way, noting that

> the State is under a duty to provide respondent with such training as an appropriate professional would consider reasonable to ensure his safety and to facilitate his ability to function free from bodily restraints. It may well be unreasonable not to provide training when training could significantly reduce the need for restraints or the likelihood of violence. (p. 324)

The same logic would seem to apply to correctional settings where the treatment of special needs offenders may be (a) essential to their effective participation in prison programs (which may be directly related to their short- and long-term liberty interests), (b) necessary to keep them out of punitive segregation (thereby avoiding unnecessary restraints), and (c) helpful in minimizing their involvement in and vulnerability to prison violence.[5]

Too Much Treatment?: The Right to Refuse

One tension in the standards governing the treatment of vulnerable offenders concerns allegedly invasive and abusive therapy administered in criminal justice settings. Critics of mental health care in jails and prisons often argue that as many professional

---

[5]Cf. Cohen & Dvoskin (1992), who list among the overriding reasons for mental health treatment in correctional settings "maximiz[ing] each inmate's ability to participate in rehabilitative programs within the prison" and "to help keep the prison safer for staff, inmates, volunteers, and visitors" (p. 462).

sins have been committed in the name of treatment as in cases in which treatment has been withheld (e.g., Kittrie, 1973; Stefan, 1992) The Due Process Clause of the U.S. Constitution provides all citizens—including special needs offenders—with the right to some degree of procedural protection in instances in which the state acts to limit their freedoms or invade their protected sphere of personal autonomy. Thus in addition to not getting what they need, vulnerable offenders are sometimes at risk of being compromised or harmed by too much therapeutic intervention, delivered in a form that is unwanted or counterproductive. Legal analyses of standard-of-care issues thus must include consideration of the procedural mechanisms by which certain kinds of treatment can be declined or refused.

The Supreme Court first examined the right of a prisoner to refuse mental health treatment in a pre-*Youngberg* case. Larry Jones was serving a prison term in a Nebraska correctional facility when he was transferred to a mental hospital. He challenged the transfer, arguing that inadequate procedures had been used in the decision-making process by which he was moved. In *Vitek v. Jones* (1980) the Court essentially agreed. It noted first that even prisoners retained a limited liberty interest in which "a major change in the conditions of confinement.... should not be imposed without the opportunity for notice and an adequate hearing" (p. 488). The Court also concluded that the prison's decision to characterize Jones as a mentally ill patient and transfer him to a mental hospital had "some stigmatizing" consequences. When "coupled with the subjection of the prisoner to involuntary behavior modification as a treatment for mental illness" (p. 494), the changed living conditions and accompanying stigma meant that the prison should be required to provide Jones with access to some kind of formal procedure through which he could challenge and perhaps avoid his transfer.

In Due Process Clause cases like this, once the courts have identified an interest or right that requires procedural protection they still must decide what kind of process is due (that is, the specific nature of the procedures needed to protect the interest at stake). In the *Vitek* case, the Court was not persuaded that the Nebraska law under which Jones was transferred had afforded him adequate procedural protection. Nebraska allowed such transfers merely on the finding by a designated physician or psychologist that the prisoner " 'suffers from a mental disease or defect' and 'cannot be given proper treatment in that facility' " (p. 483). The Court concluded that prisoners like Jones were entitled to more. It required (a) prior written notification that the transfer was being considered, (b) sufficient time to prepare for a hearing, (c) "competent help" or assistance at the hearing, (d) the opportunity to present witnesses and cross-examine those testifying against the prisoner, and (e) that the final decision be made by an independent decision maker, (f) who stated in writing his or her factual findings and reasons for ordering the transfer.[6] However, the Court

---

[6]Four of the Justices in the majority agreed that

> A prisoner thought to be suffering from a mental disease or defect requiring involuntary treatment probably has an even greater need for legal assistance, for such a prisoner is more likely to be unable to understand or exercise his rights. In these circumstances, it is appropriate that counsel be provided to indigent prisoners whom the State seeks to treat as mentally ill. (pp. 496–497)

Although Justice Powell agreed that it "is unlikely that an inmate threatened with involuntary transfer to mental hospitals" would know how to adequately protect his own interests and observed that "the

also made it clear that to avoid "unnecessary intrusion into either medical or correctional judgments," the independent decision maker "need not come from outside the prison or hospital administration" (p. 496).

Ten years later, and long after *Youngberg*'s (1982) professional-judgment standard had been articulated, the Court revisited a related issue and clarified another aspect of an inmate's right to refuse treatment. In *Washington v. Harper* (1990)—a case in which the American Psychiatric Association sided with the majority opinion and the American Psychological Association urged the opposite view—the Court set out the procedural protections required for state prisoners challenging the involuntary administration of psychotropic drugs. Overturning a Washington Supreme Court opinion that gave such prisoners the right to a judicial hearing, the U.S. Supreme Court noted that the "extent of a prisoner's right under the [Due Process Clause] to avoid the unwanted administration of antipsychotic drugs must be defined in the context of the inmate's confinement" (p. 222).

Youngberg's deferential stance to the judgments of professionals was apparent throughout the *Harper* opinion. The Court refused to question the motives of those administering the drugs: "We will not assume that physicians will prescribe these drugs for reasons unrelated to the medical needs of the patients; indeed, the ethics of the medical profession are to the contrary" (p. 223, n. 8). The Court reiterated its own often expressed view that "prison authorities are best equipped to make difficult decisions regarding prison administration" (pp. 223–224).[7] Moreover, in facilitating the forcible administration of drugs, the opinion weighed heavily the state's interest in ensuring the safety of correctional officers, administrative staff, and prisoners themselves:

> Where an inmate's mental disability is the root cause of the threat he poses to the inmate population, the State's interest in decreasing the danger to others necessarily encompasses an interest in providing him with medical treatment for his illness. (pp. 225–226)

With these issues in mind, the Court ruled that "given the requirements of the prison environment, the Due Process Clause permits the State to treat a prison inmate who has a serious mental illness with antipsychotic drugs against his will, if the inmate is dangerous to himself or others and the treatment is in the inmate's medical interest" (p. 227).[8] Moreover, rejecting "the notion that the shortcomings of spe-

---

circumstances of being imprisoned without normal access to others who may assist him places an additional handicap upon an inmate's ability to represent himself" (p. 498). he balked at the requirement that "independent assistance demands that a licensed attorney be provided" (p. 497). Thus the majority opinion in *Vitek* held only that prisoners be provided "competent help" in their pretransfer hearings.

[7]Later in the opinion the Court emphasized the "deference that is owed to medical professionals who have the full-time responsibility of caring for mentally ill inmates like respondent and who possess, as courts do not, the requisite knowledge and expertise to determine whether the drugs should be used in an individual case" (p. 230, n. 12).

[8]Justice Stevens, joined by Brennan and Marshall, disagreed with the majority view. In their dissenting opinion they observed that although the current policy required "a medical judgment as to a prisoner's mental condition and the cause of his behavior," it did *not* "require a determination that forced medication would advance his medical interest" (p. 244). Rather, they suggested, the primary purpose of forcibly administering psychotropic drugs was "to ease the institutional and administrative burdens of maintaining prison security and [to provide] a means of managing an unruly prison population and

cialists can always be avoided by shifting the decision from a trained specialist using the traditional tools of medical science to an untrained judge or administrative hearing officer" (p. 232), the Court concluded that these findings could be made internally by the appropriate prison officials. A judicial hearing was not required.

Finally, a separate but related set of involuntary treatment issues stem from the so-called sexual predator laws enacted by about a dozen states beginning in the early 1990s. These statutes seemed to many observers to blur the distinction between criminal laws that provide for specific punishments in response to specific criminal offenses, and civil laws that are designed to further a range of other public purposes but generally not through means of punishment. The sexual predator statutes provide that persons who have been convicted of a violent sex offense[9] can be incarcerated *beyond* the completion of their prison sentences if they are adjudged to suffer from a "mental abnormality" or "personality disorder" that predisposes them to "predatory acts of sexual violence."[10] Critics argued that the statutes subjected persons to a kind of double jeopardy—allowing them to be punished a second time, *after* they had already served their designated prison sentences. Moreover, the states that enacted these laws were often ambivalent about the issue of treatment. That is, they rarely provided any sex offender therapy during the term of imprisonment, and in some instances actually suggested that sexual predators were untreatable. Yet the same states later incarcerated these offenders under allegedly "nonpunitive" civil laws for the ostensible purpose of providing treatment until they were no longer a danger.

The status of the newly enacted sexual predator laws was resolved in part by the Supreme Court in a narrow 5 to 4 decision in *Kansas v. Hendricks* (1997). The Court rejected the notion that the nature and potentially indefinite duration of the confinement provided under the Kansas statute reflected a punitive intent: "Far from any punitive objective, the confinement's duration is instead linked to the stated purposes of the commitment, namely, to hold the person until his mental abnormality no longer causes him to be a threat to others" (p. 2083). The Court's opinion left unclear the issue of how exactly that threat might be abated, because it also made light of the fact that little or no treatment was apparently being provided for persons

---

preventing property damage" (pp. 244–245). And they noted further that the use of psychotropic drugs "simply to suppress an inmate's potential violence, rather than to achieve therapeutic results," as appeared to be the goal in inmate Harper's case, "may also undermine the efficacy of other available treatment programs that would better address his illness" (pp. 248–249). Such drugs may do little more than "reduce an inmate's dangerousness, not by improving his mental condition, but simply by sedating him with a medication that is grossly excessive for that purpose" (p. 249, n. 17). However, it appeared that the medication may not have been effective for even the limited purpose of controlling inmate Harper. Indeed, much of his subsequent violence may have been precipitated by his resistance to taking the drugs themselves. See p. 249, nn. 16 & 17.

[9]Under the terms of the Washington state sexual predator law, for example, "sexually violent offenses" include not only rape, rape of a child, and child molestation, but also offenses like murder, assault, kidnapping, and burglary, when the offenses are determined to have been "sexually motivated." WASH. REV. CODE § 71.09.020(4).

[10]One federal judge found the use of these terms in the Washington statute to be deliberately vague, unenlightening, and circular. He invalidated the law on the basis that it essentially allowed indefinite confinement on the basis of future dangerousness and nothing more: "Predictions of dangerousness alone are an insufficient basis to continue indefinitely the incarceration of offenders who have completed their prison terms" (*Young v. Weston*, 1995, p. 751).

the state was now authorized to hold. In fact, the opinion suggested that "treatment is not possible for this category of individuals" (p. 2084).

Justice Breyer disagreed with this reading of the psychiatric literature on the treatment of sex offenders. He and several other Justices dissented in *Hendricks*, arguing that there was evidence that sexual predators could benefit from therapy and also that the state had conceded as much. However, persons confined under Kansas's sexual predator law typically did not receive "any treatment until after [their] release date from prison and only inadequate treatment thereafter" (p. 2088). Indeed, the *Hendricks* dissenters contended that "when a State decides offenders can be treated and confines an offender to provide that treatment, but then refuses to provide it, the refusal to treat while a person is fully incapacitated begins to look punitive" (p. 2096).

Several issues were left unresolved in *Hendricks*. The Court was ambiguous about the exact conditions under which civilly committed sex offenders could be kept while under presumably "nonpunitive" confinement. For example, in Washington state persons committed under the sexual predator statute are confined in a facility that occupies part of a medium-security prison. The "residents" of this unit are not only subject to the rules and regulations of the Department of Corrections but are afforded *less* freedom and fewer privileges than the prisoners. Thus they are not permitted to move unescorted through the prison; they are denied access to work, education, and vocational training programs; and they are precluded from conjugal visiting—all things to which the prisoners at the facility are entitled. It is possible for a prisoner to serve out his entire prison sentence at this medium security prison and then to be retained under the sexual predator law as a civilly committed "resident" at the very same institution. If so, he would find that, once having "paid his debt to society" and become a resident in the special program there, he would be subjected to reduced freedoms and significantly worse conditions of confinement (*Turay v. Seling*, 1998). This kind of anomaly in the application of these laws— along with the vexing question of the nature of the treatment persons confined as sexual predators should receive—are likely to be clarified and modified in the course of subsequent litigation.[11]

---

[11]The tensions that plague this area of law are illustrated in the decision of one federal appellate court. *Neal v. Shimoda* (1997), involved a Hawaii statute requiring that even prisoners who had been accused but never convicted "of sexual misconduct in the course of an offense" needed to complete a 25-session sex offender treatment program before becoming eligible for parole. However, an offender's admission into the program was made contingent on signing a statement to the effect that he "admits and takes full responsibility" for the sexual offenses with which he had been charged. Although the Ninth Circuit left that provision intact, the panel used *Vitek* as the basis for clarifying several preliminary procedural issues. Thus, before being classified as sex offenders for purposes of the required treatment program, prisoners were entitled to notice, a hearing in which they could call witnesses and present documentary evidence in their defense, and were entitled to receive a written summary of the evidence relied on by the fact finders and the reasons for the actions taken. The two-judge majority also wrote

> Besides simply punishing offenders, Hawaii has attempted to address the causes of the behavioral deviance exhibited by its inmates in the laudable hope that these criminals will not engage in further criminal activity once they are released from custody. But any correctional treatment program administered by the State must comply with the mandates of the Constitution. (p. 833)

On the other hand, the dissenting Judge in *Neal* was concerned with the fact that "prison officials select individuals based solely on their past acts, not their current mental or behavioral condition" (p. 835). He would have invalidated the law on the basis of the purely retrospective nature of this inquiry. For a thoughtful discussion of these and related issues, see Wettstein (1992).

Statutory Provisions Directly Affecting Special Needs Inmates

The decisions of the U.S. Supreme Court and the other federal courts reviewed previously establish constitutionally required minimum standards of treatment and care. State and federal government institutions—and the officials and employees working for them—cannot lawfully provide special needs offenders with treatment and care that fall below these basic standards. However, Congress and state legislatures also can pass laws that *expand* the rights of institutionalized persons. They can also enact legislation that affects the procedures by which these rights are implemented—and do so in ways that may make enforcement of constitutional protections easier or more difficult.

Civil Rights of Institutionalized Persons Act

In 1980, Congress passed the Civil Rights of Institutionalized Persons Act (CRIPA), which gave legislative authority for the U.S. Department of Justice (DOJ) to safeguard the constitutional rights of persons confined in state institutions, including prisons. The law gave the U.S. attorney general the power to sue in cases of "egregious or flagrant conditions which deprive persons of any right, privilege or immunity secured or protected by the Constitution or laws of the United States" (42 U.S.C. § 1997).

CRIPA represented a significant advance in the effort to safeguard the rights of special needs prisoners. Indeed, one of the authors (CH) worked on an early CRIPA case in which the U.S. Department of Justice effectively litigated on behalf of prisoners at Washington state's maximum security prison at Walla Walla (*Hoptowit v. Ray*, 1982). The power and resources of the federal government were effectively harnessed in upholding constitutional rights against state officials who were reluctant to enforce them and who vigorously resisted attempts to improve prison conditions for special needs prisoners and others.

Yet placing significant authority in the hands of the Department of Justice bestowed CRIPA with both a substantial strategic benefit and a potential political burden. On the one hand, the DOJ is uniquely positioned to press federal constitutional claims in cases in which state officials may be heavily influenced by local political pressures and public sentiments that are hostile to the rights of groups as unpopular as criminal offenders. However, the DOJ itself is to some degree influenced by the political agenda of the executive branch it serves.

For example, soon after CRIPA was passed, the issues of crime and punishment were intensely politicized (e.g., Beckett, 1997). At a national level, the federal government was implicated in these law and order debates and its willingness to sue on behalf of state prisoners was compromised. Thus the civil rights division of DOJ during the Reagan–Bush years showed little enthusiasm for CRIPA, at times reversing positions and agreements that their own attorneys had labored to fashion (e.g., Alexander, 1984; Cornwell, 1988; Hayden, 1997).[12] Although, under a new

---

[12]Apparently responding to concerns about the costs of increasing levels of prisoner litigation, Congress empowered courts to stay prisoner litigation for 90 days pending exhaustion of internal prison grievance procedures and provided for the certification of such procedures by the Department of Justice

federal administration, the statute has been employed more vigorously in recent years, uncertainties remain. Indeed, as long as crime and punishment issues continue to be exploited for political gain CRIPA and other laws designed to protect the rights of special needs and other offenders are likely to operate with variable force and effect.

The Americans With Disabilities Act

The most powerful legal tool currently available to prisoners (or any other person) with disabilities is the Americans With Disabilities Act, commonly known as the ADA. The ADA is a federal statute that was designed to "provide a clear and comprehensive national mandate for the elimination of discrimination against individuals with disabilities." To accomplish this purpose in state and local governments, the ADA prohibits any "public entity" from subjecting any "qualified individual with a disability" to discrimination on the basis of disability.

The ADA defines discrimination very broadly, beyond the "intent to discriminate" normally associated with racial prejudice (such as purposefully excluding minorities from public facilities and institutions). Discrimination under the ADA occurs when a person with a disability is unable to get access to a government program or facility. For example, a building with only stairs at the entrance is inaccessible to a person who uses a wheelchair; a school lecture is inaccessible to a person who is deaf; written regulations are inaccessible to a person who is blind. The ADA requires government agencies to provide access to their programs for people with disabilities by making all reasonable modifications that do not create an undue financial or administrative burden or do not result in a fundamental alteration of the program. Thus, the building must have a ramp, the lecture must include a sign language interpreter (if a deaf or hearing-impaired person is in the audience), and the written regulations must be accessible through alternative formats, such as Braille or computer-speech recognition programs.

In one sense, the application of the ADA to the criminal justice system seems straightforward. Historically, prisons have been places in which people with certain kinds of disabilities were often overrepresented. Like many other parts of society, correctional facilities nonetheless continued to discriminate against persons with disabilities, in large part simply by ignoring their special needs. And, because disabled prisoners are so completely dependent on the institutions in which they are incarcerated, such discimination is felt acutely. For example, prisoners who use wheelchairs face discrimination when they cannot enter their cell because the door is too narrow; once in the cell their bed and toilet may be inaccessible because grab bars are not installed. If they are deaf, they may not hear emergency warnings, be able to participate in parole or disciplinary hearings, or be able to communicate with their doctor. And they are denied the limited freedom to seek or create alternative ways of meeting these needs.

The inability to participate in prison programs also may adversely affect prisoners' ability to obtain parole, and in at least one state a prisoner's disability itself

---

(DOJ). However, the DOJ was slow to approve such procedures and, by the early 1990s, only a few state prison systems had obtained such certification (Sturm, 1993, p. 738).

was grounds for denial of parole (e.g., *Rowe v. Fauver*, 1982). One district court succinctly summarized an all too common situation in prison:

> [The] straitened circumstances under which these inmates live are contrary to reason and common sense. Physically handicapped inmates must either manage as best they can, with virtually no special assistance, in physical environments which pose extreme difficulties for them, or spend their days vegetating, denied access to virtually all the programs and activities available to non-disabled inmates. . . . In short, [the Department of Corrections] provides essentially no accommodations for handicapped inmates which would enable them more effectively to function and contend with their desperately onerous situations in prison. (*Ruiz v. Estelle*, 1980, p. 1340)

Until recently, many prison systems failed to provide adequate accommodation to the needs of disabled prisoners. Yet they vehemently opposed the federal government's attempt to prohibit disability discrimination in their institutions. They contended that the ADA simply was not intended to protect state prisoners, and some courts agreed with them. Indeed, in the case that brought this issue before the Supreme Court, some 34 states filed briefs opposing the application of the ADA to prisons. However, in a unanimous opinion the Court held that the language of the ADA "unmistakably includes State prisons and prisoners within its coverage" (*Pennsylvania Department of Corrections v. Yeskey*, 1998, p. 1956).

The states had argued that Congress's seemingly universal definition of a public entity as "any department, agency, special purpose district or other instrumentality of a State . . . or local government" did *not* include prisons. The thrust of the states' argument was that Congress did not think it was protecting prisoners when it enacted the ADA. Therefore, they claimed, some additional affirmative indication of its intent to include disabled prisoners was required before the ADA could be applicable. Had the Supreme Court accepted that argument in *Yeskey*, *all* laws of general application, including the Civil Rights Acts, would have been void in prisons. Such a ruling would truly have created an "iron curtain drawn between the Constitution and the prisons of this country" (*Wolff v. McDonnell*, 1974, pp. 556–557). Fortunately, the Supreme Court disagreed.

Prison Litigation Reform Act

In 1996, Congress passed the Prison Litigation Reform Act (PLRA),[13] allegedly responding to complaints that federal judges had "coddled" prisoners and entertained frivolous inmate lawsuits. The several components of this sweeping law each limit a different aspect of prisoners' rights litigation. Some provisions of the Act discourage prisoners from claiming constitutional violations by making it more difficult for prisoners to file lawsuits and limiting the fees attorneys can recoup in these proceedings. Other provisions narrow the scope of inquiry and intervention that a federal court can use to address the totality of conditions or treatment at a facility. With respect to a court's ability to oversee prison practices over an extended period of time, the Act requires them to periodically determine that the relief in question (a) has been narrowly drawn, (b) is necessary to correct the violation of a federal right, and (c) represents the least intrusive means of redressing the violation.

---

[13] 8 U.S.C.A. § 3626(c)(1) (West Supp. 1997).

Although the lower courts are still in the process of determining when and how it will be applied, the PLRA threatens to have a profound impact on prisoners' rights. One commentator noted that, as written, the Act "fundamentally alters the landscape of prisoner litigation" (Riewe, 1997, p. 119), and another predicted that the PLRA "will severely limit the ability of the federal courts to correct serious abuses suffered by prisoners, including . . . failure to provide prisoners with minimally adequate medical and mental health care" (Leven, 1996, p. 2).

One of the PLRA's most important and immediate effects has been to limit what are called "consent decrees"—binding agreements that are entered into by parties to civil rights and other kinds of cases to avoid lengthy, expensive trials and preempt likely adverse findings of fact. A high percentage of cases brought to protect the constitutional rights of inmates are resolved in this way. Indeed, numerous such consent decrees governing prison conditions and the treatment of vulnerable offenders were in force throughout the United States at the time of the PLRA's passage. However, under the terms of the Act, most state and local governments—as defendants in these cases—can request termination of their agreements and renege on commitments that they had made under existing consent decrees. Specifically, in cases lacking an explicit finding that the implemented relief "extends no further than necessary to correct the violation of the Federal right," [14] parties can move to immediately end judicial oversight. Yet, as one legal analyst complained, it was precisely this finding "that many defendants deliberately avoided by agreeing to the consent decree" in the first place (Bloom, 1998, p. 412).

Implementation: Court Orders and Institutional Change

It is important to acknowledge the special complexities that are involved in implementing judicial opinions and court orders in institutional settings. Writing in pre-PLRA times, Haney and Pettigrew (1986) nonetheless expressed concern over the fate of "numerous federal court decisions [that] have attempted to extend constitutional rights to previously unprotected groups in previously unregulated places" (p. 267), including vulnerable offenders in correctional settings. As they noted, despite stunning legal victories that "promised rights and protections to people desperately in need of them, [and] raised expectations for fair and humane treatment" (p. 268), real institutional change proceeded at an extremely slow pace, if at all.

Warren and Moon's (1994) case study tracing the history of the first "deinstitutionalization" case to order community-based treatment for mentally ill patients, *Dixon v. Weinberger*, (1975), illustrates how difficult it can be to translate courtroom success into real institutional change. In *Dixon*, implementation efforts became an "odyssey" that, as Warren and Moon put it, revealed "how a class action suit brought on behalf of mentally disabled plaintiffs can result in legal victories, yet have little impact upon the operations of a government agency" (p. 330).[15] The case study

---

[14]Prison Litigation Reform Act of 1995, Pub. L. No. 104-134, § 802(b)(2), 110 Stat. 1321, 1321-68 (1996) (codified at 18 U.S.C. § 3626).

[15]Among the representative problems they identified were implementation plans that were "consensus" documents that "reflected only a general policy and lacked specific details by which progress could be measured," providing only "vague timetables" for achieving key goals in which "interim steps for meeting these goals also were not outlined" (Warren & Moon, 1994, p. 338).

provided a sobering example of what the authors called "the pitfalls of good process." That is,

> In many ways *Dixon* is a model of good process. The parties preferred negotiation over court orders, the plaintiffs always accepted concrete services rather than paper victories, and experts participated in shaping the course of change. Yet these efforts were largely unsuccessful. (p. 352)

Among other things, these authors emphasized (a) the importance of taking local politics and attitudes toward outside expertise into account; (b) recognition of the way in which "socially stigmatized and politically powerless" consumers of the services in question must somehow be involved in the legal reforms themselves (p. 354); and (c) preserving the ability of oversight panels, committees, or special masters to both provide technical assistance and "act as a strong external critic" when necessary (p. 355).

Haney and Pettigrew (1986) suggested a programmatic model of judicial implementation designed to maximize the amount of institutional change brought about by court orders protecting vulnerable inmates. Although their suggestions were made before the PLRA changed the landscape of prisoners' rights litigation, many of them still apply. They included conceiving of institutional changes as applied behavior modification and developing elaborate case-specific plans for transforming institutional settings; the optimal use of mediation and other forms of nonadversarial dispute resolution that would include staff and public education and more participatory decision making; and finally, an emphasis on implementation as the most critical stage of institutional change on behalf of vulnerable populations, including an acknowledgment not only of the substantial intellectual and economic resources that must be devoted to this task but also a concession of its fundamentally experimental nature and the need to develop a broad and accessible database of "what works."

Haney and Pettigrew (1986) noted that even though the crucial nexus had been established between the needs of vulnerable inmates and the power of the courts to protect them, what remained undeveloped was "the procedural technology to protect those rights in the special institutional settings in question" (p. 276). Although current trends in Supreme Court prison doctrine and the passage of the PLRA[16] threaten to limit the scope and frequency of judicial intervention into correctional institutions on behalf of special needs and other offenders, these suggestions provide a blueprint of sorts for effective court-ordered change.

In light of a decade and a half's worth of additional experience with litigation designed to effect institutional reform, we offer this brief addendum to Haney and Pettigrew's suggestions. The first is to note that, notwithstanding the formal power of courts to hold recalcitrant prison officials in contempt, correctional systems and individual institutions are almost impossible to significantly change without good-faith cooperation on the part of a significant number of employees. Before, during, and after litigation has commenced, hearings and trials are conducted, and legal

---

[16] The PLRA's Section 3626(a), as amended, prohibits courts from granting prospective relief unless the court finds that the relief is "narrowly drawn, extends no further than necessary to correct the violation of the Federal right, and is the least intrusive means necessary to correct the violation." In the context of the current discussion, it appears to move courts in the opposite direction from the one they should be traveling.

victories obtained, negotiated agreements always represent a promising alternative to continued courtroom confrontations. To the extent that prison officials come to understand that judicial decrees have the potential to increase badly needed resources, improve working conditions, and enable them to operate better institutions, court-ordered reform is more likely to succeed. In a related way, it is advisable for court orders to require prison officials to generate their *own* plans for correcting the constitutional violations that have been identified at trial. Even though these plans often must be substantially modified with input from other parties, this process invests officials in the task of devising proactive plans for change. Indeed, the U.S. Supreme Court has now required that courts give state prison systems an opportunity to present their own remedial plans. Thus the state should have the first chance to "correct the errors made in the internal administration of their prisons." (See *Lewis v. Casey,* 1996, p. 362.)

In addition, we believe that effective institutional change usually requires the long-term involvement of a special master or monitor empowered to engage in independent fact finding and to make change-oriented recommendations to the parties as well as the overseeing court. Especially in large systems, special masters are needed not only to inform the parties and the court about the amount of progress being made toward court-ordered changes but also to provide wardens and other prison officials with much-needed information that they might not otherwise have about conditions, widespread institutional practices, and other treatment-related issues. Moreover, the work of special masters must often be supplemented by the presence of outside experts who are needed to assist in identifying nonobvious problems and devising solutions that are often overlooked by persons who have become accustomed to the status quo approach. Finally, the continued, long-term, hands-on involvement of plaintiffs' attorneys and judges themselves is another important ingredient in most successful models of effective judicially created institutional change.

Three Case Studies on the Rights of Special Needs Offenders

To illustrate the application of some of these constitutional doctrines and suggestions for effective institutional change, we discuss three relatively recent California prison cases involving special needs offenders. All three are cases in which the authors directly participated, one of us (CH) as an expert witness, the other (DS) as one of the attorneys of record.

Systemwide Deliberate Indifference: Coleman v. Wilson (1995)

When Ralph Coleman entered the California Department of Corrections in the late 1980s, he was diagnosed as having a major mental illness. In fact, his mental illness appeared to have played an important role in the crimes for which he was incarcerated. He was sent to a medical facility within the prison system and, eventually, to a new maximum security prison that had just opened in a rural area of the state. Once there Coleman realized that he would not be able to receive any real treatment for his psychological problems. Indeed, the "mental health program" at this prison consisted of one master's level psychologist who was responsible for not only treating the 3500 inmates who were housed there but also for spending 20% to 30% of his time preparing psychological evaluations for the agency that determined whether prisoners were suitable for parole. This psychologist would later testify that his daily routine at the prison consisted of "running as fast as I can putting out as many fires as I could." He candidly admitted that psychotic patients "of course" did not receive adequate treatment or care, and that many stayed in their cells for long periods of time without receiving any attention from the staff.[17] Coleman worried about his worsening mental state, especially since he now had no hope of receiving treatment in the prison where he was confined. He filed a civil rights lawsuit seeking transfer to an institution where he could obtain ongoing therapy.

Legal claims like Coleman's rarely succeed. Ordinarily, as long as there is some kind of treatment that is theoretically available, prisons are typically in a position to argue that "professional judgment" has been exercised in the decision whether to provide it. Moreover, as we noted earlier, proving that Coleman and others like him had been measurably harmed by the prison's failure to provide any specific kind and amount of treatment is often very problematic. And, if cases like Coleman's make it past the initial legal hurdles where they are usually dismissed, prison administrators can simply transfer the prisoner to another facility where marginally better treatment is available. Although the individual prisoner's lot is improved, the larger issue of inadequate treatment becomes moot and little in the system changes. In this case, however, Coleman would not only eventually prevail but he would watch over a several year period as his original, individual claim was transformed into a major class action lawsuit that would affect the lives of tens of thousands of California prisoners.

One reason for Coleman's unexpected, dramatic success was coincidental. Unbeknownst to him, shortly before he filed his lawsuit an elaborate study of the mental health needs of California prisoners was completed (Norman & Cotton & Associates, 1989). The state legislature had provided generous funding for the study and high-ranking officials of the Department of Corrections had participated in its design and implementation. It was easily the most sophisticated and comprehensive study of its kind ever conducted in the state prison system, and its results were unsettling. It showed that an estimated 27.1% of California prisoners were suffering from a "severe mental disorder" *and* were experiencing current symptomatology within a month of being interviewed. In addition, nearly 7% of the prisoner population had current symptoms and severe mental disorders that were *undetected* by the prison authorities. In the large California prison system this would translate into nearly 10,000 prisoners who were suffering from severe mental disorders that authorities had failed to identify and, perforce, neglected to address with any meaningful treatment.[18]

Although they had participated in the planning and oversight of the research that uncovered these facts, Department of Corrections officials quickly attempted to discredit its findings. Indeed, in deposition testimony given in advance of Coleman's impending civil rights class action trial, the head of the prison system challenged

---

[17] This quote and others have been taken from documents filed with the court in the three cases that we examine.

[18] The mere fact that prisoners had been identified or detected by prison authorities as suffering from mental disorders did not mean that their problems were being handled appropriately. In fact, despite their psychiatric classification status, fully 64% of the *identified* group reported that they had not received mental health professional services at *any* time during their present incarceration.

the study results, saying that he had spent much time visiting California prisons and had not noticed many mentally ill persons there. Nonetheless, the comprehensive statewide study was used as the starting point in the litigation to show that the mental health needs of the prisoners were substantial and that the Department of Corrections had consistently and dramatically underestimated them in its resource allocations and staffing patterns.[19]

Experts for both sides testified in pretrial proceedings that mental health resources were clearly inadequate and probably unconstitutional.[20] They acknowledged that there were prisons in the California system with more than 5000 prisoners but lacking a single staff psychiatrist. There was also little dispute that nonpsychiatrically trained physicians were inappropriately prescribing psychotropic medications; that powerful, potentially toxic medications were being administered but not properly monitored; that there were unacceptably long delays in the transfer of prisoners who needed immediate residential and inpatient care; and that many prisoners in need of immediate mental health care were being housed in segregation units instead of treatment facilities. Still, the Department of Corrections refused to settle the case and trial commenced.

In the course of trial testimony before a federal magistrate judge,[21] the head of the Department of Corrections made this remarkable concession: He had resisted developing and implementing a simple, standardized format to screen for mental illness among incoming inmates because he knew that once mentally ill individuals were identified he would be responsible for treating them.[22] The trial demonstrated that the mental health system throughout the entire department was so "seriously and chronically understaffed" that delays of up to five months for routine psychiatric examinations were not uncommon. Prisoners in need of psychiatric care were sometimes relegated to "bus therapy" in which they were shuffled back and forth between institutions but never given adequate evaluation or treatment. The understaffing had created another potentially dangerous problem: overuse and misuse of psychotropic medication in lieu of other less invasive but more labor-intensive therapy.

The proceedings also revealed that adequate record keeping—the starting point

---

[19]At the time of the lawsuit, the California prison system was estimated to house:

> Almost 10,000 prisoners with a current major mental illness, another 20,000 with other serious mental disorders, while approximately 18,000 prisoners need some form of treatment on any given day. The [Department of Corrections] currently has the capacity to house only 737 prisoners in a psychiatric hospital, and about 3,000 in residential treatment programs. In 1992, the outpatient clinical staff was less than 20% of that recommended by [the statewide prevalence study], with seven prisons lacking a staff psychiatrist, six with no mental health professional on staff, and 10 with less than one mental health clinician. (Specter, 1994, p. 110–111)

[20]As in most such cases, overcrowding had played a role in precipitating the crisis. For example, Department of Correction's data documented that between 1979 and 1986 the prisoner population had increased 139%, whereas budgeted positions for clinical staff increased a mere 29%.

[21]Cases like this often involve evidentiary hearings before a magistrate judge who makes findings of fact and recommends legal conclusions that, if they are disputed by any of the parties, are taken directly to a federal district court judge for resolution.

[22]At the California Institution for Men, for example, "screening took place in a room that was crowded with naked inmates, completely chaotic, and devoid of privacy." Screening consisted of a single question: Have you ever been admitted to a psychiatric hospital? Not surprisingly, the court found that unless an inmate explicitly asked for care or exhibited obviously bizarre behavior, their psychological needs would likely go undetected.

for meaningful therapeutic oversight—was lacking throughout the California prison system. Indeed, the court found "disorganized, untimely, and incomplete filing of medical records, insufficient charting, and incomplete or nonexistent treatment plans" and frequent instances of prisoners being transferred between institutions "without even such medical records as might exist." And finally, the magistrate judge concluded that the widespread practice of using administrative segregation in lieu of psychiatric treatment "exacerbates the underlying mental illness, induces psychosis, and increases the risk of suicide."

Applying the appropriate legal standard to the facts of the case, the court ruled that prison officials not only failed to provide appropriate care but they did so knowingly and manifesting deliberate indifference to the basic needs of the inmates. Specifically, because the Department's own data had clearly documented the growing gap between the numbers of prisoners and the mental health resources, because their own study had identified tens of thousands of mentally ill prisoners who were not receiving adequate treatment, and because the prison's mental health system was so grossly inadequate that its deficiencies must have been obvious, the magistrate ruled that the prison officials and the governor knew of these problems for years and failed to do anything about them. Holding the state responsible for these significant constitutional violations, he made sweeping recommendations for widespread injunctive relief.

Still the Department of Corrections and state's attorneys were resistant. They challenged the factual findings on which the magistrate's recommendations were based, even though their own experts had conceded most of them. They refused to implement the recommended reforms and appealed to a federal district court judge. Although the appeal delayed the implementation of necessary changes by a full year, it ultimately failed.[23] The federal district court judge who received the magistrate's findings adopted them all, and wholeheartedly supported his recommendations for injunctive relief. He further required that a special master be appointed to monitor and report on the prison system's compliance with the court-ordered remedies.

Vulnerable Prisoners in "Supermax": Madrid v. Gomez (1995)

In late 1989, the California Department of Corrections opened a "state-of-the-art" punitive segregation or "supermax" security housing unit (SHU) at Pelican Bay Prison. The prison purported to house the state's most dangerous prisoners—"the worst of the worst," as state prison officials repeatedly referred to them in press releases and statements to the public. However, this prison not only subjected inmates to near total social isolation but also completely isolated them from the natural environment and from most of the natural rhythms of life (Haney, 1997b). The SHU prisoners were confined to housing units that had no windows, and they were per-

---

[23]The timetable in cases such as this compromises their effectiveness in addressing immediate, crisis-level concerns. Coleman's individual lawsuit was certified as a class action in 1991. The trial before the magistrate began in March 1993. Approximately 11 experts testified for both sides in the course of a 39-day hearing and the magistrate issued his findings of fact and recommendations for injunctive relief about a year later, in June 1994. The federal district court with whom the state pressed their appeal decided against them in September 1995, some five years after Coleman filed his original complaint (Coleman v. Wilson, 1995).

mitted to exercise for less than an hour a day in a small, high-walled, concrete-encased "yard" that provided them with only a glimpse of skylight overhead.

Inmates in these units endured a degree of long-term, involuntary, enforced idleness that was unprecedented in American corrections. Put simply: They had virtually nothing to *do*. All prisoners were "cell fed"—twice a day meals were placed on tray slots in the cell doors to be eaten by the prisoners locked inside. They were never permitted out of their cells unless they were moving to and from showers or yard, or being escorted—in chains and accompanied by two baton-wielding correctional officers per inmate—to the law library or infirmary outside the unit. Thus with minor and insignificant exceptions, a prisoner's entire life was lived within the parameters of his 80-square foot cell, a space that was typically shared with another prisoner whose life was similarly circumscribed.

In addition to these unprecedented levels of social isolation and idleness, prisoners in these units were subjected to mistreatment and brutality at the hands of correctional officers. Indeed, a federal judge would eventually acknowledge a "tremendous potential for abuse" at the prison that stemmed in part from the guards' "nearly total control over the inmates under their supervision" (*Madrid v. Gomez*, 1995, p. 1160). He would also underscore the way in which the physical environment at the prison "reinforces a sense of isolation and detachment from the outside world, and helps create a palpable distance from ordinary compunctions, inhibitions and community norms" (*Madrid v. Gomez*, 1995, p. 1160).

But concerns over brutality amounted to more than mere abstractions: There were countless instances of excessive force at the prison including one in which a prisoner's arm was broken when staff bent it back through his tray slot, others in which guards punched prisoners in the face with closed fists and kicked them in the face and head, left them "hog-tied" or in fetal restraints for hours at a time, placed "naked or partially dressed inmates in outdoor holding cages during inclement weather" where they were "exposed to the elements as well as public view" (p. 1171), subjected prisoners to unnecessarily high numbers of "cell extractions" in which teams of guards engaged in prescribed procedures that the court characterized as "undeniably violent maneuver[s] which can involve several weapons, including 38 millimeter gas guns, tasers, short metal batons, and mace" (p. 1172) and that "routinely involved a strikingly high degree of force, and resulted in numerous injuries that were too often left unexplained by official incident reports" (p. 1173) and, finally, instances in which guards discharged firearms "unnecessarily, and in some cases, recklessly" (p. 1179–1180) and sometimes with lethal consequences.

When the two of us first toured and inspected this prison, we were shocked by the extraordinary levels of isolation and idleness imposed, by the widespread complaints about physical and mental abuse at the hands of correctional staff, and the level of psychological pain and suffering that these conditions of confinement were inflicting on the persons housed there (e.g., Haney, 1997b; Haney & Lynch, 1997). We were shocked by something else as well: the unexpectedly high number of mentally ill prisoners who seemed to be locked inside this punitive segregation unit. The Department of Correction's official position on this supermax prison indicated that it had been designed and was being used to house the system's toughest and most incorrigible prisoners. We had assumed that, in identifying the so-called "worst of the worst," the prison was engaged in some rudimentary screening process by which prisoners whose disciplinary infractions were the product of their mental illness or developmental disability were excluded from this frighteningly punitive place. We were wrong.

The psychiatrically dangerous consequences of the failure to evaluate the mental health of the persons placed in the Pelican Bay supermax unit were magnified by the prison's totally inadequate mental health monitoring and almost nonexistent therapy or treatment program. For the first several years of the prison's operation, there was one master's-level psychologist who was responsible for 3500 prisoners, nearly half of whom were locked inside the supermax. There was no effective procedure in place for knowledgeable staff to periodically monitor the psychological state of the prisoners housed there, no regular programs of therapy to address the psychiatric needs of prisoners—either preexisting problems or ones developed in response to the draconian conditions of confinement—and no effective system by which prisoners who suffered acute breakdowns could be quickly transferred into inpatient treatment facilities. In fact, prisoners who either were or became mentally ill in the punitive segregation unit were often treated more harshly than others. That is, because their psychiatric conditions made it difficult for them to conform to the extreme demands and rigid routines of the supermax environment, the resulting disciplinary infractions often led to guard mistreatment and confinement inside a newly created, so-called "violence control unit" in which conditions were even more stark and severe than in the rest of the SHU.[24]

After a lengthy trial focusing on a wide range of civil rights violations at the facility, the judge reached a series of extremely critical factual conclusions, including the view that physical environment at the prison reinforced "a sense of isolation and detachment from the outside world, and help[ed] create a palpable distance from ordinary compunctions, inhibitions and community norms" (p. 1160). He also concluded that the interior of the prison subjected prisoners to "stark sterility and unremitting monotony" (p. 1229) and expressed concern over the fact that prisoners "can go weeks, months or potentially years with little or no opportunity for normal social contact with other people" (p. 1229).

However, although the opinion recognized that "social science and clinical literature have consistently reported that when human beings are subjected to social isolation and reduced environmental stimulation, they may deteriorate mentally and in some cases develop psychiatric disturbances" (p. 1230), conceded that "many, if not most, inmates in the SHU experience some degree of psychological trauma in reaction to their extreme social isolation and the severely restricted environmental stimulation in the SHU" (p. 1235), and even acknowledged that conditions inside the SHU "may press the outer bound of what most humans can psychologically

---

[24]Unfortunately, the situation we encountered at Pelican Bay was not unique to this unit. For example:

> The lack of mental health care for the seriously mentally ill who end up in segregation units has worsened the condition of many prisoners incapable of understanding their condition. This is especially true in cases where prisoners are placed in levels of mental health care that are not intense enough, and begin to refuse taking their medication. They then enter a vicious cycle in which their mental disease takes over, often causing hostile and aggressive behavior to the point that they break prison rules and end up in segregation units as management problems. Once in punitive housing, this regression can go undetected for considerable periods of time before they again receive more closely monitored mental health care. This cycle can, and often does, repeat. (Streeter, 1998, p. 167)

tolerate" (p. 1267), the judge did not require the prison to alter or modify its general conditions of confinement.

Although constrained by the current state of Eighth Amendment law in addressing generalized conditions of confinement (Haney & Lynch, 1997), the *Madrid* court did exempt certain categories of vulnerable prisoners from placement in the Pelican Bay Security Housing Unit based on their preexisting psychological states. Thus the judge ruled that prisoners who were already mentally ill, those who suffered from chronic depression, brain damage, and mental retardation—because "such inmates are not required to endure the horrific suffering of a serious mental illness or a major exacerbation of an existing mental illness before obtaining relief" (p. 1265)—were to be excluded from this extreme form of punitive segregation. About a year after its historic decision, the *Madrid* court also ordered the state to remove prisoners meeting those diagnostic descriptions from the SHU, to implement plans for the screening and monitoring of the psychiatric condition of prisoners, and to create a special psychiatric security unit to provide treatment for acutely disturbed SHU prisoners. Specifically exempted from the removal order were prisoners suffering from the acute effects of isolation itself (sometimes called "reduced environmental stimulation syndrome") because the court had not found that "the risk of suffering a sufficiently serious degree of psychological trauma was high enough among all inmates to justify a presumptive exclusionary category based" on this syndrome alone.[25]

Protecting the Developmentally Disabled: Clark v. California *(1998)*

Mental retardation and other developmental disabilities create a special kind of vulnerability and dependency in prison. Although developmentally disabled offenders do not necessarily need "treatment" in the psychiatric sense of the word, they do need a higher level of support and protection to function safely inside a prison and specialized habilitation services to prepare them for life in the outside world. Moreover, if their special needs are not addressed explicitly, as Judge William Wayne Justice once observed, "Mentally retarded persons meet with unremitting hardships in prison" (*Ruiz v. Estelle*, 1980, p. 1344).

Unlike the *Coleman* and *Madrid* litigation, attorneys evaluating the plight of the developmentally disabled in California's massive prison system faced the additional challenge of determining how many such prisoners were affected and who they were. Although there was reason to believe that the department had known for years that there were a significant number of developmentally disabled prisoners in its penal institutions, it had done little to provide for the accommodation, protection, and provision of services to these vulnerable prisoners. Indeed, it had done virtually nothing to identify them. Lacking any systematic screening to detect developmental disability, the first step in addressing the problem was to estimate the number of such prisoners.

There was good reason to believe that the number was not small. A simple extrapolation from the population at large, where 2% to 3% of the population is

---

[25]Remedial Order Re: Exclusion from the Security Housing Unit, Madrid v. Gomez, No. C90-3094-TEH, filed December 15, 1995, at 15–16.

mentally retarded, would yield an estimate of the number of mentally retarded prisoners in California (where there are approximately 160,000 state prisoners total)—of about 4000. Applying the range of estimates derived from direct studies of other state prison systems—that found between 4% to 10%—would lead one to expect somewhere between 6400 and 16,000 mentally retarded persons incarcerated in the California Department of Corrections. And using the only California-specific empirical data to appear anywhere in the literature—Brown and Courtless's (1971) figure of 5.4% of California prisoners—would lead to a present-day estimate of more than 8600 mentally retarded prisoners.

In addition to reliably estimating the number of developmentally disabled prisoners in the California system, plaintiffs attorneys and experts demonstrated that they were less able to adapt to prison conditions than other inmates, were more likely to be beaten or raped, could not as easily comply with prison rules and procedures, did not have access to the full range of services and privileges available to other prisoners, and were disproportionately deprived of good-time credits (which indirectly increased the lengths of their prison sentences). Moreover, these negative consequences interacted with and compounded each other, so that the plight of the developmentally disabled prisoner was worsened in several significant ways. Failing to provide appropriate habilitation services meant that the mentally impaired prisoners' condition was unlikely to improve while they were incarcerated and that many of them would likely be made worse by the experience. Because they were not identified, protected, and provided services, their adjustment problems worsened. Thus as their condition deteriorated as they confronted a difficult and dangerous prison environment without the benefit of habilitation services of any kind, they were rendered more likely to behave impulsively and violently.

In *Clark v. California* (1998), attorneys representing the class of developmentally disabled prisoners housed in the Department of Corrections finally sued in federal court, alleging deprivation of constitutionally protected liberty interests and Eighth Amendment violations,[26] and relied as well on several specialized statutes, including the ADA. As they pressed their case they found the Department initially unresponsive and seemingly unsympathetic. Corrections officials claimed that there were no more than a *handful* of developmentally disabled prisoners in the entire system and, since they were readily identifiable, no special screening procedures were needed to detect them. Indeed, prison official after prison official submitted sworn deposition testimony to the effect that in the large prisons for which they were responsible—some holding many thousands of inmates—that there were *no* developmentally disabled persons. How did they know? They had not noticed any.

Reliable estimates that there were thousands of developmentally disabled prisoners in the system notwithstanding, the institutional histories of many of the plaintiffs included in the lawsuit spoke to the serious problems they faced. For example, Jack Von Gunten was a 46-year-old developmentally disabled prisoner with an IQ of 48. He has been in special education classes throughout his childhood and per-

---

[26]The Eighth Amendment does not provide the only legal protection. In *City of Cleburne v. Cleburne Living Center* (1985), the Supreme Court found that although developmental disability was not a quasi-suspect classification requiring a more exacting standard of review, people with mental retardation are subject to irrational fear and prejudice and held that discrimination against them was unlawful under the equal protection clause of the 14th Amendment.

formed at a second-grade level. At the time the litigation commenced, Von Gunten was housed in the mainline prison population but, because of his intellectual disability, was deprived of any access to any vocational programs. When he was transferred to San Quentin he quickly became the target of other prisoners who extorted money and property from him, and verbally and physically harassed and abused him. The resulting emotional trauma led him to seek psychiatric counseling at San Quentin, but he was told that none was available to him. His disability was so severe that he was unable to understand the rules that were posted at the prison and was punished for violating rules that he did not and could not understand. He often failed to keep appointments because he could not read the prison ducats or slips of paper on which the times and places were written.

James Simmons was a 45-year-old developmentally disabled prisoner whose IQ was measured at 49. He was illiterate. Prison officials who evaluated James described him as "gullible, easy prey to more sophisticated criminals . . . afflicted with a profuse mental deficiency, dependent and childlike." In part because of his disability, he also moved and talked very slowly, which frequently led correctional officers to surmise that he was under the influence of drugs. He regularly was drug-tested and strip-searched as a result. He also was frequently harassed by fellow inmates. In addition, despite the Department of Correction's own failure to provide Simmons with suitable vocational training or counseling of any kind, repeated decisions to deny him parole cited his developmental disability as one of the primary reasons.

As the litigation proceeded, numerous such case histories surfaced. In addition, the Department of Corrections was faced with expert estimates that the number of developmentally disabled in the prison system numbered into the thousands—perhaps as many as 10,000 or more, rather than the few its officials had claimed. In addition, there were a series of expert evaluations indicating that the prison system was not meeting its constitutional responsibilities to protect the mentally retarded against the special dangers they confronted in correctional institutions and was manifesting deliberate indifference to their other needs as well. However, on the eve of trial, the state entered into an agreement that was designed to remedy these problems. The agreed on reforms included implementing a valid screening procedure to accurately identify the developmentally disabled, providing for special classification and housing, and offering habilitation programs in which these inmates would be provided appropriate work and training opportunities.

Conclusion: Legal Rights in Uncertain Legal Times

Contemporary prison law is in flux. After a promising beginning in which federal constitutional standards were applied in the reform of many state prison systems, a period of retrenchment set in. This is one reason we have refrained in this chapter from attempting to provide blackletter summaries of applicable law—in these times, especially, legal doctrines are subject to rapid and unexpected transformation and, in any event, may vary not only over time but across jurisdictions. We have opted instead to discuss the basic underlying constitutional principles on which particular legal standards rest. But the good news in this otherwise sobering area of law is that special needs offenders still occupy a relatively protected constitutional position.

Deliberate indifference to the serious needs of vulnerable prisoners that results in the infliction of unnecessary suffering is still prohibited in all jurisdictions. Although the focus of constitutional inquiry has shifted to the state of mind of relevant decision makers—whether a substantial risk of serious harm has been created that prison officials were subjectively reckless in disregarding—threats to the well-being of vulnerable prisoners appear to be increasingly understood and acknowledged. And, despite questions about the wisdom of deferring to the judgments of professionals in correctional contexts, uncertainties about whether the judgments of correctional officials or mental health and treatment staff should be binding in those cases in which they conflict, and ways to reduce documented instances in which prisoners have suffered from too much intrusive intervention, legal doctrines seeking a balance of these competing interests are in place in most prison systems in the country.

The picture is equally mixed on legislative fronts. One piece of federal legislation —the PLRA—has limited prisoners' ability to sue in federal court, and two others —CRIPA and the ADA—still provide the basis for protecting special needs offenders. Indeed, as we have tried to show in our discussion of the three case studies taken from recent litigation in which we participated in California, despite uncertain, shifting, and even adverse legal precedents, it is still possible to rely on existing laws to address the plight of vulnerable prisoners, to both prevail in court and to use constitutional and legislative mandates in fashioning meaningful settlements. As we have also tried to show, however, much work remains to be done on the crucial issue of implementation and finding ways to ensure that hard-won legal victories have their intended effects.

References

Alexander, E. (1984, Fall). Justice Department retreats: The Michigan case. *National Prison Project Newsletter, 1*, 1–3.

Beckett, K. (1997). *Making crime pay: Law and order in contemporary American politics.* New York: Oxford University Press.

Bersoff, D. (1992). Autonomy for vulnerable populations: The Supreme Court's reckless disregard for self-determination and social science. *Villanova Law Review, 37*, 1569–1605.

Bloom, I. (1998). Prisons, prisoners, and pine forests: Congress breaches the wall separating legislative from judicial power. *Arizona Law Review, 40*, 389–424.

Brown, B., & Courtless, T. (1971). *The Mentally Retarded Offender.* DHEW Pub. No. (HSM) 72-90-39. Washington, DC: Government Printing Office.

Capps v. Atiyeh. (1982). 559 F. Supp. 894 (D. Ore.).

City of Cleburne v. Cleburne Living Center. (1985). 473 U.S. 432.

Civil Rights of Institutionalized Persons Act. (1980). Pub. L. No. 96-247, 94 Stat. 349 (codified as amended at 42 U.S.C. §§ 1997–1997j (1994)).

Clark v. California. (1998). No. C-96-1486 FMS (N.D. Cal.).

Cohen, F., & Dvoskin, J. (1992). Inmates with mental disorders: A guide to law and practice. *Mental & Physical Disability Law Reporter, 16*, 462–480.

Coleman v. Wilson. (1995). 912 F. Supp. 1282 (N.D. Cal.).

Cornwell, J. (1988). CRIPA: The failure of federal intervention for mentally retarded people. *Yale Law Journal, 97*, 845–862.

Dixon v. Weinberger. (1975). 405 F. Supp. 974 (D.D.C.).

Estelle v. Gamble. (1976). 429 U.S. 97.

Farmer v. Brennan. (1994). 511 U.S. 825.

Haney, C. (1997a). Psychology and the limits to prison pain: Confronting the coming crisis in Eighth Amendment law. *Psychology, Public Policy, and Law, 3*, 499–588.

Haney, C. (1997b). Infamous punishment: The psychological effects of isolation, in J. Marquart & J. Sorensen (Eds.), *Correctional contexts: Contemporary and classical readings* (pp. 428–437). Los Angeles: Roxbury.

Haney, C., & Lynch, M. (in press). Regulating prisons of the future: The psychological consequences of supermax and solitary confinement. *New York University Review of Law and Social Change. 23*, 477–570.

Haney, C., & Pettigrew, T. (1986). Civil rights and institutional law: The role of social psychology in judicial implementation. *Journal of Community Psychology, 14*, 267–277.

Haney, C., & Zimbardo, P. (1998). The past and future of U.S. prison policy: Twenty-five years after the Stanford prison experiment. *American Psychologist, 53*, 709–727.

Hayden, M. (1997). Class action, civil rights litigation for institutionalized persons with mental retardation and other developmental disabilities: A review. *Mental & Physical Disability Law Reporter, 21*, 411–421.

Helling v. McKinney. (1993). 113 S. Ct. 2475.

Hoptowit v. Ray. (1982). 682 F.2d 1237 (9th Cir.).

Hudson v. McMillian. (1992). 506 U.S. 1.

Kansas v. Hendricks. (1997). 117 S. Ct. 2072.

Kittrie, N. (1973). *The right to be different: Deviance and enforced therapy*. Baltimore: Penguin.

Leven, D. (1996). 25 years after Attica. *New York Law Journal* (September 19), 2.

Lewis v. Casey. (1996). 518 U.S. 343.

Madrid v. Gomez. (1995). 912 F. Supp. 1282 (E.D. Cal.).

Neal v. Shimoda. (1997). 131 F.3d 818 (9th Cir.).

Norman & Cotton, & Associates. (1989). *Current description, evaluation, and recommendations for treatment of mentally disordered criminal offenders: Vol. 1 Introduction and prevalence (The Stirling Report)*. Sacramento: California Department of Corrections, Office of Health Care Services.

Pennsylvania Department of Corrections v. Yeskey. (1998). 118 S. Ct. 1952.

Rhodes v. Chapman. (1981). 452 U.S. 337.

Riewe, J. (1997). The least among us: Unconstitutional changes in prisoner litigation under the Prison Litigation Reform Act of 1995. *Duke Law Journal, 47*, 117–160.

Rowe v. Fauver. (1982). 533 F. Supp. 1239 (D.N.J.).

Ruiz v. Estelle. (1980). 503 F. Supp. 1265 (S.D. Tex.), *cert. denied*, 103 S. Ct. 1438.

Specter, D. (1994). Cruel and unusual punishment of the mentally ill in California's prison: A case study of a class action suit. *Social Justice, 21*, 109–116.

Stefan, S. (1992). Leaving civil rights to the "experts": From deference to abdication under the professional judgment standard. *Yale Law Journal, 102*, 639–717.

Streeter, P. (1998). Incarceration of the mentally ill: Treatment or warehousing? 77 *Michigan Bar Journal, 77*, 166.

Sturm, S. (1993). The legacy and future of corrections litigation. *University of Pennsylvania Law Review, 142*, 639–738.

Turay v. Seling. (1998). C91-664WD (W.D. Wash.).

Veneziano, L., & Veneziano, C. (1996). Disabled inmates. In M. McShane & F. Williams (Eds.), *Encyclopedia of American Prisons* (pp. 157–161). New York: Garland.

Veneziano, L., Veneziano, C., & Tribolet, C. (1987). The special needs of prison inmates with handicaps: An assessment. *Journal of Offender Counseling, Services & Rehabilitation, 12*, 61–72.

Vitek v. Jones. (1980). 445 U.S. 480.

Warren, M., & Moon, R. (1994). Dixon: In the absence of political will, carry a big stick. *Law & Psychology Review, 18*, 327–359.

Washington v. Harper. (1990). 494 U.S. 210.

Wettstein, R. (1992). A psychiatric perspective on Washington's sexually violent predators statute. *University of Puget Sound Law Review, 15,* 597–633.

Whitley v. Albers. (1986). 475 U.S. 312.

Wilson v. Seiter. (1991). 501 U.S. 294.

Wolff v. McDonnell. (1974). 418 U.S. 554.

Young v. Weston. (1995). 898 F. Supp. 744 (W.D. Wash.).

Youngberg v. Romeo. (1982). 457 U.S. 307.

Chapter 3
NATIONAL CORRECTIONAL HEALTH CARE STANDARDS

B. Jaye Anno

Before the 1970s, little attention was paid to the health needs of juvenile and adult offenders. Historically, the courts had adopted a "hands-off" policy when it came to managing correctional facilities. They reasoned that correctional administrators were better informed about the types of programs and services that should be offered, and trusted that these officials would provide whatever care was necessary. Inmates who sought relief from the courts for denial of adequate heath care had to demonstrate that the deprivation of care amounted to cruel and unusual punishment of such a magnitude as to "shock the conscience of the court" (Anno, 1991).

During the 1970s, this judicial attitude began to change. The case that signaled the beginning of the reversal of the hands-off policy regarding prisoners' rights to medical care was *Newman v. Alabama*. In this October 1972 decision, a U.S. district court found the Alabama correctional system to be in violation of inmates' constitutional right to be free from cruel and unusual punishment by failing to provide them with adequate and sufficient medical care. In 1976, the U.S. Supreme Court ruled in *Estelle v. Gamble* that inmates had a right to receive adequate care to meet their serious medical needs. In 1977, a U.S. court of appeals specifically stated in *Bowring v. Godwin* that serious mental health needs must be addressed as well. As cited in Cohen (1988, p. 55), the court stated that "we see no underlying distinction between the right to medical care for physical ills and its psychological or psychiatric counterpart."

The 1970s was a decade characterized by social change. "The judicial activism of the courts was paralleled by the social activism of certain professional associations during that same era, which began to focus on the health needs of underserved populations such as the urban poor, rural America, minorities, women and children, and the incarcerated" (Anno, 1994, p. 375). Although the courts had determined that individuals behind bars were entitled to adequate health care, it fell to the professional associations to define what "adequate" care meant.

The first national standards developed specifically to guide the health care provided in adult prisons and jails were those of the American Public Health Association (APHA; 1976). A year later, the American Medical Association (AMA) published its standards for health services in jails (1977), and followed these in 1979 with separate sets for prisons (AMA, 1979b) and juvenile confinement facilities (AMA, 1979a). In 1977, the American Correctional Association (ACA) adopted the AMA's standards for the health portion of its standards issued for both jails and juvenile facilities (ACA, 1977a, 1977b, 1977c).

In 1983, a new organization emerged—the National Commission on Correctional Health Care (NCCHC). NCCHC is a not-for-profit 501-(c)-(3) organization whose board of directors is made up of representatives named by 37 professional associations in the fields of law, law enforcement, corrections, and medical, mental health, and dental care. Because NCCHC was an outgrowth of the AMA's early efforts to improve health services in adult and juvenile detention and correctional facilities, it adopted the AMA's standards as its own.

During that same decade, a number of other organizations published standards for correctional facilities, including the American Bar Association (ABA; 1989), the American Nurses' Association (ANA; 1985), and the American Psychiatric Association (APA; 1989). In addition, the Joint Commission on Accreditation of Healthcare Organizations (JCAHO) began to explore applying its community standards to health delivery systems in correctional facilities.

This seeming proliferation of standards by so many different groups can be confusing to the uninitiated. In reality, though, only three sets of standards currently are used to any extent by detention and correctional facilities to guide the management of their health delivery systems: Those of the ACA, those of the JCAHO, and those of the NCCHC.

The ABA's mental health standards are concerned primarily with legal issues affecting offenders who are mentally ill or retarded rather than their care and treatment, and those of the ANA solely address nursing care and responsibilities. The APHA's standards, particularly the revised version (Dubler, 1986), provide useful advice but lack an accreditation component, and hence seldom are used. Those of the AMA are obsolete, because the NCCHC has taken over the AMA's correctional health program. The APA's standards address psychiatric care but are intended to be used in conjunction with NCCHC's standards rather than on their own.

Of the three sets that are used, only those of the National Commission on Correctional Health Care are discussed in any detail. JCAHO's (1990) consolidated standards provide the most specificity regarding mental health care, but because they were designed for community facilities, they do not address issues unique to the care and treatment of mentally disordered individuals behind bars. The ACA's (1990, 1991a, 1991b) standards are specific to correctional institutions but do not differ appreciably from those of the NCCHC with respect to the health issues covered, except that the latter are considerably more detailed.

The purpose of this chapter is to review the guidelines established by the National Commission on Correctional Health Care for the care and treatment of adult and juvenile offenders with special needs. In particular, the focus is on NCCHC standards that address components of an adequate delivery system for the care and treatment of adult and juvenile offenders with mental disorders. In addition, the chapter briefly addresses the topics of measuring compliance with NCCHC standards, comparing correctional health standards with those for community facilities, and the utility of standards including the extent to which implementing national standards positively affects quality of care for adult and juvenile offenders.

NCCHC's Correctional Health Standards

The primary purpose of the National Commission on Correctional Health Care is to work with correctional institutions—jails, prisons, and juvenile detention and confinement facilities—to help them improve their health care delivery systems. One of the major ways the commission accomplishes this goal is by publishing national standards for correctional health services and offering a voluntary accreditation program to those facilities interested in complying with NCCHC's requirements.

The commission considers its standards to be minimal rather than optimal guidelines for establishing adequate health delivery systems in correctional institutions. The standards are applicable to both male and female facilities holding inmates for varying lengths of time. At present, NCCHC publishes separate sets of standards for jails (1996), for prisons (1997), and for juvenile facilities (1995a). Although many of the core standards are similar, NCCHC recognizes that health requirements may differ depending on the type of institution, the health needs of the offenders it holds, and how long they stay.

NCCHC does not have separate standards for mental health services, although in 1999, it published a companion volume to its 1997 prison standards addressing critical issues in mental health care (NCCHC, 1999). All three sets of the commission's standards assume a unified health care delivery model that includes medical, dental, and mental health services.

In the sections that follow, NCCHC's current requirements from its juvenile (1995a), jail (1996), and prison (1997) health standards are compared, particularly those standards that apply to mental health services. To distinguish the separate sets, standards from the juvenile edition are designated with a "Y" for youth, those from the jail edition are designated with a "J," and those from the prison edition are designated with a "P."

In addition to differences in content, there may be differences between the sets in emphasis as well. All NCCHC standards are designated either as "essential," which means a facility must meet all aspects of the standard to be accredited, or as "important," which means that a facility has some choice about whether a particular standard will be complied with. Regardless of type, an institution must meet all applicable essential standards and 85% of the important ones applicable to it to attain accreditation. Any differences in emphasis of standards among the three sets is pointed out as well.

Finally, although I am aware of the special terminology used in the juvenile justice field, it seems unnecessarily redundant to constantly use both the adult and juvenile terms. Thus in this chapter the terms *inmate* and *offender* are intended to include youths who are detained or placed in juvenile facilities as well as adult jail detainees and those adults committed to state correctional facilities. Similarly, child care workers are included as custody or correctional staff as those terms are used in this chapter.

Administrative Issues

All three sets of NCCHC standards require there to be a single individual designated as the health authority, who is responsible for overseeing the health delivery system (essential: Y-01, J-01, P-02). If this individual is not a clinician, there also must be a designated responsible physician who has final authority over clinical decisions. At the time of the last survey, in about a third of the state prison systems, mental health services were operated separately from medical and dental services (Anno, 1991). Thus the NCCHC prison standards state that where mental health services are under a separate organizational structure, there also must be a designated mental health authority and a designated mental health clinician.

Medical autonomy also is addressed by all three sets of NCCHC standards (essential: Y-02, J-02, P-03). The intent is to ensure that clinical decisions made by health providers (e.g., physicians, dentists, psychologists) are not overruled by custody staff whether for security, punitive, or financial reasons. The caveat is that the care ordered must be necessary to meet inmates' serious health needs. If it is, correctional staff are prohibited under this standard from denying or unnecessarily delaying the needed care.

The three sets further require at least quarterly administrative meetings between the health authority and the person responsible for the facility or their designees to discuss health services, including mental health care (essential: Y-04, J-03, P-04). In addition, the jail and prison sets require monthly health services staff meetings to discuss administrative and procedural issues. Although not explicitly stated, there is an expectation that where mental health services are operated separately from medical services, both groups will invite representatives from the other group to their meetings, or at least share their meeting minutes so that each group can stay informed about the other one. Further, all three sets require statistical reports (annually for juvenile facilities and monthly for prisons and jails) that outline the type and frequency of services offered and where they were provided (i.e., on-site or in the community).

Another obligation common to the sets of standards regardless of type is to develop and maintain policy and procedure manuals that govern the care provided (essential: Y-03, J-04, P-05). In a unified system, a facility should have a policy and procedure statement that addresses each standard in the set it uses unless the standard never applies (e.g., pregnancy counseling would be not applicable if the facility never holds females). If mental health services are organized separately, though, it is necessary to have a separate policy manual that addresses administrative and personnel issues for mental health staff in addition to those standards specific to the care and treatment of mental health clients.

A quality improvement program is an essential requirement of all three sets of NCCHC standards (Y-05, J-05, P-06). Where facilities are large enough, a multidisciplinary quality improvement committee must meet at least quarterly to design, conduct, and/or review the results of quality improvement studies. In a unified system, mental health representatives are members of the quality improvement committee and mental health topics are included as subjects for review. If mental health services are separate and not included in the larger committee, there should be a quality improvement program that focuses just on mental health issues. The prison standards include an additional requirement that the work of all practicing physicians be reviewed at least annually through a peer review process (important: P-13). By definition, this standard applies to psychiatrists.

Another essential standard common to all three sets is the necessity of communication between health and custody staff regarding patients with special needs, including those with serious mental disorders or developmental disabilities (Y-25, J-07, P-08). This standard requires health staff to notify custody personnel if any of their patients have special needs that should be taken into account prior to any decisions by custody staff regarding housing or program assignments, disciplinary measures, or admissions to or transfers from institutions. For adults, the jail and prison standards also require consultation before assigning inmates to work. It is important to note that health staff need not reveal an individual's diagnosis. Rather, they should state the specific restriction that should be taken into account. For example, an individual on psychotropic medication might be restricted from working in an environment with elevated temperatures. One who is retarded might be restricted from jobs that require adherence to complex instructions.

Personnel Issues

An essential requirement regardless of the type of facility is ensuring that health staff have the proper credentials for the tasks they perform (Y-18, J-17, P-18). If individuals need to be licensed, certified, or registered to provide care in the community, this standard says that such requirements apply to health professionals providing care to inmates as well. In some states, there are no licensure or certification requirements for certain mental health staff such as bachelor's- or master's-level psychologists, substance abuse counselors, mental health technicians, and so forth. Where that is the case, such individuals need not be licensed, certified, or registered to work in correctional facilities either. What is not permitted under NCCHC standards, though, is a two-tiered system where licensure or certification is required for mental health staff to provide services in the community but not required for them to provide similar services to those behind bars.

In addition, all three sets of NCCHC standards state that all qualified mental health professionals must receive a minimum of 12 hours of continuing education or staff development annually (essential: Y-21, J-18, P-19). Newly hired mental health staff also must receive a formal orientation that reviews similarities and differences between a correctional and a community setting, as well as the characteristics and special needs of the patients they will serve (Y-21, J-25, P-25). In adult facilities, this is an important standard, but orientation must be provided within the first 90 days of employment. In the juvenile standards, this is an essential requirement, but no time frame is specified for completing the orientation of new staff. The prison set contains an additional important standard, which specifies that health administrative and support staff also receive at least 12 hours of continuing education or staff development appropriate to their positions (P-26). All mental health staff must have written job descriptions specific to their positions that define their duties and responsibilities (essential: Y-19, important: J-22, P-23).

Another essential standard common to all three sets is health training for child care workers or correctional officers (Y-22, J-19, P-20). Because custody staff are with inmates around the clock, they often are in the best position to observe changes in an individual's appearance or behavior, and are usually the first responders when there is an emergency. Thus they need to know how to recognize signs and symptoms of serious mental illness and suicidal behavior, as well as what to do when an emergency occurs. In small facilities without any full-time health staff, the juvenile and jail standards require that there be a designated health-trained staff member who coordinates the health delivery system (essential: Y-20; important: J-24). This issue is not addressed in the prison standards because virtually all prisons are of sufficient size to employ at least one full-time health professional.

None of the sets of NCCHC standards permit inmates to serve as health care workers by rendering direct patient care, scheduling health care appointments, or handling medical or mental health records (essential: Y-24, J-21, P-22). Such practices were common in the past when there were insufficient numbers of paid staff to handle these tasks, but years of experience showed that putting some inmates in charge of others' health care led to extortion and exploitation. In recent years, compliance with this standard has been problematic in some facilities that use inmate peers as health educators, or to lead support groups, or to serve as "buddies" for inmates who may be suicidal. Current editions of the NCCHC standards permit such exceptions providing the inmate workers are appropriately trained and supervised and serve as adjuncts to, rather than substitutes for, professional staff.

Both the jail (J-23) and the prison (P-24) sets contain an important standard requiring a written staffing plan that ensures a sufficient number of health staff of varying types is available "to provide adequate evaluation and treatment consistent with contemporary standards of care" (NCCHC, 1996, 29; 1997, 29). The Commission does not dictate specific health staffing patterns for correctional facilities, because there are too many variables that affect staffing that differ from institution to institution. Rather, it is incumbent on the jail or prison to demonstrate that the staffing it has in place is sufficient to meet inmates' serious health needs.

Support Services

Another essential standard common to all three sets of NCCHC standards is the management of pharmaceuticals (Y-42, J-26, P-27). Although most of this standard is directed at pharmacists and medical staff, it does specify in each set that psychotropic and behavior-modifying medications should be prescribed "only when clinically indicated (as one facet of a program of therapy) and not for disciplinary reasons." Again, this standard seeks to remedy past practices in some facilities where a substantial number of residents were kept medicated as a means of keeping the institution calm.

The need to have sufficient clinic space, equipment, and supplies is an important standard common to all three sets (Y-07, J-27, P-28). Where mental health services are provided in the facility, this standard specifies that there should be private interviewing space to see such clients and that the room should have desks and chairs available for use as well as lockable files for patient records or other confidential materials.

All facilities regardless of type need to have made advance arrangements for off-site specialty services and inpatient hospitalization when such care is not available on site (important: Y-46, J-29, P-30). This standard applies to mental health needs as well as medical ones.

Care and Treatment Issues

Seeing all new arrivals within an hour or two after they are admitted to the correctional facility to ascertain whether they have any health needs may well be the most important requirement common to all three sets (essential: Y-27, J-30, P-32). The standard on initial screening requires intake staff to ascertain whether the new arrival has any mental problems including suicidal ideation, is currently on any medications, has a history of prior or recent drug or alcohol use, or exhibits behavior suggestive of an altered mental status. Its purpose is to ensure that those individuals with serious needs are referred immediately for care. The requirements of this standard are similar in the three sets except that the prison standards state that receiving screening must be completed by qualified health professionals, whereas the jail and juvenile versions permit health trained staff to conduct the initial screening.

Information on the availability and types of health services (including mental health care) and how to access them also must be provided to new arrivals (essential: Y-28, J-31, P-31). The prison standards state that this must be done within 24 hours of admission, whereas neither the juvenile nor jail versions specify an exact time period for providing this information other than to state that it must be done "upon arrival."

The next major encounter with newly arrived inmates occurs at the time of the health assessment (essential: Y-33, J-33, P-34). In jails, this more detailed assessment must be completed on all inmates within 14 days of their arrival, whereas prisons and juvenile institutions are allowed only seven days to complete this appraisal. It includes, among other things, a review of the earlier screening results, taking vital signs, providing a "hands-on" physical exam, and taking a more extensive history regarding the use and abuse of alcohol and drugs, any suicide attempts, and any treatment for mental health problems including hospitalizations and previous medications. Again, those inmates with identified mental health needs must be referred to mental health professionals for follow-up care and treatment.

Because much of the health assessment is medical in nature, nurses, physician extenders, and physicians are the usual staff completing it. Mental health staff generally are not involved in the routine intake processing of all inmates until the time of a separate mental health evaluation. There is great variance among NCCHC's standards sets on this element, because it is not specifically addressed in the juvenile version, it is mandatory in the prison version (P-35), and it is identified as important in the jail version (J-39). Both sets of standards for adult facilities require the mental health evaluation to be completed within 14 days of an individual's arrival.

In many facilities, the mental health evaluation is a two-tiered process. Mental health workers conduct a structured interview to complete the mental health history and determine the individual's mental status. This is conducted in a manner and on a form approved by the mental health authority. Screening for retardation or developmental disability also occurs at this time. Those individuals suspected of or identified with mental health needs then are referred to mental health professionals (e.g., psychiatrists, clinical psychologists, psychometrists) for further evaluation and the development of a treatment plan as appropriate.

All three sets of NCCHC standards specify the necessity of developing a treatment plan for those offenders with special needs. This is an essential standard for jails (J-49) and prisons (P-51) and an important one for juvenile institutions (Y-47). Both the jail and prison standards state that the treatment plan is to include "instructions about diet, exercise, adaptation to the correctional environment, medication, the type and frequency of diagnostic testing, and the frequency of follow-up for medical evaluation and adjustment of treatment modality" (NCCHC, 1996, 63; 1997, 65). Individuals with special or serious mental health needs or who are developmentally disabled are specifically mentioned in the jail and prison standards as among those requiring treatment plans. Juvenile standard Y-47 states only that youths who are potentially suicidal or psychotic need such plans, but it has an additional important standard on the care of the physically or mentally disabled juvenile (Y-51) that requires treatment plans for any mental disability.

NCCHC's three sets of standards all mandate that offenders have the opportunity daily to request assistance to meet their nonemergency health needs (essential: Y-31, J-34, P-37). These requests must be documented, triaged, and acted on by qualified health professionals. Individuals with health concerns are scheduled to be seen at sick call, which is defined as "care for an ambulatory inmate with health care requests that are evaluated and treated in a clinical setting" (NCCHC, 1996, 47; 1997, 49). In essence, sick call is equivalent to an office visit in a community setting.

NCCHC standards differ dramatically in their specifications for sick call. In the juvenile version, sick call must be held once a week in facilities with fewer than 25 inmates and five days per week in institutions with more than 100 youths (essential: Y-32). In contrast, the jail standards require sick call to be held one day a week if the population is fewer than 100 and five days per week if it exceeds 200 (essential: J-35), whereas the prison standards state that nurse sick call must be held daily regardless of the facility's size (essential: P-38). In addition, the prison standards state that a physician must be "on site seeing patients a minimum of three and one half hours per week per 100 inmates" (NCCHC, 1997, 49).

It is not clear how these specifications for frequency of sick call apply to mental health services, because the need for such services is considerably less than the need for medical services in almost all institutions. As to timeliness of care, though, the adult versions indicate that generally nonemergency requests for care should be triaged within 24 hours, and the inmate should be seen by a qualified health professional within the next 24 hours (or 72 hours if on a week-end). This specification would apply to mental health care as well as medical care.

None of the sets of NCCHC standards permit physicians to use standing orders for prescription medications (important: Y-48, J-41, P-43). Instead, direct orders are required (essential: Y-35, J-37, P-40).

All facilities must have arrangements to provide emergency services and to train staff in the procedures for notifying appropriate personnel and arranging transportation to the emergency health care facility when necessary (essential: Y-34, J-36, P-41). Psychiatric emergencies and suicide attempts must be addressed in the facility's procedures as well as medical emergencies.

Continuity of care from admission to discharge should be provided (important: Y-49, J-42, P-44), and all treatment should occur in private with due consideration of the patient's dignity and feelings (important: Y-45, J-08, P-09). Both sets of standards for adult facilities explicitly recognize that for certain patients who may be disruptive or a high security risk, custody staff may need to be present during the health encounter. Under these circumstances an attempt should be made to provide either auditory or visual privacy. For mental health encounters, auditory privacy is paramount.

Health Promotion and Disease Prevention

An important standard found in all three sets is the need to offer health education programs and training in self-care skills to inmates (Y-14, J-44, P-46). Alcohol and drug problems, prevention of sexual and other physical violence, and stress management are among the suggested topics. For juveniles, the standards also recommend health education in family planning (important: Y-58).

All three sets of standards address tobacco use in correctional facilities but differ somewhat in their requirements (important: Y-13, J-48, P-50). For juveniles, tobacco in any form is prohibited as it is in the community. For adults, the jail standards state that all health care areas should be smoke free and that there should be non-smoking areas in inmate communal facilities such as housing, dining, and recreation areas. The prison standards require that smoking be prohibited in all indoor areas of the facility, but would permit smoking out of doors if the prison had such a policy.

Special Needs and Services

Where institutions have infirmaries, *essential* requirements of all three sets of NCCHC standards are that they be staffed around the clock by qualified health personnel under the direction of an RN, that a physician be on call 24 hours a day, and that admission to and discharge from the inpatient facility occur only on the order of a physician or other provider where permitted by law (essential: Y-36, J-50, P-52). The scope of services provided must be in writing, and separate inpatient records must be kept. A manual of nursing procedures is required also, and patients must be within sight or sound of health personnel at all times. The definition of an infirmary includes inpatient mental health facilities as well as medical ones.

If the correctional institution segregates certain individuals, whether for disciplinary or administrative reasons, NCCHC standards require health staff to be more proactive with these inmates to ensure that they continue to have access to health services. The three sets of standards differ somewhat in their specifications, though. The juvenile version addresses only those youths removed from general population owing to behavioral problems. This essential standard (Y-39) requires health staff to evaluate such individuals daily to ensure that their health status has not declined and to document these encounters in the individual's medical record. In addition, the discussion to this standard recommends that the upper limit for segregating juveniles be set at 24 hours or less.

In contrast, the jail standards do not define a time limit for segregation. They state that anyone who is segregated regardless of reason should be seen by health staff a minimum of three times per week. This is an important standard in the jail version and does not require that segregation rounds be noted in the individuals' charts (J-43).

The prison version has separate standards depending on the type of segregation imposed. If an inmate is placed in segregation for administrative reasons, health staff must make rounds at least three times per week but need not document these visits in individual charts (important: P-45). If, however, the inmate is placed in disciplinary segregation, he or she must be seen daily by health personnel, and these encounters must be documented in the individual's health record (essential: P-39). Both of these prison standards impose an additional requirement of notifying health staff whenever anyone is placed in either type of segregation so they can check the inmates' medical and mental health records to ensure that there are no contraindications to such placement.

In most facilities regardless of type, segregation rounds are conducted by medical staff. None of NCCHC's sets of standards address the frequency with which mental health staff should visit individuals in segregation. Obviously, individuals on a mental health caseload should be seen at whatever frequency is specified in their treatment plan no matter where they are housed in the institution. Mental health professionals should be aware, though, that segregation may exacerbate feelings of anxiety or depression and may lead to a decline in individuals' mental status. For this reason, I recommend that mental health staff make rounds of segregation inmates at least weekly. This is in addition to the rounds made by medical personnel. The purpose of these rounds is simply to check on inmates' mental status and need not be a lengthy process. If any problems are identified, the individual should be scheduled to be seen in a clinical setting.

All facilities regardless of type must have procedures in place to manage individuals in need of treatment for intoxication or withdrawal. This is an essential standard in all three sets (Y-29, J-52, P-54), but is particularly applicable to juvenile detention facilities and adult jails where individuals usually arrive directly from the community. For the most part, individuals placed in adult prisons or juvenile correctional facilities are coming from another institution and no longer are in need of detoxification or in danger of undergoing withdrawal. Nonetheless, all facilities must have procedures in place to manage intoxication and withdrawal owing to the possibility of inmates obtaining alcohol or drugs while behind bars. Medical supervision by a psychiatrist or other physician specialist is required. In addition, all facilities regardless of type should have programs in place to manage individuals with alcohol or other drug problems (important: Y-50, J-54, P-56).

Although seldom discussed, sexual assault is a not uncommon occurrence behind bars. Both sets of NCCHC standards for adult facilities recognize this and state that jails and prisons should have policies and procedures in place to treat victims of sexual assault both medically and psychologically (important: J-55, P-57). After the victim has been physically examined, a mental health professional should evaluate the inmate to determine whether crisis intervention counseling and long-term follow-up are needed.

Suicide prevention is a mandatory component of all three sets of standards (essential: Y-37, J-51, P-53). There must be a written plan that addresses staff training, identification of potential suicide risk, monitoring those individuals deemed to be at risk, referral of suicidal individuals to appropriate mental health providers and facilities, evaluation of the extent of risk by a mental health professional, appropriate housing and supervision for suicidal individuals, communication between custody and health staff, intervention when a suicide is in progress, notification of appropriate individuals, reporting procedures, and an after-the-fact review of any suicide or serious suicide attempt to determine whether changes in procedures are needed. In addition, the standards for adult facilities have added a requirement for critical incident debriefing for inmates and personnel who may have witnessed or responded to a suicide in progress.

Health Records

All three sets of NCCHC standards deem it essential that there be a standardized and uniform health record format and that the record contain documentation of all clinical testing, findings, and encounters (Y-59, J-58, P-60). The standards recommend, but do not require, a unified health record system. If, however, medical, mental health, or dental services each maintain their own charts, copies of relevant information—including major health problems, medications, and allergies—must be kept in all charts and updated continuously.

The need to maintain confidentiality of the health records and their contents is another essential standard found in all three sets (Y-60, J-59, P-61). The health records must be kept separately from individuals' custody records, and access to the health records and the information they contain must be controlled by the health authority consistent with applicable local, state, and federal laws. Certain information from the health record may be shared with custody staff when necessary to preserve the health and safety of that inmate, other inmates, or staff members (important: Y-08; essential: J-60, P-62). Custody staff should be told if an individual is suicidal or mentally ill or retarded, but there seldom is a need to reveal any details regarding individuals' specific mental conditions.

Correctional institutions also should have policies and procedures in place regarding the transfer of health records or health information (important: Y-61, J-62, P-64), as well as specifying how and how long such records must be maintained after individuals have left the facility (important: Y-62, J-63, P-65). Both sets for adult institutions contain an additional standard requiring the health record to be provided during all clinical encounters for reference and documentation by health staff (important: J-61, P-63).

Medical–Legal Issues

An essential component of all three sets of NCCHC standards is the appropriate use of therapeutic restraints (Y-40, J-64, P-66). Policies and procedures are required that specify "the type(s) of restraints that may be used and when, where, how, and for how long" (NCCHC, 1995a, 38; 1996, 83; 1997, 83). All three sets call for the use of soft restraints only, but differ as to who can order restraints and how long they should be used. The juvenile standards state that the facility's policy should specify who can authorize the use of restraints for therapeutic purposes, whereas both of the adult sets restrict authorization to a physician or another health provider where permitted by law. Under the juvenile standards, duration in restraints should not exceed two hours without involving a mental health professional to develop a plan for alternate intervention strategies. The jail standards state that an order for restraints generally should not exceed 24 hours, which is reduced to 12 hours in the prison standards. All three versions specify that individuals in restraints should be checked at least every 15 minutes.

It is important to note that these standards address the use of restraints as part of a treatment regimen. Health staff should not have any involvement in restraining individuals for custody reasons except to monitor their health status periodically.

The adult standards apply the same criteria noted previously to the use of therapeutic seclusion (essential: J-64, P-66)—in other words, there must be policies and procedures governing its use, use is authorized only by a physician or other health professional where permitted by law, individuals must be checked every 15 minutes, the duration should not exceed 12 (prison) or 24 (jail) hours, and seclusion should not be used for disciplinary reasons. The juvenile standards are silent regarding the use of therapeutic seclusion.

Both of the sets of standards for adult facilities permit the use of forced psychotropic medication in an emergency situation (essential: J-65, P-67), but this topic is not discussed in the juvenile standards. Under the adult standards, there must be policies and procedures that "include requirements for authorization by a physician and specification of the duration of the regimen; when, where, and how the procedures may be used; and treatment plan goals for less restrictive treatment alternatives as soon as possible" (NCCHC, 1996, 84; 1997, 84). The discussion indicates that psychotropic medication should be forced only in an emergency situation when the individual poses an imminent or immediate threat to self or others and only after all less restrictive measures have been used.

An important component of all three sets of standards is the prohibition against health staff involvement in collecting information for forensic purposes (Y-66, J-66, P-68). Correctional administrators often are tempted to use their own health staff to collect information that may be used against inmates, but this poses an ethical dilemma for providers if they use their professional skills to harm rather than help their patients. Examples in the mental health arena include performing psychological or psychiatric evaluations of inmates for use in adversarial proceedings or to determine parole eligibility. Neither of these examples is unethical unless the provider is in a treating relationship with the inmate. In these cases, the NCCHC standards recommend that the services of an outside provider be obtained.

The prison standards contain an additional prohibition against health staff participating in executions in any way (important: P-69). This prohibition is not applicable to jails or juvenile facilities because executions do not occur in those settings. For mental health staff, the primary involvement would occur in determining whether an inmate was sufficiently competent to be executed. NCCHC's (1995b) position is that such decisions should be made by mental health professionals who are not in a treating relationship with the condemned prisoner.

All three sets of NCCHC standards extend to inmates the same right to informed consent regarding proposed health treatments, examinations, and procedures that they would have in the community. This is designated as important in the jail (J-67) and prison (P-70) standards but essential in the juvenile version (Y-63). Because laws regarding informed consent differ among jurisdictions, NCCHC recommends that the advice of legal counsel be sought regarding establishing appropriate policies and procedures.

A related standard recognizes inmates' right to refuse treatment (essential: Y-64; important: J-68, P-71). This right generally is extended to mental health patients as well unless such refusals result in danger to self or others. Again, it is wise to consult legal counsel in drafting policies and procedures regarding inmates' right to refuse treatment, because there is specific case law that provides guidance about when and how an individuals' refusal of psychiatric inpatient care or medications may be overridden. Inmates retain certain due process rights even behind bars.

Finally, all three sets of NCCHC standards state that any research involving inmates as participants must be "consistent with established ethical, medical, legal, and regulatory standards for human research" (important: Y-65, J-69, P-72). It is important to note that this standard does not prohibit behavioral research providing that the methodology employed meets applicable guidelines for using human participants.

Other Issues

All three versions of NCCHC's standards also contain additional requirements governing the delivery of health care such as environmental health and safety, kitchen sanitation and food handlers, diet, exercise, dental care, personal hygiene, and so forth. However, such requirements generally do not apply to mental health care unless the facility is a free-standing mental health inpatient unit.

Measuring Compliance With NCCHC Standards

Although many correctional institutions choose to use the NCCHC's standards simply as guidelines in establishing their health care delivery systems, an increasing number seek formal accreditation of their health services as a way to measure the extent of their compliance with national recommendations. The National Commission on Correctional Health Care offers a voluntary accreditation program for interested facilities.

The accreditation process begins when facility staff submit an application that provides some basic information about their medical, dental, and mental health services. The next step is to complete a self-survey questionnaire, which is the facility's own assessment of the extent of its compliance with NCCHC's standards. After a period of consultation between the facility's staff and the commission's staff, when it appears on paper that a sufficient number of standards have been complied with, the commission schedules an on-site survey to measure the extent of actual compliance with standards.

NCCHC's survey teams are made up of correctional health professionals. The exact make-up of the team depends on the type of facility under review, its health mission, and its size. A small facility may be reviewed by just an administrator and a physician over the course of a single day. Larger facilities can expect a two- to three-day survey with additional team members such as psychologists, nurses, and dentists participating. Facilities with special mental health missions such as psychiatric inpatient care or programs for developmentally disabled individuals can anticipate that professionals in these areas will participate in the review process.

Following the on-site survey, the team submits a report of its findings to the commission's staff. The report is presented to an accreditation committee that meets three times a year. This committee has the responsibility of making the final decisions regarding a facility's accreditation status.

A Comparison of Correctional and Community Health Standards

As noted previously, the standards used most frequently to guide the delivery of health services in correctional facilities are those of the American Correctional Association (ACA) or those of the National Commission on Correctional Health Care. Because both of these sets of standards were based on those developed in the 1970s by the American Medical Association, the topics covered are quite similar, but those of the NCCHC are considerably more detailed.

The primary difference between these two sets of national correctional standards is one of emphasis. The ACA's standards address all aspects of managing correctional facilities, of which health services is only one component. In contrast, the NCCHC's standards are devoted solely to defining requirements for the care and treatment of offenders' health needs. This difference in emphasis carries over to the accreditation process. An NCCHC accreditation team usually spends as much time on-site reviewing just the delivery of health care as an ACA team spends reviewing all programs and services (e.g., classification, food services, library services, inmate housing, disciplinary programs, work and school activities, correctional staff training, health care). Because their mission is different, the make-up of ACA and NCCHC accreditation teams differs as well. ACA generally uses experienced correctional managers to review all services, including health care. Such individuals can determine whether health care policies and procedures are in place, but they are not in a position to comment on the appropriateness of such policies or on the quality of care provided. In contrast, NCCHC's accreditation teams are made up of administrators and clinicians working in correctional health care. Because of these differences, many of the better managed correctional facilities seek accreditation from both organizations.

With the exception of the federal prison system, few correctional facilities use the community standards developed by the JCAHO. In part, this may be because JCAHO standards are more difficult to meet. Although the topics covered by JCAHO and NCCHC are similar, JCAHO's standards are considerably more detailed. As an example, in its consolidated standards manual, JCAHO (1990) has separate sections devoted to alcoholism and other drug-dependence services, forensic services, and mental retardation and developmental disability services, whereas NCCHC has only a couple of standards addressing each of these topics. On the other hand, JCAHO standards do not address any of the unique aspects of providing care and treatment for offenders in a correctional setting such as health training for correctional staff, autonomy of clinical decisions, use of offenders as health workers, health evaluation of inmates in administrative or disciplinary segregation, sexual assault, the role of health staff in executions, and so forth, all of which are addressed in NCCHC standards. As a result, many correctional health professionals believe that JCAHO's standards are not as relevant to their environment as the standards of NCCHC.

Another reason JCAHO's standards are not used as frequently in corrections as those of the ACA and the NCCHC is because of cost considerations. It is not just that JCAHO has more requirements for health services but also that its accreditation process costs two to three times that of correctional accrediting bodies for the same size facility.

Utility of National Correctional Health Standards and Impact on Quality of Care

The purpose of national correctional health standards is to provide guidance in establishing adequate health care delivery systems to meet the serious needs of adult and juvenile offenders. To date, NCCHC has been very successful in achieving this purpose. Accreditation provides significant protection against class action suits alleging that the *system* of care is inadequate.

This does not mean, however, that the care provided in accredited facilities is always of the highest quality. NCCHC considers its standards to be minimal guidelines, and some accredited facilities barely meet the standards, whereas others far exceed the requirements needed for accreditation. In addition, even in a system that exceeds national standards, this does not guarantee that all staff will follow the established policies and procedures or that all clinical staff will be equally skilled in providing care and treatment. What accreditation does do, however, is to help ensure that there is a quality review system in place to help identify problems in service delivery so that corrective action can be implemented.

Conclusion

Mental health services are an integral part of any correctional health delivery system, whether operated separately or as part of a unified health system. National standards provide useful guidance in establishing and maintaining adequate services to treat the special needs of mentally disordered adult and juvenile offenders. Although greater attention should be paid in the future to quality of care issues in national correctional health standards, the existing standards are useful in identifying the key aspects of an adequate health care delivery system.

Fortunately, the commission revises its standards about every five years. Since its first standards were published in 1987, each successive edition has provided more extensive recognition of the importance of mental health care behind bars and more emphasis on quality of care. As noted previously, a companion volume to the NCCHC's 1997 prison standards was published in 1999 that discusses their applicability to mental health care in greater detail (NCCHC, 1999).

Given the commission's commitment to a unified health delivery system, it is unlikely that it will publish separate standards for mental health services in the future, but I expect subsequent editions of its standards to continue to emphasize the need for quality mental health care for incarcerated adults and adolescents.

References

American Bar Association. (1989). *ABA criminal justice mental health standards*. Washington, DC: Author.

American Correctional Association. (1977a). *Manual of standards for adult local detention facilities*. Laurel, MD: Author.

American Correctional Association. (1977b). *Manual of standards for juvenile detention facilities and services*. Laurel, MD: Author.

American Correctional Association. (1977c). *Manual of standards for juvenile training schools and services*. Laurel, MD: Author.

American Correctional Association. (1990). *Standards for adult correctional institutions* (3rd ed.). Laurel, MD: Author.

American Correctional Association. (1991a). *Standards for adult local detention facilities* (3rd ed.). Laurel, MD: Author.

American Correctional Association. (1991b). *Standards for juvenile training schools* (3rd ed.). Laurel, MD: Author.

American Medical Association. (1977). *Survey questionnaire for the accreditation of medical care and health services in jails*. Chicago: Author.

American Medical Association. (1979a). *Standards for health services in juvenile correctional facilities*. Chicago: Author.

American Medical Association. (1979b). *Standards for health services in prisons*. Chicago: Author.

American Nurses' Association. (1985). *Standards of nursing practice in correctional facilities*. Kansas City, MO: Author.

American Psychiatric Association. (1989). *Psychiatric services in jails and prisons*. Washington, DC: Author.

American Public Health Association. (1976). *Standards for health services in correctional institutions*. Washington, DC: Author.

Anno, B. J. (1991). *Prison health care: Guidelines for the management of an adequate delivery system*. Chicago: National Commission on Correctional Health Care.

Anno, B. J. (1994). Standards for the delivery of mental health services in a correctional setting. In Rosner, R. (Ed.), *Principles and practice of forensic psychiatry* (pp. 375–379). New York: Chapman & Hall.

Bowring v. Godwin. (1977). 551 F.2d 44 (4th Cir.).

Cohen, F. (1988). *Legal issues and the mentally disordered prisoner*. Washington, DC: National Institute of Corrections.

Dubler, N. N. (Ed.). (1986). *Standards for health services in correctional institutions* (2nd ed.). Washington, DC: American Public Health Association.

Estelle v. Gamble. (1976). 429 U.S. 97.

Joint Commission on Accreditation of Healthcare Organizations. (1990). *Consolidated standards manual*. Oakbrook Terrace, IL: Author.

National Commission on Correctional Health Care. (1995a). *Standards for health services in juvenile detention and confinement facilities*. Chicago: Author

National Commission on Correctional Health Care. (1995b). Position statement on competency for execution. *Journal of Correctional Health Care*, 2 (1), 75.

National Commission on Correctional Health Care. (1996). *Standards for health services in jails*. Chicago: Author.

National Commission on Correctional Health Care. (1997). *Standards for health services in prisons*. Chicago: Author.

National Commission on Correctional Health Care. (1999). *Correctional mental health care: Standards & guidelines for delivering services*. Chicago: Author.

Newman v. Alabama. (1972). 349 F. Supp. 285 (M.D. Ala.), *aff'd*, 503 F. 2d 1320 (5th Cir. 1974), *cert. denied*, 421 U.S. 948 (1975).

Part II

Treating Disordered Offenders

Chapter 4
TREATING CONDUCT DISORDER, ANTISOCIAL, AND PSYCHOPATHIC PERSONALITIES

Carl B. Gacono, Ron J. Nieberding, Amy Owen, John Rubel,
and Robert Bodholdt

In more than 50 years of evaluating and treating conduct disorder (CD), antisocial personality disorder (ASPD), and psychopathic patients in various outpatient, hospital, and correctional settings, and training others to do the same (Gacono, 2000; Gacono & Meloy, 1994), we are continually surprised by the misuse of the terms antisocial personality disorder and psychopathy. Despite more than 30 years of published research on psychopathy (Hare, 1966, 1996), clinicians continue to confuse ASPD with psychopathy—inappropriately viewing them as synonymous (Losel, 1998). These conditions evolved along separate theoretical paths and manifest empirically measurable and clinically relevant differences—the differences are not merely semantic.

Conduct disorder and antisocial personality disorder (American Psychiatric Association, 1968, 1980, 1994) evolved from a social deviancy model (Robins, 1966) and the term sociopathy (American Psychiatric Association, 1952). Sociopathy is an antiquated term lacking contemporary clinical meaning. Used in the original *DSM*, sociopathy included a variety of conditions such as sexual deviation, alcoholism, and "dyssocial" and "antisocial" reactions. The antisocial reaction was similar to the classic psychopath (Jenkins, 1960), describing individuals who were

> always in trouble, profiting neither from experience nor punishment and maintaining no loyalties ... are frequently callous and hedonistic ... emotional immaturity with lack of a sense of responsibility, lack of judgment, and an ability to rationalize their behavior so that it appears warranted, reasonable, and justified. (American Psychiatric Association, 1952, p. 38)

In *DSM-II* "sociopath" was replaced by antisocial personality disorder (American Psychiatric Association, 1968), and gradually characteristics of the traditional psychopath disappeared (Cleckley, 1976; Hare, 1996; Meloy, 1988).

The *DSM* conceptualization of conduct disorder and ASPD has relegated the disorder to primarily *behavioral* criteria. Conduct disorder is a juvenile prerequisite for an adult ASPD diagnosis. Predominantly a male diagnosis, low base rates for CD and ASPD make such labels clinically useful in community settings. In forensic, correctional, or institutional treatment settings, where base rates commonly exceed 50% (Gacono & Meloy, 1994), a CD or ASPD diagnosis adds little to clinical understanding or treatment planning.[1]

The views expressed in this chapter are solely the authors' and may or may not reflect the opinions of any past, present, or future institutional affiliations. We wish to extend appreciation to Dr. Lynne Bannatyne for her helpful comments and suggestions. We are also grateful to Dr. Richard Rasulis for helping us navigate the research internet on Conduct Disorder.

[1]Community base rates for CD are 3% to 5% of school age children with a male to female ratio

Unlike CD and ASPD, the traditional concept of psychopathy (Cleckley, 1976; Hare, 1996; Meloy, 1988)[2] made up of trait and behavioral criteria. As measured by the Psychopathy Checklists (Forth, Kosson, & Hare, in press; Hare, 1991; Hart et al., 1995), psychopathy contains two stable, oblique factors characterized by egocentricity, callousness, and remorselessness (Factor 1) and an irresponsible, impulsive, thrill-seeking, unconventional, and antisocial lifestyle (Factor 2). Factor 1 includes such traits as glibness, superficial charm, grandiosity, pathological lying, conning–manipulative, shallow affect, lack of empathy and remorse, and correlates with narcissistic and histrionic personality disorders, low anxiety, low empathy, and self-report measures of Machiavellianism and narcissism (Harpur, Hare, & Hakstian, 1989; Hart & Hare, 1989). Factor 2 includes patterns of proneness to boredom, impulsivity, and irresponsibility and correlates most strongly with criminal behaviors, lower socioeconomic background, lower IQ and less education, self-report measures of antisocial behavior, and the diagnosis of conduct disorder and antisocial personality (Hare, 1991; Harpur et al., 1989). Most criminal psychopaths meet the criteria for ASPD, whereas most individuals with ASPD are not psychopaths.

The traditional concept of psychopathy transcends cultural bias associated with CD and ASPD (Cooke, 1998; Murphy, 1976). Most cultures have names for individuals diagnosed with psychopathy. For example, in Eskimo cultures the word "kunlangeta" describes "a man who . . . repeatedly lies and cheats and steals things and does not go hunting and, when the other men are out of the village, takes sexual advantage of many women—someone who does not pay attention to reprimands and who is always being brought to the elders for punishment" (Murphy, 1976, p. 1026). It is interesting to note that the prescribed "treatment" for the "kunlangeta" consists of "push(ing) him off the ice when nobody else was looking" (p. 1026)—that is, if he did not push you off first.

The overwhelming majority of NATO countries (see Cooke, 1998) share a traditional definition of psychopathy similar to that measured by Hare's Psychopathy Checklists (Cooke, 1998; Hare, 1991). The evolving worldwide consensus can be attributed to the empirical work of Hare and his colleagues. Contrary to earlier beliefs that supported the social deviancy model underlying *DSM*'s CD and ASPD diagnosis, Hare and others have demonstrated that psychopathic traits can be reliably rated (Hare, 1991).

The relationship between psychopathy level and risk of future behavior has been repeatedly demonstrated. High Psychopathy Checklist scores have been associated with increases in quantity and variety of offenses committed (Hare & Jutai, 1983), frequency of violent offenses (Hare & McPherson, 1984), reoffense rates (Hare, McPherson, & Forth, 1988), poor treatment response (Ogloff, Wong, & Greenwood, 1990; Rice, Harris, & Cormier, 1992), and institutional misbehavior (Gacono, Meloy,

---

of between 4 : 1 to 9 : 1. ASPD rates are 5.8% of males and 1.2% of females with 45% to 75% in forensic settings.

[2]The Hare Psychopathy Checklist-Revised (PCL-R; Hare, 1991) is a 20-item, 40-point scale (≥ 30 = psychopathy). The mean PCL-R score for a combined prison population is 23.37 ($SD = 7.96$); forensic psychiatric population, 20.56 ($SD = 7.79$). The Psychopathy Checklist: Screening Version (PCL:SV; Hart, Cox, & Hare, 1995) is a 12-item, 24-point scale (≥ 18 suggests psychopathy). It is a screening tool, not a substitute for the PCL-R. The Psychopathy Checklist:Youth Version (PCL:YV; Forth, Kosson, & Hare, in press) is modified for adolescent offenders.

Sheppard, Speth, & Roske, 1995; Gacono, Meloy, Speth, & Roske, 1997).[3] These robust findings do not seem to be biased by culture, gender, and the presence or absence of a major mental disorder (Cooke, 1998). Psychopathy level is currently considered an essential component of risk assessment (Bodholdt, Richards, & Gacono, 2000).

Patients with psychopathic traits and behaviors significantly impact the therapeutic milieu—hospital (Gacono, Meloy, Sheppard, Speth, & Roske, 1995) or correctional facility (Ogloff et al., 1990; Rice et al., 1992). Psychopathy level *must* be identified and controlled when attempting to treat or evaluate treatment of CD and ASPD patients (Gacono, 1998). Not only do the individual failures of psychopathic individuals affect treatment outcome data, but their attitudes and behaviors ripple through the treatment milieu, negatively affecting the progress of other patients (Kosson, Steuerwald, Forth, & Kirkhart, 1997). Concurrent diagnoses, such as sexual paraphilia, substance abuse, cognitive impairment, or Axis-I functional psychoses also affect treatment effectiveness with ASPD patients (Losel, 1998; Rice & Harris, 1997).

Program integrity must be considered when evaluating treatment outcome (Losel, 1998). Politics and treatment do not mix (Moretti et al., 1997). Despite good intentions, correctional programming frequently lacks skilled clinicians, adequate facilities, or, in a misguided fashion, offers external rewards, such as sentence reduction, for treatment participation. *All* these factors can contribute to decreased treatment effectiveness (see Burns & Nolen-Hoeksema, 1992; Critis-Christoph et al., 1991; Falvey & Hebert, 1992; Mallinckrodt & Nelson, 1991; Orlinsky & Howard, 1980; Stein & Lambert, 1984, 1995). Frequently, more influenced by politics than scientific rigor, bureaucratic interest in presenting positive treatment outcome can influence findings, making them less reliable than data collected in independently controlled studies. Even when effective, treatment programs can be discontinued solely for political reasons (Rice, 1997).

In the following section we discuss the prevalence and developmental course of conduct disorder (CD) and appropriate treatment interventions.

Conduct Disorder (CD)

Terms, such as *violent tendencies, acting out, conduct problems, aggressiveness, antisocial behavior,* and *juvenile delinquency* have been used as labels for conduct disorder (CD). CD has long been associated with behaviors such as aggressive acts, theft, vandalism, fire setting, lying, truancy, and running away (Kazdin et al., 1989), and is included along with attention-deficit hyperactivity disorder (ADHD) and oppositional defiant disorder (ODD) in the "Attention-Deficit and Disruptive Behavioral Disorders" section of *DSM-IV* (American Psychiatric Association, 1994). Although a certain degree of adolescent acting out is expected, a CD diagnosis is

---

[3]Rorschach findings have provided convergent validity to other trait and behavioral measures finding that psychopathic ASPDs produce more indices associated with borderline personality organization (Gacono, 1990), are more narcissistic (Gacono, Meloy, & Heaven, 1990), and show less attachment and anxiety (Gacono & Meloy, 1991) than nonpsychopathic ASPDs.

reserved for significant antisocial behavior that is clearly beyond the realm of "nor-mal" functioning (Kazdin, 1987).

The *DSM-IV* (American Psychiatric Association, 1994) allows for coding CD as mild, moderate, or severe depending on symptom frequency and impact on others, and allows the clinician to designate a childhood or adolescent onset. Evaluating severity and age of onset provides some discrimination to this otherwise heteroge-neous diagnosis. Conduct disorder captures a wide range of psychologically diverse children (Gacono & Meloy, 1994). A CD diagnosis based on a history of physical fighting, cruelty to animals, using a weapon in more than one fight, and forcing someone into sexual activity likely describes a different child than one who is clas-sified as CD by virtue of running away from home at least two times, often being truant from school, and having stolen without confrontation of the victim on more than one occasion. In addition, CD can be diagnosed in adults ($\geq$18) who do not meet ASPD criteria.

Prevalence and Course

Despite low base rates in community samples (<18 years; 6–16% for males and 2–9% for their female counterparts; American Psychiatric Association, 1994, p. 88), CD constitutes a frequent diagnosis: Approximately 33% to 50% of referrals to child and adolescent clinics (Eppright, Kashani, Robinson, & Reid, 1993; Kazdin, 1987; Robins, 1991; Shamsie & Huchly, 1991). Base rates for CD within juvenile correc-tional facilities assuredly exceed both community and clinic populations (Forth & Burke, 1998).

Like most disorders, the course of CD is variable. Early onset is a poor prog-nostic indicator and places the individual at increased risk for other problems such as adult ASPD; substance abuse; and poor work, marital, and occupational adjust-ment (Kazdin, 1987). A consistent and unremitting display of antisocial behavior over time, under socialized patterns (Henn, Bardwell, & Jenkins, 1980; Quay, 1987; Schmidt, Solant, & Bridger, 1985), low levels of anxiety (McBurnett et al., 1991; Quay & Love, 1977; Walker et al., 1991), or concurrent hyperactivity (August, Stewart, & Holmes, 1983; Leober, Brinthaupt, & Green, 1990) also foreshadow a chronic course (Frick, 1998).[4]

Literature Review

Our literature review focused on published research for a 10-year period (1987–1997). The PsychLit database was assessed using the following keywords: conduct disorder, treatment, treatment outcome, juvenile delinquency, juvenile offenders, be-havioral treatment, cognitive–behavioral treatment, psychodynamic–psychoanalytic treatment, milieu therapy, therapeutic community, and psychopharmacology. Using all possible combinations of these qualifiers yielded a total of 162 citations during the 10-year period. After excluding studies examining substance abuse, concurrent

---

[4]In a prospective longitudinal study of 137 substance-abusing adolescents, onset of deviant behavior at or before age 10, the diversity of deviant behaviors, and more extensive pretreatment drug use best predicted progression to adult antisocial personality disorder (Myers, Stewart, & Brown, 1998).

diagnosis of ADHD, and case studies, the number of citations was reduced to 25. Summary studies, meta-analytic studies, available books and book chapters published in the past 10 years, were included in the review.

A European-based review (Losel, 1998) was also examined to provide cross-cultural breadth to the chapter. Last, only "empirical" studies using "treatment groups" were included in our final review ($N = 9$). A listing of these references and relevant summary articles is presented in Table 4.1.

Cognitive–Behavioral Treatment

Over the past decade, cognitive–behavioral approaches have dominated the research literature in the treatment of CD children and adolescents. Cognitive treatment strategies, although differing somewhat in form and substance, essentially focus on cognitive processes as mediators of behavior and emotion (Barley, 1986). In this view, disordered behavior and emotion are largely consequences of various cognitive deficiencies—for example, irrational beliefs and thinking errors. Behavioral interventions, in contrast, are largely based on operant, classical, or social learning paradigms. Faulty learning sets the stage for behavioral and emotional difficulties. As a consequence, behavioral change, through modification of the relationship between target behaviors and the factors that elicit or maintain them, becomes the focus of treatment. Many argue that clinical practice often requires combining cognitive and behavioral approaches (Barley, 1986).

Clinical evaluation of this approach is well-represented by the work of Kazdin and colleagues (Kazdin, 1993, 1995; Kazdin et al., 1987; Kazdin et al., 1989). These investigators examined the effectiveness of Problem Solving Skills Training (PSST), a specific and didactically presented skill-based training program. PSST was provided with and without in vivo practice sessions, and compared to nondirective relationship therapy (RT). PSST was found to more effectively decrease externalizing, aggressive behaviors, and overall behavioral problems relative to RT, although sustained benefits were suspect (Kazdin et al., 1989). Despite progress, most PSST, RT, and, control children continued to evidence conduct problems (Kazdin et al., 1987). In a related study of 29 pre-adolescents in a day treatment setting (Kendall et al., 1990), cognitive–behavioral treatment led to significant behavioral improvements.

Aggression Replacement Training (ART), a multimodal, psychoeducational approach (that includes structured learning exercises, such as anger-control training and moral education) was found to be effective with aggressive and assaultive youth in reducing the frequency and intensity of acting out and impulsivity, as well as increasing prosocial interactions (Glick & Goldstein, 1987). Postrelease functioning was rated as improved in four of six areas measured. The lack of significant differences in work and school functioning, however, casts some doubt on the generalizability and maintenance of other therapeutic gains. Finally, Lipsey's (1991) meta-analysis of more than 400 juvenile program evaluations found that behavioral, skill-oriented, and multi-modal methods produced the largest effects with the greater impact in community settings (less psychopathy) relative to institutional settings.

Table 4.1—*Summary of CD Treatment Literature (1987–1997)*

Author(s)	Control Type[a]	N	Setting	Treatment	Outcome[b]	1[c]	2[c]
Cognitive–Behavioral Approaches							
Glick et al. 1987	Yes	60	Residential	ART	Pos	Y	N
Kazdin et al. 1987	Yes	56	Inpatient	PSST/RT	Pos	Y	Y
Kazdin et al. 1989	No	112	Outpatient	PSST/PSST-P	Pos	Y	Y
Kazdin 1995	No	105	Outpatient	PSST/PMT	Pos	Y	N
Kendall et al. 1990	No	29	Day-treat.	CB v.s. PD	Pos	Y	N
Family-Based Approaches							
Borduin et al. 1993	No	176	Outpatient	MST vs. IT	Pos	Y	N
Henggeler et al. 1992	Yes	84	Outpatient	MST	Pos	Y	N
Milieu/Therapeutic Community Approaches							
Leeman et al. 1993	Yes	57	Corr. Inst.	EQUIP	Pos	Y	N
Mann-Feder 1996	No	288	Residen. Tx	TC vs. TE	Pos	N	N
Psychoanalytic/Psychodynamic Approaches							
Fonagy et al. 1994	No	135	Archival	23% of CD group improved			
Summary/Meta-Analytic Studies							
Andrews et al. 1990	Meta-analysis of 80 treatment programs						
Campbell et al. 1995	Review of Pharmacological Treatment						
Diamond et al. 1996	Review of Family-based treatment research						
Garrett 1985	Meta-analysis of 111 studies, Residential Tx						
Greenwood 1994	Review article on CD Tx						
Izzo & Ross 1990	Meta-analysis of Rehab. Programs for juveniles						
Kazdin 1987	Review article on Tx, including family Tx						
Lipsey 1991	Meta-analysis based on 400 programs						
Lock & Strauss 1994	Summary of In-patient Treatment for CD						
Offord & Bennett 1994	Literature review, Outcome, Tx efficacy						
Robins 1991	Review article						
Shamsie & Huchy 1991	Summary of CD literature						

[a]Type of treatment: ART = Aggression Replacement Training, PSST = Problem Solving Skills Training, PSST-P = PSST with in vivo practice, RT = Relationship Therapy, PMT = Parent Management Training, CB = Cognitive Behavioral, PD = Psychodynamic, MST = Multisystemic Therapy, IT = Interpersonal Therapy, EQUIP = Equipping Youth to Help One Another (a multi-component group treatment program), TC = Therapeutic Community, TE = Token Economy.
[b]Positive Outcome (POS).
[c]1, Follow-up, 2, *DSM* criteria were used to determine diagnosis.

Therapeutic Community

Milieu and therapeutic environments have been used extensively in community set-tings (Fagan, 1991; Izzo & Ross, 1990; Mann-Feder, 1996; Mendel, 1995) and to a lesser extent in correctional settings (Leeman et al., 1993; Selman, 1986). Although these programs may differ in regard to specific therapeutic interventions, most are characterized by a comprehensive and interactive treatment philosophy. This philos-ophy involves three salient conditions, including distribution of responsibility and decision-making power; clarity of programming and treatment goals; and a high level of staff–patient interaction (Gunderson, 1978).

Comparing a therapeutic community with a modified token economy, Mann-Feder (1996) found an overall trend toward improvement in both groups. Leeman et al. (1993) evaluated a hybrid program, which combined aspects of ART and a mod-ified version of the Positive Peer culture group format with incarcerated juveniles. Experimental participants showed significant improvements in institutional conduct and recidivism rates (Leeman et al., 1993).

Family-Based Approaches

Although not typically used in correctional settings, family-based approaches aimed at addressing the behavioral and psychological manifestations of CD have gained prominence over the past decade. Our literature review yielded a total of four family therapy studies, including one comprehensive review (Diamond et al., 1996).

Most notable among family-based interventions is Multisystemic Therapy (MST), a highly individualized family and home-based treatment that has its foun-dations in the social–ecological model of development (Henggeler et al., 1992; also see Henggeler & Borduin, 1990). In a controlled study of 84 juvenile offenders, Henggeler et al. (1992) reported substantial improvements (fewer arrests and in-creased family cohesion) in both the research participants and their families. In a related study (Borduin, Mann, Cone, & Henggeler, 1995), MST was more effective than individual therapy for preventing criminal behavior and violent offending among a high-risk group of 176 juveniles with prior criminal histories. Kazdin (1987) also discussed a family-based integrative approach, Functional Family Therapy, that has its roots in systems theory and behaviorism. No studies were found, however, that assessed this intervention.

Dumas's (1989) work supported the efficacy of family approaches presented within the context of a formal therapeutic program. Although not conclusive, prelim-inary findings suggest that family-based interventions affect CD, at least milder or less ingrained CD (Diamond et al., 1996).[5]

Additional Therapeutic Approaches

Although well-controlled studies are scarce, psychoanalytic treatment, psychophar-macology, and hospital-based treatment are among the remaining approaches used

---

[5]Gacono and Elliott (cited in Gacono & Meloy, 1988) reported short-term success treating CD males using a multifamily treatment group format based on Yochelson and Samenow's (1977) criminal thinking model.

with CD. Fonagy and Target (1994), in a non-experimental design, reported 23% of disruptive CD children demonstrated improvement as a result of psychoanalytic treatment. In a theoretical article, Sherwood (1990) suggested that successful psychodynamic treatment of CD patients includes confronting the adolescents' narcissism, a view shared by earlier theorists (Aichhorn, 1925).

Campbell and Cueva (1995) provided a useful overview of psychopharmacological intervention with CD individuals. They view CD as behaviorally heterogeneous, with pharmacological intervention rightly targeting "symptoms" involving aggression. Whereas aggressive subtype distinctions are increasingly being identified, generalized findings suggest mixed results for lithium; methylphenidate (Ritalin) may be superior to both lithium and placebo; some support for the efficacy of carbamazepine, despite side effects; and some support for clonidine's effectiveness. The authors conclude that the GABA-ergic system should be studied more extensively for its potential role in aggressive behavior (Campbell & Cueva, 1995).

Psychopharmacological interventions with CD patients have typically occurred within hospital settings (Wells & Faragher, 1993). In reviewing the literature between 1980–1991, Lock and Strauss (1994) found that, despite the large number of CD patients referred to inpatient psychiatric facilities, systematic outcome studies have not been published.

In contrast to the preponderance of pharmacotherapy studies targeting fairly specific symptoms (e.g., aggression, rage), Klein et al., (1997) describe preliminary but encouraging results with methylphenidate on more global measures of CD. Similarly, central serotonergic function is increasingly being implicated as moderating a number of temperamental aspects of antisocial behavior commonly relegated to the domain of personality and personality disorder, including social affiliativeness, disagreeableness, affective instability, aggression, and impulsivity (Constantino, Morris, & Murphy, 1997; Fava, 1997; Kavoussi, Armstead, & Coccaro, 1997; Knutson et al., 1998; Kristiansson, 1995; Miller et al., 1996). Of particular interest in this regard have been selective serotonin reuptake inhibitors and atypical neuroleptics.

Summary of CD Outcome Literature

There are few well-controlled, empirical studies within correctional settings that contain either short- or long-term outcome measures such as rates of institutional adjustment and reoffense. Only two studies included female CD participants—a surprising finding, because Glasser's (1965) "reality therapy" began with adolescent females incarcerated at the California Youth Authority (Horne & Glaser, 1993). Fewer than 50% of the identified studies had adequate control groups. Only three of the reviewed studies used *DSM* CD criteria, thus adding to the diagnostic heterogeneity of their research participants. Finally, none of the CD treatment studies addressed or controlled for psychopathy level, despite its adaptation for adolescent offenders (Forth, Hart, & Hare, 1990; Forth et al., in press; Smith, Gacono, & Kaufman, 1997). This oversight clearly limits the generalizability of the findings.

Despite methodological limitations, several treatments such as family-based approaches (especially MST), problem solving, and some psychopharmacological agents, show promise—especially when carried out within community settings (Offord & Bennett, 1994). Preventive strategies also appear promising for some individuals. Given the approximate cost of incarceration for a juvenile ($35,000 per year; Greenwood, 1994) and perhaps an even greater emotional cost, increased emphasis on research related to prevention and treatment is clearly warranted.

Antisocial Personality Disorder (ASPD)

An antisocial personality disorder diagnosis relies primarily on behavioral criteria (American Psychiatric Association, 1994, p. 648). From 1987 (American Psychiatric Association, 1987) to 1994 (American Psychiatric Association, 1994) only minor changes in the ASPD diagnostic criteria have been made. Two items (irresponsible parenting and failure to sustain a monogamous relationship) have been deleted, and two *DSM-III-R* items related to irresponsible behavior have been collapsed.

Unlike the CD diagnosis, antisocial personality disorder criteria do not provide guidelines for coding severity. This is unfortunate because determining severity has been clinically useful with CD patients. A conduct disorder history is a necessary but insufficient requirement for an adult ASPD diagnosis (American Psychiatric Association, 1994, p. 787). The relationship between ASPD and psychopathy is not defined in the *DSM-IV.*

Prevalence and Course

ASPD community base rates are approximately 3% for males and 1% for females (American Psychiatric Association, 1994, p. 648). Estimates within clinical settings have varied from 3% to 30%, with estimates much higher for correctional settings (Stevens, 1994). The nature of the treatment setting often predicts the severity of character pathology. Outpatient centers tend to treat the less violent and more neurotic. Psychiatric hospitals tend to treat those who display concurrent mental illness and exhibit lower levels of psychopathy. Prisons are more likely to manage or treat chronic offenders and the criminally dangerous—with the frequency of severe ASPDs (psychopathy) dependent on security level; the higher the security the greater number of psychopaths.

ASPD has a chronic course, although some of the antisocial behaviors and substance abuse decrease in severity around the fourth decade, at least for nonpsychopathic patients (Hare, 1991). Psychopaths, who make up a small percentage of ASPDs, continue on a chronic course of criminal, and particularly violent, offending (Hare & McPherson, 1984; Serin, 1991). Psychopathy predicts higher reoffense rates (Hart, Kropp, & Hare, 1988) and a higher risk for violence, even after the age when this behavior typically decreases in nonpsychopathic offenders (Hare & McPherson, 1984).

Although the clinical picture for most CD and ASPD patients varies, therapeutic pessimism towards psychopathic patients is warranted (Gacono, 1998, 2000). Psychopathic individuals are pathologically narcissistic (Gacono et al., 1990), do not attach (Meloy, 1988), experience deficits in anxiety and affect (Gacono & Meloy 1991), exhibit impaired empathy and remorse, are often impulsive, are unable or unwilling to tolerate frustration, do not trust, and exhibit high rates of all types of misbehavior within the institutional setting (Gacono et al., 1995; Gacono, Meloy,

Speth, & Roske, 1997). As a consequence, they have little ability to form a working alliance with a therapist (Meloy 1995; Strasburger, 1986). In controlled studies, treatment response has been dismal (Ogloff et al., 1990; Rice et al., 1992; Rice, Harris, & Quinsey, 1990).

Several studies document improved prognosis for ASPD patients (likely not psychopathic; PCL-R $\geq$ 30) who are co-diagnosed with an Axis I disorder (Anderson & Brauer, 1985; Gabbard & Coyne, 1987; Shea, Widiger, & Klein, 1992; Weiss, Davis, Hedlund, & Cho, 1983). Woody, McLellan, Luborsky, and O'Brien (1985) found depression to be associated with a positive prognosis in ASPD patients with a substance abuse history; however, treatment success is relative as patients with ASPD generally demonstrate a poorer response to alcohol abuse treatment than do patients without ASPD (Poldrugo & Forti, 1988; Schuckit, 1985). Gabbard and Coyne (1987) found 70% of their ASPD patients left treatment prematurely; histories of felony arrest and conviction, repeated lying, and an unresolved legal situation at admission all related to negative treatment response. Positive response was related to the presence of anxiety and an Axis I diagnosis of depression (both contraindicated in psychopathy; Meloy, 1988).

Other Axis I psychotic disorders may also influence recidivism and treatment response in ASPD patients. Yet even within mentally disordered samples, high psychopathy levels correlate with increased misbehavior, recidivism, and poor treatment response (Gacono et al., 1995; Gacono et al., 1997; Rice & Harris, 1992; Rice, Harris, Lang, & Bell, 1990).

Literature Review

Our literature review was conducted via the PsychLit database and focused on published research between 1987–1997. Keywords used included several general topics: *antisocial personality disorder, offender, psychopathy, treatment,* and *outcome,* and more specific indicators such as *behavioral treatment, cognitive–behavioral treatment, psychodynamic* or *psychoanalytic treatment, milieu therapy,* and *therapeutic community.* The key words *ASPD* and *treatment* produced 85 citations during the 10-year period. After excluding studies examining chemical dependency treatment, psychopharmacological interventions, case studies, and articles using quasi-experimental designs, the number was reduced to three. Summary and meta-analytic studies and available books and book chapters were also reviewed. A summary of these key references is provided in Table 4.2.

Cognitive–Behavioral

Authors such as Yochelson and Samenow (1976, 1977) and Walters (1990) believe specific cognitive distortions contribute to and maintain antisocial behavior. Many of these ideas follow from the work of Ellis (1962) and Rational Emotive Therapy (RET or REBT). Ellis stated he developed RET based partially on his experiences treating persons with delinquency and antisocial problems (Barley, 1986). From this perspective, successful rehabilitation requires offenders to change their "criminogenic" thinking, which incidently often involves changing behavior directly by

Table 4.2—*Summary of ASPD and Psychopathy Treatment Literature (1987–1997)*

Author(s)	Control Group	N	Setting	Outcome Controlled	Follow-up	Psychopathy
Cognitive–Behavioral Approaches						
Walters 1990	—[a]	—	Cor	—	n/a	n/a
Henning et al. 1996	Yes	55	Cor	Pos	Yes	No
Family-Based Approaches: No relevant studies were found.						
Milieu/Therapeutic Community						
Ogloff et al. 1990	Yes	80	Cor	Pos	Yes	Yes
Rice et al. 1992	Yes	176	Cor	Pos	Yes-10 yr	Yes
Meta-Analytic/Summary Articles						
Andrews et al. 1990	Meta-analysis of 80 studies					
Gendreau et al. 1990	Summary article of meta-analytic findings					
Rice 1997	Summary of research on violent offenders					

[a]No data available.

means of engaging participants in various therapeutic exercises and homework assignments. A common format involves explicitly focusing on "criminal thinking errors" via psychoeducation, journaling, and group psychotherapy. Patients are instructed to monitor and chronicle their thinking patterns, without editing, on a daily basis. Journal entries thus provide the structure for later therapeutic intervention.

A related treatment approach, Relapse Prevention (Marlatt & Gordon, 1985), has also been associated with successful correctional treatment programs (Andrews et al., 1990). Of particular importance is identifying high-risk situations and developing specific strategies for dealing with such situations. These and other issues related to relapse prevention were addressed in less than 25% of the studies reviewed.

Henning and Frueh (1996) studied the impact of a cognitive–behavioral treatment program that targeted criminal thinking. A non-treatment control group ($N = 141$) was compared to a treatment group ($N = 55$). Significant recidivism differences were observed between groups (treatment group = 50%; control group = 70%). Although these results appear impressive, failing to randomize group assignments, using recidivism as the sole outcome measure, and the lack of an ethnically representative sample limit their generalizability.

Therapeutic Communities

Therapeutic communities were developed in psychiatric settings in England during the late 1940s (Jones, 1956; McCord, 1982). Members of a therapeutic community care materially and emotionally for one another, follow the rules of the community, submit to the authority of the group, and suffer sanctions imposed by the group

(Jones, 1956). Therapeutic communities continue to be recommended for addictions, mentally disordered offenders, and criminal offenders (Bratter, Collabolleta, Fossbender, Pennacchia, & Rubel, 1985; DeLeon, 1985).

Not unlike the CD literature, most studies reviewed pertaining to therapeutic communities failed to assess for level of psychopathy. An exception is found, however, in Ogloff et al. (1990), who compared treatment groups within a therapeutic community program. PCL-R identified psychopaths (Hare, 1991) showed less clinical improvement, displayed lower levels of motivation, and were discharged from the program earlier than non-psychopaths. Rice et al. (1992) conducted a retrospective evaluation of the efficacy of a maximum security therapeutic community program (10 years duration) in reducing recidivism among mentally disordered offenders. Treated offenders were matched with untreated offenders on variables most consistently related to recidivism (i.e., age, criminal history, and offense category). The relationships among treatment, psychopathy, and both criminal and violent recidivism were assessed. Psychopathic patients who participated in the therapeutic community exhibited higher rates of recidivism than did the psychopaths that did not. The opposite result was obtained for nonpsychopathic patients who tended to benefit from treatment.

These latter two well-designed studies contribute to the literature because psychopathy level is assessed and controlled, and, in the Rice et al. (1992) study, longitudinal outcomes are measured. Certainly, clinicians using the therapeutic community modality should reevaluate its use with psychopathic patients.

Summary of the ASPD/Psychopathy Outcome Literature

Lillyquist (1980) distinguished between three levels of outcome research. The simplest and most popular design identifies characteristics or behaviors that distinguish recidivists from nonrecidivists. A more sophisticated design uses the interactionist model in an attempt to determine which patient profits most from a given therapy in a specific setting. The most sophisticated evaluation considers not only personal and situational variables of participants but also analyzes the program structure including staffing patterns and administrative influence. Based on our reviews, between 60% to 70% of the CD and ASPD treatment studies published during the past decade are at best characterized by the first level of outcome research.

Lillyquist (1980) proposed five research outcome criteria:

1. Control or comparison groups must be used.
2. There must be precisely defined experimental variables and clear description of the treatment procedure.
3. There should be a measurement of the targeted behavior before and after treatment.
4. Follow up studies should be conducted over a considerable period of time.
5. Appropriate statistical tests should be used to verify that group differences are not due to chance.

With few exceptions (i.e., three to four studies), the studies we reviewed failed to meet these criteria.[6] For example, only two studies of adult offenders controlled for psychopathy level. No CD study controlled for this factor. Despite limitations in various research designs, moderate support exists for the efficacy of cognitive–behavioral approaches (Andrews et al., 1990; Losel, 1998; e.g., challenging criminal thinking patterns, relapse prevention strategies)—particularly within a therapeutic community with nonpsychopathic ASPDs.

Future Directions for Practice and Research

Had our chapter focused solely on treating psychopathy it would have been brief. Simply stated, at this time there is *no empirical* evidence to suggest that psychopathy is treatable (Meloy, 1995). In fact, "milieu therapy" has been linked to higher rates of violent reoffense in psychopathic patients (Rice et al., 1992). Currently, institutional *management* rather than treatment per se is the state of the art for psychopathy.

Treatment potential for nonpsychopathic CD and ASPD patients may be better. There is some specific evidence and, from the broader offender treatment literature, much "inferential" evidence concerning treatment amenability for nonpsychopathic CD and ASPD patients (see Tables 4.1 and 4.2). Studies that focus on treating "symptoms" such as substance abuse, aggressive behavior, and conduct problems, although not specifically addressing underlying character pathology, allow clinicians to infer what might work with these patients (Rice & Harris, 1997).

The failure to account for character pathology (Reid, 1978) is curious and may originate from a general pessimism toward treating CD and ASPD patients (therapeutic nihilism; Lion, 1978; Meloy, 1988), devaluation of a patient group that confronts the clinician's narcissism (Richards, 1993), and studies written by and for an unsophisticated, clinical audience. Assessing character pathology is essential (Reid, 1978) for understanding individual differences, meaningful interpretation of treatment outcome, and for providing adequate levels of patient care. Rather than ignoring or falling prey to character pathology, staff must be trained to understand it.

In the following section we review guidelines and caveats, and offer suggestions for future programming, research, and treatment. Based on our literature review and clinical experience, we offer the following treatment suggestions and identify contraindications for treatment. We let the often-cited dictum from Paul (1967, p. 110) guide the remainder of our discussion: "What treatment, by whom, is most effective for this individual with that specific problem, and under which set of circumstances?"

When Not to Treat

Although seldom posed as a question, the clinician needs to assess treatability before initiating treatment. Even in difficult cases in which "political and bureaucratic pressures force the clinician to 'treat' untreatable patients with ASPD" (Meloy, 1995,

---

[6]Wong and Elek (1990) found that none of the studies reviewed met their six criteria for a good study: (a) a valid measure of psychopathy, (b) an assessment of diagnostic reliability, (c) a detailed description of the treatment program, (d) the use of reliable and objective measures of treatment outcome, (e) a follow-up period of at least one year, and (f) the use of an appropriate control group.

p. 2277), assessment can guide the development of management strategies that reduce the risk of violence to staff and others. When considering treatment over management, the clinician must first consider if adequate assessment resources are available. The PCL-R (Hare, 1991) is the standard for assessing psychopathy; however, few staff are adequately trained in this procedure, and psychopathy level must be weighed against a backdrop of other variables relevant to assessment of violence potential or treatment amenability (Gacono, 1998; Meloy & Gacono, 1995). An assessment of cognitive strengths and weaknesses as well as personality functioning determined by instruments such as the MMPI-2 and Rorschach should also be considered. Several personal and intrapsychic factors to consider as militating against a contract for treatment (vs. management) in patients elevated in psychopathy include

1. Sadistic aggressive behavior in the patient's history that resulted in serious injury, maiming, or death to the victim;
2. A complete absence of any remorse, justification, or rationalization for such behavior;
3. Intelligence greater than or less than two standard deviations from the mean;
4. A historical absence of any capacity, or inclination, to form a bond or an emotional attachment to another person; and,
5. An atavistic fear of predation felt by experienced clinicians when in the patient's presence without any overt behavior precipitating such a countertransference reaction. (Meloy, 1988, p. 323)

Additional questions that must be answered by the treatment team before treating CD and ASPD patients include, Is the treatment setting secure enough to contain the ASPD patient's psychopathy level? What personality characteristics, gleaned from clinical research on patients with ASPD or psychopathy, are relevant to treatment planning with this patient? What transference and countertransference is likely to be elicited by this patient (Meloy, 1995; Kosson et al., 2000)?

So the initial assessment points in the direction of treatment. Six principles (Meloy, 1995) that guide the treatment of CD, ASPD, or psychopathic patients are

1. During the initial diagnostic workup, psychopathy level should be determined, with a clinical focus on attachment capacity and superego disturbance.
2. Treatable Axis I mental or substance abuse disorders should be identified.
3. Situational factors impacting the antisocial behaviors should be delineated.
4. Current and future legal status of the patient should be identified or predicted.
5. Treatment should only begin in those cases in which safety of patient and clinician are ensured.
6. Countertransference reactions must be acknowledged and understood because they provide insight into the patient's inner world. (Meloy, 1995, p. 2290)

In all cases, evaluation precedes treatment. Assessment as described in this chapter is meant to be considered an ongoing process, whereby patient presentation at any point in time may warrant reconsidering fundamental aspects of the contract for treatment (Gacono, 2000). Starting again from the beginning is very often preferable to allowing, for example, a brief well-delineated intervention to lapse into a poorly-delineated course of long-term therapy; such is a risk commonly encountered following crisis intervention.

Which Treatment Approach

Cognitive–behavioral techniques and social learning principles make up the most frequently used methods for treating this population (e.g., Bandura, 1986; Mischel, 1973). Cognitive–behavioral techniques are best implemented within a clear and consistent treatment philosophy (Glasser, 1965; Wexler, Falkin, & Lipton, 1990). Other essential treatment ingredients include the following:

1. Clear and unambiguous program rules and consequences are established at the beginning of treatment and consistently enforced. Treatment with offenders assumes they have abused their status and privileges in society. Staff must determine nonnegotiable rules and consequences, and through therapeutic confrontation expose maladjustive, irresponsible behavior. Confrontation attacks the dysfunctional aspects of behavior, penetrates justifications, stimulates evaluation of behavior, promotes acceptance of responsibility, challenges patients to mobilize their resources, and defines a direction toward growth and development. (Bratter, 1976)
2. Practical life skills and cognitive skills are taught congruent with participants' psychosocial developmental levels (e.g., Ross, Fabiano, Ewles, 1988). Life skills, deficits in reading, work, sexuality, finances, health and wellness, and personal hygiene can be remediated through specific curriculum designed for offenders (e.g., Conger, 1973a, 1973b), as can cognitive skills geared toward problem recognition and problem solving, goal setting and motivations, social perspective taking and empathy. (Fabiano, Robinson, & Porporino, 1990)
3. A heavy emphasis on identifying and modifying participants' cognitive distortions and criminal lifestyle patterns (Walters, 1990). Treatment must address antisocial values and thinking and the associated features of criminal peer associations, impulsivity, substance abuse, affective deficits, and insensitivity to aversive consequences. (Andrews et al., 1990)
4. Awareness of behavioral–emotional impact on family–victims and an increased tolerance for accompanying affect.
5. Opportunities for treatment continuity throughout incarceration, supervised release and community aftercare are established and readily available. (Gacono, 1985)

Research *suggests* cognitive–behavioral techniques are more effective in the initial phases of treatment. Cognitive interventions (Gacono, 1985; Gacono & Meloy, 1988) strengthen the CD or ASPD patient's weakened ego functions (i.e., anger management, decreased impulsivity) through confrontation of chronic dynamic–cognitive–behavioral patterns (Gacono & Meloy, 1988, 1994). As noted in Figure 4.1, anger is used consciously (cognitively) by CD and ASPD patients to control the

```
                                    GRANDIOSITY
                                    PRETENTIOUSNESS
                                    ENTITLEMENT

                                                              CONTROL

                    ANGER
                    POWER THRUST
                    REGAINING CONTROL

    ZERO STATE
    WORTHLESSNESS
    LOSS OF CONTROL
```

Figure 4.1.   The relationship between Cognitive Style and Unconscious Defensive Process.
Note: Adapted from Gacono & Meloy, 1988, 1994.

external world through intimidation of others. At the same time, anger unconsciously
defends against feelings of inner worthlessness, while supporting a grandiose self-
image and associated attitudes such as entitlement. Confrontation of criminal thinking first stimulates, then counters the escalation of anger while interrupting its defensive functions. The nonpsychopathic ASPD patient subsequently experiences a
primitive anxiety–depression or what Yochelson and Samenow (1977) called the
"zero state" and Wishnie (1977) labeled an "inner state of anxiety." Confrontation
coupled with support allows the patient to gradually tolerate this experience; support
and cognitive restructuring combined with "in vivo" exposure leads to increased
mastery. Increased tolerance for dysphoria and other negative aspects of the self
decreases their intensity as "high-risk" stimuli toward relapse. It also decreases the
need for defensive grandiosity, while allowing for more realistic self and other appraisal. Similar but not equivalent dynamic–cognitive processes operate in psychopathic CDs and ASPDs; however, they are generally not responsive to intervention.

Interruption and restructuring of these "defensive processes" creates a foundation for concurrent or later specific psychodynamic, relationship-oriented therapy
addressing childhood physical and sexual abuse, increased affect tolerance, and identity growth. Interactive rather than mutually exclusive cognitive therapies create new
and more adaptive coping systems, and dynamic therapies reduce the toxic energy
that fueled the older maladaptive strategies (Gacono & Meloy, 1988, 1994).

Early in treatment, action-oriented interventions aimed at consciousness raising,
dramatic relief, and environmental reevaluation maximize the receptivity of CD and
ASPD patients to change (Prochaska, Di Clemente, & Norcross, 1992). Treatment
providers can use supportive confrontations and interpretations, bibliotherapy, role
playing, empathy training, and other procedures to facilitate these processes. Aichhorn (1925), who based his treatment model on psychoanalytic theory, observed the
need to establish a narcissistic transference with juvenile delinquents and suggested
an action-oriented treatment that presented the delinquent with an idealized and more
powerful version of themselves. This noncorruptible figure could be internalized,
identified with, and over time attached to. Documented techniques and manuals (e.g.,

Chambless et al., 1996; Linehan, 1993) are necessary for guiding work with non-psychopathic CD and ASPD patients; however, the treatment of these patients should not be reduced solely to "re-education."

Although there is no established pharmacological treatment for CD and ASPD patients, certain symptoms and behaviors can be treated. In patients with concurrent Axis I disorders such as anxiety, depression, or schizophrenia, medications may reduce symptomatology and increase treatment participation. Certain medications may also inhibit modes of violence (see Eichelman, 1988; Meloy, 1995).

Therapy Process: Managing Threats to Integrity and Who Should Treat

Although important, techniques may only account for 15% of the variance in psychotherapy outcome research (Duncan & Moynihan, 1994). Common therapeutic variables, especially the working alliance, are critical to successful treatment (Lion, 1978; Strupp, 1996). Because experienced clinicians better understand transference, countertransference (relationship elements) and resistance, well-trained *experienced* clinicians are increasingly viewed as superior service providers (Burns & Nolen-Hoeksema, 1992; Critis-Christoph et al., 1991; Falvey & Hebert, 1992; Mallinckrodt & Nelson, 1991; Orlinsky & Howard, 1980; Stein & Lambert, 1984, 1995; Strupp, 1997). Successful management of multiple forces that otherwise work to distort or disable therapy process is essential for positive treatment outcome. This therapeutic complexity is also more effectively addressed by seasoned clinicians (Burns & Nolen-Hoeksema, 1992; Critis-Christoph et al., 1991; Falvey & Hebert, 1992; Mallinckrodt & Nelson, 1991; Orlinsky & Howard, 1980; Stein & Lambert, 1984, 1995; Strupp, 1997).

Correctional settings are rarely viewed as inculcating a devotion to sound research and practice. Ethical and professional dilemmas abound (see Weinberger & Sreenivasan, 1994). The recent shift away from a guiding correctional tenet involving rehabilitation, supervision by clinically unsophisticated, nonclinical administrators, and unclear professional roles contribute to the devaluation of the treatment providers themselves, as well as their professional roles. Ethical conflicts arise as professionals are asked to perform correctional duties such as participating in armed escort of patients. Clinicians may be advised by various levels of administration that confidentiality applies under no circumstance, and that in fact the client is not the person receiving treatment but instead the institution paying the salary. There may be little tolerance for dialogue on these issues, and it is not uncommon for certain types of clinicians to abandon their professional identity in favor of career considerations. As these "professionals" move into non-clinical positions, career aspirations often supersede advocacy for ethical professional practice. These "career shifts" are not lost on the inmate population; a fragile foothold can be lost for treatment.[7] When evaluating professional practice in a correctional setting, which includes approved clinical

---

[7]To our knowledge there have been no systematic studies examining characterisitics and credentials of psychologists who promote out of their clinical roles—beyond the institutional level—in the Federal Correctional System. It would be interesting to ascertain if they are licenced, how many maintain advanced diplomate status, and whether their degress are other than traditional PsyDs or PhDs in clinical psychology. Although not inclusive, these indices do suggest incorporation of a professional identity and should be held by those who guide clinical practice within an institutional setting.

internships, regulatory agencies should evaluate as rigorously and subsequently offer opinions as strongly concerning these basic "ethical" issues as they do for more "politically attractive" ones. Clinical staff in institutional settings are dependent on direct support from their parent disciplines when attempting to maintain ethical practice.

Various countertransference issues can also distort the treatment enterprise. Clinicians must have emotional maturity and psychological awareness to manage a myriad of real and intense emotional reactions stimulated by CD and ASPD patients (see Kosson et al., 2000; Lion, 1978; Meloy, 1988; Strasburger, 1986). Typical countertransference reactions stimulated in these populations should be anticipated and managed (Kosson et al., 2000; Meloy, 1988). Meloy (1988) articulated eight common countertransference reactions observed through interactions with CD and ASPD patients and their clinicians: "therapeutic nihilism" (Lion, 1978), "illusionary treatment alliance," "fear of assault or harm" (Strasburger, 1986), "denial and deception," "helplessness and guilt" (Strasburger, 1986), "devaluation and loss of professional identity," "hatred and wish to destroy" (Strasburger, 1987), and "assumption of psychological complexity." "Therapeutic nihilism" (Lion, 1978), for example, resulted from a belief that all ASPD patients are untreatable by virtue of their diagnosis, whereas its opposite reaction, "illusory treatment alliance," involved the belief that a treatment alliance exists, when, in actuality, there is no realistic bond between patient and therapist (p. 326). As countertransference can disrupt the therapeutic work with CD and ASPD patients, acknowledging, understanding, and managing its impact is essential to successful treatment (Kosson et al., 2000).

Resistance or transference is frequently experienced and has been discussed elsewhere (Bursten, 1972; Meloy, 1988). Meloy (1988) discussed four predictable patterns of resistance, "manipulative cycling," "deceptive practice," "malignant pseudoidentification," and "sadistic control," that can be anticipated and confronted. Enabling is a potent family dynamic that, when confronted and altered within the CD patient's family system, can reduce resistance. "Projective identification" (Grotstein, 1980) is a psychodynamic process that explains enabling; it involves the externalization of intrapsychic dynamics of one or more of the patients' caregivers, whereby control of the patient's emotions or behavior helps maintain the caregiver's psychological equilibrium. Transference-like countertransference must be anticipated, confronted, and managed in these patients; when ignored they impede therapy, disrupt the milieu and, in extreme cases, result in assaults, inappropriate staff involvement, or even death (Gacono, 2000; Gacono et al., 1995).[8]

Countertransference and transference combine to form intense interpersonal dynamics that affect the milieu and dyadic relationships.[9] Staff splitting highlights problems associated with treating severe character disorders, particularly CD and ASPD

---

[8]In studying a group of patients who malingered the insanity defense we found that 100% were diagnosed with psychopathy (PCL-R $\geq$ 30) and physically violent. Thirty-nine percent were sexually involved with or married female staff.

[9]The salient nature of the psychopath's interpersonal style allowed Kosson and his colleagues (Kosson, Steuerwald, Forth, & Kirkhart, 1997) to develop the Interpersonal Measure of Psychopathy (IM-P). The IM-P is a 21-item scale assessing psychopathy level based on interpersonal dynamics during an interview. The IM-P correlates with the PCL-R total score; its strongest correlations are with the interpersonal, affective components of psychopathy (Factor 1). The IM-P holds promise as an assessment tool for quantifying a patient's psychopathy level (see Kosson et al., 2000).

patients. Through splitting (Grotstein, 1980), the intrapsychic dynamics of the "borderline organized" patient are externalized and can be seen in staff through their polarized opposite and conflicting perceptions toward the patient. The patient's internal world is divided into "all good" and "all bad"; once externalized, staff perceptions mirror the patient's inner dynamics. As staff perceptions are translated into differential treatment, therapeutic progress is stymied or regresses. Splitting can be curtailed by relying on empirical assessment data in forming and maintaining treatment strategies (rather than subjective opinion). Informed staff communication, unified team member confrontations of the patient's behavior, the use of structure with immediate consequences for antisocial attitudes and behaviors, and controlling staff–patient contact are all means of "containing" therapeutic process in this population and of isolating attempts to undermine or derail treatment (Kosson et al., 2000).

Given the frequency of "negative process" in even less character-disordered populations (Binder & Strupp, 1997), one can only estimate the impact of countertransference and resistance on treatment outcomes in this population. Unfortunately, the least experienced clinicians (Burns & Nolen-Hoeksema, 1992; Falvey & Hebert, 1992; Stein & Lambert, 1995) or those drawn to these populations for the wrong reasons (Richards, 1993) are often found treating CD and ASPD patients. Qualified supervision is essential to treating these patients and maintaining program integrity.

Finally, the integration of community resources, volunteers, and ex-offenders as a supportive adjunct to treatment (or what Gacono, 1985, p. 20, labeled a "multi-agency treatment modality") is a desirable bridge to establish a sense of connectedness to the prosocial world, to foster hope, and in providing an expanded "treatment team" (Chaiken, 1989; Gacono, 1985). It is imperative that adjunct providers receive training to provide treatment goals consistent with the primary treatment team. This "it takes a village approach" parallels research investigating effects of a number of contextual variables affecting the unfolding of CD, such as aggravating effects of drug use and mitigating effects of positive interpersonal relationships (Capaldi, Chamberlain, Fetrow, & Wilson, 1997).

Most Effective

Clinicians must answer three questions regarding their treatment interventions (Howard, Moras, Brill, Martinovich, & Lutz, 1996):

1. Does it work under experimental and rigorous methodological conditions?
2. Does it work in the real, day-to-day world of clinical practice?
3. Does it work for this particular client?

Question 1 can be answered by efficacy studies, considered as the standard for outcome research (Jacobson & Christensen, 1996). Efficacy studies are characterized by therapy of a brief and fixed duration, manualized treatment, single disorders, and random assignment. Efficacy studies have good internal validity, but findings may not be generalizable to real-world settings. Question 2 can be addressed via effectiveness studies (e.g., Seligman, 1996), which look at therapy as it is actually delivered under less controlled conditions. Effectiveness studies are characterized by complex disorders, including patients with multiple diagnoses, and flexible treatment

based on clinical judgment. Question 3 is periodically assessed by the treating therapist for each client. Surprisingly, given the captive nature of this population and
the huge amount of money available for treatment and supervision (community,
parole, institution), there are few efficacy studies with CD, ASPD, and psychopathic
patients.

Most published efficacy studies are poorly designed quasi-experimental procedures. Their conclusions are often anecdotal, suggestive, not conducive to generalization, and difficult to replicate. Little attention has been given to the patient's
perceptions of treatment, and no studies, of which we are aware, have addressed the
underlying process change mechanisms that work in various situations (e.g., Drozd
& Goldfried, 1996; Watson & Greenberg, 1996). Finally, there is little agreement
about what standardized measures need to be collected to allow for comparative data
analyses between different settings and information from larger databases (McLellan
& Durell, 1996).

This Individual With That Specific Problem

Based on his work with families of antisocial personalities, Lykken (1995) suggested
that it is naive to think the same treatment approach will be equally effective for a
CD inner-city, minority youth and a CD upper middle-class, suburbanite, Caucasian
youth (Reid, 1978). We concur.

Not only do the CD and ASPD diagnoses capture a diverse population, comorbidity of Axis I psychological and substance abuse problems further obscures the
clinical treatment picture (e.g., Hiller, Knight, & Simpson, 1996; Losel, 1998). Statements concerning treatment effectiveness must be made in the context of unique and
specific group characteristics, varying behavioral patterns and conditions, types of
intervention (Beutler, 1991; Beutler, Kim, Davison, Karno, & Fisher, 1996), and skill
level of the treating clinicians. Treatment planning with ASPD and CD clients should
take into account the trait-like quality of interpersonal reactance present in these
populations—in other words, the indwelling tendency to respond oppositionally to
external demands (Beutler & Consoli, 1992). Based on the client's level of reactance,
the therapist is in a better position to determine the clinical utility regarding the use
of directive, non-directive, self-directed, and paradoxical interventions.

Assessment strategies that detect the quantitative and qualitative distinctions
among these diverse populations are essential for meaningful treatment planning and
subsequent treatment intervention (Gacono, 1998). The PCL-R (Hare, 1991) is perhaps the most useful assessment instrument available for this purpose. This procedure
provides an estimate of treatability based on the total score, as well as individual
items whose scores can guide specific treatment recommendations (Gacono, 1998,
2000).

Given that careful observation is a first step in developing and modifying hy-
potheses (Bednar, Burlingame, & Masters, 1988), we have noticed that quantitative
differences in psychopathy level (PCL-R; Hare, 1991) appear correlated with the
level of treatment necessary to promote prosocial behavior. For many CD or ASPD
nonsexual-offending patients who score in the mild range (PCL-R < 19), treatment
involvement of one to two years creates an opportunity for change. Those in the
moderate range (PCL-R = 20–27) may need a highly structured treatment regimen

lasting two to five years. Future research may suggest specific Factor 1 and Factor 2 profiles that correlate with treatment success or failure. There is currently nothing the behavioral sciences can offer for treating those with psychopathy (PCL-R $\geq$ 30; e.g., Hare, 1992; Ogloff et al., 1990); however, some can be managed and in some cases psychopharmacology may decrease impulsivity and violence.

Finally, no studies have adequately investigated the effects of race, social class, and gender bias on treatment effectiveness with CD and ASPD patients—despite the profound manner in which these biases impact clinical judgment and treatment outcome (Garb, 1997).

Under Which Set of Circumstances

In terms of treatment efficiency and cost–benefit ratios, group therapy is the major treatment modality promulgated for this population. Residential settings and therapeutic communities are popular, and in some cases necessary for initial phases of treatment (Kernberg, 1984; Potts, Barley, Jones, & Woodhall, 1986; Shamblin, 1986). Although patients provide input into the communities' daily functioning, treatment effectiveness requires sound staff-provided structure and guidance (Rubel, Bratter, Smirnoff, Hartwig-Thompson, & Baker, 1982; Shamblin, 1986). Personally meaningful reinforcers dispensed following desirable behavior may also enhance treatment compliance and decrease antisocial acting out for some patients (e.g., Mathias, 1996).

Little attention has been paid to combined treatment modalities. We have found that group therapy, judiciously supplemented by individual supportive and psychodynamic treatment and self-help approaches, can be highly effective for some CD and ASPD nonpsychopathic patients. For example, a model treatment readiness program developed by CBG and sponsored by the San Diego County Juvenile Probation Department combined family therapy with confrontation of criminal thinking errors in treating CD male adolescents and their families. Families met in multifamily treatment groups focusing on confrontation of family enabling and identifying and altering criminal thinking in the adolescent. Family enabling was affected by the youthful offender stating in front of the entire group and other families that the main reason for his criminal activity was the need for excitement and stimulation and not because of peer pressure; often, parents are amazed or shocked that this could be so. Families were able to acknowledge their shame and dysphoria and curtail enabling patterns that supported acting out in the CD patient. Individual family sessions continued to be the focus of the larger group, also teaching new strategies for interacting. Family therapy combined with residential treatment, medication, and concurrent play therapy can also help some CD children.

Careful and thorough assessment is essential for identifying individuals who can benefit from combined treatments, providing a timetable for implementing interventions, monitoring treatment progress, and providing treatment outcome data. Unfortunately, relevant assessment receives little attention in many treatment programs.

Final Reflections

Comparing recent (Losel, 1998; Meloy, 1995) and earlier writings (Reid, 1978; Reid, Dord, Walter, & Bonner, 1986; Yochelson & Samenow, 1977), the reader may be struck by similarities, and by implication, the lack of progress in empirically demonstrating treatment efficacy with CD and ASPD patients. Despite the growing numbers of these patients, treatment approaches that address character pathology are more often discussed than evaluated. When evaluated, methodology is often lacking. The quality of treatment research, with several notable exceptions (Ogloff et al., 1990; Rice et al., 1992), has not kept pace with the mental health professionals' ability to evaluate and predict.

As researchers and clinicians, we are nonetheless vulnerable to the popular battlecry "Do something!" with, to, or about this growing population. As such, some of us may feel compelled to advocate for simple solutions to some of the most complex of human problems, not unlike the countertransference reactions described previously. Had the data directed us along an easy, universal, or cookbook-styled course, we would have been delighted to present that course. We expect that progress in working with this population will evolve as a series of small things brought together.

This chapter targets empirically-based and controlled studies of psychosocial interventions with CD and ASPD patients. Can these patients be successfully treated? If so with what methods? Treatment proponents, often influenced more by countertransference than empirical data,[10] are overly optimistic, and detractors cite the absence of empirical data or negative findings to support their positions. Historically, public policy mirrors clinical disagreement, vacillating between habilitation and retribution.

When posed as a yes–no dichotomy, questions concerning treatment amenability cannot be answered. We believe many of these patients can be successfully treated —although the process is arduous—others managed, and a smaller group must be viewed, at least for the present, as untreatable. As clinicians, our task is to identify, through assessment and treatment matching factors that correlate with treatment success in ASPD patients (Gacono, 1998, 2000; Gacono & Hutton, 1994; Meloy & Gacono, 1995). Applying one treatment or management approach to all CD and ASPD patients ensures treatment failure (Reid, 1978). As clinicians we can do better.

In the final analysis, we cannot realistically and ethically imply that all CD and ASPD individuals benefit from treatment. Neither can we imply that nothing works (Martinson, 1974). What we can say is that something seems to work for some members of this population some of the time. As forensic clinicians, we must do better.

References

Aichhorn, A. (1925). *Wayward Youth.* New York: Viking Press.

American Psychiatric Association. (1952). *Diagnostic and statistical manual of mental disorders.* Washington, DC: Author.

American Psychiatric Association. (1968). *Diagnostic and statistical manual of mental disorders* (2nd ed.). Washington, DC: Author.

---

[10]Richards (1993) described mental health workers as "benign narcissists" (p. 292) and discussed the unique challenges to their belief systems (countertransference) when working with the antisocial and psychopathic patients (also see Meloy, 1988, 1995; Strasburger, 1986).

American Psychiatric Association. (1980). *Diagnostic and statistical manual of mental disorders* (3rd ed.). Washington, DC: Author.

American Psychiatric Association. (1987). *Diagnostic and statistical manual of mental disorders* (3rd ed., rev.). Washington, DC: Author.

American Psychiatric Association. (1994). *Diagnostic and statistical manual of mental disorders* (4th ed.). Washington, DC: Author.

Anderson, W., & Brauer, B. (1985). Clients with MMPI high D-Pd: Therapy implications. *Journal of Clinical Psychology, 41,* 181–188.

Andrews, D. A., Zinger, I., Hoge, R. D., Bonta, J., Gendreau, P., & Cullen, F. T. (1990). Does correctional treatment work? A clinically relevant and psychologically informed meta-analysis. *Criminology, 28,* 369–405.

August, G., Stewart, M., & Holmes, C. (1983). A four-year follow-up of hyperactive boys with and without conduct disorder. *British Journal of Psychiatry, 143,* 192–198.

Bandura, A. (1986). *Social foundations of thought and action: A social cognitive theory.* Englewood Cliffs, NJ: Prentice-Hall.

Barley W. D. (1986). Behavioral and cognitive treatment of criminal and delinquent behavior. In W. Reid, D. Dorr, J. Walker, & J. Bonner (Eds.), *Unmasking the psychopath: antisocial personality and related syndromes* (pp. 159–190). New York: W. W. Norton.

Bednar, R. L., Burlingame, G. M., & Masters, K. S. (1988). Systems of family treatment: Substance or semantics? *Annual Review of Psychology, 39,* 401–434.

Beutler, L. E. (1991). Have all won and must all have prizes? Revisiting Luborsky, et al.'s verdict. *Journal of Consulting and Clinical Psychology, 59,* 226–232.

Beutler, L. E., & Consoli, A. J. (1992). Systematic eclectic psychotherapy. In J. Norcross & M. Goldfried (Eds.), *Handbook of psychotherapy integration* (pp. 268–299). New York: Basic Books.

Beutler, L. E., Kim, E. J., Davison, E., Karno, M., & Fisher, D. (1996). Research contributions to improving managed health care outcomes. *Psychotherapy, 33,* 197–206.

Binder, J. L., & Strupp, H. H. (1997). "Negative process": A recurrently discovered and underestimated facet of therapeutic process and outcome in the individual psychotherapy of adults. *Clinical Psychology: Science and Practice, 4,* 121–139.

Bodholdt, R., Richards, H., & Gacono, C. (2000). Assessing psychopathy in adults: The Hare Psychopathy Checklist-Revised (PCL-R) and Psychopathy Checklist Screening Version (PCL:SV). In C. B. Gacono (Ed.), *The Clinical and Forensic Assessment of Psychopathy: A Practitioner's Guide* (pp. 55–86). Mahweh, NJ: Erlbaum.

Borduin, C. M., Mann, B. J., Cone, L., & Henggeler, S. (1995). Multisystemic treatment of serious juvenile offenders: Long term prevention of criminality and violence. *Journal of Consulting and Clinical Psychology, 63,* 569–578.

Bratter, T. (1976). Confrontation groups: The therapeutic community's gist to psychotherapy. In P. Vamos & J. Devlin (Eds.), *The first world conference on therapeutic communities* (pp. 164–174). Montreal: Portage Press.

Bratter, T. E., Collabolletta, E. A., Fossbender, A. J., Pennacchia, M. C., & Rubel, J. G. (1985). The American self-help residential therapeutic community: A pragmatic treatment approach for addicted character-disordered individuals. In T. E. Bratter & G. C. Forrest (Eds.), *Alcoholism and substance abuse: Strategies for clinical intervention* (pp. 461–507). New York: Free Press.

Burns, D., & Nolen-Hoeksema, S. (1992). Therapeutic empathy and recovery from depression in cognitive–behavioral therapy: A structural equation model. *Journal of Consulting and Clinical Psychology, 60,* 441–449.

Bursten, B. (1972). The manipulative personality. *Archives of General Psychiatry, 26,* 318–321.

Campbell, M., & Cueva, J. E. (1995). Psychopharmacology in child and adolescent psychiatry: A review of the past seven years. Part II. *Journal of the American Academy of Child and Adolescent Psychiatry, 34,* 1262–1272.

Capaldi, D., Chamberlain, P., Fetrow, R., & Wilson, J. (1997). Conducting ecologically valid prevention research: Recruiting and retaining a "whole village" in multimethod, multi-agent studies. *American Journal of Community Psychology, 25,* 471–492.

Chaiken, M. R. (1989). *Prison program for drug-involved offenders.* N C J 118316. Washington, DC: National Institute of Justice.

Chambliss, D. L., Sanderson, W. C., Shoham, V., Johnson, S. B., Pope, K. S., Crits-Christoph, P., Baker, M., Johnson, B., Woody, S. R., Sue, S., Beutler, L., Williams, D. A., & McCurry, S. (1996). An update on empirically validated therapies. *The Clinical Psychologist, 49,* 5–18.

Cleckley, H. (1976). *The Mask of Sanity* (5th ed.). St. Louis MO: Mosby.

Cooke, D. (1998). Psychopathy across cultures. In D. Cooke, A. Forth, & R. Hare (Eds.), *Psychopathy: theory, research and implications for society* (pp. 13–45). NATO ASI Series, Netherlands: Kluwer Academic.

Conger, D. (1973a). *Life skills coaching manual.* Prince Albert, Saskatchewan, Canada: Saskatchewan Newstart.

Conger, D. (1973b). *Readings in life skills.* Prince Albert, Saskatchewan, Canada: Saskatchewan Newstart.

Constantino, J., Morris, J., & Murphy, D. (1997). CSF 5-HIAA and family history of antisocial personality disorder in newborns. *American Journal of Psychiatry, 154,* 1771–1773.

Critis-Christoph, P., Baranckle, K., Kurcias, J., Beck, A., Carroll, K., Perry, K., Luborsky, L., McLellan, A., Woody, G., Thompson, L., Gallagher, D., & Zitrin, C. (1991). Meta-analysis of therapist effects in psychotherapy outcome studies. *Psychotherapy Research, 1,* 81–92.

Deleon, G. (1985). The therapeutic community: Status and evolution. *The International Journal of the Addictions, 20,* 823–844.

Diamond, G. S., Serrano, A. C., Dickey, M., & Sonis, W. (1996). Current status of family-based outcome and process research. *Journal of the American Academy of Child and Adolescent Psychiatry, 35,* 6–16.

Drozd, J. F., & Goldfried, M. R. (1996). A critical evaluation of the state-of-the-art in psychotherapy outcome research. *Psychotherapy, 33,* 171–180.

Dumas, J. E. (1989). Treating antisocial behavior in children: Child and family approaches. *Clinical Psychology Review, 9,* 197–222.

Duncan, B. L., & Moynihan, D. W. (1994). Applying outcome research: Intentional utilization of the client's frame of reference. *Psychotherapy, 31,* 294–301.

Eichelman, B. (1988). Toward a rational pharmacotherapy for aggressive and violent behavior. *Hospital and Community Psychiatry, 39,* 31–39.

Ellis, A. (1962). *Reason and emotion in psychotherapy.* Seacus NJ: Lyle Stuart.

Eppright, T. D., Kashani, J. H., Robinson, B. D., & Reid, J. C. (1993). Comorbidity of conduct disorder and personality disorders in an incarcerated juvenile population. *American Journal of Psychiatry, 150,* 1233–1236.

Fabiano, E., Robinson, D., & Porporino, F. (1990). *A preliminary assessment of the Cognitive Skills Training Program: A component of Living Skills programming: Program description, research findings and implementation strategy.* Ottawa: Correctional Service of Canada.

Fagan, J. (1991). Community-based treatment for mentally disordered juvenile offenders. *Journal of Clinical Child Psychology, 20,* 42–50.

Falvey, J., & Hebert, D. (1992). Psychometric study of the clinical treatment planning simulations (CTPS) for assessing clinical judgment. *Journal of Mental Health Counseling, 14,* 490–507.

Fava, M. (1997). Psychopharmacological treatment of pathological aggression. *Psychiatric Clinics of North America, 20,* 427–51.

Fonagy, P., & Target, M. (1994). The efficacy of psychoanalysis for children with disruptive disorders. *Journal of the American Academy of Child and Adolescent Psychiatry, 33,* 45–55.

Forth, A., & Burke, H., (1998). Psychopathy in adolescence: Assessment, violence, and developmental precursors. In D. Cooke, A. Forth, & R. Hare (Eds.), *Psychopathy: theory, research and implications for society* (pp. 205–227). Netherlands: Kluwer Academic.

Forth, A., Hart, S., & Hare, R. (1990). Assessment of psychopathy in male young offenders. *Psychological Assessment: A Journal of Consulting and Clinical Psychology, 2,* 342–344.

Forth, A., Kosson, D., & Hare, R. (in press). *The Psychopathy Checklist: Youth version.* Unpublished Test Manual, Multihealth Systems.

Frick, P. (1998). Callous-unemotional traits and conduct problems: Applying the two-factor model of psychopathy to children. In D. Cooke, A. Forth, & R. Hare (Eds.), *Psychopathy: theory, research and implications for society* (pp. 161–187). NATO ASI Series, Netherlands: Kluwer Academic.

Gabbard, G., & Coyne, T. (1987). Predictors of response of antisocial patients to hospital treatment. *Hospital and Community Psychology, 38,* 1181–1185.

Gacono, C. B. (1985). Mental health work in a county jail: A heuristic model. *Journal of Offender Counseling, 5,* 16–22.

Gacono, C. B. (1990). An empirical study of object relations and defensive operations in antisocial personality. *Journal of Personality Assessment, 54,* 589–600.

Gacono, C. B. (1998). The use of the Psychopathy Checklist-Revised (PCL-R) and Rorschach for treatment planning with antisocial personality disordered patients. *International Journal of Offender Therapy and Comparative Criminology, 42,* 49–64.

Gacono, C. B. (2000). Suggestions for the implementation and use of the Psychopathy Checklists in forensic and clinical practice. In C. B. Gacono (Ed.), *The clinical and forensic assessment of psychopathy: A practitioner's guide* (pp. 175–202). Mahweh, NJ: Erlbaum.

Gacono, C. B., & Hutton, H. E. (1994). Suggestions for the clinical and forensic use of the Hare Psychopathy Checklist-Revised (PCL-R). *International Journal of Law and Psychiatry, 17,* 303–317.

Gacono, C. B., & Meloy, J. R. (1988). The relationship between cognitive style and defensive process in the psychopath. *Criminal Justice and Behavior, 15,* 472–483.

Gacono, C. B., & Meloy, J. R. (1991). A Rorschach investigation of attachment and anxiety in antisocial personality. *Journal of Nervous and Mental Disease, 179,* 546–552.

Gacono, C. B., & Meloy, J. R. (1994). *The Rorschach assessment of aggressive and psychopathic personalities.* Hillsdale, New Jersey: Erlbaum.

Gacono, C. B., Meloy, J. R., & Heaven, T. (1990). A Rorschach investigation of narcissism and hysteria in antisocial personality. *Journal of Personality Assessment, 55,* 270–279.

Gacono, C. B., Meloy, J. R., Sheppard, K., Speth, E., & Roske, A. (1995). A clinical investigation of malingering and psychopathy in hospitalized insanity acquittees. *Bulletin of the American Academy of Psychiatry and the Law, 23,* 387–397.

Gacono, C. B., Meloy, J. R., Speth, E., & Roske, A. (1997). Above the law: Escapes from a maximum security forensic hospital. *Bulletin of the American Academy of Psychiatry and the Law, 25,* 547–550.

Garb, H. N. (1997). Race bias, social class bias, and gender bias in clinical judgment. *Clinical Psychology: Science and Practice, 4,* 99–120.

Gendreau, P., & Andrews, D. A. (1990). Tertiary prevention: What the meta-analyses of the offender treatment literature tell us about "what works." *The Canadian Journal of Criminology, 32,* 173–184.

Glasser, W. (1965). *Reality therapy: A new approach to psychiatry.* New York: Harper & Row.

Glick, B., & Goldstein, A. P. (1987). Aggression replacement training. *Journal of Counseling and Development, 65,* 256–262.

Greenwood, P. W. (1994). What works with juvenile offenders: A synthesis of the literature and experience. *Federal Probation, 58,* 63–67.

Groltstein, J. (1980). *Splitting and projective identification.* New York: Aronson.

Gunderson, J. (1978). Defining the therapeutic process in psychiatry milieus. *Psychiatry, 41,* 327–355.

Hare, R. D. (1966). Psychopathy and choices of immediate and delayed punishment. *Journal of Abnormal Psychology, 71,* 25–29.

Hare, R. D. (1991). *The Hare Psychopathy Checklist-Revised.* Toronto, Canada: Multi-Health Systems.

Hare, R. D. (1992). *A model treatment program for offenders at high risk for violence.* Ottawa: Research Branch, Correctional Services of Canada.

Hare, R. D. (1996). Psychopathy: A clinical construct whose time has come. *Criminal Justice and Behavior, 23,* 25–54.

Hare, R. D., & Jutai, J. (1983). Criminal history of the male psychopath: Some preliminary data. In K. Van Dusen & S. Mednick (Eds.), *Prospective studies of crime and delinquency* (pp. 225–236). Boston: Klyuner Mijhoff.

Hare, R. D., & McPherson, L. (1984). Violent and aggressive behavior by criminal psychopaths. *International Journal of Law and Psychiatry, 7,* 35–50.

Hare, R. D., McPherson, L., & Forth, A. (1988). Male psychopaths and their criminal careers. *Journal of Consulting and Clinical Psychology, 56,* 710–714.

Harpur, T., Hare, R., & Hatistian, R. (1989). Two factor conceptualization of psychopathy: Construct validity and assessment implications. *Psychological Assessment: A Journal of Consulting and Clinical Psychology, 1*(11), 6–17.

Hart, S., & Hare, R. (1989). Discriminant validity of the Psychopathy Checklist in a forensic psychiatric population. *Psychological Assessment: A Journal of Consulting and Clinical Psychology, 1*(1), 211–218.

Hart, S., Cox, & Hare, R. D. (1995). *The Hare Psychopathy Checklist: Screening Version.* North Tonawanda, New York: Multihealth Systems.

Hart, S. D., Kropp, P., & Hare, R. D. (1988). Performance of male psychopaths following conditional release from prison. *Journal of Consulting and Clinical Psychology, 56,* 227–232.

Henggeler, S. W., & Borduin, C. M. (1990). *Family therapy and beyond: A multisystemic approach to treating the behavior problems of children and adolescents.* Pacific Grove, CA: Brooks/Cole.

Henggeler, S. W., Melton, G. B., & Smith, L. A. (1992). Family preservation using multisystemic therapy: An effective alternative to incarcerating serious juvenile offenders. *Journal of Consulting and Clinical Psychology, 60,* 953–961.

Henn, F. A., Bardwell, R., & Jenkins, R. L. (1980). Juvenile delinquents revisited. *Archives of General Psychiatry, 37,* 1160–1163.

Henning, K. R., & Frueh, B. C. (1996). Cognitive-behavioral treatment of incarcerated offenders. *Criminal Justice and Behavior, 23,* 523–541.

Hiller, L. M., Knight, K., & Simpson, D. D. (1996). An assessment of comorbid psychological problems in a residential criminal justice drug treatment population. *Psychology of Addictive Behaviors, 10,* 181–189.

Horne, A. M., & Glaser, B. A. (1993). Conduct disorders. In R. T. Hammerman, C. G. Last, & M. Hersen (Eds.), *Handbook of prescriptive treatments for children and adolescents* (pp. 85–101). Boston: Allyn & Bacon.

Howard, K. I., Moras, K., Brill, P. L., Martinovich, Z., & Lutz, W. (1996). Evaluation of Psychotherapy: Efficacy, effectiveness, and patient progress. *American Psychologist, 51,* 1059–1064.

Izzo, R., & Ross, R. (1990). Meta-analysis of rehabilitation programs for juvenile delinquents: A brief report. *Criminal Justice and Behavior, 17,* 134–142.

Jacobson, N. S., & Christensen, A. C. (1996). Studying the effectiveness of psychotherapy: How well can clinical trials do the job? *American Psychologist, 51,* 1031–1039.

Jenkins, R. (1960). The psychopathic or antisocial personality. *Journal of Nervous and Mental Disease, 131,* 318–334.

Jones, M. (1956). The concept of a therapeutic community. *American Journal of Psychiatry, 113,* 647–650.

Kavoussi, R., Armstead, P., & Coccaro, E. (1997). The neurobiology of impulsive aggression. *Psychiatric Clinics of North America, 20,* 395–403.

Kazdin, A. E. (1987). Treatment of antisocial behavior in children: Current status and future directions. *Psychological Bulletin, 102,* 187–203.

Kazdin, A. E. (1993). Treatment of conduct disorder: Progress and directions in psychotherapy research. *Development & Psychopathology, 5,* 277–310.

Kazdin, A. E. (1995). Child, parent and family dysfunction as predictors of outcome in cognitive–behavioral treatment of antisocial children. *Behavior Research and Therapy, 33,* 271–281.

Kazdin, A. E., Bass, D., Siegel, T., & Thomas, C. (1989). Cognitive–behavioral therapy and relationship therapy in the treatment of children referred for antisocial behavior. *Journal of Consulting and Clinical Psychology, 57,* 522–535.

Kazdin, A. E., Esveldt-Dawson, K., French, N. H., & Unis, A. S. (1987). Problem-solving skills training and relationship therapy in the treatment of antisocial child behavior. *Journal of Consulting and Clinical Psychology, 55,* 76–85.

Kendall, P. C., Reber, M., McLeer, S., & Epps, J. (1990). Cognitive–behavioral treatment of conduct-disordered children. *Cognitive Therapy & Research, 14,* 279–297.

Kernberg, O. (1984). *Severe personality disorders: Psychotherapeutic strategies.* London: Yale University Press.

Klein, R., Abikoff, H., Klass, E., Ganeles, D., Seese, L., & Pollack, S. (1997). Clinical efficacy of methylphenidate in conduct disorder with and without attention deficit hyperactivity disorder. *Archives of General Psychiatry, 54,* 1073–1080.

Knutson, B., Wolkowitz, O., Cole, S., Chan, T., Moore, E., Johnson, R., Terpstra, J., Turner, R., & Reus, V. (1998). Selective alteration of personality and social behavior by serotonergic intervention. *American Journal of Psychiatry, 155,* 373–379.

Kosson, D., Gacono, C., & Bodholdt, R. (2000). Assessing psychopathy: Interpersonal aspects and clinical interviewing. In C. B. Gacono (Ed.), *The clinical and forensic assessment of psychopathy: A practitioner's guide* (pp. 203–230). Mahweh, NJ: Erlbaum.

Kosson, D. S., Steuerwald, B. L., Forth, A. E., & Kirkhart, K. J. (1997). A new method for assessing the interpersonal behavior of psychopathic individuals: Preliminary validation studies. *Psychological Assessment, 9,* 89–101.

Kristiansson, M. (1995). Incurable psychopaths? *Bulletin of the American Academy of Psychiatry and Law, 23,* 555–62.

Leeman, L. W., Gibbs, J. C., & Fuller, D. (1993). Evaluation of a multi-component group treatment program for juvenile delinquents. *Aggressive Behavior, 19,* 282–292.

Lillyquist, M. J. (1980). Understanding and changing criminal behavior. Englewood Cliffs, NJ: Prentice Hall.

Linehan, M. M. (1993). *Cognitive–behavioral treatment of borderline personality disorder.* New York: Guilford Press.

Lion, J. (1978). Outpatient treatment of psychopaths. In W. Reid (Ed.), *The Psychopath: A comprehensive study of antisocial disorders and behaviors* (pp. 286–300). New York: Brunner/Mazel.

Lipsey, M. W. (1991). Juvenile delinquency treatment: A meta-analytic inquiry into the variability of effects. In T. Cook (Ed.), *Meta-analysis for explanation: A casebook.* New York: Russell Sage Foundation.

Lock, J., & Strauss, G. D. (1994). Psychiatric hospitalization of adolescents for conduct disorder. *Hospital and Community Psychiatry, 45,* 925–928.

Loeber, R., Brinthaupt, V., & Green, S. (1990). Attention deficits, impulsivity, and hyperactivity with or without conduct problems: Relationships to delinquency and unique contextual factors. In R. M. McMahon & R. D. Peters (Eds.), *Behavior disorders of adolescence: Research, intervention, and policy in clinical and school settings* (pp. 39–61). New York: Plenum Press.

Losel, F. (1998). Treatment and management of psychopaths. In D. Cooke, A. Forth, & R. Hare (Eds.), *Psychopathy: theory, research and implications for society* (pp. 303–354). Netherlands: Kluwer Academic, NATO ASI Series.

Lykken, D. T. (1995). *The antisocial personalities*. Hillsdale, NJ: Erlbaum.

Mallinckrodt, B., Nelson, M. (1991). Counselor training level and the formation of the psychotherapeutic working alliance. *Journal of Counseling Psychology, 38*, 135–138.

Mann-Feder, V. R. (1996). Adolescents in therapeutic communities. *Adolescence, 31*, 17–28.

Marlatt, G., & Gordon, J. (Eds.). (1985). *Relapse prevention: Maintenance strategies in the treatment of addictive behaviors*. New York: Guilford Press.

Martinson, R. (1974). What works? Questions and answers about prison reform. *The Public Interest, 35,* 22–54.

Mathias, R. (1996). Specialized approach shows promise for treating antisocial drug abuse patients. *NIDA Notes, 11*, 10–11, 14.

McBurnett, K., Lahey, B. B., Frick, P. J., Risch, C., Loeber, R., Hart, E. L., Christ, M. A., & Hanson, K. S. (1991). Anxiety, inhibition, conduct disorder in children: II. Relation to salivary cortisol. *Journal of the American Academy of Child and Adolescent Psychiatry, 30*, 192–196.

McCord, W. (1982). *The psychopath and milieu therapy: A longitudinal study*. New York: Academic Press.

McLellan, A. T., & Durell, J. (1996). Outcome evaluation in psychiatric and substance abuse treatments: Concepts, rationale, and methods. In L. I. Sederer & B. Dickey (Eds.), *Outcome assessment in clinical practice* (pp. 34–44). Baltimore: Williams & Wilkins.

Meloy, J. R. (1988). *The psychopathic mind: origins, dynamics, and treatment*. Northvale, NJ: Aronson.

Meloy, J. R. (1995). Antisocial personality disorder. In G. Gabbard (Ed.), *Treatments of Psychiatric Disorders, 2nd Edition* (pp. 2273–2290). Washington, DC: American Psychiatric Press.

Meloy, J. R., & Gacono, C. B. (1995). Assessing the psychopathic personality. In J. Butcher (Ed.), *Clinical foundations of personality assessment* (pp. 410–422). New York: Oxford University Press.

Mendel, S. (1995). An adolescent group within a milieu setting. *Journal of Child & Adolescent Group Therapy, 5,* 47–51.

Miller, S., Mortensen, E., Breum, L., Alling, C., Larsen, O., Bige Rasmussen, T., Jensen, C., & Bennicke, K. (1996). Aggression and personality: Association with amino acids and monoamine metabolites. *Psychological Medicine, 26*, 323–331.

Mischel, W. (1973). Toward a cognitive social learning reconceptualization of personality. *Psychological Review, 80,* 252–283.

Moretti, M., Emmrys, C., Grizenko, N., Holland, R., Moore, K., Shamsie, J., Hamilton, H. (1997). The treatment of conduct disorder: Perspectives from across Canada. *Canadian Journal of Psychiatry, 42*, 637–648.

Murphy, J. (1976). Psychiatric labeling in cross-cultural perspective. *Science, 191,* 1019–1028.

Myers, M. G., Stewart, B. A., & Brown, S. A. (1998). Progression from conduct disorder to antisocial personality disorder following treatment for adolescent substance abuse. *American Journal of Psychiatry, 155*, 479–485.

Offord, D. R., & Bennett, K. J. (1994). Conduct disorder long-term outcomes and intervention effectiveness. *Journal of the American Academy of Child and Adolescent Psychiatry, 33,* 1069–1078.

Ogloff, J. R., Wong, S., & Greenwood, A. (1990). Treating criminal psychopaths in a therapeutic community. *Behavioral Sciences and the Law, 8,* 181–190.

Orlinsky, D., & Howard, K. (1980). Gender and psychotherapeutic outcomes. In A. M. Brodsky & R. T. Hare-Mustin (Eds.), *Women and psychotherapy*, (pp. 3–34), New York: Guilford Press.

Paul, G. (1967). Strategy of outcome research in psychology. *Journal of Consulting Psychology, 31,* 109–119.

Poldrugo, F., & Forti, B. (1988). Personality disorders and alcohol treatment outcome. *Drug and Alcohol Dependence, 21,* 171–176.

Potts, L., Barley, W., Jones, K., & Woodhall, P. (1986). Comprehensive inpatient treatment of a severely antisocial adolescent. In W. Reid, D. Dorr, J. Walker, & J. Bonner (Eds.), *Unmasking the psychopath: Antisocial personality and related syndromes* (pp. 231–255). New York: W. W. Norton.

Prochaska, J. O., DiClemente, C. C., & Norcross, J. C. (1992). In search of how people change: Applications to addictive behaviors. *American Psychologist, 47,* 1102–1114.

Quay, H. C. (1987). Institutional treatment. In H. C. Quay (Ed.), *Handbook of Juvenile Delinquency*, (pp. 118–138). New York: Wiley.

Quay, H. C., & Love, C. T. (1977). The effect of a juvenile diversion program on rearrests. *Criminal Justice and Behavior, 4,* 377–396.

Reid, W. (1978). Diagnosis of antisocial syndromes. In W. Reid (Ed.), *The psychopath: A comprehensive study of antisocial disorders and behaviors* (pp. 3–6). New York: Brunner/Mazel.

Reid, W., Dord, D., Walter, J., & Bonner, J. (1986). *Unmasking the psychopath: Antisocial personality and related syndromes.* New York: W. W. Norton.

Rice, M. E. (1997). Violent offender research and implications for the criminal justice system. *American Psychologist, 52,* 414–423.

Rice, M. E., & Harris, G. (1992). A comparison of criminal recidivism among schizophrenic and nonschizophrenic offenders. *International Journal of Law and Psychiatry, 15,* 397–408.

Rice, M. E., & Harris, G. T. (1997). The treatment of mentally disordered offenders. *Psychology, Public Policy, and Law, 3,* 126–183.

Rice, M. E., Harris, G., & Cormier, C. (1992). An evaluation of a maximum security therapeutic community for psychopaths and other mentally disordered offenders. *Law and Human Behavior, 16,* 399–412.

Rice, M. E., Harris, G., Lange, C., & Bell, V. (1990). Recidivism among male insanity acquittees. *The Journal of Psychiatry and Law, 18,* 379–403.

Rice, M. E., Harris, G., & Quinsey, V. L. (1990). A follow up of rapists assess in a maximum security psychiatric facility. *Journal of Interpersonal Violence, 5,* 435–440.

Richards, H. (1993). *Therapy of substance abuse syndromes.* Northvale, NJ: Aronson.

Robins, L. (1966). *Deviant children grown up: A sociological and psychiatric study of sociopathic personality.* Baltimore: Williams & Wilkins.

Robins, L. (1991). Conduct disorder. *Journal of Child Psychology and Psychiatry, 32,* 193–212.

Ross, R. R., Fabiano, E. A., & Ewles, C. D. (1988). *International Journal of Offender Therapy and Comparative Criminology, 32,* 29–35.

Rubel, J. G., Bratter, T. E., Smirnoff, A. M., Hartwig-Thompson, L., & Baker, K. G. (1982). The role of structure in the professional model and self-help concept of the therapeutic community: Different strokes for different folks? *International Journal of Therapeutic Communities, 3,* 218–232.

Schmidt, K., Solant, M. V., & Bridger, W. H. (1985). Electrodermal activity of undersocialized aggressive children: A pilot study. *Journal of Child Psychology and Psychiatry, 25,* 653–660.

Schuckit, M. (1985). The clinical implications among alcoholics. *Archives of General Psychiatry, 42,* 1043–1049.

Seligman, M. E. (1996). Science as an ally of practice. *American Psychologist, 51,* 1072–1079.

Selman, R. D. (1986). A therapeutic milieu for treating the antisocial, substance abusing adolescent. In Reid, W., D. Dorr, J. Walker, & J. Bonner (Eds.), *Unmasking the psychopath: Antisocial personality and related syndromes* (pp. 221–230). New York: W.W. Norton.

Serin, R. C. (1991). Psychopathy and violence in criminals. *Journal of Interpersonal Violence, 6,* 423–431.

Shamblin, W. (1986). Inpatient treatment of antisocial youth. In treatment of antisocial syndromes: The therapist's feelings. In W. Reid, D. Dorr, J. Walker, & J. Bonner (Eds.), *Unmasking the psychopath: Antisocial personality and related syndromes* (pp. 208–220). New York: W.W. Norton.

Shamsie, J., & Huchly, C. (1991). Youth with conduct disorder: A challenge to be met. *Canadian Journal of Psychiatry, 36,* 405–414.

Shea, M. T., Widiger, T. A., & Klein, M. H. (1992). Comorbidity of personality disorders and depression: Implications for treatment. *Journal of Consulting and Clinical Psychology, 60,* 857–868.

Sherwood, V. R. (1990). The first stage of treatment with the conduct disordered adolescent: Overcoming narcissistic resistance. *Psychotherapy, 27,* 380–387.

Smith, A., Gacono, C., & Kaufman, L. (1997). A Rorschach comparison of psychopathic and nonpsychopathic conduct disordered adolescents. *Journal of Clinical Psychology, 53,* 289–300.

Stein, D., & Lambert, M. (1984). On the relationship between therapist experience and psychotherapy outcome. *Clinical Psychology Review, 4,* 127–142.

Stein, D., & Lambert, M. (1995). Graduate training in psychotherapy: Are therapy outcomes enhanced? *Journal of Consulting and Clinical Psychology, 63,* 182–196.

Stevens, G. F. (1994). Prison clinician's perceptions of antisocial personality disorder as a formal diagnosis. *Journal of Offender Rehabilitation, 20,* 159–185.

Strasburger, L. (1986). Treatment of antisocial syndromes: The therapist's feelings. In W. Reid, D. Dorr, J. Walker, & J. Bonner (Eds.), *Unmasking the psychopath: Antisocial personality and related syndromes* (pp. 208–220). New York: W.W. Norton.

Strupp, H. H. (1996). The tripartite model and the Consumer Reports study. *American Psychologist, 51,* 1017–1024.

Strupp, H. H. (1997). Research practice, and managed care. *Psychotherapy, 34,* 91–94.

Walker, J. L., Lahey, B. B., Russo M. F., Frick, P. J., Christ, M. A., McBurnett, K., Loeber, R. K., Stouthamer-Loeber, M., & Green, S. M. (1991). Anxiety, inhibition, and conduct disorder in children. I: Relations to social impairment. *Journal of the American Academy of Child and Adolescent Psychiatry, 30,* 187–191.

Walters, G. D. (1990). *The criminal lifestyle: Patterns of serious criminal conduct.* Newbury Park, CA: Sage.

Watson, J. C., & Greenberg, L. S. (1996). Pathways to change in the psychotherapy of depression: Relating process to session change and outcome. *Psychotherapy, 33,* 262–274.

Weinberger, L., & Sreenivasan, S. (1994). Ethical and professional conflicts in correctional psychology. *Professional Psychology: Research and Practice, 25,* 161–167.

Weiss, M. A. J., Davis, D., Hedlund, J. L., & Cho, D. (1983). The dysphoric psychopath: A comparison of 524 cases of antisocial personality disorder with matched controls. *Comprehensive Psychiatry, 24,* 355–369.

Wells, P., & Faragher, B. (1993). In-patient treatment of 165 adolescents with emotional and conduct disorders: A study of outcome. *British Journal of Psychiatry, 162,* 345–352.

Wexler, H. K., Falkin, G. P., & Lipton, D. S. (1990). Outcome evaluation of a prison therapeutic community for substance abuse treatment. *Criminal Justice and Behavior, 17,* 71–92.

Wishnie, H. (1977). *The impulsive personality*. New York: Plenum Press.

Wong, S., & Elek, D., (1990). *The treatment of psychopathy a review*. Unpublished manuscript, Department of Psychology, University of Saskatchewan, Saskatoon, Saskatchewan, Canada.

Woody, G. E., McLellan, T., Luborsky, L., & O'Brien, C. P. (1985). Sociopathy and psychotherapy outcome. *Archives of General Psychiatry, 42*, 1081–1086.

Yochelson, S., & Samenow, S. (1976). *The criminal personality, Volume 1: A profile for change*. New York: Jason Aronson.

Yochelson, S., & Samenow, S. (1977). *The criminal personality, Volume 2: The change process*. New York: Jason Aronson.

Chapter 5
TREATING SUBSTANCE ABUSE DISORDERS

C. Aaron McNeece, David W. Springer, and Elizabeth M. Arnold

In the war on drugs, at least three points have become increasingly clear: (a) incarceration in and of itself does little to break the cycle of illegal drug use and crime; (b) offenders sentenced to incarceration for substance-related offenses exhibit a high rate of recidivism once they are released; and (c) drug abuse treatment has been shown to be demonstrably effective in reducing both drug abuse and drug-related crime (Drug Court Clearinghouse and Technical Assistance Project [DCCTAP], 1996, p. 8).

Treatment for substance abuse addiction is seen as a key component in preventing reoffenses. More than a million persons are in custody or under community supervision who need drug treatment, yet only one in ten is receiving the needed services (Gerstein & Harwood, 1990). This is ironic because substance abuse is a long-standing problem in many cities throughout the nation, and each year $38 billion are spent on cocaine consumption alone. Three quarters of the funds for the United State's highly publicized "war on drugs" goes to domestic enforcement, and only 7% is dedicated to treatment (RAND, 1994). The relatively low priority for treatment partially accounts for the increasing number of offenders arrested on drug-related charges and for the current "revolving-door" phenomenon in our prisons.

The issue of how these individuals, juvenile and adult offenders who have substance abuse problems, should be treated in the justice system is an increasingly important issue. This chapter focuses on current efforts aimed at treating the large number of adult and juvenile offenders with substance abuse disorders who are involved in the criminal justice system. Research has demonstrated that involuntary treatment of offenders is just as effective as voluntary treatment (NIDA, 1999). We describe the assessment of offenders, various treatment modalities, and we discuss settings and programs; we then review approaches to monitoring offenders. We explore the issue of what constitutes "effective" treatment. Finally, we recommend future research and practice regarding substance-abusing criminal offenders.

Adult–Juvenile Differences

In much of the discussion in this chapter we describe substance abuse phenomena that are common to both adults and juveniles. The reader should keep in mind, however, that there are some substantial differences in these client populations. Because juveniles are experiencing rapid physiological, psychological, and sociocultural development, treatment strategies designed for adults may need to be adapted to take into account these developmental issues. Viewing presenting problems by a substance-abusing juvenile from a developmental framework provides a more inclusive perspective for mental health professionals (McNeece & DiNitto, 1998). Because the legal status of juveniles is different from adults, they are treated in a different system that operates under a different set of rules (Schwartz, 1989). Effective intervention with juveniles requires familiarity with the legal system, awareness of specialized assessment and treatment approaches, and knowledge of community, individual, peer, and family factors that contribute to substance abuse (Jenson, 1997).[1]

Assessment

"Assessment is the act of determining the nature and causes of a client's problem" (Lewis, Dana, & Blevins, 1994, p. 71). It is the first active phase of treatment. There are various ways to go about conducting a thorough substance abuse assessment. Information may be gathered through a substance use history or a biopsychosocial assessment, or by administering appropriate measurement tools to the client. The worker–client interaction that takes place while conducting a substance use history contextualizes information that is lost through self-report, pencil-and-paper methods. However, what is gained by administering assessment tools such as the widely used Michigan Alcoholism Screening Test (MAST) is an account of the problem in a standardized manner with a reliable and valid tool. Regardless of the method used, it is imperative that the worker attempt to understand the client's substance abuse problems from the client's perspective, taking into account the client's cultural background and avoiding preconceived notions.

The complete substance use history should include an assessment of the following areas of the client's life: history of presenting problem; history of substance use and abuse; medical history; living arrangements; marital status; family history (which may include a genogram); religious–spiritual history; work history; legal history; sexual history; and mental status examination (i.e., appearance and behavior; mood and affect; thought content and process; speech patterns; immediate and remote memory; orientation to person, place, and time; insight and judgment).

Standardized assessment tools that address substance use problems may provide additional information not obtained otherwise. Some available assessment instruments are the Index of Drug Involvement (IDI), the Addiction Severity Index (ASI), the Drug Use Screening Inventory-Revised (DUSI-R), the Comprehensive Drinker Profile (CDP), the Michigan Alcoholism Screening Test (MAST), the Substance Abuse Subtle Screening Inventory (SASSI), and the Offender Profile Index (OPI).

The Index of Drug Involvement (IDI; Faul & Hudson, 1997) is a 25-item scale intended to measure the severity of a client's problem with drug abuse. Items are measured on a 7-point Likert scale. Like many of Hudson's instruments, scores on the IDI range from 0 to 100. Higher scores indicate more problematic drug use. A clinical cutting score of 30 may be useful in interpreting the score and making clinical decisions, where the higher the score, the more likely that inpatient treatment might be warranted. However, Faul and Hudson (1997) suggested that this cutting score be interpreted with caution until these study findings can be replicated with a larger clinical sample. Reliability estimates are excellent, with a coefficient alpha of .97 and a low SEM value (2.86), as are validity estimates at .60 or greater.

The Addiction Severity Index (ASI; McLellan, Luborsky, Woody, & O'Brien, 1980; McLellan et al., 1985) is a structured interview that is accompanied by a

---

[1]For a full discussion of adult/juvenile differences, see McNeece and Roberts (1997).

numerical scoring system. It is one of few standardized instruments that addresses drugs other than alcohol. It addresses seven areas of functioning: medical status, employment status, drug use, alcohol use, legal status, family and social relationships, and psychological status (McLellan et al., 1980). The ASI has a follow-up version that has helped practitioners and researchers measure client progress and assess program effectiveness. The fact that the ASI addresses legal status may make it particularly useful for mental health professionals working with substance abusing offenders.

The Drug Use Screening Inventory-Revised (DUSI-R; Tarter & Hegedus, 1991) is a 159-item multidimensional pencil-and-paper instrument, measured on a dichotomous (yes–no) scale, that has recently been created to assess the severity of problems of adolescents and adults. Like the ASI, this instrument addresses areas other than substance abuse. The 10 domains on the DUSI-R address drug and alcohol use, behavior patterns, health status, psychiatric disorder, social competence, family system, school performance–adjustment, work adjustment, peer relationships, and leisure–recreation. The information obtained from the completed DUSI-R can be used to develop an individualized treatment plan. However, scores do not indicate specific types of treatment. That decision is left to the clinical judgment of the practitioner. The authors of this instrument report those using it are able to classify adults and adolescents with *DSM-IV* substance disorders and those with no psychiatric disorders.

The Comprehensive Drinker Profile (CDP; Lewis et al., 1994) addresses various aspects of the client's life, including basic demographic information, family and employment history, history of drinking, pattern of alcohol use, alcohol-related problems, severity of dependence, social aspects of use, associated behaviors, medical history, and motivations for drinking and treatment. The CDP has incorporated the Michigan Alcoholism Screening Test (MAST; Selzer, 1971), which is known to most substance abuse mental health professionals. The MAST is a 24-item, dichotomous (yes–no) measure that addresses drinking habits with demonstrated empirical qualities (W. R. Miller, 1976; Selzer, Vinokur, & Van Rooijen, 1974). The instrument is usually self-administered (pencil and paper) and then scored. Two shorter versions of the MAST also exist: The Short MAST (SMAST) contains 13 items and the Brief MAST contains 10 items (Pokorny, Miller, & Kaplan, 1972). These shorter versions are often used with slower readers, which may be relevant for those working with clients in the criminal justice system. Internal consistencies are excellent for both the long (alpha = .95) and short (alpha = .93) forms of the MAST, and the instrument also has excellent known-groups validity (Fischer & Corcoran, 1994).

The Substance Abuse Subtle Screening Inventory (SASSI; G. A. Miller, 1985; G. A. Miller, Miller, Roberts, Brooks, & Lazowski, 1997) is a 67-item pencil-and-paper instrument. This instrument is different from those described previously in that most of the true–false items on the one side of the tool do not directly inquire about alcohol or drug use. Rather, the reverse side of the SASSI consists of items that inquire directly about alcohol and drug use. These items on the reverse side were formerly called the Risk Prediction Scales (Morton, 1978). Collectively, these two sides provide items that possess face validity and more subtle items that are empirically derived. The SASSI is unique in that it is accompanied by a set of decision rules to determine if the client fits the profile of a chemically dependent person, and other guidelines help determine if a respondent is an abuser but not dependent. An additional strength of the tool is that separate guidelines are used to score results for men and women.

The OPI is a widely used classification instrument designed to determine which type of drug-abuse intervention (long-term residential, short-term residential, intensive outpatient, regular outpatient, or urine monitoring only) to use with particular offenders (Inciardi, McBride, & Weinman, 1993). Research on approximately 900 clients indicated that the results obtained by matching clients with treatment on the basis of the OPI were no better than results for clients who were simply assigned to receive urinalysis monitoring (Hepburn, Johnston, & Rogers, 1993).

All of the standardized measurement instruments described earlier—except for the OPI—have good reliability and validity estimates reported by their authors, and in most cases, their utility has been demonstrated by other researchers (McNeece & DiNitto, 1998). However, it is never wise for a practitioner to rely solely on self-report measures when determining diagnostic impressions and course of treatment, because it is relatively easy for respondents to present themselves as they wish to be perceived by others on such measures. Thus clinical decisions should be supplemented by a thorough biopsychosocial history, which should include information gathered from external sources such as spouses or parents.

Following a complete assessment, the mental health professional is in a position to form a diagnostic impression. Professionals can more easily communicate with one another about a client's problem by referring to a specific diagnosis to describe the client's problem. In addition, a diagnosis can provide clarity to the treatment plan in terms of what the problem is and the appropriate goals and objectives for the client to achieve to alleviate the problem.

One common diagnostic framework often used by substance abuse mental health professionals and other helping professionals is the *Diagnostic and Statistical Manual of Mental Disorders-IV* (*DSM-IV*; American Psychiatric Association, 1994). The *DSM-IV* operates on a multiaxial system. Each person is evaluated on each of five axes, with Axis I addressing clinical syndromes such as substance abuse and dependence. The *DSM-IV* makes a clear distinction between substance use, abuse, and dependence. "The essential feature of Substance Dependence is a cluster of cognitive, behavioral, and physiological symptoms indicating that the individual continues use of the substance despite significant substance-related problems" (American Psychiatric Association, 1994, p. 176). The symptoms of substance dependence are similar across the various categories of substances, of which there are 11 total: alcohol; amphetamine or similarly acting sympathomimetics; caffeine; cannabis; cocaine; hallucinogens; inhalants; nicotine; opioids; phencyclidine (PCP) or similarly acting arylcyclohexylamines; and sedatives, hyponitics, or anxiolytics.

In comparison to substance dependence, "the essential feature of substance abuse is a maladaptive pattern of substance use manifested by recurrent and significant adverse consequences related to the repeated use of substances" (American Psychiatric Association, 1994, p. 182). A key difference between the two diagnoses is that the criteria for substance abuse do not include physical tolerance, withdrawal symptoms, or a pattern of compulsive use.

Once the practitioner has conducted a thorough assessment and has developed a diagnostic impression, a decision must be made about what type of treatment modality and treatment setting are most appropriate for the client. A discussion of how the practitioner can use available information to reach this complex decision follows. For example, in the section later in the chapter that discusses whether in-patient versus outpatient is warranted for a client, we provide some guidelines to aid the practitioner in reaching such a decision. In addition, various treatment modalities are discussed along with relevant outcome research. This is accompanied by a syn-opsis of the effectiveness of different treatment settings and programs, including more recent developments (such as juvenile assessment centers and drug courts) in dealing with substance abusing offenders.

Approaches to Treatment

Several different modalities (individual, family, and group) may be used to treat persons with substance abuse problems. Of course, these approaches are not mutually exclusive. They are often used in conjunction with one another when treating the substance abusing client.

Consider the client who is being treated in an agency setting for substance dependence. A combination of individual, family, and group therapy approaches will address more aspects of his or her functioning than will one of these approaches alone.

Individual Therapy

Traditionally, the preference in chemical dependency treatment has been group ther-apy, with individual therapy used to supplement the group when warranted. Individ-ual therapy might address areas such as depression, faulty cognitions (often referred to in the field as "stinking thinking"), "using" behaviors, and sexual dysfunctions. This modality usually entails "talk therapy" between a client and clinical psychol-ogist, social worker, or substance abuse mental health professional. The practitioner may devote one-on-one time with the client early on in treatment to encourage the client to consider group treatment and other aspects of the helping process.

Group Therapy

Group therapy is often the treatment of choice by chemical dependency mental health professionals and can take the form of support groups, psychoeducational groups, and interactional therapeutic groups. Such groups can be conducted in outpatient and inpatient settings, including settings within the criminal justice system, and can be closed-ended or open-ended. Although approaches to group therapy may vary, ac-cording to Flores (1988),

> most professionals who work with alcoholics and addicts on a sustained basis agree that group therapy offers the chemically dependent individual unique opportunities (1) to share and to identify with others who are going through similar problems; (2) to understand their own attitudes toward addiction and their defenses against giving up alcohol and drugs by confronting similar attitudes and defenses in others; and (3) to learn to communicate needs and feelings more directly. (p. 7)

Working with group members in the criminal justice system takes on a different connotation than working with members in the community. In the criminal justice setting, the group worker is bound by structural constraints, policies, and laws. Nevertheless, the primary objective remains the same. The worker should focus on the strengths of the individual, consider group exercises that will emphasize these strengths, and foster the concept of cohesion within the group. Cohesiveness is defined by Festinger (1950) as "the resultant of all the forces acting on all the members to remain in the group" (p. 274). Cohesiveness is essential if the group is to remain intact and reach a productive working stage where constructive confrontation accompanied with high levels of self-disclosure takes place in a supportive environment.

These principles also apply to support groups that are often made available for parents, spouses, siblings, and other family members. Multifamily groups are an effective way to make use of group and family dynamics to facilitate change. Several families come together in a group setting, where they share their problems, confront members within their own family and in other families, and serve as a source of support. The worker facilitating the multifamily group needs skills in both group and family work. Members soon discover that other people (and in this case entire families) have experienced many of the same problems, a phenomenon referred to by Yalom (1994) as "universality."

In the case of work with juvenile substance abusers in agency and juvenile justice settings, forms of positive peer culture (PPC) are often used to facilitate group treatment. This method, developed by Harry Vorrath, was heavily influenced by a peer-oriented treatment model called guided group interaction. According to Vorrath and Brendtro (1985), "PPC is a total system for building positive youth subcultures" (p. xx). Consider the following case example taken from Vorrath and Brendtro (1985), which illustrates how PPC might work for youth with substance abuse problems:

> A group home for troubled girls had severe drug abuse problems. The result of the many attempts to suppress the activity was a cold war between staff and youth. Suspicion, searches, and restriction became commonplace. That was a year ago. Now staff members no longer police students for drugs, and the climate of intrigue is gone. As a new girl enters, her peers confiscate any drugs she may have and tell her, "We don't have to use dope around here." Drug problems are dealt with openly in a helpful, matter-of-fact way. Group members state with strong conviction that when a person has good feelings about herself she no longer needs to get high on drugs. (p. xix)

The earliest recorded study of PPC was conducted by the Minnesota Department of Corrections, which studied more than 700 youth who had been paroled from a Minnesota PPC program (Minnesota Department of Corrections, 1973). Their findings were favorable, indicating a success rate of 81.5 percent and fewer than a one-fifth (18.5%) recidivism rate in a two-year follow-up. Subsequent analysis of the Minnesota study revealed problems with the research methodology, however (Sarri & Selo, 1974). Since that time, other studies have found that PPC is an effective modality across different problem areas, including increased feelings of self-worth and reduced delinquent values and attitudes (Michigan Department of Social Services, 1983) and a reduction in asocial behavior (McKinney, Miller, Beier, & Bohannon, 1978). However, no studies were found that specifically addressed the effectiveness of PPC with substance-abusing clients.

According to Jackson and Springer (1997), a special type of group that can be formed in juvenile justice settings is the *therapeutic gang*. This type of group functions as an incarcerated gang. Although one reason for the worker to form a therapeutic gang may be to improve security within the facility, the major purpose is to assist these clients in finding positive alternatives to the negative attitudes, behaviors, and values that they are typically accustomed to. To effectively implement the therapeutic gang, the worker must have a working knowledge of both group and gang dynamics.

As indicated earlier, there are many forms of group treatment with chemically dependent clients. Nevertheless, Brandsma and Pattison's (1985) review of about 30 studies generally indicated a positive outcome of using group therapy in a chemical dependency treatment program as well as a need to further empirically demonstrate the effectiveness of this modality. This is further supported by Solomon (1982), who notes a lacuna in the literature comparing group with individual treatment for alcoholics, and comparing different approaches to conducting groups.

Family Therapy

A truism in substance dependency is that families are critical factors to consider when developing a treatment plan for the client (Smith & Springer, 1998). Working with the individual client without examining the family structure, dynamics, and roles that are influenced by and influence the client's substance dependency is often insufficient. The relationship between adolescent substance use and family system characteristics—parental behaviors is supported in the literature (Anderson & Henry, 1994; Denton & Kampfe, 1994), revealing that family drug use, family composition, family interaction patterns, and family boundaries are all correlated with an increased risk of adolescent substance use. The most commonly used family treatment approach with substance abuse is structural—strategic family therapy (Smith & Springer, 1998). Developed by Salvador Minuchin and his associates (Minuchin, 1974; Minuchin & Fishman, 1981), this approach incorporates family development and a family-systems conceptual framework. Studies addressing the efficacy of structural family therapy with youth have revealed positive results when used with drug-abusing families (Fishman, Stanton, & Rosman, 1982; Szapocznik, Kurtines, Foote, Perez-Vidal, & Hervis, 1986).

A recent study (Joaning, Quinn, Thomas, & Mullen, 1992) compared the effectiveness of family systems therapy, adolescent group therapy, and family drug education. Tentative findings of the study reveal that family systems therapy was more effective in stopping adolescent drug abuse when compared to group therapy or family drug education, producing twice the number of drug-free clients than family drug education and three times the number when compared to group therapy. Marital or couples therapy has also shown promising effects for alcohol-using clients, but the short-term benefits appear to be more amplified than do long-term results (National Institute on Alcohol Abuse and Alcoholism, 1990).

Self-Help Programs

Alcoholics Anonymous (AA), founded by William ("Bill W.") Wilson and Robert ("Dr. Bob") Holbrook Smith, is an abstinence-based 12-step program that maintains that alcoholism is a disease that can be coped with but not cured. Thus according to the AA philosophy, there are recovering alcoholics but not cured or ex-alcoholics.

Other self-help 12-step programs, such as Narcotics Anonymous (NA), follow the same conceptual framework. AA and NA meetings are held in both adult and juvenile secured correctional settings. Additional self-help groups include Routine Recovery and Women's Sobriety.

There are three parts of these 12-step programs: surrender steps, integrity steps, and serenity steps (Brundage, 1985). The surrender steps require an acknowledgment of a substance dependence problem (whether alcohol or drugs) and that such a problem is destructive to the member's life. The member surrenders to a "higher power," which is not necessarily synonymous with God or any similar deity. Integrity steps allow members to apologize for difficulties caused to others as a result of their drug or alcohol use. The last three steps in 12-step programs collectively form the serenity steps and are concerned with the member maintaining a drug-free life.

One study examined the effectiveness of 12-step programs with adolescents (Alford, Koehler, & Leonard, 1991). Their findings indicated that Alcoholics Anonymous benefited adolescents who were able to understand and accept AA principles and traditions. However, the lack of a comparison group in the study requires that these findings be interpreted with caution and not generalized to all adolescents. In general, studies of the effectiveness of AA tend to focus on middle- and upper-class populations with rather stable lives before the onset of a drinking problem (Alexander, 1990). Inpatient substance abuse treatment programs throughout the United States continue to be based on a disease model that uses the 12-step approach. However, there is a significant lacuna in the research literature on the effectiveness of such programs (Abadinsky, 1990). Others have criticized AA for its lack of credible research supporting an abstinence-oriented "disease" model (W. R. Miller & Hester, 1980; Ogborne & Glasser, 1985).

The authors question the blanket use of prescribing AA and NA programs to all substance abusing offenders. Should the offender who is a substance user (i.e., has engaged in "experimental" use of one drug) be told that he or she has a disease and has to attend 90 NA meetings in 90 days, or would this approach better serve those who meet criteria for substance or polysubstance dependence? This question is particularly salient for juvenile offenders, because it is our experience that adolescents often experience more difficulty "buying into" the disease model. This issue needs to be explored further by helping professionals working with this population.

Psychoeducational Approaches

In many corrections settings, adult and juvenile offenders are required to complete educational classes as a part of treatment. In the justice system, two main types of educational programs for offenders exist: didactic educational programs and psychoeducational programs.

Didactic educational programs closely resemble a seminar or class. In these programs, offenders are presented with information about substance abuse and its effects. Offenders may learn about topics such as the physical effects of drug and alcohol abuse or the impact of substance abuse on family members, or they may be provided information about substance abuse treatment. In didactic educational programs, offenders are expected to listen to the information provided, and although there may be some interaction, the presenter is the focus of the program and interaction is generally minimal.

Psychoeducational programs combine "the presentation of didactic information to increase knowledge with a variety of other techniques to help clients make desired changes and to provide support" (McNeece & DiNitto, 1994, p. 117). In these programs, the emphasis is not solely on the facilitator but group interaction is encouraged. Structured exercises such as role plays, group discussion on specific topics, and homework assignments are generally part of psychoeducational programs.

The major objectives of psychoeducational approaches include development of motivation and commitment to treatment through recognition of the addiction history, stages of recovery, and the impact of drug use on physical health and vocational and social functioning; the enhancement of life skills (e.g., managing a checkbook, time management) and communication skills; AIDS education and prevention activities; relapse prevention skills, including recognition of signs and symptoms of relapse, avoidance of active drug users, identification of high-risk situations, and strategies for managing a lapse or relapse; and development of an aftercare plan that incorporates use of community treatment resources (Peters, 1993, p. 53).

Educational programs are a key component in many types of drug treatment but are seldom used as a primary treatment modality. Educational programs are used in the majority of settings in which offenders receive treatment, including jails, residential programs, and outpatient programs. However, because these programs are used in conjunction with other programs, few researchers have evaluated educational programs by themselves; most studies have examined the effectiveness of multifaceted programs that include education as one component.

Pharmacotherapy

There are various types of drugs that may be used to help an alcoholic or addict recover from their addiction following detoxification. Such drugs include, but are not limited to, disulfiram—better known as Antabuse—methadone, levo-alpha-acetylmethadol (LAAM), and naltrexone. These four drugs are briefly reviewed, as are some available outcome studies regarding their use in treatment.

Disulfiram

Disulfiram, better known by its trade name Antabuse, has been used to treat alcoholics. Clients usually take disulfiram once a day. It does not reduce the desire to drink. Rather, it deters those taking it from drinking because they know that they will become extremely ill if they do consume alcohol. Even products that contain alcohol, such as mouthwash, can bring about symptoms. Disulfiram–alcohol reactions might include symptoms such as increased pulse, sweating, a severe headache, and vomiting. Some deaths have even been reported. Thus it is important that a client is completely detoxified before starting disulfiram. The criminal justice system has been supportive about the use of the drug, ordering many clients to take it when appropriate. Clients report to their probation or parole officer to take the drug under supervision, and some officers make the client crush the aspirin-size pill and mix it with a liquid so that the client cannot "cheek their meds" until leaving the office when the drug can be spit out. Outcome studies on the use of disulfiram have been equivocal, with some authors (e.g., Fuller et al., 1986) doubting its usefulness and others (McNichol & Logsdon, 1988) giving a more positive review of its benefits in treatment.

Methadone

Methadone was approved by the U.S. Food and Drug Administration in 1972 for the purpose of treating opioid addiction (Retig & Yarmolinsky, 1995). It is a synthetic narcotic drug that appears to be helpful in deterring addicts from pursuing illegal activities to support their drug habits. There are approximately 750 to 800 methadone clinics operating in the United States (Ling, Rawson, & Compton, 1994). Nevertheless, a great deal of controversy remains. Hanson and Venturelli (1995) summarize some advantages and disadvantages of methadone maintenance:

> The advantages of methadone over other forms of maintenance therapy are (1) It can be administered orally. (2) It acts in the body 24 to 36 hours, compared to heroin's action of 4 to 8 hours. (3) It causes no serious side effects at maintenance doses. (4) At sufficient dose levels, methadone will almost completely block the effects of heroin. (5) When taken orally, it does not produce substantial euphoric effects. Disadvantages of methadone maintenance include (1) The person taking it may develop dependence. (2) It will not prevent the addict from taking other drugs that may interfere with treatment and rehabilitation. (p. 486)

Methadone is considered cost-effective in the sense that it may contribute to reduced crime (Ling, Rawson, & Compton, 1994). Nevertheless, some communities refuse to have a methadone clinic for fear of attracting heroin users to their area. There are more available outcome studies about the effectiveness of methadone maintenance than about other types of pharmacotherapy, and in spite of controversies surrounding this treatment, it generally produces positive outcomes (Gerstein & Harwood, 1990) because these programs tend to be effective in reducing drug use and criminality (Snair, 1989), especially when combined with psychosocial services (McLellan, Arndt, Metzger, Woody, & O'Brien, 1993).

LAAM

Approved by the U.S. Food and Drug Administration in 1993, levo-alpha-acetylmethadol (LAAM) is a methadone analog with longer lasting effects than methadone used to treat narcotic addicts (Gerstein & Harwood, 1990), and clients generally take it three days a week (Prendergast, Grella, Perry, & Anglin, 1995). Thus LAAM may be best used with clients who warrant fewer clinic visits, whereas methadone might be better suited for clients in need of daily clinical contact. Although long-term studies on the effectiveness of LAAM are sparse, it has generally been found to be equally effective to methadone in terms of reduced heroin use, employment rates, and arrest rates (McNeece & DiNitto, 1998). It appears that clients feel more normal when taking LAAM in comparison to methadone.

Naltrexone

An improved version of the drug naloxone (Witters & Venturelli, 1988), naltrexone (trade name ReVia) is useful in treating a narcotic overdose because it reverses respiratory depression produced by narcotics. Where methadone is a substitute for narcotic drugs, naltrexone reverses their effects. Witters and Venturelli (1988) stated, "Naltrexone is best suited for adolescent heroin users with relatively short experience with heroin, for recently paroled prisoners who have been abstinent while incarcerated, and for persons who have been on methadone maintenance who wish to go off, but who are afraid of relapsing to heroin" (p. 331). Naltrexone has recently been found to enhance treatment outcomes of alcoholics and cocaine addicts (the University of Florida College of Medicine, 1992; cited in McNeece & DiNitto, 1998), but more long-term studies are needed.

Each of these drug therapies should not be used in isolation. Clients should be closely monitored when participating in these drug therapies, especially in the early stages of treatment. One means of monitoring the progress of drug therapy is through case management services.

Case Management

Case management activities originated in early 20th-century social work practice that provided services to disadvantaged clients. Most descriptions of case management include at least six primary functions: (a) identification and outreach to people in need of services; (b) assessment of specific needs; (c) planning for services; (d) linkage to services; (e) monitoring and evaluation; and (f) advocacy for the client system (Ridgely, 1996). Workers are increasingly engaging in case management activity in their work with substance abusing offenders.

The importance of workers providing case management services for substance abusing clients in the criminal justice setting is supported by Martin and Inciardi (1993), who stated that "drug-involved criminal justice clients often face a wider spectrum of problems than other populations targeted by case management, including the life disruptions associated with police and court processing, the perceived stigma of a criminal record, the possibility of lost freedom through incarceration, and the disruptions caused in work, school, and family activities" (p. 89). They go on to argue that if case management is combined with legal sanctions to enforce participation in treatment, it is more likely that clients will remain in treatment and thus receive needed services. Treatment Alternatives to Street Crime (TASC) programs (discussed at length later in this chapter) have successfully implemented this notion (Inciardi & McBride, 1991). Others also support the use of case management services, because it has been shown to encourage substance abusers to remain in treatment and reach treatment goals (Kofoed, Tolson, Atkinson, Toth, & Turner, 1986).

As the prevalence of HIV increases in the drug-abusing population, it is imperative that case managers address this multifaceted problem in their work with clients. One study (Batki, 1990; cited in Beeder & Millman, 1997) revealed improved outcomes in clients whose case management included interdisciplinary communication and treatment procedures, such as medical treatment of HIV symptoms and treatment of neuropsychiatric syndromes associated with AIDS. Beeder and Millman (1997) responded to controversy around HIV testing in early stages of substance abuse recovery by noting their experience, which suggests that if the need for the test is presented in a tactful, empathic manner then clients do not leave treatment prematurely. They go on to highlight that making the diagnosis of HIV or AIDS early in treatment can help clients use their resources and live an abstinent, responsible life.

There is a lack of empirical evidence to support case management as an effective intervention (Babor et al., 1991, cited in Jenson, 1997). However, one recent study (Jenson et al., 1994, cited in Jenson, 1997) followed 93 delinquent youths who received case management services in the Utah corrections system, indicating that the most common activity of case managers was coordinating substance abuse services.

Acupuncture

Acupuncture is a form of ancient Chinese medicine that has been used for the past 20 years to treat addictions. The use of acupuncture involves inserting four or five needles into an individual's ear for approximately 45 minutes. Acupuncture is believed to reduce the physical signs of withdrawal, including cravings, body aches, headaches, nausea, sweating, and muscle cramping. Supporters of acupuncture also claim it relieves depression, anxiety, and insomnia (Turnabout ASAP, 1997). The needles are believed to produce a powerful response that helps decrease the desire for drugs and alcohol, thus helping the brain regain its chemical balance. Once this crucial balance is restored, the abuser, it is hoped, will become more introspective and receptive to therapy (Edwards, 1993).

The use of acupuncture to treat chemical dependency was discovered by accident by Dr. H. L. Wen, a Hong Kong neurosurgeon. He was preparing an opium addicted patient for surgery using electroacupuncture as analgesia when the patient discovered his withdrawal symptoms had subsided (Singer, 1996).

The first substance abuse facility known to use acupuncture with substance abusers is Lincoln Hospital Substance Abuse Center in South Bronx, New York. Acupuncture is used at Lincoln Hospital to treat a large number of persons with addictions—250 clients a day in 1993 (U.S. GAO, 1996). Dr. Michael Smith of Lincoln Hospital, one of the pioneers of acupuncture use with drug addicts in the United States, has worked with Dr. Wen to try to locate precisely the most important acupuncture points to assist in managing withdrawal symptoms. Acupuncture also has become particularly popular among "drug court" programs in the United States. There seems to be no reason other than the first drug court in Miami used acupuncture. Others followed suit.

Despite anecdotal reports of success, few empirical studies exist that have examined the effectiveness of acupuncture in treating addictions. Two studies have examined the use of acupuncture with inner-city, cocaine-dependent methadone clients. Margolin, Avants, Chang, and Kosten (1995) found that the majority (90%) of participants in an eight-week course of treatment remained abstinent for more than one month. However, 50% of those individuals studied did not complete the program, which is a problem experienced by others researching this topic. Bullock, Umen, Colliton, and Olander (1987) conducted a blinded placebo study, and despite payment for program completion only 52% of those receiving the treatment and 2.5% of the placebo group completed the study. The study's results are limited by the large dropout rate, but the results were nonetheless promising: Six months after program completion, none of the participants had to be admitted for detoxification and only 26% admitted to consuming alcohol. These statistics are promising when compared to the control group, 98% of whom had been admitted for detoxification or reported alcohol use.

Avants, Margolin, Chang, Kosten, and Birch (1993) found that among regular crack users who had been using an average 10 years, six weeks of treatment reduced the frequency of use and cravings. Others (Brewington, Smith, & Lipton, 1994; Lipton, Brewington, & Smith, 1990) have found that although acupuncture can produce reductions in self-reports of day-to-day cocaine use among chronic crack users, the urinalysis results of participants did not differ from those of the control group.

Although these studies provide limited optimism for the use of acupuncture as a promising treatment modality for addictions, some researchers (McLellan, Grossman, Blaine, & Haverkos, 1993; Moon & Latessa, 1994) have asserted that the majority of the studies on this topic do not meet commonly accepted empirical standards and overestimate the evidence from well-controlled studies of acupuncture's effectiveness. The National Institute on Drug Abuse (NIDA) has been involved in technically evaluating the effectiveness of acupuncture as a legitimate form of substance abuse treatment. In addition to NIDA approval, to surpass investigational status the promoters of acupuncture must convince the FDA that acupuncture needles are safe and effective for use in substance abuse treatment (Singer, 1996). Thus far, NIDA has yet to support the use of acupuncture, and its position has been clearly articulated:

> It was disturbing to the panel to note that acupuncture treatment for opiate dependence had been critically evaluated in the 1970's and 1980's but that there had been very little methodologically solid work in the area during those two decades. Meanwhile, acupuncture procedures have been accepted and expanded over the same period of time and are now used in the treatment of cocaine and alcohol dependence. While some studies have emerged that were experimentally and clinically reasonable, the consensus was that much of the fundamental work remains to be done and that after two decades of contemporary use in the field of addiction, there is no compelling evidence for the efficacy of acupuncture in the treatment of either opiate or cocaine dependence. (McClellan et al., 1993, p. 575)

However, NIDA has agreed to participate in research on acupuncture and has funded studies at Lincoln Hospital, the University of Miami, and Hennepin County Medical Center in Hennepin County, Minnesota. The first national study to begin in late 1997 is being conducted by researchers from Columbia University (Singer, 1996). Such empirical testing is necessary for acupuncture to gain credibility from researchers and treatment professionals. Singer (1996) has argued that acupuncture has demonstrated some measure of success but has yet to be accepted as a legitimate form of substance abuse treatment. He argued that acupuncture is held to a "higher standard" than other types of treatment because of its fundamental conflict with Western medicine and philosophy.

Treatment Settings and Programs

In addition to the various types of treatment described previously, substance abuse treatment may be provided in a number of different settings. The most common treatment settings are discussed in the following pages.

Inpatient and Residential Programs

Individuals with substance abuse problems involved in the justice system can be referred to inpatient or residential treatment programs for their substance abuse problems in several ways. A judge can court-order a person to treatment, a worker at a juvenile assessment center (JAC) or juvenile addictions receiving facility (JARF; discussed later in the chapter) can refer a youth to such a program, or inpatient treatment can be mandated as part of probation.

A diagnosis for the client is warranted to justify admission into an inpatient or residential facility. The client should exhibit a high degree of medical risk, suicidal or homicidal threat, or a high likelihood of injury by neglect to warrant inpatient admission. Current health care policy and the fragmentation of community-based service networks make inpatient treatment an expensive and overused form of care (Schwartz, 1989).

Inpatient treatment has changed drastically over recent years. The era of 28-day treatment programs is almost extinct. The cost of such programs is too high for most people to pay for out of pocket, and third-party payers overwhelmingly no longer reimburse for such services. Inpatient programs typically provide respite for family, drug education, group encounters with peers, and individual treatment, which may include a pharmacological component.

Longer inpatient (residential) programs for offenders, such as therapeutic communities, also exist. Once admitted into such facilities, clients are encouraged to form close emotional ties with other patients. When successful, adolescents will perceive themselves as part of a group of peers who act as a support network (Obermeier & Henry, 1989). If third-party payers are involved, a dual diagnosis of the child or adolescent is required to warrant payment for such treatment. For example, in addition to demonstrating that a diagnosis of a substance abuse problem (e.g., polysubstance dependence) is warranted, the practitioner or agency must also be able to identify and justify an Axis I diagnosis in the *DSM-IV* (American Psychiatric Association, 1994).

There is little doubt that extended residential communities are necessary for seriously disturbed children and adolescents. When children or adolescents chronically endanger themselves with their drug and alcohol use, extended residential treatment may be the desired alternative because of its ability to provide 24-hour monitoring of behavior (Downey, 1991). The same holds true for adults.

One residential model that has been implemented throughout the country are restitution centers, which control and provide support for residents who must pay victim restitution out of earnings from community work. One such program is the Griffin Diversion Center in Georgia, which was established in the early 1970s. Residents typically work eight hours a day, maintain the center's operations, complete community service on weekends, attend classes or therapy sessions in the evenings, provide routine drug testing, participate in sports tournaments, and organize food and clothing drives (DiMascio, 1995).

Outpatient Programs

An alternative to the more expensive and restrictive inpatient and residential care described earlier is outpatient treatment. This approach is being increasingly used because, as already noted, third-party payers typically demand dual diagnoses to reimburse for inpatient or residential treatment. For example, in addition to demonstrating that a diagnosis of a substance abuse problem (e.g., polysubstance dependence) is warranted, the practitioner or agency must also be able to identify and justify an Axis I diagnosis in the *DSM-IV* (American Psychiatric Association, 1994).

This practice has resulted in an increased use of intensive outpatient programs (IOPs) and partial hospitalization programs (PHPs) in the field, both of which allow the youth to return home each night with his or her family rather than "live" at the facility. In general, a PHP, also referred to as day treatment, is more intense compared with an IOP. One distinct difference between the two approaches is that a client typically attends day treatment Monday through Friday during the day (for example, from 8 a.m. to 4 p.m.), whereas a client in an IOP might only attend three nights a week for three hours each night. Otherwise, IOPs and PHPs provide the same services as inpatient or residential treatment at lower costs. Thus goal-oriented and planned short-term treatment is being favored over longer term treatment approaches (Wells, 1994).

Inpatient Versus Outpatient Treatment

There is no evidence to suggest that inpatient treatment is any more effective with most substance abusing clients than outpatient treatment (Gerstein & Harwood, 1990; Hepburn, Johnston & Rogers, 1993; NIAAA, 1997). Indeed, some parents who avail themselves of extended inpatient treatment for their children may do so more for themselves than for their children, because the treatment period acts as a respite. And for improvements gained in inpatient programs to be maintained, critics of this approach suggest that children and adolescents need changes to occur while in their home settings. Changes that occur within an inpatient setting frequently occur within a vacuum; the typical frustrations and challenges that might encourage alcohol and drug use and abuse are absent in an inpatient setting. Thus improvements seen in the hospital do not necessarily extend to home settings (Joaning, Gawinski, Morris, & Quinn, 1986). One study (Friedman & Utada, 1983) found that outpatient settings devoted more staff time to individual and family therapy than residential programs that had a heavier emphasis on art therapy, group therapy, vocational training, and medical services.

Regarding the treatment of cocaine (and crack) dependence, a condition that practitioners are likely to encounter among juvenile and adult offenders, Gold (1997) provided guidelines to use in determining whether inpatient or outpatient treatment is warranted. Gold argued that outpatient treatment is the preferred modality for cocaine abusers for some of the following reasons: Cocaine use can typically be stopped abruptly without medical risk; life is more "normal" in an outpatient setting than the inpatient, and returning the client to a normal life is a key goal of treatment; the cost of outpatient care is lower; there is less stigma and disruption to one's life in outpatient care than with the inpatient; and it is certain that outpatient care will be needed anyway because of the risk of relapse. However, Gold said that

> when drug use is severe, or if outpatient care is not possible or has failed in the past, hospitalization is called for. While not a complete listing, indications for inpatient care include:

1. Chronic crack, freebase, or intravenous use
2. Concurrent dependency on other addictive drugs or alcohol
3. Serious concurrent medical or psychiatric problems
4. Severe impairment or psychological or neurological functioning
5. Insufficient motivation for outpatient treatment
6. Lack of family and social supports
7. Failure in outpatient treatment. (p. 191)

We have chosen cocaine use to illustrate the issues that must be addressed in the inpatient versus outpatient debate because the use of this drug is common among offenders. However, this guideline can be applied to most substances when considering whether inpatient or outpatient treatment is warranted for a client.

Therapeutic Communities

Therapeutic communities (TCs) may be considered to fall under the realm of residential programs or jail treatment programs. The therapeutic community is a residential treatment environment that provides an around-the-clock learning experience in which the drug user's changes in conduct, attitudes, values, and emotions are implemented, monitored, and reinforced on a daily basis (DeLeon, 1986). Typically, a TC is highly structured, lasting anywhere from 3 to 15 months. However, because of the confrontational nature of the community, it is common for residents to leave within the first three months of the program (Goldapple, 1990).

The treatment philosophy is that substance abuse is a disorder of the whole person, that the problem lies in the person and not the drug, and that the addiction is but a symptom and not the essence of the disorder (Pan, Scarpitti, Inciardi, & Lockwood, 1993). The primary goal of the TC approach is to lead the client to a responsible, substance-free life. Although individual, family, and group therapy may be components of the TC, the cornerstone of the program is the peer encounter that takes place in the group process. Rules of the community are specific and enforced by the residents themselves. In general, the TC staff are themselves recovering substance abusers who have successfully completed treatment in a therapeutic community.

Most research indicates that offenders who leave therapeutic communities do not fare significantly better with postrelease drug and crime experiences when compared to their counterparts who did not participate in a therapeutic community (McNeece & Daly, 1997). Gerstein and Harwood (1990) found that therapeutic community programs, when closely linked to community-based supervision and treatment programs, can significantly reduce rearrest rates. However, Gerstein and Harwood (1990) were careful to point out the limitations of available research on the effectiveness of therapeutic communities:

> Conclusions about the effectiveness of TCs are limited by the difficulties of applying standard clinical trial methodologies to a complex, dynamic treatment milieu and a population resistant to following instructions. Randomized trials or natural experiments in the community, which would permit a well-controlled comparison of clients admitted to TC treatment versus an equivalent group ... Currently, the strongest conclusions on the effectiveness of TCs are based on nonrandomized or nonexperi-

mental but rigorously conducted studies of clients seeking admission to therapeutic communities. (p. 156)

Therapeutic communities are commonly used in correctional settings (Lipton, Falkin, & Wexler, 1992). To develop a sense of community among TC participants and to minimize any negative peer influence from inmates not involved with treatment, many TC programs are arranged so that participants are isolated from the general population. Implementing therapeutic communities in correctional settings has been hindered at times by a reluctance to provide long-term therapeutic services, by philosophical opposition to the use of staff who themselves are former offenders, to coercive treatment strategies, and by the need for specialized staff training and technical assistance (Peters, 1993).

Juvenile Assessment Centers (JACs) and Juvenile Addiction Receiving Facilities (JARFs)

Unfortunately, the nation's juvenile justice system is currently strained and faces many difficulties in dealing with serious juvenile offenders. Historically, there has existed a lack of adequate resources nationwide to provide treatment for youth in the juvenile detention system. Bazemore (1993) commented on this phenomenon, arguing that "detention in many Florida counties had come to represent a holding center or dumping ground for runaways, homeless adolescents, probation violators, minor offenders, and other youth who lack appropriate supervision" (p. 31). In response to the rise in juvenile delinquency and truancy and the inability to effectively deal with this population, some states (e.g., Florida, Colorado, Kansas) have adopted legislation that mandates establishing community assessment centers, often referred to as a juvenile assessment center (JAC).

In Florida, for example, the juvenile assessment centers are authorized by the Florida Legislature (39.0471, F.S. 1995) as follows:

> The Department [of Juvenile Justice] shall work cooperatively with substance abuse facilities, mental health providers, law enforcement agencies, schools, health services providers, and other entities involved with children to establish a juvenile justice assessment center in each service district. The assessment center shall serve as a central intake and screening for children referred to the department. Each juvenile justice assessment center shall provide services needed to facilitate initial screening of children, including intake and needs assessment, substance abuse screening, physical and mental health screening, and diagnostic testing, as appropriate. The entities involved in the assessment center shall make the resource for the provision of these services available at the same level to which they are available to the general public.

Each juvenile assessment center (JAC) has as a similar objective to serve as a centralized intake system in which law enforcement officers can bring youth charged with truancy, felonies, and misdemeanors. Although these centers can be organized differently, they should have as their cornerstone multidisciplinary screening and assessment systems. The centers are designed to help ensure that the youths' service needs are addressed in disposition recommendations, link at-risk or troubled youth and their families with needed services, and track the outcomes of these problem-identification and program-linking activities.

Youth are brought into a JAC through a secure sally port, a designated area between the assessment center and outside world; and they are fingerprinted and photographed, allowing law enforcement officers to drop off a youth in custody and return to patrol (often inside of 10 minutes). The JAC staff assess and determine what should be done with the youth. Some assessment centers are using the Problem Oriented Screening Instrument for Teenagers (POSIT), which is designed to identify problems in any functional area (including substance abuse) requiring further assessment or treatment. From the initial screening, a determination is made regarding the necessity of an in-depth assessment. Following all assessments, if the youth meets detention criteria, the youth is transported to the juvenile detention center. Otherwise, the youth may be placed in nonsecure detention or another suitable facility, be placed on home detention, or released outright to a parent, guardian, or responsible adult. Youth are assigned case managers to monitor their progress through the system, including follow-up assessment and disposition. Various services are provided in the centers, including detoxification, physical and mental health screening, referrals, and urinalyses. The centers are typically operated through a collaborative effort from different components of the juvenile justice system and other human service agencies.

Typically, if the initial screening and assessment indicate the presence of substance use then the youth is referred for a more in-depth substance abuse assessment. Some JACs have a substance abuse assessment team housed in the center to perform this function. Others have complete detoxification units, often called a Juvenile Addiction Receiving Facilities (JARF). The JARF can either be located in the same building as the JAC or may be located close by but in a separate facility. If a youth is brought to a JAC by an arresting officer and the youth appears to be intoxicated, then the youth may be transferred to the JARF for detoxification. Although the JAC is strictly a juvenile justice enterprise, the JARF has affiliations with juvenile justice but often is a community-based center. Therefore, the JARF also accepts youth for admission who have not been charged with any offense but are in need of detoxification or substance abuse treatment.

Travis County Juvenile Court in Austin, Texas, has recently developed a JAC to serve that area. There is a unique aspect about this JAC, however. The impetus for its development came from a group called the Juvenile Offender Substance Abuse Treatment Services (JOSATS) Network. JOSATS is a federal demonstration project sponsored by the Center for Substance Abuse Treatment (CSAT). The primary goal of JOSATS is to reduce recidivism and substance abuse relapse among juvenile offenders by combining substance abuse treatment, ancillary services, and juvenile justice supervision. Although data about its effectiveness is pending, the network's potential in helping substance abusing juvenile offenders seems promising.

At least one pilot study to date (Dembo & Brown, 1994) has indicated that the assessment center concept as implemented in Tampa, Florida, has the ability to identify multiple-problem, high-risk youth. The study involved 110 truant youth brought to the Tampa JAC in January 1993. The majority of these youth were males who ranged in age from 9 to 18 years, with an average age of 14. According to the study, just under half (45%) had a history of one or more arrests on a delinquency charge. An analysis of POSIT results revealed that 96% of these youth indicated a potential problem in peer relations; 82% indicated a potential problem in "mental health status"; and 33% to 47% had a potential problem involving substance abuse, physical health, family relations, and vocational status.

McNeece et al. (1997) were involved in an in-depth study of six Juvenile Assessment Centers/Juvenile Assessment Receiving Facilities in Florida. Results indicated that the primary presenting problems among youth involved peer relations, family relations, mental health, substance abuse, physical health, and school–vocational issues. JARFs provided short-term stabilization, and sometimes detox. However, assessments were placed in a youth's file but often were not used to help make appropriate referrals, and staff did not have the resources to provide adequate follow-up case management services. One judge referred to this process as "assessment to nowhere." In addition, turf wars between agencies in the JACs sometimes hindered interagency information sharing.

These findings suggest that changes in juvenile justice policy are needed to promote interagency cooperation within the JACs, and assessments need to be better used to help make timely referrals. Increased funding is needed for additional staff and resources if the JACs and JARFs are to operate effectively. Juvenile assessment centers and juvenile addictions receiving facilities are key components in the current movement in the juvenile justice system to create multiagency facilities that process delinquents and at-risk youth. An understanding of these centers will no doubt be a significant tool in workers' repertoire who find themselves employed by agencies serving this population.

Juvenile Boot Camps

Shock incarceration is derived from the "scared straight" model. Under this approach, juvenile offenders are incarcerated for a brief period (Parent, 1989). Juvenile boot camps based on a military model are usually small in size; they stress discipline, physical conditioning, and strict authoritarian control (McNeece, 1997). It is precisely these characteristics that have made these camps popular with both politicians and the general public.

Some criminal justice researchers argue that boot camps do not make a long-term impact on juveniles because they do not meet the needs of offenders, and that in fact rearrest rates of boot camp graduates are similar to those of inmates (MacKenzie, 1994; cited in DiMascio, 1995). A recent report conducted by the Florida Department of Juvenile Justice indicates that arrest rates at Florida's six boot camps averaged between 63% to 74% for the first 60 boot camp graduates. The results were similar to comparison groups in other programs. Likewise, the Florida Juvenile Justice Advisory Board released a study indicating a 45% rearrest rate for all youth ($N = 317$) who went through the state's six boot camps during a six-month period. As a result of these findings, the Florida legislature reexamined the state's boot camps in the 1998 legislative session (Kaczor, 1997).

Treatment Alternatives to Street Crime (TASC)

In the attempt to combat substance abuse in communities, alternatives other than incarceration have been tried in recent years. One of the most widely known alternatives is Treatment Alternatives to Street Crime (TASC), a program initially funded in 1972 by federal money. TASC targets offenders who appear to have the potential to benefit from treatment and do not pose significant safety risks to communities with supervision (Lipton, 1995). The purpose of TASC is to identify, assess, refer for treatment, and conduct follow-up on drug offenders. Initially, many TASC programs were operated independently of the court and treatment systems (McNeece & Daly, 1997). Offenders in TASC programs are not incarcerated, but rather are treated outside the court system in community-based programs. Each offender is assigned a case manager who assists in gaining access to treatment, provides linkages to other needed community services, and reports back to the appropriate court officials about the offender's progress.

The monitoring function of the case manager is one of the hallmarks of TASC. Case managers attempt to get to know clients and generally visit them while the offender is in treatment. For offenders who do not comply with the program, TASC does not have its own enforcement team and must rely on the police to arrest those who are noncompliant. Although TASC case managers may use the threat of incarceration as a tool to enhance compliance, they are likely to give offenders who are noncompliant with the program another chance (Young, Dynia, & Belenko, 1996).

During the past decade the TASC model has adapted to the changing nature of both drug use and crime. In some cases the TASC model has been extended beyond that of a "bridge" between the criminal justice and substance abuse treatment systems to that of a "network" that identifies the multiple needs of criminal justice clients and manages the linkage of clients with multiple services originating from multiple systems (Swartz, 1993).

The National Institute on Drug Abuse's Treatment Outcome Prospective Study examined the impact of TASC programs on criminal offenders' posttreatment behavior compared to a voluntary control group. In the six-month period following program completion, TASC participants were comparable to the control group in regard to drug use, criminal involvement, and employment. The most significant predictor of criminal reinvolvement was a history of predatory crime and arrest before beginning treatment. In addition, the case management services were found to encourage continued treatment participation (Collins & Allison, 1993).

One of the initial funding sources for TASC programs, the Law Enforcement Assistance Administration (LEAA), required that those agencies receiving funding conduct independent evaluations. From 1972 to 1982, more than 40 evaluations were conducted. The majority of independent evaluators found that TASC programs had effectively intervened with clients to reduce drug abuse and criminal activity, linked the criminal justice and treatment systems, and identified previously untreated drug-dependent offenders (Cook & Weinman, 1985).

A more recent study of narcotic-addicted offenders in TASC programs (Hubbard, Collins, Rachal, & Cavanaugh, 1988) found support for two commonly held beliefs regarding offenders and drug treatment: The high level of structure of programs such as TASC may provide the necessary environment for offenders to discontinue drug use, and offenders mandated for treatment tend to stay in treatment longer, which is believed to enhance treatment outcomes. In Washington and Oklahoma TASC was evaluated, and encouraging results were found; recidivism rates were 14% and 19%, respectively.

Direct federal funding for TASC ceased in the 1980s, but this and other similar programs continue to exist (McNeece & Daly, 1997). One such offshoot is the Treatment Alternative Programs (TAP). In Wisconsin, an evaluation of TAP showed less favorable results than previous studies: 43% of offenders were rearrested, and 23% of those rearrested were arrested on alcohol or drug charges (Van Stelle, Mauser, & Moberg, 1994).

Drug Court

A promising and innovative alternative to combat the growing substance abuse problem in this country is the establishment of diversionary programs known as drug courts. The mission of treatment-oriented drug courts is to eliminate substance abuse and the resulting criminal behavior. (There are other drug courts that are used only to facilitate the speedy processing of drug offenders.) Drug court is a "team effort that focuses on sobriety and accountability as the primary goals" (National Association of Drug Court Professionals [NADCP], 1997, p. 8). The team of professionals generally includes the state attorney, public defender, pretrial intervention or probation staff, treatment providers, and the judge, who is considered the central figure in the team.

According to the Drug Courts Program Office of the U.S. Department of Justice (1997), there are 10 key components of drug courts:

1. Drug courts integrate alcohol and other drug treatment services with justice system case processing.
2. Using a nonadversarial approach, prosecution and defense counsel promote public safety while protecting participants' due process rights.
3. Eligible participants are identified early and promptly placed in the drug court program.
4. Drug courts provide access to a continuum of alcohol, drug, and other related treatment and rehabilitation services.
5. Abstinence is monitored by frequent alcohol and other drug testing.
6. A coordinated strategy governs drug court responses to participants' compliance.
7. Ongoing judicial interaction with each drug court participant is essential.
8. Monitoring and evaluation measure the achievement of program goals and gauge effectiveness.
9. Continuing interdisciplinary education promotes effective drug court planning, implementation, and operations.
10. Forging partnerships among drug courts, public agencies, and community-based organizations generates local support for drug court effectiveness.

These criteria constitute an "ideal" model of drug court, and few meet all of these standards. In practice, drug courts are defined by (a) their treatment-oriented, nonadversarial philosophy; (b) their focus on nonviolent offenders with substance abuse problems; and (c) the use of judicial oversight to monitor offenders' behavior and to ensure compliance with the court's recommendations for treatment. In general, an offender is placed in a drug court program for 9 to 12 months. On successfully completing that program, the offender will be continued on probation or some form of court supervision for another year. In some jurisdictions, the offender's criminal record may be expunged if all of the court's conditions for treatment are satisfied (Arnold, Valentine, McInnis & McNeece, 2000).

The role of the judge is crucial in the operation of a drug court. Judges may openly admonish (or praise) clients for their behavior during courtroom proceedings. Beyond that, judges may issue court orders requiring that a client attend treatment, submit to urinalysis, seek employment, meet with a probation officer, avoid associations with drug-abusing friends, and so forth. Failure to comply with these judicial decrees may result in a finding of contempt, landing the offender in jail or transferring him or her to a regular criminal court. Judges are provided with continuous feedback on the offender's performance by the other drug court participants. There is little room for the offender to "fall through the cracks" in this system.

Drug courts have generally processed offenders in two ways: (a) through the use of deferred prosecution (adjudication is deferred, and the defendant enters treatment); or (b) through a postadjudication process by which the case is adjudicated but sentencing is withheld while the defendant is in treatment (U.S. GAO, 1995).

Drug courts tend to be a nonadversarial process (Goldkamp, in press). In 1989, the first drug court was established by Janet Reno, the then sitting state attorney for the Eleventh Judicial Circuit (Miami). Among other things, drug court was an attempt on the part of the legal and judicial system to focus on substance abuse recovery rather than on the merits of a given case. The result was a collaborative, nonadversarial relationship among court professionals.

The Miami Drug Court has served as a model for the development of other drug courts. It has been exemplary in many ways: (a) the comprehensive nature of services provided; (b) the range of available public agencies; and (c) the personal attention provided to each offender by the presiding judge. It was noted that most defendants actually want the treatment provided, implying that the defendants perceive drug court as a useful program (Finn & Newlyn, 1993). In its first three years of operation, approximately 60 percent of offenders who were diverted to the drug court program successfully completed the requirements for drug court graduation (Finn & Newlyn, 1993).

The Miami Drug Court appears to have reduced recidivism among participants, *and* the program tends to be cost-effective. In an 18-month period beginning in 1990, 67% of drug court defendants were not rearrested. Those who were rearrested had an average first arrest time of 235 days compared to 79 days for other offenders arrested on felony charges during the same time period (Curriden, 1994). Finally, the Miami Drug Court also reduced the cost to the taxpayer. It costs $30,000 to house an offender in the Dade County jail compared to $3000 per offender in drug court (Drug Strategies, 1997).

Patterned after the Miami Drug Court, new drug courts developed in Oakland, California, and Portland, Oregon. Although these courts incorporated aspects of the Miami Court, they made changes to fit their communities' needs (Goldkamp, in press). Although drug courts "vary widely in scope, organization, and points of intervention, all treatment drug courts developed in recent years share an underlying premise that drug possession and use is not simply a law enforcement/criminal justice problem but a public health problem with deep roots in society" (U.S. Department of Health and Human Services [DHHS], 1996, p. 1).

The great expanse of the drug court movement is a result, in part, to the federal money made available by the attorney general of the United States under Title V of the Violent Control and Law Enforcement Act of 1994. These grants helped establish drug courts nationwide. As a result, the number of drug courts, the scope of services, and the range of addicted populations served increased (DCCTAP, 1997). Three hundred and twenty-five drug courts now exist in 48 states, the District of Columbia, Guam, and Puerto Rico, as well as 13 Native American tribal courts (DCCTAP, 1997).

To date, the research that has been conducted on drug courts and other diversion or intervention programs is scant (Farabee, Simpson, Dansereau, & Knight, 1995; Hepburn & Albonetti, 1994; Huddleston, 1996, 1997; McBride & Inciardi, 1993; Moon & Latessa, 1994). Few single-site studies and only one multisite study (Goldkamp, in press) on drug courts have been conducted (McNeece, Valentine, McInnis, Mayfield, & Lipovetsky, 1997).

Recently, drug courts have begun to acknowledge and address the needs of special populations and issues. Some examples are juvenile drug courts, drug courts for women (Drug Strategies, 1997), night drug courts (Smith, Davis, Laszlo, & Goretsky, 1994), and the application of drug court to judicial settings such as family courts, where crack cocaine users who are involved in domestic violence and dependency cases are offered treatment (Office of the State Courts Administrator [OSCA], Supreme Court of Florida, 1996). In addition, there is interest in expanding drug courts to the federal court system, where 60% of all inmates are sentenced for drug offenses (Drug Strategies, 1997).

Common indicators of effective drug courts are retention in the drug court program, lowered criminal recidivism, and recovery from substance abuse. Based on a March 1995 survey of 33 drug courts, 35% of offenders enrolled in drug court programs graduated from the program; 27% did not complete the program; and 37% of those enrolled in the program were still active (U.S. GAO, 1995). Regarding recidivism, a team of independent evaluators found that of 48 offenders who completed the 15-month program in the Stillwater, Oklahoma, drug court, only two reoffended within 18 months after program completion. That is a success rate of 96%, perhaps one of the best rates in the country (Huddleston, 1996).

But not all outcome research has been so favorable. To draw conclusions about the effectiveness of drug courts in treating substance abuse, researchers often look to probationers as a comparison group. These probationers are generally drug offenders who are either ineligible for drug court, do not have access to a drug court, or elect not to enter a drug court program. Hepburn and Albonetti (1994) compared recidivism rates for individuals on probation, some of whom received treatment and drug testing and others of whom received drug testing only. Those who received both treatment and drug testing were most similar to drug court clients, and those who were only drug tested were most similar to traditional probation offenders. Hepburn and Albonetti (1994) found no significant differences in revocation of probationary status between those who were tested only and those who received treatment as well.

Besides being interested in the retention of offenders in the drug court program, its effectiveness in substance abuse recovery, and lowered criminal recidivism rates, researchers are concerned with factors such as inclusion criteria for drug court participants, the role of judicial supervision, and the impact of individual motivation in drawing conclusions about the effectiveness of drug court programs. Targeting "high risk offenders" for treatment, for example, maximizes cost savings, because these offenders are believed to be most likely to reoffend. "High risk" may not be those offenders with serious or extensive criminal histories but those who have more serious drug problems (Moon & Latessa, 1994).

Judicial supervision may also have beneficial effects on reducing recidivism among drug court participants. In a recent three-year study in Oklahoma, Huddleston (1997) compared 48 graduates and 62 nongraduates of a drug court with 47 program graduates and 41 nongraduates of an alternative sentencing precursor to drug court. The study compared recidivism rates between these two groups to determine the effectiveness of cognitive therapy and other quality control systems. Findings suggest that there were beneficial effects of judicial supervision in decreasing recidivism rates. Judicial supervision in drug courts, combined with cognitive therapy, increased the success rate for defendants (96%), whereas decreasing failures (2%), compared to 74% and 39%, respectively, for the comparison group (Huddleston, 1997).

This rapid evolution of form and substance represents a missed opportunity to document and analyze a potentially fundamental innovation as it develops. Having failed to respond to the initial and more basic questions posed by the drug court phenomenon, research now faces more difficult problems exploring the nature and testing the effects of the change in progress.

Research that provides a comprehensive description of a model program, including historical (contextual) information and attitudinal data of drug court professionals and offenders, is lacking. Additional research is needed on the unique collaborative dynamic seminal to drug courts. A recent Department of Justice study suggested that better coordinated drug court strategies were needed, including education and training for police and other drug court professionals, improvement in communication and information flow from drug court staff to police, and a support and monitor function for the police working with drug court offenders (NADCP & Office of Community Oriented Policing Services, U.S. Department of Justice, 1997). This is consistent with the 1996 Hart poll indicating that police chiefs, by a margin of two to one, support treatment for drug offenders over prosecution and incarceration (Drug Strategies and the Police Foundation, 1996). This demonstrates law enforcement's interest in alternatives to incarceration and the need for police training in drug court procedures. Research in this area may clarify at least part of the collaborative dynamics inherent in drug courts and provide a research agenda for the future.

Monitoring the Substance Abusing Offender's Probation

The main method of monitoring offenders who have not been sentenced to prison is probation. Probation, in combination with therapy, support, and surveillance, is the most common type of treatment used as an alternative to incarceration (Lipton, 1995). With regular probation, an offender lives at home and receives periodic monitoring. Many offenders with substance abuse problems are sentenced to intensive supervision probation (ISP), a more restrictive type of probation than traditional probation. ISP is a method of monitoring that can be used as an alternative to incarceration. ISP requires that the offender and probation officer keep in close contact, which generally includes random home visits to ensure compliance with the requirements of the program. In addition, the offender may have to perform community service, maintain employment, adhere to a curfew, and submit to urine drug testing. Compared to basic probation, ISP is generally more expensive and requires that probation officers have smaller caseloads to accommodate the increase in supervision of the offender. ISP, though, may be more cost-effective than basic probation in the long-run, when the alternative for offenders is prison or jail (Edna McConnell Clark Foundation, 1995). ISP is less costly than incarceration even when the cost of supervision is included.

Urine Drug Testing

Urine drug testing in the criminal justice system is a surveillance method designed to detect whether offenders are currently using drugs or alcohol. The offender must provide a urine sample, which is tested for the presence of specific drugs. Two main types of detection are commonly used: immunoassays and chromatography (Timrots, 1992). Immunoassays use antibodies to detect whether the specimen has higher qualities of the drug being tested than a calibrator with a known quantity of the drug. If the quantity is higher than the calibrator, the test is considered positive for that particular drug.

A second more expensive type of testing is chromatography. This procedure involves separating and identifying the components of the urine. Gas chromatography–mass spectrometry is a type of chromatography that is believed to be one of the most effective types of drug testing but is very expensive—generally between $25 and $100 per test (Timrots, 1992).

Urine drug testing is used in the criminal justice system with offenders in three main ways: (a) as an adjunct to community supervision; (b) as an assessment tool for offenders entering the system; and (c) as an assessment of drug use during mandated drug treatment. Providing drug testing serves several purposes in the criminal justice system: it informs judges of the offenders' current drug use as a consideration for bail-setting or sentencing; it indicates whether the offender is complying with a mandate to be drug free; and it identifies those offenders who are in need of treatment (Timrots, 1992). Relying on self-report is insufficient in most cases because offenders have a strong incentive to report that they are drug free regardless of whether they have used drugs. Those who continue to use drugs may have any number of sanctions imposed, depending on their legal jurisdiction or corrections facility. Offenders who test negative for drugs may be tested less frequently or may no longer be required to continue testing (Nurco, Hanlon, Bateman, & Kinlock, 1995).

Monitoring offenders on probation or parole for continued drug use is a continual challenge for those providing community-based supervision to this population. In some cities—for example, Baltimore—positive drug screens (four in Baltimore) are considered violations of parole (Nurco et al., 1995). The need for such monitoring nationwide is crucial because it is estimated that more than half of all persons on community supervision are involved in the sale and/or use of drugs (Nurco, Hanlon, & Kinlock, 1990). With drug use believed to be associated with an increase in criminal behavior (Anglin, 1988), assisting offenders in maintaining a drug-free lifestyle may reduce the likelihood of further criminal behavior. One study found no difference in recidivism between a group that received drug monitoring and treatment and a group that received drug monitoring only (Hepburn & Albonetti, 1994). The authors acknowledge that it is unclear, though, whether the failure of treatment to affect recidivism is a reflection of the treatment implementation or intensity or the result of using probationers for the sample.

Turner, Petersilia, and Deschenes (1994) noted that anecdotal evidence suggests that many corrections officials are not sold on the benefits of random drug testing as a deterrent or a diagnostic technique. Given problems with failure to revoke probationary status and a lack of treatment options when someone does have a positive drug screen, Turner et al. recommend that the following questions be asked before establishing widespread use of drug testing for those under community supervision:

1. How do probation–parole agencies implement drug testing orders?
2. How many drug dependent offenders have testing conditions revoked?
3. How many offenders are actually tested, with what frequency and results?
4. How does the justice system respond to positive drug tests?
5. Do such tests result in added probation–parole conditions, referrals to treatment programs, or revocation?
6. What impact do Intensive Supervision Probation/Parole (ISP) programs with drug testing have on offender recidivism, as measured by official records of technical violations and new arrests?
7. How do jurisdictions differ on these dimensions? (p. 233)

Using drug testing as a part of an initial assessment for offenders entering the court or corrections systems is a relatively new phenomena. Some programs have asked offenders to submit to urine drug screens at the time of arrest. Those that test positive may be released but asked to submit to drug monitoring as a condition of their pretrial release. The aim of this form of monitoring is to increase the likelihood that the offender will abstain from future drug use and appear at the next scheduled court appearance (State of Florida, 1994). The use of testing in jails may be rare, as a national study found that only 3% of jails report screening offenders at the time of admission (Peters, May, & Kearns, 1992). However, this figure is much lower than the recent findings of the National Institute of Justice Drug Use Forecasting (DUF) program. This program calculates the percentage of offenders arrested in certain cities throughout the country who have positive urine drug screens at the time of arrest. Recent DUF data reveals that the percentage of male inmates testing positive for any drug ranged from 51% to 83% (Office of National Drug Control Policy, 1997).

For offenders mandated to treatment or those who agree to treatment as a part of their court proceedings, urine drug screens may be required to ensure compliance with treatment. Court and corrections officials will generally want to know if the offender is complying with treatment and remaining abstinent from drugs. In programs in which access to treatment may be limited by available space or funding, those who do not comply may be discharged from treatment. Those who do not successfully complete treatment and continue to have positive drug screens may be sent back to court for sanctions.

For urine drug testing to serve a useful purpose, protocols for positive tests must be in place. If no sanctions are established and no treatment is available, the usefulness of drug testing is difficult to determine. However, urine drug testing is still believed to be a more reliable measure of continued substance abuse, because most offenders tend to underreport their drug use (Wish, Toborg, & Bellassai, 1988).

In addition, a sophisticated process for collecting urine specimens must be in place. Chavaria (1992) advocated for a totally randomized system of collection whereby the offender can potentially be required to provide a specimen seven days a week. The code-a-phone system is an example of a randomized system for collecting specimens from offenders. With this system, each offender is assigned a number and must call in and listen to a recording each day to see if his or her number is on the recording. If the number is on the recording, the offender must provide a urine specimen the next day.

Drug testing for inmates at various points in the legal and corrections system is becoming more prevalent. The federal government has encouraged uniform drug testing of incarcerated offenders. Florida is one state that has responded to such requests. In 1993, the Florida legislature passed the Inmate Substance Abuse Testing Program for offenders in state prisons. The purposes of this project are to identify offenders in need of drug treatment, to discourage drug use, and to increase the number of inmates referred and treated for substance abuse (Department of Community Affairs, Division of Housing and Community Development, State of Florida, 1997).

Drug testing appears to serve a useful purpose in monitoring offenders with substance problems. However, drug testing alone is not sufficient to keep offenders from using drugs and reoffending. The best approach may be to combine random drug testing with forms of rehabilitative drug treatment to address the addiction and, it is hoped, minimize the likelihood that the individual will engage in future criminal behavior (Graboski, 1986).

Future Directions for Research and Practice

Discussions of this type seem to beg the question, "Where do we go from here?" We present some thoughts about future directions for treatment, drug policy, and research.

Redefining Treatment

We should consider carefully redefining chemical dependency treatment. One of the problems with the current definition is that the "disease concept" of chemical dependency is based on an assumption that four decades of medical and social science research has failed to support—that chemical dependency is a disease in the same sense that pneumonia or a kidney infection or arthritis is a disease and that a specific treatment would bring the problem under control. In fact, addiction to drugs is not at all like most other "diseases." Arthritics do not choose to have arthritis, and they cannot choose to stop being arthritic. Drug abusers, on the other hand, do choose, at least in the beginning, to use drugs. More often than many of us suspected, they also choose to stop using drugs or to cut down on their use to manageable levels. Although initially popular because it did help reduce the stigmatization that came with being labeled an "addict," treatment professionals are beginning to realize that the disease model can be more of a hindrance than a help. It allows the addict to avoid responsibility, and it steers us into blind alleys in our research efforts.

Taking Treatment Seriously

In addition to providing adequate funding for treatment, we have recently begun paying attention to the *quality* of treatment. Much of what has passed for treatment through the end of the 20th century and into the 21st has been unworthy of the name. Methadone maintenance programs infrequently provide any educational or therapy services. "In-jail counseling" very often means only that weekly AA meetings are held for inmates. Family therapy sometimes means only that the spouses of clients are included in the infrequent chats that are called "therapy" in those programs. Vocational development frequently means only that a client was told of a job possibility on the other side of town.

Making Treatment "User Friendly"

One of the other major problems with current treatment options is that most addicts just do not participate. One of the problems with the early research literature was that almost all of the research was conducted on a tiny minority of drug abusers who were (a) trapped in the criminal justice system and *forced* into treatment, or (b) more highly motivated than the majority to *voluntarily* seek treatment. Treatment is not user friendly in the sense that those persons seeking treatment are often in danger of being arrested, losing their jobs, or losing custody of their children. Drug treatment programs funded with public money tend to have the same type of stigma associated with other publicly funded welfare programs (McNeece & DiNitto, 1998). The United States has developed a "two-tier" system of care, one for the poor under public sponsorship and one for those who can pay with private insurance or out-of-pocket funds. The private tier developed primarily from private hospital units that originally focused almost exclusively on the medical treatment of alcoholism. The origins of the public tier are found in the federal government's "wars" on crime and poverty beginning in the late 1960s, and in many ways it is still an adjunct to the criminal justice system. Private programs are too expensive for all but the very rich or the well-insured. Most insurance companies and HMOs will put such severe limits on chemical dependency treatment that clients will be paying well over 50% of total program costs. It is our position that public policy should both guarantee amnesty for all classes of drug users seeking treatment and provide funding for all addictions treatment.

One impetus for such a paradigm shift in our U.S. drug policy might be found in the AIDS epidemic. HIV/AIDS represents such a potentially catastrophic public health problem that American values, which have helped to maintain a separate and unequal two-tier system may be beginning to change. The connection between drug abuse and HIV/AIDS seems obvious to even the most casual observer, and it seems equally obvious that this nation cannot afford to provide anything less than the most modern, state-of-the-art drug treatment to *all* drug abusers (regardless of cost) if we are to deal effectively with the HIV/AIDS problem.

Public policy should also require that treatment be "culturally appropriate," because one of the major problems in the past century is that middle-class, protestant treatment models do not attract or effectively serve large numbers of Hispanic, Native American, African American, and other minority drug abusers. Public policy also should be sensitive to "gender-relevant" treatment, getting beyond the simplistic assumption that any given treatment is equally useful for both males and females. A portion of the funding should be set aside specifically for child care and for other ancillary services for women in treatment. The GAO recently reported that there were only 15 beds available in the entire state of Massachusetts for pregnant drug abusers. In New York, 54 of 78 treatment programs surveyed denied treatment to pregnant women (U.S. GAO, 1990).

Linking Treatment With Harm Reduction

When agencies are forced to precisely define measurable objectives by which their accomplishments would be evaluated, they usually discover that it is much easier to be successful with harm-reduction strategies rather than curative approaches. The federal government should make the receipt of federal funding contingent on the repeal of a number of state laws, including those that prohibit the free distribution of needles and syringes to intravenous drug users. The harm-reduction approach may also benefit clients in other ways. Alcoholics who previously considered their battle with alcoholism as a zero-sum game may begin to work on cutting down on their drinking, no longer doomed to "failure" because of their inability to achieve total abstinence.

Making Aftercare a Priority

It seems strange that relatively few programs make provisions for working with clients after treatment, beyond a referral to Alcoholics Anonymous or Narcotics Anonymous, despite the fact that researchers have known for decades that most addicts relapse repeatedly after leaving treatment (see Marlatt, 1985, for a review of studies). This shortcoming is even more surprising when one considers the ample evidence that has been available for years regarding the relationship between well-designed aftercare–community support and better outcomes (Currie, 1993; Ito & Donovan, 1986; Stark, 1992). Although the economic benefits of treatment have been well-documented and the importance of aftercare in maintaining sobriety is equally well-established, there has not been as much focus on the economic benefits that aftercare adds above and beyond treatment. However, because the benefit–cost ratio for drug treatment is typically 10:1 or better (Belenko & Peugh, 1998), and because aftercare is far less costly than the initial treatment, it becomes obvious that aftercare is well worth the investment. As Langenbucher (1996) argued, the problem is not how to pay for treatment and aftercare services but how to get people to *use* those services. Effective and appropriate aftercare and community services are essential to maximizing the benefits of treatment and are well worth the costs.

Linking Treatment to Work

As early as 1972 the Vera Institute of Justice in New York City developed a "supported work" program for addicts called the Wildcat Service Corporation (WSC) (Friedman, 1978). During the next four years WSC put more than 4000 exaddicts and exoffenders to work. They were successfully placed with the Board of Education, the public libraries, youth therapy agencies, the Bronx district attorney, and Mount Sinai Hospital. They painted schools and Head Start centers, renovated buildings in the South Bronx, worked as messengers and translators, and did maintenance work for the police department. About one-third of the WSC workers graduated to non-subsidized employment. The most astounding discovery was that among an experimental and control group, those who worked at least half time were much more likely to cut down on their drug use. Research also established that the taxpayers got back $1.12 for every $1 put into the program (Friedman, 1978). A larger experiment by the Manpower Demonstration Research Corporation (MDRC) with an even more difficult and hard to place group of addicts was successful in making them more productive and less criminal through subsidized employment, saving the taxpayers several thousand dollars per client (MDRC, 1980). Such successes should be used to convince Congress to provide funding to guarantee subsidized employment, where needed, for every recovering addict.

Research

We have made considerable progress from the early days of alcoholism research when most of those efforts studied White men in voluntary programs (McNeece & DiNitto, 1998). However, our research still shows equivocal results with enough frequency to make most observers somewhat skeptical of treatment efficacy. For years we have been urged to match patients to appropriate treatment, but the latest results indicate that matching makes little difference in treatment outcomes (NIAAA, 1997). An alternative explanation, however, is that we simply have not learned which factors are important to consider in matching patients to treatment. It still seems that one could make a good case for further studies of culturally appropriate treatment. Culture and ethnicity were factors not considered in project MATCH (NIAAA, 1997). It seems obvious from looking at the national- and international-level data on substance abuse that the rates of abuse and addiction vary greatly between cultures.

Another avenue of research that is being pursued with more vigor is the study of individuals who have been successful in terminating an addiction, usually without treatment (Stewart, 1998). If we can determine the common characteristics, if any, of "self-quitters," perhaps we can identify those that have the potential for being transferable via education or training, and incorporate that strategy into our treatment approaches.

Medical–biophysical research will no doubt continue research into the genetic factors associated with addiction. Whether that research eventually leads to the development of a "magic pill" is highly doubtful. Even it that miracle does happen, it would appear to be years away.

Outcome Research: Determining Effectiveness

Although substance abuse treatment for offenders varies across programs, facilities, and locations, the National Task Force on Correctional Substance Abuse Strategies (1991) noted that "effective programs" have common characteristics: clearly defined missions, goals, admission criteria, and assessment strategies for those seeking treatment; support and understanding of key agency administrators and staff; consistent intervention strategies supported by links with other agencies as the offender moves through the system; well-trained staff who have opportunities for continuing education; and ongoing evaluation and development based on outcome and process data. One of the main issues of contention among researchers and substance abuse providers has been an operational definition of the term "effective treatment." The Treatment Outcome Working Group, a meeting of treatment and evaluation experts sponsored by the Office of National Drug Control Policy (ONDCP), has established some results and outcomes that define effective treatment:

1. Reduced use of the primary drug
2. Improved functioning of drug users in terms of employment
3. Improved educational status
4. Improved interpersonal relationships
5. Improved medical status and general improvement in health
6. Improved legal status
7. Improved mental health status
8. Improved noncriminal public safety factors (ONDCP, 1996).

Although some of these desired outcomes are not pertinent to incarcerated offenders receiving treatment, they are appropriate long-term goals following release. Failure to accomplish several of these goals will most likely result in involvement in future drug use and criminal activity and subsequent incarceration.

One issue of contention in evaluating drug treatment methods and programs for criminal offenders is that recidivism tends to be defined in terms of rearrest rates. Offenders who successfully complete treatment may continue to use drugs but may not be rearrested. If recidivism is defined only as rearrest, an unknown percentage of inmates may continue to have substance abuse problems. Recidivism statistics may actually underestimate the actual rate of continued substance abuse among offenders. One alternative to gaining a better estimate of continued drug use is to examine the substance use level and productivity after treatment completion (Van Stelle et al., 1994). However, continuing to monitor offender behavior posttreatment is difficult unless the offender is mandated to have follow-up through probation or parole and urine drug testing.

Changing Resource Allocation

Freeing up most of the resources we spend on drug interdiction, law enforcement, the courts, and incarceration would allow us to make substantial progress in improving treatment and in making treatment available to those who need it. Reducing the number of people arrested and incarcerated for drug possession and other minor drug offenses would also allow the police to concentrate their efforts on more serious crimes, thus making communities safer.

The decline of U.S. inner cities and the consequent deterioration of the quality of life for poor and minority individuals are to a large degree responsible for the epidemic of drug abuse. It is foolish to believe, in the face of declining economic opportunities, that either the threat of criminal punishment or the promise of a short-term treatment program will cause teenagers and young men to avoid lives of crime and involvement with drugs. In the long run, stable families, safe neighborhoods, and economically viable cities are the keys to slowing both drug use and crime.

References

Abadinsky, H. (1993). *Drug abuse: An introduction* (2nd ed.). Chicago: Nelson-Hall.

Alexander, B. K. (1990). Alternatives to the war on drugs. *Journal of Drug Issues, 20*(1), 1–27.

Alford, G. S., Koehler, R. A., & Leonard, J. (1991). Alcoholics Anonymous—Narcotics Anonymous model inpatient treatment of chemically dependent adolescents: A two-year outcome study. *Journal of Studies on Alcohol, 52,* 118–126.

American Psychiatric Association. (1994). *Diagnostic and statistical manual of mental disorders* (4th ed.). Washington, DC: Author.

Anderson, A. R., & Henry, C. S. (1994). Family system characteristics and parental behaviors as predictors of adolescent substance use. *Adolescence, 29*(114), 405–420.

Anglin, M. D. (1988). The efficacy of civil commitment in treating narcotic addiction. In C. G. Leukefeld & F. M. Tims (Eds.), *Compulsory treatment of drug abuse: Research and clinical practice* (NIDA Research Monograph No, 86). Rockville, MD: National Institute on Drug Abuse.

Arnold, E. M., Valentine, P. V., McInnis, M., & McNeece, C. A. (2000). Evaluating drug courts: An alternative to incarceration. In G. L. Mays & P. R. Gregware (Eds.), *Courts and justice: A reader, second edition.* Prospect Heights, IL: Waveland Press.

Avants, S. K., Margolin, A., Chang, P., Kosten, T., & Birch, S. (1993). Acupuncture for the treatment of cocaine addiction: Investigation of a needle puncture control. *Journal of Substance Abuse Treatment, 12*(3), 195–205.

Bazemore, G. (1993). Formal policy and informal process in the implementation of juvenile justice reform. *Criminal Justice Review, 18*(1), 26–45.

Beeder, A. B., & Millman, R. B. (1997). Patients with psychopathology. In J. H. Lowinson, P. Ruiz, R. B. Millman, & J. G. Langrod (Eds.), *Substance abuse: A comprehensive textbook* (3rd ed.). Baltimore: Williams & Wilkins.

Belenko, S., & Peugh, J. (1998). Fighting crime by treating substance abuse. *Issues in Science and Technology, 15*(1), 53–60.

Brandsma, J. M., & Pattison, E. M. (1985). The outcome of group psychotherapy with alcoholics: An empirical review. *American Journal of Drug and Alcohol Abuse, 11*(1&2), 151–162.

Brewington, V., Smith, M., & Lipton, D. (1994). Acupuncture as a detoxification treatment: An analysis of controlled research. *Journal of Substance Abuse Treatment, 11*(4), 289–307.

Brundage, V. (1985). Gregory Bateson, Alcoholics Anonymous, and stoicism. *Psychiatry, 48,* 40–51.

Bullock, M. L., Culliton, P. D., & Olander, R. T. (1989). Controlled trial of acupuncture for severe recidivist alcoholism. *The Lancet, 8,* 1435–1439.

Bullock, M. L., Umen, A. J., Culliton, P. D., & Olander, R. T. (1987). Acupuncture treatment of alcohol recidivism: A pilot study. *Alcoholism: Clinical and Experimental Research, 11*(3), 292–295.

Chavaria, F. R. (1992). Successful drug treatment in a criminal justice setting: A case study. *Federal Probation, 56*(1), 48–52.

Collins, J. J., & Allison, M. (1993). Legal coercion and retention in drug abuse treatment. *Hospital and Community Psychiatry, 34*(12), 1145–1149.

Cook, L. F., & Weinman, B. A. (1985). *TASC program brief.* Washington, DC: Bureau of Justice Assistance, Office of Justice Programs, U.S. Department of Justice.

Curriden, M. (1994, May). Drug courts gain popularity. *ABA Journal,* 16–18.

Currie, E. (1993). *Drugs, the cities, and the American future.* New York: Hill & Wang.

DeLeon, G. (1986). The therapeutic community for substance abuse: Perspective and approach. In D. DeLeon & J. T. Zeigenfuss (Eds.), *Therapeutic communities for addictions: Readings in theory, research and practice* (pp. 5–18). Springfield, IL: Charles C. Thomas.

Dembo, R., & Brown, R. (1994). The Hillsborough County juvenile assessment center. *Journal of Child & Adolescent Substance Abuse, 3*(2), 25–43.

Denton, R. E., & Kampfe, C. M. (1994). The relationship between family variables and adolescent substance abuse: A literature review. *Adolescence, 29*(114), 475–495.

Department of Community Affairs, Division of Housing and Community Development, State of Florida. (1997). *Drug control and system improvement program: Annual report, state fiscal years 1991 through 1996.* Tallahassee, FL: Author.

DiMascio, W. M. (1995). *Seeking justice: Crime and punishment in America.* New York: Edna McConnell Clark Foundation.

Downey, A. M. (1991). The impact of drug abuse upon adolescent suicide. *Omega Journal of Death and Dying, 22*(4), 261–275.

Drug Court Clearinghouse and Technical Assistance Project. (1996, May). *Fact sheet* (Tech. Rep). Washington, DC: American University.

Drug Court Clearinghouse and Technical Assistance Project. (1997, May). *Drug courts: 1997 overview of operational characteristics and implementation issues* (Tech. Rep). Washington, DC: American University.

Drug Strategies. (1997). *Cutting crime: Drug courts in action.* Washington, DC: Author.

Drug Strategies and the Police Foundation (1996). *Drugs and crime across America: Police chiefs speak out.* Washington, DC: Author.

Edna McConnell Clark Foundation. (1995). *Seeking justice: Crime and punishment in America.* New York: Author.

Edwards, B. (1993, June 23). Drug court's success rate outstanding. *Tampa Tribune,* p. 1–2.

Farabee, D. J., Simpson, D. D., Dansereau, D., & Knight, K. (1995). Cognitive inductions into treatment among drug users on probation. *The Journal of Drug Issues, 25,* 669–682.

Faul, A. C., & Hudson, W. W. (1997). The Index of Drug Involvement: A partial validation. *Social Work, 42*(6), 565–572.

Festinger, L. (1950). Informal social communication. *Psychologicial Review, 57,* 271–282.

Finn, P., & Newlyn, A. K. (1993, June). Miami's "drug court": A different approach. *National Institute of Justice Focus.* Washington, DC: NIJ.

Fischer, J., & Corcoran, K. (1994). *Measures for clinical practice: A sourcebook. Volume 2* (2nd ed.). New York: Free Press.

Fishman, H. C., Stanton, M. D., & Rosman, B. (1982). In M. D. Stanton, T. C. Todd, & Associates (Eds.), *The family therapy of drug abuse and addiction.* New York: Guilford Press.

Flores, P. J. (1988). *Group psychotherapy with addicted populations.* New York: Haworth Press.

Friedman, L. (1978). *The Wildcat experiment: An early test of supported work in drug abuse rehabilitation.* Washington, DC: NIDA.

Friedman, A. S., & Utada, A. (1983). High school drug use. *Clinical Research Notes*. Washington, DC: U.S. Government Printing Office, National Institute on Drug Abuse.

Fuller, R. K., Branchey, L., Brightwell, D. R., Derman, R. M., Emrick, C. D., Iber, F. L., James, K. E., Lacoursiere, R. B., Lee, K. K., Lowenstam, I., Maany, I., Neiderhiser, D., Nocks, J. J., & Shaw, S. (1986). Disulfiram treatment of alcoholism: A veterans administration cooperative study. *Journal of the American Medical Association, 256*(11), 1449–1455.

Gerstein, D. R., & Harwood, H. J. (Eds.). (1990). *Treating drug problems (Vol. 1)*. Washington, DC: National Academy Press.

Gold, M. S. (1997). Cocaine (and crack): Clinical aspects. In J. H. Lowinson, P. Ruiz, R. B. Millman, & J. G. Langrod (Eds.), *Substance abuse: A comprehensive textbook* (3rd ed.). Baltimore: Williams & Wilkins.

Goldapple, G. (1990). *Enhancing retention: A skills-training program for drug dependent therapeutic community clients*. PhD Dissertation, Florida State University.

Goldkamp, J. S. (in press). Challenges for research and innovation: When is a drug court not a drug court? In C. Terry (Ed.), *Judicial change and drug treatment courts: Case studies in innovation.*

Grabowski, J. (1986). *Acquisition maintenance cessation and re-acquisition: Overview and behavioral perspective of relapse and tobacco use*. (Research monograph series). Washington, DC: National Institute on Drug Abuse.

Hanson, G., & Venturelli, P. (1995). *Drugs and society* (4th ed.). Boston: Jones and Bartlett.

Hepburn, J. R., & Albonetti, C. A. (1994). Recidivism among drug offenders: A survival analysis of the effects of offender characteristics, type of offense, and two types of intervention. *Journal of Quantitative Criminology, 10*(2), 159–179.

Hepburn, J. R., Johnston, W., & Rogers, S. (1993). *Success of drug testing and drug treatment with probationers*. National Institute of Justice, National Criminal Justice Reference Service (NCJ No. 149020).

Hubbard, R. L., Collins, J. J., Rachal, J. V., & Cavanaugh, E. R. (1988). The criminal justice client in drug abuse treatment, In C. G. Leudefeld & F. M. Times (Eds.), *Compulsory treatment of drug abuse: Research and clinical practice* (NIDA Research Monograph 86, pp. 57–80). Rockville, MD: National Institute on Drug Abuse.

Huddleston, W. (1996). CBT/Payne and Logan County, Oklahoma Drug Court 18 Monthly Recidivism Study of Graduates and A.T.T.A.C. Program (Precursor to D.C.) 3 Year Recidivism Study of Graduates. *Cognitive-Behavioral Treatment Review, 5*(3&4), 9.

Huddleston, W. (1997). Summary of drug court evaluation: Recidivism study. *Cognitive-Behavioral Treatment Review & CCI News, 6*(1/2), 16–17.

Inciardi, J. A., & McBride, D. C. (1991). *Treatment Alternatives to Street Crime (TASC): History, experiences, and issues*. Rockville, MD: National Institute on Drug Abuse.

Inciardi, J. A., McBride, D. C., & Weinman, B. A. (1993). *Offender profile index: A user's guide*. National Institute of Justice, National Criminal Justice Reference Service (NIJ No. 148829). Washington, DC: NIJ.

Ito, J. R., & Donovan, D. M. (1986). Aftercare in alcoholism treatment: a review. In W. R. Miller & N. Heather (Eds.), *Treating addictive behaviors: Processes of change*. New York: Plenum Press.

Jackson, M. S., & Springer, D. W. (1997). Social work practice with African-American juvenile gangs: Professional challenge. In C. A. McNeece & A. R. Roberts (Eds.), *Policy and practice in the justice system* (pp. 231–248). Chicago: Nelson-Hall.

Jenson, J. M. (1997). Juvenile delinquency and drug abuse: Implications for social work practice in the justice system. In C. Aaron McNeece & A. R. Roberts (Eds.), *Policy and practice in the justice system* (pp. 107–123). Chicago: Nelson-Hall.

Joaning, H., Gawinski, B., Morris, J., & Quinn, W. (1986). Organizing a social ecology to treat adolescent drug abuse. *Journal of Strategic and Systemic Therapies, 5*, 55–66.

Joaning, H., Quinn, W., Thomas, F., & Mullen, R. (1992). Treating adolescent drug abuse: A comparison of family systems therapy, group therapy, and family drug education. *Journal of Marital and Family Therapy, 18*(4), 345–356.

Kaczor, B. (1997, June 22). Legislators let down by boot camps. *Tallahassee Democrat,* p. 3B.

Kofoed, L., Tolson, R., Atkinson, R., Toth, R., & Turner, J. (1986). Outpatient treatment of patients with substance abuse and coexisting psychiatric disorders. *American Journal of Psychiatry, 143,* 867–872.

Langenbucher, J. W. (1996). Socioeconomic analysis of addictions treatment. *Public Health Reports, 111*(March/April), 135–137.

Lewis, J. A., Dana, R. Q., & Blevins, G. A. (1994). *Substance abuse counseling: An individualized approach* (2nd ed.). Pacific Grove, CA: Brooks/Cole.

Ling, W., Rawson, R. A., & Compton, M. A. (1994). Substituting pharmacotherapies for opioid addiction: From methadone to LAAM and Buprenorphine. *Journal of Psychoactive Drugs, 26*(2), 119–128.

Lipton, D. S. (1995). *The effectiveness of treatment for drug abusers under criminal justice supervision.* Washington, DC: National Institute of Justice Research Report, U.S. Department of Justice.

Lipton, D., Brewington, V., & Smith, M. (1990, August). *Acupuncture and crack addicts: A single-blind placebo test of efficacy.* Presentation at Advances in Cocaine Treatment, NIDA Technical Review Meeting.

Lipton, D. S., Falkin, G. P., & Wexler, H. K. (1992). Correctional drug abuse treatment in the United States: An overview. In C. Leukefeld & F. Tims (Eds.), *Drug abuse treatment in prisons and jails.* National Institute on Drug Abuse, Research Monograph Series, No. 118. Washington, DC: U.S. Government Printing Office.

Manpower Demonstration Research Corporation. (1980). *Summary and findings of the national supported work demonstration.* New York: Ballinger.

Margolin, A., Avants, S. K., Chang, P., & Kosten, T. R. (1995). Acupuncture for the treatment of cocaine dependence in methadone-maintained patients. *The American Journal on the Addictions, 2*(3), 194–201.

Marlatt, G. A. (1985). Relapse prevention: Theoretical rational and overview of the model. In G. A. Marlatt & J. R. Gordon (Eds.), *Relapse prevention: maintenance strategies in the treatment of addictive behaviors.* New York: Guilford Press.

Martin, S. S., & Inciardi, J. A. (1993). Case management approaches for criminal justice clients. In J. A. Inciardi (Ed.), *Drug treatment and criminal justice, 27* (pp. 81–96). Newbury Park, CA: Sage.

McBride, D. C., & Inciardi, J. A. (1993). The focused offender disposition program: Philosophy, procedures, and preliminary findings. *The Journal of Drug Issues, 23*(1), 143–160.

McKinney, F., Miller, D. J., Beier, L., & Bohannon, S. R. (1978). Self-concept, delinquency, and positive peer culture. *Criminology, 15*(4), 529–538.

McLellan, A. T., Arndt, I. O., Metzger, D. S., Woody, G. E., & O'Brien, C. P. (1993). The effects of psychosocial services in substance abuse treatment. *Journal of the American Medical Association, 269*(15), 1953–1959.

McLellan, T., Grossman, D., Blaine, J., & Haverkos, H. (1993). Acupuncture treatment for drug abuse: A technical review. *Journal of Substance Abuse Treatment, 19,* 569–576.

McLellan, A. T., Luborsky, L., Cacciola, J., Griffith, J., Evans, F., Barr, H. L., & O'Brien, C. P. (1985). New data from the Addiction Severity Index: Reliability and validity in three centers. *The Journal of Nervous and Mental Disease, 173*(7), 412–423.

McLellan, A. T., Luborsky, L., Woody, G. E., & O'Brien, C. P. (1980). An improved diagnostic instrument for substance abuse patients: The Addiction Severity Index. *The Journal of Nervous and Mental Disorders, 168,* 26–33.

McNeece, C. A. (1997). Future directions in justice system policy and practice. In C. A. McNeece & A. R. Roberts (Eds.), *Policy and practice in the justice system* (pp. 263–269). Chicago: Nelson-Hall.

McNeece, C. A., & Daly, C. M. (1997). Treatment and intervention with chemically involved adult offenders. In C. A. McNeece & A. R. Roberts (Eds.), *Policy and practice in the justice system* (pp. 69–86). Chicago: Nelson-Hall.

McNeece, C. A., & DiNitto, D. M. (1998). *Chemical dependency: A systems approach.* 2nd ed. Boston: Allyn and Bacon.

McNeece, C. A., & Roberts, A. R. (Eds.). (1997). *Policy and practice in the justice system.* Chicago: Nelson Hall.

McNeece, C. A., Springer, D. W., Shader, M. A., Malone, R., Smith, M. A., Touchton-Cashwell, S., & Antalek, M. (1997). An evaluation of juvenile assessment centers in Florida. Tallahassee: Florida State University, Institute for Health and Human Services Research.

McNeece, C. A., Valentine, P. V., McInnis, M., Mayfield, E. L., & Lipovetsky, K. (1997). An evaluation of drug courts in Florida. Tallahassee: Florida State University, Institute for Health and Human Services Research.

McNichol, R. W., & Logsdon, S. A. (1988). Disulfiram: An evaluation research model. *Alcohol Health and Research World, 12*(3), 202–209.

Michigan Department of Social Services. (1983). *The institution centers: Objectives and progress.* Lansing, MI: Institutional Services Division, O.C.Y.S.

Miller, G. A. (1985). *The substance abuse subtle screening inventory manual.* Bloomington, IN: SASSI Institute.

Miller, G. A., Miller, F. G., Roberts, J., Brooks, M. K., & Lazowski, L. (1997). *The SASSI-3.* Bloomington, IN: Baugh Enterprises.

Miller, W. R. (1976). Alcoholism scales and objective measures. *Psychological Bulletin, 83,* 649–674.

Miller, W. R., & Hester, R. K. (1980). Treating the problem drinker: Modern approaches. In W. R. Miller (Ed.), *The addictive behaviors* (pp. 11–141). New York: Pergamon.

Minnesota Department of Corrections. (1973). *The Red Wing training school follow-up study.* Minneapolis, MN: Research Division.

Minuchin, S. (1974). *Families and family therapy.* Cambridge, MA: Harvard University Press.

Minuchin, S., & Fishman, H. C. (1981). *Family therapy techniques.* Cambridge, MA: Harvard University Press.

Moon, M. M., & Latessa, E. J. (1994). Drug treatment in adult probation: An evaluation of an outpatient and acupuncture program. *Journal of Evaluation and Program Planning, 17*(2), 217–226.

Morton, L. A. (1978). *The Risk Prediction Scales.* Indianapolis, IN: Department of Mental Health, Division of Addiction Services.

National Association of Drug Court Professionals & The Office of Community Oriented Policing Services, U.S. Department of Justice. (1997). *Community policing and drug courts/community courts: Working together within a unified court system.* Alexandria, VA: Author.

National Association of Drug Court Professionals Drug Court Standards Committee. (1997, January). *Defining drug courts: Key components.* Washington, DC: Author.

National Institute on Alcohol Abuse and Alcoholism. (1990). *Seventh special report to the U.S. Congress on alcohol and health.* Rockville, MD: U.S. Department of Health and Human Services.

National Institute on Alcohol Abuse and Alcoholism (1997). Patient-treatment matching. *Alcohol Alert No. 36,* 1–4.

National Institute on Drug Abuse. (1999). *Principles of drug addiction treatment: A research-based guide.* NIH Publication No. 99-4180. Washington, DC: Author.

National Task Force on Correctional Substance Abuse Strategies. (1991). *Intervening with substance-abusing offenders: A framework for action.* Washington, DC: U.S. Department of Justice, National Institute of Corrections.

Nurco, D. N., Hanlon, T. E., Batemna, R. W., & Kinlock, T. W. (1995). Drug abuse treatment in the context of correctional surveillance. *Journal of Substance Abuse Treatment, 12*(1), 19–27.

Nurco, D. N., Hanlon, T. E., & Kinlock, T. W. (1990). Offenders, drugs, crime and treatment (Draft). Washington, DC: U.S. Department of Justice, Bureau of Justice Assistance.

Obermeier, G. E., & Henry, P. B. (1989). Adolescent inpatient treatment. *Journal of Chemical Dependency, 2*(1), 163–182.

Office of National Drug Control Policy. (1996, March). *Treatment protocol effectiveness study.* Washington, DC: U.S. Government Printing Office.

Office of National Drug Control Policy. (1997, February). *The national drug control strategy: 1997* (NCJ Publication No. 163915). Washington, DC: U.S. Government Printing Office.

Office of State Courts Administrator, Supreme Court of Florida. (1996, September). *Gaining momentum: A model curriculum for drug courts.* Tallahassee, FL: Author.

Ogborne, A. C., & Glaser, F. B. (1985). Evaluating Alcoholics Anonymous. In T. E. Bratter & G. G. Forrest (Eds.), *Alcoholism and substance abuse* (pp. 176–192). New York: Free Press.

Pan, H., Scarpitti, F. R., Inciardi, J. A., & Lockwood, D. (1993). Some considerations on therapeutic communities in corrections. In J. A. Inciardi (Ed.), *Drug treatment and criminal justice, 27* (pp. 30–43). Newbury Park, CA: Sage.

Parent, D. (1989). *Shock incarceration: An overview of existing programs.* Washington, DC: Department of Justice, National Institute of Justice.

Peters, R. H. (1993). Drug treatment in jails and detention settings. In J. A. Inciardi (Ed.), *Drug treatment and criminal justice, 27* (pp. 44–80). Newbury Park, CA: Sage.

Peters, R. H., May, R. L., & Kearns, W. D. (1992). Drug treatment in jails: Results of a nationwide survey. *Journal of Criminal Justice, 20,* 283–295.

Pokorny, A. D., Miller, B. A., & Kaplan, H. B. (1972). The Brief MAST: A shortened version of the Michigan Alcoholism Screening Test (MAST). *American Journal of Psychiatry, 129*(3), 342–345.

Prendergast, M. L., Grella, C., Perry, S. M., & Anglin, M. D. (1995). Levo-alpha-acetylmethodal (LAAM): Clinical, research, and policy issues of a new pharmacotherapy for opioid addiction. *Journal of Psychoactive Drugs, 27*(3), 239–247.

RAND. (1994). *Projecting future cocaine use and evaluating control strategies* (RB-6002). Santa Monica, CA: Author.

Retig, R. A., & Yarmolinsky, A. (Eds.). (1995). *Federal regulation of methadone treatment.* Washington, DC: National Academy Press.

Ridgely, M. S. (1996). Practical issues in the application of case management to substance abuse treatment. In H. A. Siegal & R. C. Rapp (Eds.), *Case management and substance abuse treatment: Practice and experience* (pp. 1–20). New York: Springer.

Sarri, R., & Selo, E. (1974). Evaluation process and outcome in juvenile corrections: A grim tale. In P. O. Davidson, F. W. Clark, & L. A. Hamerlynch (Eds.), *Evaluation of community programs.* Champaign, IL: Research Press.

Schwartz, I. (1989). Hospitalization of adolescents for psychiatric and substance abuse treatment: Legal and ethical issues. *Journal of Adolescent Health Care, 10*(6), 473–478.

Selzer, M. L. (1971). The Michigan Alcoholism Screening Test: The quest for a new diagnostic instrument. *American Journal of Psychiatry, 127,* 1653–1658.

Selzer, M. L., Vinokur, A., & Van Rooijen, L. A. (1974). Self-administered Short Michigan Alcoholism Screening Test (SMAST). *Journal of Studies on Alcohol, 15,* 276–280.

Singer, J. A. (1996, Spring). *An analysis of acupuncture therapy for the treatment of chemical dependency and its struggle for legitimacy.* New York: State University of New York at Stony Brook.

Smith, B. E., Davis, R. C., Laszlo, A. T., & Goretsky, S. R. (1994, August). *Drug night courts: The Cook County experience.* Washington, DC: Bureau of Justice Assistance.

Smith, T. E., & Springer, D. W. (1998). Treating chemically dependent children and adolescents. In C. A. McNeece & D. M. DiNitto (Eds.), *Chemical dependency: A systems approach* (2nd ed.). Boston: Allyn & Bacon.

Snair, J. R. (1989). *Report on evaluation research review conducted for the governor's study commission on crime prevention and law enforcement.* Tallahassee: Florida State University.

Solomon, S. D. (1982). Individual versus group therapy: Current status in the treatment of alcoholism. *Advances in Alcohol and Substance Abuse, 2*(1), 69–86.

Stark, M. J. (1992). Dropping out of substance abuse treatment: A clinically oriented review. *Clinical Psychology Review, 12,* 93–116.

State of Florida, Advisory Council on Intergovernmental Relations. (1994). *Community corrections: A review of current policy and programs* (Monograph). Tallahassee, FL: Author.

Stewart, C. (1998). *A study of "self-quitters" and smokers.* PhD dissertation, Florida State University, Tallahassee.

Swartz, J. (1993). The next 20 years: Extending, refining, and assessing the model. In J. A. Inciardi (Ed.), *Drug Treatment and Criminal Justice* (pp. 127–148). Newbury Park, CA: Sage.

Szapocznik, J., Kurtines, W. M., Foote, F. H., Perez-Vidal, A., & Hervis, O. (1986). Conjoint versus one-person family therapy: Further evidence for the effectiveness of conducting family therapy through one person with drug-abusing adolescents. *Journal of Consulting and Clinical Psychology, 54,* 395–397.

Tarter, R. E., & Hegedus, A. M. (1991). The drug use screening inventory: Its application in the evaluation and treatment of alcohol and other drug abuse. *Alcohol Health and Research World, 15*(1), 65–75.

Timrots, A. (1992). *Fact sheet: Drug testing in the criminal justice system.* Rockville, MD: Drugs & Crime Data Center and Clearinghouse.

Turnabout ASAP. (1997). *Acupuncture treatment for substance abuse.* Santa Monica, CA: Rand.

Turner, S., Petersilia, J., & Deschenes, E. P. (1994). The implementation and effectiveness of drug testing in community supervision: Results of an experimental evaluation. In D. L. MacKenzie & C. D. Uchida (Eds.), *Drugs and crime: Evaluating public policy initiatives* (pp. 231–252). Thousand Oaks, CA: Sage.

U.S. Department of Health and Human Services. (1996). *Treatment drug courts: Integrating substance abuse treatment with legal case processing* (DHHS Publication No. SMA 96-3113). Washington, DC: U.S. Government Printing Office.

U.S. General Accounting Office. (1990). *Drug-exposed infants: A generation at risk.* Washington, DC: General Accounting Office.

U.S. General Accounting Office. (1995, May). *Drug courts: Information on a new approach to address drug-related crime* (GAO/GGD Publication No. 95-159BR). Washington, DC: U.S. Government Printing Office.

U.S. General Accounting Office. (1996, June). *Cocaine treatment: Early results from various approaches* (GAO/HEHS-96-80). Washington, DC: U.S. Government Printing Office.

Van Stelle, K. R., Mauser, E., & Moberg, D. P. (1994). Recidivism to the criminal justice system of substance-abusing offenders diverted into treatment. *Crime and Delinquency, 40*(2), 175–196.

Vorrath, H. H., & Brendtro, L. K. (1985). *Positive peer culture* (2nd ed.). New York, NY: Aldine De Gruyter.

Wells, R. A. (1994). *Planned short-term treatment.* New York: Free Press.

Wish, E. D., Toborg, M., & Bellassai, J. (1988). *Identifying drug users and monitoring them during conditional release* (National Institute of Justice briefing paper). Washington, DC: U.S. Department of Justice, National Institute of Justice.

Witters, W., & Venturelli, P. (1988). *Drugs and society* (2nd ed.). Boston: Jones and Bartlett.

Yalom, I. D. (1994). *The theory and practice of group psychotherapy* (4th ed.). New York: Basic Books.

Young, D., Dynia, P., & Belenko, S. (1996, November). *How compelling is coerced treatment? A study of different mandated treatment approaches*. Paper presented at the annual meeting of the American Society of Criminology, Chicago.

Chapter 6
TREATING PATIENTS FOUND NOT GUILTY BY REASON OF INSANITY

Randall T. Salekin and Richard Rogers

Patients found not guilty by reason of insanity (NGRI patients) cause apprehension and concern for mental health professionals regarding their effective inpatient treatment, release, and aftercare in the community. Effective treatment and management of NGRI patients is especially challenging, because the verdict presents dual and possibly conflicting mandates to clinicians: beneficial treatment without undue constraints versus community safety. Favoring one mandate at the expense of the other generates serious problems, such as lack of a therapeutic progress or undue risk to the community. Developing a model that integrates both of these concepts is critical for successfully treating and managing these patients (Zonana & Norko, 1996). Overshadowing the treatment of NGRI patients are two related debates: (a) the appropriateness of the not guilty by reason of insanity defense itself, and (b) the standard to be used for NGRI verdicts.

The treatment of NGRI patients can only be understood in the context of the insanity defense itself and the remarkable ambivalence that it engenders in both public and professional arenas. Much of the public fear and foreboding is related to misperceptions of the insanity defense (Perlin, 1996; Silver, Cirincione, & Steadman, 1994). Perlin (1996) outlined common myths regarding the insanity defense: It (a) is overused; (b) is limited to murder cases; (c) presents no risk to the defendant pleading insanity; (d) results in a quick release from custody; (e) is a ploy by criminal defendants "faking" insanity; (f) results in a financially driven "battle of the experts"; and (g) is inappropriately used by attorneys to obtain unwarranted acquittals. The public image of a wealthy person evading justice is likely to have a chilling effect on their tolerance of his or her postacquittal treatment and eventual release.

Empirical evidence has shown that these claims are less than accurate. In reality, the insanity defense is used in less than 1% of cases (Callahan, Steadman, McGreevy, & Clark, 1991; Steadman, Monahan, Harstone, Kantorowski-Davis, & Robbins, 1982), is frequently unsuccessful, and generally results in lengthy stays in restrictive maximum security facilities for longer periods than defendants convicted on similar crimes (Silver, 1995; Steadman, 1980, 1985). The insanity plea carries considerable risk because a failed defense is tantamount to a conviction. Moreover, if the defense fails, prison terms are significantly longer than comparable cases in which the defense is not raised (Perlin, 1996). The defense is most frequently pled in cases involving minor property crimes and is much less frequently used in crimes involving a victim's death (Steadman, 1985). In direct contrast to public perceptions, most cases do not involve a battle of the experts. Generally, both state and defense experts agree about both the severity of the defendant's mental illness and his or her criminal responsibility (Ogloff, Schweighofer, Turnbull, & Whittemore, 1992; Zonana, Bartel, Wells, Buchanan, & Getz, 1990; Zonana & Norko, 1996). According to Perlin (1996), feigned insanity is rarely attempted and often unsuccessful. Data from Rogers (1986) compiled across multiple sites found a prevalence of definite malingering to be rare (4.5%).

Debates regarding insanity standards have overshadowed treatment programs for NGRI patients. With respect to insanity standards, available data (Rogers, Seman, & Clark, 1986; Wettstein, Mulvey, & Rogers, 1991) suggest that specific standards are likely to have little effect on clinical determinations of criminal responsibility. For example, Ogloff (1991) found that mock jurors do not appreciate the legal nuances found in specific insanity standards. Instead, jurors focused on general issues when making decisions, such as the defendant's history of mental illness, expert testimony on the NGRI patient's disorder, and whether or not the defendant intended to harm. Whatever the standard used, once a person is adjudicated NGRI, most people believe that they are entitled to receive treatment for their disorders (Hans, 1986).

Yet we lack research on the treatment of these persons. This may be partially attributable to the fact that the indefinite commitment of NGRI patients is more punishment than treatment (Szasz, 1963). As German and Singer (1976) concluded, "No group of patients has been more deprived of treatment, discriminated against, or mistreated than persons acquitted of crimes on the grounds of insanity" (p. 1074). In this regard, Quinsey (1988) also concluded that the treatment of mentally disordered offenders receives very little attention in the literature both by itself and in comparison to other forensic issues (e.g., the prediction of dangerousness).

Despite this, treatment of NGRI patients remains a crucial responsibility for mental health professionals and society as a whole. Judge David Bazelon described the issue well when he stated, "Our collective conscience does not allow punishment where it cannot impose blame" (American Bar Association Criminal Justice Mental Health Systems, 1989, p. 324). Although we recognize the imperfections with the insanity defense and the concerns regarding its misuse, the very nature of this verdict would suggest that treatment of NGRI patients is both necessary and proper. In essence, we contend that NGRI patients require treatment that will allow them to return to live in the community without restrictions but, at the same time, without undue risk to the public.

The purpose of this chapter is to present specific information regarding the treatment needs of NGRI patients and to suggest modalities for providing that treatment. We also furnish information regarding follow-up of NGRI patients and what issues should be considered before NGRI patients are released to the community. A natural starting point for the chapter is a description of NGRI patients' characteristics with special attention to their treatment needs. We begin with demographic and psychiatric characteristics of NGRI patients.

Demographic and Clinical Characteristics of NGRI Patients

A necessary precondition to treatment planning for NGRI patients is the examination of background and psychiatric data as a basis for clinical intervention. Research now exists on the demographic and clinical characteristics of NGRI patients across 16 states and two Canadian provinces. The goal of this review is to provide a clear picture of the NGRI patients' treatment needs to formulate a more reasoned and informed approach to effective treatment. First, we summarize the extensive research of Callahan, Steadman, McGreevy, and Robbins (1991). Second, we augment Callahan et al.'s research with our own literature review.

Callahan Study

Callahan and her colleagues (1991) compiled data on nearly one million felony indictments, spanning 49 counties and eight states. In addition to providing descriptive data on insanity pleas (9.3 per 1000) and resulting acquittals (2.6 per 1000), they supplied important data on 2565 NGRI patients. The great majority were male (86.5%), with an average age of 32.1 years. They were balanced between Black (42.6%) and White (50.4%) ethnic backgrounds. Most NGRI patients had been previously arrested (70.2%) and had psychiatric histories that included hospitalization (82.0%). As expected, primary diagnoses were made up of schizophrenic disorders (67.9%), other psychotic or mood disorders (16.0%), mental retardation (4.8%), and other mental disorders (4.5%). In addition, small numbers had a primary diagnosis of personality disorder (3.5%) or substance abuse (2.7%).

Literature Review

In Table 6.1, we present data from 23 studies on a total of 3136 NGRI patients. Similar results were found across these studies to that of the Callahan et al. (1991) study. The majority of the NGRI patients were male (79.1%), with an average age of 33.6 years. The acquittees were composed of 39.1% Black and 51.6% White ethnic backgrounds. Approximately half of the NGRI patients had been previously arrested (51.2%). Most had psychiatric histories that included hospitalization (66.2%). As expected, primary diagnoses were made up predominantly of psychotic disorders (66.8%). Slightly more than half of the NGRI patients (53.5%) had a schizophrenic disorder. Present to a lesser extent were other psychotic or mood disorders (17.3%) and mental retardation (4.5%). Surprisingly, a substantial minority had a primary diagnosis of personality disorder (19.8%), one half of which carried the diagnosis of antisocial personality disorder (APD). Although not a primary diagnosis, approximately two thirds of the NGRI patients had substance abuse problems. Seventy-four percent of the index crimes committed by the NGRI patients were violent in nature.

Psychotic disorders, with one exception, were the predominant diagnostic category. In a small sample of 25 cases, Phillips and Pasewark (1980) found that 48% had personality disorders, and only 36% had schizophrenia. It is likely that this sample does not adequately represent NGRI acquittees in Connecticut. In fact, Zonana et al. (1990) has shown that major mental illness is more prevalent than personality disorders among NGRI patients in Connecticut.

Nonetheless, personality disorders are the second most frequent diagnosis, making up approximately 19.8% of the acquittees. Nearly 10% of the NGRI patients meet the criteria for a diagnosis of APD. The results of this study would indicate that the view that holds that the NGRI defense is the last refuge of sociopathic individuals who manipulate mental health and criminal justice systems to escape confinement in a penitentiary may only hold true for very few of the defendants.

Important gender differences were noted with regard to NGRI patients' diagnostic picture. Specifically, differences were found in the diagnostic frequency of

Table 6.1—*Background and Diagnostic Characteristics of NGRI Patients*

Authors	Background Data				Diagnostic Data (%)								% Violent Crime
	N	Age	% Male	% Hosp	Psychot	Scz	Organ	Mood	MR	PD	APD	SA Hx	
Bogenberger et al. (1987)	107	29	94	22	64	51	3	13	6	7	—	—	52
Cooke & Sikorski (1974)	167	37	87	44	68	—	—	—	—	25	—	—	91
Criss & Racine (1980)	223	38	85	66	74	66	1	2	1	22	6	81	81
Gacono et al. (1995)	18	34	100	—	72	39	17	23	0	100	55	88	83
Greenland (1979)	103	31	78	53	47	—	—	—	7	—	—	—	95
Heilbrun, Griffin-Heilbrun, & Griffin (1988)	41	39	0	78	—	34	20	20	0	10	10	76	94
Hodgins, Hebert, & Baraldi (1986)	29	38	0	100	79	57	4	—	4	—	—	—	100
Linhorst & Dirks-Linhorst[a] (1997)	797	33	88	—	78	—	—	—	—	44	23	49	52
Morrow & Petersen (1966)	44	34	100	34	45	—	14	—	14	—	—	—	47
Norwood, Nicholson, Enyart, & Hickey (1991)	61	34	92	96	74	59	2	10	—	—	2	13	75
Pasewark, Jeffrey, & Bieber (1987)[b]	36	32	100	100	64	64	3	7	3	8	0	3	54
Petrila (1982)	67	31	—	79	68	—	8	2	8	5	0	—	60
Phillips & Pasewark (1980)	25	28	92	61	40	36	—	—	—	48	—	—	20

Study	N	Scz	Psychot	Mood	% Hosp	SA Hx	Organ	MR	PD	APD			
Rice & Harris (1990)	53	33	—	75	66	—	—	—	—	13	—	—	100
Rogers & Bloom (1982)[b]	440	31	91	85	67	61	6	6	5	—	—	3	5	55
Seig, Ball, & Menninger (1995)	149	33	75	—	67	—	—	20	—	—	4	40	74
Shah, Greenberg, & Convit (1994)	62	41	84	—	90	—	3	2	0	0	0	68	95
Silver, Cohen, & Spodiak (1989)	127	31	100	59	71	71	6	3	8	8	—	—	69
Steadman (1980)	278	34	86	38	68	—	—	—	—	3	13	—	90
Steadman et al. (1983)	110	33	97	40	—	—	—	—	—	—	—	—	76
Wettstein & Mulvey (1988)	137	34	82	67	65	57	2	11	2	4	—	—	77
Zonana, Bartel, Wells, Buchanan, & Getz (1990)	62	32	50	75	68	49	11	12	—	16	—	61	85
Average[c]	3136	33.6	79.1	65.1	66.8	53.7	7.1	10.1	4.5	20.9	10.6	48.4	73.9

Note. All numbers represent percentages of NGRI patients. All categories are primary diagnoses. SA Hx = the total percentage of patients with substance abuse histories. N = the number of NGRI patients; % Hosp = prior psychiatric hospitalizations; Psychot = any type of psychotic disorder; Scz = schizophrenia; Organ = organic disorder; Mood = all mood disorders; MR = Mental retardation; PD = All Personality Disorders; APD = Antisocial Personality Disorder; violent crime = violent index crime.

[a] These diagnoses were grouped as "major mental illness" with psychotic disorders being prominent.

[b] Formal diagnosis of substance abuse rather than a history.

[c] Average = averages for each of the columns with the exception of N which is the total number of NGRI patients.

disorders and in the potential for future dangerousness, which may suggest different treatment needs for female versus male NGRI patients. With regard to Axis I diagnoses, females were more likely than males to be diagnosed with mood disorders, although still constituting only a minority of NGRI patients. These data suggest a need for women's treatment programs emphasizing mood disorders. Few women were diagnosed ASPD. This is consistent with the literature, which shows a lower prevalence of this disorder and psychopathy in women (Salekin, Rogers, & Sewell, 1997). Moreover, Axis II disorders in general were rarely diagnosed in females. When personality disorders were diagnosed, they tended to be borderline personality disorders. These gender differences suggest a need for treatment approaches for women designed to increase self-management of intense, labile emotion, interpersonal conflict, and identity confusion (Linehan, 1993). The less extensive criminal history and lower potential for repetitive violence suggest that treatment for many female NGRI patients may safely take place in relatively low-security settings.

One inescapable conclusion from these data is that most persons acquitted by reason of insanity were seriously mentally ill at the time of their entry into forensic mental health systems. As for locus of treatment issues, it is significant to note that in a substantial minority of the cases, relatively trivial offenses were overshadowed by severe disorders. More specifically, about one fourth of acquittees (26%) have minor or nonviolent offenses, but severe mental disorders; in such cases, security issues may pose less risk and treatment needs may assume greater importance.

Typically, NGRI treatment programs tend to be generic and not focused on the demographic and clinical profiles of NGRI patients. Rather, their presumed dangerousness appears to override all other considerations, except possibly the need to exact some retribution despite a "not guilty" determination (Hans, 1986; Quinsey, 1988). Thus the primary societal concern for NGRI patients is for a secure environment, regardless of such an environment's ability to foster appropriate treatment interventions. We contend that if a greater emphasis were given to treatment, issues of dangerousness prediction would require less attention.

Treatment of NGRI Patients

Current treatment of NGRI patients has favored a top-down approach in which general programs are devised and NGRI patients' are served solely within the realm of the program's offerings. In contrast, a bottom-up perspective details the treatment needs of NGRI patients and then attempts to tailor interventions to these needs. In this section, we explore patient needs from a bottom-up perspective in an effort to tailor treatment to specific clinical needs. The basic goals of treatment are fourfold: (a) diagnose and treat the mental disorder, (b) reduce the risk of dangerousness, (c) prepare the NGRI patient for the community, and (d) monitor his or her adjustment in the community.

The research data currently available on NGRI patients offer a starting point for such treatment programs. The majority of NGRI patients warrant a diagnosis of schizophrenia, frequently complicated with substance abuse and personality disorders. Certainly, with one half to two thirds of most NGRI cohorts diagnosed with schizophrenia and a similar percentage of the acquittees diagnosed with substance abuse problems, these two areas seem like important targets for treatment. Moreover,

ASPD and the related syndrome of psychopathy (Salekin, Rogers, & Sewell, 1996) are likely to complicate the management of NGRI patients.

NGRI patients are often characterized by severe symptomatology and less-than-optimum treatment response. Because of their frequent Axis I–Axis II disorders, state-of-the-art treatment is needed to alleviate acute symptomatology, maintain stability of patients' functioning, and prepare NGRI patients for community living. Once in the community, NGRI patients should continue to be monitored for symptomatology and general adjustment.

Though treatment strategies and techniques used with NGRI patients are often identical to those used with nonforensic patients, the context and settings in which health services are delivered are frequently unique. Treating NGRI patients has an explicit goal of minimizing future criminal activity. Treating NGRI patients also differs from nonforensic populations in that motivation for treatment is externally imposed and monitored. Therapeutic progress is often less important than compliance with treatment, and lack of treatment compliance often results in immediate sanctions. We first begin our review with specific treatment approaches to symptomatology common among NGRI patients. We then discuss five treatment-related issues that are frequently emphasized in preparing clinicians for NGRI treatment services.

Treating NGRI Patients With Psychotic Symptomatology

The majority of NGRI patients are found nonresponsible on the basis of delusions and hallucinations. More specifically, Rogers (1986) found among defendants assessed as insane that delusions played a major role in 82.3% and hallucinations in 35.2% of the cases. Our own review also shows a high prevalence of psychotic symptomatology. Therefore, effective treatment of psychosis is equally important to both the clinical status of the patient and public safety. Because the majority of NGRI patients were strongly influenced by psychotic symptoms in committing often violent crimes, the compelling logic is that these same psychotic symptoms must be competently managed and treated to preclude further violent acts. From a preventative perspective, careful monitoring of psychotic symptoms for signs of possible decompensation is a crucial element of treatment.

Psychopharmacologic treatment has been shown to be very effective at ameliorating active psychotic symptomatology (Jacobsen, 1986; Kane & Freeman, 1994; Richelson, 1996). Neuroleptics, in general (e.g., Thorazine, Prolixin, Haloperidol, Mellaril, and Trilafon), have been most commonly used in treating psychotic disorders (Bezchlibnyk-Butler & Jeffries, 1996; Breslin, 1992; Pickar et al., 1992). New-generation medications shown to be highly effective with psychotic disorders include Clozapine, Risperidone, Olanzapine, Sertindole, and Quetiapine (Richelson, 1996). These new-generation medications have been shown to also have an impact on aggressive and violent behavior in psychotic patients. For example, Dalal, Larkin, Leese, and Taylor (1999) examined the effectiveness of Clozapine in reducing psychotic symptoms, reducing serious violent behavior, and facilitating discharge of 50 patients with schizophrenia in a forensic hospital facility. For patients who continued Clozapine treatment for a minimum of 12 months, the majority showed symptom reduction, and this symptom reduction was associated with a reduction in violence and a higher rate of discharge. Volavka and Citrome (1999) and Citrome and Volavka

(2000) have also found that atypical antipsychotic medications (Clozapine, Risperidone, and Quetiapine) reduce psychotic symptoms and aggression in schizophrenic patients.

Psychotherapy has also been an effective means of treating psychotic symptoms independently or more commonly in combination with psychopharmacologic treatment (e.g., Breier & Strauss, 1983; Lowe & Chadwick, 1990; Paul & Lentz, 1977). For instance, Breier and Strauss (1983) have demonstrated that self-control methods in psychotic disorders can be an effective form of treatment. According to Breier and Strauss, the self-regulation process consists of three phases: (a) awareness of psychotic or prepsychotic behavior by self-monitoring, (b) recognition of certain behaviors as a signal of disorder by self-evaluation, and (c) employment of self-control methods. The most common methods of control are self-instruction and change in activity level. Meichenbaum (1977) has suggested that coping self-talk statements could be used to guide schizophrenic patients' attention. Detecting early signals that may herald the onset of psychotic symptoms and noting the sequences of events often followed by symptoms are particularly important. As noted by Rice, Harris, and Quinsey (1996), effective treatment of NGRI patients with combined pharmacological and psychotherapy treatments requires extensive planning and commitment of resources.

Treating NGRI Patients With Mood Disorders

Treating depression in NGRI patients deserves special attention. Although only a minority of the NGRI patients have mood disorders as a primary diagnosis, substantial numbers have moderate to severe symptoms at the time of the offense (28.8% depressive and 15.9% manic symptoms; Rogers, 1986). Still other NGRI patients acquire depressive symptoms in the course of their postacquittal hospitalization (Hambridge, 1990). Much of this depression is related to the realization of (a) the crimes that they have committed and (b) their indefinite and lengthy hospitalizations. In fact, improvement in psychotic symptoms actually may increase depression in NGRI patients. That is, as psychotic symptoms abate, many NGRI patients begin to experience guilt and subsequent depression for the act(s) that led to their hospitalization.

A new class of 5-HT antidepressants have, at least preliminarily, shown considerable success with depressed patients. Such drugs include Mirtazipine, Nefazodone, and Venlafaxine. These drugs are less likely than tricylic drugs to have adverse effects and are less lethal if overdosed (Frazer, 1994; Nelson, 1997). Although these new drugs are promising, pharmacological treatment of more recalcitrant forms of depression often requires either cyclic antidepressants or monoamine oxidase inhibitors. Finally, electroconvulsive therapy can be useful for cases of major depression that have not responded adequately to drug treatment (Fink, 1987; Nelson, 1997).

For bipolar disorders, the treatment with the most empirical support is lithium carbonate and more recently Valproate or Carbamazepine. According to Gerner and Stanton (1992), the overall noncompliance and nonresponse rate to lithium in bipolar disorder is relatively high. However, Valproic acid is increasingly receiving support as an effective medication for bipolar disorders and is less likely to produce adverse effects in patients (Gerner & Stanton, 1992). Moreover, Valproate appears to be indicated in rapid cycling bipolar disorders more so than lithium carbonate. Long-term treatment is critical for NGRI patients with mood disorders given the substantial relapse rates (Rice et al., 1996).

We contend that psychotherapeutic approaches for treating depressed NGRI patients should include cognitive–behavioral therapy (CBT). CBT has proven successful across diverse clinical settings (Beck, Rush, Shaw, & Emery, 1979; Elkin et al., 1989; Meichenbaum, 1977; Persons, 1989; Scott, Williams, & Beck, 1995). More recently, CBT has been found to be effective with bipolar disorders (Satterfield, 1999; Zaretsky, Segal, & Gemar, 1999). Treatments using cognitive–behavioral approaches should focus on self-control and problem solving skills for NGRI patients. In addition, CBT should be used to correct negative or distorted self-schemas and beliefs that depressed NGRI patients may have. Meichenbaum (1977) has suggested that self-talk can be a useful strategy to change depressive thought patterns, and this cognitive strategy may also help bipolar patients better regulate their emotions. Other concrete treatment components for bipolar disorder focus on prevention of mood cycles, early detection of cycle onset, and mood stabilization during cycles. Interpersonal therapy might also be used, and although effective for depression there is less empirical research supporting its effectiveness for bipolar disorder (Weissman, 1994).

Treatment of Substance Abuse Among NGRI Patients

Clinical data on NGRI patients indicate that substance abuse is often a secondary diagnosis and an important treatment issue. In many psychotic patients, substance abuse may precipitate decompensation or impede further progress. Although rarely the central diagnostic issue for defendants found NGRI (Rogers, 1986), addressing substance abuse problems plays a critical role in their effective treatment. In cases of adjudicated NGRI patients, nearly one half warrant a secondary diagnosis of a substance abuse disorder. Moreover, the acquisition of use of illegal substances constitutes an additional offense. For NGRI patients in particular, rearrests typically constitute a treatment failure.

Miller (1982) recommended the use of alcohol-sensitizing drugs and behavioral treatment with high-risk patients. The positive effects may be limited, however, to persons with alcohol disorders whose problem drinking is confined to a few risk situations. Moreover, Moncrieff and Drummond (1997) argued that there is little evidence thus far that pharmacological treatment for alcohol problems is effective. These results were based on 16 studies that examined the effect of such drug treatments as Acomprosate, Natrexone, Bromocriptine, selective serotonin re-uptake inhibitors, and Buspirone. Ross and Lightfoot (1985) reviewed the literature on the treatment of alcohol-abusing offenders and found that aversion therapy, behavioral training in self-control, relaxation, communication, assertion, social skills, and family therapy were effective forms of treatment. Dimeff and Marlatt (1995) have shown that relapse prevention training is an effective way to prevent the drinking cycle. There is no reason to believe that relapse prevention would not work with other forms of drug abuse. General cognitive–behavioral strategies that have NGRI patients focus on the antecedents to their drug use and acquisition of self-control and problem-solving skills would be beneficial. Stacy (1997) has shown that cognitions often lead to increased drug use and that relapse prevention can provide a useful means of treating substance abusers. Unfortunately, many studies have not considered dually diagnosed offenders as is typically found with NGRI samples. NGRI patients with substance abuse problems would benefit maximally from treatment programs that addressed their substance abuse problems and other Axis I disorders concurrently.

Treating Anxiety Disorders in NGRI Patients

Rogers (1986) found severe or pervasive anxiety in 28.9% of defendants evaluated clinically as insane. It is important to note that the presence of psychotic symptoms does not preclude anxiety. Little is known of whether this anxiety serves to inhibit psychotically based behavior or, conversely, facilitate such behavior. Rogers and Wettstein (1985) found low levels of anxiety among most NGRI patients, but higher levels among treatment failures.

Although only evidenced in a minority of the NGRI patients, anxiety can be a distressing problem for these individuals. In the case of NGRI patients, some may be diagnosed with posttraumatic stress disorder given that they often are traumatized by the events that lead to their hospitalization (e.g., Hambridge, 1990).

Behavior therapy for anxiety disorders and panic disorders has been shown to be efficacious (Barlow, 1988; Chambless & Goldstein, 1980; Foa & Tillmanns, 1980; Fyer, Mannuzza, & Endicott, 1987; Koback, Greist, Jefferson, Katzelnick, & Henk, 1998; Nietzel & Bernstein, 1981; Silverman et al., 1999; Turner, 1984; Wolpe, 1990). According to Suinn (1990) and Wolpe (1990), anxiety management training that includes both induced anxiety and relaxation is recommended for those who have generalized anxiety that is manifested primarily by affective symptoms. Suinn (1990) and Wolpe (1990) contend that stress inoculation and systematic desensitization should be considered for persons whose symptoms are primarily in the cognitive domain. Others (e.g., Foa, Wilson, Foa, & Barlow, 1991) have suggested thought-stopping as a way in which patients can deal with intrusive anxiety-evoking thoughts and obsessions, by preventing such thoughts from entering his or her mind. Still others (e.g., Borkovec & Mathews, 1988; Ost, 1987) prescribe more generalized treatment, such as intensive relaxation training, in the hope that learning to relax when beginning to feel tense will keep anxiety from spiraling out of control. With this treatment, patients are taught to relax away tensions, responding to incipient anxiety with relaxation rather than alarm. This strategy has been found to be very effective in alleviating anxiety symptoms (Borkovec & Roemer, 1994; Borkovec & Whisman, 1996).

Treating NGRI Patients Who Lack Life Skills

Life skills deficits are an important and pervasive problem for NGRI patients. Given the low educational attainment of NGRI patients, programs designed to increase their knowledge and general skills is likely to prove useful in allowing acquittees to be more adaptive in their communities (Rice et al., 1996). One method that can improve educational attainment is a contingency management approach to literacy and mathematical skills (Ayllon & Milan, 1979). Such programs are likely to have positive effects with regard to attaining employment once released. In addition, token economy programs that emphasize vocational and educational training in prison settings have been shown to reduce postrelease recidivism (Milan, 1987). With the high rate of unemployment among NGRI patients, developing job skills appears to be necessary before community release. Researchers (e.g., Furman, Geller, Simon, & Kelly, 1979; Kelly, Laughlin, Clairborne, & Patterson, 1979; Shady & Kue, 1977; Twentyman, Jensen, & Kloss, 1978) have shown that such programs have been highly successful in helping individuals obtain employment.

Another important component to the successful integration of patients into the community is appropriate follow-up to ensure that these individuals are able to maintain their employment in the community. Peckman and Muller (1999) followed-up seven schizophrenic patients living in a community to address the problems they face when entering the work force, which included (a) interpersonal, (b) episodic and unpredictable symptoms, (c) treatment interventions, and (d) inappropriate values. The patients provided the following useful coping strategies to successfully cope with work-related problems: (a) openness with employer, (b) taking on tasks step by step, and (c) positive self-talk. These schizophrenic patients offered many creative and practical solutions: (a) support (either by hotline or on-going workshops), (b) education for employers and the community, (c) personal training (problem-solving, money management, social skills), and (d) environmental stability. NGRI patients are likely to require assistance in the areas pinpointed by these patients with schizophrenia.

Teaching Social Skills to NGRI Patients

The treatment of choice for socially inadequate behavior is social skills training. In brief, social skills training involves a variety of techniques that are used to change a person's social behavior in particular social situations (Rice et al., 1996). Use of behavioral components such as role playing, modeling, feedback, and coaching would likely prove useful for NGRI patients who require social skills training. Meta-analytic studies (Benton & Schroeder, 1990; Corrigan, 1991) have shown that social skills training can improve postrelease social functioning of schizophrenic and other seriously mentally ill patients with long-term effects. Strong support is marshaled for the conclusion that social skills training is beneficial for both low-functioning schizophrenic patients and higher functioning patients with other diagnoses (Benton & Schroeder, 1990; Corrigan, 1991; Mueser, Levine, Bellack, Douglas, & Brady, 1990; Rice, Harris, Quinsey, & Cyr, 1990). As Rice et al. (1996) highlighted, precautions should be taken to ensure that the unit policies do not admonish or punish the NGRI patients for socially appropriate assertive behaviors acquired in social skills training programs.

Managing Anger, Aggression, and Violence With NGRI Patients

NGRI patients who display aggression pose a serious management problem. Anger, by itself, is a potential risk factor for violence among mentally disordered individuals

(Novaco, 1994). Deffenbacher (1999) outlined cognitive–behavioral interventions for anger reduction. These strategies include enhancing one's self-awareness through using record-keeping, role plays, and behavioral experiments in which the individual attends to experiential and behavioral elements of their behavior. NGRI patients may experience increased efficacy in lowering anger as they become able to initiate coping strategies when they are aware of themselves and the triggers of their anger.

Other strategies proposed by Deffenbacher include the avoidance of anger-provoking events, distancing one's self emotionally from provocative cues (until one is able to deal more rationally with a problem), and taking time-outs. In addition, relaxation interventions that focus on emotional and physiological arousal may be helpful in training NGRI patients to lower arousal and increase a sense of calmness and control, thereby increasing their overall coping capacity.

Stress-inoculation training has been shown to be a particularly effective method of controlling anger (e.g., Novaco, 1977, 1997; Robins & Novaco, 1999). Novaco's stress-inoculation training program involves teaching patients to monitor anger, to observe its relationship to antecedent cognitions and environmental events, and to control experiences of anger when they arise, including the use of self-instructional techniques (Meichenbaum, 1975, 1977). Outcome studies found this approach to be effective with diverse groups suffering anger problems (Feindler, Marriott, & Iwata, 1984; Nomellini & Katz, 1983; Schlichter & Horan, 1981). Other studies have shown that the reduction of institutional aggression is an obtainable goal with the use of behavioral therapy (Etscheidt, 1991; Rice, Harris, Varney, & Quinsey, 1989; Wong, Slama, & Liberman, 1987; Wong, Woosley, Innocent, & Liberman, 1988).

Rice et al. (1989) outlined several classes of interventions to reduce assaultiveness. These interventions include (a) psychopharmacologic treatment, (b) seclusion and mechanical restraint, (c) behavioral treatment, and (d) staff training. As the authors acknowledge, psychopharmacological treatment and mechanical restraints are unlikely to be successful without other treatments. Within a behavioral paradigm, they recommended that specific consequences be set up for problem behaviors and inpatient reinforcement be arranged for prosocial behaviors that are incompatible with assaultiveness. In addition, they recommended staff training in verbal calming and defusing skills be combined with fair and reasonable management policies. Furthermore, Harris and Rice (1994) have suggested that effective prosocial models enhance the likelihood of improvement among forensic patients.

Problems of assaultiveness, property destruction, possession of weapons, and suicidal threats are extremely important to placement decisions of NGRI patients (Rice et al., 1996). Even the rare occurrence of these behaviors is likely to mean that the patient will not be considered for community discharge. Thus the successful reduction of physical aggression is inevitably a high priority for the patient as well as for proper and safe management of treatment facilities.

NGRI patients diagnosed as ASPD or as psychopathic can pose serious management and risk problems for other patients and staff. Gacono, Meloy, Sheppard, Speth, and Roske (1995) provided data on NGRI patients classified as both psychopathic and malingerers ($n = 18$). They found that this group of NGRI patients, when compared to other NGRI patients, posed numerous problems to staff, including problems with management, sexual intimacy with staff, verbal and physical assaultiveness, illicit drugs, and escape potential.

Rice et al. (1996) suggested the following interventions for APD forensic patients: (a) problem-solving combined with social skills training, (b) moral reasoning, (c) academic programs that emphasize democratic teaching methods with instructors as good role models, (d) contingency management procedures to reduce conflict at work and attitudes toward work, and (e) deliberately contrived opportunities for interactions with prosocial models. For both (c) and (e), they suggested that models be selected because of their interpersonal skills and be trained in how to respond to antisocial comments and rationalizations for law violation.

Monitoring NGRI Patients' Progress in Treatment

Planned monitoring of NGRI patients' treatment progress is crucial to their evaluation and subsequent treatment modifications. Rogers, Harris, and Wasyliw (1983) were the first to assess systematically NGRI patients' progress in treatment. These authors assessed 32 NGRI outpatients in court-mandated treatment for patterns of psychopathology at the Isaac Ray Center. Using the SCL-90 (Derogatis, 1977) and the SADS-C (Spitzer & Endicott, 1978), they compared self-report and interview-based methods and found that the self-report method (SCL-90) elicited greater symptom severity on initial evaluations. In general, they found that NGRI patients manifested mild to moderate severity of psychopathology, with a substantial endorsement of depressive and aggressive symptoms. Given the low frequency of psychotic symptoms and mild-to-moderate impairment, Rogers et al. concluded that the NGRI patients were placed appropriately in outpatient treatment. However, as Rogers et al. observed, the sample was somewhat constrained because five NGRI patients were rehospitalized before data collection was completed, and therefore these patients were dropped from the analyses.

The treatment program at the Isaac Ray Center was comprised of an eclectic, problem-oriented treatment model that incorporates psychopharmacological and psychotherapeutic approaches. The authors assessed the observed psychopathology of the NGRI patient at two specified intervals ($M = 6.6$ months) in their mandatory treatment. They found a moderate degree of similarity between the observed symptoms and the patient's self-report and that most patients remained stable in their psychological impairment. However, three patients demonstrated a marked improvement, two others manifested substantial decompensation in their psychological functioning as rated by the global assessment scale of the SADS-C. Also, marked discrepancies between self-report and interviews were noted for certain symptoms (e.g., depressed feelings, obsessions and compulsions, the experience and expression of anger, agitation, and the severity of delusions). Given the potential relationship between these symptoms and dangerous behavior, such inconsistencies constitute a special concern for treating high-risk NGRI patients.

An obvious conclusion from this study is that multiple sources of data over specific periods of time is extremely useful in the monitoring of NGRI patients. In particular, discrepancies between observed versus self-reported symptoms is relevant to risk assessment among NGRI patients. These data could be further augmented through collateral interviews with family members and significant others within the NGRI patients' immediate environment.

Issues Specifically Related to NGRI Patients

In the section that follows we discuss five treatment-related issues to prepare clinicians for NGRI treatment services. With this special population, psychologists should
be aware of the difficult aspects of treatment that might affect their own perspective
of what constitutes treatment and how outcome should be measured. Furthermore
mental health professionals will need to consider what factors might affect their
patient's perspective of treatment, client-therapist relationship, and outcome.

Security Versus Treatment

A good starting point for addressing treatment issues specifically related to NGRI
patients is to highlight the security versus treatment concern. Both inpatient and
outpatient insanity treatment programs must balance security and compliance issues
with individual treatment needs. Forensic inpatient facilities must emphasize security,
which is characterized as minimizing escape risk and recidivism while ensuring the
safety of patients and staff against the possibility of violent behaviors. The escape
of even one NGRI patient is unacceptable to most forensic facilities, even if no
violence occurs. This zero-tolerance perspective is reinforced by negative media,
further limitations on other NGRI patients, and threats to continued funding for the
treatment program and the facility. As a result, the institutionalized NGRI patient
may experience restricted movement, tight control over emotional expression, and
highly controlled patient-to-patient interactions. In addition, many safety policies
may be imposed as real or symbolic protections.

Outpatient NGRI patients are monitored carefully regarding treatment compliance and possible decompensation. Missed appointments typically fall within the
security concerns and are often interpreted as a need for protective or punitive actions. In this regard, court or review-board sanctions may be imposed because of a
failure to keep outpatient appointments.

Treatment needs of NGRI patients, although important, are addressed only after
security concerns. Clinicians have a professional responsibility to protect both the
NGRI patient and others. An NGRI patient rearrested for a violent offense is likely
to impede any progress in treatment and result in lengthy institutionalization. Although role conflicts arise, the forensic clinician can avert some potential conflicts
by outlining the parameters of the relationship and by clearly explaining how treating
NGRI patients differs from more typical therapist–client relationships. In defining
the NGRI therapeutic relationship, we advocate a written contract of mutual responsibilities *before* beginning treatment.

Psychological Health Versus Stabilization

Traditionally, forensic treatment goals have emphasized attaining therapeutic change
and psychological growth within the individual patient (Cavanaugh, Wasyliw, &
Rogers, 1985; Garfield & Bergin, 1994; Zonana & Norko, 1996). Creating an optimal
therapeutic environment, allowing the development of genuineness, accurate empathy, and positive regard between the clinician and the patient is essential to the

treatment process (Cavanaugh et al., 1985; Garfield & Bergin, 1994). In many cases, the overriding goal is improved functioning with a concomitant reduction of distress.

The treatment of chronically mentally disordered persons has given rise to clinical management as a goal in itself (Cavanaugh et al., 1985; Zonana & Norko, 1996). Interventions with both institutionalized and ambulatory NGRI patients often fall in the category of stabilization rather than continued progress. Clinical management typically takes center stage because of the following factors: (a) limited resources for more active treatment, (b) a lack of intrinsic motivation for change by some NGRI patients, (c) repeated failures of treatment to produce any further improvements, and (d) administrative–legal constraints on treatment. Especially on an outpatient basis, one primary goal of NGRI treatment is stabilization, although we believe that attempts to go beyond this level of treatment are necessary.

Motivation Versus Apathy: Resistance to Treatment

Psychological treatment classically involves an individual who desires change, is aware of internal conflicts, and voluntarily seeks treatment (Cavanaugh et al., 1985; Garfield & Bergin, 1994). Within the forensic system, treatment is imposed on involuntary NGRI patients, who frequently are unwilling participants in the treatment process. Whereas the motivation in traditional psychotherapy is generally internal (e.g., increase self-awareness or reduce stress), NGRI patients understandably are motivated by external issues, such as increased liberty and eventual discharge. The NGRI patient may actively seek treatment because of an awareness that released patients have "demonstrated" to the staff that they had benefited from treatment. Whether such motivation is simply a manipulation of staff is a matter of perspective. We would submit that all persons trapped in an adversarial setting are likely to find methods to extricate themselves. The task for forensic clinicians is to understand and empathize with the various motivations of NGRI patients. Although many mental health professionals may feel uncomfortable with patient perceptions of staff (e.g., jailor or probation officer), understanding their perspectives will facilitate rapport and possible treatment alliance.

Therapists' Negative Feelings and Treatment of the NGRI Patient

The therapist's negative feelings toward violent NGRI patients has received increasing attention (Cavanaugh et al., 1985; Zonana & Norko, 1996). Some index crimes (e.g., a mother's killing of her own children) may evoke strong negative feelings that negates a therapeutic relationship. Although not prevalent in NGRI populations, assaults on clinicians or the perceived risk of such assaults may also impede treatment. Violent patients may elicit severe reactions in the clinician that interfere with treatment. For example, a therapist may be unduly rigid in setting limits and overly cautious in writing reports on a potentially aggressive patient. Conversely, a therapist may not be aware of his or her attempts to appease a violent patient and avoid any confrontation or direct feedback. Thus a difficult aspect of treating NGRI patients is confronting the issues of the patient's dangerousness and the therapist's personal reactions to it (Cavanaugh et al., 1985; Zonana & Norko, 1996). Consulting with colleagues when treating violent patients is likely to be an effective strategy for dealing with this problem (Madden, Lion, & Penna, 1977).

The Agency Problem

Monahan (1980) described agency in terms of a clinician's primary responsibilities and perceived role. In the forensic arena, agency is likely to affect psycholegal opinions and influence the course of treatment (Rogers, 1987). Many clinicians perceive themselves as agents of the court or forensic facility. In these instances, the clinicians' primary responsibility is to further the goals and objectives articulated by these facilities within the framework of ethical practice. Other clinicians will perceive themselves as agents of the patients. Their goals will be to fulfill the patients' needs within the framework of existing legal procedures and ethical practice.

Rogers (1986) argued that agency is likely to have subtle but real influences on how NGRI patients are evaluated. We believe that staff at forensic facilities should discuss openly their position on agency. If possible, a consensus should be achieved and disseminated on how agency is addressed at each facility. We speculate that many professional dilemmas arise from a lack of clarity regarding this issue.

A concrete example of agency problems emerges from confidentiality. In most forensic settings, limits are placed on confidentiality, with reporting relationships preestablished with courts or review boards. The question of how much to divulge regarding a patient's status clearly reflects the issue of agency. Clinicians who perceive themselves as agents of the courts are likely to produce extensive documentation. Those who view themselves as agents of the NGRI patients are more likely to invoke a "need-to-know" position and provide only essential information.

Dangerousness and Discharge

One of the most serious public concerns with regard to the insanity defense has been the real and perceived risks posed by the return of NGRI patients to the community (Tellefsen, Cohen, Silver, & Dougherty, 1992). This concern has presented numerous problems for mental health professionals. "Solutions" have included both increased security and longer periods of institutionalization as sincere efforts for protecting society. However, outcome studies, such as Baxstrom (e.g., Steadman & Cocozza, 1974), suggest that this concentration on security is sometimes unwarranted. Patients involuntarily placed in maximum-security facilities posed little risk when released by court order to less secure facilities and the community (Steadman & Cocozza, 1974). Nevertheless, risk assessment will and should continue to be an important component of NGRI patients' readiness to return to the community.

Two new measures of risk assessment for forensic patients were recently developed. Rice (1997) outlined how violence research could be used to make better predictions with regard to the dangerousness of NGRI patients, thereby increasing public safety. Rice described the Violence Risk Assessment Guide (VRAG) that performed well at predicting violent criminal behavior among male NGRI patients who previously had committed a violent crime. Based on two cross validations, Rice concluded that the VRAG's performance was robust across different follow-up periods. She surmised that use of the VRAG would lead to fewer new victims and fewer new violent crimes. In addition, a second measure of dangerousness, the HCR-20, was developed for risk assessments with forensic patients. Although validation studies are ongoing, the preliminary results appear promising (Webster, Douglas, Eaves, & Hart, 1997).

Rice suggested that violent recidivism among mentally disordered offenders is related to the same variables as found among nonmentally disordered offenders. Rice and her colleagues have shown that psychopathy is associated with a moderate likelihood of future violence. In a meta-analysis conducted by Salekin et al. (1996) psychopathy was shown to be a moderate predictor of violent recidivism. Although psychopathy is rarely considered a mental disorder for purposes of insanity acquittal, some NGRI patients who have committed a violent offense warrant this classification (Rice et al., 1990). The empirical data strongly suggest that violent recidivism would be reduced, and public safety thereby enhanced, by release decisions based on risk of future violence. It is important to note that preliminary data suggests that psychopathy may be less predictive among female psychopaths than their male counterparts (Salekin, Rogers, Ustad, & Sewell, 1998).

Cohen, Spodak, Silver, and Williams (1988) examined the adjustment of NGRI patients who were released into the community. Based on both actuarial and clinical predictors, a model for forensic release decisions was derived from data on 127 NGRI patients, a matched control of 127 convicted felons, and a comparison group of 135 mentally disordered prison transfer patients. These authors measured two outcome indicators: (a) rearrests within five years after release and (b) overall functioning in the community during a two and one half year period after release.

The first discriminant analysis accurately predicted 75% of those rearrested using the following six variables: adjustment in hospital, clinical assessment of hospital staff, Global Assessed Scale score at release, functioning before their offense, heroin addiction, and birth order. A second discriminant function analysis identified seven variables that accurately predicted the overall functioning of 80.4% of the NGRI patients. Variables associated with successful outcome after release differed between the NGRI and prison groups. The two discriminant analyses illustrated that statistical models can combine actuarial, clinical, and criminological data to determine the likelihood of success after release for NGRI patients. Several variables evidenced utility in determining release readiness, including adjustment in the hospital, clinical assessment of patient involvement, Global Assessed Scale score at release, and functioning before their offense. The first three variables related to the patient's progress at the hospital. Other variables (i.e., marital status, severity of offense, working before hospitalization, birth order, and heroin addiction) also predicted outcome but were not related to patient stay.

Eisner (1989) developed a specialized measure to determine the readiness of NGRI patients to return to the community. The instrument is designed to assess the patient's disorder, behavior, and medication. In addition, it focuses on the NGRI patients' acknowledgement of mental disorder and of criminal behavior and acceptance of treatment. Although this measure appears to assess relevant components regarding readiness of NGRI patients to be released, it has not been formally tested. Therefore the measure is of little use at this point since there is no empirical foundation to base decisions on (Rogers & Salekin, 1998).

Reforms in the Locus of Treatment

Two of the major reforms that have been enacted attempt to make significant changes in the locus of treatment. The GBMI alternative would place more people in state prisons in which mental health services would be mandated. The Oregon approach using a Psychiatric Security Review Board (PSRB) tends to emphasize outpatient treatment after inpatient treatment.

In 1975, Michigan was the first state to enact a GBMI verdict, with its primary goal being to decrease the number of insanity acquittals (Steadman, 1985). Michigan legislators hoped to use the new verdict to prevent the early release of dangerous NGRI patients by offering Michigan juries a substitute for the insanity verdict (Smith & Hall, 1982). Following the GBMI determination, a sentence is imposed and the defendant is committed to prison, where he or she is to be provided treatment by either corrections or mental health professionals when psychiatrically indicated. In practice, this statute changes the locus of control for treatment from the mental hospital to the prison. In fact, the new verdict has failed in its intended purpose (Smith & Hall, 1982; Steadman, 1985): The volume of NGRI cases has remained comparable to pre-GBMI levels. In effect, what has been created is simply another class of offenders for whom mental health treatment is mandated. The GBMI group tends to resemble the inmates more than NGRI patients, especially with more sex-related offenses, which are rarely found in NGRI populations (Smith & Hall, 1982).

Perlin (1996) argued that GBMI statutes do little to ensure effective treatment for offenders with mental disabilities. The director of the state correctional or mental health facility is mandated to provide a GBMI inmate with such treatment as he or she "determines necessary"; however, the GBMI inmate is not ensured treatment "beyond that available to other offenders" (Slobogin, 1985, p. 513). One comprehensive study of the GBMI verdict in Georgia revealed that only 3 of the 150 GBMI defendants were being treated in hospitals (Steadman et al., 1993, p. 195).

The Oregon program developed an independent review board that would balance the treatment needs of NGRI patients with community protection. The major innovation in this approach was to remove decisions of release away from both the criminal courts and the treating staff for the release and monitoring of NGRI patients. Oregon's reform attempted to shift the locus of treatment to the community.

Rogers and Bloom (1982) suggested that the program may have effected a change in locus of treatment with many benefits and few costs. For one cohort of NGRI patients studied, the mean length of hospitalization before conditional release under the review board's jurisdiction was 363 days. This number is substantially less than the 670 days for NGRI patients in New York (Steadman, 1985). However, the New York patients tended to have more serious offenses, and in both Oregon and New York states, length of hospitalization was related to seriousness of criminal offense.

Conclusions

Despite its importance, treating NGRI patients has been a relatively unresearched and undeveloped facet of forensic psychology. Necessary security constraints often impede the optimal treatment of NGRI patients. Although treatment of NGRI patients has tended to be generic, we have advocated greater attention to individualized needs and specific treatment interventions. Empirical reviews of NGRI patient data confirm commonly held diagnostic perceptions. Most NGRI patients have severe mental disorders with psychosis featured prominently. Alcohol and drug abuse are very common as secondary diagnoses that substantially complicate treatment. It is surprising to note that small but appreciable numbers were found insane without an Axis I disorder, at least at the time of their postacquittal admission to forensic facilities.

Treatment programs must target the specific symptoms and needs of individual NGRI patients. Of special concern is identifying symptoms and associated features that signal possible decompensation or recidivism. In this context, four basic goals were proposed: (a) diagnose and treat the mental disorder, (b) reduce the risk of dangerousness, (c) prepare the NGRI patients for discharge, and (d) monitor their adjustments in the community.

Two recurring themes in this chapter must be considered in NGRI patient treatment: individualization and balancing. As previously noted, individualization reflects on the basic need to augment actuarial data with specific characteristics of particular NGRI patients that predict both treatment success as well as failure. Balancing reflects the equilibristic efforts presented by conflicting forces from the criminal justice and mental health systems, public concerns, and patient needs.

References

American Bar Association Criminal Justice and Mental Health Division. (1989). *American Bar Association Criminal Justice and Mental Health Standards*. Washington, DC: Author.

Ayllon, T., & Milan, M. A. (1979). *Correctional rehabilitation and management: A psychological approach*. Chichester, England: Wiley.

Barlow, D. H. (1988). *Anxiety and its disorders: The nature and treatment of anxiety and panic*. New York: Guilford Press.

Beck, A. T., Rush, A. J., Shaw, B. F., & Emery, G. (1979). *Cognitive therapy of depression*. New York: Guilford Press.

Benton, M. K., & Schroeder, H. E. (1990). Social skills training with schizophrenics: A meta-analytic evaluation. *Journal of Consulting and Clinical Psychology, 58*, 741–747.

Bezchlibnyk-Butler, K. Z., & Jeffries, J. J. (1996). *Clinical handbook of psychotropic drugs*. Toronto: Hogrefe & Huber.

Bogenberger, R. P., Pasewark, R. A., Gudeman, H., & Beiber, S. L. (1987). Follow-up of insanity acquittees in Hawaii. *International Journal of Law and Psychiatry, 10*, 283–295.

Borkovec, T. D., & Mathews, A. (1988). Treatment of nonphobic anxiety disorders: A comparison of nondirective, cognitive, and coping desensitization therapy. *Journal of Consulting and Clinical Psychology, 56*, 877–884.

Borkovec, T. D., & Roemer, L. (1994). Generalized anxiety disorder. In M. Hersen & R. T. Ammerman (Eds.), *Handbook of prescriptive treatments for adults* (pp. 261–281). New York: Plenum Press.

Borkovec, T. D., & Whisman, M. A. (1996). Psychosocial treatment for generalized anxiety disorder. In M. Marissakalian & R. E. Prien (Eds.), *Long-term treatment of anxiety disorders* (pp. 171–199). Washington, DC: American Psychiatric Association.

Breier, A., & Strauss, J. S. (1983). Self control in psychotic disorders. *Archives of General Psychiatry, 40*, 1141–1145.

Breslin, N. A. (1992). Treatment of schizophrenia: Current practice and future promise. *Hospital and Community Psychiatry, 43*, 877–885.

Callahan, L. A., Steadman, H. J., McGreevy, M. A., & Robbins, P. C. (1991). The volume and characteristics of insanity defense pleas: An eight-state study. *Bulletin of the American Academy of Psychiatry and Law, 19,* 331–338.

Cavanaugh, J. L., Wasyliw, O. E., & Rogers, R. (1985). Treatment of mentally disordered offenders. In J. O. Cavenar (Ed.), *Psychiatry* (pp. 1–27). Philadelphia: J.B. Lippincott.

Chambless, D., & Goldstein, A. (1980). The treatment of agoraphobia. In A. Goldstein & E. B. Foa (Eds.), *Handbook of behavioral interventions: A clinical guide* (pp. 332–415). New York: Wiley.

Citrome, L., & Volavka, J. (2000). Management of violence in schizophrenia. *Psychiatric Annals, 30,* 41–52.

Cohen, M. I., Spodak, M. K., Silver, S. B., & Williams, K. (1988). Predicting outcome of NGRI patients released to the community. *Behavioral Sciences and the Law, 6,* 515–530.

Cooke, G., & Sikorski, C. R. (1974). Factors affecting length of hospitalization in persons adjudicated not guilty by reason of insanity. *Bulletin of the American Academy of Psychiatry and Law, 8,* 251–261.

Corrigan, P. W. (1991). Social skills training in adult psychiatric populations: A meta-analysis. *Journal of Behavior Therapy and Experimental Psychiatry, 22,* 203–210.

Criss, M. L., & Racine, D. R. (1980). Impact of change in legal standard for those adjudicated not guilty by reason of insanity 1975–1979. *Bulletin of the American Academy of Psychiatry and Law, 8,* 261–271.

Dalal, B., Larkin, E., Leese, M., & Taylor, P. J. (1999). Clozapine treatment of long-standing schizophrenia and serious violence: A two-year follow-up study of the first 50 patients treated with clozapine in Rampton high security hospital. *Criminal Behaviour and Mental Health, 9,* 168–178.

Deffenbacher, J. L. (1999). Cognitive–behavioral conceptualization and treatment of anger. *Journal of Clinical Psychology, 55,* 295–309.

Derogatis, L. R. (1977). *The SCL-90, R Version manual: Scoring administration and procedures for the SCL-90.* Baltimore: Johns Hopkins University Press.

Dimeff, L. A., & Marlatt, G. A. (1995). Relapse prevention. In R. K. Hester & W. R. Miller (Eds.), *Handbook of alcoholism treatment approaches: Effective alternatives* (pp. 176–194). Toronto: Allyn & Bacon.

Eisner, H. R. (1989). Returning the not guilty by reason of insanity to the community: A new scale to determine readiness. *Bulletin of the American Academy of Psychiatry and Law, 17,* 401–403.

Elkin, I., Shea, M. T., Watkins, J. T., Imber, S. D., Sotsky, S. M., Collins, J. F., Glass, D. R., Pilkonis, P. A., Leber, W. R., Docherty, J. P., Fiester, S. J., & Parloff, M. B. (1989). NIMH treatment of depression collaborative research program: 1. General effectiveness of treatments. *Archives of General Psychiatry, 46,* 971–983.

Etscheidt, S. (1991). Reducing aggressive behavior and improving self-control: A cognitive–behavioral training program for behaviorally disordered adolescents. *Behavioral Disorders, 16,* 107–115.

Feindler, E. L., Marriott, S. A., & Iwata, M. (1984). Group anger control training for high school delinquents. *Cognitive Therapy and Research, 8,* 299–399.

Fink, M. (1987). Convulsive therapy in affective disorders: A decade of understanding and acceptance. In H. Y. Metzler (Ed.), *Psychopharmacology: The third generation of progress* (pp. 1071–1076). New York: Plenum Press.

Foa, E. B., & Tillmanns, A. (1980). The treatment of obsessive-compulsive neurosis. In A. Goldstein & E. B. Foa (Eds.), *Handbook of behavioral interventions: A clinical guide* (pp. 416–500). New York: Wiley.

Foa, E. B., Wilson, R., Foa, E. B., & Barlow, D. H. (1991). *Stop obsessing! How to overcome your obsessions and compulsions.* New York: Bantam Books.

Frazer, A. (1994). Antidepressant drugs. *Depression, 2,* 1–19.

Furman, W., Geller, M., Simon, S. J., & Kelly, J. A. (1979). The use of a behavioral rehearsal procedure for teaching job interviewing skills to psychiatric patients. *Behavior Therapy, 10,* 157–167.

Fyer, A. J., Mannuzza, S., & Endicott, J. (1987). Differential diagnosis and assessment of anxiety: Recent developments. In H. Y. Meltzer (Ed.), *Psychopharmacology: The third generation of progress* (pp. 1177–1191). New York: Raven.

Gacono, G. B., Meloy, J. R., Sheppard, K., Speth, E., & Roske, A. (1995). A clinical investigation of malingering and psychopathy in hospitalized NGRI patients. *Bulletin of the American Academy of Psychiatry and Law, 23,* 387–397.

Garfield, S. L., & Bergin, A. E. (1994). *Handbook of psychotherapy and behavior change* (3rd ed.). New York: John Wiley.

German, J. R., & Singer, A. C. (1976). Punishing the not guilty: Hospitalization of persons acquitted by reason of insanity. *Rutgers Law Review, 29,* 1011–1083.

Gerner, R. H., & Stanton, A. (1992). Algorithm for patient management of acute manic states: Lithium, Valproate, or Carbamazepine? *Journal of Clinical Psychopharmacology, 12,* 57–63.

Greenland, C. (1979). Crime and the insanity defense, an international comparison: Ontario and New York state. *Bulletin of the American Academy of Psychiatry and Law, 7,* 125–137.

Hambridge, J. A. (1990). The grief process in those admitted to regional secure units following homicide. *Journal of Forensic Sciences, 35,* 1149–1154.

Hans, V. P. (1986). An analysis of public attitudes toward the insanity defense. *Criminology, 4,* 393–415.

Harris, G. T., & Rice, M. E. (1994). The violent patient. In R. T. Ammerman & M. Hersen (Eds.), *Handbook of prescriptive treatments for adults* (pp. 463–486). New York: Plenum Press.

Heilbrun, K., Griffin-Heilbrun, P. G., & Griffin, N. (1988). Comparing females acquitted by reason of insanity, convicted, and civilly committed in Florida: 1977:1984. *Law and Human Behavior, 12,* 295–311.

Hodgins, S., Hebert, J., & Baraldi, R. (1986). Women declared insane: A follow-up study. *International Journal of Law and Psychiatry, 8,* 203–216.

Jacobson, E. (1986). The early history of psychotherapeutic drugs. *Psychopharmacology, 89,* 138–144.

Kane, J. M., & Freeman, H. L. (1994). Towards more effective antipsychotic treatment. *British Journal of Psychiatry, 165,* 22–31.

Kelly, J. A., Laughlin, C., Clairborne, M., & Patterson, J. (1979). A group procedure for teaching job interviewing skills to formerly hospitalized psychiatric patients. *Behavior Therapy, 10,* 299–310.

Kobak, K. A., Greist, J. H., Jefferson, J. W., Katzelnick, D. J., & Henk, H. J. (1998). Behavioral versus pharmacological treatments of obsessive compulsive disorder: A meta-analysis. *Psychopharmacology, 136,* 205–216.

Linehan, M. M. (1993). *Cognitive-behavioral treatment of borderline personality disorder.* New York: Guilford Press.

Linhorst, D. M., & Dirks-Linhorst, P. A. (1997). The impact of insanity acquittees on Missouri's public mental health system. *Law and Human Behavior, 21,* 327–338.

Lowe, C. F., & Chadwick, P. D. (1990). Verbal control of delusions. *Behavior Therapy, 21,* 461–479.

Madden, D. J., Lion, J. R., & Penna, M. W. (1977). Assaults on psychiatrists by patients. *American Journal of Psychiatry, 133,* 422–429.

Meichenbaum, D. (1975). Self-instructional methods. In F. Kanfer & A. Goldstein (Eds.), *Helping people change.* New York: Pergamon Press.

Meichenbaum, D. (1977). *Cognitive-behavioral modification: An integrative approach*. New York: Plenum Press.

Milan, M. A., (1987). Token economy programs in closed institutions. In E. K. Morris & C. J. Braukmann (Eds.), *Behavioral approaches to crime and delinquency: A handbook of application, research, and concepts* (pp. 195–222). New York: Plenum Press.

Miller, W. R. (1982). Treating problem drinkers: What works? *The Behavior Therapist, 5,* 15–18.

Monahan, J. (1980). *Who is the client? The ethics of psychological intervention in the criminal justice system*. Washington, DC: American Psychological Association.

Moncrieff, J., & Drummond, D. C. (1997). New pharmacologic treatments for alcohol abusers. *Addiction, 92,* 939–947.

Morrow, W. R., & Petersen, D. B. (1966). Follow-up on discharged offenders—"Not Guilty by Reason of Insanity" and "Criminal Sexual Psychopaths." *Journal of Criminal Law, Criminology & Police Science, 57,* 31–34.

Mueser, K. T., Levine, S., Bellak, A. S., Douglas, M. S., & Brady, E. U. (1990). Social skills training for acute psychiatric inpatients. *Hospital and Community Psychiatry, 41,* 1249–1250.

Nelson, J. C. (1997, February). *Recently marketed antidepressants*. Paper presented at the ASCP President's Day weekend meeting, Barbados.

Nietzel, M. T., & Bernstein, D. A. (1981). Assessment of anxiety and fear. In M. Hersen & A. S. Bellack (Eds.), *Behavioral assessment: A practical handbook* (2nd ed., pp. 135–147). New York: Pergamon Press.

Nomellini, S., & Katz, R. C. (1983). Effects of anger control training on abusive patients. *Cognitive Research and Therapy, 7,* 57–67.

Norwood, S., Nicholson, R. A., Enyart, C., & Hickey, M. L. (1991). Characteristics and outcomes of NGRI patients in Oklahoma. *Behavioral Sciences and the Law, 9,* 487–500.

Novaco, R. W. (1977). Stress innoculation: A cognitive therapy for anger and its application to a case of depression. *Journal of Consulting and Clinical Psychology, 45,* 600–608.

Novaco, R. W. (1994). Anger as a risk factor for violence among the mentally disordered. In J. Monahan & H. J. Steadman (Eds.), *Violence and mental disorder* (pp. 21–60). Chicago: University of Chicago Press.

Novaco, R. W. (1997). Remediating anger and aggression with violent offenders. *Legal and Criminological Psychology, 2,* 77–88.

Ogloff, J. R. P. (1991). A comparison of insanity defense standards on juror decision making. *Law and Human Behavior, 15,* 509–521.

Ogloff, J. R. P., Schweighofer, A., Turnbull, S. D., & Whittemore, K. (1992). In J. R. P. Ogloff (Ed.), *Law and psychology: The broadening of the discipline* (pp. 171–207). Durham, NC: Carolina Academic Press.

Ost, L-G. (1987). Applied relaxation: Description of a coping technique and review of controlled studies. *Behavioral Research and Therapy, 25,* 397–409.

Pasewark, R. A., Jeffrey, R., & Bieber, S. (1987). Differentiating successful and unsuccessful insanity pleas defendants in Colorado. *Journal of Psychiatry and Law, 15,* 55–71.

Paul, G. L., & Lentz, R. J. (1977). *Psychosocial treatment of chronic mental patients: Milieu versus social learning programs*. Cambridge, MA: Harvard University Press.

Peckham, J., & Muller, J. (1999). Employment and schizophrenia: Recommendations to improve employability for individuals with schizophrenia. *Psychiatric Rehabilitation Journal, 22,* 399–402.

Perlin, M. L. (1996). The insanity defense: Deconstructing the myths and reconstructing the jurisprudence. In B. D. Sales & D. W. Shuman (Eds.), *Law, mental health, and mental disorder*. Pacific Grove, CA: Brooks/Cole.

Persons, J. B. (1989). *Cognitive therapy in practice: A case formulation approach*. New York: W. W. Norton.

Petrila, J. (1982). The insanity defense and other mental health dispositions in Missouri. *International Journal of Law and Psychiatry, 5,* 81–101.

Phillips, B. L., & Pasewark, R. A. (1980). Insanity plea in Connecticut. *Bulletin of the American Academy of Psychiatry and Law, 8,* 325–344.

Pickar, D., Owen, R. R., Litman, R. E., Konicki, E., Gutierrez, R., & Rapaport, M. H. (1992). Clinical and biological response to clozapine in patients with schizophrenia. *Archives of General Psychiatry, 49,* 345–353.

Quinsey, V. L. (1988). Assessments of the treatability of forensic patients. *Behavioral Sciences and the Law, 6,* 443–452.

Rice, M. E. (1997). Violent offender research and implications for the criminal justice system. *American Psychologist, 52,* 414–423.

Rice, M. E., & Harris, G. T. (1990). The predictors of insanity acquittal. *International Journal of Law and Psychiatry, 13,* 217–224.

Rice, M. E., Harris, G. T & Quinsey, V. L. (1996). Treatment of forensic patients. In B. D. Sales & S. A. Shah (Eds.), *Mental health and law: Research, policy and services* (pp. 141–189). Durham, NC: Carolina Academic Press.

Rice, M. E., Harris, G. T., Quinsey, V. L., & Cyr, M. (1990). Planning treatment programs in secure psychiatric facilities. In D. Weisstub (Ed.), *Law and mental health: International perspectives* (pp. 162–230). New York: Pergamon Press.

Rice, M. E., Harris, G. T., Varney, G. W., & Quinsey, V. L. (1989). *Violence in institutions: Understanding, prevention, and control.* Toronto: Hans Huber.

Richelson, E. (1996). Preclinical pharmacology of neuroleptics: Focus on new generation compounds. *Journal of Clinical Psychiatry, 57,* 4–11.

Robins, S., & Novaco, R. W. (1999). Systems conceptualization and treatment of anger. *Journal of Clinical Psychology, 55,* 325–337.

Rogers, J. L., & Bloom, J. D. (1982). Characteristics of persons committed to Oregon's Psychiatric Security Review. *Bulletin of the American Academy of Psychiatry and the Law, 10,* 15–164.

Rogers, R. (1986). *Conducting insanity evaluations.* New York: Van Nostrand Reinhold.

Rogers, R. (1987). Ethical dilemmas in forensic evaluations. *Behavioral Sciences and the Law, 5,* 149–160.

Rogers, R., Harris, M., & Wasyliw, O. E. (1983). Observed and self-reported psychopathology in NGRI acquittees in court-mandated outpatient treatment. *International Journal of Offender Therapy and Comparative Criminology, 27,* 143–149.

Rogers, R., & Salekin, R. T. (1998). Beguiled by Bayes: A reanalysis of Mossman and Hart's estimates of malingering. *Behavioral Sciences and the Law, 16,* 147–153.

Rogers, R., Seman, W., & Clark, C. C. (1986). Assessment of criminal responsibility: Initial validation of the R-CRAS with the M'Naghten and GBMI standards. *International Journal of Law and Psychiatry, 9,* 67–75.

Rogers, R., & Wettstein, R. M. (1985). Relapse in NGRI outpatients: An empirical study. *Journal of Offender Therapy, 29,* 227–236.

Ross, R. R., & Lightfoot, L. O. (1985). *Treatment of the alcohol-abusing offender.* Springfield, IL: Thomas.

Salekin, R. T., Rogers, R., & Sewell, K. W. (1996). A review and meta-analysis of the Psychopathy Checklist and Psychopathy Checklist—Revised: Predictive validity. *Clinical Psychology: Science and Practice, 3,* 203–315.

Salekin, R. T., Rogers, R., & Sewell, K. W. (1997). Construct validity of psychopathy in a female offender sample: A multitrait-multimethod evaluation. *Journal of Abnormal Psychology, 106,* 576–585.

Salekin, R. T., Rogers, R., Ustad, K. L., & Sewell, K. W. (1998). Psychopathy and recidivism: Generalizing across genders. *Law and Human Behavior, 22,* 109–128.

Satterfield, J. M. (1999). Adjunctive cognitive-behavioral therapy for rapid-cycling bipolar disorder: An empirical case study. *Psychiatry: Interpersonal and Biological Processes, 62,* 357–369.

Schlichter, K. J., & Horan, J. J. (1981). Effects of stress inoculation on the anger and aggression management of institutionalized juvenile delinquents. *Cognitive Therapy and Research, 5,* 359–369.

Scott, J., Williams, J. M. G., & Beck, A. T. (1995). *Cognitive therapy in clinical practice: An illustrative casebook.* New York: Routledge.

Seig, A., Ball, E., & Menninger, J. A. (1995). A comparison of female versus male insanity acquittees in Colorado. *Bulletin of the American Academy of Psychiatry and Law, 23,* 523–532.

Shady, G. A., & Kue, S. G. (1977). Preparing the hardcore disadvantaged for employment: Social skills orientation course—An evaluation. *Canadian Journal of Criminology and Corrections, 19,* 303–309.

Shah, P. J., Greenberg, W. M., & Convit, A. (1994). Hospitalized insanity acquittees' level of functioning. *Bulletin of the American Academy of Psychiatry and Law, 22,* 85–93.

Silver, E. (1995). Punishment or treatment: Comparing the lengths of confinement of successful and unsuccessful insanity defendants. *Law and Human Behavior, 19,* 375–388.

Silver, E., Cirincione, C., & Steadman, H. J. (1994). Demythologizing inaccurate perceptions of the insanity defense. *Law and Human Behavior, 18,* 63–70.

Silver, S. B., Cohen, M. I., & Spodiak, M. K. (1989). Follow-up after release of insanity acquittees, mentally disordered offenders, and convicted felons. *Bulletin of the American Academy of Psychiatry and Law, 17,* 387–400.

Silverman, W. K., Kurtines, W. M., Ginsburg, G. S., Weems, C. F., Rabian, B., & Serafini, L. T. (1999). *Journal of Consulting and Clinical Psychology, 67,* 675–687.

Slobogin, C. (1985). A rational approach to responsibility. *Michigan Law Review, 83,* 513–620.

Smith, G., & Hall, J. (1982). Evaluating Michigan's guilty but mentally ill verdict: An empirical study. *University of Michigan Journal of Law Reform, 16,* 77–114.

Spitzer, R. L., & Endicott, J. (1978). *Schedule of Affective Disorders and Schizophrenia-Change Version (SADS-C).* New York: Biometrics Research.

Stacy, A. W. (1997). Memory activation and expectancy as prospective predictors of alcohol and marijuana use. *Journal of Abnormal Psychology, 106,* 61–73.

Steadman, H. J. (1980). Insanity acquittals in New York state, 1965–1978. *American Journal of Psychiatry, 137,* 321–326.

Steadman, H. J. (1985). Insanity defense research and treatment of NGRI patients. *Behavioral Sciences and the Law, 3,* 37–48.

Steadman, H. J., & Cocozza, J. J. (1974). *Careers of the criminally insane.* Lexington, MA: Lexington Books.

Steadman, H. J., Keitner, L., Braff, J., & Arvanites, T. M. (1983). Factors associated with a successful insanity plea. *American Journal of Psychiatry, 140,* 401–405.

Steadman, H. J., McGreevy, M. A., Morrissey, J. P., Callahan, L. A., Robbins, P. C., & Cirincione, C. (1993). *Before and after Hinckley: Evaluating the insanity defense reform.* New York: Guilford Press.

Steadman, H. J., Monahan, J., Hartstone, E., Kantorowski-Davis, S., & Robbins, P. C. (1982). Mentally disordered offenders: A national survey of patients and facilities. *Law and Human Behavior, 6,* 31–38.

Steadman, H. J., Pasewark, R. A., Hawkins, M., Kiser, M., & Bieber, S. (1983). Hospitalization length of NGRI patients. *Journal of Clinical Psychology, 39,* 611–614.

Suinn, R. M. (1990). *Anxiety management training.* New York: Plenum Press.

Szasz, T. S. (1963). *Law, liberty, and psychiatry.* New York: MacMillan.

Tellefsen, C., Cohen, M. I., Silver, S. B., & Dougherty, C. (1992). Predicting success on conditional release for NGRI patients: Regionalized versus nonregionalized hospital patients. *Bulletin of the American Academy of Psychiatry and Law, 20,* 87–99.

Turner, S. M. (1984). *Behavioral theories and treatment of anxiety.* New York. Plenum Press.

Twentyman, C. T., Jensen, M., & Kloss, J. D. (1978). Social skills training for the complex offender: Employment seeking skills. *Journal of Clinical Psychology, 34,* 320–326.

Volavka, J., & Citrome, L. (1999). Atypical antipsychotics in the treatment of the persistently aggressive psychotic patient: Methodological concerns. *Schizophrenia Research, 35 Supplement,* 23–33.

Webster, C. D., Douglas, K., Eaves, D., & Hart, S. D. (1997). *The HCR-20 Scheme: The assessment of dangerousness and risk.* Burnaby, British Columbia, Canada: Simon Fraser University.

Weissman, M. M. (1994). Psychotherapy in the maintenance treatment of depression. *British Journal of Psychiatry, 165,* 42–50.

Wettstein, R. M., & Mulvey, E. (1988). Disposition of insanity acquittees in Illinois. *Bulletin of the American Academy of Psychiatry and the Law, 16,* 11–24.

Wettstein, R. M., Mulvey, E., & Rogers, R. (1991). Insanity defense standards: A prospective comparison. *American Journal of Psychiatry, 148,* 21–27.

Wolpe, J. (1990). *The practice of behavior therapy.* New York: Pergamon Press.

Wong, S. E., Slama, K. M., & Liberman, R. P. (1987). Behavioral analysis and therapy for aggressive psychiatric and developmentally disabled patients. In L. H. Roth (Ed.), *Clinical treatment of the violent person* (pp. 20–53). New York: Guilford Press.

Wong, S. E., Woosley, J. E., Innocent, A. J., & Liberman, R. P. (1988). Behavioral treatment of violent psychiatric patients. *Psychiatric Clinics of North America, 11,* 569–579.

Zaretsky, A. E., Segal, Z. V., & Gemar, M. (1999). Cognitive therapy for bipolar depression: A pilot study. *Canadian Journal of Psychiatry, 44,* 491–494.

Zonana, H., Bartel, R. L., Wells, J. A., Buchanan, J. A., & Getz, M. A. (1990). Part II: Sex differences in persons found not guilty by reason of insanity: Analysis of data from the Connecticut NGRI registry. *Bulletin of the American Academy of Psychiatry and Law, 18,* 129–142.

Zonana, H., & Norko, M. A. (1996). Mandated treatment. In W. Sledge and A. Tasman (Eds.), *Clinical challenges in psychiatry* (pp. 249–291). Washington, DC: American Psychiatric Press.

Part III

Treating Developmentally and Learning Disabled Offenders

Chapter 7
TREATMENT AND CARE FOR OFFENDERS WITH MENTAL RETARDATION

Kenneth Day and Thomas Berney

There are adult and juvenile offenders who have a full scale IQ of less than 70 (a score that equates to two standard deviations from the mean of normal distribution) and who broadly fulfill the criteria for mental retardation in the two major systems of classification, *DSM-IV* and *ICD-10*. Mental retardation, however, invariably involves more than a simple cognitive impairment. Additional definitive criteria include adaptive behavior, social functioning, the level of emotional maturity, and the presence of other disabilities (most notably communication). Some with an IQ in the borderline range of 70 to 85 may find their needs better met within mental retardation services, whereas others of similar ability may find the mainstream services, for persons of normal intelligence, more suitable. The most important determining factor is the pattern of need of that individual at that time.

Mentally retarded offenders share many features in common with nonretarded offenders but they differ significantly from other mentally disordered offenders (Robertson, 1981). The typical offender with mental retardation is a youth or young male of mild to borderline intelligence. A high percentage show evidence of sociopathy or other personality disorders (Day, 1993).

Although there is also a relationship between mental retardation, epilepsy, and aggression, it is not straightforward (Creaby, Warner, Jamil, & Jawad, 1993) or closely linked with criminality. Indeed, studies have failed to demonstrate any significant association (Deb & Hunter, 1991; Lund, 1990; Richardson, Koller, & Katz, 1985), although in some mentally retarded offenders, epilepsy can be an important, unrecognized, treatable contributory factor (Milne & O'Brien, 1997).

The mentally retarded offender's background is often characterized by a poor urban environment and a family of limited ability. He is likely to have suffered significant psychosocial deprivation, to have exhibited a range of behavioral problems during childhood and adolescence, and to have spent substantial periods in some form of residential care or schooling (Day, 1988, 1995; Lund, 1990; Richardson et al., 1985). Within his home there will have been little to offset his disability to help him develop a protective degree of self-esteem, or any occupational or recreational framework to fill his time. The greater degree of everyday dependency, the need for continuing care and supervision, and the difficulty in achieving an occupational role or any measure of success all combine to hinder and distort the process of individuation. The mentally retarded adolescent has difficulty in attaining a place in a normal peer-group and becomes the willing follower of a more able, delinquent gang or of criminal family members, ready to be used by them and to accept "dares" in a search for status or acceptance (Day, 1990a). The mentally retarded adolescent's ineptness then makes him or her the most likely to be caught. The majority of mentally retarded adult offenders are first convicted in their teenage years, and there is a clear and significant link between unstable upbringing and a history of behavior disturbance in childhood and subsequent offending behavior (Lund, 1990; Richardson et al., 1985).

Under-socialization, poor internal controls, and faulty social learning are frequently compounded by educational underachievement, poor social and occupational skills, and low self-esteem (Day, 1990a). Minor physical disabilities, which may identify the individual, will reduce his self-confidence and impair his social integration (Day, 1990a). Although a study of adolescents with mental retardation in secure provision found them to be particularly weak on the communication and socialization domains of the Vineland Adaptive Behavior Scale, this finding applied also to those of normal ability. However, compared with their normal peers, they were more likely to be disciplined for poor hygiene, a failure to follow rules, and assaults both on other inmates and on staff; suicidal acts and ideation were less frequent (Hall & Bernal, 1995; Smith, Algozzine, Schmid, & Hennly, 1990).

An unexpected and spontaneously violent temperament may have its roots in a behavioral phenotype. Some argue that an autistic spectrum disorder might partially explain such violence—one example is Asperger's syndrome, characterized by a normal ability and fluent syntactical speech but with an "active-but-odd" style of social relationship (Mawson, Grounds, & Tantam, 1985; Wing, 1991). Unfortunately, the debate is based on insufficient information and confounded by conflicting definitions of the autistic spectrum disorders. Where violence does arise, it is from a variety of causes that reflect poor communication, interference with an obsession, a sense of being threatened, a misapprehension of normal limits or behavior, egocentrism, and a concretely simple social logic (Baron-Cohen, 1988). For example, in cases known to the authors, the use of a literal, fairy-tale logic is frequent, leading to a disproportionate response, oblivious to the serious nature of an action. For example, setting fire to a house was the natural way to stop the use of satellite television for one patient; stabbing became the first response to discourage a boyfriend's unwanted intimacy in another; and assisted suicide was a solution to social difficulty for a third. In addition, there can be the complete handing over of responsibility to others: "If I kill myself, it'll be your fault because you didn't. . . ." The absence of systematic studies puts an undue weight on such individual examples.

Finally, heightened irritability may simply be the result of physical or psychiatric disorder or the adverse effect of concomitant medication. Although this applies across the whole field of mental retardation, these factors are less readily recognized in autism because of the unusual responses and limited communication.

An association between mental retardation, criminality, and additional sex chromosomes (both X and Y), first suspected in the 1960s, remains far from proven. Although retrospective and prospective studies have confirmed an above average height, conflicting results have been found in relation to cognitive skills, behavior problems, and offending behavior (Day, 1993). There is no evidence to suggest that offending behavior has a higher prevalence in the Fragile X syndrome; instead social anxiety is the predominant characteristic.

The rest of this chapter will review specific offender types within the mentally retarded offender population, explore identification and assessment issues of concern when working with mentally retarded offenders, review treatment modalities, and consider other important treatment issues. The chapter concludes with a discussion of future research needs.

Characteristics of Specific Types of Offender

Female offenders are unusual and invariably grossly disturbed individuals who present a wide range of behavioral difficulties and who are extremely difficult to help (Day, 1993a). The few available studies reveal a markedly different picture from the male with promiscuity, behavior problems, and self-neglect being the principle reasons for institutional care. Conventional offenses are uncommon among women, and there is a high incidence of self-wounding and mutilation, attempted suicide and indiscriminate aggressive acts to property and persons (Day, in press; McKerracher & Dacre, 1966; Robertson, 1981; Walker & Roberts, 1992). Female offenders with mental retardation may also commit the rare and unusual crime of baby stealing (d'Orban, 1976, 1990). Family backgrounds are invariably grossly disturbed and characterized by promiscuity, illegitimacy, incest, criminal behavior in the male members, mental illness, and severe psychosocial deprivation. There are no specific reports on treatment and management, and this is an area that urgently requires both service development and research. The strategies and services described in the latter half of this chapter refer essentially to managing male offenders, but some aspects may be helpful in managing female offenders.

Studies of sex offenders with mental retardation, in both adult and adolescent populations, show significant differences from nonretarded sex offenders (Day, 1994, 1997; Gilby, Wolf, & Goldberg, 1989). Those with mental retardation show a far greater spread of offense type, offending against both males and females and adults and children—a victim's age and sex seeming to be largely a matter of circumstance and opportunity rather than the indication of a particular sexual preference. Serious offenses are uncommon and a high proportion of offenses can be categorized as "nuisance offenses," including public masturbation, exhibitionism, voyeurism, and minor indecent assault. Heterosexual offenses rarely occur in the context of an established or developing relationship or with a consenting partner, and alcohol is hardly ever a precipitating factor. Poor impulse control, poor adaptive behavior skills, social ineptness, sexual inexperience and naiveté, and the lack of normal sexual outlets are the most common underlying causes. The majority of serious offenses are committed by individuals with a sociopathic personality disorder and a history of other offending and antisocial behavior. True sexual deviancy appears to be uncommon. Adolescents who sexually abuse others often have a past history of themselves being sexually abused. Although emotional elements, such as anger and resentment, occur, the symptoms of posttraumatic stress disorder are very unusual (Balogh et al., in press).

Arsonists with mental retardation tend to be passive inadequate individuals, with poor verbal skills, who have difficulty interacting at an emotional level with others and who use fire-setting as a communicative vehicle in response to conflict and stress (Bradford, 1982; Clare, Murphy, Cox, & Chaplin, 1992; Geller & Bertsch, 1985; Jackson, Glass, & Hope, 1987; McKerracher & Dacre, 1966; O'Sullivan & Kelleher, 1987).

Delinquency, vandalism, and property offenses are usually rooted in faulty upbringing, poor parenting models, and delinquent contamination to which mentally retarded youths are particularly vulnerable. Occasionally solitary delinquent acts occur as a consequence of poor self-control or frustration (Day, 1990a) Offenses involving physical violence are uncommon, but a substantial number of mentally retarded offenders show a low frustration tolerance, often in association with organic brain damage and sometimes epilepsy (Day, 1990a, 1993).

Identification and Assessment

Early identification of underlying mental retardation is essential to enable appropriate treatment measures to be implemented, but there is a widespread failure in the legal system to recognize the presence of mental retardation because of the inexperience of the police and other agencies. This problem is beginning to be addressed in training in the United States (Wood & White, 1992) and in the United Kingdom, where it has assumed some medico–legal importance with the introduction of new laws governing the validity of statements made by mentally retarded persons to the police (Clare & Gudjonsson, 1991; Gudjonsson, 1992; Gudjonsson, Clare, Rutter, & Pearse, 1993; Schilit, 1979).

Comprehensive assessment forms the basis of the treatment plan. Information should be obtained from as many sources as possible. The key elements are the same as those for other mentally disordered offenders and are dealt with in other chapters. In mental retardation particular attention should be paid to the circumstances surrounding the offense, the offenders concept of right and wrong, understanding of the offense and the possible consequences to self and others, level of mental retardation, evidence of brain damage, personality features, and the presence of psychiatric illness (Day, 1990a). Psychological assessment, including IQ, educational attainments, adaptive behavior, and personality profile should always be carried out together with a structured analysis of the offense cycle. Physical investigations should include genetic assessment to exclude a genotypic abnormality and EEG studies if brain damage or epilepsy is suspected.

Regular assessments of dangerousness and the risk of further offending are crucial in shaping the treatment plan, assessing progress, and in making the eventual decision to discharge. As in all mentally disordered offenders a past history of violence and previous offenses, evidence of ruthlessness and poor compliance with treatment are key predictors of increased risk (Day, 1990a; Duggan, 1997; Prins, 1993; Royal College of Psychiatrists, 1996). In mental retardation, particularly important factors to consider are evidence of poor self control, low frustration tolerance, unpredictability, emotional coldness, poor understanding of the offense, the level of support and supervision at the time of the offense, and in sex offenders, offender typology (Day, 1997).

We have found the following clinical indicators useful, particularly in early adolescence, in differentiating sexual abuse by a perpetrator from sexual experimentation. Abuse is suggested where there is

- A significant difference in age or where the partner is prepubertal,
- A power differential between the perpetrator and the partner—for example, the partner is more retarded than the perpetrator,
- A level of knowledge that shows inappropriate sophistication,
- Ritualistic behavior or other indicators of sexual deviancy,
- A pattern of activity that persists over time or over a number of partners.

These indicators have to be substantiated. Their use must take into account the perpetrators disabilities; for example, autism may mean a person simply is unaware of his partner's distress if it is not explicit.

Treatment Modalities

A large number and range of treatment programs have been described for offenders with mental retardation. They can be grouped into programs in institutional settings, programs in community settings, and offense-specific programs.

Treatment Programs in Institutional Settings

Institutional treatment is indicated if the offense is a serious one; if the offender is deemed to pose a significant danger to the public; where there is a general need for care, training, supervision, and control that cannot be properly provided in the community; where an in-depth assessment is required; and for those persistent multiple offenders who have proved unresponsive to other treatment approaches (Day, 1990a, 1997). Institutional care may also be necessary if it is impossible to meet the offender's general and specific treatment needs in the community because of a lack of specialist personnel and facilities.

It is not surprising that the first treatment programs were developed in institutional settings. They usually comprise a comprehensive package of personal, occupational, and social skills training, including further education, underpinned by a token economy program that aims to link behavior with its consequences by the systematic issue of tokens or points contingent on appropriate behavior that can be exchanged for a range of backup reinforcers. One of the first such programs was developed at the Murdoch Center, North Carolina (Burchard, 1967). Offenders were admitted to a special 12-bed unit with comprehensive facilities and exposed to an intensive program comprising a package of practical skills training with systematically issued tokens to reinforce socially desirable behavior. Tokens could be used to purchase a variety of goods and privileges from a tariff that ranged from 5 to 10 for food items to 1500 for trips to town and visits home. Undesirable behavior was punished immediately by the loss of a specified number of tokens, with, additionally, time-out for nonviolent and seclusion for violent behavior. An over-arching and rather complex behavior credit system provided a further incentive for good behavior. A maximum of seven behavior credits was awarded each day. Credits were lost for time-out or for seclusion but could be repurchased using tokens on the same day. Those with the maximum number of credits paid for a particular privilege using tokens at the standard rate whereas those with fewer credits had to pay more. Purchase of trips and other outside privileges required the maximum number of credits. Positive behavioral changes occurred in the unit, but no follow up studies were carried out.

Subsequent programs have all contained the same essential elements of a controlled environment, high staffing ratios, highly trained and experienced nursing and care staff, intensive support from a multiprofessional team, and a comprehensive package of teaching and training. A number of schemes have extended the residential provision to enable phased rehabilitation and longer term care where this is necessary (Day, 1988, 1990b; Denkowski & Denkowski, 1984; Denkowski, Denkowski, & Mabli, 1983; Fidura, Lindsey, & Walker, 1987; Lund, 1992; Sandford, Elsinger, & Grainger, 1987). The principal variation is to be found in the precise nature of the token economy program and its application and can be as varied as any monetary scheme invoking performance-related pay. In some schemes tokens or points are issued immediately following the behavioral event, in others on a daily or weekly basis; in some the scheme applies to all aspects of behavior, in others it is differentially targeted on antisocial behavior. One such point-based scheme separates behavior into training and social components (Denkowski & Denkowski, 1984; Denkowski et al., 1983). Training points are earned for habilitative behavior (washing, room cleaning, class attendance, etc.) and can be used to purchase low-value reinforcers such as cigarettes, extra snacks, and time off from activities. Social points, earned at a specified rate per hour by refraining from antisocial behavior, can be used to purchase off-site activities and other highly desirable reinforcers. Antisocial behavior results in deduction from the balance of social points: physical aggression brings time-out as well. The points value of targeted behavior is periodically adjusted on an individual basis when behavioral objectives are not being obtained or are too easily exceeded. The achievement of at least 80% of the available social points and less than five time-outs in a consecutive 30-day period entitles the patient to move from a closed unit to an open unit. Any significant lapse in antisocial behavior results in a partial or complete return to the closed unit. Again positive improvements while participating in the program were reported, but there was no follow-up.

Another scheme uses a three-stage approach (Sandford et al., 1987). In the first (assessment) stage a set number of tokens are available daily, which can be earned for all aspects of behavior. In stage two, tokens are awarded only for problem areas and social stamps are awarded for obtaining a specified daily number of tokens and for participating in skills training. Stage three requires acquiring a predetermined number of weekly points to purchase a variety of privileges and goods. After a short assessment period at stage one, patients progress to stage two. Progress to stage three depends on accumulating a specified number of social stamps. Consistent failure at stage three results in a return to stage two. This scheme was evaluated using a matched control group. After six months the treatment group showed considerable improvements in the domains of social skills and difficult behavior, and these were maintained six months after discharge. The control group showed no improvements over the same period.

A further variation involves a weekly incentive scheme based on five grades (Day, 1988, 1990b, 1997). Each grade attracts a range of privileges, including pocket money, social activities, visits to the community, and home leave—with grade one carrying the least and grade five the most. Offenders enter the scheme on grade three and normally rise or fall by one grade at a time. These are decided at a weekly meeting attended by all the unit's staff and based on standards of self-care, cooperativeness, attitude to other residents and staff, application to work, work output, and behavior outside the unit and, eventually, outside the hospital. Below grade three a change in grading can be achieved in one week. But it requires four weeks of good behavior on grade three to rise to grade four, and another four weeks good behavior on grade four before rising to grade five. Offenders attend the weekly grading meetings to discuss their grades, defend their problem behavior, and receive praise and encouragement for appropriate behavior. The scheme recently has been modified to provide additional incentives for those who remain on grade five continuously for weeks or more and to make a distinction between remuneration for work and rewards for good social behavior. The success of this approach suggests that the more elaborate procedures of other schemes may be unnecessary (Day, 1988, 1990b). For the small number of patients who cannot cope with a weekly scheme, because of their immaturity or lower level of intellectual functioning, a daily points system proved more suitable. However, most were able to move on to the weekly incentive scheme in due course (Day, 1990b). In a retrospective assessment of 20 offenders who had completed the program, 55% showed a good response, 30% a fair response, and 15% a poor response (Day, 1988).

In addition to their primary role, token economy schemes are invaluable in providing a framework for the general running of specialist units and in facilitating individual counseling about problem behavior and other matters. They are able to operate with a high degree of fairness because the whole group is subject to the same living and working environment and provide an excellent basis for social learning. Institutional programs have been criticized on the grounds that a blanket, whole-environment approach ignores individual needs and that it is difficult to transfer the skills acquired to the normal environment and the individually tailored treatment packages that are advocated (Holland & Murphy, 1990). However, the two approaches are by no means incompatible, and individualized packages of social and personal skills training, further education, counseling, and offense-specific interventions are essential features of most institutional schemes. There is also evidence that carefully phased rehabilitation can overcome the problem of transfer of skills.

Very few units are dedicated to treating the adolescent with mental retardation, particularly in the mild and borderline range of ability, and none are described in the literature. Mentally retarded adolescents tend to flounder in the verbal environment of the mainstream adolescent unit or where it is difficult for them to make progress comparable to their more sophisticated peers, and they provide an easy butt for their esteem-building humor. Fraser and Stephenson Houses, in Northumberland, United Kingdom, are residential, psychiatric units for assessing and treating adolescents whose IQ falls in an approximate range of 60 to 80. One is open and one secure and, as with all adolescent units, the approach is multidisciplinary and multiagency, including education and social work input. Staffing encompasses psychiatry, psychology, and occupational, art, and music therapists. Treatment is multimodal, with a strong emphasis on family work essential to the patient's rehabilitation in the community. Many will relapse if they return to an environment identical to the one they left. Such family work is designed to help parents and relatives to understand, supervise, and support their delinquent children (Firth et al., in press).

Such hospital units provide the resource to remove a patient from his delinquent peer group. Within a well-structured, supervised, and supportive setting, the person can acquire and rehearse the skills that enable them to change their style of life and establish new relationships.

The adolescent unit is complemented by a system of specialist residential schools. However, there are key differences in that the schools are geared to long-term care with a different emphasis on relationships; the input is less intensive and therapeutic; and the ability to control, detain, and tolerate a pupil is more limited.

Treatment Programs in the Community

The majority of offenders with mental retardation can be managed in the community supported by the social, probation, and specialist psychiatric services. Many continue to live with their families while attending local programs, but some require an out-of-home placement either because they need more structure and support or because of disruptive family relationships.

The same principles of treatment and care apply in the community as in institutions but their implementation requires good interagency collaboration. Liaison and success depend crucially on the availability of specialist services including trained and experienced personnel.

A highly successful, community-based Special Offenders Service in Lancaster County, Pennsylvania, established in 1980 involves a combined, integrated approach from both the mental health—mental retardation and probation services (White & Wood, 1988; Wood & White, 1992). Both adults and juveniles are served, and most clients have a substantial record of previous criminal behavior. The emphasis is on personal responsibility and accountability, increasing self-esteem and improving social competence. The team sees clients, initially daily and then weekly, for counseling and support; all crises are dealt with immediately. The intensive treatment and rehabilitation program includes work orientation, social skills training, time management and, where appropriate, involvement of the family. Clients are rewarded for positive changes in behavior and counseled about any difficulties that arise. All are subject to probation or parole, which reinforces compliance, the ultimate sanction being the threat of a return to court and imprisonment. The scheme carries around 40 to 50 clients annually; the average duration of probation is 30 months and a parole of 6 to 23 months. The service has proved highly successful: over ten years (1982–1992) the recidivism rate has averaged 5% compared with the equivalent national rate of 60% (Wood & White, 1992).

Delinquents are deficient in social skills (Sarason, 1968) and social training is an important component of treatment programs for offenders. These range from the very specific training in how to stand, talk, and what phrases to use or avoid, to the more general ability to deal with different social situations, including how to cope with a group of friends, parents, or the police. The development of peer relationship skills requires practice with a peer group with sufficient structure, supervision, and support to allow mistakes to be retrieved. After rehearsal within the treatment group, counseling and support helps the clients translate the use of these techniques within their own peer group. Further (adult) education helps the offender acquire some of the academic skills that he or she lacks—both literacy and some occupational skills. This can be a substantial help to the development of self-esteem. There is an associated need for sexual education, counseling, and contraceptive advice.

Some clinicians advocate a constructional approach, which attempts to establish attractive, acceptable alternative repertoires to antisocial behavior rather than just focusing on maladaptive behavior (Cullen, 1993; Dana, 1993; Donnellan, LaVigna, Negri-Shoultz, & Fassbender, 1988). This involves identifying as far as possible the factors causing and driving the offending and establishing alternative behaviors that achieve similar consequences, including environmental manipulation. This approach would appear to be particularly useful in delinquency.

Specialized Treatment Programs for Specific Offenders

Until recently the main emphasis in treatment has been on containment and general programs of training. These aimed to improve social and academic skills as well as emotional maturity and they remain an important component of management. As more has been learned about the characteristics of particular types of mentally retarded offenders, there has been an increasing focus on interventions specific to the offense, often derived from those used with offenders of normal ability. Such interventions are still in their infancy but programs have been described for sex offenders (Cox-Lindenbaum & Lindenbaum, 1994; Foxx, Bittle, Bechtel, & Livesay, 1986; Griffiths, Hingsburger, & Christian, 1989; Haaven, Little, & Petre-Miller, 1990; Lund, 1992; Swanson & Garwick, 1990), arsonists (Clare, Murphy, Cox, & Chaplin, 1992), and violent and aggressive offenders (Benson, 1994; Cullen, 1993). It is important to stress, however, that a holistic approach that addresses all aspects of an offenders functioning is essential and that offense-specific interventions are only one, albeit important, component of a comprehensive treatment program (Day, 1990a, 1997).

Sex Offenders

Sex offenders constitute between a third and a half of the patients admitted to specialist treatment units for mentally retarded offenders. Studies have suggested an incidence of four to six times higher than that in nonretarded offenders (Day, 1993).

Sex Education

Deficient and distorted knowledge about sex and sexual behavior is an important underlying etiologic factor in all mentally retarded sex offenders. Providing accurate information, correcting cognitive distortions, and teaching responsible sexual behavior is a key component in treatment. Sex education packages developed for general use in mental retardation are suitable for providing basic knowledge (Craft, 1987; Johnson, 1984; Kempton, 1988) but need to be supplemented with more specific programs covering, for example, laws and social codes relating to sexual behavior (Charman & Clare, 1992). Training in social and sexual skills is crucial. Most mentally retarded sex offenders have major defects in their understanding of male and female sexuality and in relationship and courtship skills (Forchuk, Martin, & Griffiths, 1995). Early forms of training packages were limited by their emphasis on the correct verbal response. Later programs sought to overcome this with a combination of social skills training, problem solving, and modeling, which assists offenders to make their own decisions and develop coping mechanisms to deal with the many diverse situations that can arise and unfold in a sexual relationship (Valenti-Hein & Mueser, 1990). A major difficulty is the limited opportunity available to use and further develop the skills learned in the group setting into every day life situations with an appropriate peer group of the opposite sex (Day, 1997).

Sex Behavior Management Programs

Approaches that have been used successfully with nonretarded sex offenders have been adapted for use with mentally retarded offenders (Cox-Lindenbaum & Lindenbaum, 1994; Griffiths et al., 1989; Haaven et al., 1990; Knopp, 1984; Lund, 1992; Swanson & Garwick, 1990). Although helpful for all groups of sex offenders they are particularly indicated in those whose behavior may be part of a general antisocial disorder with poor impulse control (Day, 1997). Their aim is to assist offenders to recognize, acknowledge, and accept responsibility for their problems; to change their attitude toward sexual behavior; to teach them to recognize high-risk situations; and to develop coping and avoidance strategies to enable them to gain control over their sexual behavior. Most programs adopt a group approach and use a range of cognitive–behavioral techniques, including peer group pressure, confrontation, victim empathy, and a detailed analysis of the "offense cycle." They usually last from one to three years and require a high level of patient cooperation and motivation.

Good results have been reported for most programs, but there are few long-term studies. One community-based multicomponent program reported that there was no recurrence of antisocial sexual behavior in 30 clients admitted to the program over a period of up to five years (Griffiths, Quinsey, & Hingsburger, 1989). Another reported that 9 of 15 clients who had been admitted to an outpatient group therapy program had not reoffended over a 30-month period and that only two had been rearrested for committing another sexual offense (Swanson & Garwick, 1990). A more long-term study reported the outcome of 16 mentally retarded individuals with histories of serious sexual problems subject to a similar residential treatment program. Over a five-year period, six had been discharged to community facilities and none had reoffended in the follow-up period, which averaged 2.1 years. Another four had moved to less restrictive settings, and five remained in active treatment (Lund, 1992). Another study reported on the 10-year follow-up of 62 patients admitted to an inpatient program using arousal control and cognitive restructuring, monitored by plethysmography, coupled with group therapy, anger management, social skills training, general rehabilitation, and relapse prevention (Haaven et al., 1990). The therapeutic treatment milieu encouraged personal responsibility, an accountability for all behaviors, and an understanding of its effects on other people. Their recidivism rate was 23% for sex offenses and 44% for all crimes—the lowest rates being in those patients in treatment for longer than a year. They did not provide the specific rates for different types of sexual offense or for different offender groups. In all four studies the IQ range of the participants fell in the range of 55 to 85.

Antiandrogen Drugs

Properly used and controlled antilibidinal drugs can bring substantial therapeutic benefit and play an important role in a management program. The principal indications are as follows (Day, 1997):

- As an adjunct to other treatments to facilitate concurrent therapy and to enable behavioral and socialization programs to be undertaken,
- To control sexually deviant impulses and behavior and to provide relief from intrusive fantasies and paraphilia,

- As the principle therapeutic intervention in patients who have failed to respond to other treatment approaches and who continue to pose serious problems to their own well being and the safety of others.

They are sometimes useful as an initial short-term measure in patients posing a serious risk while a detailed assessment is being undertaken and other treatment methods explored and implemented. They may also be used to provide additional control at times of particular stress.

The aim is to reduce sex drive to a level at which the patient can control and to facilitate his or her participation in sex behavior management programs: dosages should be carefully monitored and titrated accordingly. Treatment usually requires a lengthy period and eventual withdrawal should be carefully phased (Day, 1997). In the United Kingdom cyproterone acetate is currently the drug of choice, whereas in North America medroxyprogesterone acetate is more widely used. Both are highly effective in reducing sex drive and sex response in patients with mental retardation. The drugs are contraindicated in patients with thromboembolic disease or liver dysfunction and should be used with caution in patients with diabetes mellitus. The risk of affecting bone and testicular maturation means that they should not be used in patients under 18 years of age or where their development is incomplete. Excellent reviews are available of the indications and dosage of these and newer drugs, including goserilin acetate (Clarke, 1989; Cooper, 1995).

The use of antiandrogens should always be discussed in detail with patients and their families and consent (preferably written) obtained (Griffiths et al., 1989). Antiandrogens should not be given to mentally retarded offenders against their will other than in exceptional circumstances. In the authors' experience the majority is usually willing to undertake treatment and is able to give informed consent.

Treatment of Deviant Sexual Behavior

Little is known about the characteristics and likely response to treatment of the small number of mentally retarded sex offenders who show true sexual deviancy or paraphilia (Day, 1997). There are reports of the successful use of covert desensitization, aversion therapy, and satiation therapy in the treatment of pedophilia, exhibitionism, and fetishism (Clare, 1993; Griffiths et al., 1989; Murphy, Coleman, & Haynes, 1983; Swanson & Garwick, 1990). However, a review of 13 papers found that most were single case studies and concluded that, although high success rates were reported, the experimental design in most was insufficiently rigorous to enable an adequate evaluation to be made (Foxx et al., 1986). Good results have been reported with the use of antiandrogens drugs in cases of pedophilia, exhibitionism, and fetishism in the mentally retarded (Clare, 1993; Murphy et al., 1983; Myers, 1991).

Fire Setters

Fire setting is overrepresented in this population. Management presents significant problems, the recidivism rate is high, and some form of institutional care is inevitable (Day, 1993). Remarkably little attention has been paid to specific treatment interventions. Management strategies should help the arsonist to understand his or her offense cycle and the emotional and other antecedents to fire setting, improve his or her interactive communication skills, and teach him or her coping strategies that include avoidance and escape, anger management, and relaxation (Jackson et al., 1987; Stewart, 1993). Success has been reported using this approach for the treatment of an arsonist with mild mental retardation (Clare et al., 1992). Much more evaluative research is needed on this and other treatment methods. Specific interventions must be combined with sensible general measures to minimize the risk of further fire setting episodes such as close supervision, removal from high stress situations, and a complete ban on personal matches and lighters coupled with frequent personal searches.

Violent Offenders

Reducing anxiety and improving control over anger and other emotional disturbance is an important therapeutic measure in managing many of the offenders with mental retardation, particularly those displaying aggression.

Anger Management and Self-Regulation Procedures

The use of anger management in mental retardation has been pioneered by Benson (Benson, 1992, 1994). Training combines relaxation therapy with self-instructional and problem-solving training, carried out either in groups or with the individual, to improve interpersonal functioning and the self-control of anger. Initially training focuses on identifying feelings, contextual and precipitating events, and the activation of anger. Then the patient is taught verbal self-regulation in the form of coping self-statements such as "take it easy" or "stay cool." These techniques are used in problem solving or training using role play with examples from everyday life such as criticism from friends or individuals at work, teasing, and so forth.

Psychopharmacotherapy

The use of medication in mental retardation without evidence of a specific mental illness tends to be frowned on today because of the previous overprescription of neuroleptics in institutions. However, judiciously used, drugs can be a valuable adjunct to treatment and management. They are indicated in offenders who are impulsive, unpredictable, and have difficulty in controlling aggressive feelings. They may be used as an interim measure while assessment is taking place, to help control episodes of extreme aggressive behavior, to facilitate cooperation with behavioral and social training programs or on a longer term basis as an adjunct to other forms of treatment.

The neuroleptics, certain antiepileptics, such as carbamazepine, valproate and lamotrigene, and lithium are all effective in selected patients (Crabbe, 1994; Tyrer, in press). Choice depends on the individual, antiepileptics being the preferred choice, for example, in some patients with established organic brain damage whereas lithium should only be used in situations in which it is possible to control drug intake and monitoring facilities are available. Carbamazepine diminishes aggression in a proportion of people with mental retardation, not necessarily only in those with epilepsy nor, where epilepsy is present, in those with poor seizure control (Laminack, 1990; Langee, 1989). Indeed, an improvement in seizure control can occasionally make aggression worse, perhaps because frequent seizures sometimes decrease affective reactivity or create a state of confused compliance. Furthermore, the drugs themselves may occasionally produce a range of disturbance including psychosis, depression, and aggression. Although the benzodiazepines have been particularly criticized (Commander, Green, & Prendergast, 1991; Sheth, Goulden, & Ronen, 1994), most drugs can produce unexpected adverse behavioral change, particularly in this population with an underlying brain disorder.

The value of lithium in the control of aggression in mentally retarded people is well-established (Spreat, Behar, Renesk, & Niazzo, 1989). It is at its most effective where there is overactivity and stereotypy, but is less likely to be helpful for those who are male or socially withdrawn (Tyrer, Walsh, Edwards, Berney, & Stephens, 1984). There are conflicting reports of its effect on epilepsy—an increased frequency of psychomotor seizures (Jus et al., 1973) being counterbalanced by the more positive report of a reduction of aggressive and assaultive behavior (Morrison, Erwin, Fianturco, & Gerber, 1973).

The older neuroleptics should be used cautiously because of the dangers of parkinsonism and tardive dyskinesia. It is to be hoped that the newer neuroleptics, such as risperidone and clozapine, might be as effective and less likely to cause adverse side effects (Cohen & Underwood, 1994).

Aggression is sometimes the result of extreme anxiety, even amounting to panic. In these patients Beta-adrenergic blockers (propranolol, pindolol) can reduce the number of aggressive episodes (Ruedrich, Grush, & Wilson, 1990; Williams, Mehl, Yudofsky, Adams, & Roseman, 1982) and seem most useful either where there is an organic underlay or where there are signs of sympathetic overarousal such as pupillary dilatation, tachycardia, palmar sweating, pallor, and a more sustained sensory hyperacuteness. There may also be a more general effect in autism that can take some weeks to take effect (Ratey et al., 1987). They are nonsedative and, although including asthma, depression, and hypotension, adverse effects are relatively mild and infrequent.

Drug regimes should be carefully planned and monitored. They should commence with a small dose, which is gradually increased to avoid adverse effects and an overshoot of an effective level. The regimen should ensure that a particular drug is given in an adequate dose and for a sufficient length of time before being discarded as ineffective. A paradoxical increase in aggression as a result of cerebral disinhibition may occur on low dosage and usually indicates increasing the dose rather than stopping the drug. In general, drugs used as mood stabilizers should not be given in combination (Day, 1990a, 1990b).

Other Treatment Issues

Other factors that affect the response to treatment include the nature of the population and the services available.

Comorbidity and Dual Diagnosis

Between one quarter and one third of mentally retarded offenders have a history of mental illness, often psychosis. The possibility of an associated mental illness should always be explored and, if present, treated appropriately. However, in contrast to other mentally disordered offenders, mental illness is rarely a direct cause of criminal behavior in the mentally retarded. When it is, this is usually readily apparent and treatment of the underlying mental illness should be the main focus of the treatment plan and may be all that is necessary.

Alcohol is also rarely a factor—a reflection of the low use of alcohol by mentally retarded individuals and perhaps also the different etiology of much of their offending. However, at least one study has reported a high incidence of alcohol and substance abuse in mentally retarded sex offenders. Alcohol and drug history should always be thoroughly explored, its contribution to, or relationship with the offense carefully assessed, and an appropriate management program implemented.

Treatment of any coexisting physical disorder is an important component of the treatment program. These conditions have often been neglected, and further improvements are usually possible through corrective procedures. Skilled counseling can also assist adjustment problems.

Epilepsy frequently coexists with mental retardation. It is often suggested that violence might be ictal, representing an automatism (Gedye, 1989; Monroe, 1970) but this is rare (Treiman, 1991); a confusional misinterpretation of the environment during impaired consciousness being more usual. However, most epilepsy-related aggression is peri-ictal (occurring either in the prodrome or during the postictal period) or inter-ictal, being less clearly linked to actual seizural events. Apart from the well-recognized irritability, epilepsy may exacerbate any other psychopathology, including disinhibition, autism, or hyperactivity. All these states can be improved with better seizure control, which can make a substantial difference to the longer-term course of the offending. The first hurdle is to make the diagnosis. A study of 100 offenders admitted to a comprehensive, national forensic service found that 10% had unrecognized epilepsy and that, although epilepsy had been identified in another 8%, it was inadequately treated. These patients largely fell in the mild range of mental retardation. Their epilepsy appears to have been overlooked because their past history of events and environmental disturbance was more than enough to explain their offending behavior without seeking organic pathology (Milne & O'Brien, 1997). This has to be balanced against the risk of overdiagnosis of epilepsy, particularly when encouraged by the broad therapeutic spectrum of antiepileptic medication.

Families and Caregivers

Families and caregivers often need help in understanding and adjusting to the situation as well as advice on handling a whole range of other practical problems. Their support and cooperation can be critical to the success of treatment. Family therapy, whether conjoint or separate, may be indicated in some cases. In others, where the family is grossly dysfunctional, the emphasis might have to be on insulating the offender against the adverse influences of his or her family. An important element of many residential programs is the removal of a person from the indulgent or exploitative embrace of their family and peers. Only very substantial change that can withstand a return to the seduction of the previous haunts. Patterns of family behavior, rooted in long-standing relationships, have to be changed or else a new, out-of-home placement found. This may extend to providing a legal framework with the person living under some form of community order.

Specialist Services

Offenders with mental retardation differ significantly from other mentally disordered offenders in the origins, nature, and presentation of their offending behavior and in their treatment and care needs. They are disadvantaged and vulnerable in generic forensic psychiatry settings and require specialist services (Day, 1995). Such services have been developed since the 1960s, but growth has been slow and there is still an overall shortage of resources (Day, 1993; Santamour & Watson, 1982). Treatment units vary considerably in size and scope from small single units to larger complexes offering a range of facilities and treatment programs (Day, 1995). A model specialist comprehensive service has been described by Day (Day, 1993). The key components are

- Appropriately trained and experienced staff,
- Specialist treatment programs,
- Specialist community-based services for assessment, treatment, aftercare, and continuing care, including support personnel and a range of residential and day facilities,
- Open inpatient assessment and treatment units for less serious offenders and for rehabilitation,
- Inpatient assessment and treatment units with varying levels of security for the more dangerous offenders,
- Long-term secure facilities for continuing care,
- Rehabilitation programs and group homes, and
- Adolescent facilities that should be distinct from those for adults and linked to a broader adolescent service to ensure an appropriate and continuous pathway of treatment and rehabilitation.

Specialist forensic services can only be developed successfully on a regional basis. A certain critical mass of patients is essential to ensure therapeutic and financial viability and to enable a fully comprehensive range of services to be provided. Good multiagency cooperation is essential in planning, developing, and implementing, and a single provider is preferred to ensure continuity of care (Day, 1995).

In the United Kingdom a three-tier model of care has evolved, comprising high-security provision at the national level, medium-security provision at the regional level, and a range of services at the local level, including inpatient treatment units, aftercare, rehabilitation, and continuing care, provided by the health, social, and probation services (Day, 1993). A recent major review of services for mentally disordered offenders supported continuing this system but called for greater integration between agencies and improved local services and reaffirmed the need for specialist provision for mentally retarded offenders (Department of Health & Home Office, 1992). The current greatest deficit is the lack of appropriate provision for habilitation and aftercare, which means that offenders often have to stay too long in treatment units. It also increases the likelihood of breakdown and reoffending after discharge.

Appropriately trained staff at all levels are crucial to a successful service. This is reflected in the increasing number of specialist postgraduate training courses for nurses and other staff in the management of mentally retarded offenders in the United Kingdom and the United States. A subspecialty of the forensic psychiatry of mental retardation is now emerging in the United Kingdom (Royal College of Psychiatrists, 1997).

Prognosis and Outcome

Most treatment programs report significant improvements during the course of the treatment and during the immediate follow-up period, but longer term studies show a low but persistent tendency toward recidivism, particularly in sex offenders and arsonists, although few go on to commit serious offenses (Day, 1994; Soothill & Gibbens, 1987). The majority reoffend during the first year after discharge (Day, 1988), but in one 15-year follow-up study, 20% of patients did not reoffend until four years or more after discharge (Gibbens & Robertson, 1983; Soothill & Gibbens, 1987). Reconviction rates may be reduced substantially by court diversion schemes (Brier, 1994) and, on their own, paint an unduly pessimistic picture. Global assessments indicate a rather better outcome. Although 55% of Day's offender group were reconvicted following discharge (and nearly half more than once) 70% were rated as reasonably well or well-adjusted, using a range of social adjustment measures at their last follow-up contact (Day, 1988).

Good outcome is associated with an adequate period of inpatient treatment and good aftercare, including stable residential placements, regular daytime occupation, supervision, and support (Craft, 1984; Day, 1988). A poor outcome is associated with a poor response to inpatient treatment and a history of previous convictions (Day, 1988; Gibbens & Robertson, 1983; Payne, McCabe, & Walker, 1974). Offenders against the person appear to have a better prognosis than do property offenders (Day, 1988; Payne et al., 1974) perhaps because of real differences between the two groups. Offenses against the person are essentially problems of self-control and immaturity with the potential to respond to treatment, whereas property offenses are more a function of overall lifestyle and subcultural influences to which the offender frequently returns on discharge (Day, 1988).

Primary prevention is essential and lies more in the realm of social policy than psychiatry (Day, 1995). It includes the societal support to enable adequate parenting of a child who may often be both unusually demanding and relatively unrewarding to rear. The child then requires a specialized education on a broad front that encompasses many of the elements that a normal child acquires unthinkingly from his or her parents, peers, and environment. Sex education is particularly important in the context of social relationships. An innovative school prevention program devised in Lancaster County, Pennsylvania, is awaiting evaluation. All mentally retarded pupils are taught about the law, the consequences of breaking the law, how to avoid being exploited by others, and they are tutored in decision making and problem solving

(Wood & White, 1992). Child protection measures are essential to interrupt the recurrent cycles of abuse that characterize many of these families. Secondary prevention includes adequate support and supervision, the avoidance of situations that expose the individual to temptation or risk, and prompt intervention at the first signs of problems, however minor.

Areas for Future Research

More basic research is needed in all aspects of care and treatment in the field of mentally retarded offenders, including epidemiology, offender typologies, treatment modalities and their efficacy, preventative measures, and models of service provision. Research to date has tended to focus on certain specific groups of offenders, leaving major gaps in knowledge. More research is particularly needed into the characteristics and management of arsonists, true sexual deviants, and female offenders.

The increasing number of therapeutic approaches, ranging from medication to aromatherapy, often expensive and sometimes harmful, makes it increasingly important to acquire some firm knowledge of their relative effectiveness. The efficacy of a treatment may sometimes depend on the zeal and charisma of a therapist who may be unaware of their relevance—for example, a behaviorist may discount the interpersonal skills acquired earlier, with a psychotherapist. Independent evaluation is needed to identify these covert elements. An additional problem is the difficulty in comparing like with like, because unspecified selection procedures color a program's character and results. In reviewing the results of a treatment program for sex offenders, for example, it is not helpful to lump together people who are predominantly exhibitionists with those whose offenses include violent assault.

The development of community programs is likely to produce a greater network of care that should have a positive impact on the rehabilitation of offenders. In most studies the follow-up period is limited to a year or two, and there is a need for long-term studies to ascertain whether improvements in the short term are maintained. Research is also needed on the characteristics of the substantial number of patients who fail to respond to treatment measures and become recidivists. This should specifically examine the outcome of the different subgroups, including the relationships among different behavioral phenotypes, aggression, and offending.

References

American Psychiatric Association. (1994). *Diagnostic and statistical manual of mental disorders* (4th ed.). Washington, DC: Author.

Balogh, R., Bretherton, K., Whibley, S., Berney, T., Graham, S., Richold, P., Worsley, C., & Firth, H. (in press). Sexual abuse in children and adolescents with learning disabilities. *Journal of Intellectual Disability Research.*

Baron-Cohen, S. (1988). An assessment of violence in a young man with Asperger's syndrome. *Journal of Child Psychology and Psychiatry and Allied Disciplines, 29*(3), 351–360.

Benson, B. (1992). *Teaching anger management to persons with mental retardation.* Worthington, OH: IDS.

Benson, B. (1994). Anger management training: A self controlled programme for persons with mild mental retardation. In N. Bouras (Ed.), *Mental Health in Mental Retardation* (pp. 224–232). Cambridge: Cambridge University Press.

Bradford, J.-M. (1982). Arson: A clinical study. *Canadian Journal of Psychiatry, 27*(3), 188–193.

Brier, N. (1994). Targeted treatment for adjudicated youth with learning disabilities: Effects on recidivism. *Journal of Learning Disabilities, 27*(4), 215–222.

Burchard, J. D. (1967). Systematic socialisation: A programmed environment for the rehabilitation of anti-social retardates. *Psychosocial Record, 17*, 461–476.

Charman, T., & Clare, I. (1992). Education about the laws and social rules relating to sexual behaviour: An education group for male sex offenders with mild mental handicaps. *Mental Handicap, 20*, 74–80.

Clare, I. C. (1993). Issues in the assessment and treatment of male sex offenders with mild learning disabilities. Special Issue: Paraphilias. *Sexual and Marital Therapy, 8*(2), 167–180.

Clare, I., & Gudjonsson, G.-H. (1991). Recall and understanding of the caution and rights in police detention among persons of average intellectual ability and persons with a mild mental handicap. Division of Criminological and Legal Psychology First Annual Conference (1991, Canterbury, England). *Issues in Criminological and Legal Psychology, 1*(17), 34–42.

Clare, I. C. H., Murphy, G. H., Cox, D., & Chaplin, E. H. (1992). Assessment and treatment of fire setting: A single case assessment. *Criminal Behaviour in Mental Health, 2*, 253–268.

Clarke, D. J. (1989). Antilibidinal drugs and mental retardation: A review. *Medicine Science and the Law, 29*, 136–148.

Cohen, S. A., & Underwood, M. T. (1994). The use of clozapine in a mentally retarded and aggressive population. *Journal of Clinical Psychiatry, 55*(10), 440–444.

Commander, M., Green, S. H., & Prendergast, M. (1991). Behavioural disturbances in children treated with clonazepam. *Developmental Medicine and Child Neurology, 33*(4), 362–363.

Cooper, A. J. (1995). Review of the role of two antilibidinal drugs in the treatment of sex offenders with mental retardation. *Mental Retardation, 33*(1), 42–48.

Cox-Lindenbaum, D., & Lindenbaum, L. (1994). A modality for treatment of aggressive behaviour and sexual disorders in people with mental retardation. In N. Bouras (Ed.), *Mental Health in Mental Retardation* (pp. 244–254). Cambridge: Cambridge University Press.

Crabbe, H. (1994). Pharmacotherapy in mental retardation. In N. Bouras (Ed.), *Mental Health in Mental Retardation* (pp. 187–204). Cambridge: Cambridge University Press.

Craft, A. (Ed.). (1987). *Mental handicap and sexuality: Issues and perspectives.* Tunbridge Wells, UK: Costello Press.

Craft, M. (1984). Should one treat or gaol psychopaths. In M. Craft & A. Craft (Eds.), *Mentally Abnormal Offenders* (pp. 384–396). London: Balliere Tindall.

Creaby, M., Warner, M., Jamil, N., & Jawad, S. (1993). Ictal aggression in severely mentally handicapped people. *Irish Journal of Psychological Medicine, 10*(1), 12–15.

Cullen, C. (1993). The treatment of people with learning disabilities who offend. In K. Howells & C. R. Hollin (Eds.), *Clinical approaches to the mentally disordered offender* (pp. 145–163). Chichester, UK: John Wiley.

Dana, L. (1993). Treatment of personality disorder in persons with mental retardation. In R. J. Fletcher & A. Dosen (Eds.), *Mental health aspects of mental retardation* (pp. 281–290). New York: Lexington Books.

Day, K. (1988). A hospital based treatment programme for male mentally handicapped offenders. *British Journal of Psychiatry, 153*, 635–644.

Day, K. (1990a). Mental retardation: Clinical aspects and management. In R. Bluglass & P. Bowden (Eds.), *Principles and practice of forensic psychiatry* (pp. 399–418). Edinburgh: Churchill Livingstone.

Day, K. (1990b). Treatment of anti-social behaviour. In A. Dosen, A. van Gennep, & G. J. Zwanikken (Eds.), *Treatment of mental illness and behavioural disorder in the mentally retarded* (pp. 103–122). Leiden, Netherlands: Logon.

Day, K. (1993). Crime and mental retardation: A review. In K. Howells & C. R. Hollin (Eds.), *Clinical approaches to the mentally disordered offenders* (pp. 111–144). Chichester, UK: John Wiley.

Day, K. (1994). Male mentally handicapped sex offenders. *British Journal of Psychiatry, 165* (Supplement Number 318), 630–639.

Day, K. (1995). Specialist psychiatric services for mentally retarded offenders. In R. J. Fletcher, D. McNelis, & L. Fusaro (Eds.), *Proceedings of the International Congress II on the Dually Diagnosed* (pp. 102–106). New York: National Association for the Dually Diagnosed.

Day, K. (1997). Sex offenders with learning disabilities. In S. G. Read (Ed.), *Psychiatry in learning disability* (pp. 278–306). London: W.B. Saunders.

Day, K. (2000). *Aggressive behaviour in mildly mentally retarded women.* Unpublished manuscript.

Deb, S., & Hunter, D. (1991). Psychopathology of people with mental handicap and epilepsy. 3. Personality-disorder. *British Journal of Psychiatry*, 830–834.

Denkowski, G. C., & Denkowski, K. M. (1984). Community based residential treatment models for mentally retarded adolescent offenders. In J. M. Berg (Ed.), *Perspectives and progress in mental retardation: Volume I, social psychological and educational aspects* (pp. 303–311). Baltimore: University Park Press.

Denkowski, G. C., Denkowski, K. M., & Mabli, J. (1983). A 50-state survey of the current status of residential treatment programs for mentally retarded offenders. *Mental Retardation, 21*(5), 197–203.

Department of Health, & Home Office. (1992). *Review of health and social services for mentally disordered offenders and others requiring similar services: Final summary report* (CM2088). London: HMSO.

Donnellan, A., LaVigna, G. W., Negri-Shoultz, N., & Fassbender, L. L. (1988). *Progress without punishment. Effective approaches for learners with problems.* New York: Teachers College Press.

d'Orban, P. T. (1976). Child Stealing: A typology of female offenders. *British Journal of Criminology, 16*, 275–281.

d'Orban, P. T. (1990). Kidnapping, abduction and child stealing. In R. Bluglass & P. Bowden (Eds.), *Principles and practice of forensic psychiatry* (pp. 797–804). Edinburgh: Churchill Livingstone.

Duggan, C. (Ed.). (1997). *Assessing risk in the mentally disordered* (Vol. 170, Suppl. 32). London: British Journal of Psychiatry.

Fidura, J. G., Lindsey, E. R., & Walker, G. R. (1987). A special behavior unit for the treatment of behavior problems of persons who are mentally retarded. *Mental Retardation, 25*, 107–111.

Firth, H., Balogh, R., Berney, T., Bretherton, K., Graham, S., & Whibley, S. (in press). The psychopathology of sexual abuse in young people with a learning disability. *Journal of Intellectual Disability Research.*

Forchuk, C., Martin, M. L., & Griffiths, M. (1995). Sexual knowledge interview schedule reliability. *Journal of Intellectual Disability Research, 39*, 35–39.

Foxx, R. M., Bittle, R. G., Bechtel, D. R., & Livesay, J. R. (1986). Behavioural treatment of the sexually deviant behaviour of mentally retarded individuals. *International Review of Research in Mental Retardation, 14*, 291–317.

Gedye, A. (1989). Episodic rage and aggression attributed to frontal lobe seizures. *Journal of Mental Deficiency Research, 33*(5), 369–379.

Geller, J., & Bertsch, G. (1985). Fire setting behavior in the histories of a state hospital population. *American Journal of Psychiatry, 142,* 464–468.

Gibbens, T. C. N., & Robertson, G. (1983). A survey of the criminal careers of Hospital Order patients. *British Journal of Psychiatry, 143,* 362–375, 370–375.

Gilby, R., Wolf, L., & Goldberg, B. (1989). Mentally retarded adolescent sex offenders. A survey and pilot study. *Canadian Journal of Psychiatry, 34*(6), 542–548.

Griffiths, D., Hingsburger, D., & Christian, R. (1989). Treating developmentally handicapped sexual offenders: The York Behavior Management Services Treatment Programme. *Psychiatric Aspects of Mental Retardation Reviews, 4,* 49–52.

Griffiths, D. M., Quinsey, V. L., & Hingsburger, D. (1989). *Changing inappropriate sexual behavior: A community based approach for persons with developmental disabilities.* Baltimore: Paul Brookes.

Gudjonsson, G. (1992). *The psychology of interrogations, confessions and testimony.* Chichester, UK: John Wiley & Sons.

Gudjonsson, G., Clare, I., Rutter, S., & Pearse, J. (1993). *Persons at risk during interviews in police custody: The identification of vulnerabilities.* London: HMSO.

Haaven, J., Little, R., & Petre-Miller, D. (1990). *Treating intellectually disabled sex offenders: A model residential programme.* Orwell VT: Safer Society Press.

Hall, I., & Bernal, J. (1995). Asperger's syndrome and violence. *British Journal of Psychiatry, 166* (Feb.), 262.

Holland, T., & Murphy, G. (1990). Behavioural and psychiatric disorder in adults with mild learning difficulties. *International Review of Psychiatry, 2,* 117–135.

Jackson, H. F., Glass, C., & Hope, S. (1987). A functional analysis of recidivistic arson. *British Journal of Clinical Psychology, 26,* 175–185.

Johnson, P. R. (1984). Community based sexuality programmes for developmentally handicapped adults. In J. M. Berg (Ed.), *Perspectives and progress in mental retardation: Volume I* (pp. 313–321). Baltimore: University Park Press.

Jus, A., Villeneuve, A., Gautier, J., Pires, A., Côté, J. M., Jus, K., Velleneuve, R., & Perron, D. (1973). Some remarks on the influence of lithium carbonate on patients with temporal lobe epilepsy. *International Journal of Clinical Pharmacology, Therapeutics and Toxicology, 1*(7), 67–74.

Kempton, W. (1988). *Life horizons (sex education for persons with special needs).* Santa Monica, CA: James Stanfield.

Knopp, F. H. (1984). *Retraining adult sex offenders: Methods and model.* Orwell, VT: Safer Society Press.

Laminack, L. (1990). Carbamazepine for behavioral disorders. *American Journal of Mental Retardation, 94,* 563–564.

Langee, H. R. (1989). A retrospective study of mentally retarded patients with behavioral disorders who were treated with carbamazepine. *American Journal on Mental Retardation, 93*(6), 640–643.

Lund, J. (1990). Mentally retarded criminal offenders in Denmark. *British Journal of Psychiatry, 156,* 726–731.

Lund, C. A. (1992). Long term treatment of sexual behaviour problems in adolescent and adult developmental disabled persons. *Annals of Sex Research, 5*(5–31).

Mawson, D. C., Grounds, A., & Tantam, D. (1985). Violence and Asperger's syndrome: A case study. *British Journal of Psychiatry, 147,* 566–569.

McKerracher, D. W., & Dacre, A. J. I. (1966). A study of arsonists in a special security hospital. *British Journal of Psychiatry, 112,* 1151–1154.

Milne, E., & O'Brien, G. (1997). Epilepsy in learning disabled offenders—Prevalence, diagnosis and impact of treatment. *Epilepsia, 38* (Supp. 3), 111.

Monroe, R. (1970). *Episodic behavioural disorders: A psychodynamic and neurophysiologic analysis.* Cambridge, MA: Harvard University Press.

Morrison, S. D., Erwin, C. W., Fianturco, D. T., & Gerber, C. J. (1973). Effect of lithium on combative behaviour in humans. *Diseases of the Nervous System, 34,* 186–189.

Murphy, W. D., Coleman, E. M., & Haynes, M. R. (1983). Treatment and evaluation issues with the mentally retarded sex offender. In J. G. Greer & I. R. Stuart (Eds.), *The sex aggressor: Current perspectives on treatment* (pp. 22–41). New York: Van Nostrand Rheinhold.

Myers, B.-A. (1991). Treatment of sexual offenses by persons with developmental disabilities. *American Journal on Mental Retardation, 95*(5), 563–569.

O'Sullivan, G. H., & Kelleher, M. J. (1987). A study of fire setters in the south west of Ireland. *British Journal of Psychiatry, 151,* 818–823.

Payne, C., McCabe, S., & Walker, N. (1974). Predicting offender patients' reconvictions. *British Journal of Psychiatry, 125,* 60–64.

Prins, H. (1993). A service provision and facilities for the mentally disordered offender. In K. Howells & C. R. Hollin (Eds.), *Clinical approaches to the mentally disordered offender* (pp. 35–67). Chichester, UK: John Wiley & Sons.

Ratey, J. J., Mikkelsen, E., Sorgi, P., Zuckerman, S., Polakoff, S., Bemporad, J., Bick, P., & Kadish, W. (1987). Autism: The treatment of aggressive behaviors. *Journal of Clinical Psychopharmacology, 7*(1), 35–41.

Richardson, S. A., Koller, H., & Katz, M. (1985). Relationship of upbringing to later behaviour disturbance of mildly mentally retarded young people. *American Journal of Mental Deficiency, 90,* 1–8.

Robertson, G. (1981). The extent and pattern of crime amongst mentally handicapped offenders. *Journal of the British Institute of Mental Handicap, 90,* 1–8.

Royal College of Psychiatrists. (1996). *Assessment and clinical management of risk of harm to other people* (CR53). London: Author.

Royal College of Psychiatrists. (1997). *Educational policy* (Occasional Paper 36). London: Author.

Ruedrich, S., Grush, L., & Wilson, J. (1990). Beta adrenergic blocking medications for aggressive or self-injurious mentally retarded persons. *American Journal on Mental Retardation, 95*(1), 110–119.

Sandford, D. A., Elsinger, R. H., & Grainger, W. (1987). Evaluation of a residential behavioural programme for behaviourally disturbed mentally retarded young adults. *American Journal of Mental Deficiency, 91,* 431–434.

Santamour, M. B., & Watson, P. S. (1982). *The retarded offender.* New York: Praeger.

Sarason, I. G. (1968). Verbal learning, modeling, and juvenile delinquency. *American Psychologist, 23,* 254–266.

Schilit, J. (1979). The mentally retarded offender and criminal justice personnel. *Exceptional Children, 46*(1), 16–22.

Sheth, R. D., Goulden, K. J., & Ronen, G. M. (1994). Aggression in children treated with clobazam for epilepsy. *Clinical Neuropharmacology,* 332–337.

Smith, C., Algozzine, B., Schmid, R., & Hennly, T. (1990). Prison adjustment of youthful inmates with mental retardation. *Mental Retardation, 28*(3), 177–181.

Soothill, K. L., & Gibbens, T. C. N. (1987). Recidivism of sexual offenders: a reappraisal. *British Journal of Criminology, 18,* 267–276.

Spreat, S, Behar, D., Renesk, B., & Niazzo, P. (1989). Lithium carbonate for aggression in mentally retarded persons. *Comprehensive Psychiatry, 111*(6), 505–511.

Stewart, L. A. (1993). Profile of female firesetters: Implications for treatment. *British Journal of Psychiatry, 163,* 248–256.

Swanson, C. K., & Garwick, G. B. (1990). Treatment for low-functioning sex offenders: Group therapy and interagency coordination. *Mental Retardation, 28*(3), 155–161.

Treiman, D. M. (1991). Psychobiology of ictal aggression. In D. B. Smith, D. M. Treiman, & M. R. Trimble (Eds.), *Neurobehavioral problems in epilepsy. Advances in neurology* (Vol. 55). New York: Raven Press.

Tyrer, S. (in press). Psychopharmacological approaches. In A. Dosen & K. Day (Eds.), *Handbook of treatment of mental illness and behaviour disorders in mentally retarded children and adults*. Washington: American Psychiatric Press.

Tyrer, S. P., Walsh, A., Edwards, D. E., Berney, T. P., & Stephens, D. A. (1984). Factors associated with a good response to lithium in aggressive mentally handicapped subject. *Progress in Neuro-Psychopharmacology and Biological Psychiatry, 8*(4–6), 751–755.

Valenti-Hein, D., & Mueser, K. (1990). *The dating skills programme: Teaching sociosexual skills to adults with mental retardation*. Worthington, OH: IDS.

Walker, C. E., & Roberts, M. C. (1992). Handbook of clinical child psychology (2nd ed.).

White, B. L., & Wood, H. (1988). The Lancaster County mentally retarded offenders programme. In J. A. Stark, F. J. Menolascino, M. H. Albarelli, & V. C. Gray (Eds.), *Mental retardation and mental health: Classification, diagnosis, treatment services* (pp. 402–408). New York: Springer Verlag.

Williams, D. T., Mehl, M. D., Yudofsky, S., Adams, D., & Roseman, B. (1982). The effect of propranolol on uncontrolled rage outbursts in children and adolescents with organic brain dysfunction. *Journal of the American Academy of Child and Adolescent Psychiatry, 21*(2), 129–135.

Wing, L. (1991) The relationship between Asperger's syndrome and Kanner's autism. In U. Frith (Ed.), *Autism and Asperger's syndrome* (pp. 93–121). Cambridge: Cambridge University Press.

Wood, H. R., & White, B. L. (1992). A model for rehabilitation and prevention for offenders with mental retardation. In R. W. Conley, R. Luckasson, & G. N. Bouthilet (Eds.), *The criminal justice system and mental retardation: Defendants and victims* (pp. 153–165). Baltimore: Brookes.

World Health Organization. (1992). *ICD 10. The ICD 10 classification of mental and behavioural disorders: Clinical descriptions and diagnostic guidelines*. Geneva: Author.

Chapter 8
TREATING OFFENDERS WITH EDUCATIONAL DISABILITIES

Robert B. Rutherford Jr., Heather M. Griller-Clark, and Cindy Wheeler Anderson

Individuals with educational disabilities are those whose intellectual, physical, learning, or emotional disabilities and academic-skill deficits entitle them to special education services. The delivery of these services is mandated by the Individuals With Disabilities Education Act (IDEA; 1990), which superseded the Education for All Handicapped Children Act of 1975. This federal law mandates that all disabled persons *under the age of 22* have the right to a free and appropriate public education adjusted to meet their individual needs. Furthermore, incarcerated youth with disabilities are guaranteed special education services not only in accordance with IDEA but also in accordance with Section 504 of the Rehabilitation Act of 1973, the Americans With Disabilities Act (ADA; 1990), the Fourteenth Amendment to the U.S. Constitution, and various state laws (McIntyre, 1993).

Although the IDEA provides the right to a free and appropriate education for all handicapped individuals, including those who are incarcerated, the role of special education programming in corrections has only recently been recognized (Rutherford, Nelson, & Wolford, 1985). This is significant, considering that students with learning disabilities, mild to moderate mental retardation, and emotional and behavioral disorders are considerably more prevalent in correctional institutions than in the public school population (Murphy, 1986).

As you read this chapter it is important to keep in mind several basic concepts about adult and juvenile offenders with educational disabilities. First, correctional special education is an emerging field. In fact, it was only in the past decade that offenders with disabilities started to receive attention. Second, there is no single "right" way to provide special education services to offenders. The process of special education is as individualized as the students themselves. Therefore, the research supports numerous effective practices for providing education to offenders. Finally, there is a difference in philosophy between corrections and education. The primary role of corrections is to provide public safety through confinement and punishment, whereas the role of education is to liberate. This juxtaposition can be seen in the way education is either supported or inhibited in institutional settings. This population is challenging anyway, but the added constraints of some correctional policies and institutionalization make successfully treating adult and juvenile offenders with educational disabilities even more difficult.

To understand the role of special education in treating offenders with disabilities, this chapter focuses primarily on the characteristics and overrepresentation of youth with educational disabilities in adult and juvenile corrections. Although it is recognized that adults older than 22 may benefit from special education, these services are not required under the IDEA. Therefore, this chapter describes how special education laws affect corrections, the prevalence and characteristics of those 22 and younger in both juvenile and adult corrections, the links between disability and delinquency, and best practices in correctional special education.

Special Education Laws and Corrections

To understand the importance of providing special education services in juvenile and adult detention centers, jails, correctional institutions, and camps it is necessary to understand special education law. In 1975, Congress passed the Education for All Handicapped Children Act (Public Law No. 94-142), which mandated that all handicapped children and youth between the ages of 3 and 22 are entitled to a free and appropriate education. Education is made up of those individualized special education and related services necessary to enable the student to benefit from an education. Over the years Congress has amended and reauthorized the law, which as already noted is now known as the IDEA (Public Law No. 105-17).

In addition to the IDEA, two other federal statutes prohibit discrimination against persons with disabilities. Section 504 of the Rehabilitation Act of 1974 and the ADA provide protections to children and youth with disabilities. In response to the federal mandates, every state has revised its own laws to reflect the obligations set forth in the IDEA.

The Individuals With Disabilities Education Act

One of the most important principles of the IDEA is that special education services are an entitlement for all eligible children and youth with disabilities, regardless of the individual's location or legal status. Thus special education services, and the procedural protections of the law, must be provided to eligible individuals under age 22 years in the public schools, as well as in the various institutional settings in which these students may be found (Keating & Warboys, 1997). Specifically, the IDEA Amendments of 1997 (Public Law No. 105-17) mandate that appropriate special education services must be provided in juvenile and adult correctional facilities.

The categories of disabilities covered under the IDEA and state laws include

- Mental retardation,
- Specific learning disabilities,
- Emotional disturbance,
- Deafness and hard of hearing,
- Speech and language impairments,
- Visual impairments,
- Orthopedic impairments,
- Autism,
- Traumatic brain injury,
- Other health impairments,
- Deafness-blindness, and
- Multiple disabilities.

Although any of these disabilities may be found among those incarcerated in the juvenile and adult criminal justice systems, by far the most prevalent disabilities are mental retardation, learning disabilities, and emotional disturbance.

Individuals with disabilities are entitled to seven basic services under the IDEA. First is *screening, identification, and referral*, where, if students are suspected of having a disability, they are referred for assessment to determine if they are eligible for special education services. Correctional education providers must actively seek out potentially eligible or previously identified special education students.

Second, those individuals who are identified as potentially disabled have a right to a *comprehensive evaluation* to determine the nature and extent of the disability and what educational services are necessary to compensate for it. Each student is to be assessed in all areas related to the suspected disability by qualified persons and a written assessment report must be provided.

Third, the student is entitled to an *Individualized Education Program (IEP)*. The IEP process is at the heart of state and federal special education law. The IEP is developed by a special IEP team that analyzes the student's needs and determines what should be done to meet those needs. The IEP team must include (a) a school administrator or his or her designated representative; (b) the student's teachers; (c) the parent, guardian, or parent surrogate; (d) in some cases, the students; and (e) the individuals who participated in the assessment. The IEP team may also include, at the discretion of the parent or school, anyone else who has knowledge or expertise needed to help develop the IEP. The IEP team must provide a written plan specifying exactly what services the individual will receive, how these services will be provided, what the goal and immediate objectives of each service or educational component are, and what specific means will be used to accomplish these goal and objectives.

Fourth, special education must involve *individually tailored services* for each student. The education agency must have available a full continuum of services and placements to meet each student's needs. Decisions regarding educational placement must follow the determination of what the individual needs and the development of the IEP to meet those needs. Within the concept of individualized programming, the student with disabilities in corrections has the right to appropriate special education services in the least restrictive setting possible within the structure of the institution. Whenever possible, disabled students should be educated with students without disabilities, and removal from the regular educational environment should occur only when there is no other way to deliver services to the student.

Fifth, in addition to special education services, federal and state laws mandate that students with disabilities also receive *related services*, which are corrective and supportive services designed to assist a student with a disability to benefit from special education. Although not exhaustive, the most common related services found in correctional settings are speech pathology and audiology, psychological services and counseling, and health and medical screening and services.

Sixth, the IDEA and state laws include numerous *procedural protections* to ensure that the special education process operates fairly and properly. The procedures and timelines for the special education screening and assessment process and the IEP itself are designed to ensure that parents, guardians, or surrogate parents are full participants with the power to consent or withhold consent to all proposed actions. Due process procedures are in place when disputes occur.

Seventh, the IDEA requires that a transition plan be developed and specific

transition services be provided for students with disabilities. From a corrections perspective, *transition* refers to a special education program component aimed at bridg-
ing the gap between the schooling provided in the correctional facility and school,
work, family, or independent living on return to the community (Coffey & Gemignani, 1994).

Section 504 of the Rehabilitation Act of 1973

Section 504 of the Rehabilitation Act of 1973 is the basic civil rights provision
pertaining to discrimination against individuals with disabilities. It states, quite simply, that "no otherwise qualified handicapped individual in the United States shall,
solely by reason of his handicap, be excluded from participation in, be denied the
benefits of, or be subjected to discrimination under any program or activity receiving
federal financial assistance" (Coffey, Procopiow, & Miller, 1989, p. 41).

Education programs in correctional facilities are covered directly by the federal
requirements implementing Section 504. In addition to prohibiting discrimination,
correctional education agencies are required to take affirmative steps to eliminate
discrimination. These steps include locating and identifying students with disabilities,
conducting appropriate evaluations, providing a free appropriate education to eligible
students, and conforming to procedural safeguards.

The Americans With Disabilities Act

The Americans With Disabilities Act (ADA) of 1990 is a civil rights act that prohibits
state and local governments and their subdivisions from discriminating against individuals on the basis of disability. Although the ADA is closely aligned with Section
504, the ADA also requires that all public entities (including correctional facilities)
with 50 or more employees conduct a self-evaluation of their programs, services,
and activities to ensure that they are fully accessible, that barriers are removed in a
timely manner, and that the institution's policies and procedures do not have the
effect of discriminating against individuals with disabilities (Kincaid, 1993).

Prevalence and Overrepresentation of Educational Disabilities
in the Justice System

Estimates of the prevalence of persons 21 years of age and younger in correctional
facilities who are in need of special education vary widely (Rutherford, Bullis, Anderson, & Griller-Clark, 2000). There are several reasons for this discrepancy in
prevalence estimates, including inconsistencies in defining handicapping or disabling
conditions, inadequate special education screening and assessment procedures, problems implementing special education programs in correctional settings, inadequate
funding, failure to obtain prior school records, and administrative policies that place
institutional security above education (Kerr, Nelson, & Lambert, 1987; Leone, 1986;
Leone, Rutherford, & Nelson, 1991; Rutherford et al., 1985; Warboys & Shauffer,
1986). For example, several states commit youthful offenders identified as mentally

retarded to a separate mental health system rather than a correctional system. As a consequence, these states do not have youthful offenders classified as mentally retarded within their corrections system. States may also separate youthful offenders identified as having emotional or behavioral disorders and commit them in mental health facilities.

Furthermore, there is considerable overlap between disabilities (Kauffman, 1997; Wood & Lazzari, 1997). For example, an individual may be diagnosed with both learning disabilities and emotional disturbance, or learning disabilities and attention deficit disorder (ADD) or attention deficit hyperactivity disorder (ADHD). In fact, considerable overlap exists between learning disabilities and ADHD. Approximately 33% of youth with learning disabilities also have ADHD (Wood & Lazzari, 1997). In addition, approximately 50 to 70% of youth with learning disabilities or emotional disturbance have ADD (Kauffman, 1997). According to diagnostic criteria, however, youth whose primary handicapping condition meets criteria for other categories, like learning disabilities or emotional disturbance, are ineligible for classification under ADD or ADHD (Barkley, 1991). Therefore, prevalence estimates of ADD, ADHD, and other co-occurring disorders cannot be measured accurately.

In addition to the inconsistencies in defining disabilities, there are inconsistencies in the legal age for differentiating delinquent and adult criminal behavior. For example, most states define 18 as the age of majority, but California places many individuals under the age of 25 in juvenile facilities (Bullock & McArthur, 1994). The lack of a standard procedure for defining individuals with disabilities in juvenile and adult corrections, policies that place security above education, and the overall lack of reliable prevalence research in juvenile correctional special education all contribute to the discrepancies in prevalence estimates (Nelson, Rutherford, & Wolford, 1987; Rider-Hankins, 1992).

These discrepancies also indicate the need for standardized definitions, and for more reliable methods of assessment and record keeping within the juvenile and adult criminal justice systems. According to Murphy (1986), variability in identifying and labeling disabled juvenile offenders limits the conclusions that may validly be drawn from existing prevalence rates. In fact, because many juvenile and adult institutions do not have effective procedures in place for identifying youth with disabilities, the percentages reported may actually understate the prevalence of disabilities among incarcerated youth (Warboys, Burrell, Peters, & Ramiu, 1994). Nevertheless, the research leaves no doubt that large numbers of offenders are disabled and in need of special education services and that this number is increasing (Leone, 1994). Although a full range of disabling conditions exists in correctional facilities, by far the most common conditions are learning disabilities, mental retardation, and emotional disturbance (Leone et al., 1991; Nelson et al., 1987; Rutherford & Wolford, 1992).

Learning Disabilities

Learning disabilities are the most prevalent disability among children and youth in the general school population. It is also among the most overrepresented population in corrections. It has been reported that anywhere from 9 to 76% of students in special education programs in juvenile corrections are identified as learning disabled

(Nelson & Rutherford, 1989). Currently 68% of youth receiving special education services in the California Youth Authority (2000) are learning disabled. The prevalence of youth with learning disabilities is estimated to be 11% of the total juvenile offender population (Warboys et al., 1994). In contrast, public school statistics report the prevalence of learning disabilities to be approximately 5% (Sikorski, 1991; Warboys et al., 1994). The research is clear: learning disabilities have emerged as the largest disability category in both correctional institutions and public schools.

The term *learning disability* incorporates several different disorders (Warboys et al., 1994). It is not a term used to define temporary or minor learning problems. The most common characteristic identifying a learning disability is a significant discrepancy between achievement and overall ability (Baca & Cervantes, 1989). According to the federal definition, as outlined in the 1997 Amendments to the IDEA, the term specific learning disability means

> A disorder in one or more of the basic psychological processes involved in understanding or using language, spoken or written, which may manifest itself in an imperfect ability to listen, think, speak, read, write, spell or do mathematical calculations. Such term includes such conditions as perceptual disabilities, brain injury, minimal brain dysfunction, dyslexia, and developmental aphasia. Such term does not include a learning problem that is primarily the result of visual, hearing, or motor disabilities, of mental retardation, of emotional disturbance, or of environmental, cultural, or economic disadvantage. (Individuals With Disabilities Education Act Amendments, 1997)

Although there is no proven cause and effect relationship between learning disabilities and delinquency, there are a number of characteristics that may account for the overrepresentation of learning-disabled individuals in correctional institutions. For example, individuals with learning disabilities commonly display hyperactivity, perceptual motor impairment, lack of emotional control, poor general coordination, disorders of attention, impulsivity, poor memory, difficulty reading, writing, spelling, and doing arithmetic, and problems in directionality (Coffey et al., 1989). In addition, adolescents with learning disabilities have been found to commit significantly higher numbers of self-reported violent acts, used significantly more marijuana and alcohol, and have significantly more school discipline problems than their nondisabled peers (Casey & Keilitz, 1990). Furthermore, data from the National Center for State Courts suggests that learning-disabled youth may be adversely treated in the juvenile justice system because of their greater difficulty in understanding the justice process and extricating themselves from the system (Sikorski, 1991).

Mental Retardation

Offenders with mild to moderate mental retardation are also disproportionately represented in the criminal justice system. Santamour and West (1979) found that the prevalence of mental retardation in corrections was three times that found in the general population. Furthermore, a meta-analysis of the prevalent literature on juvenile offenders with disabilities found the overall weighted prevalence estimate for offenders with mental retardation to be 12.6% (Casey & Keilitz, 1990). In contrast, public school statistics report the prevalence of mental retardation to be 1.61% of the school-age population (Sikorski, 1991). This contrast has ignited concern in the form of legislation, standards, and greater attention to the issue, and has provided some education and treatment support for offenders with mental retardation. However, Santamour contended that the majority of individuals with mental retardation who encounter the justice system still suffer gross injustice. He stated, "People with mental retardation are more likely than those without retardation to be arrested, to be convicted, to be sentenced to prison, and to be victimized in prison" (Santamour, 1987, p. 106).

The relationship between mental retardation and criminal behavior has long been under examination. In the early nineteenth century, mental retardation was thought to be caused solely by biological factors. It was at this time that theorists tried to link mental retardation with criminality, poverty, insanity, and general moral and physical degeneration (Kauffman, 1997; Santamour, 1987). More recently, theorists have shifted their focus to the effects of environmental factors on mental retardation and have questioned whether mental retardation predisposes an individual to commit criminal acts (Santamour, 1987). Although there is no cause-and-effect relationship between mental retardation—or any other disability—and delinquency, some of the social disadvantages and characteristics associated with disabling conditions may lead to increased likelihood of contact with the criminal justice system (Leone et al., 1991). Offenders with mental retardation may experience disadvantages because they

- May not understand the implications of the rights being read to them;
- May confess quickly when arrested and say what they think another person wants to hear;
- May have difficulty communicating with a lawyer and other court personnel;
- May not be recognized as mentally retarded by lawyers and other court personnel;
- Are more likely to plead guilty, are more often convicted of the arresting offense, and are less likely to plea bargain for a reduced sentence than a person without retardation;
- Are less likely to have their sentences appealed;
- Are less likely to receive pretrial psychological examinations;
- Are less frequently placed on probation or in other diversionary noninstitutional programs;
- Once in a correctional facility, are slower to adjust to the routine, have more difficulty learning regulations, and accumulate more rule infractions, thus limiting access to special programs and parole opportunities;
- Are less likely to take part in rehabilitation programs;
- Are often the recipients of practical jokes and sexual harassment in correctional institutions; and
- Are more frequently denied parole and serve longer sentences than non-retarded offenders incarcerated for the same crimes. (Santamour, 1987, pp. 110–111)

Mental retardation is not a unitary concept. It is defined as "significantly subaverage general intellectual functioning existing concurrently with deficits in adaptive behavior, and manifested during the development period" (Grossman, 1983, p. 11). Mental retardation is usually classified into four levels: mild, moderate, severe, or profound. Mild mental retardation includes individuals with IQs from 50 to 75.

Profound mental retardation includes individuals with IQs below 25 (Wood & Lazzari, 1997). Although a higher proportion of individuals with mild or moderate mental retardation is found in corrections than in the general population, individuals with severe and profound developmental disabilities are rarely found in correctional facilities because they are diverted to community and residential programs shortly after arrest (Santamour, 1987), and because they are unlikely to have the opportunity to commit criminal offenses and be incarcerated (Nelson, 1987).

Emotional Disturbance

Individuals with emotional disturbance are also significantly overrepresented in correctional institutions. These individuals are commonly referred to as emotionally disturbed, seriously emotionally disturbed, emotionally handicapped, or behaviorally disordered. Morgan's (1979) survey of 204 juvenile correctional administrators indicated that 16.2% of juvenile offenders were identified as seriously emotionally disturbed. Other studies have provided estimates of emotional disturbance in juvenile offenders between 16.2% and 50% (Murphy, 1986). A recent review of the literature reports the prevalence of emotional disturbance in juvenile offenders at 20% (Warboys et al., 1994). In contrast, the prevalence of emotional disturbance in public schools is reported between 2% and 5% (National Mental Health Association, 1993). As these statistics suggest, there is a higher degree of emotional disturbance among youth in juvenile corrections than among youth in public schools (Eisenmann, 1991; Kauffman, 1989; Murphy, 1986; Nelson & Rutherford, 1989).

Once again, however, there is no direct relationship between emotional disturbance and juvenile delinquency. Although delinquent behavior is typically considered to reflect social maladjustment, a large number of delinquents are diagnosed as having serious emotional disturbance (Warboys et al., 1994). Rutherford and Wolford (1992) suggested that this overrepresentation is a result of the fact that individuals who exhibit antisocial or acting-out behavior are more likely to come into contact with the juvenile or adult criminal justice systems.

There are several characteristics of delinquent youth that are strongly correlated with serious emotional disturbance. These characteristics include problems in school; low verbal intelligence; parents who are alcoholic or who are frequently arrested; family reliance on welfare or poor management of income; broken, crowded, or chaotic homes; erratic and inadequate parental supervision; parental and sibling indifference or hostility toward the youth; and substance abuse (Kauffman, 1997; Leone et al., 1991; Rutherford & Wolford, 1992). Although the effects of these characteristics and others can be seen in the behavior of all children during stressful moments, it is the frequency and intensity of these behaviors that indicates an emotional disturbance (Baca & Cervantes, 1989). Emotional disturbance is defined in the IDEA as

> A condition exhibiting one or more of the following characteristics over a long period
> of time and to a marked degree, which adversely affects educational performance: a)
> an inability to learn which cannot be explained by intellectual, sensory, or health
> factors; b) an inability to build or maintain satisfactory interpersonal relationships
> with peers and teachers; c) inappropriate types of behavior or feelings under normal
> circumstances; d) a general pervasive mood of unhappiness or depression; and e) a

tendency to develop physical symptoms or fears associated with personal or school problems. The term includes children who are schizophrenic or autistic. The term does not include children who are socially maladjusted, unless it is determined that they are seriously emotionally disturbed. (Individuals With Disabilities Education Act, 1990)

Some of the characteristic behaviors used in determining emotional disturbance for individuals include depression; hypochondria; regression; overly dependent behavior; compulsive behavior; being accident-prone; feelings and moods that are out of proportion to the provocation or situation in which they occur; conversations with self or imaginary figures; extreme anxiety; strong uncontrollable fears or frequent crying; seeming distracted, dreamy, or extremely withdrawn; and exhibiting aggressive behavior (Baca & Cervantes, 1989).

As stated previously, it is not the existence of these behaviors that indicate emotional disturbance but the frequency and intensity of the behaviors. Furthermore, although the existence of learning disabilities, mental retardation, or emotional disturbance does not predispose an individual to delinquency, the relationship between disabilities and delinquency is apparent.

Links Between Disability and Delinquency

In a discussion of the link between disability and delinquency, Keilitz and Dunivant (1987) and Fink (1990) enumerate that learning and behavioral disabilities among youthful offenders have been attributed to three theories of causation: school failure theory (Murray, 1976; Post, 1981), susceptibility theory (Murray, 1976), and differential treatment theory (Keilitz, Zaremba, & Broder, 1981). In addition, Larson (1988) proposed an alternative metacognitive-deficits hypothesis to explain why youth with disabilities are more likely than nondisabled youth to be incarcerated. Although there is limited empirical evidence to support any single theory of overrepresentation, a combination of these factors is probably the best explanation for the high number of disabled offenders found in the criminal justice system.

School Failure Theory

School failure theory holds that intellectual, learning, and emotional disabilities lead to school failure, which influences negative self-image, which in turn results in school dropout and delinquency. This theory implies that school suspension and dropout increase a disabled youth's opportunities for delinquent behavior. Because of the disabled youth's school failure, the accompanying characteristics of slow learning and disciplinary problems may cause the youth to be labeled as a problem student and classed together with other behavior-problem students. Thus this negative labeling and grouping may lead to a decline in attachment to school and to teachers as significant adults, resulting in diminished social control and increased socially troublesome behavior (Keilitz & Dunivant, 1987). This theory is an extrapolation of Cohen's (1955) sociologically based "middle-class measuring rod" explanation of delinquency. Larson (1988) pointed out that, although the need for school achievement is aspired to by all social classes, disabled youth often fail to achieve in school.

Thus it is believed that disabled youth seek out delinquent-prone peer groups to meet their needs for recognition and achievement (Larson, 1988).

Susceptibility Theory

It is suggested by susceptibility theorists that disabled individuals possess certain cognitive and personality characteristics that predispose them to criminal behavior. This view asserts that disabilities are frequently accompanied by "a variety of socially troublesome personality characteristics" (Murray, 1976, p. 26). These characteristics include such behaviors as an inability to anticipate the consequences of one's behavior, lack of impulse control, poor perception of social cues, irritability, suggestibility, and a tendency to act out. As such, these disorders are thought to directly contribute to delinquent and criminal behavior by susceptibility theorists (Keilitz & Dunivant, 1987).

Differential Treatment Theory

Differential treatment theorists assert that learning and emotionally disabled offenders and their nondisabled, delinquent peers engage in the same rate and kind of delinquent behaviors. The striking difference, however, is that teachers, social workers, and other juvenile justice officials treat disabled youth differently, which increases the likelihood of their arrest and adjudication. That is, there are distinctive characteristics that are believed to cause disabled offenders to have different arrest, adjudication, and disposition outcomes than their nondisabled delinquent peers. The differential arrest hypothesis is that disabled youth are more likely to be apprehended by the police because they lack the abilities to plan strategies, avoid detention, interact appropriately in encounters with the police, or comprehend police questions and warnings.

Support for this hypothesis comes primarily from research by Keilitz and his colleagues (Keilitz & Dunivant, 1987; Keilitz & Miller, 1980; Keilitz et al., 1981), who found that disabled youth were adjudicated at about twice the rate as their nondisabled peers even when both groups self-reported similar types and rates of delinquent behavior. As a consequence, the researchers concluded that differential treatment was an explanation for the much higher incidence of adjudication of disabled youth.

This theory also suggests that certain characteristics correspond with disabilities (i.e., social abrasiveness, irritability, a lack of self-control), bringing about more severe treatment by probation officers, attorneys, judges, and other justice officials. Accordingly, the differential disposition hypothesis proposes that offenders with disabilities are more likely to be committed to correctional facilities than nondisabled offenders adjudicated on the same charges because of their inherent lack of cognitive and social skills (Keilitz & Dunivant, 1987).

Metacognitive Deficits Hypothesis

The metacognitive deficits hypothesis (Larson, 1988) is based on a preliminary investigation indicating that disabled youth's problem-solving strategies are less well-developed than those of socially competent high school students. This hypothesis suggests that ineffective social cognitive problem-solving increases the risk of delinquency among disabled youth. This research was prompted by a lack of empirical evidence supporting other theories of overrepresentation, which led to an in-depth investigation of the social skills and associated problem-solving skills of disabled youth in corrections (Larson, 1988).

Summary of Links Between Disability and Delinquency

Although little conclusive empirical evidence supports any particular theory, some evidence upholds the differential treatment theory at least in the correctional setting. According to studies conducted by Buser (1985), Buser, Leone, and Bannon (1987), and Walter (1988) within Maryland juvenile and adult correctional facilities, disabled offenders are charged with a disproportionate number of disciplinary infractions. They also contend that disabled offenders in the adult system spend more time in disciplinary confinement, serving longer sentences than nondisabled offenders. Despite this fact, the probable cause of delinquency among youth with disabilities, as well as the noted overrepresentation of disabled youthful offenders in the juvenile justice system, is probably best explained by some combination of these theories (Leone et al., 1991). The question of whether a youth's school failure is a symptom of psychological and emotional problems or adverse home environments, or whether school failure leads to such problems is almost unanswerable (Coffey, 1998). Nevertheless, providing educational services in correctional settings increases the odds for school success of both adult and juvenile offenders.

Educational Services in Adult and Juvenile Corrections

The types of facilities in which youthful offenders are incarcerated within the juvenile and adult criminal justice systems include (a) pretrial detention centers and jails administered by city, county, or state law enforcement agencies; (b) juvenile correctional institutions administered by the state; (c) state adult correctional facilities; and (d) publicly or privately operated camps and specialized treatment facilities. It must be emphasized that each of these types of facilities, despite their operational differences, are required to provide the seven basic special education services as outlined in the IDEA.

Pretrial Detention Centers and Jails

Pretrial detention centers and jails are designed to confine juvenile and adult offenders who have been arrested and are awaiting preliminary and dispositional court hearings. In addition, individuals occasionally are sentenced to detention or jail for brief periods of custody. As Roush (1993) noted, a problem that interferes with the continuity of educational programming for adjudicated youth in detention is the high mobility and indeterminant amount of time they spend in these facilities. The duration of confinement varies widely from one program to the next. Although pretrial confinement of several days or weeks is typical, incarceration of several months to a year is becoming more commonplace as the nature of many criminal offenses has become more serious.

Although few jails offer educational programs, most detention centers provide some level of school programming for youthful detainees. However, because the placement and length of stay for delinquent youth in detention centers are determined by the juvenile court rather than by educators, appropriate and comprehensive educational services rarely are provided. It has been especially difficult for detention center staff to provide special education services because of the high student turnover, short stays, and problems with obtaining educational records and IEPs of youth with disabilities.

Juvenile Correctional Institutions

Another type of facility, juvenile correctional institutions, are state-operated secure facilities that generally house sentenced juvenile offenders for periods of several months to several years, depending on the severity of the youth's crime and his or her behavior while incarcerated. These "reform" or "training" schools range from unfenced minimum security facilities to maximum security prison-type settings. Most states operate one or more juvenile correctional institutions where juvenile court judges or the correctional agency assigns youth to facilities based on age, prior criminal record, type of offense, length of sentence, or place of residence within the state. Educational needs are rarely, if ever, considered directly in facility assignment (Gerry, 1985).

Some level of educational programming is almost universally present in state juvenile correctional institutions. Unless students have obtained a high school diploma or GED, they are expected to be enrolled in school. Although special education services are provided in most juvenile facilities, most programs do not adequately meet the needs of students with disabilities (Leone, 1994; Rutherford et al., 1985; Rutherford, Nelson, & Wolford, 1986).

Adult Correctional Institutions

These types of facilities are also state-operated and house adult and youthful offenders who have been tried and convicted in adult courts. With the increase in violent and other serious crimes among young people, more and more of these youth are being remanded to the adult criminal justice system (Parent, Dunworth, McDonald, & Rhodes, 1997). Many adult facilities have youthful offender units where juveniles convicted of adult crimes are placed apart from the adult population "out of sight and sound." Although some general education classrooms are available in adult facilities, special education programming has been virtually nonexistent.

Adult correctional institutions usually are overcrowded, and the number of youthful offenders is rising. Although youthful offenders make up approximately 20% to 30% of the population of adult correctional facilities (Gerry, 1985), there has been a reluctance on the part of correctional administrators to provide comprehensive special education services to eligible youth. The recent amendments to the IDEA (Public Law No. 105-17, 1997) reaffirms the mandate for providing special education in adult, as well as juvenile, corrections. And comprehensive guidelines such as *Programming for Mentally Retarded and Learning Disabled Inmates: A Guide for Correctional Administrators* (Coffey et al., 1989) and *The Corrections Connection: Special Education in the Criminal Justice System* (Western Regional Resource Center, 1993) have been developed to assist in designing and implementing special education services in adult corrections.

Camps and Specialized Treatment Centers

These public and private facilities generally have less offenders assigned to them than detention centers and state correctional facilities. They include county probation camps or ranches where youth spend equal amounts of time working and going to school; local and state boot camps that provide quasi-military training to first-time offenders; and secure-care programs for youth with specialized treatment needs, such as sex offender, violent offender, drug addiction, or seriously emotionally disturbed offender programs. Although services in camps and treatment facilities are often individualized and focus on specific treatment needs (Bobal, 1984), special education is generally not provided to youth with disabilities in these types of alternative programs (Quinn & Rutherford, 1997).

Best Practices in Correctional Special Education

It is important to keep in mind that there is no single effective correctional special education program; rather there are a number of "best practices" that address both academics and behavior. However, these practices, which are critical to implementing meaningful educational services for disabled students, are often missing in corrections. The literature highlights six essential components of effective correctional special education programs for adults and juveniles. These components include (a) procedures for conducting functional assessments of the skills and learning needs of offenders with disabilities; (b) a flexible curriculum that teaches functional academic, social, and daily living skills; (c) effective and efficient instructional techniques; (d) programs and procedures for the transition of youth with disabilities between correctional programs and the community; (e) comprehensive systems for providing both institutional and community services to offenders with disabilities; and (f) availability of appropriate staff, resources, and procedural protections for students with disabilities (Rutherford & Howell, 1997; Rutherford et al., 1985).

Functional Assessment

A traditional assessment is an integral part of the processing of offenders for purposes of classification and placement within the correctional system. Assessment typically takes place in a central diagnostic or classification center where the offender receives medical, psychological, intellectual, and achievement evaluations. Achievement evaluations, which are usually standardized, one-time, and group administered, are usually used for institutional demographic reports and rarely for assigning offenders to specific programs or institutions. These traditional assessment and classification procedures in correctional settings have had limited value in identifying offenders with disabilities or in inspiring educational programming for such offenders.

A functional assessment, on the other hand, identifies skill deficits that interfere with a student's educational achievement and social–emotional adjustment. This assessment should be based on the student's needs in relationship to the curriculum taught in the education program, rather than on global achievement or ability measures. Assessment should be a continuous rather than a static process, and results should be used to make systematic adjustments in the student's educational program (Howell, Fox, & Morehead, 1993).

Assessing a student's needs to determine special education eligibility and develop educational treatment plans is an essential component of effective programming for offenders with disabilities. Functional assessment procedures should be tailored to the needs of the student and the curriculum of the school. Assessment materials and procedures should be selected, administered, and interpreted in ways that allow for adequate disability screening, determination of special education program eligibility, and the development of a functional education plan.

In a review of special education interventions that work—that is, those that have been validated and demonstrate substantial effect sizes, Forness, Kavale, Blum, and Lloyd (1997) pointed out that systematic formative evaluation procedures have been shown to significantly increase students' school achievement. Formative evaluation involves monitoring and charting discrete units of student academic progress across time. Fuchs and Fuchs (1986), in a meta-analysis of studies using curriculum-based data collection procedures at least twice each week, found that the integration of formative evaluation with instruction significantly raised typical achievement outcome scores for youth with disabilities.

In addition, Fuchs and Fuchs (1997) have found Curriculum-Based Measurement (CBM) useful in identifying students with disabilities. CBM (Deno, 1985) is a methodology for cataloging academic competence and progress in which specific procedures for sampling curricula, administering and scoring assessments, and summarizing and interpreting data results are outlined (Deno & Fuchs, 1987). Marston (1989) further substantiated that CBM produces reliable and valid information about a student's academic standing at a given point in time. When performance is measured routinely, CBM monitors academic progress reasonably well.

Functional Curriculum

Traditional educational curricula in correctional institutions are often not designed for youthful offenders with disabilities. Because fewer than 20% of juvenile and adult offenders will complete high school or receive the GED (Coffey, 1983), the focus of many correctional education programs on obtaining high school course credits or preparing for the GED is of limited value for the majority of students. Emphasis is often placed on moving to higher grade levels or scoring higher on standardized tests rather than on acquiring functional skills. Rutherford et al. (1985) question the validity of such a focus for offenders with disabilities, who often lack the functional skills to find a job or live independently in their communities.

A functional educational curriculum is one that allows the program to meet a student's individual needs. Such a curriculum focuses on developing functional job-related, daily living, and social skills. Youth with disabilities in corrections frequently need to learn basic reading and mathematics skills, as well as how to follow directions, find a job, live on a budget, use a telephone, purchase goods and services, interact appropriately with others, read a newspaper, use appropriate language, run simple computer programs, and so forth.

In addition, developing work, job, and career-related skills is critical for the eventual success of most students with disabilities. Although most correctional programs do not provide comprehensive vocational programs on site, the development of basic work skills, coupled with job-related social and life-skills training, is a valuable component of a correctional special education curriculum. Opportunities for institutional work experience, part-or full-time employment, and access to vocational training programs in the community when students transition out are important adjuncts to an effective and functional curriculum.

A functional curriculum as outlined by Fredericks (1997) includes instruction in social skills, independent living, leisure, and vocational skills that will facilitate independence and foster productivity. This curriculum is taught as a partial substitute for academic classes and focuses on social situations that the student is currently experiencing. For example, in the money management area of the independent living curriculum, the principles and strategies of keeping a budget are taught. Then the student's actual budget becomes the teaching tool. It is the integration of the academic and the practical that creates a functional curriculum.

Goldstein (1988) offered another example of a functional curriculum in which instruction in a variety of social skills is integrated into the regular academic curriculum. His *Prepare Curriculum* offers a series of coordinated psychoeducational courses designed to teach prosocial competencies to incarcerated youth. These courses provide a curriculum for developing interpersonal skills, moral reasoning, problem solving, situational perception, anger control, stress management, empathy, and cooperation (Goldstein, 1988).

Effective and Efficient Instruction

Youth with educational disabilities in corrections display very real academic and social limitations that demand special education interventions, services, and supports. It would be incorrect and an overgeneralization to assert that by providing these services to these youth they will all be successful in their return to community settings. However, there are validated instructional strategies that when offered in a comprehensive and integrated manner can have a positive, preventive effect on a portion of this population while they are in custody, and later on their return to the community to maintain these positive behaviors over time (Walker & Bullis, 1995; Wolf, Braukmann & Ramp, 1987).

Functional instruction means using positive and direct instructional strategies in correctional education programs to teach academic and social skills. Teachers should be accountable for delivering instruction that specifically addresses short-term objectives and performance standards specified in the defined school-wide curriculum. In addition, teachers must systematically monitor student progress toward mastery of those objectives and standards, in the appropriate sequence and according to student needs. This is accomplished by ensuring the alignment of instruction with plans based on assessment instruments that are themselves aligned with the curriculum.

This sort of alignment requires (a) a curriculum, (b) appropriate assessment, and (c) effective instruction. Therefore, the use of functional assessment procedures and a functional curriculum are not the only prerequisites for alignment. In their review of special education interventions that work, Forness et al. (1997) found that direct instruction interventions that focus on teaching objectives also are needed. Direct instruction involves teaching essential academic and social skills in the most effective and efficient manner possible (Carnine, Silbert, & Kameenui, 1990). The effectiveness of this approach has been supported by large-scale experimental studies with instructionally naive students (Gersten, Becker, Heiry, & White, 1984; Guthrie, 1977) and by studies that investigated the characteristics of effective teachers (Rosenshine & Stevens, 1986). According to Rosenshine (1979):

> Direct instruction refers to high levels of student engagement within academically focused, teacher-directed classrooms using sequenced materials. It refers to teaching activities focused on academic matters where goals are clear to students; time allocated for instruction is sufficient and continuous; content coverage is extensive; student performance is monitored; questions are at a low cognitive level and produce many correct responses; and feedback to students is immediate and academically oriented. In direct instruction, the teacher controls instructional goals, chooses material appropriate for the student's ability level, and paces the instructional episode. Interaction is characterized as structured, but not authoritarian; rather, learning takes place in a convivial academic atmosphere. (p. 17)

White (1988) conducted a meta-analysis of 25 studies on the effectiveness of direct instruction programs with special education students. A substantial percentage of the outcomes significantly favored direct instruction with an average magnitude of effect of .84 standard deviation units. Not a single outcome measure in any of the 25 studies significantly favored the comparison treatment. The effects were not restricted to a particular disability, age group, or skill area. The studies that investigated academic outcomes in reading and math, as well as measures of intellectual ability and readiness skills, consistently demonstrated the effectiveness of direct instruction.

Another aspect of effective and efficient instruction involves the use of behavior modification or applied behavior analysis strategies for intervention and evaluation in the correctional classroom. This systematic, performance-based method of changing student behavior calls for specifying observable and measurable social, academic, daily living, and vocational behaviors and evaluating the effects of positive and direct instructional strategies on changing these behaviors.

Behavioral interventions derived from applied behavior analysis (Baer, Wolf, & Risley, 1968) and social learning theory (Bandura, 1969) emphasize the use of overt, objectively observable behaviors as dependent measures. Behavioral interventions include both behavior enhancement procedures and behavior reduction procedures. Behavior enhancement procedures include tangible, token, activity, and social reinforcement, as well as contracting and modeling. Behavior reduction procedures, which have been empirically validated for at-risk and disabled students in schools and correctional settings, include differential reinforcement, extinction, response cost, and time-out (Nelson & Rutherford, 1988).

Forness et al. (1997) identify behavior modification as a special education intervention that works. They point out Skiba and Casey's (1985) meta-analysis of 41 intervention studies with behaviorally disordered children and youth that found that treatments based on a behavioral approach appear to be consistently powerful across analyses. The latter authors found that reinforcement, aversive procedures (i.e., time-out and response cost), behavioral consultation, and cognitive behavior modification were consistently powerful and stable. Robinson, Smith, Miller, and Brownell (1999) conducted an additional analysis of the cognitive behavior modification research literature and found equally strong effect sizes for this behavioral intervention technique.

Over the past several decades, thousands of studies have demonstrated that behavioral interventions are effective in increasing desired behaviors and reducing undesired behaviors across students of all ages, cultures, and psychological characteristics (Rutherford & Nelson, 2000). There is no evidence that behavioral procedures work differently for students with disabilities in corrections than for any other group. Researchers and practitioners apply and adjust behavioral interventions as required by the individual characteristics of each pupil. This ability to conduct formative evaluations and to adjust intervention procedures while interventions are in progress is a major strength of the behavioral approach.

Meta-analyses for techniques for systematically enhancing reading comprehension (e.g., strategy training, visual representations, or organizational cues; Talbot, Lloyd, & Tankersley, 1994) and for the use of mnemonics (e.g., keyword, pegword, or acoustic representations; Mastropieri & Scruggs, 1989) produced mean effect sizes above one standard deviation. Forness et al. (1997) suggested that these instructional interventions are among the most powerful special education interventions.

Transition

The need for transition or reentry services for offenders with disabilities in correctional programs is acute. The transition or transfer of students and their educational records through the justice system is a critical component of effective special education programming. Services are needed that link correctional education programs to the student's previous public school program, as well as to the educational and community services needed to support the offender following incarceration. Transition is generally the most neglected component of correctional education programs (Griller, Rutherford, Mathur, & Anderson, 1997). Cooperation between the public schools, community agencies, and correctional education programs seldom occurs. Identifying offenders with disabilities often is slowed by the difficulty in obtaining previous educational records, and institutional educational records are rarely forwarded to educational or vocational programs in the community once the offender returns to the community (Lewis, Schwartz, & Ianacone, 1988). In addition, no single agency accepts the responsibility for providing transition services.

The responsibility for transition must be shared by the correctional education staff as well as by the public schools and other community-based programs that transfer students. In their review of transition programs in juvenile corrections, Coffey and Gemignani (1994) found that effective transitional services include the following components: interagency coordination, preplacement joint planning, transfer of records before a student's move from one jurisdiction to another, and specific prerelease transitional programs including social skills, independent living skills, and vocational skills training, as well as instruction in law-related education.

Most authors agree that offenders with disabilities need special assistance during transition periods (Edgar, Webb, & Maddox, 1987; Leone, Walter, & Edgar, 1990). This is because of several factors. First, special-needs youth have greater social, emotional, and learning needs than their nondisabled peers (Pollard, Pollard, & Meers, 1994). Second, there is great variation in the types of transition services and interventions delivered (Halloran & Simon, 1995; Kochhar & West, 1995; Taymans, Corbey, & Dodge, 1995). For example, some programs focus on movement from school to postschool activities, some focus on vocational training, and some focus on continuing education or independent living, whereas others include all of these. Third, a continuum of care, including partnerships between schools, families, communities, and businesses that link school-based learning with work-based learning, has not been fully established (Halloran & Simon, 1995).

For these reasons, Edgar (1991) contended that a new approach to transition services for special needs youth is needed. The Juvenile Corrections Interagency Transition Model presents step-by-step strategies that help facilitate the smooth transition of juvenile offenders from corrections to the community. These strategies include establishing interagency awareness, communication, cooperation, and efficient transfer of school records (Webb, Maddox, & Edgar, 1991).

Comprehensive Systems

Comprehensive systems for providing coordinated special education services to offenders with disabilities often do not exist either within the correctional institution or before or following incarceration. Developing comprehensive systems means balancing the often competing priorities of staff within the institution and of professionals in the various juvenile justice, educational, and community agencies with whom offenders with disabilities come into frequent contact.

Correctional programs have three functions: "custody and supervision," where offenders are monitored and their movement restricted; "work," where offenders make restitution, maintain the institution, and conform to the work ethic; and the "provision of programs" (including education), where offenders receive appropriate services and engage in meaningful activities to occupy their time. Providing meaningful special education services to offenders with disabilities involves balancing these often competing priorities and maintaining effective communication and cooperation among staff responsible for these youth.

Comprehensive and coordinated linkages also do not exist between the courts, the public schools, correctional education programs, and after-care programs. Interagency communication and cooperation must be established where juvenile and criminal court judges make sentencing and placement decisions that take into account the special education needs of disabled offenders, and where parole and after-care programs are linked to the correctional education program to ensure continuous and meaningful special education services.

A system for providing "wraparound" programming (Eber, 1997) should be implemented where comprehensive, cooperative, and coordinated services, both within the institution and within the community, are implemented to effectively serve students with disabilities in the justice system. Wraparound is a process for developing realistic behavior plans for students with disabilities, which involve all domains of the student's life. Within the institution, special and general education teachers, treatment staff, and custody personnel, as well as correctional and correctional education administrators, work cooperatively to provide effective custody, treatment, and education to disabled offenders. Wraparound in the community involves linking representatives of the correctional facility with families, public schools, work sites, parole offices, and specialized treatment facilities to provide continuous and meaningful special education services.

Appropriate Staff, Resources, and Procedural Protections

As pointed out previously, a significant proportion of youth in correctional settings are disabled. Therefore, a significant proportion of the correctional education staff needs to be composed of certified special education teachers and custodial and treatment staff must have extensive training in how to serve students with disabilities. In addition, special education programs in juvenile and adult correctional facilities must focus on providing a full continuum of educational services, including instruction in academics, social skills, independent living skills, and vocational skills. Finally, procedural protections including notification of initial evaluation and eligibility, IEP development, and review and revision of IEP's must be provided to special education students and their parents or guardians.

Given the assumption that special education procedural requirements are in the student's best interest, the promise of the special education mandate under IDEA is not being met in many correctional programs. In a number of facilities, especially in jails and adult correctional institutions, there are no certified teachers, and offenders with disabilities are not identified, evaluated, or provided with appropriate special education services. In most juvenile and adult facilities, a full continuum of special education services is not in place for students with disabilities, and if they are available, they are often markedly inferior to those found in the public schools. If we as a society are to change the future for youthful and adult offenders with disabilities we have to rely not only on our current knowledge base of what is working in the criminal justice system but also examine those factors and trends that appear to *not* be working. The correctional education experience for those with educational disabilities can be positive—especially if residential and educational staff are willing to share, exchange, and pool their knowledge and professional experiences (Coffey, 1998).

Future Directions for Correctional Special Education

Emerging trends are likely to affect educating and treating juveniles and youthful offenders with disabilities. For example, in the past 10 years there has been a substantial increase in the contracting of private for-profit programs to provide correctional services. This trend suggests that programs in juvenile corrections are becoming more polarized. Today, public facilities are more likely to house either serious offenders or offenders with special problems in restrictive settings. Private facilities, on the other hand, are being used to house the large number of adjudicated youth in community placements whose problems are less severe. How these private providers will respond to the educational needs of incarcerated persons who are 21 or under is unknown.

A significant trend in juvenile corrections in the early 1990s was a move toward the use of indeterminate sentencing of young offenders. Most states authorized indeterminate sentencing and allowed juvenile correctional agencies discretion regarding a youth's stay in the correctional facility. An opposite trend has emerged over the past several years in a number of states toward the increased use of determinate or fixed sentences for certain types of juvenile and adult crime. Some state laws have removed discretion from juvenile and adult court judges and mandated that offenders serve set sentences. This creates education problems. As a result of determinate sentencing, correctional personnel have less discretion as to when offenders should be released. Thus offenders with fixed sentences have less incentive to take part in education, treatment, and other rehabilitation services.

Moreover, the number of offenders in juvenile correctional facilities has increased markedly in most states (Center on Crime, Communities, and Culture, 1997). Concurrently, a major shift in public attitude toward youth crime has led to a "get tough" policy in many states in which juvenile offenders are sentenced to longer and more severe penalties. As part of this policy, more youths are being tried as adults and sentenced to adult correctional facilities. As a result, adult correctional systems are increasingly responsible for providing special education services to youthful offenders with disabilities. Although juvenile corrections in most states generally provide some level of special education programming for youthful offenders with disabilities, appropriate special education services in adult corrections is virtually nonexistent. In recent hearings on the reauthorization of the IDEA, many state departments of corrections lobbied to exempt adult corrections from the mandates of the law. Although the IDEA Amendments of 1997 (Public Law No. 105-17) reaffirm that those with disabilities in both adult and juvenile corrections are entitled to special education services, adult systems are now exempted from providing transition planning and transition services to inmates whose sentences go beyond age 22. In addition, if a youth with a disability is convicted as an adult and incarcerated in an adult program, the IEP team may modify the youth's IEP or placement "if the state demonstrates a bona fide security or compelling penological intent that cannot be otherwise accommodated" (IDEA Amendments, 1997, p. 58; Keating & Warboys, 1997).

This is unfortunate because, as Nelson pointed out, "the majority of persons incarcerated in this country are young and poorly educated, both in the amount of schooling received and levels of functional academic and social competence attained" (1987, p. 15). A significant proportion of these offenders have educational disabilities according to state and federal definitional criteria. If best practices in correctional special education are not systematically and comprehensively implemented, young offenders with disabilities will not acquire appropriate living skills to help them, once released, stay out of prison.

References

Americans With Disabilities Act. (1990). Public Law No. 101-336, 42 U.S.C. §§ 12101–12213.

Baca, L. M., & Cervantes, H. T. (1989). *The bilingual special education interface.* Columbus, OH: Merrill.

Baer, D. M., Wolf, M. M., & Risley, T. R. (1968). Some current dimensions of applied behavior analysis. *Journal of Applied Behavior Anaylsis, 1,* 91–97.

Bandura, A. (1969). Principles of behavior modification. New York: Holt.

Barkley, R. A. (1991). Attention deficit hyperactivity disorder. *Psychiatric Annals, 21*(12), 725–733.

Bobal, C. M. (1984). An unconventional approach to providing education services to violent offenders. In R. Mathais, P. De Muro, & R. Allison (Eds.), *Violent juvenile offenders: An anthology* (pp. 273–281). San Francisco: National Council On Crime and Delinquency.

Bullock, L. M., & McArthur, P. (1994). Correctional special education: Disability prevalence estimates and teacher preparation programs. *Education and Treatment of Children, 17*(3), 347–355.

Buser, C. E. (1985). *The relationship between educational handicaps and disciplinary infractions in an adult male prison setting.* Unpublished masters thesis, University of Maryland, College Park.

Buser, C. E., Leone, P. E., & Bannon, M. E. (1987). Prison segregation units and the educational rights of handicapped inmates: Problems and some potential solutions. *Issues in Correctional Training and Casework, 3,* 1–3.

California Youth Authority. (2000). *Monthly Special Education Reports.* Sacramento: Department of the Youth Authority.

Carnine, D., Silbert, J., & Kameenui, E. J. (1990). *Direct instruction reading* (2nd ed.) New York: Macmillan

Casey, K., & Keilitz, I. (1990). Estimating the prevalence of learning disabled and mentally retarded juvenile offenders: A meta-analysis. In P. E. Leone (Ed.), *Understanding troubled and troubling youth* (pp. 82–101). Newbury Park, CA: Sage.

Center on Crime, Communities, and Culture. (1997). *Education as crime prevention: Providing education to prisoners.* New York: Author.

Coffey, O. D. (1983). Meeting the needs of youth from a correctional viewpoint. In S. Braaten, R. B. Rutherford, & C. D. Kardash (Eds.), *Programming for adolescents with behavioral disorders* (pp. 79–84). Reston, VA: Council for Children With Behavioral Disorders.

Coffey, O. D. (1998). Collaboration between education and treatment for at-risk and delinquent youth: Administrative issues and considerations. In B. I. Wolford, C. M. Nelson, & R. B. Rutherford (Eds.), *Shakertown Symposium III: Building collaboration between education and treatment for at-risk and delinquent youth.* Richmond, KY: National Coalition for Juvenile Justice Services.

Coffey, O. D., & Gemignani, M. G. (1994). *Effective practices in juvenile correctional education: A study of the literature and research 1980–1992.* Washington, DC: National Office for Social Responsibility.

Coffey, O. D., Procopiow, N., & Miller, N. (1989). *Programming guide for mentally retarded and learning disabled offenders: A guide for correctional administrators.* Washington, DC: U.S. Department of Justice.

Cohen, A. K. (1955). *Delinquent boys.* New York: Free Press.

Deno, S. L. (1985). Curriculum-based measurement: The emerging alternative. *Exceptional Children, 52,* 219–232.

Deno, S. L., & Fuchs, L. S. (1987). Developing curriculum based measurement systems for data-based special education problem solving. *Focus on Exceptional Children, 19*(8), 1–16.

Eber, L. (1997). Improving school-based behavioral interventions through use of the wrap-around process. *Reaching Today's Youth, 1*(2), 32–36.

Edgar, E. B. (1991). Providing ongoing support and making appropriate placements: An alternative to transition planning for mildly handicapped students. *Preventing School Failure, 35*, 36–39.

Edgar, E. B., Webb, S. L., & Maddox, M. (1987). Issues in transition: Transfer of youth from correctional facilities to public schools. In C. M. Nelson, R. B. Rutherford, & B. I. Wolford (Eds.), *Special education in the criminal justice system* (pp. 251–272). Columbus, OH: Merrill.

Education for All Handicapped Children Act. (1975). Public Law No. 94-142, 20 U.S.C. § 1401.

Eisenmann, R. (1991). Conduct disordered youth: Insights from a prison treatment program. *Beyond Behavior, 2*(1), 3–4.

Fink, C. M. (1990). Special education students at risk: A comparative study of delinquency. In P. E. Leone (Ed.), *Understanding troubled and troubling youth* (pp. 61–81). Newberry Park, CA: Sage.

Forness, S. R., Kavale, K. A., Blum, I. M., & Lloyd, J. W. (1997). Mega-analysis of meta-analysis: What works in special education and related services. *Teaching Exceptional Children, 29*, 4–10.

Fredericks, H. D. (1997). An education perspective. In C. M. Nelson, R. B. Rutherford, & B. I. Wolford (Eds.), *Shakertown Symposium II: Comprehensive and collaborative systems that work for troubled youth: A national agenda* (pp. 68–89). Richmond, KY: National Coalition for Juvenile Justice Services.

Fuchs, L. S., & Fuchs, D. (1986). Effects of systematic formative evaluation: A meta-analysis. *Exceptional Children, 53*, 199–208.

Fuchs, L. S., & Fuchs D. (1997). Use of curriculum-based measurement in identifying students with disabilities. *Focus on Exceptional Children, 30*(3), 1–16.

Gerry, M. (1985). *Monitoring the special education programs of correctional institutions: A guide for special education monitoring staff of state education agencies.* Washington, DC: National Association of State Directors of Special Education.

Gersten, R., Becker, W. C., Heiry, T. J., & White, W. A. T. (1984). Entry IQ and yearly academic growth of children in Direct Instruction programs: A longitudinal study of low SES children. *Education Evaluation and Policy Analysis, 6*, 109–121.

Goldstein, A. P. (1988). *The Prepare Curriculum.* Champaign, IL: Research Press.

Griller, H. M., Rutherford, R. B., Mathur, S. R., & Anderson, C. W. (1997, July). *A model transition program for juvenile offenders.* Paper presented at the 52nd International Correctional Education Association Conference, Houston, TX.

Grossman, H. J. (Ed.). (1983). *Classification in mental retardation.* Washington, DC: American Association on Mental Deficiency.

Gutherie, J. T. (1977). Follow through: A compensatory education experiment. *The Reading Teacher, 31*(2), 240–244.

Halloran, W. D., & Simon, M. Y. (1995). The transition services requirement: A federal perspective on issues, implications and challenges. *The Journal for Vocational Special Needs Education, 17*, 94–97.

Howell, K. W., Fox, S., & Morehead, M. K. (1993). *Curriculum-based evaluation* (2nd ed.). Belmont, CA: Brooks/Cole.

Individuals With Disabilities Education Act. (1990). Public Law No. 101-476, 20 U.S.C. § 1400.

Individuals With Disabilities Education Act Amendments. (1997). Public Law No. 105-17, 20 U.S.C. §1400.

Kauffman J. M. (1989). *Characteristics of children's behavior disorders* (4th ed.). Columbus, OH: Merrill.

Kauffman, J. M. (1997). *Characteristics of emotional and behavioral disorders of children and youth* (6th ed.). Upper Saddle River, NJ: Prentice-Hall.

Keating, S., & Warboys, L. (1997). IDEA Amendments limit special education rights of incarcerated youth. *Youth Law News*. San Francisco: Youth Law Center.

Keilitz, I., & Dunivant, N. (1987). The learning disabled offender. In C. M. Nelson, R. B. Rutherford, & B. I. Wolford (Eds.), *Special education in the criminal justice system* (pp. 120–137). Columbus, OH: Merrill.

Keilitz, I., & Miller, S. L. (1980). Handicapped adolescents and young adults in the justice system. *Exceptional Education Quarterly, 2*, 117–126.

Keilitz, I., Zaremba, B. A., & Broder, P. K. (1981). Learning disabilities and juvenile delinquency. In L. D. Savitz & N. Johnston (Eds.), *Contemporary criminology* (pp. 95–104). New York: Wiley.

Kerr, M. M., Nelson, C. M., & Lambert, D. L. (1987). *Helping adolescents with learning and behavior problems*. Columbus, OH: Merrill.

Kincaid, J. M. (1993). The rights of special education students in correctional facilities. In Western Regional Resource Center (Ed.), *The corrections connection: Special education in the criminal justice system* (pp. 1–13). Eugene, OR: Author.

Kochran, C. A., & West, L. L. (1995). Future directions for federal legislation affecting transition services for individuals with special needs. *The Journal for Vocational Special Needs Education, 17*, 85–93.

Larson, K. A. (1988). A research review and alternative hypothesis explaining the link between learning disabilities and delinquency. *Journal of Learning Disabilities, 21*, 357–363, 369.

Leone, P. E. (1986). Teacher training in corrections and special education. *Remedial and Special Education, 7*(3), 41–47.

Leone, P. E. (1994). Education services for youth with disabilities in a state-operated juvenile correctional system: Case study and analysis. *Journal of Special Education, 28*(1), 43–58.

Leone, P. E., Rutherford, R. B., & Nelson, C. M. (1991). *Special education in juvenile corrections*. Reston, VA: Council for Exceptional Children.

Leone, P. E., Walter, M. B., & Edgar, E. B. (1990). Multidisciplinary perspectives on the transition of troubled youth to community settings: Results from a delphi survey. In B. I. Wolford, C. J. Miller, & P. Lawrenz (Eds.), *Transitional services for troubled youth* (pp. 5–11). Richmond: Eastern Kentucky University.

Lewis, K. S., Schwartz, G. M., & Ianacone, R. N. (1988). Service coordination between correctional and public school systems for handicapped juvenile offenders. *Exceptional Children, 55*, 66–70.

Marston, D. (1989). Curriculum-based measurement: What is it and why do it? In M. R. Shinn (Ed.), *Curriculum-based measurement: Assessing special children* (pp. 18–78). New York: Guilford Press.

Mastropieri, M. A., & Scruggs, T. E. (1989). Constructing more meaningful relations: Mnemonic instruction for special populations. *Educational Psychology Review, 1*(2), 83–111.

McIntyre, T. (1993). Behaviorally disordered youth in correctional settings: Prevalence, programming, and teacher training. *Behavioral Disorders, 18*(3), 167–176.

Morgan, D. J. (1979). Prevalence and types of handicapping conditions found in juvenile correctional institutions: A national survey. *Journal of Special Education, 13*, 283–295.

Murphy, D. M. (1986). The prevalence of handicapping conditions among juvenile delinquents. *Remedial and Special Education, 7*(3), 7–17.

Murray, C. (1976). *The link between learning disabilities and juvenile delinquents: Current theory and knowledge* (Publication No. 241-093-2134). Washington, DC: U.S. Government Printing Office.

National Mental Health Association. (1993). *All systems failure*. Alexandria, VA: Author.

Nelson, C. M. (1987). Handicapped offenders in the criminal justice system. In C. M. Nelson, R. B. Rutherford, & B. I. Wolford (Eds.), *Special education in the criminal justice system* (pp. 2–17). Columbus, OH: Merrill.

Nelson, C. M., & Rutherford, R. B. (1988). Behavioral interventions with behaviorally disordered students. In M. C. Wang, M. C. Reynolds, & H. J. Walberg (Eds.), *Handbook of special education: Research and practice* (Vol. 2, pp. 125–153). New York: Pergamon Press.

Nelson, C. M., & Rutherford, R. B. (1989, September). *Impact of the correctional special education training (C/SET) project on correctional special education.* Paper presented at the CEC/CCBD National Topical Conference on Behavioral Disorders, Charlotte, NC.

Nelson, C. M., Rutherford, R. B., & Wolford, B. I. (Eds.). (1987). *Special education in the criminal justice system.* Columbus, OH: Merrill.

Parent, D., Dunworth, T., McDonald, D., & Rhodes, W. (1997). *Key legislative issues in criminal justice: Transferring serious juvenile offenders to adult courts.* Washington, DC: U.S. Department of Justice, Office of Juvenile Justice and Delinquency Prevention.

Pollard, R. R., Pollard, C. J., & Meers, G. (1994). Determining effective transition strategies for adjudicated youth with disabilities: A national delphi study. *Journal of Correctional Education, 45,* 190–195.

Post, C. H. (1981). The link between learning disabilities and juvenile delinquency: Cause, effect and "present solutions." *Juvenile and Family Court Journal, 32,* 58–68.

Quinn, M. M., & Rutherford, R. B. (1997). *Alternative programs for students with social, emotional, and behavioral problems.* Reston, VA: Council for Children with Behavioral Disorders.

Rehabilitation Act. (1973). Public Law No. 93–12, 87 Stat. 335.

Rider-Hankins, P. (1992). Review of the research: The educational process in juvenile correctional schools. American Bar Association; Special Committee on Youth Education for Citizenship. (ERIC Document Reproduction Service, No. 349346)

Robinson, T. R., Smith, S. W., Miller, M. D., & Brownell, M. T. (1999). Cognitive behavior modification of hyperactivity-impulsivity and aggression: A meta-analysis of school-based studies. *Journal of Educational Psychology, 91,* 195–203.

Rosenshine, B. (1979). Content, time, and direct instruction. In P. L. Peterson & H. J. Wahlberg (Eds.), *Research on teaching: Concepts, findings, and implications.* Berkley, CA: McCutchan.

Rosenshine, B., & Stevens, R. (1986). Teaching functions. In M. C. Wittrock (Ed.), *Handbook of research on teaching* (3rd ed., pp. 376–391). New York: Macmillan.

Roush, D. W. (1993). A juvenile justice perspective. In C. M. Nelson, R. B. Rutherford, & B. I. Wolford (Eds.), *Shakertown Symposium II: Comprehensive and collaborative systems that work for troubled youth: A national agenda* (pp. 29–60). Richmond, KY: National Coalition for Juvenile Justice Services.

Rutherford, R. B., Bullis, M., Anderson, C. W., & Griller-Clark, H. M. (in press). *Youth with disabilities in the correctional system: Prevalence rates and identification issues.* Washington, DC: American Institutes for Research.

Rutherford, R. B., & Howell, K. W. (1997). Education program assessment: MacLaren Children's Center School. Los Angeles: Los Angeles County Department of Child and Family Services.

Rutherford, R. B., & Nelson, C. M. (2000). Management of aggressive and violent behavior in schools. In E. L. Meyen, G. A. Vergason, & R. J. Whelan (Eds.), *Educating students with mild disabilities: Strategies and methods* (2nd ed., pp. 71–92). Denver, CO: Love.

Rutherford, R. B., Nelson, C. M., & Wolford, B. I. (1985). Special education in the most restrictive environment: Correctional/special education. *Journal of Special Education, 19,* 59–71.

Rutherford, R. B., Nelson, C. M., & Wolford, B. I. (1986). Special education programming in juvenile corrections. *Remedial and Special Education, 7*(3), 27–33.

Rutherford, R. B., & Wolford, B. I. (1992). Handicapped youthful offenders. In L. M. Bullock (Ed.), *Exceptionalities in children and youth* (pp. 196–219). Needham Heights, MA: Allyn and Bacon.

Santamour, M. B. (1987). The criminal justice system. In C. M. Nelson, R. B. Rutherford, & B. I. Wolford (Eds.), *The mentally retarded offender* (pp. 106–118). Columbus, OH: Merrill.

Santamour, M. B., & West, B. (1979). *Retardation and criminal justice: A training manual for criminal justice personnel.* Washington, DC: President's Committee on Mental Retardation and the New Jersey Association for Retarded Citizens, New Brunswick.

Sikorski, J. B. (1991). Learning disorders and the juvenile justice system. *Psychiatric Annals, 21*(12), 742–747.

Skiba, R., & Casey, A. (1985). Interventions for behavior disordered students: A quantitative review and methodological critique. *Behavioral Disorders, 10,* 239–252.

Talbott, E., Lloyd, J. W., & Tankersley, M. (1994). Effects of reading comprehension interventions for students with learning disabilities. *Learning Disability Quarterly, 17,* 223–232.

Taymans, J. M., Corbey, S., & Dodge, L. (1995). A national perspective of state level implementation of transition policy. *Journal of Vocational Special Needs Education, 17,* 98–102.

Walker, H. M., & Bullis, M. (1995). A comprehensive services model for troubled youth. In C. M. Nelson, B. I. Wolford, & R. B. Rutherford (Eds.), *Comprehensive and collaborative systems that work for troubled youth: A national agenda* (pp. 122–148). Richmond, KY: National Coalition for Juvenile Justice Services.

Walter, M. E. (1988). *A study of cognitive and behavioral differences between educationally handicapped and nonhandicapped male youth.* Unpublished doctoral dissertation, University of Maryland, College Park.

Warboys, L., Burrell, S., Peters, C., & Ramiu, M. (1994). *California juvenile court special education manual.* San Francisco: Youth Law Center.

Warboys, L., & Shauffer, C. (1986). Legal issues in providing special education services to handicapped inmates. *Remedial and Special Education, 7*(3), 34–40.

Webb, S. L., Maddox, M., & Edgar, E. B. (1991). *Juvenile Corrections Interagency Transition Model.* Seattle: University of Washington.

White, W. A. T. (1988). A meta-analysis of effects of direct instruction in special education. *Education and Treatment of Children, 11,* 364–374.

Wolf, M. M., Braukmann, C., & Ramp, K. (1987). Serious delinquent behavior as a part of a significantly handicapping condition: Cures and supportive environments. *Journal of Applied Behavior Analysis, 20,* 347–359.

Wood, J. W., & Lazzari, A. M. (1997). *Exceeding the boundaries: Understanding exceptional lives.* Orlando, FL: Harcourt Brace.

Part IV

Treating High-Risk Offenders

Chapter 9
MANAGING AND TREATING VIOLENT OFFENDERS

Ralph C. Serin and Denise L. Preston

Assessing, treating, and managing violent individuals have become an increasing preoccupation of mental health professionals, in both correctional and forensic jurisdictions. It appears that all segments of society are affected because perpetrators and victims reflect a broad range of cultural and socioeconomic situations. Violent individuals include youth and adults, who are referred for assessment and treatment within both community and institutional settings. Chronic or persistently violent offenders typically have earlier onset of delinquent and criminal behavior, with a greater incidence over their life span (Moffitt, 1993a). It is important that *violence* be defined as a phenomenon distinct from *delinquency* and *criminality*. This is so that intervention for delinquency and criminality not be seen as sufficient for violent offenders, either in terms of treatment targets or theoretical underpinnings. This is not to imply, however, that managing violent clients cannot be informed by risk–need principles reflected in the psychology of criminal conduct (Andrews & Bonta, 1994).

Although there have been significant gains in the area of risk assessment and prediction of dangerousness (Quinsey, Harris, Rice, & Cormier, 1998; Steadman et al., 1993; Webster, Harris, Rice, Cormier, & Quinsey, 1994), these have failed to lead to comparable advances in intervention for violent offenders (Rice, Harris, & Quinsey, 1996). Also, there appears to be parallel research with violent juveniles and adults, but few concerted efforts to integrate best practices from each area. At the same time, reviews regarding the treatment of violent individuals have highlighted the complexity of the task (Tolan & Guerra, 1994) but provided little assistance to clinicians regarding best practices. Notwithstanding some signs of encouragement, the current status appears to be that we are now asking better questions, but are still not in a position to provide definitive answers regarding treatment efficacy. It is also notable that interdisciplinary initiatives that integrate theoretical approaches, assessment strategies, and interventions are beginning to be emphasized (Howell, 1995).

For the purpose of this chapter, violent behavior is considered the intentional and malevolent physical injuring of another without adequate social justification (Blackburn, 1993a). Within this definition there is provision for perpetrators to be anger-motivated or goal-oriented (Buss, 1961; Zillman, 1979). Anger is therefore not a prerequisite to offender violence (Novaco & Welsh, 1989), but is a common antecedent. Although threats and psychological injury are not included in this definition, this is not intended to mitigate their harmful effects on the victim. It should be noted that this definition excludes self-injurious behavior that is prevalent among offenders (Sherman & Morschauser, 1989), because intervention for this group is beyond the scope of this chapter. Because sexual offenders and perpetrators of spousal abuse have some relatively distinct treatment needs, they too were excluded from this

We would like to acknowledge the assistance of Nicola Epprecht in the completion of this chapter.

review. We decided instead to better reflect the current state of the art with respect to the treatment of violent offenders.

Within the developmental or adolescent literature in particular, there has been a virtual explosion of services aimed at reducing juvenile violence (Tolan & Guerra, 1994). Much of the work, however, has been in mobilizing community resources for preventing violence in what might be viewed as primary or secondary intervention (Tolan & Guerra, 1994). This work is critical in an overall model for preventing, treating, and managing violent behavior of individuals, but this chapter will focus mainly on tertiary intervention strategies—on individual and psychological factors (Madden, 1987), with an acknowledgment of the importance of social and societal factors.[1]

The purpose of this chapter is to highlight research that will assist clinicians who deliver services to violent offenders by providing clarity regarding issues that have an impact on treatment effectiveness. This will include issues related to definitions, the identification of treatment targets, models for intervention, treatment resistance, measurement of treatment gain, and program effectiveness. The emphasis will be on psychological treatments for violent behavior although pharmacological interventions will be summarized. Specific assessment issues will be described in the context of program and supervision issues, not risk assessment per se. Also, guidelines for incorporating treatment information into risk management decisions for violent offenders will be discussed.

There have been several impediments to progress in the area of treatment of violent offenders. These include problems with definition, restrictive conceptual models, weak research methodology, overreliance on self-report indexes of treatment needs and treatment gain, and the lack of outcome studies. These difficulties are not unique to this population (Quinsey, Rice, Harris, & Lalumière, 1993), but the perception by the public of an epidemic in the increase of violence and intolerance for treatment failures (false negatives) suggest much work is required regarding communication and public policy.

Defining Violent Offenders

A major impediment in treating violent offenders has been confusion over the definition of this population. Perhaps related to this has been the failure to recognize violent individuals as being heterogeneous. This lack of homogeneity requires them to be differentially managed, whether in terms of sanctions by the courts (Coordinating Council on Juvenile Justice and Delinquency Prevention, 1996), intervention strategies (Tolan & Guerra, 1994), or community supervision and risk-management requirements (Quinsey & Walker, 1992).

Violent offenders are usually defined in terms that are not mutually exclusive such as criminal convictions (e.g., assaults), attitudes (e.g., hostility), emotions (e.g., anger), and victim selection (e.g., spousal assault). Previous failures to specifically delineate types of violent offenders obscures treatment needs and confounds program-effectiveness research. For example, predominantly instrumentally aggressive clients are unlikely to show substantive gains in an arousal management-based

---

[1]Interested readers are referred to Tolan and Guerra (1994).

anger control program. Further, even observable and measurable changes within the program may well be unrelated to reductions in future violence. This might imply the program to be ineffective when more accurately, the program would not be effective for instrumentally violent clients.

Although not as sophisticated as the typology research with sex offenders (Knight & Prentky, 1990), there have been efforts to develop typologies for violent offenders. Some have included offense types (Dietz, 1987) and others have reflected detailed clinical reviews (Toch, 1969). More recently, cognitive style has been described as potentially useful in differentiating among violent offenders (Novaco & Welsh, 1989). This work is similar to research by Dodge and his colleagues (Crick & Dodge, 1994), who emphasize social-processing deficits in violent juveniles. Tolan and Guerra (1994) distinguished adolescent violent offenders according to patterns of their use of violence. They determined four distinct types: situational, relationship, predatory, and psychopathological. Most important, they suggested that these different types of violence can be distinguished in terms of their stability, prevalence, causes, and preferred intervention. Situational violence incorporates setting, environmental cues, and social factors. Although they do not specify how they arrived at their estimates, Tolan and Guerra (1994) suggested that more than 25% of the violence perpetrated by adolescents in the United States is situational. Relationship violence reflects interpersonal conflict and incorporates psychological and social factors. Estimated prevalence rates for adolescents are about 25%. Predatory violence denotes instrumental or goal-oriented violence, often in the context of criminality and gang activities. The prevalence rate for violent adolescents has been estimated at about 5%. Psychopathological violence, the least prevalent at less than 1 percent, reflects repetitive violence across settings, mainly because of the individual's neuropsychological deficits.

The scheme proposed by Tolan and Guerra (1994) extends earlier research attempting to define violent individuals by linking type of violence to type of intervention. Their work illustrates the utility of differentiated intervention, noting that violent offenders will not have the same onset, causes, treatment needs, and treatment response. Although lacking empirical support, it provides an important focus that was previously lacking in the treatment literature on violent offenders. This work is also consistent with a problem-based definition of violent offenders (Rice, Harris, Quinsey, & Cyr, 1990).

Treatment Considerations

The following sections deal with issues specific to violent offenders that affect treatment efficacy. These issues are intended to guide clinicians to identify key questions to consider when developing programs for violent offenders.

Treatment Needs–Targets

Literature reviews of risk factors in chronically violent or aggressive individuals yield such problems as hostility (Megargee, 1976), impulsivity (Henry & Moffitt, 1997), substance abuse (Pihl & Peterson, 1993), major mental disorders (Monahan, 1997), psychopathy (Hart & Hare, 1997), social information processing deficits (Dodge & Schwartz, 1997), and experience of poor parenting (Patterson, Reid, & Dishion, 1992) or neglect as a child (Widom, 1997). As well, follow-up studies (Zamble & Quinsey, 1997) and problem surveys (Rice, et al., 1990) point to anger as an important proximal risk factor for violence. These results illustrate the complexity of factors that must be considered in developing a general theory of violent behavior in formulating a theory about individual cases and in responding to violence through intervention.

Integrating Contributions From Developmental Literature

In designing interventions for violent adult offenders, the developmental literature has proven informative. This literature reflects a high level of sophistication and provides a good model (Tolan & Guerra, 1994). Moreover, many persistently violent adults would have likely received a diagnosis of conduct disorder as a child. Although this information is not available in either retrospective or prospective studies of offenders, it is implied from clinical experience and follow-up studies of juveniles (Robins, 1978). This suggests that interventions proven effective with conduct-disordered children may have utility for antisocial and violent adults.

Kazdin (1993) made specific recommendations regarding the development of treatment programs for conduct disorder. These apply equally to residential (inpatient) and community (outpatient) programs in both mental health and correctional jurisdictions. These include the development of subtypes to identify points for treatment; the development of manuals with specific and concrete guidelines to better assess program integrity and facilitate replication; the consideration of small scale (individual) and group designs to generate promising techniques; the consideration of multiple measures of treatment outcome; and the consideration of such issues as duration of treatment and the relative and combined efficacy of treatment combinations.

The developmental literature relevant to conduct disorder also prescribes a multifaceted intervention approach emphasizing skills acquisition (Kazdin, 1993), but is cognizant of cognitive processing or neuropsychological deficits (Moffitt, 1993b; Quay, 1993). This is consistent with the broader correctional programming literature (McGuire, 1995) and the sex offender treatment literature (Marques, Day, Nelson, & West, 1994). Related to maintenance, treatment programs within the correctional and sex offender domains address proximal or process issues, but it is recognized that gains diminish over time. This suggests the importance of a maintenance perspective and not a treatment cure (Dodge, 1993; Kazdin, 1993; Quinsey et al., 1998) for persistently violent individuals. Related to this, a study with violent juveniles by Guerra and Slaby (1990) illustrated that their experimental intervention, which was skills-based and targeted aggressive beliefs, was most effective posttreatment, but the gains did not generalize to yield reduced recidivism rates. This highlights the need for programs, particularly those intervening with higher risk, treatment-resistant individuals, to focus on both process measures of treatment gain and multiple outcome measures.

Finally, the developmental literature also provides some encouraging evidence regarding treatment effectiveness, notably in the area of family interventions. They are all skill-based, but vary somewhat in focus from parental training (Patterson, 1986) to family organization (Szapocznick & Kurtines, 1993) and family systems (Henggler, Melton, & Smith, 1992). These interventions are quite resource intensive and the extent to which they might be applied to residential settings and case-based interventions for adults is unclear.

Risk and Treatment Intensity

The strategy for determining treatment intensity for violent offenders is not well-defined. The work in the general area of treatment of offenders (Andrews et al., 1990; Rice & Harris, 1997) and antisocial adolescents (Kazdin, 1987) provides some specific guidelines. For instance, the broader correctional treatment literature equates intensity with risk (McGuire, 1995), with higher risk offenders requiring more intensive intervention (Andrews & Bonta, 1994). This matching of treatment intensity to risk underscores the importance of reliable and valid risk assessments.[2]

Treatment intensity must balance frequency of sessions, duration of sessions, and program integrity. Clinicians' resilience and mental health must also be considered in determining treatment intensity because persistently violent offenders are a challenging group. The setting in which treatment is provided also complicates the issue of treatment intensity, because it is far more difficult to provide higher intensity programs in the community than in inpatient facilities. The advantages and disadvantages of residential versus community-based treatment will be discussed in the next section (Robinson, 1996).

The range and chronicity of the treatment needs, then, not criminal convictions, should determine the ideal length of a program for violent offenders. It may not necessarily be the case that longer is better (Lochman, 1985). Whether a four-month program is preferred to a six-month program or half or full day sessions are preferred are empirical questions, yet the decisions are most typically determined by operational requirements.

Residential Versus Community-Based Programs

As stated earlier, it is more difficult to provide intensive treatment in the community than in institutions. Often, consultants who have other work demands provide community-based programs. Offenders have family and employment requirements that limit their availability. As well, noncompliance with respect to attendance and homework in community sessions is markedly higher (Meichenbaum & Turk, 1987). A final concern for community programs is how to deal with high-risk offenders, particularly if program participation is conscripted and the agency cannot refuse the offender.

Conversely, residential programs provide increased control to clinicians. Compliance is higher, although attendance and punctuality are far from perfect. Longer programs are more easily accommodated, as are programs that require more frequent sessions. Residential programs can also use milieu treatment or token economies that

---

[2]See Quinsey et al. (1998) for a scholarly review of assessment issues germane to violent offenders.

specifically address offender motivation (Agee, 1979). Also, institutional programs increasingly seem to focus on high-risk situations as an important aspect of treatment. Applying relapse prevention to violent offender treatment is appealing, but there is little empirical evidence for its uncritical use with the various different types of violent offenders (Prisgrove, 1993).

A disadvantage of residential or inpatient programs is that treatment effects seldom generalize across settings (Quinsey et al., 1998). Thus, an advantage of community or outpatient treatment is the opportunity to practice, in vivo, new skills. Perhaps for this reason, in other types of programming community sites have yielded greater results (Robinson, 1996). Community programs are also less costly.

Treatment Resistance

A final consideration in developing interventions for violent offenders relates to their interpersonal characteristics. In discussing treatment intensity, it was noted that persistently violent offenders are a challenging group. They tend to be described as treatment resistant. When compared to other offenders, they tend to be less motivated for treatment, more resistant or noncompliant while in treatment, have higher attrition rates, demonstrate fewer positive behavioral changes while in treatment, and demonstrate higher recidivism rates posttreatment. This is particularly true for those who are also psychopaths (Ogloff, Wong, & Greenwood, 1990; Rice et al., 1992). Offender noncompliance or attrition poses practical and methodological problems and has implications for treatment efficacy. Accordingly, those who intervene with persistently violent offenders must make every effort to motivate them to commit themselves to treatment. Related to this is the delivery of treatment in ways that will maximize the likelihood that these individuals will make significant behavioral changes.

Several authors have suggested specific strategies for engaging treatment-resistant clients (Jenkins, 1990; Kanfer & Schefft, 1988; Miller & Rollnick, 1991; Murphy & Baxter, 1997). The choice of the strategies used by therapists will depend on clients' state of readiness for change (Prochaska, DiClemente, & Norcross, 1992).

To assist clients to shift their "motivational balance" in favor of the benefits of change versus those of the status quo, therapists should challenge clients' views and the likely consequences of maintaining their current behavior and potential advantages of changing. This could be done by completing a cost–benefit analysis of the short-term and long-term advantages and disadvantages of completing versus not completing a violent offender treatment program. This analysis should include the perspectives of offenders, their families and significant others, friends, victims, victims' families and significant others, and society in general. This helps offenders to see the discrepancy between their current behavior and important personal goals (Preston & Murphy, 1997).

Some of the techniques for therapeutic engagement of treatment-resistant clients may be contraindicated when applied to psychopaths (Baumeister, Smart, & Boden, 1996). Psychopaths have a diminished capacity to form meaningful interpersonal relationships, although they can effectively mimic such a capacity, so interventions that place a heavy emphasis on developing a therapeutic alliance between therapists and clients are more likely to fail with psychopathic clients. Moreover, such treatments may be risky to therapists because they may perceive a false sense of personal safety with psychopaths (Meloy, 1995). Psychopathic clients can also be manipulative, and therapists must be persistent in setting and enforcing limits on their relationships with psychopaths. This is also one principle of effective correctional programming (Andrews et al., 1990).

Treatment Programs

It should be clear from the review thus far that interventions for chronic or persistently violent offenders must be multimodal and reflect proximal (individual) and distal (societal, cultural, familial) risk factors for violence. The distal factors imply primary and secondary interventions and proximal factors have been addressed by tertiary-level interventions. Tolan and Guerra (1994) provided an excellent review of primary and secondary interventions for violent juveniles. Because the focus for this review is on chronically violent youth and adults, as discussed earlier, only a review of tertiary-level pharmacological and psychological programs will be provided.

Pharmacological Interventions

At this time, no medication has been developed or approved specifically for treating violent behavior.[3] Several classes of psychotropic medications, however, have been used with some success with specific types of violent individuals. Antidepressants have been used to treat children and adolescents diagnosed with depression with agitation and attention deficit/hyperactivity disorder, and adults who are violent as a result of depression, personality disorders, brain injury, dementia, and schizophrenia. There have been cases, however, in which patients have shown an increase in suicidality or aggression following treatment with antidepressants.

Lithium, used primarily in treating bipolar disorder, has been shown to reduce violence in children and adolescents with conduct disorder and episodic dyscontrol and in children, adolescents, and adults who are developmentally delayed. It has also reduced violence in adults who have brain injuries, personality disorders, or schizophrenia, as well as those diagnosed with schizoaffective and organic mood disorders. Lithium has, however, also been shown to increase aggression in patients with temporal lobe epilepsy. It can also lower the seizure threshold for those with temporal lobe epilepsy and organic mental disorders. As well, lithium can cause toxic neurological reactions at therapeutic doses and is contraindicated in those with cardiovascular, renal, and thyroid disease.

Antipsychotics, because of their sedative effects, are used primarily for the acute management of violent behavior, usually resulting from a psychotic episode. Such violence may be related to delusions, hallucinations, or thought disorders. Antipsychotics are contraindicated for violence resulting from drug intoxication or with-

---

[3]See Corrigan, Yudofsky, and Silver (1993) and Karper and Krystal (1997) for comprehensive reviews of pharmacological interventions for violent behavior. This section is a summary of these two reviews.

drawal because they lower the threshold for seizures. For the same reason, they are contraindicated for those with epilepsy. Antipsychotics are not recommended for long-term managing of violent behavior because prolonged sedation profoundly affects patients' quality of life; may exacerbate dyscontrol, rage, and violence; and are associated with serious neurological side effects. The latter is associated with patient noncompliance with medication.

Antianxiety, anxiolytic, or sedative medications are also used primarily for the acute management of violent behavior. Because they increase seizure thresholds and are associated with few side effects, they are often the medication of choice in emergency situations. They have been shown to be effective with those demonstrating violent behavior as a result of alcohol withdrawal and acute psychosis as well as those exhibiting manic agitation and episodic temper outbursts. They are contraindicated for elderly people or those with liver dysfunction. As well, prolonged use may result in confusion, memory problems, sedation, depression, hypotension, and dependency.

Antihypertensive medications, most notably beta-blockers, have reduced aggressiveness and impulsivity in children and adolescents with intermittent explosive disorder, conduct disorder, and attention-deficit disorder. They have also been effective with adults with neurological impairments, chronic organic brain syndromes, and mental retardation. They have fewer neurological side effects than antipsychotic medications; thus, they may be better tolerated by those with organic mental disorders. Antihypertensives are not recommended for those with asthma, diabetes, and cardiovascular or lung disease. In rare cases they may also cause or exacerbate depression.

Anticonvulsant medications have been shown to have an impact on the aggressive behaviors of those with brain damage, particularly those with abnormal electroencephalograms. They have reduced aggression in some patients with dementia, some who are developmentally delayed and some who have organic mental disorders or impulse control problems. They can, however, cause side effects such as agranulocytosis and liver function abnormalities.

Although positive reports about the impact of medication on violent behavior are encouraging, this literature is plagued with numerous methodological problems, including small sample sizes, lack of control groups, failure to use double-blind procedures, noncompliance, and poor diagnostic accuracy. As well, although medication may have an impact on certain biological causes of violent behavior, on its own it is rarely effective in reducing violence over the long-term. This is primarily because medication cannot eliminate the numerous psychosocial causes of violence. Clearly, for those whose violence can be partially attributed to biology, an integrated approach using both pharmacological and psychological interventions would be most effective. The vast majority of violent offenders, however, would neither require nor benefit from pharmacological treatment. For them, psychological interventions should have some utility.

Psychological Interventions

Evidence from juvenile and adult studies with offenders consistently underscore the relative importance of behavior modification, cognitive–behavioral training, and social skills training to reduce antisocial behavior, and in some cases, violence. Psychotherapy and social casework have not proved effective at reducing antisocial behavior (Kazdin, 1993; Quinsey et al., 1998). In the juvenile literature, multidimensional programs such as those involving family systems have had the greatest impact, but the results are often confounded by such factors as intensity and caseload level (Tolan & Guerra, 1994).

When provided, descriptions of programs for violent offenders lead one to conclude that different clinicians label similar interventions differently. For instance, some programs are described as social skills training, yet target several different components—for example, assertion, self-control (arousal reduction), and social anxiety (Henderson, 1989). Other social skills programs, however, target specific areas, such as social withdrawal (Quinsey & Varney, 1977), conversational skills (Rice, 1983), and assertion (Marshall, Keltner, & Marshall, 1981). Within these studies there are assumptions that theoretically relate patients' poor social skills to violent behavior. Although it is likely that these targets all fall within a cluster of interactional skill deficiencies, it is not clear that all violent offenders are equally deficient in these areas (Henderson, 1989).

Under the rubric of treatment programs for violent offenders the most common category is that of anger management or anger control. Although the specific treatment components vary somewhat across programs and settings, it is common to see components to address arousal levels and some review or rehearsal of alternative thinking. Stress inoculation is advocated by Novaco (1975) and more cognitively based programs often refer to Ellis's (1977) irrational beliefs. More recently it appears that both components are incorporated into programs, although it is uncertain which contributes greatest to treatment gain, or the manner in which they may interact.

The components of a stress inoculation program typically consider awareness of hierarchy of individual anger cues; relationship between self-statements and anger level; model of anger and measurement of parameters (intensity, duration, frequency, behavioral outcome); reappraisal of anger situations; self-instructional coping aids; relaxation training to reduce arousal level and facilitate self-control; and skills practice. All of these strategies are aimed at reducing the arousal level of an individual. The view is that increased arousal equals reduced anger control. Arousal reduction involves systematic relaxation or distraction or imagery techniques (although our experience is that offenders feel awkward about practicing to mastery). Learning to recognize and control arousal decreases the likelihood of aggressive responses in perceived conflict situations. Increasingly, communication and assertion skills have been incorporated into this approach, although the core elements are cognitive preparation, skill acquisition, and application practice.

Ellis's (1977) approach more specifically emphasizes the role of cognitions, notably irrational beliefs, in the provocation and maintenance of anger levels. Offenders are taught that their irrational beliefs result in increased arousal (anger) and that their arousal precipitates aggressive behavior. Intervention targets the thought-to-feeling link, challenging offenders to refute irrational beliefs, presumably decreasing the likelihood of aggressive responses.

Implicit in the proliferation of anger control programs is that violent offenders are angry and that their level of anger exceeds that of nonviolent offenders (Hunter, 1993). Accordingly, reduced levels of anger are anticipated to result in less frequent and optimally less violent behavior. This is a curious notion in that violence is relatively infrequent, unreliably measured, and often appears to be motivated for reasons other than anger (Henderson, 1984, 1986). Perhaps for this last reason recent programs have included skills practice in the areas of social skills, assertion, problem solving, and empathy. With respect to the latter, the cognitive (perspective-taking) and behavioral (responding to perspective-taking) components of empathy are taught and practiced, with the hope that the emotional component (vicarious emotional response to perspective-taking) will follow.

Organizing intervention in sections that relate to self-regulation issues and cognitive deficiencies in violent offenders may be instructive in developing working models for assessment and intervention. These two approaches imply that most violence can be attributed to (a) high arousal–poor self-regulation (Novaco, 1976) or (b) poor problem-solving skills in the context of conflict situations (Slaby & Guerra, 1988).

Self-Regulation Strategies

Among the various treatment targets described in programs for violent offenders are arousal reduction techniques (Levey & Howells, 1990), interpersonal skill acquisition, (e.g., social skills, assertion, problem-solving; Guerra & Slaby, 1990; Henderson, 1989), and cognitive distortions (Ellis, 1977; Rokach, 1987). Some authors have incorporated several of these components into a more comprehensive package (Goldstein & Keller, 1987). Also, it has been suggested that treatment programs vary according to their emphasis on cognitive or behavioral deficiencies (Kennedy, 1990) and this may relate to approaches used to measure treatment gain. Again, many studies are multifaceted in their assessment of treatment gain (Kennedy, 1990; Kolko, Loar, & Sturnick, 1990).

Cutting across various prison settings and populations, evidence exists to support the application of relaxation training or stress inoculation to anger control issues (Hughes, 1993; Hunter, 1993; Kennedy, 1990; Rokach, 1987; Schlichter & Horan, 1981; Serin & Kuriychuk, 1994; Stermac, 1987). These studies replicate findings with nonoffender samples (Deffenbacher, 1992), where improved relaxation facilitates anger control. It is not clear, however, that arousal reduction strategies are necessarily superior to skills acquisition in the areas of social interactions or problem solving (Kennedy, 1990; Moon & Eisler, 1983) or cognitive coping skills (Deffenbacher, Story, Brandon, Hogg, & Hazaleus, 1988). Additional research is required before conclusions can be made regarding the differential treatment effects of components of typical anger control programs. Such research will need to ensure that offenders with pretreatment deficits are matched to the relevant area and that attentional controls are available (Guerra & Slaby, 1990; Henderson, 1989; Kolko et al., 1990).

Some programs target impulsivity, yet these appear to reflect a problem-solving strategy with a delay or pause feature comparable to self-instructional training (Camp, Blom, Herbert, & Van Doorninck, 1977). One novel application has been Rokach's (1987) use of a forced delay feature as part of a process reviewing simulated social situations. This is consistent with research highlighting the central role latency (impulsivity) plays in the expression of cognitive schema (Dodge & Newman, 1981). That is, pausing may inhibit expression of negative thoughts and facilitate generation of alternative responses.

Cognitive Processing Strategies

Novaco and Welsh (1989) described the importance of appraisals and expectations in viewing potentially provocative events and promoting an aggressive response. Prior beliefs or schema influence automatic processing of information, which is an important form of cognitive processing. Research with adult offenders has demonstrated irrational beliefs (Ford, 1991) and attributional biases (Serin, 1991) in violent offenders. Research in the area of juvenile violence has highlighted the critical role information processing deficits play in determining and maintaining aggressive behavior (Crick & Dodge, 1994; Dodge & Frame, 1982; Slaby & Guerra, 1988). Aggressive juvenile offenders have been found to be deficient in social problem-solving skills and to espouse many beliefs supporting aggression. Specifically, they tend to define problems in hostile ways, adopt hostile goals, seek less confirmatory information, generate fewer alternative solutions, anticipate fewer consequences for aggressive solutions, and choose less effective solutions. This work has prompted investigations into the efficacy of interventions developed to improve the information processing skills of human participants (Lochman & Lenhart, 1993).

Although several examples of these efforts can be found in the developmental literature for aggressive and delinquent youth (Feindler, Marriott, & Iwata, 1984; Hains, 1989), the most ambitious effort with juvenile offenders described the utility of a problem-solving strategy that targeted biased thinking skills (Guerra & Slaby, 1990). The intervention consisted of 120 aggressive adolescents, equally divided by gender, being randomly assigned to a 12-week cognitive mediation training, attention control, or no-treatment control. The cognitive mediation training specifically targeted the deficits noted previously by Slaby and Guerra (1988). Those familiar with the psychology of criminal conduct (Andrews & Bonta, 1994) will note this is a specific application of targeting thoughts that maintain violent criminal behavior. Pre- and posttreatment assessment incorporated measures of social cognition (beliefs about aggression), behavior ratings, self-report, and recidivism (24 months). Posttreatment gains for the treatment group were noted in terms of increased skills in solving social problems, reduced support of aggressive beliefs, and reduced aggressive behaviors (based on blind raters). The inference is that these sociocognitive factors regulate aggressive behavior, yet recidivism rates for the treated individuals, although reduced, were not significantly lower than the control groups.

Several studies have examined the efficacy of cognitive–behavioral interventions for aggressive adult offenders. Hunter (1993) offered a 10-week anger management program to 28 incarcerated male offenders who had a propensity for interpersonal violence. She compared them to a control group of 27 inmates. The intervention included relaxation therapy, stress management, conflict resolution, and cognitive therapy, the latter targeting errors in thinking (hostile and aggressive thoughts), irrational beliefs, and negative self-talk. Offenders in both groups completed pre- and posttreatment self-report measures pertaining to personality, cognitions, behaviors, and social desirability and researchers recorded other behavioral indexes, including institutional infractions. She found that treated offenders showed significant gains relative to nontreated offenders across self-report and behavioral ratings. No follow-up data are available, however, and the total sample is only 55 offenders.

Hughes (1993) provided a 12-week anger management program to 52 incarcerated adult offenders and attempted to compare them to a control group of 27 offenders. The latter were men who either dropped out of the program after one or two sessions, or who opted not to participate in the program for a variety of reasons. The program, described as both educational and experiential, consisted of relaxation therapy, assertiveness training, moral reasoning, problem-solving, and rational emotive therapy. Offenders in the treatment group completed a number of self-report measures pre- and posttreatment. Also for the treatment group, Hughes (1993) completed behavioral ratings of role plays pre- and posttreatment. Offenders in the control group completed pretreatment self-report measures only. Hughes (1993) attempted to gather posttreatment data from the control group, but few of them agreed to complete the tests. Finally, four years after program completion he gathered staff ratings of treated offenders' ability to cope with anger, anxiety, and various problem situations and obtained recidivism data. Hughes (1993) found that treated offenders reported posttreatment gains regarding anger scores, irrational beliefs, and in role plays. However, there was no difference in recidivism rates between the treated and nontreated groups.

Kennedy (1990) compared the relative efficacy of stress inoculation treatment to a behavioral skills treatment (Goldstein & Keller, 1987) with a sample of 37 incarcerated adult offenders. The former involved training in cognitive strategies for dealing with the four stages of conflict (preparing for provocation, impact and confrontation, coping with arousal, and reflecting on the provocation), relaxation training, and imagery, and the latter involved teaching social skills such as assertiveness and empathy through the use of modeling, role-plays, feedback, and transfer training. Offenders completed several self-report measures both pre- and posttreatment. As well, Kennedy (1990) completed pre- and posttreatment behavioral ratings of structured role plays, and reviewed offender files for relevant incident reports. She found that offenders showed posttreatment gains on several of the measures. However, she also completed an interim assessment of treatment gain and found that order of presentation of treatment had no effect. The greatest treatment gain occurred in the initial phase of treatment, regardless of which treatment was offered first.

An intensive two-year correctional program in Vermont that focuses on criminal thinking in violent offenders has demonstrated a reduction in violent recidivism relative to an untreated group (Bush, 1995). Some innovations in the program include the use of a therapeutic milieu, the use of "thinking reports," and the use of paraprofessional staff (trained correctional officers). The program has now been delivered for nine years and has incorporated a complementary community aftercare component.

An overview of these programs is presented in Table 9.1. It should be noted that all programs report some treatment effects, but few provide the rigor (i.e., control groups) to conclude that intervention for violent adults reduces violent recidivism. Quinsey et al. (1998) also noted that the relationship between response to treatment and subsequent dangerousness has yet to be demonstrated empirically. Nonetheless, they stated that theoretically based, empirically driven programs, appropriately implemented, should be developed, delivered, and evaluated. They and others (Serin, 1998) also suggested that treatment should be reconceptualized as a mechanism for enhanced risk management through continuing intervention in the community.

Lastly, in 1996 the Correctional Service of Canada developed an intensive treatment demonstration program for incarcerated persistently violent adult offenders (Serin, 1995). The treatment program is intense, involving four group sessions and one individual session per week for 16 weeks. Treatment is provided by two staff members—a doctoral-level registered psychologist and a bachelor's-level therapist. Based on a review of the literature, treatment targets include motivation for treatment and behavior change, aggressive beliefs, cognitive distortions, arousal management, impulsivity, conflict resolution, problem-solving, assertiveness, empathy enhancement, and relapse prevention.

Measuring treatment needs includes measures of treatment readiness, personality, impulsivity, anxiety, anger, attachment, aggressive beliefs, social problem-solving, empathy, relapse prevention, and social desirability. About half of the tests are available in the public domain and the rest were developed specifically for the treatment program. Most are self-report measures, whereas some constitute a structured, tape-recorded interview with a formal scoring protocol. The interview consists largely of vignette assessments of attributional biases (Dodge & Newman, 1981). The vignette measures also assess problem-solving skill deficits, aggressive beliefs, and empathy. These are dynamic behavioral ratings and have recently been demonstrated to predict violent recidivism (Bettman, 1997). On an on-going basis, the impact of program content on knowledge and skills acquisition is assessed through self-report measures, and staff complete weekly behavioral ratings to measure motivation, attentiveness, comprehension, participation, attitude, and skills implementation. For each of the domains rated by staff, there is a 5-point Likert scale with behavioral descriptors for each rating. The two program staff discuss each domain for each participant and arrive at their ratings by consensus.

Measurement of Treatment Gain–Program Evaluation (Outcomes)

One major shortcoming of this literature on the treatment of violent offenders is the overreliance on self-report measures of treatment gain. Concerns regarding the veracity of uncorroborated self-report in offender samples have been expressed elsewhere (Rogers, 1986; Shapiro, 1991), and efforts to control for social desirability or intelligence appear warranted. Self-report information is important because it reflects offenders' self-perceptions (Blackburn, 1993a), yet it may be an insufficient measure of treatment gain given the demand characteristics, the reality that intervention is often accepted under duress, and where less than favorable posttreatment reports have significant negative consequences. Related to the concern about self-report instruments is that most have been developed for nonoffender populations (Novaco, 1994), lack validity scales, and have such transparent items that interpreting posttreatment improvement without corroborating indexes of gain may be at best speculative (Hughes, 1993). A related concern is that some violent offenders receive higher scores posttreatment, which suggest greater problems on self-report measures of anger, aggressiveness, and hostility (Novaco, 1994; Selby, 1984; Serin & Kuriychuk, 1994). Baseline measures or within-subjects comparisons are warranted so that individual offender's improvement may be considered.

Meloy (1995) highlighted the importance of dystonic affect (i.e., depression and anxiety) as requisite to therapeutic gain because they indicate a capacity for concern over one's actions and empathy for others. Conversely, Meloy noted the absence of such emotion in primary psychopaths may be a distinguishing factor in their poor response to treatment. Also, Gerstley et al. (1989) commented on the facilitative role

Table 9.1—*Summary of Adult Violent Treatment Outcome Studies*

Study	Research Participants	Treatment Attributes	Evaluation	Outcome
Rokach (1987)	51 treated incarcerated male offenders, 44 controls with violent criminal history and self-report anger problems	Anger management, cognitive–behavioral, short-term (27 hours), group format	Nonrandom referrals, partially matched controls, pre- and posttest self-reports, non-blind posttreatment interviews, no recidivism data	Positive within treatment effects, no recidivism data
Stermac (1987)	Offenders remanded to METFORS[a] for psychiatric assessment, 20 treated and 20 controls with anger problem	Anger management, cognitive–behavioral, short-term (12 hours), group format	Randomly assigned, control group, pre- and posttest self-report measures, no recidivism data	Some positive within-treatment effects, no recidivism data
Kennedy (1990)	Canadian provincially incarcerated males referred for anger management, 19 treated and 18 controls	Anger management, cognitive–behavioral, short-term (60 hours), group format	Nonrandom, unmatched delayed treatment control group, pre- and posttest self-report measures, blind behavioral ratings of role plays, 2 month follow-up assessing institutional misconducts	Positive within-treatment effects and mixed findings regarding institutional misconducts
Rice, Harris, & Cormier (1992)	176 treated mentally disordered male offenders and 146 matched controls with violent histories	Intensive two-year therapeutic community therapy, group therapy, 80 hours per week	Nonrandom, matched controls, retrospective 10 year follow-up measuring general and violent recidivism	No significant overall treatment effects, but treated psychopaths exhibited higher failure rates than untreated psychopaths

Hughes (1993)	Federally incarcerated male offenders, 52 treated and 27 controls with violent criminal histories	Cognitive–behavioral, anger management, short-term (24 hours), group format	Referrals served as nonrandom, not-matched controls, pre- and posttest self-report measures, role plays, coping ability ratings, four-year follow-up assessing time to rearrest, and recidivism	Positive within-treatment effects, mixed results regarding effects on recidivism
Hunter (1993)	Federally incarcerated males, 28 treated, 27 controls with violent histories	Cognitive–behavioral anger management, short-term (10 weeks), group format	Nonrandom, unmatched waiting list controls, pre- and posttest self-report measures, two-month follow-up assessing institutional misconducts	Positive within-treatment effects and posttreatment effects
Smiley, Mulloy, & Brown (1997)	134 treated federally incarcerated male offenders with violent index offense, 14,500 controls	Cognitive–behavioral violent offender personality disorder program, group therapy, eight months	Nonrandom, control group not matched, unspecified follow-up period, recidivism: success or failure on conditional release	No posttreatment effects
Bush (1995)	81 treated violent male offenders and 287 male controls, both from Vermont Department of Corrections	Cognitive self-change program, targets attitudes, beliefs, and thoughts; supportive of violence, group format, six-month to two-year institution component and one-year community component	Nonrandom, control group not matched, one- to three-year postcommunity treatment follow-up period, recidivism: arrest or parole violation	Positive treatment effects; recidivism rate was twice as high for untreated group than for treated group (more than seven months in treatment)

Note. [a]Metropolitan Toronto Forensic Service.

of therapeutic alliance in treating antisocial males. These issues might be profitably considered in post hoc comparisons of offenders who show posttreatment gain versus those who do not.

The use of recidivism rates as a measure of treatment gain has been debated (Blackburn, 1993a), yet for offender populations the expectation of increased community safety and reduced violent recidivism is often their *raison d'être*. Multiple outcome measures are also recommended to detect partial successes that may be obscured by dichotomous success–fail definitions, as are survival analyses to control for unequal release times (Chung, Schmidt, & Witte, 1991).

Treatment outcome should be measured in a number of ways. For residential or institutional settings, intermediate measures of treatment gain include reductions in the frequency and severity of institutional infractions, especially verbal threats and physical assaults. An increase in the number of participants seeking and maintaining institutional employment would also be an intermediate gain. So too, would increased compliance with correctional treatment plans, transfers to reduced security institutions, and the granting of parole or discretionary release. For community or outpatient settings, intermediate measures of treatment gain include seeking and maintaining employment and compliance with community supervision. Long-term measures of outcome include increase in time to reoffend, reduction in the severity of reoffenses, and reduction in violent recidivism rates.

Some of the intermediate targets may assist clinicians to answer questions about the effectiveness of a new program before outcome data are available. For instance, after providing the Correctional Service of Canada's treatment demonstration program for persistently violent offenders to two groups of offenders, the program staff were able to report a 50% reduction in institutional infractions for the six months during the program relative to the previous six months for offenders in the program. Other notable outcomes for the program included improved employment posttreatment and transfers to reduced security (Preston & Murphy, 1997). It remains to be determined whether such intermediate gains are predictive of reduced recidivism.

Pre–post treatment changes on self-report measures are also important intermediate indexes of treatment gain, yet they have not proved particularly effective predictors of outcome with offender populations (Rice & Harris, 1997). Social desirability, transparent items, and historical items contribute to concerns about reliance on offenders' self-report as indexes of treatment gain. With this in mind, alternative strategies for use by clinicians to assess treatment readiness, interpersonal style, and treatment performance have been developed. The interpersonal style measure includes clinician ratings of offender characteristics such as motivation, victim stance, callousness, and problem-solving ability. The treatment-performance measure includes clinician ratings of knowledge of program content, understanding of criminality, skills acquisition, and skills application. Preliminary data regarding these behaviorally anchored rating scales are encouraging (Kennedy & Serin, 1997; Serin & Kennedy, 1997), and research on the use of these measures of treatment responsivity with different offender populations is proceeding.

Differential Treatment

A theme throughout this chapter is the heterogeneity of violent offenders. It should be apparent, then, that the current array of interventions reviewed fail to adequately address the range of treatment needs. It is also a clinical reality that few settings have the resources to provide multiple programs for different types of violent offenders. Also, although appealing from a methodological viewpoint, the operational juggling required to match offenders to specific treatment modules based on pretreatment assessment is quite arduous. Such a strategy also necessitates the use of open groups, and this might interfere with the group dynamics and cohesion. This is because not all offenders would receive all treatment components. Notwithstanding these problems, improvements in the prescription of programs to better match the treatment needs of different violent offenders' remains an important goal.

From the treatment responsivity research (Kennedy & Serin, 1997), it is clear that program effectiveness will be increased relative to the extent to which programs are prescriptively applied to offenders. Perhaps using a more comprehensive assessment protocol to determine different types of violent offenders and their specific treatment needs will lead to more differentiated programming. If offenders are inappropriately assigned to a specific treatment program, then demonstration of treatment effectiveness will be markedly impaired. The issue is more what type of program works for which offender(s).

Managing Violent Offenders

From a clinical perspective, implicit in the delivery of programs for violent offenders is the expectation that such programming will lead to reductions in violent recidivism. Regrettably, the evidence is far from compelling, certainly for groups of persistently violent offenders. What then are the implications for risk management of violent offenders' posttreatment? For those programs that focus on relapse prevention, the offense cycle provides a mechanism to discover antecedents or proximal factors to an offender's use of violence. For those programs that use comprehensive risk appraisals, there is an opportunity for the clinician to make recommendations regarding the required intensity and nature of community aftercare and supervision. This can include both treatment requirements and recommendations regarding treatment noncompliance.

Yet not all offenders benefit equally from treatment, and abstinence of violence may be an unrealistic expectation. For the highest risk offenders, the potential contribution of treatment must be considered judiciously. In this regard, developing explicit decision rules to assist clinicians against unbridled optimism would be advantageous (Serin, 1998). These guidelines could assist decision makers in integrating pretreatment ratings of risk and responsivity with posttreatment ratings of treatment gain to determine an offender's reintegration potential and a reasonable risk-management strategy for the duration of his sentence. We are currently engaged in an effort to develop and validate such a scheme.

Summary

Notwithstanding the concern about violent offenders, there exists a surprisingly small body of literature describing effective treatment efforts, particularly in contrast to other groups such as those convicted of sexual offenses and spousal abuse offenses.

Most published studies do report treatment gains, but this has mainly been restricted to self-reports and has not generalized to improved recidivism rates. To date, measuring treatment efficacy has been confounded by this overreliance on self-report questionnaires, the absence of control groups, and problems in defining violent offenders. This chapter has provided several schemes to assist clinicians and researchers in improving the current state of violent offender programming. The most impressive studies regarding both methodology and outcome are from the juvenile literature and reflect comprehensive multisystemic programs. Efforts should be initiated to better incorporate best practices from the juvenile literature into treatment programs for violent adult offenders. The juvenile literature also places greater emphasis on skill acquisition in the areas of family dynamics and problem-solving than the emphasis with adults on arousal management. Models, then, that integrate arousal level, self-regulation, and cognitive style may prove helpful as clinicians strive to provide programs for an array of different types of violent offenders. Multimethod assessments of treatment needs, risk, and treatment gain are also recommended. With respect to management issues, pretreatment risk appraisals, and decision rules regarding treatment response are essential.

References

Agee, V. L. (1979). *Treatment of the violent incorrigible adolescent.* Lexington, MA: Lexington Books.

Andrews, D. A., & Bonta, J. (1994). *The psychology of criminal conduct.* Cincinnati, OH: Anderson.

Andrews, D. A., Zinger, I., Hoge, R. D., Bonta, J., Gendreau, P., & Cullen, F. T. (1990). Does correctional treatment work? A clinically relevant and psychologically informed meta-analysis. *Criminology, 28,* 369–404.

Baumeister, R. F., Smart, L., & Boden, J. M. (1996). Relation of threatened egotism to violence and aggression: The dark side of high self-esteem. *Psychological Bulletin, 103,* 5–33.

Bettman, M. D. (1997, June). *Social problem-solving, attitudes, and the prediction of recidivism risk.* Paper presented at the annual conference of the Canadian Psychological Association, Toronto, Canada.

Blackburn, R. (1993a). *The psychology of criminal conduct.* Chichester, England: John Wiley & Sons.

Bush, J. (1995). Teaching self-risk management to violent offenders. In J. McGuire (Ed.), *What works: Reducing reoffending: Guidelines from research and practice* (pp. 139–154). Chichester, England: John Wiley & Sons.

Buss, A. H. (1961). *The psychology of aggression.* New York: Wiley.

Camp, B. W., Blom, G. E., Herbert, F., & Van Doorninck, W. J. (1977). "Think aloud": A program for developing self-control in young aggressive boys. *Journal of Abnormal Child Psychology, 5,* 157–169.

Chung, C. F., Schmidt, P., & Witte, A. D. (1991). Survival analysis: A survey. *Journal of Quantitative Criminology, 7,* 59–98.

Coordinating Council on Juvenile Justice and Delinquency Prevention. (1996). *Combating violence and delinquency: The national juvenile justice action plan summary.* Washington, DC: Office of Juvenile Justice and Delinquency Prevention, U.S. Department of Justice.

Correctional Service of Canada. (1996, March). *Standards and guidelines for the provision of services to sex offenders*. Ottawa: Public Works and Government Services Canada.

Correctional Service of Canada. (1997). *Basic facts about corrections in Canada. 1997 edition*. Ottawa: Public Works and Government Services Canada.

Corrigan, P. W., Yudofsky, S. C., & Silver, J. M. (1993). Pharmacological and behavioral treatments for aggressive psychiatric inpatients. *Hospital and Community Psychiatry, 44*, 125–133.

Crick, N. R., & Dodge, K. A. (1994). A review and reformulation of social information-processing mechanisms in children's social adjustment. *Psychological Bulletin, 1*, 74–101.

Deffenbacher, J. L. (1992, March). *Cognitive–behavioral approaches to anger reduction*. Proceedings of XXIV Banff international conference on the behavioral sciences.

Deffenbacher, J. L., Story, D. A., Brandon, A. D., Hogg, J. A., & Hazaleus, S. L. (1988). Cognitive and cognitive-relaxation treatments of anger. *Cognitive Therapy and Research, 12*, 167–184.

Dietz, P. E. (1987). Patterns in human violence. In L. E. Hales & A. J. Francis (Eds.), *Psychiatry Update: APA Annual Review, Vol. 6*. Washington, DC: American Psychological Association.

Dodge, K. A. (1993). The future of research on the treatment of conduct disorder. *Development and Psychopathology, 5*, 311–319.

Dodge, K. A., & Frame, C. L. (1982). Social-cognitive biases and deficits in aggressive boys. *Child Development, 53*, 620–635.

Dodge, K. A., & Newman, J. P. (1981). Biased decision making processes in aggressive boys. *Journal of Abnormal Psychology, 90*, 375–379.

Dodge, K. A., & Schwartz, D. (1997). Social information processing mechanisms in aggressive behaviour. In D. M. Stoff, J. Breiling, & J. D. Maser. (Eds.), *Handbook of antisocial behavior* (pp. 171–180). New York: John Wiley & Sons.

Ellis, A. (1977). *Anger—How to live with and without it*. Secaucus, NJ: Citadel Press.

Feindler, E. L., Marriott, S. A., & Iwata, M. (1984). Group anger control training for junior high school delinquents. *Cognitive Therapy and Research, 8*, 299–311.

Ford, B. D. (1991). Anger and irrational beliefs in violent inmates. *Personality and Individual Differences, 12*, 211–215.

Gerstley, L., McLellan, T., Alterman, A., Woody, G., Luborsky, L., & Prout, M. (1989). Ability to form an alliance with the therapist: A possible marker of prognosis for patients with antisocial personality disorder. *American Journal of Psychiatry, 146*, 508–512.

Goldstein, A. P., & Keller, H. (1987). *Aggressive behavior: Assessment and intervention*. New York: Pergamon Press.

Guerra, N. G., & Slaby, R. G. (1990). Cognitive mediators of aggression in adolescent offenders: Intervention. *Developmental Psychology, 26*, 269–277.

Hains, A. A. (1989). An anger-control intervention with aggressive delinquent youths. *Behavioral Residential Treatment, 4*, 213–230.

Hart, S. D., & Hare, R. D. (1997). Psychopathy: Assessment and association with criminal conduct. In D. M. Stoff, J. Breiling, & J. D. Maser. (Eds.), *Handbook of antisocial behavior* (pp. 22–35). New York: John Wiley & Sons.

Henderson, M. (1984). Prison inmates' explanations for interpersonal violence: Accounts and attributions. *Journal of Consulting and Clinical Psychology, 52*, 789–794.

Henderson, M. (1986). An empirical typology of violent incidents reported by prison inmates with convictions for violence. *Aggressive Behavior, 12*, 21–32.

Henderson, M. (1989). Behavioral approaches to crime. In K. Howells and C. R. Hollin (Eds.), *Clinical approaches to violence* (pp. 25–37). London: John Wiley & Sons.

Henggeler, S. W., Melton, G. B., & Smith, L. (1992). Family preservation using multisystemic therapy: An effective alternative to incarcerating serious juvenile offenders. *Journal of Consulting and Clinical Psychology, 60*, 953–961.

Henry, B., & Moffitt, T. E. (1997). Neuropsychological and neuroimaging studies of juvenile delinquency and adult criminal behavior. In D. M. Stoff, J. Breiling, & J. D. Maser. (Eds.), *Handbook of antisocial behavior* (pp. 280–288). New York: John Wiley & Sons.

Howell, J. C. (Ed.). (1995). *Guide for implementing the comprehensive strategy for serious, violent, and chronic juvenile offenders*. Washington, DC: Office of Juvenile Justice and Delinquency Prevention, U.S. Department of Justice.

Hughes, G. V. (1993). Anger management program outcomes. *Forum on Corrections Research, 5, 1,* 5–9.

Hunter, D. (1993). Anger management in the prison: An evaluation. *Forum on Corrections Research, 5,* 3–5.

Jenkins, A. (1990). *Invitations to responsibility: The therapeutic engagement of men who are violent and abusive*. Adelaide, South Australia: Dulwich Centre.

Kanfer, F. H., & Schefft, B. K. (1988). *Guiding the process of therapeutic change*. Champaign, IL: Research Press.

Karper, L. P., & Krystal, J. H. (1997). Pharmacotherapy of violent behavior. In D. M. Stoff, J. Breiling, & J. D. Maser. (Eds.), *Handbook of antisocial behavior* (pp. 436–444). New York: John Wiley & Sons.

Kazdin, A. E. (1987). Treatment of antisocial behavior in children: Current status and future directions. *Psychological Bulletin, 102,* 187–203.

Kazdin, A. E. (1993). Treatment of conduct disorder: Progress and directions in psychotherapy research. *Development and Psychopathology, 5,* 277–310.

Kennedy, S. M. (1990). *Anger management training with adult prisoners*. Unpublished manuscript.

Kennedy, S. M., & Serin, R. C. (1997). Treatment responsivity: Contributing to effective correctional programming. *International Community Corrections Association Journal, 7,* 46–52.

Knight, R. A., & Prentky, R. A. (1990). Classifying sexual offenders: The development and corroboration of taxonomic models. In W. L. Marshall, D. R. Laws, & H. E. Barbaree (Eds.), *The handbook of sexual assault: Issues, theories, and treatment of the offender* (pp. 27–52). New York: Plenum Press.

Kolko, D. J., Loar, L. L., & Sturnick, D. (1990). Inpatient social–cognitive skills training groups with conduct disordered and attention deficit disordered children. *Journal of Child Psychology and Psychiatry and Allied Disciplines, 31,* 737–748.

Levey, S., & Howells, K. (1990). Anger and its management. *Journal of Forensic Psychiatry, 1,* 305–327.

Lochman, J. E. (1985). Effects of different treatment lengths in cognitive behavioral interventions with aggressive boys. *Child Psychiatry and Human Development, 16,* 45–56.

Lochman, J. E., & Lenhart, L. A. (1993). Anger coping intervention for aggressive children: Conceptual models and outcome effects. *Clinical Psychology Review, 13,* 785–805.

Madden, D. J. (1987). Psychotherapeutic approaches in the treatment of violent persons. In L. H. Roth (Ed.), *Clinical treatment of the violent person*. New York: Guilford Press.

Marques, J. K., Day, D. M., Nelson, C., & West, M. A. (1994). Effects of cognitive–behavioral treatment on sex offender recidivism: Preliminary results of a longitudinal study. *Criminal Justice and Behavior, 21,* 28–54.

Marshall, P. C., Keltner, A. A., & Marshall, W. L. (1981). Anxiety reduction, assertive training and enactment of consequences: A comparative treatment study in the modification of nonassertion and social fear. *Behavior Modification, 5,* 85–102.

McGuire, J. (Ed.). (1995). *What works: Reducing reoffending: Guidelines from research and practice*. Chichester, England: John Wiley & Sons.

Megargee, E. I. (1976). The prediction of dangerous behavior. *Criminal Justice and Behavior, 3,* 3–21.

Meichenbaum, D., & Turk, D. C. (1987). *Facilitating treatment adherence: A practitioner's guidebook*. New York: Plenum Press.

Meloy, J. R. (1995). Treatment of antisocial personality disorder. In G. Gabbard (Ed.), *Treatments of psychiatric disorders: The DSM-IV Edition* (pp. 2273–2290). Washington, DC: American Psychiatric Press.

Miller, W. R., & Rollnick, S. (1991). *Motivational interviewing: Preparing people to change addictive behavior.* New York: Guilford Press.

Moffitt, T. E. (1993a). Adolescence-limited and life-course-persistent antisocial behavior: A developmental taxonomy. *Psychological Review, 100*, 674–701.

Moffitt, T. E. (1993b). The neuropsychology of conduct disorder. *Developmental Psychopathology, 5*, 135–151.

Monahan, J. (1997). Major mental disorders and violence to others. In D. M. Stoff, J. Breiling, & J. D. Maser (Eds.), *Handbook of antisocial behavior* (pp. 92–100). New York: John Wiley & Sons.

Moon, J. R., & Eisler, R. M. (1983). Anger control: An experimental comparison of three behavioral treatments. *Behavior Therapy, 14*, 493–505.

Murphy, C. M., & Baxter, V. A. (1997). Motivating batterers to change in the treatment context. *Journal of Interpersonal Violence, 12*, 607–619.

Novaco, R. W. (1975). *Anger control.* Toronto: D. C. Heath.

Novaco, R. W. (1976). The function and regulation of the arousal of anger. *American Journal of Psychiatry, 133*, 1124–1128.

Novaco, R. W. (1994). Anger as a risk factor for violence among the mentally disordered. In J. Monahan & H. J. Steadman (Eds.), *Violence and mental disorder: Developments in risk assessment* (pp. 21–59). Chicago: University of Chicago Press.

Novaco, R. W., & Welsh, W. N. (1989). Anger disturbances: Cognitive mediation and clinical prescriptions. In K. Howells and C. R. Hollin (Eds.), *Clinical approaches to violence* (pp. 39–60). London: John Wiley & Sons.

Ogloff, J. R. P., Wong, S., & Greenwood, A. (1990). Treating criminal psychopaths in a therapeutic community program. *Behavioral Sciences and the Law, 8*, 181–190.

Patterson, G. R. (1986). Performance models for antisocial boys. *American Psychologist, 41*, 432–444.

Patterson, G. R., Reid, J. B., & Dishion, T. J. (1992). *Antisocial boys: A social interactional approach, Vol. 4.* Eugene, OR: Castalia.

Pihl, R. O., & Peterson, J. B. (1993). Alcohol/drug use and aggressive behavior. In S. Hodgins (Ed.), *Mental Disorder and Crime.* Newbury Park, CA: Sage.

Preston, D. L., & Murphy, S. (1997). Motivating treatment-resistant clients in therapy. *Forum on Corrections Research, 9, 2*, 39–43.

Prisgrove, P. (1993). A relapse prevention approach to reducing aggressive behavior. In S. A. Gerrall & W. Lucas (Eds.), *Serious violent offenders: Sentencing, psychiatry and law reform* (pp. 179–191). Canberra: Australian Institute of Criminology.

Prochaska, J. O., DiClemente, C. C., & Norcross, J. C. (1992). In search of the structure of change. In Y. Klar, J. D. Fisher, J. M. Chinsky, & A. Nadler (Eds.), *Self-change: Social psychological and clinical perspectives* (pp. 87–114). New York: Springer-Verlag.

Quay, H. C. (1993). The psychobiology of undersocialized aggressive conduct disorder: A theoretical perspective. *Development and Psychopathology, 5*, 165–180.

Quinsey, V. L., Harris, G. T., Rice, M. E., & Cormier, C. A. (1998). *Violent offenders: Appraising and managing risk.* Washington, DC: American Psychological Association.

Quinsey, V. L., Rice, M. E., Harris, G. T., & Lalumière, M. L. (1993). Assessing treatment efficacy in outcome studies of sex offenders. *Journal of Interpersonal Violence, 8*, 512–523.

Quinsey, V. L., & Varney, G. W. (1977). Social skills game: A general method for the modeling and practice of adaptive behaviors. *Behavior Therapy, 8*, 278–281.

Quinsey, V. L., & Walker, W. D. (1992). Dealing with dangerousness: Community risk management strategies with violent offenders. In R. DeV. Peters (Ed.), *Aggression and violence throughout the life span* (pp. 244–262). Newbury Park, CA: Sage.

Rice, M. E. (1983). Improving the social skills of males in a maximum security psychiatric setting. *Canadian Journal of Behavioural Science, 15*, 1–13.

Rice, M. E., & Harris, G. T. (1997). The treatment of adult offenders. In D. M. Stoff, J. Breiling, & J. D. Maser (Eds.), *Handbook of antisocial behavior* (pp. 425–435). New York: John Wiley & Sons.

Rice, M. E., Harris, G. T., & Cormier, C. A. (1992). An evaluation of a maximum-security therapeutic community for psychopaths and other mentally disordered offenders. *Law and Human Behavior, 16*, 399–412.

Rice, M. E., Harris, G. T., & Quinsey, V. L. (1996). Treatment for forensic patients. In B. D. Sales & S. A. Shah (Eds.), *Mental health and law: Research, policy and services* (pp. 141–189). Durham, NC: Carolina Academic Press.

Rice, M. E., Harris, G. T., Quinsey, V. L., & Cyr, M. (1990). Planning treatment programs in secure psychiatric facilities. In D. N. Weisstub (Ed.), *Law and mental health: International perspectives, Vol. 5* (pp. 162–230). New York: Pergamon Press.

Robins, L. (1978). Sturdy predictors of adult antisocial behavior: Replications from longitudinal studies. *Psychological Medicine, 8*, 611–622.

Robinson, D. (1996). Factors influencing the effectiveness of cognitive skills training. *Forum on Corrections Research, 8, 3*, 6–9.

Rogers, R. (1986). *Clinical assessment of malingering and deception.* New York: Guilford Press.

Rokach, A. (1987). Anger and aggression control training: Replacing attack with interaction. *Psychotherapy, 24*, 353–362.

Schlichter, K. J., & Horan, J. J. (1981). Effects of stress inoculation on the anger and aggression management skills of institutionalized juvenile delinquents. *Cognitive Therapy and Research, 5*, 359–365.

Selby, M. J. (1984). Assessment of violence potential using measures of anger, hostility, and social desirability. *Journal of Personality Assessment, 48*, 531–544.

Serin, R. C. (1991). Psychopathy and violence in criminals. *Journal of Interpersonal Violence, 6*, 423–431.

Serin, R. C. (1995). *Persistently violent (non-sexual) offenders: A program proposal.* Research Report R-42. Ottawa: Correctional Service of Canada.

Serin, R. C. (1998). Treatment responsivity, intervention and reintegration: A conceptual model. *Forum on Corrections Research, 10, 1*, 29–32.

Serin, R. C., & Kennedy, S. (1997). *Treatment readiness and responsivity: Contributing to effective correctional programming.* Research Report R-54. Ottawa: Correctional Service of Canada.

Serin, R. C., & Kuriychuk, M. (1994). Social and cognitive processing deficits in violent offenders: Implications for treatment. *International Journal of Law and Psychiatry, 17*, 431–441.

Shapiro, D. L. (1991). *Forensic psychological assessment: An integrative approach.* Boston: Allyn and Bacon.

Sherman, L. G., & Morschauser, P. C. (1989). Screening for suicide risk in inmates. Special issue: Jail suicide: A comprehensive approach to a continuing national problem. *Psychiatric Quarterly, 60*, 119–138.

Slaby, R. G., & Guerra, N. G. (1988). Cognitive mediators of aggression in adolescent offenders: 1. Assessment. *Developmental Psychology, 24*, 580–588.

Smiley, W. C., Mulloy, R., & Brown, S. (1997). Treatment in violent offenders: Reducing the risk to reoffend. *Forum on Corrections Research, 9*(2), 44–47.

Steadman, H. J., Monahan, J., Robbins, P. C., Applebaum, P., Grisso, T., Klassen, D., Mulvey, E. P., & Roth, L. (1993). From dangerousness to risk assessment: Implications for appropriate research strategies. In S. Hodgins (Ed.), *Mental disorder and crime* (pp. 39–62). Newbury Park, CA: Sage Publications.

Stermac, L. E. (1987). Anger control treatment for forensic patients. *Journal of Interpersonal Violence, 1*, 446–457.

Szapocznik, J., & Kurtines, W. M. (1993). Family psychology and cultural diversity: Opportunities for theory, research, and application. *American Psychologist, 48* (4), 400–407.

Toch, H. (1969). *Violent men*. Chicago: Aldine.

Tolan, P., & Guerra, N. (1994). *What works in reducing adolescent violence: An empirical review of the field*. Boulder: Center for the Study and Prevention of Violence, Institute for Behavioral Sciences, University of Colorado, Boulder.

Webster, C. D., Harris, G. T., Rice, M. E., Cormier, C., & Quinsey, V. L. (1994). *The violence prediction scheme: Assessing dangerousness in high risk men*. Toronto: Centre for Criminology, University of Toronto.

Widom, C. S. (1997). Child abuse, neglect, and witnessing violence. In D. M. Stoff, J. Breiling, & J. D. Maser (Eds.), *Handbook of antisocial behavior* (pp. 159–170). New York: John Wiley & Sons.

Zamble, E., & Quinsey, V. L. (1997). *The criminal recidivism process*. New York: Cambridge University Press.

Zillman, D. (1979). *Hostility and aggression*. Hillsdale, NJ: Erlbaum.

Chapter 10
TREATING JUVENILE SEX OFFENDERS

Judith V. Becker and Bradley R. Johnson

Over the past decade, an increased emphasis has been placed on identifying, treating, and assessing outcome with adolescent sexual offenders. A sex offender can be defined in many ways, but ultimately he or she is an individual who has committed overt sexual acts that are contrary to existing sexual mores in their society (Gebhard, Gagnon, Pomeroy, & Christenson, 1964). There was a time when many believed that exploitative adolescent sexual behaviors should be dismissed or ignored as experimental, playful, or just part of growing up. Yet it is likely that 20 to 30% of rapes and 30 to 50% of child molestations are committed by adolescents (Becker, Cunningham-Rathner, & Kaplan, 1986; Davis & Leitenberg, 1987; Matthews, 1987). There is also a growing awareness that prepubescent children may commit what some would consider sexual offenses (Hunter, 1993). No longer can we take a "kids will be kids approach" to overt sexual offenses committed by youngsters.

The *Diagnostic and Statistical Manual of Mental Disorders*, 4th Edition (American Psychiatric Association, 1994) defines paraphilias as recurrent, intense sexually arousing fantasies, sexual urges, or behaviors generally involving (a) nonhuman objects, (b) the suffering or humiliation of one's self or one's partner, or (c) children or other nonconsenting persons. To be so categorized these fantasies or behaviors need to occur over a minimal period of at least six months. The individual with a paraphilia may also have normal sexual arousal to nonparaphilic fantasies or, in some cases, may find the paraphilic fantasies obligatory for sexual arousal. Many paraphilias develop at an earlier age than once thought, often during the teenage years (Abel, Mittelman, & Becker, 1985). For example, Abel et al. (1985) showed that 74% of homosexual pedophilia begins under the age of 19. Even cases of extreme sadistic paraphilias have been documented starting in early adolescence (Johnson & Becker, 1997).

Before 1980, there were only 19 major papers published on the topic of adolescent sexual offenders (Barbaree, Hudson, & Seto, 1993); however, a recent informal survey by the authors shows more than 160 major articles on this topic. This increased amount of literature in a relatively short time likely correlates to an increase of individuals in the mental health communities who have gained an interest and expertise in evaluating and treating youthful sexual offenders. In fact, the authors estimate that there are more than 1000 mental health professionals in the United States who provide services to this population.

In 1986, the National Task Force on Juvenile Sexual Offending was formed to begin the task of creating "standards" in the field. They published their preliminary report in 1988 (National Adolescent Perpetrator Network, 1988) and a revised report (National Adolescent Perpetrator Network, 1993) five years later. In 1984, the Association for the Treatment of Sexual Abusers was established with only a handful of members. It is now an international, multidisciplinary organization with nearly 1800 members. This and other organizations frequently have conferences and workshop presentations updating what is known on working with both adult and adolescent sexual offenders, and each year our knowledge base expands.

There is no empirically derived unitary profile of an adolescent sexual offender. They come from all racial, ethnic, religious, and socioeconomic groups. However, what is known is that about 70% of adolescent sexual offenders come from two parent homes, most attend school and achieve average grades, and less than 4% suffer from a major mental illness (Schwartz & Cellini, 1995). In 1991, the Safer Society (National Adolescent Perpetrator Network, 1993) showed the median age of juvenile offenders to be between 14 and 15, fewer than 10% of adolescent offenders to be female, more than one third of the offenses having involved force, and more than 90% having known their victim(s).

We feel it is important to increase our knowledge of adolescent sexual offenders so that a better job can be done to identify offenders as early as possible and refer them for treatment. It is likely that the way people behave sexually is the product of multiple factors, including biological predisposition, environmental exposures, and learned behaviors based on life experiences. Assessments and treatment plans need to address each of these factors. This chapter will present a brief review on assessing the juvenile offender and a more detailed description of what is known about treatment. We will mention treatments that have been tried and focus on treatments that have been scientifically or clinically shown to be successful.

Assessing Juvenile Offenders

To develop appropriate treatment strategies that are custom made to the offender, it is vital that a thorough and appropriately conducted evaluation occur. The motivation behind sexual behaviors by children and adolescents is often hard to delineate. It may range from exploration to well thought out and purposeful behavior to gratify one's sexual desires. When a youthful sexual offender has been referred for an evaluation, it is the job of the assessor to determine the probability that a deviant sexual act occurred, the reason for its occurrence, and whether or not there is need for intervention.

Interviewing a juvenile sexual offender without doing one's homework can have dramatic consequences. It is important to review as much background information on the youth as possible before meeting with him or her. This should include the police reports, reports by the probation officer and court, prior psychological or psychiatric evaluations–treatment notes, victim statements, prior offender statements, school records, and letters from individuals who know the offender well.

Too often interviewers feel they can decide whether a sexual offense has actually occurred and can predict whether an adolescent sexual offender needs treatment based on a brief clinical interview and by administering psychometric testing. This is false. Indeed, there is no specific test, biological or psychological in origin, that can determine whether an individual has committed a specific sexual offense or predict possible recidivism. Rather, we believe that completing a thorough clinical evaluation based on an interview is the most important part of the assessment of a sexual offender. Experience and training in interviewing and treating children and adolescents is imperative. Even individuals who are trained in interviewing and treating adult sexual offenders may not adequately be able to conduct child or adolescent interviews or offer treatment in an appropriate or helpful manner.

A complete psychological–psychiatric evaluation needs to be undertaken during the interview that allows the evaluator to gain the necessary bio-psycho-social information necessary to form a comprehensive and individualized treatment plan. The assessment should include a detailed statement of the offender's account of the alleged crime or act. It is important to gain data on who they were with when the offense happened as well as what their thoughts were before, during, and after the offense. Experience helps the evaluator know when to inquire for further details and when to ask about behaviors that are commonly seen with specific types of paraphilic acts. It is important that the youth understand that the evaluator has spoken with many others about similar situations, placing the youth at ease to talk about sexual material. This same concept will also serve well during treatment.

Although we do not have empirically derived and agreed on models to explain the etiologies of sex offending, the assessment should gather all information that may be part of the causal sequence leading up to sexual or nonsexual reoffending. Thus we believe that it is important to obtain

- A history of present and past psychiatric illnesses and treatments;
- A family psychiatric history;
- A social history;
- A medical history including such things as past surgical procedures, chronic medical illnesses, acute traumatic injury, head trauma, history of seizures, and history of loss of consciousness;
- History of current and past medications and other medical treatments;
- A developmental history, learning such things as whether the child was the product of a planned pregnancy, if the mother had exposures to alcohol, drugs, or abuse during the pregnancy, and if there were any complications with the delivery;
- Information about the temperament of the youth as he or she was a developing infant and toddler;
- A history of interactions with other children and adults while growing up;
- A history of educational development, including whether they have been referred for special education services or have learning disabilities;
- An employment history;
- Family history and functioning;
- Future plans for employment, education, and family;
- Emotional, physical, and sexual abuse history;
- The current living arrangements, and social and financial support;
- Legal problems history;
- History of gang involvement;
- History of violent behaviors;
- Alcohol and substance abuse history; and
- A detailed sexual history, including when puberty began, when the adolescent first became aware of his or her own sexuality (for a male, when he became aware of obtaining erections and when the erections correlated with sexual stimuli or fantasies), how the adolescent's sexual relationships developed (such as when the adolescent experienced his or her first crush and romantic kiss, and how the adolescent first learned about sex), the nature of his or her first type of sexual contact (such as prolonged kissing, touching, oral sexual

contact, anal sexual contact, and actual intercourse), and if there have been multiple sexual contacts.

It is important that the interviewer not make preconceived assumptions about the individual he or she is evaluating regarding their sexual history. In a nonthreatening manner, the evaluator can ask about both heterosexual and homosexual fantasies and contacts, the age range of their sexual fantasies, and whether they are of a consensual or nonconsensual nature. In addition, the interviewer should question about the youth's exposure to sexually explicit materials such as magazines, movies, the Internet, and toll telephone calls. This information will become helpful in addressing how to interrupt the deviant fantasies or actions as part of treatment.

Finally, it is important to ask the youth in a nonthreatening and nonjudgmental way about common paraphilias. One should ask youths how old they were the first time they ever fantasized about engaging in a specific paraphilic behavior, as well as the first time that they engaged in the actual behavior. For older youth, one may even need to ask about less common paraphilic behaviors. If the youth has committed a violent sexual act or has been arrested previously for unrelated violent behaviors, it is important to also question about sexual fantasies connected with such things as assault, torture, control, and even killing. It is important that all of the offender's paraphilias be addressed in treatment rather than just the obvious or assumed one.

A thorough evaluation should include a detailed mental status examination, including their concentration and memory abilities. One should assess the youth's general fund of knowledge and intelligence as well as insight and judgment. As part of this evaluation, the interviewer may even wish to include a formal screening mental status test to rule out cognitive impairments that would hinder more abstract forms of treatment.

Comprehensive Treatment

The treatment plan for a juvenile sex offender should follow from the comprehensive assessment of the juvenile and his or her family and be individualized to meet the needs of the offender. We propose a model of comprehensive treatment outlined in this section that is based on our experience and treatment outcome data in the literature, which is presented later in this chapter.

Becker and Kaplan (1993), Becker and Hunter (1997), and Pithers et al. (1995) have all provided detailed descriptions of treatment modalities that have been used to treat juvenile sex offenders. Following is a description of modalities that have been used with both prepubescent and pubescent youth who have sexual behavior problems or who have committed sexual offenses.

Gray and Pithers (1993) described a relapse prevention model in treating sexually aggressive adolescents and children. Their model is based on the premise that offense precursors can be identified and addressed. Like adult offenders, juvenile offenders often make decisions that place them in high-risk situations to engage in sexually inappropriate behaviors. The risk of lapsing or relapsing increases once the youth is in a high-risk situation. The role of their sexual fantasies is also important. If the juvenile fantasizes and masturbates to inappropriate sexual thoughts, he or she increases the likelihood that the abusive or deviant sexual fantasies will increase in frequency and intensity. Eventually, cognitive distortions develop that are then used to justify the offender's inappropriate sexual behaviors.

Treatment within this model consists of an internal self-management dimension and an external, supervisory dimension. The internal self-management consists of having the juveniles identify and discuss their risk factors and identify and learn coping strategies to use when faced with a risk factor. For example, an adolescent may seek out sexually explicit magazines if he or she is at home alone. Looking at the magazine causes the adolescent to become sexually stimulated and fantasize about deviant thoughts. They may be at a higher risk to offend at that moment. They could learn to not be alone or discard the sexually explicit materials they have access to to help decrease their risk.

The external, supervisory dimension involves having the juvenile meet with his or her care providers, selective family members, probation officers, and selected community advocacy members, and provide them with a disclosure of the relapse process. This "prevention team" is there to assist in supporting the juvenile as well as supervising, which works to assist in diminishing the risk of a relapse. The external, supervisory component allows for developing a collaborative relationship between the therapist and those people with whom the juvenile interacts.

Becker and Hunter (1997) outlined the components of a treatment program that has been used with both residentially placed juveniles as well as those treated on an outpatient basis. Because many juveniles who have committed sexual offenses tend to deny or minimize their behavior, the first step involves having the youth accept responsibility for his or her behavior. There are many reasons why a youth is not totally forthcoming in discussing the sexual offense(s), including shame, fear of consequences, embarrassment, and not wanting to be stigmatized. The reasons for denial need to be explored and processed. The juvenile needs to be instructed that ultimately it is in his or her best interest to "unburden" themselves by acknowledging and accepting responsibility for his or her behaviors.

The juvenile is also educated about what benefits may accrue to him or her by participating in treatment. The primary goal of treatment is to prevent further victimization from occurring. Juveniles are provided with an understanding of the nature of adolescent sexual perpetration, including its causes and treatment. Other treatment goals include increasing social competence so that the juvenile will develop age-appropriate consensual relations with peers as well as assessing and treating whatever dysfunctions there may be within the family. Rehearsing in role play on how to relate socially with age-appropriate peers, for example, could help reduce the risk of reoffense of an adolescent who has been sexual with a younger child because they are more comfortable socially with children than same-aged peers.

In many cases, youth receive individual therapy as well as group therapy and family therapy. The authors recommend using a multimodal treatment program based in part on cognitive–behavioral techniques. Cognitive restructuring assists adolescents in understanding their thoughts, feelings, or events that contributed to their inappropriate sexual behavior. This component of therapy focuses on identifying and then correcting those patterns of thinking that are considered to be inappropriate. For example, some juveniles believe that females want to be raped. Other juveniles believe that if a child does not resist, the child actually wants to be sexual with them. These errors in their thinking need to be identified and the concepts corrected.

This can be done individually, but group therapy allows an avenue for one adolescent to confront and teach another youth how their thinking has not been correct.

Values clarification therapy is used to focus on a discussion of sexual values and providing clarification and ultimately assists the youth in the cessation of destructive exploitative relationships in promoting healthy and age-appropriate ones. Many youth have not as yet made decisions regarding the age that they wish to wait to engage in sexual intercourse, for example, and may need to discuss their options in therapy. This allows the adolescent to weigh the pros and cons of their choices and make decisions that will positively affect their futures.

Teaching general impulse control techniques assists the juvenile in acquiring skills related to the development of improved sexual impulse control. This component focuses on teaching the youth how to interrupt the impulsive sexual thoughts that he or she might have that could potentially lead to heightened inappropriate sexual arousal and eventual acting out behavior. These techniques are similar to what is taught, for example, to adolescents who suffer from attention deficit–hyperactivity disorder. The use of medications to help with impulsivity may even need to be considered.

Empathy training provides the juveniles with an understanding of the impact that their behavior has had on their victim(s). This component of treatment is designed to help the adolescent develop an understanding of empathy and consciousness toward other people. This can be empirically challenging in youth who are developing antisocial-like behaviors and personalities. One may start this process by describing what he or she did to the victim and discuss how this may have emotionally or physically affected the victim in both the acute and the chronic situation. If an offender has been sexually abused in the past, he or she could relate how this victimization affected him or her and then relate these feelings to how their victim(s) may have felt.

Anger management assists the adolescents in identifying those stimuli, including individuals and environments, to which they have responded with anger or physical or verbal aggression. Because in a number of cases it has been our experience that youth have acted out sexually because they did not properly handle their anger, it is important that youth learn to identify those situations and stimuli that serve as risk factors and learn how to cope with them in a pro social manner. One way to do so is to help the youth learn to appropriately communicate their feelings. Other methods include helping the adolescent gain insight into the causes of their anger or the use of relaxation exercises to deal with specific anger-provoking situations. We often use role play in either individual or group therapy to use concrete examples of how to defuse anger and to teach anger management.

Sexual education should provide a basic understanding of human sexuality and relationships. The ultimate goal of this component of treatment is to promote healthy, consensual, age-appropriate relationships and when they are at an age and maturity to be responsible for those relationships. Discussion is important to help the adolescent make decisions about how far sexual relationships should go at their age, given their cultural background and moral beliefs. In addition, the adolescent should review or learn aspects of pubertal development, aspects of human reproduction, basic male and female anatomy, and causes–symptoms of sexually transmitted diseases.

Although some youth can be treated on an outpatient basis, others may need to receive treatment while in residential care if they represent too high a risk or danger to society. Although at the present time there is no scientifically validated risk-assessment instrument for juvenile sex offenders, it is hoped that future research will provide such an empirically based risk assessment instrument.

Adjunctive forms of therapy that would be used also depend on the individually assessed needs of the juvenile. These might include assistance with education, basic vocational–living skills, as well as family therapy. Juveniles who have comorbid psychological or psychiatric problems also may benefit from psychiatric, psychological, and medical interventions.

Biological Intervention

Because treating sexual offenders needs to be multimodal in approach, there are occasions when biological treatment should be considered. In past years, such treatments meant using medications with unwarranted or even potentially dangerous side effects as well as using surgical procedures. These types of interventions, although occasionally helpful with adults, have been felt to be inappropriate for adolescent offenders, and therefore biological interventions have often not been addressed in treatment models for adolescents. However, medical research in this area, although in its infancy, is increasing at a rapid pace.

For years, there was a great deal of focus placed on hormones and their effects on human sexual behavior. Therefore, research was done looking at the use of antiandrogens and a variety of hormonal agents as part of a pharmacologic approach to reducing paraphilic behaviors. Using antiandrogens can suppress libido, decreasing paraphilic fantasies as well as behaviors. However, until an adolescent has actually completed puberty, including their growth spurt, antiandrogens are contraindicated. It is often recommended that antiandrogens or other hormonal agents not be used before the age of 16 (Bradford, 1993) and only in difficult cases in which other less invasive treatments have failed.

With adolescents, it is important to take a look at other pharmacologic agents that may be beneficial in reducing sexually deviant fantasies and behaviors that can both be effective and safe. Many different agents have been tried, including antipsychotic medications, antiseizure medications, mood stabilizers, and antidepressants. No single medication appears to work for every offender and, indeed, a tailor-made approach may be necessary.

Recently, there has been a great deal of interest in the relationship that paraphilias may have with obsessive–compulsive spectrum disorders. In the popular media, the term *obsession* is often used to represent an excessive preoccupation. Could some paraphilic behaviors for certain offenders be obsessive in nature? It is also debated whether sexual paraphilias may have a compulsive or an impulsive origin. However, it is likely to be quite variable in that some specific paraphilic behaviors may be compulsive, some may be impulsive, and many others may be obsessional, depending on the individual and situation. If this is the case, using agents commonly used to treat obsessive–compulsive disorder may be helpful with some adolescent sexual offenders.

Over the past ten years, there has been an increased number of reports suggesting that serotoninergic antidepressants, in particular serotonin (5-Hydroxytryptamine; 5-HT) reuptake inhibitors may decrease fantasies and behaviors (Federoff, 1993). Animal research data suggests that decreased central serotonin activity may actually disinhibit or promote male sexual behavior (Tucker & File, 1983). If a decreased central serotonin neurotransmission increases sexual behavior in animals, is it possible that this model can be translated to humans? In fact, although there are few studies yet that look at chemically increasing serotonin levels in adolescents for treating sexual paraphilias, we have seen a number of adolescent offenders who show improvement when treated with selective serotonin reuptake inhibitor medications (Johnson & Becker, 1997).

To this time, the serotoninergic agent that has been looked at most closely is fluoxetine (Bianchi, 1990; Emmanuel, Lydiard, & Ballenger, 1991; Lorefice, 1991; Perilstein, Lipper, & Friedman, 1991). Because chemical agents such as fluoxetine not only are helpful treatments for obsessive–compulsive spectrum disorders as well as depression, one could hypothesize that they are not only decreasing the impulsive, compulsive, or obsessional nature of the paraphilias, but may also be decreasing comorbid depression, which may be increasing the risk factors associated with paraphilic behaviors. Kafka (1995) suggested that other serotoninergic agents such as Lithium, clomipramine, buspirone, fluvoxamine, and sertraline may also be effective in treating patients with paraphilias and related disorders.

Although the selective serotonin reuptake inhibitors are frequently prescribed to adolescents and even to young children in today's medical world, we are not aware of any double-blind or placebo-controlled studies of their use on outpatient sexual offenders or with adolescent sex offenders. In addition, we recommend that the use of medications, including selective serotonin reuptake inhibitors, should never be considered the sole therapy. Their effectiveness is likely to be variable and also associated with individual medication compliance. It still remains to be determined whether the use of these agents will be helpful in the long run to adolescent sexual offenders. It is possible that they will be effective with certain subgroups of adolescent and adult sexual offenders. However, these subgroups have yet to be determined, if they exist at all.

Many adolescent sexual offenders may suffer from other comorbid psychiatric conditions. Psychopharmacologic intervention may be necessary to treat such disorders as depression, impulse-control disorders, anxiety, psychosis, bipolar disorder, or post traumatic stress disorder. Because these comorbid problems may be complicating factors to the adolescent sexually offending, the treatment for these disorders may improve their chances of decreased recidivism. Often overlooked is the comorbid presentation of behavioral problems such as attention deficit–hyperactivity disorder, oppositional-defiant disorder, or conduct disorder. It is well-known that these disorders improve with treatments such as stimulants, antidepressant medications, and mood stabilizers.

Work is being done to better establish the neurobiological underpinnings of sexual paraphilias. Hypersexual behaviors have often been related to hypothalamic, limbic, or cortical damage (Ball, 1968; Cooper, 1987; Demerdash et al., 1991; Kolarsky et al., 1967; Kott, 1977; Langevin et al., 1988; Mohan, Salo, Nagaswami, 1975; Signer & Cummings, 1987). Langevin et al. (1988) showed that right temporal horn dilation as seen on head scans is also associated with sexual aggression. As more is learned about how the brain structure and neurotransmitters are related to paraphilic behaviors, we are likely to learn better how to use pharmacologic agents in treating paraphilias. One can begin to see why a detailed medical history is important to obtain on individuals who will receive treatment, because this may help the evaluating physician determine what type of medications may be helpful to try as part of treatment.

The use of surgical castration (i.e., removal of testes) has been debated as a biologic intervention to be used with male sexual offenders. However, it is our opinion that this type of treatment should never be used for adolescents and that there are alternative and less invasive treatments for most adults.

The use of biological treatments can be helpful when used in addition to psychotherapeutic interventions but should not be ordered by the court except on the recommendation of a physician after he or she has completed an appropriate medical evaluation. Pharmacologic agents have side effects and medical risk. They should only be administered under appropriate medical supervision and with the use of informed consent received from the adolescent as well as his or her parent or legal guardian.

A History and Research View of Treatment Programs for Adolescents and Children

Although some youth can be treated on an outpatient basis, others may need to receive treatment while in residential care if they represent too high a risk or danger to society. It is important that communities have available a continuum of placements and services for juvenile offenders ranging from outpatient treatment on one end of the scale to day treatment or secure residential placement on the other.

The few reports in the literature that describe other treatment programs are for the most part descriptive in nature, involve small sample sizes, and do not provide long follow-up periods. The literature for the most part describes the treatment of postpubescent adolescents as opposed to prepubescent. To date, those studies describing the treatment of prepubescent youth do not provide treatment outcome data. We will review some of the treatment programs that have described their protocols and treatment modalities in the literature.

Johnson and Berry (1989) described the Support Program for Abuse Reactive Kids (SPARK), which was begun at the Child Sexual Abuse Center at Children's Institute International. This program was described as being for children under 13 years of age who have initiated sexually abusive behavior with other children. The goals of the program are to extinguish sexually abusive behavior, gather data on this population, and improve understanding of the etiology. Children are accepted into this program if they have acted in a sexual way with other children, if they used force or coercion to obtain the participation of other children, if there was an age differential of at least two years for children nine years and older, and if there is a pattern of sexually overt behavior in the children's history. The individuals in this program are treated in groups. There are separate groups for child perpetrators, their siblings who have been victimized, and their siblings who have not been victimized. Children are grouped according to gender and ages, 5 to 7, 8 to 10, and 11 to 13. The groups meet weekly for an hour and a half. The authors noted that there are generally 42 weeks of group therapy in a one-year period. The treatment involves having the children master many skills to move them away from their offending behavior, including social skills, impulse control, perspective taking, problem-solving, and cognitive strategies for behavior control. The children also explore issues including betrayal, trust, secrecy, loss of self-esteem, and powerlessness.

Pithers and colleagues (1995) described a treatment program in Vermont in which children, ages 6 to 12, and their parents meet separately in groups for one hour and then meet together for a half hour. The group activities are highly structured. The treatment is 32 weeks in duration and covers establishing safety rules; accountability for behavior; recognition, management, and expression of emotions; empowerment; healthy sexual development; cognitive distortions; victim empathy; grief work; personal victimization issues; decision making; and relapse prevention. The authors have developed an empirically derived taxonomy. A cluster analysis was used to subtype 127 prepubescent children on behavioral, demographic, and psychometric data. (Gray, Pithers, Busconi, & Houchens, 1997). Five subtypes emerged: sexually aggressive, nondisordered, highly traumatized, rule breakers, and abuse reactive. Sixty-five percent of the children were male and 35% female. These authors reported that female children were overrepresented in the nondisordered and rule-breaker subtypes, whereas males were overrepresented in the sexually aggressive and abuse-reactive subtypes.

Eight-six percent of these children with sexual behavior problems had been sexually abused themselves, and 55% had been physically maltreated. The average age at which they had been sexually abused was 4.02. The average number of victims these children had victimized was 2.02. Children in the sexually aggressive subtype had engaged in more acts of sexual behaviors involving penetration than did the youths in the other subtypes.

Children differed as to psychiatric diagnosis by subtype. Highly traumatized abuse reactive subtypes had more psychiatric diagnoses. Sexually aggressive and abuse reactive subtypes were more likely to receive a diagnosis of conduct disorder, whereas the abuse reactive children were more likely to be diagnosed as oppositional defiant. Ninety-one percent of the highly traumatized children were diagnosed as posttraumatic syndrome disorder.

The authors in comparing the relative efficacy of modified relapse prevention and expressive therapy reported that 75% of the highly traumatized children benefited from the relapse prevention, whereas those receiving the expressive therapy tended to decompensate clinically. Additional outcome data is needed to evaluate the effectiveness of these treatments by subtypes.

Bonner, Walker, and Berliner (1997) compared cognitive behavior therapy (CBT) to dynamic play therapy (DPT) with children younger than 12 years of age who had sexual behavior problems. Each child received 12 sessions of either form of therapy. The parents of the children also received an intervention consistent with the type of therapy their children received. The CBT therapy directly addressed the children's sexual behaviors and consisted of sexual behavior rules, disclosure, impulse control, sex education, and prevention of abuse. In the DPT, the children's sexual behavior was not addressed directly. Those sessions focused on encouraging the expression of feelings, providing an accepting environment, and improving the children's social interactions. These authors report that both treatment approaches were effective in reducing the children's inappropriate sexual behaviors. Research is ongoing to determine if treatment impacted differently based on certain demographic characteristics and type of sexual behavior problem.

Several single-case descriptions of the treatment of adolescent offenders appear in the literature. Burgess, Hartman, McCormack, and Grant (1988) described a case of a 14-year-old who raped a 21-year-old neighbor. In discussing treatment implications, they noted that this youth had initially been victimized and then went on to become a sexual victimizer. A four-phase treatment plan was suggested. Phase I involved individual therapy focused on establishing an alliance and building trust as well as dealing with cognitive–behavioral components of impulse control. Phase II focused on eliciting the youth's sexual and aggressive fantasies to neutralize the potential for him to act them out. Phase III focused on his own early abuse and exploitation. Phase IV focused on increasing social skill capacity. No treatment outcome or follow-up data were presented.

Darou (1992) described the treatment of a 14-year-old boy who at age 9 had been sexually molested by his father. At age 13 this youth was found "lying on top" of a 4-year-old. Later that year, he fondled preteenage girls. Darou described one session of the treatment that involved a story-telling technique. No treatment outcome or follow-up data were presented.

Several uncontrolled studies with follow-up data appear in the literature. Kahn and Lafond (1988) presented an overview of treatment sessions for adolescent sex offenders who were incarcerated in a medium-security correctional facility. Most of the youth had committed what were described as "hands-on" (fondling or penetration as opposed to "hands-off," voyeurism and exhibitionism) sexually aggressive acts. Fifty percent of the incarcerated youth had disclosed they had been sexually abused themselves. Treatment issues that were addressed in this program included breaking through denial; addressing the offender's own history of victimization; confronting attitudes that support victimization; teaching social skills; and altering deviant arousal patterns. Preliminary recidivism data indicated that 9% of the youth who had been released from the facility committed sex offenses and 8% committed nonsexual offenses. The authors noted, however, that these results are preliminary given that some youth had been released for only a few weeks and others for as long as six years.

McConaghy, Blaszczynski, Armstrong, and Kidson (1989) reported on two studies in which they compared and evaluated adult sex offender's response to treatment versus adolescent sex offender's response. Participants in the first study were randomly assigned to ten sessions of covert sensitization and ten sessions of imaginal desensitization. In the second study, participants were assigned to imaginal desensitization, biological treatment with the antiandrogen Medroxyprogesterone acetate, or a combination of imaginal desensitization and Medroxyprogesterone acetate. Results indicated that in the first study, response to covert sensitization was inferior to the imaginal desensitization intervention. In the second study, no significant differences were found between responses to either the imaginal desensitization, Medroxyprogesterone acetate, or the combination of imaginal desensitization plus Medroxyprogesterone acetate. The authors hypothesized that adolescents may have had a higher relapse rate because they experienced more serious and complex conditions, or the adolescent sexual offender's urges were under more direct hormonal control. These authors recommended more intensive follow-up treatment as part of the management of adolescent sex offenders.

Becker, Kaplan, and Kavoussi (1988) described the effectiveness of a community-based treatment program. Twenty-four male adolescents between the ages of 13 and 18 underwent therapy that included verbal satiation (a type of therapy in which the adolescent repeats the deviant fantasy outlined to the point of boredom), cognitive restructuring, covert sensitization, social skills, anger control, relapse prevention, values clarification, and sex education. Of the 24 participants, 11 had male victims and 13 had female victims. For those youth who had male victims, the treatment was successful in assisting them in reducing their arousal to deviant stimuli. This was also true for those who had female victims, although this was not demonstrated statistically. One participant evidenced more sexual arousal posttreatment. This study assessed only the impact of the treatment on deviant arousal, which was assessed one week after the youth completed the treatment program, and long-term follow-up was not done.

Kaplan, Morales, and Becker (1993) were interested in assessing the impact of one component of their multicomponent treatment program, specifically verbal satiation and whether or not this decreased deviant arousal. They investigated the use of verbal satiation to modify a typical sexual arousal. Fifteen adolescents who had offended against children underwent eight 30-minute verbal satiation sessions. Verbal satiation specifically is a technique in which the offender is taught how to use deviant thoughts in a repetitive manner to the point of satiating himself with the very stimulus that he may have used to become aroused. In other words, the sexual stimuli may actually become boring to the offender. Results indicated there was an overall decrease in participant's "deviant arousal" as measured by penile plethysmography for 14 of the 15 adolescents who underwent this treatment. However, only 5 of the 15 adolescents experienced what the authors deemed a clinically significant decrease in deviant arousal. The authors found that the younger the age of the adolescent and the closer the victim and offender were in age, the less successful the procedure. Satiation was the first component of a multicomponent treatment used by these authors to treat adolescent offenders.

Becker and Kaplan (1993) described a treatment program for male adolescent offenders. Treatment was on an outpatient basis. The treatment program was a modification of a multicomponent cognitive behavioral program that had been evaluated on an adult sex offender population. Adolescents were admitted to the program if they acknowledged having engaged in deviant sexual behavior or the sex offense was documented either by the victim's statement, a reliable valid witness, or a court finding. Treatment consisted of the following components:

- Verbal satiation, teaching the adolescent to use his or her deviant fantasies in a repetitive manner to the point of boring or fatiguing the very stimuli that had previously been arousing. Once adolescents completed the verbal satiation, they entered a 40-week closed-group treatment led by a male and female cotherapist team. Group sessions were one hour in duration. Group size consisted of between 7 to 10 adolescents;
- Cognitive restructuring, consisting of confronting the adolescent with his or her maladaptive beliefs;
- Covert sensitization, teaching the adolescent to recognize his or her own thought processes and behaviors that place the youth at risk to abuse, and to interrupt the thought processes and behavior by substituting negative consequences;
- Skills training, consisting of teaching the adolescent how to manage his or her angry impulses. Also, given that many of the adolescents have difficulty in establishing peer relationships, social interactional skills are taught;

- Sex education; and
- Relapse prevention, consisting of developing with each youth his or her own plan to prevent relapse.

Of the 300 adolescents evaluated by the authors, 68.3% entered treatment. Attendance was a problem in that only 27.3% of the youth attended 70 to 100% of scheduled therapy sessions. Becker (1990) provided follow-up data on 80 of these youths. In many instances, the youths were followed for as long as two years. Recidivism data was obtained by interviewing the youth, a family member when available, and the referral source when available. Nine percent of the youth had sexually reoffended.

It is important for clinical researchers to assess treatment outcome by category of sex offender. Hagan and Cho (1996) assessed recidivism rates of adolescent rapists and adolescents who had molested children. One hundred adolescents who had committed serious sex offenses received mandatory treatment within a state-operated juvenile correctional facility. The program consisted of group therapy, sex education, behavioral management, and what the authors described as individual and family therapy "at times." The average amount of time to treatment completion was eight months. Follow-up data was obtained by a Department of Corrections record review to determine whether the youths had further convictions. Follow-up data ranged from two to five years. Results indicated the child sex offender group did not differ significantly from the rapist group regarding sexual reoffending. Although 10% of the rapists reoffended, 8% of the child molesters sexually reoffended. Also, the groups did not statistically differ on reconviction for nonsex offenses. Twenty-seven percent of the rapists were reconvicted for nonsex offenses compared to 19% of the child molester group.

Although this study is important in that it provides data on treatment outcome and two categories of adolescent sex offenders, a limitation involves the fact that only conviction data was obtained. Adolescents may commit offenses for which they are never arrested or, if arrested, never convicted.

The longest follow-up study conducted to date using a large sample size was provided by Schram, Milloy, and Rowe (1991). They provided data on a follow-up study of 197 male juvenile sex offenders who participated in an offense-specific treatment program at ten project sites. Official arrest and conviction data were obtained. Follow-up data ranged from 5 to 9.8 years. Although 12.2% were arrested for new offenses, 10.2% were convicted. A higher percentage of arrests and convictions occurred for nonsexual offenses; 50.8% of these juveniles committed nonsex offenses and 47.7 were convicted for new nonsexual offenses. The offenders presented the most danger to public safety during the first year they had been released from an institution or had completed the treatment program. They also posed a greater risk of offending as juveniles than as adults. Institutionalized youth were significantly more likely than those receiving outpatient treatment to commit new offenses during their first year at risk. Sexual recidivists compared to nonsexual recidivists were more likely to evidence a history of truancy, thinking errors, and to have had at least one prior conviction for a sexual offense. They were also more likely to evidence deviant sexual arousal patterns.

Although these studies have reported on the efficacy of specialized treatment programs for juvenile sex offenders, Lab, Shields, and Schondel (1993) argued that the growth of sex offender treatment programs has proceeded without adequate knowledge about what might be the appropriate intervention for any one particular youth. These authors conducted a retrospective case file review of 155 youth, 46 of whom had been assigned to and received treatment in a court-based sexual offender treatment program (SOT) and 109 who received nonsexually specific interventions. It is important to note that youth were not randomly assigned to either category of intervention. Rather, they were assigned based on a risk score, where low and medium youth risk were placed in the SOT program and high-risk youth to the traditional community agencies. Results indicated that there was no statistical difference in both sexual recidivism rate and nonsexual recidivism rate for those receiving the SOT program and those receiving the nonspecific interventions. Sexual recidivism rates were low for both groups in that 2.2% of the SOT group sexually reoffended compared to 3.7% of those receiving the nonspecific intervention. Furthermore, 24% of the SOT group committed other nonsexual offenses compared to 18% of those receiving nonspecific interventions. Although this was not a controlled outcome study and data was obtained from case files, the results are intriguing in that recidivism rates were low for both groups.

The only controlled therapy outcome study that these authors were able to locate in the literature was one conducted by Borduin, Henggeler, Blaske, and Stein (1990). These authors compared the efficacy of a Multi Systemic Therapy (MST) to Individual Therapy (IT). The exact nature of the MST varied for each family but in general targeted deficits in the adolescent's cognitive processes, family relations, peer relations, and school performance. IT consisted of promoting insight, building a warm relationship, and providing social support for school attendance. Sixteen youth were randomly assigned to either the MST or IT. Follow-up data ranged on average 36 months. Recidivism data was obtained by a search of juvenile court records to determine rearrest history. The data indicate that clearly the MST was much more effective in reducing recidivism in that 12.5% of the youth who received MST were rearrested for sex offenses compared to 75% of those who received IT. Fewer of the sex offenders who received MST were arrested for nonsex offenses (25%) compared to the youth who received IT (50%). The authors acknowledge that given the small sample size, their study should be considered tentative. Although this is the only control-therapy outcome study in the literature, an issue to be considered is that arrest data were used as the only measure of recidivism. Future studies should consider a review of arrest data as well as interviewing youth under a certificate of confidentiality.

Conclusions and Future Directions

Juvenile sex offenders represent a heterogeneous population. To date, most of the articles that have appeared in the literature have been descriptive in nature. The majority of the literature on juvenile sex offenders involves postpubescent male offenders. Although juvenile females have also committed sexual offenses, they do not appear to enter the juvenile justice system as readily as male offenders do and very little has been written regarding female sex offenders. Another population where there is a dearth of literature is prepubescent children who have sexual behavior problems or engage in sexual offenses that have been defined as illegal.

Future clinical research should address the following areas: (a) development of theories to further elucidate the etiologies of juvenile sex offending behavior; (b) development of typologies and classification systems for prepubescent and postpubescent male offenders as well as female offenders, particularly focusing on factors that place youth at risk for developing sexual behavioral problems or committing sexual offenses; (c) further development of treatment interventions for different classifications of juvenile sexual offenders; and (d) treatment outcome studies with long-term follow-ups.

It is of utmost importance that our society be able to identify those youth at risk for recidivating and those youth at risk for committing violent offenses as early as possible. Quinsey, Rice, and Harris (1995) discussed an actuarial approach to predicting sexual recidivism among known adult sex offenders. These authors found that rapists were more likely to recidivate than child molesters. Also, psychopathy, measures of previous criminal history, and phallometric indexes of deviant sexual interests were found to be useful predictors of sexual recidivism. It is hoped that such prediction approaches will be developed in the future for juveniles who have committed sexual offenses or who have committed violent offenses.

References

Abel, G., Mittelman, M., & Becker, J. (1985). Sex offenders: Results of assessment and recommendations for treatment. In S. Ben-Aaron, S. Hucker, & C. Webster (Eds.), *Clinical criminology: Current concepts* (pp. 191–205). Toronto: M & M Graphics.

American Psychiatric Association. (1994). *Diagnostic and statistical manual of mental disorders* (4th ed.). Washington, DC: Author.

Ball, J. R. (1968). A case of hair fetishism, transvestitism, and organic cerebral disorder. *Acta Psychiatry Scandinavian, 44*, 249–254.

Barbaree, H. E., Hudson, S. M., & Seto, M. C. (1993). Sexual assault in society: The role of the juvenile offender. In H. E. Barbaree, W. L. Marshall & S. M. Hudson (Eds.), *The Juvenile Sex Offender* (pp. 10–11). New York: Guilford Press.

Becker, J. V. (1990). Treating adolescent sexual offenders. *Professional Psychology: Research and Practice, 21*(5), 362–365.

Becker, J. V., Cunningham-Rathner, J., & Kaplan, M. S. (1986). Adolescent sexual offenders: Demographics, criminal and sexual histories, and recommendations for reducing future offenses. Special issue: the prediction and control of violent behavior: II. *Journal of Interpersonal Violence, 1*, 431–435.

Becker, J. V., & Hunter, J. A. (1997). Understanding and treating child and adolescent sexual offenders. In T. H. Ollendick & R. J. Prinz (Eds.), *Advances in Clinical Child Psychology, 19* (pp. 177–197). New York: Plenum Press.

Becker, J. V., & Kaplan, M. S. (1993). Cognitive behavioral treatment of juvenile sex offenders. In H. E. Barbaree, F. Hudson, & W. Marshall (Eds.), *The juvenile sex offender* (pp. 264–277). New York: Guilford Press.

Becker, J. V., Kaplan, M. S., & Kavoussi, R. J. (1988). Measuring effectiveness of treatment for the aggressive adolescent sexual offender. In R. A. Prentky & V. L. Quinsey (Eds.), *Human sexual aggression: Current prospectives* (pp. 215–222). New York: Academy of Science.

Bianchi, M. (1990). Fluoxetine treatment of exhibitionism (letter). *American Journal of Psychiatry, 147*, 1089–1090.

Bonner, B., Walker, C. E., & Berliner, L. (1997). Research update: Children with sexual behavior problems: Two treatment approaches found effective. *The Link, 6*, 7.

Borduin, C. M., Henggeler, S. W., Blaske, D. M., & Stein, R. J. (1990). Multisystemic treatment of adolescent sexual offenders. *International Journal of Offender Therapy and Comparative Criminology, 34*(2), 105–113.

Bradford J. M. W. (1993). The pharmacological treatment of the adolescent sex offender. New York: Guilford Press.

Burgess, A. W., Hartman, C. R., McCormack, A., & Grant, C. A. (1988). Child victim to juvenile victimizer: Treatment implications. *International Journal of Family Psychiatry, 9*(4), 403–416.

Cooper, A. J. (1987). Medroxyprogesterone Acetate (MPA) treatment of sexual acting out in men suffering from dementia. *Journal of Clinical Psychiatry, 48*, 368–370.

Darou, W. G. (1992). An intervention with an adolescent incest victim/abuser. *The Canadian Journal of Counseling, 26*(3), 152–156.

Davis, G., & Leitenberg, H. (1987). Adolescent sex offenders. *Psychological Bulletin, 101*, 417–427.

Demerdash, A., Shaalan, M., & Midami, A. (1991). Sexual behavior of a sample of females with epilepsy. *Epilepsia, 32*, 82–85.

Emmanuel, N. P., Lydiard, R. B., & Ballenger, J. C. (1991). Fluoxitine treatment of voyeurism (letter). *American Journal of Psychiatry, 148*, 950.

Federoff, J. P. (1993). Serotoninergic drug treatment of deviant sexual interests. *Annals of Sex Research*, 105–121.

Gebhard, P., Gagnon, J., Pomeory, W., & Christenson, C. (1964). *Sex offenders: An analysis of types.* New York: Harper & Row.

Gray, A. S., & Pithers, W. D. (1993). Relapse prevention with sexually aggressive adolescents and children: Expanding treatment and supervision. In H. E. Barbaree, F. Hudson, & W. Marshall (Eds.), *The juvenile sex offender* (pp. 289–319). New York: Guilford Press.

Gray, A. S., Pithers, W., Busconi, A. J., & Houchens, P. (1997). Children with sexual behavior problems: An empirically derived taxonomy. *Association for the Treatment of Sexual Abusers*, 10–11.

Hagan, M. P., & Cho, M. E. (1996). A comparison of treatment outcomes between adolescent rapists and child sexual offenders. *International Journal of Offender Therapy and Comparative Criminology, 40*(2), 113–122.

Hunter, J. A. (1993). *The clinical diagnosis and treatment of juvenile sex offenders.* Prepared under a grant by the National Center on Child Abuse and Neglect for use by the National Training Program on Effective Treatment Approaches in Child Sexual Abuse. (Available from author)

Johnson, B. J., & Becker, J. V. (1997). Natural born killers: The development of the sexually sadistic serial killer. *Journal of the American Academy of Psychiatry and Law, 25*, 335–348.

Johnson, T. C., & Berry, C. (1989). Children who molest: A treatment program. *Journal of Interpersonal Violence, 4*(2), 185–203.

Kafka, M. P. (1995). Current concepts in the drug treatment of paraphilias and paraphilia-related disorders. *CNS Drugs, 3*, 9–21.

Kahn, T. J., & LaFond, M. (1988). Treatment of the adolescent sexual offender. *Child and Adolescent Social Work, 5*(2), 135–148.

Kaplan, M. S., Morales, N., & Becker, J. V. (1993). The impact of verbal satiation on adolescent sex offenders: A preliminary report. *Journal of Child Sexual Abuse, 2*(3), 81–88.

Kolarsky, A., Freund, K., & Machek, J. (1967). Male sexual deviation: Association with early temporal lobe damage. *Archives of General Psychiatry, 17*, 735–743.

Kott, J. A. (1977). Neurological diseases causing hypersexuality. *MAHS, 11*, 71–72.

Lab, S. P., Shields, G., & Schondel, C. (1993). Research note: An evaluation of juvenile sex offender treatment. *Crime and Delinquency, 39*(4), 543–553.

Langevin, R., Bain, J., Wortzman, G., et al. (1988). Sexual sadism: Brain, blood, and behavior. *Annals of the New York Academy of Science, 528*, 163–171.

Lorefice, L. F. (1991). Fluoxetine treatment of a fetish (letter). *Journal of Clinical Psychiatry, 52*, 41.

Matthews, R. (1987). *Female sexual offenders: Treatment and legal issues.* Minneapolis, MN: Genesis II.

McConaghy, N., Blaszczynski, A., Armstrong, M. S., & Kidson, W. (1989). Resistance to treatment of adolescent sex offenders. *Archives of Sexual Behavior, 18*(2), 97–107.

Mohan, K. J., Salo, M. W., & Nagaswami, S. (1975). A case of limbic system dysfunction with hypersexuality and fugue state. *Diseases of the Nervous System, 36*, 621–624.

National Adolescent Perpetrator Network. (1988). Preliminary report from the National Task Force on juvenile sexual offending. *Juvenile and Family Court Journal, 39*(2), 5–67.

National Adolescent Perpetrator Network. (1993). The revised report from the National Task Force on juvenile sexual offending. *Juvenile and Family Court Journal, 44*, 1–120.

Perilstein, R. D., Lipper, S., & Friedman, L. J. (1991). Three cases of paraphilias response to fluoxetine treatment. *Journal of Clinical Psychiatry, 52*, 169–170.

Pithers, W. D., Becker, J. V., Kafka, M., Morenz, B., Schlank, A., & Leombruno, P. (1995). Children with sexual behavior problems, adolescent sexual abusers, and adult sexual offenders: Assessment and treatment. *American Psychiatric Press Review of Psychiatry, 14*, 779–819.

Quinsey, V. L., Rice, N. E., & Harris, G. P. (1995). Actuarial prediction of sexual recidivism. *Journal of Interpersonal Violence, 10*(1), 85–105.

Schram, D. D., Milloy, C. D., & Rowe, W. E. (1991). *Juvenile sex offenders: A follow-up study of reoffense behavior.* Washington, DC: Urban Policy Research.

Schwartz, B. K., & Cellini, H. R. (1995). *The Sex Offender Corrections, Treatment and Legal Practice.* Kingston, NJ: Civic Research Institute.

Signer, S. S., & Cummings, J. L. (1987). Erotomania and cerebral dysfunctions. *British Journal of Psychiatry*, 151–275.

Tucker, J. C., & File, S. E. (1983). Serotonin and sexual behavior. In D. Wheatley (Ed.), *Psychopharmacology and sexual disorders* (pp. 22–49). British Association for Psychopharmacology (Monograph IV). Oxford: Oxford University Press.

Chapter 11
RESEARCH ON THE TREATMENT OF ADULT SEX OFFENDERS

Marnie E. Rice, Grant T. Harris, and Vernon L. Quinsey

Victimization studies suggest that sexual crimes are common; some indicate that women in North America have at least a one in five chance of being raped in their adult lives (Russell & Howell, 1983). During childhood, the risk of being sexually victimized may be even higher, especially for girls (Peters, Wyatt, & Finkelhor, 1986). Few of the perpetrators, even those who are convicted, end up in prison for these offenses. Furthermore, by the time an offender is convicted, he is likely to have committed many offenses against many victims (Abel et al., 1987).

Almost all adult sex offenders are men (Abel, Rouleau, & Cunningham-Rathner, 1986), although there is an emerging literature about the small group of female sex offenders (Ellis, 1998; Kaplan & Green, 1995; O'Connor, 1987). Those offenders who are charged, convicted, and sentenced to prison represent an increasingly biased group of offenders. In general, those who are imprisoned have committed more offenses and more serious offenses than offenders who are not. In North America, sex offenders make up an increasing proportion of persons held in custody. In some states, there are more persons in prison convicted of sex offenses than of any other category of offenses (Morris & Tonry, 1990). In Canada, a sex offense was the admission offense of 10.7% of the offenders admitted to the Correctional Service of Canada in 1990 to 1991, compared to 8.9% in 1986 to 1987 (Porporino & Motiuk, 1991). The records of a sample of federal offenders showed that there were many more persons who had committed sex offenses at some time in the past; in fact, 18.9% of the incarcerated population were sex offenders. Among incarcerated sex offenders, the largest group (40%) were rapists (i.e., men who had sexually assaulted adult women). A smaller percentage were child molesters (i.e., men who had committed "hands-on" offenses against prepubertal or pubescent children). Of these, 21% were extrafamilial offenders and 6% were incest offenders. Most of the remainder (28%) had offended against both children and adults.

Only a tiny fraction of incarcerated sex offenders have committed less serious sexual offenses such as exhibitionism, indecent exposure, voyeurism or frottage, although these offenses account for a large percentage of officially recorded offenses, and offenders apprehended for these offenses form a sizeable proportion of those in many outpatient treatment programs (Abel & Rouleau, 1990; Berlin et al., 1991; Maletzky, 1991a; Marshall, Eccles & Barbaree, 1991; Miner & Dwyer, 1995). There is a small literature on the evaluation of treatment outcome for exhibitionists (e.g., Langevin et al., 1979; Lindsay, Marshall, Neilson, Quinn, & Smith, 1998; Maletzky, 1991a; Marshall et al., 1991). Treatment approaches have been very similar to those used for offenders who have committed more serious offenses, and the limited outcome data available give little reason to believe that treatment efficacy is any different for these offenders than for offenders who have committed more serious "hands-on" sexual acts (e.g., Berlin et al., 1991; Maletzky, 1991a; Marshall et al., 1991).

Because sexual offenses involving physical contact (rape and child molesting) are of greatest concern to the public, because almost all of the treatment outcome data pertain to men who have been apprehended for these offenses, and because almost all incarcerated sex offenders are child molesters and rapists, we will restrict our discussion of treatments primarily to those for these two groups.

The idea that sex offenders, or many of them, at least, suffer from a mental disorder and should receive treatment has been debated at length. In the United States, the diversion of sex offenders from the criminal justice system to the mental health system began with the enactment of the first "sex psychopath" statute in Michigan in 1937. Between then and the early 1970s, an increasing number of states passed such laws. Then, over a span of several years, many such laws were repealed. One reason for the repeals was that to justify what was in many cases indeterminate detainment, it was necessary to provide for such due process considerations as treatment and annual reviews of dangerousness (Carter & Prentky, 1993). Many mental health professionals, who saw both treatment and predicting recidivism as enterprises in which there was little or no expertise, were not unhappy to see the laws repealed.

Most recently, however, public concern about serious reoffenses by released sex offenders has led to a trend towards reenactment of special laws to indefinitely detain and treat the most serious sex offenders (usually child molesters, rapists, and sexual murderers) who qualify for the label "sexual predator" (e.g., KAN. STAT. ANN. 859-29a02(b) (1994)). Contrary to the earlier laws, which were viewed as a less severe sanction than prison (Monahan & Davis, 1983), the most recent laws are designed to detain the most serious offenders beyond the end of whatever sentence they received, while at the same time providing for treatment (in most cases) and periodic reassessment of dangerousness.

Only a minority of sex offenders held in either prisons or psychiatric settings suffer from such major mental disorders as schizophrenia or other psychoses (Sturgeon & Taylor, 1980), and most sex offender treatment programs specifically exclude acutely psychotic offenders (Marques, Day, Nelson, & West, 1993; Pithers, Martin, & Cumming, 1989). Under the old sexual psychopath laws, the diagnosis most commonly responsible for a designation as a "mentally disordered" sex offender was a sexual deviation or paraphilia (almost always pedophilia or sexual sadism) in the *Diagnostic and Statistical Manual of Mental Disorders* (American Psychiatric Association, 1968, 1980, 1987). Although a diagnosis of antisocial personality disorder is very common among sex offenders, it was often not sufficient to qualify for a classification as a "mentally disordered" sex offender (Monahan & Davis, 1983). Because rapists often did not qualify as mentally disordered under the older laws, treatment programs for sex offenders have included far fewer rapists than would be expected by their proportions in the criminal justice system. However, under the new sexual predator laws, it is recognized that antisocial personality will be common, that the prognosis is poor, that treatment needs will be long-term, and that the treatments required will be very different from those suited to other civilly committed persons (e.g., The Community Protection Act passed in Washington state in 1990; WASH. § 71.09.010). Thus under the newer laws, more rapists will likely be included in treatment.

There remains, however, a small group of sex offenders who suffer from major mental illness. Based on our clinical experience, in the absence of empirical work on this issue, we recommend that the acute symptoms of psychosis be dealt with before starting any specialized treatment designed to lower the risk of sexual recidivism. Once these symptoms are under control or in remission, however, the targets for intervention for psychotic sex offenders are the same as those for any other sex offenders. Part of the rationale for this recommendation is that there is evidence that the predictors of reoffending for sex offenders in general are the same as those for sex offenders in psychiatric institutions (Hanson & Bussière, 1998).

Review of Treatment Outcome Literature for Sex Offenders

In view of the importance of finding effective treatment for sex offenders, the remainder of this chapter reviews the treatment outcome literature for these offenders. Unfortunately, there has been surprisingly little controlled research on the topic. In the following section, we examine the major treatment approaches for sex offenders and review what is known about outcome for each type of treatment. It is important for scientific and social policy purposes to note that our goal is to determine whether evidence exists that particular treatments have *specific* effects (beyond such effects of expectancy as a placebo effect, for example) on sex offender recidivism. We will not include uncontrolled reports or studies using outcome measures unrelated to recidivism. We also omit most unpublished studies and studies that included a "comparison" group acknowledged by the authors to be so different from the treated group that it should not be used to draw conclusions about the effectiveness of treatment (e.g., Berliner, Schram, Miller, & Millog, 1995; Hall, 1995a; Miner & Dwyer, 1995). Although distinctions between various types of treatment are not always clear cut, we discuss treatment outcome under three main headings: nonbehavioral psychotherapy, pharmacological and surgical treatments, and behavioral and cognitive–behavioral therapies.

Nonbehavioral Psychotherapy

At least until very recently, the most common form of treatment for child molesters and rapists has been some form of group or individual nonbehavioral psychotherapy (Quinsey, 1977, 1984). Unfortunately, in much of the literature, the treatment is not well described and seems to have been unstructured. Moreover, few nonbehavioral psychotherapy treatments have been evaluated in any controlled fashion. Those few programs that have been subject to any controlled evaluation have provided no evidence that this form of treatment has reduced the likelihood of subsequent offending among child molesters or rapists. Frisbie (1969) and Frisbie and Dondis (1965) examined treated "sexual psychopaths" from Atascadero, a maximum security psychiatric hospital in California, comparing their outcomes with those of untreated sex offenders sent elsewhere after assessment at Atascadero. The program's philosophy was humanistic, and patient government of the program was encouraged. Staff were encouraged to accept the patients without condoning their sexual misconduct, the milieu was permissive, and group therapy was combined with school, recreation, and leisure activities. The treated and untreated groups were neither randomly assigned nor matched; nevertheless, new sexual offending was higher among the treated than the untreated men.

Sturgeon and Taylor (1980) followed a later cohort of 260 men also treated at Atascadero, but released in 1973. The sexual and nonsexual violent reoffending of these offenders was compared to that of untreated sex offenders who were released from prison in the same year. The untreated group included more rapists, and the untreated men were younger, had spent longer times incarcerated for the current offense before release, and had more serious violent and nonviolent criminal histories (but less serious histories of sexual offenses) than the treated group. The treated men had fewer reconvictions for sexual offenses, but there were no differences for non-sexual violent offenses. As well, when rapists and child molesters were considered separately, there were no differences for either sexual or nonsexual violent reoffenses.

Undoubtedly, the best controlled study of the treatment outcome studies for nonbehavioral treatments is of men treated at the J. J. Peters Institute (Romero & Williams, 1983). Probationers (more than 80% were rapists or child molesters) were randomly assigned to either intensive probation or to psychodynamic group psycho-therapy plus probation. Offenders assigned to psychotherapy had nonsignificantly higher rates of rearrest for sexual offenses than those assigned to intensive super-vision alone. As well, among just those who completed more than 40 weeks of treatment (thought by the psychotherapists to be optimal), the treated participants were significantly more likely to be rearrested for a sex offense. Although the authors stress that those men who received intensive probation may have received individual "treatment" from their probation officers, a carefully planned evaluation of what was thought by the treatment providers to be an effective treatment showed no effects in reducing sexual recidivism.

In summary, the results of studies of humanistic and psychodynamic treatments have been negative. Similar to findings for offenders in general (Andrews et al., 1990) these treatments, it seems, do not reduce sexual reoffending by rapists and child molesters. Even more discouraging is the suggestion that they may even in-crease the likelihood of subsequent sex offenses.

Surgical and Pharmacological Treatments

There is no empirical basis to support the use of nonbehavioral psychotherapy treat-ments for adult sex offenders. We next look at surgical and pharmacological treat-ments.

Surgical Treatments

Although now uncommon in North America or Europe, castration (surgical removal of the testes) has been studied in nonhuman animals and was used extensively in Europe until fairly recently to reduce sex drive and recidivism in sex offenders. Castration might also reduce aggression in general. The animal evidence conclusively demonstrates that castration eventually reduces sex drive to a marginal level in adult vertebrates, and also reduces general aggression in some species. However, exactly how long it takes to affect sex drive in humans and other mammals is largely un-known. Castration has several unpleasant physical and psychological side effects on humans, including depression, hot flashes, difficulty in concentration, osteoporosis, and more feminine distribution of body fat and body hair. Physical side effects, other than osteoporosis (which may be favorably influenced by medication), are generally small and not serious. Cosmetic surgery can normalize physical appearance and even correct erectile impotence by implanting prostheses. Although there is good evidence that castration reduces sex drive, how it affects overt sexual behavior (especially human sexual behavior), and aggression more generally, over time is largely unknown (Freund, 1980). For example, many castrated men experience sexual urges for a considerable time after surgery, and about 10% are still able to engage in sexual intercourse 10 years later without prostheses (Cornu, 1973; Langeludde, 1963, both reported in Freund, 1980). Nevertheless, the intervention may be considered successful if it decreases sex drive sufficiently that the offender refrains from acting on deviant urges without any concomitant increase in aggression more generally.

Most of the human studies of the effects of castration have been completely uncontrolled, and many have included men who are not now considered to be sex offenders (for example, homosexuals who prefer adult male partners). Freund (1980) reviewed available studies of castration. In general, he found that the sexual recidivism rates among castrated offenders were low despite the fact that those offenders considered for castration were at high risk for reoffending. In one partially controlled study, Cornu (1973; reported in Freund, 1980) compared the postcastration recidivism of 121 male sex offenders (Freund did not report how this was defined) in Switzerland with that of 50 men also recommended for the procedure, but who refused. In a 5- to 30-year follow-up, 7% of the castrated and 52% of the uncastrated men committed another sexual offense (although the definition of sexual reoffending was quite broad and included publishing pornography, for example). There was little difference in the previous history of sexual offenses between the two groups. Although the differences in outcome were striking, those who were recommended but refused may have been different from those who agreed in ways that made them a higher risk group (for example, they may have been less likely to admit they had a problem). In another study (Wille & Beier, 1989), 104 voluntarily castrated sex offenders in the Federal Republic of Germany were compared with 53 men who applied for the procedure, but did not undergo castration. Most (36) of these 53 withdrew their consent before surgery. The postoperative sexual recidivism rate for the castrated men was 3% compared to 46% for the comparison sample. On the basis of current evidence, we concur with Freund (1980), who concluded that, in spite of the lack of well-controlled studies, castration can virtually abolish sexual reoffending in those freely consenting nonpsychotic offenders whose offenses were endocrinologically related (evidenced by high hormone levels, intrusive sexual fantasies, and the absence of nonsexual crimes).

In another partially controlled study of the effects of castration, Stürup (1968; see also Stürup, 1972) studied the long-term outcome of 38 men who had committed rape of either adult women or female children and had been treated in a social therapy program at Herstedvester Institution in Denmark. Eighteen men were castrated before release, and another 18 men were not (two other men were never released). Over a follow-up period lasting up to 25 years, one of the castrated and three of the noncastrated men were charged with further sex crimes. All those castrated had applied for permission to have the surgery performed, and a review panel had agreed that each was a suitable case. There was no evidence that those considered for the procedure had worse sexual offense histories, and the uncastrated men had more psychiatric symptoms. Although Stürup reported that in general he considered the results of castration to be very positive, it would be difficult to recommend the procedure based on these results (see also Gunn, 1993).

In conclusion, it seems beyond doubt that castration reduces sexual drive and can reduce the risk of sexual reoffending among offenders whose offenses are limited to sexual ones and who regard themselves as having freely consented. The issue of consent for the procedure has practical as well as legal–ethical implications, especially for incarcerated offenders or offenders who are given a choice between castration and incarceration (Alexander, Gunn, Taylor, & Finch, 1993; Maletzky, 1997). Offenders who were castrated under coercion might, for example, illicitly take testosterone or other anabolic steroids to undo the effects of castration. Although this has not apparently been much of a problem so far (Stürup, 1968, reported that one rapist in his study obtained testosterone), anabolic steroids are now available from the underground market and are often used by body builders and other athletes (Brower, 1993). In any case, no one has argued that castration is appropriate for the large proportion of offenders (especially incarcerated offenders) who are personality-disordered or have histories of nonsex offenses in addition to their sexual ones (see Eastman, 1993).

Although castration is the main surgical approach to treatment, there are animal studies and, among humans, case reports, of successful alteration of sex drive among sex offenders using stereotoxic brain surgery (of sites in the hypothalamus). However, the theoretical and empirical bases for such procedures in humans are still too weak to warrant serious consideration (see Freund, 1980, for a review of human and animal work in this area).

Pharmacological Treatments

Recently, pharmacotherapy for sex offenders has been much more widespread than surgery, especially in North America. Cyproterone acetate (CPA) and medroxyprogesterone acetate (MPA) are the two most popular medications for reducing deviant sexual behavior. Both are used to obtain the sex-drive reduction of surgical castration but with fewer ethical concerns, because the effects are completely reversible on their withdrawal. Both drugs are progesterone derivatives, and both reduce the level of circulating testosterone, although the mechanisms of action are somewhat different. Bradford and Pawlak (1993a, 1993b) studied CPA mostly with child molesters. It reduced testosterone and other hormone levels, and compared to no drug or placebo, CPA was reported to have reduced overall arousal and, in some cases, arousal (measured phallometrically) to deviant stimuli differentially. Self-reports of sexual fantasies, sexual interest, sex drive, and masturbation were also reduced. There was no assessment of effects on sexual reoffending.

Although the reduction in sex drive that accompanies these compounds is correlated with dose, the relationship (in humans particularly) appears to be far from perfect. In addition, as we mentioned with regard to castration, low-plasma testosterone is not necessarily accompanied by reduced sexual activity (Cooper, 1987; Freund, 1980). Furthermore, both drugs have side effects in addition to reducing sex desire, and most men dislike taking the drugs. Common complaints include fatigue, weight gain, headaches, loss of body hair, depression, and gastrointestinal problems. These drug treatments are regarded by sex offenders as one of the least desired therapies (Langevin, Wright, & Handy, 1988).

There have been almost no controlled outcome studies of either CPA or MPA in reducing sexual reoffending among child molesters or rapists. In one evaluation (Emory, Cole, & Meyer, 1992; Meyer, Cole, & Emory, 1992), 40 men treated with MPA were compared with 21 men offered drug treatment but who refused. Most of the individuals in the study were child molesters and the remainder were rapists, voyeurs, and exhibitionists. Both groups of offenders were outpatients and received group therapy, individual therapy, and sometimes family therapy. All admitted their offenses, and reported having overwhelming deviant fantasies. Most offenders were self-referred or referred by their physicians, although a few (mostly in the comparison group) were referred by their lawyers. Offenders who admitted their offenses but blamed substance abuse were excluded, as were offenders with histories of serious antisocial behavior. Although all participants who started MPA treatment remained on it for at least six months, the expectation was that they would remain on the drug much longer (up to five years). However, 29 of the 40 offenders dropped out of the MPA treatment prematurely, and 10 of these later reoffended. Also, seven of the men reoffended while taking MPA. Thus 18% of the men started on MPA reoffended while on the drug, but 43% of the men started on MPA reoffended before the end of the study. By comparison, 12 of the 21 or 58% of those who refused MPA reoffended while receiving other therapies. The recidivism rates (which included both self-reported and official arrests for sex offenses) were not significantly different, and recidivism for all offenders was surprisingly high considering that they were relatively low-risk, and highly motivated to begin with. Moreover, as we discuss further later in the chapter, agreeing to and continuing to take MPA is rare, so that agreeing to and persisting with the treatment may serve as a "filter" selecting especially low-risk, highly motivated offenders.

In another evaluation (Fedoroff, Wisner-Carlson, Dean, & Berlin, 1992), 46 paraphiliacs (including 29 pedophiles) were treated as outpatients for five years with either group therapy alone or group therapy plus MPA. The rate of relapse among those who had received MPA was 15%, while the relapse rate for those not receiving MPA was significantly higher at 68%. Among the pedophiles specifically, there was also a statistically significant effect in that only one who received MPA relapsed (by inviting boys to his room, for which he was not charged), whereas nine who did not receive MPA relapsed (eight of whom were arrested). However, 88 offenders were excluded from the study because they refused MPA and another 38 were excluded because they were arrested before completing five years of treatment (it is not reported how many of those were on MPA). This study suggests that among child molesters who remained in long-term psychotherapy, those who also received MPA were less likely to reoffend. The authors were cautious in their conclusions and indicated a number of methodological limitations. The research participants were not randomly assigned to receive MPA (although there were no differences between the two groups on any of the several risk factors the authors examined). Therapists were not blind as to whether or not participants received MPA. Perhaps the most serious flaw to the study, however, was the fact that offenders in the MPA plus psychotherapy condition may have been more highly motivated by virtue of their willingness to volunteer for drug treatment.

McConaghy, Blaszczynski, and Kidson (1988) compared the outcomes of 30 male sex offenders (including primarily exhibitionists and child molesters) assigned randomly to one of three groups: MPA alone, imaginal desensitization alone, or both

MPA and imaginal desensitization. The dose of MPA used in this study was lower (150 mg. administered by intramuscular injection every two weeks) than in other studies, and most men reported that they maintained appropriate heterosexual intercourse at pretreatment frequency. There were no significant differences in outcome in the one-year follow-up among the three groups. Five patients dropped out from the MPA or MPA plus imaginal desensitization groups before completing treatment.

Maletzky (1991b) compared the outcome of a group of 100 adult sex offenders (mostly rapists, child molesters, exhibitionists, and voyeurs) who received MPA as part of an outpatient treatment regime that also included behavioral, cognitive, group, and family therapy with the outcome of a group of 100 other similar offenders who received the other treatments but not MPA (and who were presumably never offered it). Despite an attempt to match the two groups, the MPA group were higher risk inasmuch as they had more extensive prior criminal histories. There was no significant difference in recidivism among the groups, although there was a trend toward higher recidivism in the follow-up period for the MPA group.

Langevin et al. (1979) attempted a study in which exhibitionists would be randomly assigned either to MPA alone, assertion training alone, or MPA plus assertion training. So many of the offenders assigned to MPA-only dropped out so that condition had to be dropped. Also, 67% of the men in the MPA plus assertion training condition quit treatment; significantly more than the 29% drop-out rate in the assertion only condition. Recidivism in a two-year follow-up did not differ among the groups despite the high dropout rate in the MPA plus assertion condition.

Finally, Hucker, Langevin, and Bain (1988) studied child molesters randomly assigned either to MPA treatment or to placebo. Of 100 eligible offenders approached, only 48 agreed to complete the initial assessment battery. Eighteen of these agreed to take part in the study. Only 11 (five MPA experimental participants and six control participants) completed a three-month trial. Although there was evidence that those on MPA showed reduced testosterone compared to placebo participants, there was no evidence that MPA changed offenders' sexual behavior.

In summary, the available evidence suggests that very few sex offenders will voluntarily accept currently available medications to reduce testosterone, and even fewer will continue to take the drugs for extended periods. However, the limited available data suggest that reoffense rates are already low among those few offenders who do remain in treatment that includes such drugs. It is important to note, however, that there is, so far, no convincing reason to believe that the drugs themselves are responsible for reducing reoffending. Just as plausible is the hypothesis that the small fraction of sex offenders who remain in treatment that includes such drugs are especially highly motivated so that fully participating in such treatment is a good predictor of success, a possibility acknowledged by the researchers themselves (Fedoroff et al., 1992).

As a final cautionary note regarding antiandrogens, Hanson and Harris (2000) reported on a group of sex offenders known to have committed a new sex offense during their time under parole supervision and a group of sex offenders (matched to the first group on several known risk factors) not known to have committed a new offense. It is interesting to note that the recidivists were more likely to have been prescribed antiandrogens than the nonrecidivists. Although it is quite likely that the men prescribed antiandrogens were perceived to be at higher risk and that is why they were prescribed the antiandrogens in the first place, this study nevertheless illustrates that including antiandrogen drugs as part of a supervision order does not mean likelihood of recidivism is thereby reduced to a low level.

There are other medications that reduce or block testosterone that, like CPA, have not yet been subject to controlled evaluation (e.g., leuprolide acetate; Dickey, 1992, gonadotropin-releasing hormone analog; Rosler & Witztum, 1998). There are also recent reports of serotonergic drugs in treating sexual deviance with the suggestion that these medications may decrease deviant sexual interests without impairing nondeviant interests (Fedoroff, 1993). There is also reason to believe, given the general popularity of several serotonergic drugs (e.g., fluoxetine) that compliance might be less problematic. Nevertheless, there have been no controlled outcome studies of the effects these drugs have on reducing sexual offending.

Behavioral and Cognitive–Behavioral Treatment

Almost every published evaluation of behavioral or cognitive–behavioral treatment shares one common treatment component—behavioral techniques to normalize deviant sexual preferences (Abel et al., 1988; Davidson, 1984; Hanson, Steffy, & Gauthier, 1993; Hildebran & Pithers, 1992; Maletzky, 1991a; Marques, Day, Nelson, & West, 1994; Marshall & Barbaree, 1988; Rice, Quinsey, & Harris, 1991; see also Furby, Weinrott, & Blackshaw, 1989; Marshall et al., 1991). The particular behavioral methods used to alter sexual preferences vary somewhat from program to program. Most techniques—covert sensitization, masturbatory reconditioning, operant conditioning, and so on—all attempt to associate aversive events with arousal to deviant stimuli or fantasies (see Maletzky, 1991a; Quinsey & Marshall, 1983, for more details on the behavioral techniques). Behavioral techniques are sometimes supplemented by having clients maintain logs of sexual fantasies as well as other psychological and behavioral precursors to sexual deviance.

Most published reports also indicate that training in social competence is a key treatment component (Abel et al., 1988; Davidson, 1984; Hanson et al., 1993; Hildebran & Pithers, 1992; Maletzky, 1991a; Marques et al., 1993; Marshall & Barbaree, 1988; Rice et al., 1991). Many contain a wide variety of such other components as sex education (Rice et al., 1991), anger management (Marshall & Barbaree, 1988), nonspecific counselling (Hanson et al., 1993), family systems therapy (Borduin, Henggeler, Blaske, & Stein, 1990), and relapse prevention (Hildebran & Pithers, 1992; Marques et al., 1994). Many contain such noncognitive–behavior elements as insight-oriented psychotherapy (Davidson, 1984) or victim awareness and empathy. Lack of standardization has some unfortunate consequences: Treatments are abandoned (or at least greatly altered) before anything is known about their effectiveness; and measures of in-program change are not reported (for exceptions see Marques et al., 1994; and Rice et al., 1991), preventing the accumulation of knowledge about the relative effectiveness of various treatment components.

Marshall and Barbaree (1988) evaluated a community-based program that combined behavioral treatments to modify sexual preferences, social skills training, relaxation training, and counselling for 68 child molesters. A comparison group was made up of men who lived too far away or changed their minds about treatment. Except for the fact that some comparison research participants had changed their minds, no information was provided about participants who dropped out of treatment.

The outcome measure was the combination of official arrests plus unofficial reports of sexual recidivism and indicated a positive effect of treatment. The authors cited official recidivism data separately (Marshall, Jones, Ward, Johnston, & Barbaree, 1991), but these yielded no statistically significant treatment effects. Marshall et al. (1991) evaluated a similar program for exhibitionists and found no statistically significant effect of treatment (see Quinsey, Harris, Rice, & Lalumière, 1993).

Hanson et al. (1993) conducted a retrospective evaluation of a program that combined the behavioral modification of sexual preferences with counseling and milieu therapy for 106 incarcerated child molesters for whom recidivism data were available. Two comparison groups were used: a group of offenders released from the institution before the program began, and a second group from the same time period as the treated individuals who did not receive treatment for a variety of administrative reasons. No information was provided about individuals who dropped out of treatment. Officially recorded convictions for sexual offenses and assault indicated no effect of treatment.

Rice et al. (1991) evaluated a combination of behavior modification for sexual preferences, social skills, and sex education for child molesters in a maximum security psychiatric institution. Fifty treated individuals were compared to a group of men who had been admitted to the institution but who did not receive treatment because of administrative reasons. There were no treatment dropouts *per se* but a significant proportion of the treatment individuals terminated treatment without having made a significant improvement in sexual preferences. Subgroups of 29 treated individuals and 18 successfully treated individuals were matched to untreated offenders on sexual deviance and sexual offending history. For none of these comparisons was there evidence of a positive effect of treatment on officially recorded sexual or violent recidivism.

Hildebran and Pithers (1992) evaluated a cognitive–behavioral program for adult rapists and child molesters. Fifty men who completed inpatient and outpatient relapse prevention treatment were compared with 40 men who dropped out before completing treatment. Men who completed treatment were significantly less likely to reoffend. However, as discussed in the section on pharmacological treatments, comparing treatment completers with treatment dropouts permits no conclusions about the efficacy of the specific treatment. Instead, completing treatment may be an indication that an offender (with or without the treatment itself) is low risk.

Borduin et al. (1990) compared community-based multisystemic therapy for adolescent sex offenders to individual therapy. The multisystemic treatment was problem-focused service aimed at family preservation by resolving school problems, social deficits, peer difficulties, and family conflict. No treatment for deviant sexual preferences was provided. Treatment assignment was random. No information was provided about treatment dropouts. Although the number of participants was small (eight in each group), officially recorded rearrest data for sexual and nonsexual offenses indicated a large positive effect of multisystemic therapy.

Nicholiachuk, Gordon, Gu, and Wong (2000) studied 283 matched pairs of treated and untreated offenders followed for a mean of six years after their release. The six- to eight-month treatment program, which occurred in a Canadian federal correctional facility, was based on cognitive–behavioral and relapse-prevention models. The untreated offenders were drawn from an archive of 2600 sex offenders incarcerated in the same region but who did not participate in the treatment program.

Sexual recidivism was lower among the treated offenders, and time series analyses showed that offense rates remained lower after 10 years. Although these results appear to be encouraging, the positive findings from this study have been called into question after it was discovered that the archive from which the matched comparison sample was drawn was likely higher risk than the treated sample despite the matching procedure (Hanson & Nicholaichuk, in press).

Marques and her colleagues have published several preliminary reports on the effectiveness of an ambitious, cognitive–behavioral program for incarcerated child molesters and rapists (Marques, 1999; Marques et al., 1993, 1994) at Atascadero State Hospital. The treatment combined relapse-prevention training, relaxation training, social skills training, stress and anger management, counseling for substance abuse problems, behavioral treatment for deviant preferences, and aftercare. Random assignment to treatment was done from a larger pool of volunteers and a second comparison group was formed by matching treatment refusers to treated individuals on age, criminal history, and offender subtype. Offenders who dropped out of the treatment group before or after treatment began were also recorded and followed. Attrition was high: 21.8% of those assigned to the treatment group dropped out before reaching Atascadero, and another 19.8% dropped out after admission to a hospital (Marques, 1999). Of the 172 participants who began treatment, the 34 who failed to complete treatment had the highest rate of reoffending (Marques, 1999; Marques et al., 1994). When offenders who completed treatment were compared with untreated volunteers, there were no significant positive effects of treatment. Some positive results of treatment were found in anaylses that controlled for differences between groups in marital status and previous treatment failure (Marques, 1999).

Three studies have evaluated the efficacy of a sex offender treatment program run in a Canadian federal correctional system treatment centre in Kingston, Ontario. It has employed behavioral and cognitive–behavioral treatment components since 1974. In addition, other psychotherapeutic components included confrontation, role playing, and supportive psychotherapy. Empathy skills training was added in 1986 and relapse prevention was added in 1989 (Quinsey, Khanna, & Malcolm, 1998). The first evaluation of this program (Davidson, 1984) compared the recidivism of 101 treated rapists and child molesters with that of a matched sample of men released before the program began. Matching variables were the age and sex of the victim and the victim's relationship to the offender. No data on attrition were provided. Compared to untreated sex offenders, treated individuals had fewer overall and assault-related convictions, equivalent sexual convictions, and more arrests for sex offenses.

In the second evaluation of this program, Quinsey, Khanna, and Malcolm (1998) compared 213 offenders who completed a treatment program with 183 offenders who were assessed as not requiring it, 52 offenders who refused to be assessed, 27 offenders who were judged to be unsuitable for participating in it (usually because they did not speak English), and 9 others who did not receive treatment for various other reasons. There were very few treatment dropouts. More than half of the sample was rearrested for some offense in the 44-month follow-up and 38% were arrested for a new violent or sexual offense. Treated offenders were the most frequently rearrested for sex offenses. Inmates judged unsuitable for treatment were rearrested least frequently, particularly for sex offenses. Inmates judged not to require treatment and those who refused treatment had fewer rearrests for sex offenses than treated individuals, although they had more rearrests for violence. After statistically controlling for the variables that predicted reoffending, the treatment program was associated with a higher rate of sexual rearrests but had no effect on violent recidivism overall. Among treated offenders, clinicians' assessment of treatment progress was unrelated to recidivism.

Looman, Abracen, and Nicholaichuk (2000) have reevaluated the effects of the treatment provided in the same program evaluated by Davidson (1984) and Quinsey et al. (1998). Looman et al. included a subset of 89 of the 213 treated offenders from the Quinsey et al. study. These 89 men were all those who were treated between 1976 and 1989 in the residential program setting for whom sufficient details about the treatment received were available, who were released before 1992, and for whom a matched untreated offender could be found. The untreated offenders were matched on age at index offense, date of index offense, and prior criminal history. However, the matching procedure was far from ideal. The controls were selected from an archive of 3000 offenders from a different part of Canada, and 63 treated men who would otherwise have been eligible for inclusion were dropped from the study because no match could be found. The archive from which the controls were selected had the same problems noted earlier for the Nicholaichuk et al. (2000) study (see Hanson & Nicholaichuk, in press). Nevertheless, the results showed a highly significant positive effect of treatment on sexual recidivism as well as a marginal effect on nonsexual recidivism.

Thus three evaluations of the same program reached very different conclusions—one finding the treatment increased risk of sexual recidivism, another finding that the same treatment decreased risk of sexual recidivism, and the third finding mixed results. Unfortunately, because of the post-hoc procedures that had to be used in all three studies to create a comparison sample, it is impossible to draw definitive conclusions from any of the studies. Perhaps the best lesson to be learned from them is that there is no good alternative to a true random-assignment study.

To date, no data compel any revision to earlier conclusions of Furby et al. (1989) about treatment in general or Quinsey et al. (1993) about cognitive–behavioral treatment in particular: The effectiveness of sex-offender treatment has yet to be demonstrated. Although there have been some studies that have obtained positive results, the strongest results have come from a group of eight adolescent offenders, and the existing data provide no evidence about just what might have been responsible for any reduction in recidivism. Thus the treatment outcome literature is profoundly unhelpful in giving clues about what might be effective with particular kinds of sex offenders. By the same token, the general lack of in-program change or process measures means that few data of theoretical value have emerged from this literature. The preferred or recommended treatment continues to evolve (e.g., Hall, Shondrick, & Hirschman, 1993; Hollin & Howells, 1991; Marshall, 1993, 1994; Marshall, Eccles, & Barbaree, 1993; Pithers, 1993) but the evolution is not based on an empirical foundation of effective treatment and has no chance to be. Just as was the case with pharmacological treatments, the available data are consistent with the contention that agreeing to and persisting with treatment over the long term serves as a filter for detecting those offenders who are less likely to reoffend, and that the specific type of treatment (so long as it is not exclusively humanistic or psychodynamic) has no specific effect on outcome.

The ongoing Marques et al. (1993, 1994, 1999) study carries the heavy burden of the field's expectations. Without question, it is a superbly designed study and will help answer the questions posed at the beginning of this chapter. Among its crucial features are

1. Clinical sophistication. The treatment program is multifaceted, targeting those aspects of sexual offenders for which there exists any evidence linking them to sexual offending and sexual recidivism. Each treatment component is linked to pre-, post-, and follow-up assessments ultimately enabling conclusions about which changes wrought by therapy are responsible for reductions in recidivism.
2. Random assignment. From a pool of sex offenders who volunteer for treatment, some are randomly selected to receive it. In addition, research participants who refuse treatment are included and matched to treated and untreated volunteers. Also, treatment dropouts are followed. This powerful design permits evaluating the specific effects of treatment versus the effects of motivation to desist from sexual offending on recidivism.
3. Reliance on "hard" outcome data. Officially recorded rates of violent, sexual, and general criminal recidivism are gathered separately. This minimizes the effects of plea bargaining and police and offender expectancies on conclusions about the effectiveness of treatment.

After over two decades of therapeutic effort, this study is one of very few methodologically sophisticated evaluations of any treatment for sex offenders. Its methodological power notwithstanding, the Marques et al. (1994) study is but a single evaluation. It appears that the question of the effectiveness of cognitive–behavioral or behavioral treatment of sex offenders will go on in the absence of a scientifically definitive answer for a long time to come. Prospects for ultimately demonstrating the efficacy of cognitive–behavioral therapy were somewhat undermined by a recent follow up of a current institutional program (Seto & Barbaree, 1999). In that study, sex offenders who showed better response to treatment (behaved well in group, did their homework, improved in empathy, understood their offense cycles, and had high quality relapse-prevention plans) were significantly more likely to reoffend violently.

General Discussion and Conclusions

Twelve of the studies reviewed were included in a meta-analysis of sex offender treatment evaluations (Hall, 1995b). Hall reported a small but statistically significant overall positive effect of treatment (Cohen's $d = .24$) and also concluded that no significant variability in effect size could be attributed to the studies' methodological quality. This latter conclusion, however, was compromised by a mischaracterization of some studies. For example, Hall reported that the control participants in a study of castration were men "not granted castration by a committee of two physicians and a lawyer" (Hall, 1995b, p. 805). In fact, the original report said something quite different: "53 applications for castration were submitted, of which only 17 cases were not granted by the authoritative commission. The larger number was cancelled by the applicants themselves before the decision of the commission was made and, in 6 cases, after the commission had given permission" (Wille & Beier, 1989, pp.

111–112)—that is, at least 68% of the control group were actually "treatment" refusers.

Further examination of the original twelve reports included in the meta-analysis showed that, in four studies (Fedoroff et al., 1992; Hildebran & Pithers, 1992; Meyer et al., 1992; Wille & Beier, 1989), all or most of the control group were men who refused or dropped out of treatment. Of the other eight, three (Borduin et al., 1990; Marques et al., 1994; McConaghy et al., 1988) used random assignment, one (Rice et al., 1991) used a matching design, and one (Hanson et al., 1993) used a control group of men from an earlier cohort of men who did not participate for administrative reasons. The comparison groups in the other three studies were more ambiguous. Two (Marshall & Barbaree, 1988; Marshall et al., 1991) used as controls men who either refused (changed their minds about treatment) or chose not to participate because they lived too far away. The comparison group in the Maletzky (1991b) study were men who did not receive MPA treatment for unspecified reasons. The mean effect size for the studies that used treatment refusers or dropouts as controls was at least .73 versus an effect size of −.01 for the studies that clearly did not. Because the use of treatment refusers or dropouts as controls produced an effect size .74 larger than studies that used randomly assigned or matched controls, Hall's analysis (1995b) provides an estimate for the nonspecific effect of volunteering for and persisting with treatment on sexual recidivism. One could argue that the appropriate inferential test for studies using treatment refusers as the control group would be to reject the null hypothesis of no treatment effect only if the entire confidence interval for d was greater than .74 (instead of the usual criterion of zero). And the effect size obtained for the five most methodologically rigorous studies indicated no effect of treatment. See also McConaghy (1999) for a discussion of other problems with the Hall meta-analysis (and a strong defense of random assignment and placebo designs).

With regard to this meta-analysis, we note that Hall (1995b) compared three classes of treatment—behavioral, cognitive–behavioral, and hormonal (including castration). He reported superiority for the latter two over behavioral. Because it seemed to contradict more comprehensive meta-analyses of treatment for offenders in general (Andrews et al., 1990; Lipsey, 1992; Lipsey & Wilson, 1993), we examined this conclusion further. Our classification of control groups yielded a more plausible explanation: None of the evaluations of behavioral treatment and all of the evaluations of hormonal interventions (that reported a positive effect) used the treatment-refusers-as-control design. Hall's (1995b) conclusions, then, may be completely compromised by confounding study quality and treatment type.

In search of empirical support for sex offender therapy, the Association for the Treatment of Sexual Abusers (ATSA), a professional association of treatment providers for sex offenders, sponsored a review of approximately 40 psychological treatments (ATSA, 2000). This meta-analysis included many methodologically weak unpublished reports (21), plus several published reports in which there was no comparison group or the comparison group were treatment dropouts (5). As well, some published reports concerned only adolescents (3) or exhibitionists (2). Thus most of the studies in the ATSA meta-analysis would not have met our criteria for inclusion in the present narrative review. Nevertheless, it is instructive to examine the results of all the studies in the ATSA meta-analysis to glean whatever can be learned.

Concerning sexual recidivism, there were three studies (the 1983 J. J. Peters study by Romero & Williams, the 1990 multisystemic treatment study by Borduin et al., and the ongoing Atascadero study by Marques and her colleagues) using random assignment ($N = 662$) indicating no effect of treatment—recidivism rates of treated and untreated offenders were identical. When offenders were assigned to treatment based on clinicians' perception of need ($N = 734$), treatment was associated with higher rates of recidivism. Treatment appeared to be associated with significantly lower rates of sexual recidivism when comparison groups comprised offenders who refused treatment or dropped out ($N = 3684$). Finally, the ATSA meta-analysis considered "incidental" designs in which offenders or therapists might not have had complete control over who got what treatment. These studies ($N = 2610$), however, yielded an effect size the same as that from studies using treatment refusers as comparison samples. Closer examination of these "incidental" studies suggested that offenders in many of the comparison groups could actually have been men who arranged to avoid treatment. In addition, interrater agreement on the categorization of study design was weak. The results for criminal recidivism in general mirrored those for specifically sexual recidivism. We conclude that this recent ATSA-sponsored meta-analysis, though admirable in intent, simply could not find enough well-designed studies to be informative (see McConaghy, 1999). At present, we must conclude that the efficacy of treatments for child molesters and rapists remains to be demonstrated.

The weakness of the treatment outcome literature underscores the need for accurate appraisals of risk. The idea that a high-risk offender (especially such serious offenders as serial sexual murderers) can be changed into a low-risk offender through treatment or through progress in treatment simply has no empirical support from the literature taken as a whole. However, to say that treatments have not been conclusively evaluated is neither to say that they do not work nor to assert that different approaches to treatment are of equivalent efficacy. The best option in these circumstances of relative ignorance is to adopt treatments that (a) fit with what is known about the treatment of offenders in general; (b) have a convincing theoretical rationale in that they are motivated by what we know about the characteristics of sex offenders; (c) have been demonstrated to produce proximal changes in theoretically relevant measures; (d) are feasible in terms of acceptability to offenders and clinicians, cost, and ethical standards; (e) are described in sufficient detail that program integrity can be measured; and (f) can be integrated into existing supervisory procedures. This last point is of special importance, because to the extent that treatment fails to reduce recidivism, supervision (including denial of community access) has to take its place.

Another implication of the outcome literature is that treating sex offenders has to be viewed not simply as a matter of providing service to offenders and protecting the public but as a matter of program development. The key to successful program development is to design interventions in such a way that their evaluation tests the theory on which they are based. Such a strategy is called "Program Development Evaluation" (Gottfredson, 1984). It is possible and even likely, in our view, that the theoretical rationales for current treatment approaches are incomplete or simply wrong. Given the results of treatment evaluations so far, the burden of proof is clearly on those who assert that the provision of sex offenders treatment reduces the likelihood of recidivism. Because there is no gold-standard method of treatment, it is ethically feasible to compare different kinds of treatment programs with each other (enabling the use of random assignment) and to compare different combinations of supervision and treatment.

Because sex offenders are by definition criminal offenders, it is reasonable to expect that principles of treatment that apply to offenders in general also apply to sex offenders. The principles of offender treatment have been conceptualized in terms of risk, need, and responsivity (Andrews et al., 1990). Andrews and his colleagues have argued that offender treatment is most effective when targeted at the criminogenic needs of high-risk cases; a similar argument, in the context of managing violent offenders, has been advanced by Quinsey and Walker (1992). However, it is also important to point out that there may be some offenders whose risk level is so high that no treatment could reasonably be expected to lower it to a level at which release to the community could be recommended (cf., Harris, Rice, & Quinsey, 1993).

As noted earlier for sex offenders, it is clear from the general literature on offender treatment that evocative, insight-oriented, nondirective, or milieu approaches have either been ineffective or have raised recidivism rates (Andrews et al., 1990; Gendreau, 1996). In particular, an evaluation of an intensive, confrontational, therapeutic community milieu therapy program for mentally disordered offenders found very high post-release rates of violent recidivism among patients (including a substantial proportion of sex offenders). The rate of recidivism among psychopathic patients (defined by Hare's Psychopathy Checklist; Hare, 1991) was higher than that of similarly psychopathic offenders sent to prison (Harris, Rice, & Cormier, 1994; Rice, Harris, & Cormier, 1992). This program is noteworthy because it involved serious offenders and was implemented with great intensity and integrity. These findings raise very serious concerns about programs that rely on these techniques for psychopathic sex offenders.

The implications of these conclusions from the literature on offender treatment must be applied to sex offender treatment programs because of the equivocal nature of sex offender outcome literature. Based on the correctional treatment literature (e.g., Andrews & Bonta, 1994; Gendreau, 1996; Zamble & Porporino, 1988), characteristics of programs that have some hope of success in reducing sex offender recidivism include a skill-based training approach emphasizing problem-solving and self-management skills; the modeling of prosocial, anticriminal behaviors and attitudes; a directive but nonpunitive orientation; a focus on modifying antecedents to criminal behavior; a supervised community component to assess and teach the offender relevant skills; and a moderately high-risk clientele.

Characteristics of programs that are likely to be ineffective or associated with increased recidivism include confrontation without skill-building; a nondirective approach; a punitive orientation; a focus on irrelevant or noncriminogenic factors (for example, building an offender's self-esteem without modifying his procriminal attitudes; Wormith, 1984); the use of highly sophisticated verbal therapies, such as insight-oriented psychotherapy, and a low-risk clientele.

The probability and type of recidivism is strongly affected by victim age, sex, and relationship to the offender; the seriousness and nature of the sex offense; and the number of previous sex offenses. There is evidence that the most important of these differences and the most relevant for the design of individual treatment programs, is the nature of the offender's sexual preferences (Hanson & Bussière, 1998). Some offenders have marked paraphilic (sexually deviant) interests in children or sadistic sexual assault. These sexual preferences can be measured with varying degrees of adequacy by offender self-report, offense history, or phallometric assessment. Undoubtedly, among offenders at least, phallometric assessments are the most valid (Harris & Rice, 1996; Harris, Rice, Quinsey, Chaplin, & Earls, 1992), although they are also undoubtedly intrusive and there are ongoing debates about the ethics of their use (e.g., McConaghy, 1989; McAnulty & Adams, 1992). Measuring these interests is important because it provides clues about the motivation underlying the offense, and an idea about the nature of possible future acts of sexual aggression. Unfortunately, phallometric assessment data can be faked and are more likely to yield misleading results when offenders are highly motivated to appear to have normal sexual preferences (Proulx, Côté, & Achille, 1993). With respect to phallometric data gathered before and after treatment, therefore, continued evidence of inappropriate sexual preferences is a bad prognostic sign, but a reduction in such interest is not necessarily a good sign. Notwithstanding recent research implicating a prenatal origin to deviant sexual preferences (Lalumière, Harris, Quinsey, & Rice, 1998), the discriminative and predictive validity of sexual preferences implies a focus for treatment. It is clear that both the development of more effective treatments for altering sexual preferences is an important step in the quest for successful treatments for sex offenders and that valid measures of sexual preferences are critical in assessing risk among these offenders.

Psychopathy is another important predictor of outcome among sex offenders, as it is among offenders in general (e.g., Hare & McPherson, 1984; Harris, Rice, & Cormier, 1991; Rice, Harris, & Quinsey, 1990; Serin, 1991). Moreover, the combination of psychopathy and sexual deviance predicts especially poor outcome (Rice & Harris, 1997). Unfortunately, although we know something about what treatments might be especially harmful for psychopaths, there are as yet no data about what might be helpful. Nevertheless, because it may eventually turn out that effective programs for psychopaths are quite different from those that work for nonpsychopaths, and because psychopathy is such an important predictor of recidivism, it is extremely important that future evaluations of treatment efficacy assess participants for psychopathy. The importance of measuring psychopathy when treating sex offenders is underscored by recent findings by Seto and Barbaree (1999). In their evaluation of treatment behavior and recidivism among sex offenders treated in a Canadian federal correctional facility, they found that men who scored higher in psychopathy and better in treatment behavior were the most likely to reoffend. Alcohol abuse is another common problem among sex offenders, as it is among offenders more generally. Alcohol abuse can, if not effectively addressed, undermine treatment effectiveness by reducing offender compliance and self-control. Thus addressing alcohol abuse in assessment and treatment is likely to be another important component of a comprehensive treatment package.

The best that can be advised based on current knowledge, then, is individualized treatment planning using the results of standardized assessments to formulate a theory of offender motivation and to choose specific interventions, including supervision, designed to prevent recidivism. Thus for an individual offender, any or all of the treatments designed to reduce sexual arousability, modify or control deviant sexual preferences, control drinking, secure employment, prevent depression, and so on, might be appropriate. These provisional recommendations cannot, however, be made with much certainty until the field has a great deal more high-quality treatment outcome research.

References

Abel, G. G., Becker, J. V., Mittelman, M., Cunningham-Rathner, J., Rouleau, J. L., & Murphy, W. D. (1987). Self-reported sex crimes of nonincarcerated paraphiliacs. *Journal of Interpersonal Violence, 2,* 3–25.

Abel, G. G., Mittelman, M., Becker, J. V., Rathner, J., & Rouleau, J. L. (1988). Predicting child molesters' response to treatment. In R. Prentky & V. L. Quinsey (Eds.), *Human sexual aggression: Current perspectives* (pp. 223–243). New York: Annals of the New York Academy of Sciences.

Abel, G. G., & Rouleau, J. L. (1990). Male sex offenders. In M. E. Thase, B. A. Edelstein, & M. Hersen (Eds.), *Handbook of outpatient treatment of adults* (pp. 271–290). New York: Plenum Press.

Abel, G. G., Rouleau, J. L., & Cunningham-Rathner, J. (1986). Sexually aggressive behavior. In J. Curran, A. L. McGarry, & S. A. Shah (Eds.), *Forensic psychology and psychiatry: Perspectives and standards for interdisciplinary practice.* Philadelphia: F. A. Davis.

Alexander, M., Gunn, J., Taylor, P. J., & Finch, J. (1993). Should a sexual offender be allowed castration? *British Medical Journal, 307,* 790–793.

American Psychiatric Association. (1968). *Diagnostic and statistical manual of mental disorders* (2nd edition). Washington, DC: Author.

American Psychiatric Association. (1980). *Diagnostic and statistical manual of mental disorders* (3rd edition). Washington, DC: Author.

American Psychiatric Association. (1987). *Diagnostic and statistical manual of mental disorders* (3rd ed., rev.). Washington, DC: Author.

Andrews, D. A., & Bonta, J. (1994). *The psychology of criminal conduct.* Cincinnati, OH: Anderson.

Andrews, D. A., Zinger, I., Hoge, R. D., Bonta, J., Gendreau, P., & Cullen, F. T. (1990). Does correctional treatment work? A clinically relevant and psychologically informed meta-analysis. *Criminology, 28,* 369–404.

Association for the Treatment of Sexual Abusers. (2000). *The 2000 ATSA report on the effectiveness of treatment for sex offenders.* Manuscript submitted for publication.

Berlin, F. S., Hunt, W. P., Malin, H. M., Dyer, A., Lehne, G. K., & Dean, S. (1991). A five-year plus follow-up survey of criminal recidivism within a treated cohort of 406 pedophiles, 111 exhibitionists and 109 sexual aggressives: Issues and outcome. *American Journal of Forensic Psychiatry, 12,* 5–27.

Berliner, L., Schram, D., Miller, L. L., & Milloy, C. D. (1995). A sentencing alternative for sex offenders: A study of decision making and recidivism. *Journal of Interpersonal Violence, 10,* 487–502.

Borduin, C. M., Henggeler, S. W., Blaske, D. M., & Stein, R. J. (1990). Multisystemic treatment of adolescent sexual offenders. *International Journal of Offender Therapy and Comparative Criminology, 34,* 105–113.

Bradford, J. M., & Pawlak, A. (1993a). Double-blind crossover study of cyproterone acetate in the treatment of the paraphilias. *Archives of Sexual Behavior, 22,* 383–402.

Bradford, J. M., & Pawlak, A. (1993b). Effects of cyproterone acetate on sexual arousal patterns of pedophiles. *Archives of Sexual Behavior, 22,* 629–641.

Brower, K. J. (1993). Anabolic steroids. *Psychiatric Clinics of North America, 16,* 97–103.

Carter, D. L., & Prentky, R. A. (1993). Forensic treatment in the United States: A survey of selected forensic hospitals. *International Journal of Law and Psychiatry, 16,* 117–132.

Cooper, A. J. (1987). Sadistic homosexual pedophilia treatment with cyproterone acetate. *Canadian Journal of Psychiatry, 32,* 738–740.

Davidson, P. R. (1984, March). *Behavioral treatment for incarcerated sex offenders: Post-release outcome.* Paper presented at the Conference on the Assessment and Treatment of the Sex Offender, Kingston, Ontario.

Dickey, R. (1992). The management of a case of treatment-resistant paraphilia with a long-acting LHRH agonist. *Canadian Journal of Psychiatry, 37*, 567–569.

Eastman, N. (1993). Surgical castration for sex offenders. *British Medical Journal, 307*, 141.

Ellis, L. (1998). Why some sexual assaults are not committed by men: A biosocial analysis. In P. Anderson & C. Struckman-Johnson (Eds.), *Sexually aggressive women* (pp. 105–118). New York: Guilford Press.

Emory, L. E., Cole, C. M., & Meyer, W. J. (1992). The Texas experience with depo provera: 1980–1990. *Journal of the Offender Rehabilitation, 18*, 125–139.

Fedoroff, J. P. (1993). Serotonergic drug treatment of deviant sexual interests. *Annals of Sex Research, 6*, 105–121.

Fedoroff, J. P., Wisner-Carlson, R., Dean, S., & Berlin, F. S. (1992). Medroxy-progesterone acetate in the treatment of paraphilic sexual disorders. *Journal of Offender Rehabilitation, 18*, 109–123.

Freund, K. (1980). Therapeutic sex drive reduction. *Acta Psychiatrica Scandinavica, 62*, 5–38.

Frisbie, L. V. (1969). *Another look at sex offenders in California.* Research Monograph No. 12. Sacramento: Department of Mental Hygiene.

Frisbie, L. V., & Dondis, E. H. (1965). *Recidivism among treated sex offenders.* Research Monograph No. 5. Sacramento: Department of Mental Hygiene.

Furby, L., Weinrott, M. R., & Blackshaw, L. (1989). Sex offender recidivism: A review. *Psychological Bulletin, 105*, 3–30.

Gendreau, P. (1996). Offender rehabilitation: What we know and what needs to be done. *Criminal Justice and Behavior, 23*, 144–161.

Gottfredson, G. D. (1984). A theory-ridden approach to program evaluation: A method for stimulating research implementer collaboration. *American Psychologist, 39*, 1101–1112.

Gunn, J. (1993). Castration is not the answer. *British Medical Journal, 407*, 790–791.

Hall, G. C. N. (1995a). The preliminary development of theory-based community treatment for sexual offenders. *Professional Psychology: Research & Practice, 26*, 478–483.

Hall, G. C. N. (1995b). Sexual offender recidivism revisited: A meta-analysis of recent treatment studies. *Journal of Consulting and Clinical Psychology, 63*, 802–809.

Hall, G. C. N., Shondrick, D. D., & Hirschman, R. (1993). Conceptually derived treatments for sexual aggressors. *Professional Psychology: Research and Practice, 24*, 62–69.

Hanson, R. K., & Bussière, M. T. (1998). Predicting relapse: A meta-analysis of sexual offender recidivism studies. *Journal of Consulting and Clinical Psychology, 66*, 348–362.

Hanson, R. K., & Harris, A. (2000). Where should we intervene? Dynamic predictors of sex offense recidivism. *Criminal Justice and Behavior, 27*, 6–35.

Hanson, R. K., & Nicholaichuk, T. (in press). A cautionary note regarding Nicholaichuk et al. (2000). *Sexual Abuse: A Journal of Research and Treatment.*

Hanson, R. K., Steffy, R. A., & Gauthier, R. (1993). Long-term recidivism of child molesters. *Journal of Consulting and Clinical Psychology, 61*, 646–652.

Hare, R. D. (1991). *The Hare Psychopathy Checklist—Revised.* Toronto: Multi-Health.

Hare, R. D., & McPherson, L. M. (1984). Violent and aggressive behavior by criminal psychopaths. *International Journal of Law and Psychiatry, 7*, 35–50.

Harris, G. T., & Rice, M. E. (1996). The science in phallometric testing of male sexual interest. *Current Directions in Psychological Science, 5*, 156–160.

Harris, G. T., Rice, M. E., & Cormier, C. A. (1991). Psychopathy and violent recidivism. *Law and Human Behavior, 15*, 625–637.

Harris, G. T., Rice, M. E., & Cormier, C. A. (1994). Psychopaths: Is a therapeutic community therapeutic? *Therapeutic Communities, 15*, 283–300.

Harris, G. T., Rice, M. E., & Quinsey, V. L. (1993). Violent recidivism of mentally disordered offenders: The development of a statistical prediction instrument. *Criminal Justice and Behavior, 20*, 315–335.

Harris, G. T., Rice, M. E., Quinsey, V. L., Chaplin, T. C., & Earls, C. (1992). Maximizing the discriminant validity of phallometric assessment. *Psychological Assessment, 4*, 502–511.

Hildebran, D. D., & Pithers, W. D. (1992). Relapse prevention: Application and outcome. In W. O'Donohue & J. H. Geer (Eds.), *The sexual abuse of children: Clinical issues, Volume 2* (pp. 365–393). Hillsdale, NJ: Lawrence Earlbaum.

Hollin, C. R., & Howells, K. (Eds.). (1991). *Clinical approaches to sex offenders and their victims.* Chichester, England: John Wiley & Sons.

Hucker, S., Langevin, R., & Bain, J. (1988). A double blind trial of sex drive reducing medication in pedophiles. *Annals of Sex Research, 1*, 227–342.

Kaplan, M. S., & Green, A. (1995). Incarcerated female sexual offenders: A comparison of sexual histories with eleven female nonsexual offenders. *Sexual Abuse: A Journal of Research and Treatment, 7*, 287–300.

Lalumière, M. L., Harris, G. T., Quinsey, V. L., & Rice, M. E. (1998). Sexual deviance and number of older brothers among sexual offenders. *Sexual Abuse: A Journal of Research and Treatment, 10*, 5–15.

Langevin, R., Paitich, D., Hucker, S., Newman, S., Ramsay, G., Pope, S., Geller, G., & Anderson, C. (1979). The effect of assertiveness training, provera and sex of therapist in the treatment of genital exhibitionism. *Journal of Behavior Therapy and Experimental Psychiatry, 10*, 275–282.

Langevin, R., Wright, P., & Handy, L. (1988). What treatment do sex offenders want? *Annals of Sex Research, 1*, 353–385.

Lindsay, W. R., Marshall, I., Neilson, C., Quinn, K., & Smith, A. H. W. (1998). The treatment of men with a learning disability convicted of exhibitionism. *Research in Developmental Disabilities, 19*, 295–316.

Lipsey, M. W. (1992). Juvenile delinquency treatment: A meta-analytic inquiry into the variability of effects. In T. D. Cook, H. Cooper, D. S. Cordray, H. Hartmann, L. V. Hedges, R. J. Light, T. A. Louis, & F. Mosteller (Eds.), *Meta-analysis for explanation* (pp. 83–126). New York: Russell Sage Foundation.

Lipsey, M. W., & Wilson, D. B. (1993). The efficacy of psychological, educational, and behavioral treatment. *American Psychologist, 48*, 1181–1209.

Looman, J., Abracen, J., & Nicholaichuk, T. P. (2000). Recidivism among treated sexual offenders and matched controls: Data from the Regional Treatment Centre (Ontario). *Journal of Interpersonal Violence, 15*, 279–290.

Maletzky, B. M. (1991a). *Treating the sexual offender.* Newbury Park, CA: Sage.

Maletzky, B. M. (1991b). The use of medroxyprogesterone acetate to assist in the treatment of sexual offenders. *Annals of Sex Research, 4*, 117–129.

Maletzky, B. M. (1997). Castration: A personal foul. *Sexual Abuse: A Journal of Research and Treatment, 9*, 1–5.

Marques, J. K. (1999). How to answer the question "Does sex offender treatment work?" *Journal of Interpersonal Violence, 14*, 437–451.

Marques, J. K., Day, D. M., Nelson, C., & West, M. (1993). Findings and recommendations from California's experimental treatment program. In C. G. N. Hall, R. Hirschman, J. Graham, & M. Zaragoza (Eds.), *Sexual aggression: Issues in etiology, assessment, and treatment* (pp. 197–214). Washington, DC: Taylor & Francis.

Marques, J. K., Day, D. M., Nelson, C., & West, M. (1994). Effects of cognitive–behavioral treatment on sex offender recidivism. *Criminal Justice and Behavior, 21*, 28–54.

Marshall, W. L. (1993). A revised approach to the treatment of men who sexually assault adult females. In G. C. Nagayama Hall, R. Hirschman, J. R. Graham, & M. S. Zaragoza (Eds.), *Sexual aggression: Issues in etiology, assessment, and treatment* (pp. 143–165). Washington, DC: Taylor & Francis.

Marshall, W. L. (1994). Treatment effects on denial and minimization in incarcerated sex offenders. *Behavior Research and Therapy, 32*, 559–564.

Marshall, W. L., & Barbaree, H. E. (1988). The long-term evaluation of a behavioral treatment program for child molesters. *Behaviour Research and Therapy, 26,* 499–511.

Marshall, W. L., Eccles, A., & Barbaree, H. E. (1991). The treatment of exhibitionists: A focus on sexual deviance versus cognitive and relationship features. *Behaviour Research and Therapy, 29,* 129–135.

Marshall, W. L., Eccles, A., & Barbaree, H. E. (1993). A three-tiered approach to the rehabilitation of incarcerated sex offenders. *Behavioral Sciences and the Law, 11,* 441–455.

Marshall, W. L., Jones, R., Ward, T., Johnston, P., & Barbaree, H. E. (1991). Treatment outcome with sex offenders. *Clinical Psychology Review, 11,* 465–485.

McAnulty, R. D., & Adams, H. E. (1992). Validity and ethics of penile circumference measures of sexual arousal: A reply to McConaghy. *Archives of Sexual Behavior, 21,* 177–186.

McConaghy, N. (1989). Validity and ethics of penile circumference measures of sexual arousal: A critical review. *Archives of Sexual Behavior, 18,* 357–369.

McConaghy, N. (1999). Methodological issues concerning evaluation of treatment for sexual offenders: Randomization, treatment dropouts, untreated controls, and within-treatment studies. *Sexual Abuse: A Journal of Research and Treatment, 11,* 183–193.

McConaghy, N., Blaszczynski, A., & Kidson, W. (1988). Treatment of sex offenders with imaginal desensitization and/or medroxyprogesterone. *Acta Psychiatrica Scandinavica, 77,* 199–206.

Meyer, W. J., Cole, C., & Emory, E. (1992). Depo provera treatment for sex offending behavior: An evaluation of outcome. *Bulletin of the American Academy of Psychiatry and Law, 20,* 249–259.

Miner, M. H., & Dwyer, S. M. (1995). Analysis of dropouts from outpatient sex offender treatment. *Journal of Psychology and Human Sexuality, 7,* 77–93.

Monahan, J., & Davis, S. K. (1983). Mentally disordered sex offenders. In J. Monahan & H. J. Steadman (Eds.), *Mentally disordered offenders: Perspectives from law and social science* (pp. 191–204). New York: Plenum Press.

Morris, N., & Tonry, M. (1990). *Between prison and probation.* New York: Oxford University Press.

Nicholaichuk, T., Gordon, A., Gu, D., & Wong, S. (2000). Outcome of an institutional sexual offender treatment program: A comparison between treated and matched untreated offenders. *Sexual Abuse: A Journal of Research and Treatment, 12,* 139–153.

O'Connor, A. A. (1987). Female sex offenders. *British Journal of Psychiatry, 150,* 615–620.

Peters, S. D., Wyatt, G. E., & Finkelhor, D. (1986). Prevalence. In D. Finkelhor (Ed.), *A sourcebook on child sexual abuse.* Beverly Hills, CA: Sage.

Pithers, W. D. (1993). Treatment of rapists: Reinterpretation of early outcome data and exploratory constructs to enhance therapeutic efficacy. In G. C. Nagayama Hall, R. Hirschman, J. R. Graham, & M. S. Zaragoza (Eds.), *Sexual aggression: Issues in etiology, assessment, and treatment* (pp. 167–196). Washington, DC: Taylor & Francis.

Pithers, W. D., Martin, G. R., & Cumming, G. F. (1989). Vermont treatment program for sexual aggressors. In D. R. Laws (Ed.), *Relapse prevention with sex offenders* (pp. 292–310). New York: Guilford Press.

Porporino, F. J., & Motiuk, L. L. (1991). *Preliminary results of national sex offender census,* Research Report No. 29. Ottawa: Correctional Service Canada.

Proulx, J., Côté, G., & Achille, P. A. (1993). Prevention of voluntary control of penile response in homosexual pedophiles during phallometric testing. *Journal of Sex Research, 30,* 140–147.

Quinsey, V. L. (1977). The assessment and treatment of child molesters: A review. *Canadian Psychological Review, 18,* 204–220.

Quinsey, V. L. (1984). Sexual aggression: Studies of offenders against women. In D. Weisstub (Ed.), *Law and mental health: International perspectives* (pp. 84–121). New York: Pergamon Press.

Quinsey, V. L., Harris, G. T., Rice, M. E., & Lalumière, M. L. (1993). Assessing treatment efficacy in outcome studies of sex offenders. *Journal of Interpersonal Violence, 8,* 512–523.

Quinsey, V. L., Khanna, A., & Malcolm, B. (1998). Recidivism among treated and untreated sex offenders. *Journal of Interpersonal Violence, 13,* 621–644.

Quinsey, V. L., & Marshall, W. L. (1983). Procedures for reducing inappropriate sexual arousal: An evaluation review. In J. G. Greer & I. R. Stuart (Eds.), *The sexual aggressor: Current perspectives on treatment* (pp. 267–289). New York: Van Nostrand Reinhold.

Quinsey, V. L., & Walker, W. D. (1992). Dealing with dangerousness: Community risk management strategies with violent offenders. In R. Peters, K. D. Craig, & V. L. Quinsey (Eds.), *Aggression and violence throughout the lifespan* (pp. 244–266). Newbury Park, CA: Sage.

Rice, M. E., & Harris, G. T. (1997). Cross validation and extension of the Violence Risk Appraisal Guide for child molesters and rapists. *Law and Human Behavior, 21,* 231–241.

Rice, M. E., Harris, G. T., & Cormier, C. A. (1992). Evaluation of a maximum security therapeutic community for psychopaths and other mentally disordered offenders. *Law and Human Behavior, 16,* 399–412.

Rice, M. E., Harris, G. T., & Quinsey, V. L. (1990). A followup of rapists assessed in a maximum security psychiatric facility. *Journal of Interpersonal Violence, 5,* 435–448.

Rice, M. E., Quinsey, V. L., & Harris, G. T. (1991). Sexual recidivism among child molesters released from a maximum security psychiatric institution. *Journal of Consulting and Clinical Psychology, 59,* 381–386.

Romero, J. J., & Williams, L. M. (1983). Group psychotherapy and intensive probation supervision with sex offenders. *Federal Probation, 47,* 36–42.

Rosler, A., & Witztum, E. (1998). Treatment of men with paraphilia with a long-acting analogue of gonadotropin-releasing hormone. *New England Journal of Medicine, 338,* 416–422.

Russell, D. E. H., & Howell, N. (1983). The prevalence of rape in the United States revisited. Signs: *Journal of Women in Culture and Society, 8,* 688–695.

Serin, R. C. (1991). Psychopathy and violence in criminals. *Journal of Interpersonal Violence, 6,* 423–431.

Seto, M. C., & Barbaree, H. E. (1999). Psychopathy, treatment behavior and sex offender recidivism. *Journal of Interpersonal Violence, 14,* 1235–1248.

Sturgeon, V. H., & Taylor, J. (1980). Report of a five-year follow-up study of mentally disordered sex offenders released from Atascadero State Hospital. *Criminal Justice Journal, 4,* 31–63.

Stürup, G. K. (1968). Treatment of sexual offenders in Herstedvester Denmark. *Acta Psychiatrica Scandinavica, 44,* 5–63.

Stürup, G. K. (1972). Castration: The total treatment. In H. L. Resnik, & M. E. Wolfgang (Eds.), *Sexual behaviors: Social, clinical and legal aspects* (pp. 361–382). London: Little, Brown.

Wille, R., & Beier, K. M. (1989). Castration in Germany. *Annals of Sex Research, 2,* 103–133.

Wormith, J. S. (1984). Attitude and behavior change of correctional clientele. *Criminology, 22,* 595–618.

Zamble, E., & Porporino, F. J. (1988). *Coping, behavior, and adaptation in prison inmates.* New York: Springer-Verlag.

Chapter 12
PREVENTING, MANAGING, AND TREATING SUICIDAL ACTIONS IN HIGH-RISK OFFENDERS

André Ivanoff and Lindsay M. Hayes

Suicide and other forms of suicidal behavior, including suicidal ideation, and direct, nonfatal self-harm, present significant problems in correctional settings. Examining the research literature, we know most about suicide in jails and adult detention facilities, somewhat less about the crises and characteristics associated with suicidal behavior in prison settings, and very little about suicide and suicidal behavior in juvenile correctional settings. Part of this knowledge comes from two comprehensive national studies of jail suicide (Hayes, 1983, 1989) and one national survey of prison suicide (Hayes, 1995a). The sole national study of suicide in juvenile institutions (Flaherty, 1980) was reissued following correction of analysis errors (Memory, 1989).

Clinical prediction of a low base-rate behavior such as suicide involves joining knowledge of demographic and individual factors with clinical assessment. This assessment must be informed by an understanding of the risk characteristics that link individuals to suicidal behavior and of the pathways that may lead those in confinement to suicide. This chapter summarizes what is known about characteristics and circumstances correlated with suicidal behavior and its prevention, management, and treatment. Our bias is empirical, weighted toward the use of well-documented and investigated methods.

The study of suicidal behavior in correctional settings has been hampered in several ways. Most obvious are problems arising from unstandardized reporting and underreporting. However the methodological problems present in the studies of suicide in confinement warrant listing because they limit our ability to anticipate, assess, and respond most effectively to suicidal behavior in these settings. First, most suicide research in prisons and jails is retrospective and descriptive, generally psychological autopsy and post hoc review. Second, few investigators use control groups when examining suicide or suicidal behaviors, making it difficult to identify characteristics that distinguish inmates who engage in these behaviors from those who do not. Base rates of demographic risk factors and maladaptive behavior patterns are often higher in correctional populations than among nonincarcerated groups; what distinguishes suicidal inmates from the general population may not distinguish them from other inmates.

Third, awareness of suicide and suicidal behavior as processes, the end result of direct and indirect pathways, is ignored when stationary indicators are used. Demographic and other static indicators suggest little about an individual at a particular point in time in a particular life situation, nor do they inform intervention (Bonner, 1992; Toch, 1975).

Inattention to causal processes and a primary focus on developing rates and profiles is evident in the correctional suicide literature. A simplistic assumption is often made that, following the initial period of high risk in jail settings, all individuals adjust and find ways of coping with life in prison. Research on the incidence and prevalence of mental disorder in jails and prisons, estimating that between 15 and 25% of jail inmates suffer from major mental disorder (Jordan, Schlenger, Fairbank, & Caddell, 1996; Teplin, 1994), suggests this may not be true for a significant number. Progress in preventing suicidal behavior in correctional settings is contingent on developing an empirical understanding of the multiple pathways or processes that lead confined individuals to suicidal behavior and suicide.

Suicidal Behavior in Correctional Settings

Staff often regard self-harm in jail and prison settings as manipulative behavior (Haycock, 1989). Although most staff will acknowledge that inmates who threaten suicide or engage in self-injurious behavior suffer from some emotional imbalance requiring special attention, too often correctional staff (with the collusion of mental health staff) conclude that the inmate is not dangerous and simply attempting to manipulate his or her environment. They often suggest that such behavior should be ignored and not reinforced through intervention or attention. In fact, it is not unusual for mental health professionals to label inmates engaging in deliberate self-harm as "manipulative" or "attention seeking," and the "truly suicidal" (i.e., more lethal means) inmates seen as "serious" and "crying for help" (Franklin, 1988). Clinicians routinely differentiate behavior they regard as "genuine" suicide attempts from other self-injurious (or nonlethal) behavior labeled as self-mutilation, suicidal gestures, manipulation, or malingering (Haycock, 1989). Such labeling, however, may reflect more about the clinician's reaction to the self-injurious behavior rather than about the inmate's risk of suicide (Thienhaus & Piasecki, 1997). A leading critic of such labeling has suggested that all staff relinquish the tendency to view self-injurious behavior by inmates according to expressed or presumed intent because the term "manipulative" is misleading and harmful to the understanding and management of self-injurious behavior (Haycock, 1992).

Other clinicians disagree and argue that self-injurious behavior displayed by "truly suicidal" versus "manipulative" inmates should result in different interventions. For suicidal inmates, prescribed interventions would include close supervision, social support, and access to or development of psychosocial resources. For inmates presumed attempting to manipulate—in other words, change their environment without suicidal intent—intervention would combine close supervision with behavior management (Bonner, 1992). There is no data, however, suggesting that such a bifurcated strategy decreases either suicide or nonfatal suicidal behaviors. Based on nonincarcerated samples, reliably assessing suicide intent—that is, does the individual truly want to die?—is difficult, as intent may shift, sometimes even during the act of self-injury. Historically, manipulative behavior was ignored or met with punitive sanctions, including isolation. Manipulative inmates may be forced to escalate their behavior to obtain attention or care and die as a result. Although some of these suicides occur either by accident or miscalculation of staff responsiveness, others result from desperate agitation and distress. Demonstrated interventions for managing and reducing the incidence of suicidal and self-harm behavior in nonincarcerated populations, whether with or without suicidal intent, include behavioral contingencies, support and validation, close monitoring, and skills training to increase basic capacities and improve emotional regulation (Linehan, 1993).

Labeling self-harm as a manipulative behavior in correctional settings is highly charged: No staff wants an inmate "getting by with something," and response to such actions is often severe. Punitive attitudes and actions toward self-harming inmates make logical sense when self-harm is viewed as challenging security. Although some argue that the problem is not in how we "label" the behavior, labeling behavior in a secure setting as manipulative has particular connotations that may unwittingly prevent inmates from receiving appropriate attention and care. Staff who feel manipulated may be more likely to react to suicidal behavior with punitive measures such as isolation or unwillingness to listen to an inmate's distress. Alternatively, behavioral contingencies may be applied that are more punitive than the inmate's behavior warrants simply as a way of setting an example for other inmates.

In the general population literature on suicidal behavior and self-mutilation, a primary reason for repetitive and often impulsive self-injury concerns *affect regulation*: This is only obliquely acknowledged in jail and prison settings. Although the majority of inmates that engage in self-injurious behavior do not go on to commit suicide, a history of such behavior places them at greater risk of suicide (Haycock, 1989; Ivanoff, Jang, & Smyth, 1996). Finally, there is little disagreement that all acts of self-injury reflect personal breakdowns resulting from crises of self-doubt, poor coping and problem-solving skills, hopelessness, and fear of abandonment (Toch, 1975), the ingredients of potentially suicidal behavior.

Who Is At Risk in Jail?

Preincarceration and demographic characteristics are usually examined first for indicators of suicidal behavior. In jail suicide, extensive and replicated reviews find that most victims are young, White, males, single or divorced, who were intoxicated on arrest (Davis & Muscat, 1993; Hayes, 1983, 1989). As previously noted, psychiatric history and a history of past suicidal behavior are also significantly linked to suicide in jail (Copeland, 1989; DuRand, Burtka, Federman, Haycox, & Smith, 1995; Farmer, Felthous, & Holzer, 1996; Marcus & Alcabes, 1993). Among detainees with a prior suicide attempt, the incidence of current mental disorder was 76% compared to nonattempters 56% (Holley, Arboleda-Florez, & Love, 1995).

The individual who engages in suicide attempts or deliberate self-harm in jail shares a similar background profile: history of psychiatric treatment, recent negative life events, and previous suicidal behavior, including recent verbalizations or gestures (Ivanoff, 1989). Other studies have found intoxication, depression, excessive stress, hopelessness, interpersonal loss, and anger to be precipitating factors in jail suicides (Bonner, 1992; Winkler, 1992).

Prisons

There are similarities in the psychological profiles of jail and prison suicides. In prisons, the reasons for suicide and other suicidal behaviors may be different than in jails; however, psychiatric history and a prior suicide attempt or self-harm episode remain the two strongest background factors linked to suicidality (Anno, 1985; California Department of Corrections, 1991; Hayes, 1995a; Ivanoff, Jang, & Smyth,

1996; White & Schimmel, 1995). Placement in segregated housing or single cells is also related (Anno, 1985; California Department of Corrections, 1991; Hayes, 1995b; Jones, 1986a, 1986b; White & Schimmel, 1995). Taken together, however, the empirical data on suicidal behavior in prisons present a more mixed picture than in jails. There is generally less agreement about demographic factors distinguishing suicidal from nonsuicidal prison inmates: age, marital status, and educational level are all inconsistent, although the criminal behavior histories among suicidal inmates are generally less severe. Suicide has been linked to longer sentences (New York State Department of Correctional Services [hereinafter NYS DOCS], 1994; Salive, Smith, & Brewer, 1989; White & Schimmel, 1995), high percentages of violent felonies (NYS DOCS, 1994), and personal crimes (Anno, 1985; Salive et al., 1989). Comparing prison inmates who engaged in deliberate self-harm or suicide attempts while in jail or prison with those who did not engage in such behavior found no differences on demographic, criminal history, or life-events factors. Homelessness and maladaptive social support (suicidal behavior, alcohol abuse, and arrest), however, among primary social network members were linked to suicidal behaviors (Ivanoff et al., 1996). Negative life events did not discriminate inmates who engaged in suicidal behavior from other inmates in this sample, inconsistent with previous research. The significant role that maladaptive social support may play in providing models for this dysfunctional behavior is consistent with other such patterns of behavior.

Juveniles

Two recent studies examined characteristics associated with suicidal behavior among confined juveniles. Suicidal ideation was associated with young age (13 or younger), female gender, White or "other" race, injected and other drug use, and sexual abuse. Suicide attempts, however, were associated with all of these risk factors plus a history of sexually transmitted diseases (Morris et al., 1995).

Rhode, Seely, and Mace (1997) found suicidal ideation among young men was most significantly correlated with current depression, major life events, poor social connections, and past suicide attempts. Among young women, however, ideation was most significantly correlated with impulsivity, current depression, and younger age. The only common correlate between both males and females was not living with a biological parent before detention (Rhode et al., 1997). Past suicide attempts among males were associated with current ideation and ineffective coping skills. Among females, major factors were major life events and impulsivity. Not residing with a biological parent prior to confinement was again the only factor significantly correlated with past attempts among both females and males. Suicidal behavior of a friend was significantly associated with past and current suicidal ideation among boys, but not girls; previous mixed findings concerning the potential influence of association or modeling on suicidal behavior limit interpretation of this result (Rhode et al., 1997).

Summation

These often mixed results suggest that searching for predictable patterns in the preincarceration backgrounds of vulnerable individuals may have limited utility. Based on the absence of differences on many background variables, such factors do not appear to readily discriminate those at risk for suicidal behavior from other inmates. As noted earlier, background factors are also limited in their ability to identify targets for intervention.

More recently, investigators have adopted the stress–vulnerability–coping model used in the general psychological literature to explain suicidal behavior in jail and prisons (Bonner, 1992; Lazarus & Folkman, 1984; Smyth, 1991). Put simply, individuals possess varying levels of vulnerability, whether biological, psychological, or socio–cultural, or a combination thereof. The vulnerabilities interact with environmental demands posed by negative life events or extreme conditions and result in varying types of maladaptation, in this case suicidal behavior and self-harm. When personal coping options or problem-solving abilities are limited, overwhelmed, or inhibited because of insufficient personal resources and skills, no solution is seen, and suicide or self-harm may be viewed as the only alternative for coping with intolerable life circumstances. This model suggests our efforts are best placed studying individuals' current emotional, cognitive, and behavioral states to identify factors associated with suicidal behavior.

Prevention and Management

The literature holds numerous examples of individual jail and prison systems that have developed effective suicide prevention programs (Cox & Morschauser, 1997; Hayes, 1994a, 1995a, 1995b; Hopes & Shaull, 1986; White & Schimmel, 1995). New York continues to experience a significant drop in the number of jail suicides following the implementation of a statewide comprehensive prevention program (Cox & Morschauser, 1997). Texas has seen a 50% decrease in the number of county jail suicides as well as almost a six-fold decrease in the rate of these suicides from 1986 through 1996, much of it attributable to increased staff training and a state requirement for jails to maintain suicide prevention policies (Hayes, 1996a). One researcher reported no suicides during a seven-year time period in a large county jail after the development of suicide prevention policies based on the following principles: screening; psychological support; close observation; removal of dangerous items; clear and consistent procedures; and diagnosis, treatment, and transfer of suicidal inmates to the hospital as necessary (Felthous, 1994).

Comprehensive suicide prevention programming has also been advocated nationally by such organizations as the American Correctional Association (ACA) and the National Commission on Correctional Health Care (NCCHC). Both groups have promulgated national correctional standards that are adaptable to individual jail, prison, and juvenile facilities. Although the ACA standards are the most widely recognized throughout the country, they provide severely limited guidance regarding suicide prevention, simply stating that institutions should have a written prevention policy that is reviewed by medical or mental health staff. ACA's broad focus on the operation and administration of correctional facilities (ACA, 1990, 1991) precludes these standards from containing needed specificity. The NCCHC standards, however, are much more instructive and offer the recommended ingredients for a suicide prevention program: identification, training, assessment, monitoring, housing, referral, communication, intervention, notification, reporting, review, and critical-incident debriefing (NCCHC, 1995, 1996, 1997). The second author, using a combination of ACA and NCCHC standards, has developed and recommended a comprehensive suicide prevention policy that addresses the following key components (Hayes, 1995a, 1995b).

Staff Training

The essential component to any suicide prevention program is properly trained correctional staff, who form the backbone of any jail or prison facility. Very few suicides are actually prevented by mental health, medical, or other professional staff because suicides are usually attempted in inmate housing units, and often during late evening hours or on weekends when program staff are not present. Suicides, therefore, must be prevented by correctional staff who have been trained in suicide prevention and have developed an intuitive sense about the inmates under their care. Correctional officers are often the only staff available 24 hours a day and form the primary line of defense in preventing suicides.

All correctional staff, as well as medical and mental health personnel, should receive eight hours of initial suicide prevention training, followed by two hours of refresher training each year. Training should cover why correctional environments are conducive to suicidal behavior, potential predisposing factors to suicide, high-risk suicide periods, warning signs and symptoms, and details of the facility's suicide prevention–response policy and procedures. In addition, all staff who have routine contact with inmates should receive standard first aid and cardiopulmonary resuscitation (CPR) training. All staff should also be trained in the use of various emergency equipment located in each housing unit. In an effort to ensure an efficient emergency response to suicide attempts, "mock drills" should be incorporated into both initial and refresher training.

Intake Screening Assessment

Screening and assessment of inmates when they enter a facility is critical to a correctional facility's suicide prevention efforts. Although there is no single set of risk factors that mental health and medical communities agree can be used to predict suicide, there is little disagreement about the value of screening and assessment in preventing suicide (Cox & Morschauser, 1997; Hughes, 1995). Intake screening for all inmates and ongoing assessment of inmates at risk is critical because research consistently reports that two thirds or more of all suicide victims communicate their intent some time before death and that any individual with a history of one or more self-harm episodes is at a much greater risk for suicide than those without such episodes (Clark & Horton-Deutsch, 1992; Maris, 1992). Intake screening may be written onto the medical screening form or on a separate form, and should obtain past suicidal ideation or attempts; current ideation, threat, plan; prior mental health treatment–hospitalization; recent significant loss (job, relationship, death of family member/close other, etc.); history of suicidal behavior by family member/close other; suicide risk during prior confinement; and arresting–transporting officer(s) belief that inmate is currently at risk. The process should also include referral procedures to mental health and medical personnel for assessment. Following the intake process, if staff hear an inmate verbalize a desire or intent to commit suicide, observe an inmate engaging in any self-harm, or otherwise believe an inmate is at risk for self-harm or suicide, known procedures should follow. Such procedures direct staff to take immediate steps ensuring that the inmate is continuously observed until appropriate medical, mental health, and supervisory assistance is obtained.

Communication

Certain behavioral signs exhibited by the inmate may be indicative of suicidal behavior and, if detected and communicated to others, may prevent a suicide. There are essentially three communication points in preventing inmate suicides: between the arresting or transporting officer and correctional staff; between and among facility staff, including medical and mental health personnel; and between facility staff and the suicidal inmate.

In many ways, suicide prevention begins at the point of arrest. What an individual says and how they behave during arrest, transportation to the jail, and at booking are crucial in detecting suicidal behavior. The scene of arrest is often a most volatile and emotional time. Arresting officers should pay close attention to the arrestee during this time; thoughts of suicide or suicidal behavior may be occasioned by the anxiety or hopelessness of the situation, and previous behavior can be confirmed by onlookers such as family and friends. Any pertinent information regarding the arrestee's well-being must be communicated by the arresting or transporting officer to correctional staff. Effective management of suicidal inmates in the facility is based on communication among correctional officers and other professional staff. Because inmates can become suicidal at any point during incarceration, correctional officers must maintain awareness, share information, and make appropriate referrals to mental health and medical staff. Facility staff must also use various communication skills with the suicidal inmate, including active listening, physically staying with the inmate if they suspect immediate danger, and maintaining contact through conversation, eye contact, and body language. Correctional staff should trust their own judgment and observation of risk behavior, and avoid being misled by others (including mental health staff) into ignoring signs of suicidal behavior. The communication breakdown between correctional, medical, and mental health personnel is a common factor found in the reviews of many inmate suicides (Anno, 1985; Appelbaum, Dvoskin, Geller, & Grisso, 1997; Hayes, 1995b; Jones, 1986b).

Housing

In determining the most appropriate housing location for a suicidal inmate, correctional officials (with concurrence from medical or mental health staff) often tend to physically isolate and sometimes restrain the individual. These responses might be more convenient for staff, but they are detrimental to the inmate because the use of isolation escalates the inmate's sense of alienation and further removes the individual from proper staff supervision. To every extent possible, suicidal inmates should be housed in the general population, mental health unit, or medical infirmary, located close to staff. Further, removal of an inmate's clothing (excluding belts and shoelaces) and the use of physical restraints (e.g., restraint chairs or boards, leather straps, straitjackets, etc.) should be avoided whenever possible, and used only as a last resort when the inmate is actively engaging in self-destructive behavior. Handcuffs should never be used to restrain a suicidal inmate. Housing assignments should be based on the ability to maximize staff interaction with the inmate, avoiding assignments that heighten the depersonalizing aspects of incarceration.

All cells designated to house suicidal inmates should be suicide-resistant, free of all obvious protrusions, and provide full visibility (Atlas, 1989; Jordan, Schmeck-peper, & Strope, 1987; Lester & Danto, 1993). These cells should contain tamper-proof light fixtures and ceiling air vents that are protrusion-free. Each cell door should contain a heavy-gauge Lexan (or equivalent grade) glass panel that is large enough to allow staff a full and unobstructed view of the cell interior. Cells housing suicidal inmates should not contain any electrical switches or outlets, bunks with open bottoms, towel racks on desks and sinks, radiator vents, or any other object that provides an easy anchoring device for hanging. Finally, each housing unit in the facility should contain various emergency equipment, including a first-aid kit, pocket mask or face shield, Ambu-bag, and rescue tool (to quickly cut through fibrous material). Correctional staff should ensure that such equipment is in working order on a daily basis.

Levels of Supervision

The promptness of response to suicide attempts in correctional facilities is often driven by the level of supervision afforded the inmate. Medical experts warn that brain damage from strangulation caused by a suicide attempt can occur within four minutes, and death within five to six minutes (American Heart Association, 1992). Standard correctional practice requires that "special management inmates," including those housed in administrative segregation, disciplinary detention, and protective custody, be observed at intervals not exceeding every 30 minutes, with mentally ill inmates observed more frequently (ACA, 1990, 1991). Inmates held in medical re-straints and "therapeutic seclusion" should be observed at intervals that do not ex-ceed every 15 minutes (NCCHC, 1995, 1996, 1997). Consistent with national cor-rectional standards and practices, two levels of supervision are generally recommended for suicidal inmates: close observation and constant observation. Close observation is reserved for the inmate who is not actively suicidal, but expresses suicidal ideation (e.g., expressing a wish to die without a specific threat or plan) or has a recent prior history of self-destructive behavior. Staff should observe such an inmate at staggered intervals not to exceed every 15 minutes (e.g., 5, 10, 7 minutes, etc.). Constant observation is reserved for the inmate who is actively suicidal, either threatening or engaging in suicidal behavior. Staff should observe such an inmate on a continuous, uninterrupted basis. Other aids (e.g., closed-circuit television, inmate companions or watchers, etc.) can be used as a supplement to, but never as a sub-stitute for, these observation levels. Finally, mental health staff should assess and interact with (not just observe) suicidal inmates on a daily basis.

Intervention

The degree and promptness of staff intervention often determines whether the victim will survive a suicide attempt. National correctional standards and practices generally acknowledge that facility policy regarding intervention should contain three primary components. First, all staff who come into contact with inmates should be trained in standard first aid procedures and cardiopulmonary resuscitation (CPR). Second, any staff member who discovers an inmate engaging in self-harm should immediately survey the scene to assess the severity of the emergency, alert other staff to call for medical personnel if necessary, and begin standard first aid or CPR as necessary. Third, staff should never presume that the inmate is dead but rather should initiate and continue appropriate life-saving measures until relieved by arriving medical personnel. In addition, medical personnel should ensure, on a daily basis, that all facility emergency response equipment is in working order.

Reporting

In the event of a suicide attempt or suicide, all appropriate correctional officials should be notified through the chain of command. Following the incident, the victim's family should be immediately notified, as well as appropriate outside authorities. All staff who came into contact with the victim before the incident should be required to submit a statement that contains their full knowledge of the inmate and incident.

Follow-Up–Administrative Review

An inmate suicide is extremely stressful for staff, who may feel angry, guilty, and even ostracized by fellow personnel and administration officials. Following a suicide, reasonable guilt is sometimes displayed by the officer who wonders, "What if I had made my cell check earlier?" When suicide or suicidal crises occur, staff affected by such a traumatic event should receive appropriate assistance. One form of assistance is Critical Incident Stress Debriefing (CISD). A CISD team, made up of professionals trained in crisis intervention and traumatic stress awareness (e.g., police officers, paramedics, fire fighters, clergy, and mental health personnel), provides affected staff an opportunity to process their feelings about the incident, develop an understanding of critical stress symptoms, and develop ways of dealing with those symptoms (Meehan, 1997; Mitchell & Everly, 1996). For maximum effectiveness, the CISD process or other appropriate support services should occur within 24 to 72 hours of the incident.

Every completed suicide, as well as each suicide attempt of high lethality (i.e., requiring hospitalization), should be examined through an administrative review process. If resources permit, clinical review through a psychological autopsy is also recommended (Spellman & Heyne, 1989). Ideally, the administrative review should be coordinated by an outside agency to ensure impartiality. The review, apart from other formal investigations that may be required to determine the cause of death, should include (a) critical review of the circumstances surrounding the incident; (b) critical review of jail procedures relevant to the incident; (c) synopsis of all relevant training received by involved staff; (d) pertinent medical and mental health services reports involving the victim; and (e) recommendations, if any, for change in policy, training, physical plant, medical or mental health services, and operational procedures.

Several recent national surveys examined the degree to which suicide prevention issues are reflected in state jail standards and in state prison policies and procedures (Hayes, 1996a, 1996b). One recent survey found that 32 states had standards regulating county and local jails, with 24 mandatory and 8 voluntary programs (Hayes, 1996a). Of the states with jail standards, only a third required suicide prevention policies, and only one state (Texas) required county jails to maintain procedures regarding six critical prevention components (staff training, intake screening, communication, housing, supervision, and intervention). Three other states had jail standards that required procedures addressing all but one of the critical components. With regard to suicide prevention policies in state and federal prison systems, a recent survey found that although 41 of 52 departments of correction (including the Federal Bureau of Prisons and District of Columbia) had a suicide prevention policy, only 15% of these agencies had procedures that contained either all or all but one critical component of suicide prevention (Hayes, 1996b).

In a recent landmark study on conditions of confinement in juvenile facilities, researchers found widespread variability using four suicide prevention assessment criteria: written procedures, intake screening, staff training, and close observation (Parent et al., 1994). Although the majority of juveniles were housed in facilities with written suicide plans, or in facilities with screening procedures, or in facilities with staff training, only 50% were in facilities with close observational procedures. Most important, only 25% of juveniles were confined in settings that met all four suicide-prevention assessment criteria. Facilities that conducted suicide screenings at admission and trained their staff in suicide prevention had lower rates of suicidal behavior among their residents. Suicidal behavior rates were higher among youth housed in isolation. Finally, although written policies providing for close observation of suicidal residents did not appear to significantly reduce the rate of suicidal behavior, it was found to be very important in reducing completed suicides because many times the policy was implemented after the risk or attempt was recognized (Parent et al., 1994).

Exemplary Programs

Why do some correctional systems experience an inordinate number of inmate suicides or deaths attributed to obvious deficiencies whereas others of comparable size are spared the tragedy? Some observers would call it good fortune, and others believe that organizational "attitude" and comprehensive policies and procedures are the keys to suicide prevention in correctional facilities (Hayes, 1997). It has been argued that negative attitudes—for example, "If someone really wants to kill themselves, there's generally nothing you can do about it"—impede meaningful jail suicide-prevention efforts. Most effective suicide prevention programs in correctional facilities have extended incident-free periods of suicide arguably related to their implementation of the following suicide prevention components: (a) suicide prevention training for correctional, medical, and mental health staff; (b) identification of suicide risk through intake screening; (c) procedures for referral to mental health or medical personnel, reassessment following crisis period; (d) effective communication between correctional, medical, and mental health staff when managing a suicidal inmate; (e) supervision and safe housing options for suicidal inmates; (f) timely medical intervention following a suicide attempt; (g) proper reporting procedures following an incident; and (h) administrative or clinical review of suicide, availability of critical incident debriefing to staff and inmates (Hayes, 1998a). But what separates exemplary programs from very good programs is "attitude." *Exemplary programs adhere to the philosophy that inmate suicide will not be tolerated.*

The Hamilton County Juvenile Court Youth Center in Cincinnati, Ohio, is one example of an exemplary program. Opened in 1995, the 160-bed facility replaced a 30-year antiquated detention center plagued with numerous physical plant problems that precipitated, in part, three youth suicides in the 1980s. The most recent suicide in the system occurred in 1986 and became the impetus for dramatic change. In addition to building a new facility, all staff received eight hours of basic suicide prevention training followed by two hours of annual training; all youth entering the facility were subjected to several layers of screening and assessment by mental health staff; all youth were observed by facility staff at 15-minute-intervals, with high-risk youth observed at 5-minute staggered intervals; and any suicide attempt, regardless of whether serious injury occurred, was subjected to an administrative review. Since the last suicide in the old facility in 1986, more than 70,000 youth have passed through the Hamilton County Juvenile Court Youth Center system. When asked to explain such a lengthy incident-free period, the superintendent remarked that it was the result of

> the cumulative impact of the worst three days of my career, those three days during and after the suicide of Dennis D. in our facility. I was at the hospital and witnessed Dennis' parents being informed by hospital staff that Dennis had died. The agony I witnessed in the face of his parents and the sense of guilt and failure that I felt as superintendent regarding his death will be something I will carry with me for the rest of my life. After Dennis' suicide, I promised myself that I would do everything possible to proactively reduce the odds of our facility ever experiencing another suicide. (quoted in Hayes, 1998a)

The Orange County Jail system in California is the 12th largest jail system in the country (Bureau of Justice Statistics, 1998). On any given day there are approximately 5400 inmates confined in five jail facilities. Since 1988, more than 800,000 inmates have passed through the jail system, with only four of those inmates committing suicide—a ratio of one suicide per 200,000 admissions (Hayes, 1998b). Although considered a "mega jail," the jail system is operated on a much smaller scale and few inmates "fall though the cracks" of needed services. For example, from the point an inmate is booked into the jail system, a series of checks and balances is initiated to identify potentially suicidal behavior. All inmates are initially screened by medical staff at intake, and the system is staffed by mental health clinicians 24 hours a day to further assess referred inmates. In addition, correctional, medical, and mental health personnel informally communicate with each other on at-risk inmates on a daily basis and attend weekly interdisciplinary staff meetings. Another example of the seriousness in which the jail system views suicide prevention is exemplified by the requirement that all correctional staff carry small laminated cards in their pockets or wallets. Each card lists the most prominent warning signs and symptoms of suicidal behavior in jail inmates and are used by staff as a continuing reminder of their responsibility to identify potentially suicidal behavior and make the appropriate referral to mental health staff. As offered by one facility commander in the Orange County Jail system,

Those cards are part of the uniform. Every time I change my uniform I have to take the card out of my breast pocket and put it into my fresh uniform. Whatever type of subliminal reminder it is, it reinforces the importance of suicide prevention to this jail administration and that deaths in custody will not be tolerated. (quoted in Hayes, 1998b)

The Hamilton County Juvenile Court Youth Center and Orange County Jail system are two very different correctional agencies, both in size and the clientele they incarcerate. Yet both agencies have exemplary suicide prevention programs in which the focal point is zero-tolerance of suicide.

Treatment

From a mental health perspective, treatment begins with crisis intervention, the immediate response to suicidal behavior. A synthesis of crisis intervention theories and principles yields six general procedures (Roberts, 1990):

1. Establishing psychological contact and beginning relationship formation,
2. Defining the problem by examining its dimensions,
3. Encouraging an exploration of emotions and feelings,
4. Exploring and assessing past attempts to cope,
5. Generating and examining alternative solutions, and
6. Taking action to restore cognitive functioning (p. 12).

Crisis intervention is different in jail and prison settings from the typical mental health setting in two important ways. First, in jail and prison settings, those responsible for direct response, and in most cases, crisis intervention, are correctional, not mental health professionals. Once professional staff have left the facility for the day, they know little of what occurs during the next 18 hours in holding facilities, crowded cell blocks, or dormitories. Necessarily, mental health staff rely on the communication of correctional staff; therefore, such individuals' ability to functionally understand the behavior of suicidal inmates is critical. We feel strongly that comprehensive prevention training for correctional staff is the primary means of suicide prevention in confined settings. Programmatic prevention efforts focusing on systemic environmental interventions such as those described earlier in this chapter have demonstrated reductions in suicide and overt suicidal behaviors in uncontrolled evaluations.

Beyond prevention and crisis intervention, however, what treatment is indicated for the suicidal individual? To begin with, there are no psychosocial or pharmacological treatments demonstrated as empirically effective in reducing suicidal behavior in jail and prison settings. Treatments discussed next represent "free world" inpatient psychiatric and outpatient mental health settings. Treatment studies targeting suicidal behaviors such as ideation and overt behavior, and other self-harm (generally referred to as self-mutilating) behaviors, have been a relatively neglected area in treatment efficacy research. This is a result in part to the risks associated with conducting research with suicidal individuals and the assumption that we already know that some treatments, or the prevailing standards of care, are better than others for treating suicidal individuals. One of the major problems in identifying treatments is the definitional ambiguity noted earlier; or, exactly what is the target of treatment? Ideation?

Impulse? Actual behavior? Suicidal behaviors, intention, and treatment targets are so variously described that generalizing existing research is fraught with problems.

Treating suicidal behaviors is usually approached in one of two ways: (a) assuming that such behaviors are symptomatic of some other (usually mental) disorder with treatment focused on the underlying disorder, or (b) assuming ideation and other suicidal behaviors can be reduced independently of other behaviors and directly targeting (whether psychosocially or biologically) suicidal behaviors. There are roughly 20 clinical trials of psychosocial and behavioral interventions for suicidal behavior. Despite the relationship between major depressive disorder and suicidal behavior, most psychosocial and pharmacological treatment trials have excluded suicidal and self-mutilating individuals, making the generalizability of these studies unknown (Stanley, personal communication, 1999).

Psychopharmacological Treatments

Despite promising data from small clinical studies, general conclusions drawn by reviewers are to proceed with caution, highlighting that pharmacotherapy should not occur without equivalent attention to psychosocial factors linked to suicidal behavior. As with psychosocial treatments for suicidal behavior, there are no published studies, or even reviews, on psychopharmacology for suicidal inmates.

Well-known, however, are studies that found reduced levels of 5-hydroxyindoleacetic acid (5-HIAA) in the cerebrospinal fluid of completed suicides, fire setters, and impulsively violent criminals (Brown & Linnoila, 1990; Coccaro, 1989). These studies are largely responsible for the dominant research on the effects of serotenergic medications in treating aggression. Although favorable effects were reported treating aggressive behavior pharmacologically, there are few studies beyond case reports or small series of uncontrolled series of studies. Recent success of newer SSRIs in treating violent behavior, including self-harm, is under examination, highlighting definitional issues: the success of SSRIs may be a result of their effects on impulsivity rather than aggression (Conacher, 1997).

In general, caramazepine, propranodol, and lithium have been most researched in the treatment of impulsivity and aggression, all drugs that interact with central serotonin systems incorporating a range of receptor and cell membrane-affecting properties. Among these drugs that show a positive effect, there is little evidence supporting the selection of any particular class of drugs (Conacher, 1997).

Unfortunately, in addressing underlying disorder, the assumption that treating depression will reduce suicide ideation has not been borne out by data (Beasley et al., 1992). Beasley et al.'s meta-analysis of fluoxetine and tricyclic antidepressants showed no significant reduction in overt suicidal behavior. The exclusion of actively suicidal individuals from initial enrollment in the study, however, may account for the absence of effect on suicidal behavior.

Ambiguous and uncertain, we are still far from clearly understanding the biochemical and neurological pathways predisposing individuals to suicidal behavior and the relationships among the behaviors, thoughts, and intentions that suicidality comprises. The contextual issues surrounding the benefits and limitations of psychotropic medications for confined suicidal individuals are similar to those for the hospitalized inpatient. If we can presume that suicidal behaviors are directly related to a set of biopsychosocial factors, understanding the relationships between suicidal behaviors and other functional domains is critical. Six medical and psychiatric conditions that may be associated with suicidal behavior include

1. Onset or exacerbation of an underlying psychiatric disorder,
2. Current life stressors that overwhelm an at-risk individual,
3. Treatment of a psychiatric disorder (e.g., adverse reaction to medication or onset of suicidal behavior as depression lifts),
4. Underlying medical condition,
5. Medical treatment (e.g., adverse reaction to drug treatment), and
6. A learned response bias or inherited predisposition toward suicidal behavior in response to stress. (Silverman et al., 1998, p. 136)

General guidelines and recommendations for pharmacotherapy with suicidal individuals have basic applicability, but fail to address the exigencies of providing service in correctional settings. Clinical signs and situations identified as requiring immediate consideration of pharmacological treatment in general inpatient settings (Silverman et al., 1998; Slaby & Dumont, 1992) are not sensitive enough for jail and prison settings. Although they follow reasonable norms of clinical care, and include acute agitation or anxiety with suicidal intent, unmanageable psychotic or manic episodes, command hallucinations, and paranoid delusions, they also include substance abuse–dependence along with a history of impulsivity or violence, excluding few in correctional settings. Heavy emphasis should be placed on the critical nature of thorough assessment, the relationship between prescriber and patient, and the treatment team's awareness of medication goals (Silverman et al., 1998; Slaby & Dumont, 1992).

Psychosocial Treatments

A review of randomized clinical trials of psychosocial and behavioral treatments for suicidal behavior found only 18 studies, with only 4 reporting positive results. The other 14 did not. Of those 4, 2 suffered from inadequate description of the intervention, leaving 2 reasonably designed studies (Linehan et al., 1991; Salkovskis, Atha, & Storer, 1990).

In these two studies, Dialectical Behavior Therapy (DBT), a cognitive–behaviorally based treatment for borderline personality disorder, demonstrated significant effects in reducing suicidal behavior among women in randomized clinical trials. DBT is a one-year outpatient program made up of weekly group-skills training and individual psychotherapy; skills-training targets include life-threatening behaviors, treatment-interfering behaviors, and quality of life behavior. Four skills modules address these issues: mindfulness, distress tolerance, emotion regulation, and interpersonal effectiveness. When compared to treatment as usual (TAU), DBT showed significant (a) decreases in suicidal behavior and self-mutilation; (b) maintenance in treatment; and (c) number of treatment days. Individuals participating in DBT engaged in fewer overall self-harm incidents than TAU subjects (Linehan, Armstrong, Suarez, Allmon, & Heard, 1991; Linehan, Heard, & Armstrong, 1993). Applications of DBT to correctional and forensic mental health settings are currently underway in more than a dozen state prison systems and forensic hospitals, as well as outpatient programs (Ivanoff, 1998).

What happens to jail and prison inmates after the crisis and after immediate treatment? There is little information available about either group. Examining the subsequent adaptation of state inmates who engaged in suicidal behavior during the first year of their incarceration, Smyth, Ivanoff, and Jang (1994) found that a second episode of self-harm during year two continued to be most strongly associated with prior psychiatric history and dysfunction among primary social network members such as alcohol abuse, arrests, and drug problems. There were general, but not uniform, decreases in psychological maladaptation (notably not in anger levels) one year into incarceration. Those with higher levels of anger one year later had more suicidal ideation.

Identifying those vulnerable or at risk because of previous suicidal behavior and providing interventions to bolster emotional skills and resources to cope with the demands of prison or jail are both part of suicide prevention. Another aspect concerns identifying the pathways out of suicide: What are the characteristics associated with subsequent adjustment following a suicidal crisis? How can we help these individuals find their niche? It is not enough to prevent only the ultimate act of suicide if the goal is to prevent harm to vulnerable individuals.

Conclusion

The belief that suicidal behavior is a symptom of some other (usually mental) disorder is extremely strong in the United States. Primary prevention efforts by the NIMH are slowly working to shift this perception toward regarding suicidal behavior as behavior that may be associated with, but not caused by, other mental health disorders. Acknowledging the interactions and direct effects of the extreme environmental conditions in correctional institutions is essential in understanding this problem.

The strongest set of recommended strategies for preventing suicidal behavior in confinement involves initial screening and subsequent environmental adaptation to address identified risk characteristics. As knowledge about these characteristics increases, screening and intervention methods will need to be refined to not only meet the needs of the institution in preventing suicide but also to assist in targeting and accessing appropriate mental health care and programming. Steps beyond environmental management, screening, and crisis management involve developing targeted group and individual skills-building approaches: What works best for whom under what circumstances?

Although the implementation of comprehensive prevention programs is universally advocated and has the potential to prevent many deaths, the effectiveness of these programs may be limited by their generic design. Effective prevention programs cannot assume and only operate as if suicide risk functions the same across all types of individuals in custody. Our response must be informed by an understanding of the individual crises that may precipitate suicidal behavior and the relationships among current behavioral factors that may affect risk. As clinical scientists we need to look for the signs, signals, indicators, and means of measuring these indicators that work across individuals for populations, or, at least for subsets of a population.

Finally, clinicians and researchers in this field share the belief that earlier intervention with suicidal individuals is linked to better prognosis for the individual and for those surrounding the suicidal individual. Over time and with practice, we have learned to attend to the environment, to the positive and negative symptoms of suicidality, and to the more subtle indicators that form the basis for clinical judgment. Our goal should be to develop methods of identification, risk assessment, and intervention based on the characteristics of both the vulnerable and the mentally disordered individuals at risk for suicide in correctional settings.

References

American Correctional Association. (1990). *Standards for adult correctional institutions* (3rd ed.). Laurel, MD: Author.

American Correctional Association. (1991). *Standards for adult local detention facilities*. Laurel, MD: Author.

American Heart Association Emergency Cardiac Care Committee and Subcommittees. (1992). Guidelines for Cardiopulmonary Resuscitation and Emergency Cardiac Care. *Journal of the American Medical Association, 268*, 2172–2183.

Anno, B. J. (1985). Patterns of suicide in the Texas Department of Corrections 1980–1985. *Journal of Prison and Jail Health, 4*(3), 82–93.

Appelbaum, K., Dvoskin, J., Geller, J., & Grisso, T. (1997). *Report on the psychiatric management of John Salvi in Massachusetts Department of Correctional Facilities: 1995–1996*. Worcester: University of Massachusetts Medical Center.

Atlas, R. (1989). Reducing the opportunities for inmate suicide. *Psychiatric Quarterly, 60*, 161–171.

Beasley, C. M., Jr., Dornseif, B. E., Bosomworth, J. C., Sayler, M. E., Rampey, A. H., Jr., Heiligenstein, J. H., Thompson, V. L., Murphy, D. J., & Masica, D. N. (1991). Fluoxetine and suicide: A meta-analysis of controlled trials of treatment for depression. *British Medical Journal, 303*(6804), 685–692.

Bonner, R. L. (1992). Isolation, seclusion, and psychosocial vulnerability as risk factors for suicides behind bars. In R. W. Maris, A. L. Berman, J. T. Maltsberger, & R. I. Yufit (Eds.), *Assessment and Prediction of Suicide* (pp. 398–419). New York: Guilford Press.

Brown, G. L., & Linnoila, M. I. (1990). CSF serotonin metabolite (5-HIAA) studies in depression, impulsivity, and violence. *Journal of Clinical Psychiatry, 51*(4), 31–34.

Bureau of Justice Statistics. (1998). *Prison and jail inmates at midyear 1997*. Washington, DC: U.S. Department of Justice.

California Department of Corrections. (1991). *Suicide prevention in the California Department of Corrections: Annual report—1990*. Sacramento: Author.

Clark, D. C., & Horton-Deutsch, S. L. (1992). Assessment of absentia: The value of the psychological autopsy method for studying antecedents of suicide and predicting future suicides. In R. Maris (Ed.), *Assessment and Prediction of Suicide* (pp. 144–182). New York: Guilford Press.

Coccaro, E. F. (1989). Central serotonin and impulsive aggression. *British Journal of Psychiatry, 155*(Suppl.), 52–62.

Conacher, G. N. (1997). Pharmacological approaches to impulsive and aggressive behavior. In C. D. Webster & M. A. Jackson (Eds.), *Impulsivity: Theory, assessment, and treatment* (pp. 394–408). New York: Guilford Press.

Copeland, A. (1989). Fatal suicide hangings among prisoners in jail. *Medicine, Science and the Law, 29*, 341–345.

Cox, J. F., & Morschauser, P. C. (1997). A solution to the problem of jail suicide. *Crisis: The Journal of Crisis Intervention and Suicide Prevention, 18*(4), 178–184.

Davis, M. S., & Muscat, J. E. (1993). An epidemiologic study of alcohol and suicide risk in Ohio jails and lockups, 1975–1984. *Journal of Criminal Justice, 21*, 277–283.

DuRand, C. J., Burtka, G. J., Federman, E. J., Haycox, J. A., & Smith, J. W. (1995). A quarter century of suicide in a major urban jail: Implications for community psychiatry. *American Journal of Psychiatry, 152*, 1077–1080.

Farmer, K. A., Felthous, A. R., & Holzer, C. E. (1996, March). Medically serious suicide attempts in a jail with a suicide-prevention program. *Journal of Forensic Sciences, JFSCA, 41*(2), 240–246.

Felthous, A. R. (1994). Preventing jailhouse suicides. *Bulletin of the American Academy of Psychiatry and Law, 22*, 477–480.

Flaherty, M. G. (1980). *An assessment of the national incidence of juvenile suicide in adult jails, lockups and juvenile detention centers.* Urbana: University of Illinois.

Franklin, R. K. (1988). Deliberate self-harm: Self-injurious behavior within correctional mental health population. *Criminal Justice and Behavior, 15*, 210–218.

Haycock, J. (1989). Manipulation and suicide attempts in jails and prisons. *Psychiatric Quarterly, 60*, 85–98.

Haycock, J. (1992). Listening to "attention seekers": The clinical management of people threatening suicide. *Jail Suicide Update, 4*(4), 8–11.

Hayes, L. M. (1983). And darkness closes in. *Criminal Justice and Behavior, 10*, 461–484.

Hayes, L. M. (1989). National study of jail suicides: Seven years later. *Psychiatric Quarterly, 60*(1), 7–29.

Hayes, L. M. (1994a). Developing a written program for jail suicide prevention. *Corrections Today, 56*(2), 182–187.

Hayes, L. M. (1994b). Juvenile suicide in confinement: An overview and summary of one system's approach. *Juvenile and Family Court Journal, 45*(2), 65–75.

Hayes, L. M. (1995a). Prison suicide: An overview and a guide to prevention. *The Prison Journal, 75*(4), 431–456.

Hayes, L. M. (1995b). *Prison suicide: An overview and guide to prevention.* Washington DC: National Institute of Corrections, U.S. Department of Corrections.

Hayes, L. M. (1996a). Jail standards and suicide prevention: Another look. *Jail Suicide/Mental Health Update, 6*(4), 1–11.

Hayes, L. M. (1996b). National and state standards for prison suicide prevention: A report card. *Journal of Correctional Health Care, 3*(1), 5–38.

Hayes, L. M. (1997). From chaos to calm: One jail system struggles with suicide prevention. *Behavioral Sciences and the Law, 15*, 399–413.

Hayes, L. M. (1998a). Model suicide prevention programs—Part II: Juvenile facilities. *Jail Suicide/Mental Health Update, 7*(4), 1–8.

Hayes, L. M. (1998b). Model suicide prevention programs—Part III. *Jail Suicide/Mental Health Update, 8*(1), 1–8.

Holley, H. L., Arboleda-Florez, J., & Love, E. J. (1995). Lifetime prevalence of prior suicide attempts in a remanded population and relationship to current mental illness. *International Journal of Offender Therapy and Comparative Criminology, 39*(3), 191–209.

Hopes, B., & Shaull, R. (1986). Jail suicide prevention: Effective programs can save lives. *Corrections Today, 48*(8), 64–70.

Hughes, D. H. (1995). Can the clinician predict suicide. *Psychiatric Services, 46*(5), 449–451.

Ivanoff, A. (1989). Identifying psychological correlates of suicidal behavior in jail and detention facilities. *Psychiatric Quarterly, 60*(1), 73–84.

Ivanoff, A. (1998). *Survey of dialectical behavior therapy programs in forensic and correctional systems: The U.S. and U.K.* Seattle: Linehan Training Group.

Ivanoff, A., Jang, S. J., & Smyth, N. J. (1996). Clinical risk factors associated with parasuicide in prison. *International Journal of Offender Therapy and Comparative Criminology, 40*(2), 135–146.

Jones, A. (1986a). Self-mutilation in prison. A comparison of mutilators and nonmutilators. *Criminal Justice and Behavior, 13*(3), 286–296.

Jones, D. (1986b). *Study of Inmate Suicides.* Frankfort: Kentucky Corrections Cabinet.

Jordan, B. K., Schlenger, W. E., Fairbank, J. A., & Caddell, J. M. (1996). Prevalence of psychiatric disorders among incarcerated women. *Archives of General Psychiatry, 53,* 513–519.

Jordan, F. B., Schmeckpeper, K., & Strope, M. (1987). Jail suicides by hanging. *American Journal of Forensic Medicine and Pathology, 8,* 27–31.

Lazarus, R. S., & Folkman, S. (1984). *Stress, appraisal and coping.* New York: Springer.

Lester, D., & Danto, B. L. (1993). *Suicide behind bars.* Philadelphia: Charles Press.

Linehan, M. M. (1993). *Skills training manual for treating borderline personality disorder.* New York: Guilford Press.

Linehan, M. M. (1998). *Dialectical behavior therapy: A model for treating the high risk, chronically suicidal patient.* Unpublished manuscript. University of Washington, Seattle.

Linehan, M. M., Armstrong, H. E., Suarez, A., Allmon, D., & Heard, H. L. (1991). Cognitive-behavioral treatment of chronically parasuicidal borderline patients. *Archives of General Psychiatry, 48,* 1060–1064.

Linehan, M. M., Heard, H. L., & Armstrong, H. E. (1993). Naturalistic follow-up of a behavioral treatment for chronically parasuicidal borderline patients. *Archives of General Psychiatry, 50,* 971–974.

Marcus, P., & Alcabes, P. (1993). Characteristics of suicides by inmates in an urban jail. *Hospital and Community Psychiatry, 44*(3), 256–261.

Maris, R. (1992). Overview of the study of suicide assessment and prediction. In R. E. A. Maris (Ed.), *Assessment and prediction of suicide* (pp. 3–22). New York: Guilford Press.

Meehan, B. (1997). Critical incident stress debriefing within the jail environment. *Jail Suicide/Mental Health Update, 7*(1), 1–5.

Memory, J. M. (1989). Juvenile suicides in secure detention facilities: Correction of published rates. *Death Studies, 13,* 455–463.

Mitchell, J. T., & Everly, G. S. (1996). *Critical incident stress debriefing: An operations manual for the prevention of traumatic stress among emergency services and disaster workers* (2nd ed.). Ellicott City, MD: Chevron.

Morris, R. E., Harrison, E. A., Knox, G. W., Tromanhauser, E., Marquis, M. A., & Watts, L. L. (1995). Health risk behavioral survey from 39 juvenile correctional facilities in the United States. *Journal of Adolescent Health, 17,* 334–344.

National Commission on Correctional Health Care. (1995). *Standards for health services in juvenile detention and confinement facilities.* Chicago: Author.

National Commission on Correctional Health Care. (1996). *Standards for health services in jails.* Chicago: Author.

National Commission on Correctional Health Care. (1997). *Standards for health services in prisons.* Chicago: Author.

New York State Department of Correctional Services. (1994). *Characteristics of suicide victims in NYSDOCS between 1986–1994.* Albany, NY: Author.

Parent, D. G., Leiter, V., Kennedy, S., Livens, L., Wentworth, D., & Wilcox, S. (1994). *Conditions of confinement: Juvenile detentions and corrections facilities.* Washington, DC: Office of Juvenile Justice and Delinquency Prevention, U.S. Department of Justice.

Rhode, P., Seeley, J. R., & Mace, D. E. (1997, Summer). Correlates of suicidal behavior in a juvenile detention population. *Suicide and Life Threatening Behavior, 27,* 164–175.

Roberts, A. R. (1990). (Ed.), *Crisis intervention handbook*. Belmont, CA: Wadsworth.

Salive, M. B., Smith, G. S., & Brewer, T. P. (1989). Suicide mortality in the Maryland state prison system, 1979 through 1987. *Journal of the American Medical Association, 262*(3), 265–369.

Salkovskis, P. M., Atha, C., & Storer, D. (1990). Cognitive-behavioral problem solving in the treatment of patients who repeatedly attempt suicide: A controlled trial. *British Journal of Psychiatry, 157*, 871–876.

Silverman, M. M., Bongar, B., Berman, A. L., Maris, R. W., Harris, E. A., & Packman, W. L. (1998). Inpatient standards of care and the suicidal patient: Part II. An integration with clinical risk management. In B. Bongar, A. Berman, R. Maris, E. Harris, & W. Packman (Eds.), *Risk management with suicidal patients* (pp. 83–109). New York: Guilford Press.

Slaby, A. (1998). Outpatient management of suicidal patients. In B. Bongar, A. Berman, R. Maris, E. Harris, & W. Packman (Eds.), *Risk management with suicidal patients* (pp. 34–64). New York: Guilford Press.

Smyth, N. (1991). The environmental preferences and adaptation of high-risk inmates: Exploring person–environment fit [Dissertation]. Albany: State University of New York at Albany.

Smyth, N. J., Ivanoff, A., & Jang, S. J. (1994). Changes in psychological maladaptation among inmate parasuicides. *Criminal Justice and Behavior, 21*, 357–365.

Spellman, A., & Heyne, B. (1989). Suicide? Accident? Predictable? Avoidable? *Psychiatric Quarterly, 60*, 173–183.

Teplin, L. (1994). Psychiatric and substance abuse disorders among male urban jail detainees. *American Journal of Public Health, 84*(2), 290–293.

Thienhaus, O. J., & Piasecki, M. (1997). Emergency psychiatry: Assessment of suicide risk. *Journal of the American Psychiatric Association, 48*(3), 293–294.

Toch, H. (1975). *Men in crisis*. Chicago: Aldine.

White, T. W., & Schimmel, D. J. (1995). Suicide prevention in federal prisons: A successful five-step program. In L. M. Hayes (Ed.), *Prison suicide: An overview and guide to prevention*. Washington, DC: National Institute of Corrections, U.S. Department of Justice.

Winkler, G. E. (1992). Assessing and responding to suicidal jail inmates. *Community Mental Health Journal, 28*(4), 317–326.

Part V

Release Planning and Aftercare

Chapter 13
RELEASE DECISION MAKING AND PLANNING

John F. Edens and Randy K. Otto

The large majority of offenders, both with and without special needs, eventually are returned to the community from correctional or forensic settings. The circumstances under which offenders return to the community vary considerably, however. Some convicted offenders who are completing jail or prison sentences return to the community under the continued supervision of the correctional system (by way of parole or probation), whereas others are under no obligation to the correctional system (i.e., those offenders who are incarcerated for their entire sentences). Similarly, offenders who have been found not guilty by reason of insanity (NGRI) and are being discharged to the community from forensic hospitals or postadjudication may continue under court jurisdiction (via conditional release) or they may be discharged outright.

Mental health professionals who work with special-needs offenders may be involved in a variety of ways with respect to release decision making. Where release of the offender is discretionary, such as in the case of NGRI acquittees who are being considered for conditional release, mental health professionals often provide considerable input into the release decision itself and can offer recommendations regarding conditions of the release, although decisions regarding the offender's release and its conditions typically are made by a quasi-judicial (e.g., parole board or psychiatric security review board) or judicial (i.e., judge) authority. In such cases, mental health professionals are called on to (a) assess the offender, (b) offer the decision maker information about the offender's appropriateness for release (considering such factors as risk for reoffending or violent behavior), and (c) provide recommendations for conditions of postrelease, such as the type of setting to which the offender should be released (e.g., independent living versus a structured group setting) or what types of treatments or interventions should be mandated as a condition of release (e.g., mental health or substance abuse treatment, sex offender treatment). Mental health professionals also may be asked to offer recommendations for special needs offenders and facilitate placements or follow-up services even in cases in which they are released into the community outright and are not subject to continued supervision by the courts, the correctional system, or the forensic mental health system.

In this chapter we provide an overview of issues germane to mental health professionals who are involved in the release decision-making process for offenders with special needs. We briefly discuss some of the history and limitations of prediction and release decision making. Then we provide an overview of strategies and methods to improve mental health professionals' decision making for offenders with special needs. Included in this discussion is a review of factors that clinicians must be aware of when making release decisions, including relevant base rates of recidivism for offender populations of interest and various risk factors (both individual and environmental–contextual) that either increase or decrease the probability of reoffending among offenders with special needs. Following this discussion of risk factors is a review of several instruments that may be used in release decision making and release planning contexts. Next we address how clinicians should structure their release recommendations and how this information should be conveyed to relevant authorities. Finally, we conclude with recommendations for future research.

A Brief History of Predictive Accuracy and Release Decision Making

Historically, evaluations of offenders' risk to engage in violent or criminal behavior have been poorly structured, unreliable, idiosyncratic, and inconsistent. Procedures and techniques have varied considerably between professionals and between and within institutions. Predictions of future risk and subsequent decisions regarding release that were based on clinical or professional inference appeared to be subjective evaluations that potentially were limited in terms of predictive accuracy. In his 1981 monograph, *The Clinical Prediction of Violent Behavior*, Monahan offered discouraging conclusions regarding the ability of mental health professionals to "predict dangerousness." Although a new generation of research, as well as reconsideration and reinterpretation of existing data, suggests that mental health professionals indeed have some ability to assess risk for violence among persons with mental disorder, their abilities are not great, and considerable error rates in terms of predictions should be expected (for reviews see Bonta, Law, & Hanson, 1998; Douglas & Webster, 1999; Monahan & Steadman, 1994; Mossman, 1994; Otto, 1992, 1994).

Aside from poor predictive accuracy, other research has suggested that mental health professionals' decision making regarding release decisions may be unduly biased by various factors, such as the personal consequences (e.g., liability and publicity) associated with the release of a patient. For example, Stevens and Brodsky (1995), using an analogue design, found that psychiatric hospital staff were significantly more likely to recommend a more restrictive security placement under "high consequence" conditions rather than "low consequence" conditions, even when high-consequence patients were considered to be no more likely to be violent or dangerous in the future. Relatedly, Poythress and Brodsky (1992) reported that, following a successful negligent-release lawsuit against staff, patient release rates dropped by approximately 50% in a forensic psychiatric hospital.

Several researchers have identified other forms of bias within the legal system that may impact (more often than not, negatively) on release decisions for special needs offenders. Feder (1994), for example, found that inmates with a recent history of psychiatric hospitalization were less likely to receive parole and more likely to serve maximum sentences, even after controlling for a variety of legal (e.g., prior imprisonments, history of violence and drug use), extralegal (e.g., race, age at release), and community support (e.g., marital status, family support, occupation) variables. Biases also affect whether a defendant will be processed through the criminal justice system or diverted to the mental health system. Hochstedler (1986, 1987) found that persons with a history of mental disorder were more likely to have criminal charges filed against them than their nondisordered counterparts, although a mental health history was positively correlated with leniency at disposition. More recent research has shown that pretrial diversion recommendations (Rogers & Bagby, 1992) and actual diversion decisions (Davis, 1994) for defendants with mental disorders are influenced by a multitude of factors, including offense seriousness, court jurisdiction, and the specific mental health professional performing the evaluation. In particular, wide variability was found in the decision making of individual psychiatrists, with some apparently being much more willing to recommend diversion than others (see also Rogers, Gillis, Dickens, & Webster, 1988).

Although several authors have argued for the positive effects of a certain degree of flexibility or latitude in individual decision making in forensic and correctional settings (e.g., Dickey, 1993), reliance on clinical judgment or other unstructured procedures to make release decisions increases the possibility of prediction errors and biased decision making, with potential negative outcomes to the public and professional alike (Borum, Otto, & Golding, 1993; Garb, 1998; Glaser, 1987). It is generally accepted that predictions based on actuarial or statistical models are more accurate (and more defensible) than are predictions based on unstructured clinical judgments (Dawes, Faust, & Meehl, 1989). This has been shown repeatedly in the prediction of violent behavior (Gardner, Lidz, Mulvey, & Shaw, 1996; Monahan, 1981; Mossman, 1994) and criminal recidivism in general (Bonta et al., 1998; M. R. Gottfredson & D. M. Gottfredson, 1988). In fact, in a number of class action lawsuits alleging unconstitutional living conditions in correctional facilities, the lack of objective criteria for classifying offenders has been cited as a source of concern. Classification systems in general and risk assessment procedures in particular were developed in many correctional settings partly in response to increased liability issues and the need to appropriately allocate resources. Although the prediction of violence remains controversial, the courts have maintained that an objective and partially valid system represents an improvement over subjective decision-making procedures in correctional settings (Clements, 1996; Monahan, 1996). For forensic hospitals in particular, the absence of well-defined and rationally and empirically supported assessment procedures places the clinician and institution at risk for malpractice litigation, particularly in cases that "go bad" (Monahan, 1993; Otto & Borum, 1997; Poythress, 1987, 1990).

Improving the Decision-Making Process

Given the previously cited limitations of predictive accuracy and subsequent liability issues related to release decision making, several authors have provided suggestions for improving this process. Poythress (1987, 1990), for example, offers a number of recommendations for structuring the evaluation and release decision-making process in institutional settings. These include (a) adoption of an assessment template or model that is used consistently by clinicians; (b) implementation of methodical evaluation of the examinee's violence history; (c) coordination of release planning with community agencies and professionals; (d) careful documentation of the evaluation process and case specific rationale; and (e) consideration of use of review boards or panels within the institution so that important decisions are not left to one clinician acting in isolation. If followed, not only do Poythress's suggestions offer the possibility of more reliable (and more valid) assessments, but they also have the potential to provide clinicians with some protection in the case of litigation (see also Monahan, 1993, for a discussion of policy and clinical strategies with respect to risk assessment). Several of these suggestions are expanded on in the following sections of this review.

Consistent with the recommendations of Poythress (1987, 1990) discussed previously, there have been significant changes over the last several years regarding how clinicians should approach the tasks of predicting recidivism and making recommendations regarding the appropriateness of release. For example, the concept of the "prediction of dangerousness" has been replaced with that of violence "risk assessment" (Steadman et al., 1993). This change in terminology is more than semantics because it reflects the field's growing emphasis on understanding the dynamic and fluid nature of risk, identifying relevant environmental and situational contributors to violence, and developing approaches to managing and minimizing risk by way of individual- and environment-centered interventions (Heilbrun, 1997; Melton, Petrila, Poythress, & Slobogin, 1997; Otto, in press; Otto & Borum, 1997). These authors suggest that clinicians use a combination of actuarial and anamnestic (i.e., individualized) approaches to assess violence risk, whereby the clinician first identifies factors from various domains that are correlated with violence potential and then reviews the examinee's history to identify unique individual factors or patterns that have been associated with past violence. Psychological tests or assessment instruments may be helpful to the degree that they assess factors that are considered to be related to recidivism (a discussion of specific instruments follows). Finally, in addition to an assessment of risk, the examiner should offer recommendations for interventions designed to decrease or control violence risk.

The recommended approach requires the clinician to engage in a number of activities that are designed to identify (a) risk of reoffending or violent reoffending and (b) interventions (both at the individual and environmental–contextual level) that will aid in controlling or minimizing risk for reoffending. For example, consider the following case scenario and the steps an examiner might take in considering release to the community.[1]

The examiner has been requested by a hospital treatment team to independently evaluate for release to the community a 20-year-old man found not guilty by reason of insanity of two counts of aggravated assault. Using a chair leg, this acquittee seriously injured two acquaintances living with him in a boarding home. The assaults occurred six weeks after the examinee, who received SSI payments because of a mental disorder, had discontinued his psychotropic medication and stopped attending a psychosocial day treatment program at the local mental health center. The assaults were precipitated in part by the examinee's paranoid beliefs that his peers were poisoning his food and conspiring to kill him. Fueling the paranoid thinking of the defendant, who was an amateur astronomer, were beliefs that his demise was being foretold by an approaching comet. Other than the index offenses, the examinee had no documented history of criminal or violent behavior. At the time of the evaluation the patient had spent two years in a forensic facility, where he received a diagnosis of paranoid schizophrenia. While hospitalized, the patient responded well to a combination of antipsychotic medication and psychosocial rehabilitation. The examinee has been cooperative with his prescribed treatment program, has shown a very good

---

[1]The following discussion of risk factors and recommended interventions is not exhaustive, as this example is offered for illustrative purposes only. Other relevant factors are discussed in subsequent sections of this chapter (see also Table 13.1) and also reviewed by Bonta et al. (1998), Gendreau, Little, and Goggin (1996), Grisso (1998), Monahan and Steadman (1994), Otto and Borum (1997), and Sandoval and Edens (1999).

adjustment in the hospital, and currently evidences no paranoid delusions or perse-cutory thinking. He has successfully managed day passes into the community and overnight visits to home over the past three months. His parents, who have been very involved with his treatment, are eager for him to live with them while he is involved in a psychosocial day treatment program.

In conducting this evaluation and planning this acquittee's release, the examiner might go through the following steps:

1. *Identification of known risk factors (i.e., empirically established) for recid-ivism and violent recidivism that are present and absent for the examinee.* The purpose of this inquiry is twofold. First, this provides the examiner with some information regarding the examinee's overall level of risk for recidi-vism. Second, identification of some of these factors facilitates the devel-opment of interventions that can be implemented to decrease or control the offender's risk. For example, even though the case scenario is circumscribed, a few empirically identified risk factors can be identified. In addition to a number of static risk factors present in this case (e.g., age, sex) the connec-tion between persecutory thinking and violence in this case mirrors a well-established empirical relationship (Link, Andrews, & Cullen, 1992; Link & Stueve, 1994; Swanson, Borum, Swartz, & Monahan, 1996). It is just as important, however, to note the absence of significant risk factors, such as drug or alcohol abuse or a history of violent and criminal behavior.

2. *Identification of empirically established risk factors for recidivism and vi-olent recidivism that are present and absent in the offender's previous, cur-rent, and proposed environments.* The purpose of this inquiry also is twofold. First, it allows the examiner to identify an absolute or relative level of risk that the examinee presents at the current time and may present in the future given environmental or contextual factors. Second, it allows the examiner to propose interventions and plans at the environmental or contextual level that will go toward controlling or reducing the offender's risk for recidivat-ing. In this case it is important to know that the offense occurred in what was probably a high stress, transient living situation, quite likely in a less than ideal neighborhood. Risk for criminal behavior (both nonviolent and violent) is higher in such environments (see, e.g., Otto, in press; Silver, Mulvey, & Monahan, 1999; Steadman et al., 1998). It is also important to note that the examinee has not engaged in violent or criminal behavior in more structured and less risky situations (e.g., during the course of hospi-talization, while in the community on day and overnight passes). An absence of other risk factors (e.g., access to prior victims) also is worth noting.

3. *Identification of examinee-specific factors for violence and recidivism.* After identifying factors that have been empirically demonstrated to be related to risk, the examiner should look to case-specific factors in an attempt to iden-tify idiosyncratic relationships or causes and effects of prior offending. Given the state of the art, there is much we do not know about offending and its causes, both at the group and individual level. Because of these limitations, the examiner should, with caution, try to identify factors that may be relevant to the particular examinee that may not necessarily be causal factors for other similar offenders. Worthy of consideration in this case are

the examinee's current and anticipated involvement in astronomy and his beliefs around these issues, given that his previous assaultive behavior was related to delusions that involved approaching comets that communicated with him.

4. *Recommendations for placement and intervention.* After this information has been assembled the examiner must come to some kind of conclusions about the examinee's risk for reoffending and identify factors that may be implemented to decrease or control this risk. In the example given previously, the examinee may be considered to be at increased risk for violent reoffending relative to the general population (given his offense history), yet at a relatively low rate of risk overall. This judgment is anchored in a number of factors offered earlier, including his lack of a criminal or violence history other than the instant offense, his positive response to medication and other interventions, his treatment compliance, the lack of access to previous victims, the availability of a supportive and structured living situation that will allow for monitoring of his adjustment, and involvement in a treatment program that would provide daily structure and allow for monitoring of medication, adjustment, and symptomatology. Thus this examinee might be a good candidate for release to the community provided certain interventions (e.g., psychotropic medication, residence with his parents, parental and client monitoring of his symptomatology and his interest in astronomy phenomena, involvement in a psychiatric day program) are conditions of his release.

Given this general framework for approaching the evaluation process, there are a number of considerations that clinicians should incorporate into their release recommendations for special needs offenders. The following sections detail critical factors that should influence release decisions, including reviews of (a) base rates of recidivism for various populations addressed in this volume; (b) various system-level and contextual–environmental factors that influence the probability of success on institutional release; (c) relevant individual-level predictor variables that have been shown to correlate with violence and recidivism, including both static and dynamic risk factors; and (d) several instruments that show considerable promise regarding their ability to aid clinicians in making informed release decisions and management recommendations. Where appropriate, these sections also detail various methodological limitations of the research that has been conducted to date on these issues. An awareness of the limitations of this literature is critical to making informed decisions regarding its applicability in any given case.

Base Rates of Recidivism

A primary factor to be considered when making release decisions for offenders with mental disorders is the base rate of recidivism for the specific offender group and how these base rates affect predictive accuracy (Meehl, 1954). Predictive power always decreases as the relative frequency of an event or outcome deviates from .5. Therefore, any attempt to ascertain the degree of risk associated with release should take into account the effect of the base rate on accuracy and error rates. To the extent that any given event is statistically rare, then the prediction in each specific case that the event will not occur will probably be the most accurate prediction. For example, if conditionally released sex offenders recidivate at a rate of .2 during the first five years after release, then a prediction that *no one* in a sample will recidivate will be accurate 80% of the time. It is unlikely that release decision-making policies based on this "high" rate of predictive accuracy would be well-received, however, given the type of error made if implemented (i.e., releasing all sex offenders, including the 20% who will recidivate). If a prediction model can be developed that accurately identifies 75% of the 20% who will reoffend but that incorrectly identifies 50% of the 80% of nonrecidivists as being likely to recidivate, then the overall rate of accuracy will only be 55%. Policy makers might find such a system to be more tolerable, however, even though overall accuracy is diminished because of the low base rate of reoffending.

Given the significant impact of base rates on predictive accuracy, a review of recidivism rates for the general population of offenders as well as for various specific offender populations discussed in this volume is warranted. These base rates serve as a starting point for evaluations of risk, which are then subsequently modified based on the various individual and environmental–contextual risk factors that are reviewed in later sections of this chapter.

The General Population of Offenders

According to Bureau of Justice Statistics (1995) data, slightly less than one half of all paroled offenders successfully complete their period of supervised release, with the majority of the "noncompleters" returning to incarceration. Similarly, Beck and Shipley (1989), in their analysis of more than half of all state prison inmates released in 1983, estimated that 63% were rearrested for a felony or serious misdemeanor within three years. Furthermore, 47% were reconvicted and 41% were returned either to jail or prison. Almost 25% had been rearrested for a violent offense by the end of 1986. Similar base rates have been reported in other large-scale studies of parole outcome (e.g., Schmidt & Witte, 1988). Results of probation outcome studies have been much more varied, primarily due to differing rates of recidivism for felony versus misdemeanor probationers (Petersilia, 1997). Approximately 75% of misdemeanor probationers successfully complete their period of supervision, whereas failure rates for felony probationers generally are more similar to parole statistics. Felony rearrest rates typically range from 40% to 60%, although rates as low as 12% have been reported (Morgan, 1993; Petersilia, 1997).

Relatively high rates of recidivism have been reported for juveniles as well. Ganzer and Sarason (1973) reported rates of approximately 20% to 30% for juvenile delinquents in Washington state. More recently, Wierson and Forehand (1995) found that approximately one third of their sample of 75 randomly selected male delinquents were rearrested over a 21-month follow-up period. Differences in recidivism rates across studies probably result from various factors, particularly the previous offense history of the samples studied (Cunneen & White, 1995), with higher rates of recidivism reported for higher risk populations. For example, Coumarelos (1994; cited in Cunneen & White, 1995) reported that about two thirds of first time offenders never appeared before the juvenile court again, whereas 50% of those with two previous arrests were arrested again. Approximately 75% of those with six previous arrests were subsequently arrested. Howell (1995) reported recidivism rates between 50% and 80% for adolescents released from state training schools (presumably "deeper end" youth). Although many juveniles desist in engaging in delinquent behavior by early adulthood, the probability of continued offending clearly increases with each subsequent arrest during adolescence (see also chap. 1, Grisso, 1998).

"Special Needs" Populations

Although a considerable body of research exists examining rates of criminal recidivism among the general population of offenders, relatively less data exist for "special needs" populations. The following sections detail the existing recidivism data for several of the specific offender groups discussed in this volume. Before reviewing these base rates, however, several methodological issues should be mentioned that influence the interpretation of this research. First, many of the studies reviewed consist of selective (rather than random or comprehensive) samples. Such studies potentially bias rates of recidivism in that those offenders considered most likely to commit new offenses or be a threat to the community may not have been conditionally released. Such studies are still informative, however, regarding rates of offending among persons viewed as, in essence, "lower risk" by parole boards or psychiatric review boards.

Second, various criteria have been used when examining the "outcome" of release decisions for offenders with mental disorders. Perhaps the most commonly used criteria in correctional outcome research are rearrest and reconviction, although rates of parole revocation, psychiatric hospitalization, and self-reports of criminal and violent behavior also have been reported in the literature. Although the criterion selected ideally should be based on the researcher's determination of what constitutes the most salient outcome, in reality outcome measures used by researchers often have been determined by matters of convenience and availability rather than theoretical significance or reliability. In particular, the use of criminal recidivism, usually defined as rearrest or reconviction over a specified follow-up period, has been criticized for various reasons. One common critique is that official records, particularly criminal justice records, are notoriously inaccurate (Doren, 1998; Maltz, 1984; Monahan, 1981, 1984). In particular, missing data in such systems may have a dramatic effect on the results of outcome research. A related concern is that official records, even if relatively accurate, do not account for nondetected violence or criminal behavior that does not result in an arrest. Although including self-report and collateral-report data routinely has been suggested as a means of increasing the accuracy of outcome measures, this rarely has been done in most circumstances. Including such information would likely result in dramatic changes in the results of such research. Recent research from the MacArthur Risk Assessment study has shown, for example, that an examination of agency records resulted in a one-year prevalence rate of only 4.5% for violent acts committed by discharged psychiatric patients. When official records were combined with patient report and collateral-informant data, however, the prevalence rate increased to 27.5% (Steadman et al., 1998).

Another concern with official records, discussed by Jones (1996), is that they confound the behavior of the individual offender with the behavior of the system itself. For example, to the extent that the police or the criminal justice system may differentially target various groups (e.g., minorities, persons from lower socioeconomic backgrounds or "high crime" neighborhoods) for rearrest, then recidivism rates will be higher in these particular groups. Similar concerns can be raised regarding parole revocation. If persons on parole or probation who are deemed high risk are assigned to increased levels of supervision, then there is an increased likelihood that violations will be detected and that they will be more likely to have their conditional release revoked than persons assigned to low-risk supervision (Latessa & Gordon, 1994; Petersilia & Turner, 1993). Other factors may influence rates of parole revocation as well. For example, even if actuarial methods are used to determine release decisions, probation–parole officers typically are permitted considerable discretion regarding responses to technical violations. As well, definitions of parole "failure" vary widely in published reports, with some researchers choosing to define persons who abscond but who are not rearrested as failures and others not doing so.

Questions also exist regarding how to conceptualize the need for hospitalization of offenders with mental disorders following release. Depending on one's frame of reference and the circumstances of the case, an inpatient psychiatric admission may represent either a positive or a negative outcome. For example, if a conditionally released NGRI acquittee with a history of schizophrenia is voluntarily rehospitalized one year postrelease because of decompensation, is this a "failure"? What if the hospitalization is involuntary but the patient has committed no crime? Similar issues exist in the case of parole failure because of technical infractions (e.g., consumption of alcohol, failure to pay costs of supervision) but not resulting from the commission of new crimes. Should a paroled sex offender, compliant with all conditions of his mandatory treatment other than testing positive for marijuana use, truly be considered a "failure" if his conditional release is revoked? The broader implication of these examples is that the use of artificial dichotomies, although easily conceptualized and analyzed statistically, may result in the loss or obfuscation of relevant information. Clearly, these are issues that go beyond methodological concerns, but the point to be made is that such issues do have a significant impact on "the criterion problem" (M. R. Gottfredson & D. M. Gottfredson, 1988) and on how results of outcome research are to be interpreted.

With these caveats in mind, the following sections review base rates of recidivism (however defined) for three specific subgroups—insanity acquittees, jail and prison inmates with severe mental disorders, and sex offenders. Data for adolescent offenders also are presented, where available.

Not Guilty by Reason of Insanity Acquittees

Outcome studies of NGRI acquittees have examined rearrest and rehospitalization rates primarily for individuals conditionally released (usually to some type of community supervision program), although a few studies also have contained participants who were released because of reaching the maximum allowable confinement time (e.g., Wiederanders, 1992). It is not surprising that investigators using longer follow-up periods generally have reported higher rates of rearrest and rehospitalization. Rates of felony rearrest for conditionally released NGRI acquittees typically range between 30 and 60% over two- to five-year follow-up periods (Bieber, Pasewark, Bosten, & Steadman, 1988; Bogenberger, Pasewark, Gudeman, & Bieber, 1987; Cohen, Spodak, Silver, & Williams, 1988; Lamb, Weinberger, & Gross, 1988; Tellefsen, Cohen, Silver, & Dougherty, 1992), although rates as low as 10% have been reported in one study (Rogers, Bloom, & Manson, 1986; however, 40% of the 165 patients had their conditional release *revoked* during this period). Lamb et al. (1988) reported on a sample of NGRI acquittees that had been accepted into a court-mandated community outpatient treatment program. Of the 79 patients (out of 101 initial referrals) accepted into their program, 32% were rearrested (72% of arrests being for violent crimes), 47% were rehospitalized, and 48% had their conditional releases revoked over a five-year follow-up, despite spending on average more than two years in secure facilities before reentering the community.

Cohen et al. (1988) reported that 54% of their 127 male NGRI acquittees were rearrested over a five-year follow-up after their conditional release from a forensic psychiatric institution. Those who had previous arrests for "serious" offenses (e.g., murder, rape, assault with intent to murder, or robbery) were more likely to be rearrested (79%) over the follow-up period than those with prior arrests for less serious offenses (47%). A subsequent study (Tellefsen et al., 1992) of the conditional release outcomes of a new sample of NGRI acquittees from this system found a similarly high rate of rearrest and rehospitalization among 60 patients who were either conditionally released directly into the community from a centralized facility or who were first discharged to a regional institution and then released into the community. Specifically, 63% of the 24 regionalized patients and 47% of the 36 non-regionalized patients were rearrested during their five-year conditional release period, with corresponding rates of rehospitalization of 79% (regionalized) and 64% (non-regionalized). Also, 58% of the regionalized patients and 31% of the nonregionalized patients had their conditional release revoked during this period.

Other investigators have reported markedly lower rates of recidivism, however. For example, Werner and Meloy (1992) reviewed the files of 24 conditionally released insanity acquittees and found that none had committed a violent act that warranted clinical or law enforcement intervention over a two-year follow-up period. Whether any nonviolent crimes were committed was not reported, however. Wiederanders (1992) is one of the few investigators to examine both conditionally and unconditionally released NGRI acquittees (a small percentage of whom were mentally disordered sex offenders however). Of those conditionally released (n = 190), only 6% were rearrested and 21% were rehospitalized, whereas 27% of the 44 unconditionally released patients were rearrested and 9% were rehospitalized over the two-year follow-up period. Although conditionally released patients had lower rearrest rates, the two groups did not differ regarding the distribution of days-before-recidivism when collapsing across the two "failure" conditions.

Maier, Morrow, and Miller (1989) reported data from the Community Preparation Service (CPS), a minimum-security forensic unit for patients either found NGRI or convicted of a sexual offense. The CPS gradually introduces patients hospitalized over extensive periods back into the community through supervised and eventually unsupervised community visits. Over a two-year period, approximately 6000 unescorted off-ground activities (typically to school, work, or home visits) had occurred, with only four recorded security breaches that were deemed significant enough to warrant placement of patients in more secure settings. Only one incident over the two-year period involved criminal behavior, during which a patient sexually assaulted a clinician on institutional grounds.

Offenders With Mental Disorders

Although generally not as intensely studied as NGRI acquittees, some investigators have examined outcome variables for offenders who are mentally ill who have been released from jail or prison. Feder (1991), reporting on a sample of 147 male inmates who required psychiatric hospitalization during imprisonment, found over an 18-month follow-up period that 64% were rearrested at least once (30% of total arrests for violent offenses) and 48% were committed to psychiatric hospitals. Furthermore, 60% of these hospital commitments were for violent or other types of criminal behavior. Similarly, Harris and Koepsell (1996) followed a sample of 27 detainees treated in a psychiatric unit of a large county jail and a matched sample of non-treated offenders from this facility. For the mentally ill individuals, 68% were rearrested within one year after being released, whereas 60% of the control participants were rearrested. There also was a nonsignificant trend for patients with psychotic disorders to be rearrested more quickly following release than nonpsychotic patients. A somewhat lower rearrest rate (49%) was reported by Draine, Solomon, and Meyerson (1994), who conducted a one-year follow-up of inmates who had received psychiatric services while in jail. Solomon and Draine (1995) reported a rearrest rate of 46% for a separate sample of 94 jail detainees with mental health problems over a one-year period. It is interesting to note that there was a nonsignificant trend for those randomly assigned to an intensive team case management program following release to be more likely to return to jail (60%) than those receiving individual case management (40%) or receiving "standard" referrals for psychiatric care (36%) following release.

Sex Offenders

According to the Bureau of Justice Statistics (1997), "On a given day in 1994 there were approximately 234,000 offenders convicted of rape or sexual assault under the care, custody, or control of corrections agencies; nearly 60% of these sex offenders are under conditional supervision in the community." In 1991, an estimated 24% of those offenders serving sentences for rape and 19% of those serving sentences for sexual assault were already on probation or parole at the time they committed the offense for which they were sent to prison (Bureau of Justice Statistics, 1997).

Several investigators have examined rates of sexual recidivism among sexual offenders, although several of the methodological limitations discussed earlier have been evident in many of the studies conducted on this particular population. Estimates of recidivism rates of sex offenders vary as a function of the follow-up period used by the investigators (higher recidivism rates are obtained when longer at-risk periods are used), the subtype of sex offender studied (there is some evidence that rapists and extrafamilial child molesters show higher rates of reoffending that intrafamilial child molesters), and the criteria used (higher estimates, of course, are reported when recidivism is defined as rearrest for a sex offense as compared to reconviction for a sexual offense). Indeed, Doren (1998) has argued that figures obtained in most sex offender recidivism studies underestimate actual recidivism rates because of limited follow-up periods, the frequency with which offenses go undetected, and the tendency for offenders to accept pleas for less serious, non-sexual offenses. He offered that more realistic estimates of long-term recidivism range from 40% to 50%.

Consistent with these findings, Furby, Weinrott, and Blackshaw (1989), in a then-comprehensive review of published studies, reported an exceedingly wide range of recidivism rates for sex offenders, ranging from less than 5% to more than 40%. The wide variability regarding samples studied, recidivism measures used, time at follow-up, and whether or not treatment was offered or required make meaningful comparisons across these disparate studies difficult. However, in a meta-analysis of 12 recent studies ($N = 1313$) comparing treatment versus various comparison conditions (e.g., no treatment or alternate treatments) for a broad range of sexual offenders, Hall (1995) reported recidivism rates for sexual offenses of 19% for treated sex offenders and 27% for comparison groups over widely varying follow-up periods (range = 1 to 28 years). Many of these treatment studies excluded the most severely impaired offenders, however, such as those who had extensive criminal histories, those who denied their offenses, or those with severe mental illnesses.

In a recent meta-analysis of 61 studies of sex offenders that used various measures of recidivism, Hanson and Bussière (1998) reported a 13% overall recidivism rate across studies using a relatively short follow-up period—five years—with higher rates reported for rapists (19%) than child molesters (13%). Quinsey, Lalumière, Rice, and Harris (1995) reported an average recidivism rate of 23% for rapists across seven studies that used varying follow-up periods and varying criteria for recidivism, and an average recidivism rate of 20% for child molesters across 17 samples that used varying follow-up periods and definitions of recidivism.

As indicated previously, higher recidivism rates are reported when offenders are followed for longer periods of time and when using more expansive definitions of recidivism. For example, Prentky, Lee, Knight, and Cerce (1997) examined the recidivism rates of 115 extrafamilial child molesters, with new charges for a physical contact sex offense being the criterion measure. Over a 25-year follow-up period, 52% of the offenders recidivated. Using a similar follow-up period, Hanson, Steffy, & Gauthier (1993) examined the recidivism rate of a sample of 197 child molesters. Using the criteria of reconviction for a sexual offense or violent offense (using the logic that persons charged with sex offenses oftentimes enter plea agreements to lesser, nonsexual charges); an overall recidivism rate of 42% was reported.

Rates for specific subgroups of sexual offenders also have been reported, although, similar to the findings of Furby et al. (1989), there seems to be considerable heterogeneity both within and between offender groups regarding recidivism rates across studies. In summarizing the existing literature, Quinsey et al. (1995) found reconviction rates for sexual offenses ranging from 10% to 36% (weighted $M = 23\%$) for seven samples (total $N = 458$) of convicted rapists over varying follow-up periods. Similarly, the weighted average sexual reconviction rate for convicted child molesters across 17 independent samples ($N = 4483$) was 20% (range = 4% to 38%) across varying follow-up periods. Same-sex child molesters displayed higher and more consistent rates of reconviction for sexual offenses (weighted $M = 35\%$; $n = 561$) than did opposite-sex child molesters (18%; $n = 1167$) and incest offenders (9%; $n = 499$). Noted earlier, the Hanson and Bussière (1998) meta-analysis reported average recidivism rates of 19% for rapists and 13% for child molesters across relatively shorter follow-up periods. Doren (1998), using broader definitions of recidivism, estimated recidivism rates of 52% and 39% for nonincest child molesters and rapists, respectively.

Although there is considerably less research on juvenile sexual offenders, recidivism rates generally appear to be lower for adolescents than for adults, with studies typically reporting rates between 3% and 15% (Brannon & Troyer, 1995; G. Davis & Leitenberg, 1987; Kahn & Chambers, 1991; Smith & Monastersky, 1986). However, rates of arrest for subsequent *nonsexual* offenses appear to be much higher, ranging between 30% and 67% across studies. These data are consistent with rates of reoffending among juvenile offenders more generally (see earlier discussion).

Summary

Based on the preceding review, a few general conclusions can be drawn. First, rates of recidivism (however defined) vary widely both within and between various offender populations. This finding illustrates both the importance of not overgeneralizing across groups and settings and the need to establish base rates of recidivism in whatever setting one is attempting to develop or validate a predictive model or assessment approach. A second general conclusion is that, although considerable variability exists, most studies tended to report recidivism rates ranging from 25% to 75%. This suggests that adequately derived predictive models may be able to produce accuracy rates that are acceptable from a policy and legal perspective. Discussed earlier, very low base-rate events are extremely difficult to predict in that the most accurate prediction generally will be that the event will not occur. However, given that recidivism rates may be closer to .5 than .05 for most offender populations, prediction models may be devised that will result in lower error rates than have been assumed in the past.[2]

Environmental–Contextual and System-Level Factors Influencing Recidivism

Given the widely varying rates of recidivism across studies of ostensibly similar offender groups (e.g., NGRI acquittee rates ranging typically from 30% to 60%), it seems clear that focusing only on the characteristics of the offender to the exclusion of the characteristics of the system in which he or she is functioning will ignore a wealth of information that is directly relevant to his or her ultimate probability of success on conditional release. As McGreevy, Steadman, Dvoskin, and Dollard (1991) have noted, there is probably no one "best" way to structure a conditional release system for all offenders with mental disorders. However, although a wealth of data does not yet exist that evaluates the effectiveness of differing release formats, several authors have identified various conditions of release that will increase the

---

[2] Attempts to predict low base-rate events usually result in the overprediction that the event will occur when it in fact does not (i.e., false positives). This high false-positive error rate has been one of the most common criticisms of attempts to predict future violence.

likelihood that a released offender will not be rearrested or require rehospitalization. Beyond the typical conditions of release used for most offenders (e.g., stable employment, prohibitions against associating with known criminals or possession of weapons), several of the most commonly required conditions of release that a clinician might recommend for various special needs offender groups include (a) involvement in outpatient treatment; (b) abstinence from alcohol and other drugs; (c) stable or supervised housing arrangements; (d) psychotropic medication compliance; and (e) mandated involvement in case management services.

Aside from specific conditions of release that may be imposed on offenders, various structural and programmatic characteristics that appear to relate to the development of successful conditional release programs have been identified. First, the intensity of supervision and services provided while on conditional release has been argued to be one of the most important factors in the successful reintegration of offenders into the community (Dvoskin & Steadman, 1994; Edens, Peters, & Hills, 1997; Griffin, Steadman, & Heilbrun, 1991; Heilbrun, Lawson, Spier, & Libby, 1994; McGreevy et al., 1991). Close supervision ostensibly results in increased compliance from the offender and increased security for the public by allowing for regular reassessment of high-risk offenders' level of functioning and potential for violence or other criminal behavior (Brown, 1996; Maier et al., 1989). For example, failure to comply with conditions of release, such as a return to drug use or lapses in adherence to prescribed medications, can be more readily detected when frequent contacts are a required part of conditional release. Failure to adhere to psychotropic medication regimens is one of the best predictors of decompensation and subsequent rehospitalization and rearrest for offenders with severe mental illnesses. There is also a growing awareness of the long-term deleterious effects of alcohol and drug abuse on offenders with mental disorders (Edens et al., 1997). A large percentage of persons with severe and persistent mental illness abuse substances, and these individuals are disproportionately represented in criminal justice populations. Furthermore, substance abuse has been shown to predict medication noncompliance, decompensation, and subsequent arrest following release (Borum, Swanson, Swartz, & Hiday, 1997; Drake, Bartels, Teague, Noordsy, & Clark, 1993).

Although some authors (e.g., Solomon & Draine, 1995; Tonry, 1990) have cautioned that increased supervision and monitoring may be used as a means of punishment and that it may actually increase the likelihood of revocation or rearrest, research on intensive supervision programs (ISPs) suggests that increased surveillance in conjunction with increased treatment services may lead to decreases in recidivism among the general population of offenders (Brown, 1996; Petersilia & Turner, 1993). Similar findings have been reported for mentally ill offenders receiving intensive case management services following conditional release (reviewed by Dvoskin & Steadman, 1994; see also Wilson, Tien, & Eaves, 1995).

A second general programmatic issue that may relate to the ultimate success of a conditionally released offender is a program's response to noncompliance–technical infractions or decompensation. In particular, the timeliness of the program's response to infractions or decompensation likely will influence outcome. For example, some states such as New York have required a formal hearing before an insanity acquittee can be recommitted (McGreevy et al., 1991), whereas others such as Oregon allow for immediate revocation and rehospitalization if conditions are violated (Bloom, Williams, & Bigelow, 1991). Aside from the speed of response, the range of response options available also will affect outcome. Successful programs usually allow for a continuum of responses to infractions, rather than simply recommitment or revocation. Such responses may include specific modifications to their orders of conditional release, such as increased supervision requirements or mandated medication compliance, or other types of civil (short-term hospital commitment) or criminal justice responses (e.g., day fines, brief jail sentences) rather than parole revocation (Griffin et al., 1991).

A third general area that will affect offenders' success following release is the extent to which they can be effectively linked to community resources (Dvoskin & Steadman, 1994; Edens et al., 1997; Jemelka, Trupin, & Chiles, 1989; Veysey, Steadman, Morrissey, & Johnsen, 1997). It is quite easy, for example, to require that an offender maintain stable housing arrangements following release. It requires considerably more effort, however, to actually provide or coordinate such services, particularly when community-based programs may not be receptive to individuals with criminal histories (Edens et al., 1997). Almost all of the most effective programs use mechanisms to coordinate the delivery of services in the community (e.g., day treatment, housing, case management). Such linkages also may improve community relations by increasing the visibility of programs and dispelling common myths and misconceptions about offenders with mental illness.

A final programmatic issue to be considered is the extent to which offenders with special needs can be reintegrated into the community gradually. In particular, paroled prison inmates with mental disorders often are released outright with little transitioning back into the community (Jemelka et al., 1989). Several NGRI programs have attempted to make this process less difficult by providing offenders progressively less restrictive placements (e.g., Maier et al., 1989), during which time their behavior and ability to effectively handle increasing levels of freedom can be continually reevaluated. As well, many prison-based substance abuse and dual diagnosis programs attempt to transition offenders into halfway houses or work release programs on release from the institution (Edens et al., 1997).

In summary, each of these related programmatic factors (level of supervision and treatment, response to violations or decompensation, linkages to community services, degree of gradual transitioning into the community) may have a dramatic effect on the likelihood of success of any released offender and should be considered by the examiner when assessing his or her risk for recidivism and determining appropriate recommendations. An awareness of these issues is critical to making informed decisions regarding the release of offenders with special needs.

Individual-Level Risk Factors

Psychologists and other behavioral scientists have devoted considerable resources to identifying empirically based risk factors and developing assessment and classification systems for criminal offenders over the past 50 years. Walters, White, and Denney (1991) noted that investigators have developed correctional assessment and classification systems based on factors such as offense history, family background, social class, personality and psychopathology, interpersonal relationships and functioning, and cognitive development. Despite the diversity of constructs that have been studied for classification and rehabilitation purposes, instruments designed specifically to predict criminal recidivism have been criticized for their tendency to focus more on historical (e.g., criminal history, escape history, juvenile delinquency) and, to a lesser degree, dispositional variables (e.g., age, gender, intelligence) that are associated with criminal offending–reoffending rather than on "dynamic" or "fluid" factors (e.g., current substance abuse, vocational skill level, relationship stability, antisocial attitudes) that may be responsive to treatment (Andrews, Bonta, & Hoge, 1990). Another criticism of these instruments is that they tend to be derived from data that is conveniently and routinely collected in criminal justice settings rather than based on any particular theoretical conceptualization of violence or criminality. Finally, some empirically based factors that may relate to recidivism risk may be objectionable from a legal or policy perspective (e.g., race, gender).

Despite the limitations of previous research, there have been significant theoretical advances in the selection of risk factors for study recently, particularly in reference to predicting violence (Monahan & Steadman, 1994). More current research has expanded on the typically used historical and dispositional variables to consider a more complex and integrated array of potential predictor domains, including greater consideration of contextual and clinical variables. Table 13.1 summarizes across these domains those risk factors that have empirical support in terms of their relation to general criminal recidivism, violent recidivism, or violent behavior more generally (i.e., violent acts not resulting in criminal charges). In the criminal justice literature there has been a similar increased focus on the significance of criminogenic (and noncriminogenic) "needs" that may place offenders at increased or decreased risk for recidivism that also are more susceptible to intervention. Recent meta-analytic investigations of the offender recidivism literature (Bonta et al., 1998; Gendreau et al., 1996) clearly reveal that dynamic "need" variables tend to correlate both with general and violent recidivism as well as or better than the more static factors that traditionally have been the focus of research.

Results of these meta-analytic investigations also point to a more controversial and as yet unresolved issue: Findings from these reviews suggest that a relatively stable group of risk factors (both dynamic and static) can be identified that appear to be equally predictive for most offenders, regardless of their mental health status.[3] The Bonta et al. (1998) study in particular concluded that variables typically presumed by psychologists and other mental health professionals to be predictive of future violence and criminality (e.g., diagnostic status, personal distress measures) were only related marginally to recidivism among released offenders with serious mental disorders and that the effects of these variables were dwarfed by those factors that have been shown to be predictive of recidivism among the general population of offenders. In essence, they concluded that mental health status is irrelevant in terms of making the most informed decision regarding risk for criminal recidivism. They do point out, however, that mentally disordered offenders in general are at lower risk for general and violent recidivism than are nondisordered offenders.

Although results of meta-analyses are informative regarding the population of

---

[3] This is not the case for sex offenders, for whom specific risk factors related to sexual deviance (e.g., phallometric assessments of deviant sexual preferences, history of prior sexual offenses, index offense committed against a stranger) have been documented that specifically predict sexual recidivism (Hanson & Bussière, 1998). In terms of general (nonsexual) recidivism, however, the same set of risk factors identified in the general offender literature appear to be equally predictive for released sex offenders.

Table 13.1—*Summary of Risk Factors for Violent and Nonviolent Offending–Reoffending*

Historical	Contextual
Arrest history (violent and nonviolent)[a]	Treatment and medication compliance
Frequency	Occupational instability–poor work ad-
Chronicity	justment[a]
Severity	Criminal–delinquent associates[a]
Diversity	Weapon availability
Juvenile delinquency[a]	Social support
Institutional adjustment[a]	Victim availability
Escape history[a]	Poor or unstable living arrangements[a]
Violence history (observer/victim/perpe-	Clinical–Mental State
trator)[a]	Psychosis
Prior psychiatric hospitalizations[a]	Delusions
Age of onset of conduct problems	Hallucinations
Family criminality	Threat–control override symptoms
Early separation from family/out of home	Substance abuse[a]
placements	Anger
Academic failure	Coocurring diagnoses
Dispositional	
Demographic variables	
Age[a]	
Gender	
Race	
Socioeconomic status	
Personality features	
Psychopathy[a]	
Antisocial personality disorder[a]	
Borderline personality disorder[a]	
Impulsiveness	
Cognitive functioning	
Judgment	
Reasoning	
Verbal skills–ability	
Neurological–CNS syndromes	

[a]Factors most strongly related to recidivism in the Bonta et al. (1998) or Gendreau et al. (1996) meta-analyses. However, several of the remaining factors listed (e.g., threat–control override symptoms) were not examined in these reviews but have been shown to predict violence or recidivism in other studies.

offenders as a whole, there are several caveats that should be kept in mind when evaluating the results of the meta-analysis conducted by Bonta et al. (1998). First, not all risk factors have been shown to be equally predictive across different sub-groups of offenders (Schmidt & Witte, 1988). For example, Wierson and Forehand (1995) reported that different factors were associated with recidivism for African American and Caucasian juvenile delinquents. Significant differences in variables predicting juvenile recidivism have been noted across urban versus rural settings as well (Heilbrun et al., 1997). Second, some mental health variables, such as a diagnosis of a schizophrenia, have been shown to positively predict violence in some studies but have been negatively associated with violence in others (Borum, 1996).

Some commentators argue that these findings result from the moderating effect of other variables and varying base rates of violence in the samples being used in these studies. More methodologically sophisticated research suggests that it is not the diagnosis of schizophrenia per se but rather the presence of "threat/control-override" symptoms (i.e., symptoms indicating the patient believes he or she is endangered by others or that external forces are taking control over his or her behavior) discussed in our earlier example that appear to be related strongly to future violence (Link & Stueve, 1994; Swanson et al., 1996). The impact of these specific symptoms were not examined in the studies included in the Bonta et al. (1998) meta-analysis. Third, the studies reviewed by Bonta and his colleagues relied exclusively on documented records of criminal behavior that led to rearrest or rehospitalization. As mentioned earlier, such studies almost certainly underestimate base rates because of nondetected violence (cf. Steadman et al., 1998). They also do not take into account those persons who are rehospitalized before committing a violent or criminal act.

Regardless of the reasons for these differing findings, it seems clear that any predictive model or assessment method developed in one setting should not be assumed to be equally predictive when it is subsequently applied to a new population. Unfortunately, several examples exist wherein risk prediction instruments developed in one particular setting or state have been adopted with only minor revisions and with no attempts to evaluate their accuracy (Wiebush, Baird, Krisberg, & Onek, 1995). Although there very well may be a "common core" of risk factors for general and violent recidivism (irrespective of mental health status of offenders), the field is clearly a long way from possessing a universally accepted set of predictors that are equally applicable across diverse forensic and correctional systems. Furthermore, even if mental health variables ultimately are not shown to be strong predictors of recidivism, examiners will still need to be aware of and assess these factors to make appropriate treatment recommendations for mentally disordered offenders who are to be released.

Assessment Instruments

Reviewed in the sections that follow are psychological assessment instruments that have been developed specifically for use with either criminal populations or potentially violent populations with respect to release decision making that assess, to varying degrees, the individual and environmental–contextual risk factors described previously. Instruments or systems designed primarily to classify and identify treatment needs of offenders entering the criminal justice system, such as the MMPI-based offender typology (Megargee & Bohn, 1979), the Adult Internal Management System (Quay, 1984), and the I-level system (Warren & Staff, 1966) are not examined in this chapter, given its focus on assessment for purposes of release decision making (see Van Voorhis, 1994, for a review of these systems). Finally, risk instruments developed for general criminal justice populations are not reviewed because they usually are used by nonmental health professionals and may not be directly relevant for release decision making for special-needs offenders (for a review of these instruments the reader is directed to Ashford & LeCroy, 1990; Hoge & Andrews, 1996; or Wiebush et al., 1995).[4] Furthermore, the information contained in these instruments often is also incorporated into the measures described later.

Readers should not consider themselves limited to instruments reviewed in this chapter, however. The classification and risk instruments mentioned previously may prove to be of some value in assessing offenders with special needs,[5] as may focused assessment instruments and standard psychological assessment measures. For example, if interested in assessing the relative risk an offender presents for reassaulting his spouse on release from jail, the examiner might consider using the Spousal Assault Risk Assessment (SARA; Kropp, Hart, Webster, & Eaves, 1995). Moreover, standard measures of psychopathology may prove helpful in some cases. For example, if assessing for release a special needs offender whose criminal offenses largely have occurred in response to paranoid thinking, standard psychological measures that assess paranoia (e.g., MMPI-2; Butcher, Dahlstrom, Graham, Tellegen, & Kaemmer, 1989; Personality Assessment Inventory; Morey, 1991) may provide valuable information. Given space constraints, the discussion that follows is limited to recently developed instruments that have been developed specifically to assess factors related to criminal and violent behavior and recidivism.

Psychopathy Checklist-Revised

The Psychopathy Checklist-Revised (PCL-R; Hare, 1991) is a 20-item instrument that assesses factors relevant to the construct of psychopathy, which is differentiated from antisocial personality disorder (see Cleckley, 1941/1982, or Hare, 1991, for a general discussion). Psychopaths are characterized by a grandiose, egocentric, and self-indulgent interpersonal style; impulsive, manipulative, and sensation-seeking behaviors; shallow affect; and a lack of remorse, guilt, and other "negative" emotions. PCL-R items are scored on a 3-point scale (0 = does not apply/not present, 1 = uncertain, 2 = applies) after completion of a record review and structured interview. Scores range from 0 to 40, with a score of 30 or greater indicative of psychopathy. The 20 items tap the previously discussed constructs and fall into two stable factors. Factor I represents interpersonal and affective characteristics of psychopathy such as lack of remorse and empathy, egocentricity, low levels of anxiety, and manipulativeness, whereas Factor II addresses behavioral and lifestyle factors such as impulsivity, social deviance, and antisocial behaviors. An abbreviated 12-item version of the PCL-R, the Psychopathy Checklist: Screening Version also is available (PCL: SV; Hart, Cox, & Hare, 1995).

The psychometric properties of the PCL-R are well-established. Adequate rates of interrater reliability, internal consistency, and test–retest reliability have been reported (see Hare, 1991, and Fulero, 1995, for detailed discussions). In addition, research consistently demonstrates the predictive validity of the PCL-R with respect to criminal behavior, and violent criminal behavior more specifically (see Hart &

---

[4] Although such instruments often include a "needs" assessment component that incorporates more dynamic variables (e.g., antisocial peers, drug abuse, living arrangements), these rarely have been evaluated in terms of their ability to predict recidivism or future violence (Bonta, 1996).

[5] Those actuarial measures based primarily on static factors correlate modestly (generally between .2 and .4) with recidivism among the general population of offenders (Gendreau et al., 1996).

Hare, 1996; Hart, Hare & Forth, 1994; Rice, 1997; Salekin, Rogers, & Sewell, 1996, for reviews and discussion of this literature).

The PCL-R and the PCL:SV are published commercially, and administration is not difficult once acceptable rates of reliability have been established. Regarding the assessment of this construct and the prediction of reoffending (particularly violent reoffending), it will be useful to the degree that the assessment of psychopathy is central to the evaluation process. Given the construct it measures, the PCL-R could be considered for use with general correctional populations as well as those with special needs, such as sex offenders or persons with severe mental illness (Hare, 1996). Because the PCL-R primarily assesses a dispositional risk factor, it may be of more limited utility with some "special needs inmates" who may be suffering from Axis I disorders and whose risk for reoffending is considered to be affected in addition by factors other than psychopathy, such as their mental state (we review the PCL-R here because it is also a central component of the VPS and the HCR-20, described later). Moreover, given preliminary research suggesting poor treatment outcomes with psychopaths (see Rice, 1997, for a review) recommendations that flow from PCL-R scores essentially will be management or dispositionally focused (i.e., release into the community as a low recidivism risk or continued incarceration as a high recidivism risk). Few treatment recommendations will be derived from an examinee's performance on the PCL-R. In addition, sensitivity and specificity of the PCL-R, although good, are not perfect, and errors in the prediction of recidivism are to be expected (i.e., a large minority of nonpsychopaths will recidivate and a significant percentage of psychopaths will not). This, in combination with questions about its utility with minority populations (Salekin et al., 1996) and females, suggests that the examiner should give careful consideration to the use of the PCL-R and presentation of PCL-R results (see also Edens, Skeem, Cruise, & Cauffman, 2000).

Violence Prediction Scheme–Violence Risk Appraisal Guide

The Violence Prediction Scheme (VPS; Webster, Harris, Rice, Cormier, & Quinsey, 1994) is an assessment method that combines actuarial and clinical data for persons whose risk for violence is at issue. The actuarial section of the VPS anchors the assessment process, whereas consideration of clinical factors allows the examiner to revise the actuarial risk assessment upwards or downwards. The actuarial component of the VPS is the Violence Risk Appraisal Guide (VRAG), which consists of 12 historical or static variables that were related to violent behavior in a sample of 618 male forensic patients (Quinsey, Harris, Rice, & Cormier, 1998). These factors include presence of psychopathy as measured by the PCL-R, early school maladjustment, personality disorder diagnosis, early age at time of offending, early separation from parents, previous failure on conditional release, history of nonviolent offending, never being married, diagnosis of schizophrenia (negatively related), injury to victim, history of alcohol abuse, and victimization of a female (negatively related). Scores on each of the 12 items are weighted, with total VRAG scores ranging from -26 to 38. Probability estimates for violent reoffending for ranges of VRAG total scores are provided over long-term follow-up periods (i.e., 7 and 10 years).

The clinical component of the VPS (the ASSESS-LIST) includes factors that are considered, in the judgment of the VPS authors, to be related to risk for violent behavior. The 10 items are concerned with the examinee's history and current adjustment, as well as release plans. The examiner determines whether each item is favorable, unfavorable, or irrelevant, in light of his or her history and current adjustment. Thus not all of the 10 items may be considered. They include history of abuse and witnessing violence; insight and prosocial–antisocial attitudes; impulsivity; social, vocational, academic, and coping skills; appropriateness of examinee's plans and expectations following release; presence, absence, or control of Axis I symptoms; availability and nature of supervision in the release environment; development of life factors that decrease violence risk (e.g., physical handicap or other limitation); institutional adjustment; sexual adjustment; and treatment involvement and progress.

The VPS authors initially offer the ASSESS-LIST "with considerable hesitation," and they consider its greater value to be as a research tool (Webster et al., 1994, p. 46). They believe that its primary usefulness may come as an "aide memoir" that will force the examiner to consider potentially relevant factors that are not in their actuarial formula (the VRAG). The authors go on to note that the ASSESS-LIST results should rarely, if ever, be used to adjust the actuarial prediction derived from the VRAG by greater than 10% in either direction. Stronger admonitions against altering risk estimates based on the VRAG have subsequently been offered by the instrument authors (Quinsey et al., 1998).

There are little data published regarding the psychometric properties of the VPS. Rates of test–retest or interrater reliability are not provided in the VPS book, but the nature of the items (at least on the VRAG) are such that interrater agreement should not prove difficult to establish; data demonstrating adequate reliability are necessary, however. The utility of the VRAG has been examined in a number of studies, and results suggest that VRAG scores are predictive of violent reoffending, at least with males who previously have been incarcerated for a violent offense (Rice, 1997; Rice & Harris, 1995; Quinsey et al., 1997; Webster et al., 1994). The VRAG also shows some utility in the prediction of recidivism among sex offenders (Belanger & Earls, 1996, cited in Rice, 1997; Rice & Harris, 1997).

The VPS is not available as a scale or instrument, but the book published by Webster et al. (1994) provides enough information such that a user-friendly version of the VRAG and ASSESS-LIST could be developed with some work on the examiner's part. It should be noted, however, that use of the VPS also requires an assessment of psychopathy via the PCL-R or PCL:SV. Thus any concerns raised with respect to the PCL-R also apply to the VRAG.

The VRAG essentially assesses for historical, static variables that have been associated with recidivism among convicted felons. As such, like the PCL-R, its main value lies in its ability to identify relative risk level for reoffending, which may aid in determining placement (e.g., release or no release; placement into a more or less secure–restrictive setting). But the VRAG and ASSESS-LIST in combination, which make up the VPS, consider both static, historical variables as well as dynamic, clinical variables, for which intervention may be considered. The VPS then may prove of some utility in determining relative risk of reoffending for populations with and without mental disorders. Furthermore, the instrument may facilitate release and treatment planning to some degree. Although use of the VRAG and ASSESS-LIST in tandem should be considered, the authors caution that actuarial risk predictions based on the VRAG should rarely, if ever, be altered by more than 10% seems important to consider. And like the PCL-R, sensitivity and specificity, although good, are not perfect. In addition, the VRAG was developed on a population of male, predominantly White, Canadian offenders and questions remain about its applicability with females and U.S. minority populations. Clinicians, of course, should consider these factors when appraising the potential utility of this instrument.

HCR-20

The HCR-20 (Webster, Douglas, Eaves, & Hart, 1997) is a checklist of risk factors for violent behavior. The 20 items, selected based on the authors' clinical experience and review of the violence literature, focus on historical factors ("H," 10 items), current clinical factors ("C," 5 items), and risk management factors ("R," 5 items) to be considered in terms of future disposition. Historical items are concerned with the examinee's violence history, relationship, work history, mental health and substance abuse history, and previous success or failure in the correctional system. Clinical factors consist of current symptomatology, impulsivity, treatment response, insight, impulsivity, and negative attitudes related to criminal, antisocial, and violent behavior. Risk-management variables address potential stressors in the environment, predicted compliance with release–discharge plans, and adequacy of discharge–release plans.

The HCR-20 is best considered as a template to guide clinicians through the risk-assessment process rather than as a test or instrument proper. The 20 items, scored on a 3-point scale (0 = no indications of factor, 1 = possible/some indications of factor, 2 = definite/clear/high indications of factor) are completed after information is gathered by the clinician. The authors note, "In most cases, file review, interview, and testing should suffice to complete the HCR-20. However, particularly for the Risk Management section, consultation with colleagues responsible for treatment or community release plans will likely be needed" (Webster et al., 1997, p. 17).

Preliminary research with the HCR-20 has been promising. Douglas (1996) and Douglas, Webster, and Wintrup (1996) reported acceptable interrater reliability. In addition, total and specific scale scores of the HCR-20 have been correlated with a history of violent charges, forensic hospitalizations, civil psychiatric hospitalizations, violence displayed in the community, and other measures of violence risk such as the VRAG and PCL-R (Douglas, 1996, 1999; Douglas et al., 1996; Douglas, Ogloff, & Nichols, 1997; Douglas, Ogloff, Nichols, & Grant, in press; Nichols, Ogloff, & Douglas, 1997; Wintrup, 1996).

The HCR-20 manual includes clear directions for administration and a coding form that can be used to facilitate administration and scoring. Like the VPS, the HCR-20 requires an assessment of psychopathy, using either the PCL-R or PCL:SV, and any caveats for these instruments apply accordingly (see earlier discussion). Because of its balance between static–historical and dynamic–clinical and environmental factors, the HCR-20 will prove of most value with offender populations with special needs in terms of release and treatment planning. Its use with the general offender population will be much more limited. Because it serves more as an assessment template than an actuarial risk prediction instrument, the HCR-20 avoids some of the criticisms that may be lodged against the PCL-R and VPS in terms of less than perfect sensitivity and specificity, but questions remain regarding its utility with minority and female populations. Furthermore, the lack of actuarial application in the HCR-29 allows for clinical judgment to play a greater role in decision making, which arguably will decrease predictive accuracy.

Level of Service Inventory-Revised

The Level of Service Inventory-Revised (LSI-R; Andrews, & Bonta, 1995) is an instrument designed to identify, by way of a standardized interview, offender and situational attributes that are relevant to level of service decisions. According to the authors, the LSI-R is "a way of systematically bringing together information important to offender treatment planning and for assigning levels of freedom and supervision" (Andrews & Bonta, 1995, p. 3). The instrument is scored after the examiner completes a detailed interview and record review. The majority of the 54 items are scored as yes–no, indicating their presence or absence. A minority of items are scored on a 0 to 3 rating scale, with 0 indicating an unsatisfactory situation with respect to the particular item and 3 indicating a satisfactory situation with no need for improvement. The 54 items are grouped into ten categories: criminal history (10), education–employment (10), financial (2), family–marital (4), accommodation (3), leisure–recreation (2), companions (5), alcohol–drug problems (9), emotional–personal (5), and attitudes–orientation (4). The items comprise both static factors as well as dynamic variables that theoretically are susceptible to change through interventions of various types. The authors noted that the LSI-R can be used to facilitate and organize a review of factors relevant to case classification and also to identify areas of concern–target behaviors and corresponding interventions, placements, or dispositions. Cut-off scores for determining appropriate types of correctional placement (e.g., halfway house, minimum security institution, maximum security institution) also are provided.

Although research to date regarding the LSI-R is somewhat limited, that which has been conducted is encouraging. The psychometric properties of the instrument have been examined, and adequate rates of interrater reliability, test–retest reliability, and internal consistency have been demonstrated (see Andrews & Bonta, 1995, for a summary). Research examining its predictive validity, the majority of which has been conducted in Canada by the instrument authors, is promising (Gendreau et al., 1996). LSI-R scores are correlated with other measures considered to be related to criminal activity such as sensation seeking, impulsivity, and indicators of psychopathy (Andrews, Bonta, Motiuk, & Robinson, 1984, cited in Andrews & Bonta, 1995; Motiuk, Motiuk, & Bonta, 1992). LSI-R scores also predict probation officers' judgments about and correctional dispositions of offenders (Andrews et al., 1984, and Bonta, Motiuk, & Ker, 1985, both cited in Andrews & Bonta, 1995). Finally, LSI-R scores are predictive of institutional adjustment of offenders, parole–probation failure, halfway house infractions, rearrest, and reincarceration (Andrews et al., 1990; Bonta & Motiuk, 1985, 1987, 1990; Coulson, Ilacqua, Nutbrown, Giulekas, & Cudjoe, 1996; Motiuk, Bonta, & Andrews, 1986). A youth version of the LSI-R has been developed (Hoge & Andrews, 1994) and a self-report version of the LSI-R, the Self-Report Inventory (SRI; Motiuk et al., 1992) exists and shows some promise.

The LSI-R is commercially published and it is easy to use. Although it assesses primarily static, historical factors, some dynamic clinical and environmental factors are addressed, suggesting that it will be of some value beyond gross decision making regarding institutional or noninstitutional disposition. Various interventions at the environmental and clinical level may be suggested by the LSI-R. Although cut scores for various kinds of institutional dispositions are offered, the authors urge caution on the part of the user. This advice is well-heeded given the limited research to date, particularly with minority and female populations.

Sex Offender Assessment Instruments

In the past few years a number of actuarial instruments have been developed that are designed to identify sex offenders at high risk for reoffending. These instruments sometimes are used to determine which convicted offenders are appropriate for extended incarceration in correctional settings or civil commitment via Sexually Violent Predator (SVP) statutes that recently have been adopted in a number of states (Cohen, 1999; Fitch, 1999).

Rapid Risk Assessment for Sexual Offense Recidivism

The Rapid Risk Assessment for Sexual Offense Recidivism (RRASOR) is an actuarial scale designed to identify the risk that convicted sex offenders present for sexual reoffending. Based on a meta-analysis of the sex offender recidivism literature (Hanson & Bussière, 1998), Hanson (1997, 1998) developed a four-item instrument focused on historical, static variables that typically are contained in an offender's administrative records: number of prior sexual offenses, age at time of return to the community, history of offending against nonfamily members, and history of offending against males. Possible scores range from 0 to 6, with higher scores representing higher risk for reoffending. With the exception of sex offense history, for which examinees can receive a score of 0 to 3, all RRASOR items are scored dichotomously.

The RRASOR has been applied to a number of different populations (Epperson, Kaul, & Hesselton, 1998; Hanson, 1997; Hanson & Thornton, in press) and has shown moderate predictive accuracy. Hanson (1997) reported an average correlation between RRASOR scores and reoffending (as assessed by arrest or conviction for another sexual offense) to be .27. In their sample of sex offenders, Epperson et al. (1998) reported a correlation of .21 between the RRASOR and sexual reoffending as measured by rearrest or reconviction. Concerns offered about the RRASOR include that there currently is no scoring manual available, it is based solely on static historical factors that are not sensitive to changes over time, it does not take into account some variables that are related to recidivism risk, and its psychometric properties are not clearly established (see Otto, Borum, & Grisso, 2000, for a more comprehensive review).

Minnesota Sex Offender Screening Tool/Minnesota Sex Offender Screening Tool-Revised

Work on the Minnesota Sex Offender Screening Tool (MnSOST/MnSOST-R; Minnesota Department of Corrections, undated) began in 1991, in response to the Minnesota Department of Corrections' call for a structured procedure to assess risk for reoffending among sex offenders (Epperson et al., 1998). Based on a review of the relevant literature, the MnSOST Task Force developed a 14-item instrument that eventually was expanded to 21 items, with weights being determined by clinical judgment. Thus the original MnSOST was not strictly an actuarially derived or developed instrument. Preliminary retrospective research using a sample of 256 sex offenders indicated that the MnSOST had modest predictive validity. Sex offenders arrested for another sexual offense on return to the community had higher MnSOST scores than those not arrested for any such offense (Epperson, Kaul, & Huot, 1995).

The Minnesota Sex Offender Screening Tool-Revised (MnSOST-R; Epperson et al., 1995) was published in 1996. It is a 16-item instrument designed to assess risk for reoffending among extrafamilial sex offenders. The 12 static–historical items consist of number of sex offense convictions and sex-offense related convictions; length of sex offending history; commitment of a sex offense while under correctional or court supervision; sex offense committed in a public place; force or threat of force used during sex offense; committed multiple sexual acts on a victim during one offense; sex offenses against teenage (13–15 year old) victims; sex offenses against strangers; adolescent antisocial behavior; drug or alcohol abuse 12 months before index offense or revocation; and employment history. The four institutional–dynamic factors are adjustment–discipline problems during incarceration; treatment for substance abuse; treatment for sex offending; and age at time of anticipated return to the community. In a sample of 387 sex offenders (123 of whom committed another offense on release to the community) MnSOST-R scores correlated .45 with reoffending (as measured by arrest for or conviction of another sex offense) over a 6-year follow-up period. The MnSOST-R has not been cross-validated, however (see Otto et al., 2000, for further discussion of this instrument).

Sex Offender Risk Appraisal Guide

The Sexual Offense Risk Appraisal Guide (SORAG; Quinsey, Harris, Rice, & Cormier, 1998) is a retrospectively developed actuarial instrument based on the post-release community adjustment of approximately 200 mentally disordered offenders with histories of rape or child molestation who had completed their sentences at a maximum-security forensic hospital. The SORAG contains 14 differentially weighted items, some of which are static and some of which are dynamic: family–parenting history, elementary school adjustment, history of alcohol abuse, marital history, history of nonviolent offenses, history of violent offenses, failure on prior conditional release, history of previous sex offense convictions, age at index offense, history of sex offenses against young girls, presence of any *DSM-III* personality disorder diagnosis, presence of *DSM-III* schizophrenia diagnosis, phallometric test results, and score on the Psychopathy Checklist-Revised.

In contrast to the RRASOR and MnSOST-R, the SORAG is used to predict violent reoffending, not simply sexual reoffending. The SORAG proved to be a moderate predictor of violent recidivism among the sample of sex offenders studies by Quinsey and his associates (1998), and it does not predict violent reoffending in sexual offenders with much more accuracy than the VRAG (see earlier discussion). These results, as well as concerns about unestablished psychometric properties (e.g., interrater reliability) have resulted in some criticism of the SORAG (see Otto et al., 2000).

Static-99

The Static-99 (Hanson & Thornton, in press) is a newly developed actuarial instrument derived from two previously existing instruments—the RRASOR (Hanson, 1997) and the Structured Anchored Clinical Judgment (SACJ; Grubin, 1998, as cited in Hanson & Thornton, in press). The Static-99 variables are historical and static in nature. Therefore, the Static-99 can be administered and scored without access to the offender because the variables of interest typically are available in an offender's record. Items consist of number of previous charges or convictions for sex offenses, number of prior sentences imposed, history of convictions for noncontact sex offenses, history of nonsexual violent offending, history of unrelated victims, history of stranger victims, history of male victims, age at time of anticipated release, and marital–relationship history. With the exception of sex offense history, all items are scored 1 or 0; possible scores range from 0 to 12.

Hanson and Thornton (in press) examined the (postdictive) accuracy of the Static-99 when applied to four different Canadian and British samples of sex offenders who had been incarcerated and released into the community. Classification accuracy was evaluated using Receiver Operating Characteristic (ROC) analyses (see Centor, 1991; Edens, Hart, Johnson, Johnson, & Olver, in press; or Hsiao, Bartko, & Potter, 1989, for further discussion). ROC analyses identified the area under the curve (AUC) of the Static-99 across the four different samples, with results ranging from .65 to .73 ($M = .70$), suggesting moderate predictive accuracy (an AUC of .50 indicates only chance accuracy for a prediction and 1.0 equals perfect accuracy). Because of its recent development there is no test manual commercially available, and questions remain regarding some of its psychometric properties (see Otto et al., 2000, for further discussion).

Sexual Violence Risk-20

The Sexual Violence Risk-20 (SVR-20; Boer, Hart, Kropp, & Webster, 1997) is not a test or actuarial technique, unlike the instruments described earlier. Rather, it is an assessment guide that directs the examiner to assess factors that are related empirically to "sexual violence," which is defined by the authors as "actual, attempted, or threatened sexual contact with a person who is nonconsenting or unable to give consent" (Boer et al., 1997, p. 9). The SVR-20 has 20 subject areas that the examiner is to review and make judgments about via clinical interview, record review, and test administration. Areas of psychosocial functioning assessed consist of sexual deviations, history of child abuse, psychopathy (as assessed by the Psychopathy Checklist-Revised), major mental illness, substance abuse, suicidal–homicidal ideation, relationship history, employment history, violent offense history, nonviolent offense history, and history of supervision failures. Aspects of sexual offending that are addressed include density of sexual offending, types of sex offenses, degree of physical harm inflicted on victims, use of weapons or threats during offenses, frequency and severity of offending, minimization and denial of offenses, and attitudes supportive of sexual offending. Finally, dispositional issues such as release plans and planning and attitudes towards interventions are considered by the examiner.

The SVR-20 is not scored but rather serves to structure the clinical assessment of the offender. The rationale for this approach is based, in part, on the theory that structured clinical assessments that direct the examiner to consider factors relevant to the questions at hand will be more reliable and valid than unstructured judgments (see Hanson, 1997, for preliminary data supporting this argument). A manual for the SVR-20 is available, and preliminary research indicates that clinical judgments based on the SVR-20 are of some value in terms of assessing recidivism risk among sex offenders (Dempster, 1999). However, more research regarding its predictive validity and psychometric properties is needed at this time.

Summary

Clearly, most of the instruments described reflect a significant advance in the field of risk assessment beyond the previous reliance on clinical judgments or purely historically based actuarial methods. These measures (except for some of the sex offender instruments) include, to varying degrees, an analysis of dynamic and situational factors that are more consistent with current thinking regarding risk assessment. Given the demonstrated importance of these variables in evaluating the likelihood of success following release (Bonta et al., 1998; Gendreau et al., 1996), further research on these and related measures clearly is warranted, particularly regarding populations of minority and female offenders. Practitioners should be cautious in considering use of such instruments, however, given current limitations associated with each (Otto, in press; Otto, 2000; Otto, Poythress, Borum, & Petrila, 1999).

Communicating Recommendations

Aside from the importance of conducting a competent evaluation of the relevant risk factors described earlier regarding release decisions, *how* this information from this procedure is provided to relevant decision makers is of critical importance (Monahan, 1996; Monahan & Steadman, 1996). A number of issues must be considered with respect to communicating results of evaluations. First, even the best instruments developed to date have significant error rates. Thus using them to classify or identify offenders will result in errors, although the rate and types of errors made will vary depending on the particular instrument, cut scores employed, and the population with which the instrument is used. Therefore it is incumbent on clinicians to communicate to the consumers of their evaluations (i.e., judges, probation boards, psychiatric review boards, hospital release boards) the limitations of their techniques and the error rates that might be expected (Grisso & Appelbaum, 1992, Melton et al., 1997; Monahan, 1981). Failure to do so arguably violates the *Ethical Principles and Guidelines* promulgated by the American Psychological Association (1992) and the *Specialty Guidelines for Forensic Psychologists* developed by the American Academy of Forensic Psychology and the American Psychology-Law Society (Committee on Ethical Guidelines for Forensic Psychologists, 1991). Mental health professionals conducting such evaluations, when offering estimates of recidivism, would do well to consider offering estimates of *relative* risk rather than predictions of dangerousness or absolute risk. Given the state of the art, this stance is more defensible. Whenever possible, the clinician should remain focused on identifying factors described earlier that increase or decrease relative risk, as well as recommending interventions or placements that can be implemented to reduce risk of reoffending. Furthermore, clinicians should consider offering intervention recommendations and assessments of violence potential in the form of conditional statements (e.g., "*If* the examinee's substance use is controlled by way of placement in a supervised living situation such as a halfway house, administration of Antabuse, participation in AA or other support groups, and continued involvement in outpatient substance abuse treatment, *then* his risk for engaging in violent behavior towards his mother is considerably decreased").

Finally, mental health professionals must remain aware that the behavior of offenders is a product of an elaborate and involved interaction between offender variables and those in the environment. As such, they must consider a variety of both individual and environmental–situational elements, ranging from employment status, to economic factors, to the availability of previous criminal partners, when communicating the results of their evaluations. Furthermore, examiners' recommendations for strategies to reduce the risk of recidivism must be just as varied as the broad array of potential risk factors that they delineate.

Future Directions

Certainly, over the past 10 years increasing attention has been paid to the prediction of criminal reoffending, assessment of violence risk, and subsequent decision making and release planning for offender populations. Although advances in the field have been made, there still has not been established a template or practice standard either for assessing violence or recidivism risk for special offender populations. Given the current state of the art, it seems that research and practice authorities from the mental health and criminology fields might be able to begin establishing standards for such activities that incorporate what is known about nonviolent offending, violent offending, mental disorder, and criminal recidivism. It is somewhat surprising that two relatively separate literatures have developed in the areas of criminal recidivism prediction (typically studied by criminologists) and violence risk assessment (typically studied by mental health professionals). How applicable the general criminal recidivism literature is to offenders with special needs (e.g., mental disorders) is not clear, and cross-pollination of these two separate but related areas should prove fruitful.

In the past few years a number of instruments have been developed that show some potential in terms of assessing risk for recidivism and violence and facilitating release planning and decision making. More research into the applied utility of these instruments is indicated because, to date, much of the research has focused on establishing the instruments' psychometric properties and predictive validity. Certainly, instruments that identify populations or persons who are at significantly greater risk for reoffending, either by way of violent or nonviolent criminal behavior, may be helpful to mental health professionals working in correctional and forensic settings. Even more helpful, however, will be the validation of instruments that assist mental health professionals in developing release and treatment plans designed to reduce offenders' recidivism and violence risk. Although a few "management-oriented" instruments and procedures have been developed recently (e.g., the *Analysis of Aggressive Behavior*; Heilbrun, 1991), there are as yet no published reports of their utility. On a related note, with a few exceptions (e.g., Draine et al., 1994; Solomon & Draine, 1995) the issue of dispositional alternatives and their value in terms of reducing rates of reoffending has not been extensively examined in jail and prison settings. Although somewhat more research has been conducted in forensic systems responsible for the supervision of NGRI acquittees, further research is clearly needed in both forensic and correctional settings regarding the impact of various dispositional alternatives.

An associated legal and social policy issue that must be addressed is how recidivism prediction and risk assessment instruments should be used, given that prediction errors always will occur. This issue is a particularly important one, given the rights at stake, and the lack of discussion is somewhat surprising. No one expects any assessment instrument to be without classification errors. Yet with rare exceptions (e.g., Grisso & Appelbaum, 1992, 1993; Litwack, 1993; Mathiesen, 1998; Webster, 1998), relatively little detailed discussion has surrounded exactly what kinds of error rates are acceptable from a legal or policy perspective, and whether and how these instruments and the information derived from them should be used in light of such inevitable inaccuracy. Consideration of such issues, from legal, social policy, and clinical practice perspectives seems necessary to determine the appropriateness, applicability, and ultimate utility of these measures in the decision-making process.

References

American Psychological Association. (1992). Ethical principles and code of conduct. *American Psychologist, 47*, 1612–1628.

Andrews, D. A., & Bonta, J. L. (1995). *The Level of Service Inventory-Revised Manual*. Toronto, Ontario: Multi-Health Systems.

Andrews, D. A., Bonta, J., & Hoge, R. D. (1990). Classification for effective rehabilitation: Rediscovering psychology. *Criminal Justice and Behavior, 17*, 19–52.

Ashford, J. B., & LeCroy, C. W. (1990). Juvenile recidivism: A comparison of three prediction instruments. *Adolescence, 25*, 441–450.

Beck, A. J., & Shipley, B. E. (1989). *Recidivism of prisoners released in 1983*. Washington, DC: U.S. Department of Justice. Also available online: http://www.ojp.usdoj.gov/bjs/abstract/rpr83.htm

Bieber, S. L., Pasewark, R. A., Bosten, K., & Steadman, H. J. (1988). Predicting criminal recidivism of insanity acquittees. *International Journal of Law and Psychiatry, 11*, 105–112.

Bloom, J. D., Williams, M. S., & Bigelow, D. A. (1991). Monitored conditional release of persons found not guilty by reason of insanity. *American Journal of Psychiatry, 148*, 444–448.

Boer, D. P., Hart, S. D., Kropp, P. R., & Webster, C. D. (1997). *Manual for the Sexual Violence Risk-20*. Vancouver British Columbia Institute Against Family Violence.

Bogenberger, R., Pasewark, R. A., Gudeman, H., & Bieber, S. L. (1987). Follow-up of insanity acquittees in Hawaii. *International Journal of Law and Psychiatry, 10*, 283–295.

Bonta, J. (1996). Risk-needs assessment and treatment. In A. T. Harland (Ed.), *Choosing correctional options that work: Defining the demand and evaluating the supply* (pp. 18–32). Thousand Oaks, CA: Sage.

Bonta J., Law, M., & Hanson K. (1998). The prediction of criminal and violent recidivism among mentally disordered offenders: A meta-analysis. *Psychological Bulletin, 123*, 123–142.

Bonta, J., & Motiuk, L. L. (1985). Utilization of an interview-based classification instrument: A study of correctional halfway houses. *Criminal Justice and Behavior, 12*, 33–352.

Bonta, J., & Motiuk, L. L. (1987). The diversion of incarcerated offenders to correctional halfway houses. *Journal of Research in Crime and Delinquency, 24*, 302–323.

Bonta, J., & Motiuk, L. L. (1990). Classification to correctional halfway houses: A quasi-experimental evaluation. *Criminology, 28*, 497–506.

Borum, R. (1996). Improving the clinical practice of violence risk assessment: Technology, guidelines, and training. *American Psychologist, 51*, 945–956.

Borum, R., Otto, R. K., & Golding, S. (1993). Improving clinical judgment and decision making in forensic evaluation. *Journal of Psychiatry and Law, 21*, 35–76.

Borum, R., Swanson, J., Swartz, M., & Hiday, V. (1997). Substance abuse, violent behavior, and police encounters among persons with severe mental disorder. *Journal of Contemporary Criminal Justice, 13*, 236–250.

Brannon, J. M., & Troyer, R. (1995). Adolescent sex offenders: Investigating adult commitment-rates four years later. *International Journal of Offender Therapy and Comparative Criminology, 39*, 317–326.

Brown, M. (1996). Refining the risk concept: Decision context as a factor mediating the relation between risk and program effectiveness. *Crime and Delinquency, 42*, 435–455.

Bureau of Justice Statistics. (1995). *Correctional populations in the United States, 1995.* Washington, DC: U.S. Department of Justice.

Bureau of Justice Statistics. (1997). *Criminal offenders statistics.* Available online: http://www.ojp.usdoj.gov/bjs/crimoff.htm.

Butcher, J. N., Dahlstrom, W. G., Graham, J. R., Tellegen, A., & Kaemmer, B. (1989). *Minnesota Multiphasic Personality Inventory (MMPI-2). Manual for administration and scoring.* Minneapolis: University of Minnesota Press.

Centor, R. M. (1991). Signal detectability: The use of ROC curves and their analyses. *Medical Decision Making, 11*, 102–106.

Cleckley, H. (1982). *The mask of sanity.* St. Louis, MO: C.V. Mosby. (Original work published 1941)

Clements, C. B. (1996). Offender classification: Two decades of progress. *Criminal Justice and Behavior, 23*, 121–143.

Cohen, F. (1999). The law and sexually violent predators—through the Hendricks looking glass. In A. Schlank & F. Cohen (Eds.), *The sexual predator: Law, policy, evaluation, and treatment* (pp. 1.1–1.13). Kingston, NJ: Civic Research Press.

Cohen, M. I., Spodak, M. K., Silver, S. B., & Williams, K. (1988). Predicting outcome of insanity acquittees released to the community. *Behavioral Sciences and the Law, 6*, 515–530.

Committee on Ethical Guidelines for Forensic Psychologists. (1991). Specialty guidelines for forensic psychologists. *Law and Human Behavior, 15*, 655–665.

Coulson, G., Ilacqua, G., Nutbrown, V., Giulekas, D., & Cudjoe, F. (1996). Predictive utility of the LSI for incarcerated female offenders. *Criminal Justice and Behavior, 23*, 427–439.

Cunneen, C., & White, R. (1995). *Juvenile justice: An Australian perspective.* New York: Oxford University Press.

Davis, G., & Leitenberg, H. (1987). Adolescent sex offenders. *Psychological Bulletin, 101*, 417–427.

Davis, S. (1994). Factors associated with the diversion of mentally disordered offenders. *Bulletin of the American Academy of Psychiatry and Law, 23*, 389–397.

Dawes, R. M., Faust, D., & Meehl, P. E. (1989). Clinical versus actuarial judgment. *Science, 243*, 1668–1674.

Dempster, R. (1999). *Prediction of sexually violent recidivism: A comparison of risk assessment instruments.* Unpublished doctoral dissertation, Simon Fraser University, Burnaby, British Columbia.

Dickey, W. J. (1993). Sentencing, parole, and community supervision. In L. E. Ohlin & F. J. Remington (Eds.), *Discretion in criminal justice* (pp. 135–174). Albany: State University of New York Press.

Doren, D. M. (1998). Recidivism base rates, predictions of sex offender recidivism, and the "sexual predator" commitment laws. *Behavioral Sciences and the Law, 16,* 97–114.

Douglas, K. S. (1996). *Assessing the risk of violence in psychiatric outpatients: The predictive validity of the HCR-20 risk assessment scheme.* Unpublished master's thesis, Simon Fraser University, Burnaby, British Columbia, Canada.

Douglas, K. S. (1999). *HCR-20 violence risk assessment scheme: Overview and annotated bibliography.* Unpublished manuscript, Simon Fraser University, Burnaby, British Columbia, Canada.

Douglas, K. S., Ogloff, J. R. P., & Nichols, T. L. (1997, August). *Assessing risk for violence among psychiatric outpatients.* Paper presented at the Annual Meeting of the American Psychological Association, Chicago.

Douglas, K. S., Ogloff, J. R. P., Nichols, T. L., & Grant, I. (1999). Assessing risk for violence among psychiatric patients: The HCR-20 violence risk assessment scheme and the Psychopathy Checklist: Screening Version. *Journal of Consulting and Clinical Psychology, 67,* 917–930.

Douglas, K. S., & Webster, C. D. (1999). Predicting violence in mentally and personality disordered individuals. In R. Roesch, S. D. Hart, & J. R. P. Ogloff (Eds.), *Psychology and law: The state of the discipline* (pp. 176–239). New York: Kluwer Academic/Plenum Press.

Douglas, K. S., Webster, C. D., & Wintrup, A. (1996, August). *The HCR-20 risk assessment scheme: Psychometric properties in two samples.* Paper presented at the Annual Meeting of the American Psychological Association, Toronto.

Draine, J., Solomon, P., & Meyerson, A. (1994). Predictors of reincarceration among patients who received psychiatric services in jail. *Hospital and Community Psychiatry, 45,* 163–174.

Drake, R., Bartels, S., Teague, G., Noordsy, D., & Clark, R. (1993). Treatment of substance abuse in severely mentally ill patients. *Journal of Nervous and Mental Disease, 181,* 606–611.

Dvoskin, J. A., & Steadman, H. J. (1994). Using intensive case management to reduce violence by mentally ill persons in the community. *Hospital and Community Psychiatry, 45,* 679–684.

Edens, J. F., Hart, S. D., Johnson, D. J., Johnson, J. K., & Olver, M. E. (in press). Use of the Personality Assessment Inventory to assess psychopathy in offender populations. *Psychological Assessment.*

Edens, J. F., Peters, R. H., & Hills, H. A. (1997). Treating prison inmates with co-occurring disorders: An integrative review of existing programs. *Behavioral Sciences and the Law, 15,* 439–457.

Edens, J. F., Skeem, J. L., Cruise, K. R., & Cauffman, E. (2000). *The assessment of juvenile psychopathy and its association with violence: A critical review.* Manuscript submitted for publication.

Epperson, D. L., Kaul, J. D., & Hesselton, D. (1998). *Final report on the development of the Minnesota Sex Offender Screening Tool-Revised (MnSOST-R).* Presented at the annual meeting of the Association for the Treatment of Sexual Abusers, Vancouver, BC, Canada, October.

Epperson, D. L., Kaul, J. D., & Huot, S. J. (1995, October). *Predicting risk for recidivism for incarcerated sex offenders: Updated development on the Sex Offender Screening Tool*

(SOST). Poster presented at the annual conference of the Association for the Treatment of Sexual Abusers, New Orleans, LA.

Feder, L. (1991). A profile of mentally ill offenders and their adjustment in the community. *Journal of Psychiatry and Law, 19,* 79–98.

Feder, L. (1994). Psychiatric hospitalization history and parole decisions. *Law and Human Behavior, 18,* 395–410.

Fitch, L. (1999, October). *Sex offender commitment in the United States.* Presentation at the Annual Meeting of the State Mental Health Program Directors—Forensic Section, Tarrytown, NY.

Fulero, S. (1995). Review of the Hare Psychopathy Checklist-Revised. In J. C. Conoley, J. C. Impara, & L. L. Murphy (Eds.), *Twelfth Mental Measurements Yearbook* (pp. 453–454). Lincoln, NE: Buros Institute.

Furby, L., Weinrott, M. R., & Blackshaw, L. (1989). Sex offender recidivism: A review. *Psychological Bulletin, 105,* 3–30.

Ganzer, V. J., & Sarason, I. G. (1973). Variables associated with recidivism among juvenile delinquents. *Journal of Consulting and Clinical Psychology, 40,* 1–3.

Garb, H. N. (1998). *Studying the clinician: Judgement research and psychological assessment.* Washington, DC: American Psychological Association.

Gardner, W., Lidz, C. W., Mulvey, E. P., & Shaw, E. C. (1996). Clinical versus actuarial predictions of violence in patients with mental illnesses. *Journal of Consulting and Clinical Psychology, 64,* 602–609.

Gendreau, P., Little, T., & Goggin, C. (1996). A meta-analysis of the predictors of adult offender recidivism: What works! *Criminology, 34,* 575–607.

Glaser, D. (1987). Classification for risk. In D. M. Gottfredson & M. Tonry (Eds.), *Prediction and classification: Criminal justice decision making* (pp. 249–292). Chicago: University of Chicago Press.

Gottfredson, M. R., & Gottfredson, D. M. (1988). *Decision making in criminal justice: Toward the rational exercise of discretion.* New York: Plenum Press.

Griffin, P. A., Steadman, H. J., & Heilbrun, K. (1991). Designing conditional release systems for insanity acquittees. *Journal of Mental Health Administration, 18,* 231–241.

Grisso, T. (1998). *Forensic evaluation of juveniles.* Sarasota, FL: Professional Resource Press.

Grisso, T., & Appelbaum, P. S. (1992). Is it unethical to offer predictions of future violence? *Law and Human Behavior, 16,* 621–634.

Grisso, T., & Appelbaum, P. S. (1993). Structuring the debate about ethical predictions of future violence. *Law and Human Behavior, 17,* 482–485.

Grubin, D. (1998). *Sex offending against children: Understanding the risk.* Police Research Series paper 99. London: Home Office.

Hall, G. C. N. (1995). Sexual offender recidivism revisited: A meta-analysis of recent treatment studies. *Journal of Consulting and Clinical Psychology, 63,* 802–809.

Hanson, R. K. (1997). *The development of a brief actuarial risk scale for sexual offense recidivism* (User Report No. 1997–04). Ottawa, ON: Department of the Solicitor General of Canada.

Hanson, R. K. (1998). What do we know about sex offender risk assessment? *Psychology, Public Policy, and Law, 4,* 50–72.

Hanson, R. K., & Bussière, M. T. (1998). Predicting relapse: A meta-analysis of sexual offender recidivism studies. *Journal of Consulting and Clinical Psychology, 66,* 348–362.

Hanson, R. K., Steffy, R. A., & Gauthier, R. (1993). Long-term recidivism of child molesters. *Journal of Consulting and Clinical Psychology, 61,* 646–652.

Hanson, R. K., & Thornton, D. (2000). Improving risk assessments for sex offenders: A comparison of three actuarial scales. *Law and Human Behavior, 24,* 119–136.

Hare, R. D. (1991). *The Hare Psychopathy Checklist-Revised manual.* Toronto: Multi-Health Systems.

Hare, R. D. (1996). Psychopathy: A clinical construct whose time has come. *Criminal Justice and Behavior, 23,* 25–54.

Harris, V., & Koepsell, T. D. (1996). Criminal recidivism in mentally ill offenders: A pilot study. *Bulletin of the American Academy of Psychiatry and Law, 24,* 177–186.

Hart, S. D., Cox, D. N., & Hare, R. D. (1995). *Manual for the Screening Version of the Psychopathy Checklist (PCL:SV).* Toronto: Multi-Health Systems.

Hart, S. D., & Hare, R. D. (1996). Psychopathy and risk assessment. Psychopathy and antisocial personality disorder. *Current Opinion in Psychiatry, 9,* 129–132.

Hart, S. D., Hare, R. D., & Forth, A. E. (1994). Psychopathy as a risk marker for violence: Development and validation of a screening version of the revised Psychopathy Checklist. In J. Monahan & H. J. Steadman (Eds.), *Violence and mental disorder: Developments in risk assessment* (pp. 81–100). Chicago: University of Chicago Press.

Heilbrun, K. (1991). *The analysis of aggressive behavior.* Richmond, VA: Department of Mental Health, Mental Retardation, and Substance Abuse Services.

Heilbrun, K. (1997). Prediction versus management models relevant to risk assessment: The importance of legal decision-making context. *Law and Human Behavior, 21,* 347–359.

Heilbrun, K., Brock, W., Waite, D., Lanier, A., Schmid, M., Witte, G., Keeney, M., Westendorf, M., Buinavert, L., & Shumate, M. (1997, August). *Risk factors for juvenile recidivism: The post-release community adjustment of juvenile offenders.* Paper presented at the Annual Meeting of the American Psychological Association, Chicago.

Heilbrun, K., Lawson, K., Spier, S., & Libby, J. (1994). Community placement for insanity acquittees: A preliminary study of residential programs and person-situation fit. *Bulletin of the American Academy of Psychiatry and Law, 22,* 551–560.

Hochstedler, E. (1986). Criminal prosecution of the mentally disordered. *Law and Society, 20,* 279–292.

Hochstedler, E. (1987). Criminal prosecution of the mentally disordered: A descriptive analysis. *Criminal Justice Review, 12,* 1–11.

Hoge, R. D., & Andrews, D. A. (1994). *The Youth Level of Service/Case Management Inventory and manual.* Ottawa, ON: Department of Psychology, Carleton University.

Hoge, R. D., & Andrews, D. A. (1996). *Assessing the youthful offender: Issues and techniques.* New York: Plenum Press.

Howell, J. (1995). *Guide for implementing the comprehensive strategy for serious, violent, and chronic juvenile offenders.* Washington, DC: Office of Juvenile Justice and Delinquency Prevention, U.S. Department of Justice.

Hsiao, J. K., Bartko, J. J., & Potter, W. Z. (1989). Diagnosing diagnoses: Receiver operating characteristic methods in psychiatry. *Archives of General Psychiatry, 46,* 664–667.

Jemelka, R., Trupin, E., & Chiles, J. A. (1989). The mentally ill in prisons: A review. *Hospital and Community Psychiatry, 40,* 481–491.

Jones, P. R. (1996). Risk prediction in criminal justice. In A. T. Harland (Ed.), *Choosing correctional options that work: Defining the demand and evaluating the supply* (pp. 33–68). Thousand Oaks, CA: Sage.

Kahn, T. J., & Chambers, H. J. (1991). Assessing reoffense risk with juvenile sexual offenders. *Child Welfare, 70,* 333–345.

Kropp, P. R., Hart, S. D., Webster, C. W., & Eaves, D. (1995). *Manual for the Spousal Assault Risk Assessment Guide* (2nd ed.). Vancouver: British Columbia Institute on Family Violence.

Lamb, R. H., Weinberger, L. E., & Gross, J. D. (1988). Court-mandated community outpatient treatment for persons found not guilty by reason of insanity: A five–year follow-up. *American Journal of Psychiatry, 145,* 450–456.

Latessa, E. J., & Gordon, J. A. (1994). Examining the factors related success or failure with felony probationers: A study of intensive supervision. In C. B. Fields (Ed.), *Innovative trends and specialized strategies in community-based corrections* (pp. 63–83). New York: Garland.

Link, B., Andrews, A., & Cullen, F. (1992). The violent and illegal behavior of mental patients reconsidered. *American Sociological Review, 57,* 1461–1500.

Link, B., & Stueve, A. (1994). Psychotic symptoms and the violent/illegal behavior of mental patients compared to community controls. In J. Monahan & H. J. Steadman (Eds.), *Violence and mental disorder: Developments in risk assessment* (pp. 137–159). Chicago: University of Chicago Press.

Litwack, T. R. (1993). On the ethics of dangerousness assessments. *Law and Human Behavior, 17,* 479–482.

Maier, G. J., Morrow, B. R., & Miller, R. (1989). Security safeguards in community rehabilitation of forensic patients. *Hospital and Community Psychiatry, 40,* 529–531.

Maltz, M. D. (1984). *Recidivism.* Orlando, FL: Academic Press.

Mathiesen, T. (1998). Selective incapacitation revisited. *Law and Human Behavior, 22,* 455–469.

McGreevy, M. A., Steadman, H. J., Dvoskin, J. A., & Dollard, N. (1991). New York state's system of managing insanity acquittees in the community. *Hospital and Community Psychiatry, 42,* 512–517.

Meehl, P. E. (1954). *Clinical versus statistical prediction: A theoretical analysis and a review of the evidence.* Minneapolis: University of Minnesota Press.

Megargee, E. I., & Bohn, M. (1979). *Classifying criminal offenders: A new system based on the MMPI.* Beverly Hills, CA: Sage.

Melton, G. B., Petrila, J., Poythress, N. G., & Slobogin, C. (1997). *Psychological evaluations for the courts: A handbook for mental health professionals and lawyers* (2nd ed.). New York: Guilford Press.

Minnesota Department of Corrections. (n.d.). *Minnesota Sex Offender Screening Tool revised (MnSOST-R).* St. Paul: Author.

Monahan, J. (1981). *The clinical prediction of violent behavior.* Washington, DC: U.S. Government Printing Office.

Monahan, J. (1984). The prediction of violent behavior: Toward a second generation of theory and policy. *American Journal of Psychiatry, 141,* 10–15.

Monahan, J. (1993). Limiting therapist exposure to *Tarasoff* liability: Guidelines for risk containment. *American Psychologist, 48,* 242–250.

Monahan, J. (1996). Violence prediction: The past twenty and the next twenty years. *Criminal Justice and Behavior, 23,* 107–120.

Monahan, J., & Steadman, H. J. (Eds.). (1994). *Violence and mental disorder: Developments in risk assessment.* Chicago: University of Chicago Press.

Monahan, J., & Steadman, H. J. (1996). Violent storms and violent people: How meteorology can inform risk communication in mental health law. *American Psychologist, 51,* 931–938.

Morey, L. C. (1991). *Personality Assessment Inventory: Professional manual.* Tampa, FL: Psychological Assessment Resources.

Morgan, K. D. (1993). Factors influencing probation outcome. *Federal Probation, 57,* 23–29.

Mossman, D. (1994). Assessing predictions of violence: Being accurate about accuracy. *Journal of Consulting and Clinical Psychology, 62,* 783–792.

Motiuk, L. L., Bonta, J., & Andrews, D. A. (1986). Classification in correctional halfway houses: The relative incremental predictive criterion validities of the Megargee-MMPI and LSI systems. *Criminal Justice and Behavior, 13,* 33–46.

Motiuk, M. S., Motiuk, L. L., & Bonta, J. (1992). A comparison between self-report and interview based inventories in offender classification. *Criminal Justice and Behavior, 19,* 143–159.

Nichols, T., Ogloff, J. R. P., & Douglas, K. S. (1997, August). *Comparing risk assessments with female and male psychiatric outpatients: The utility of the HCR-20 and PCL:SV.*

Paper presented at the Annual Meeting of the American Psychological Association, Chicago.

Otto, R. K. (1992). Predicting dangerous behavior: A review and analysis of "second generation" research. *Forensic Reports, 5*, 135–149.

Otto, R. K. (1994). On the ability of mental health professionals to "predict dangerousness": A commentary on interpretations of the "dangerousness" literature. *Law and Psychology Review, 18*, 43–68.

Otto, R. K. (in press). Assessing and managing violence risk in outpatient settings. *Journal of Clinical Psychology*.

Otto, R. K., & Borum, R. (1997). *Assessing and managing violence risk: A workshop for clinicians.* Tampa: Florida Mental Health Institute.

Otto, R. K., Borum, R., & Hart, S. D. (2000). *Professional issues in the use of actuarial instruments in sexually violent predator evaluation* (in preparation).

Otto, R. K., Poythress, N. G., Borum, R., & Petrila, J. (1999). *Assessing risk in sex offenders.* Tampa: Florida Mental Health Institute.

Petersilia, J. (1997). Probation in the United States: Practices and challenges. *National Institute of Justice Journal, 233*, 2–8.

Petersilia, J., & Turner, S. (1993). *Evaluating intensive supervision probation/parole: Results of a nationwide experiment.* Washington, DC: National Institute of Justice.

Poythress, N. G. (1987). Avoiding negligent release: A risk-management strategy. *Hospital and Community Psychiatry, 38*, 1051–1052.

Poythress, N. G. (1990). Avoiding negligent release: Contemporary clinical and risk management strategies. *American Journal of Psychiatry, 147*, 994–997.

Poythress, N. G., & Brodsky, S. L. (1992). In the wake of a negligent release lawsuit: An investigation of professional consequences and institutional impact on a state psychiatric hospital. *Law and Human Behavior, 16*, 155–173.

Prentky, R. A., Lee, A. F. S., Knight, R. A., & Cerce, D. (1997). Recidivism rates among child molesters and rapists: A methodological analysis. *Law and Human Behavior, 21*, 635–659.

Quay, H. (1984). *Managing adult inmates: Classification for housing and program assignments.* College Park, MD: American Correctional Association.

Quinsey, V. L., Harris, G. T., Rice, M. E., & Cormier, C. A. (1998). *Violent offenders: Appraising and managing risk.* Washington, DC: American Psychological Association.

Quinsey, V. L., Lalumière, M. L., Rice, M. E., & Harris, G. T. (1995). Predicting sexual offenses. In J. C. Campbell (Ed.), *Assessing dangerousness: Violence by sexual offenders, batterers, and child abusers* (pp. 114–137). Thousand Oaks, CA: Sage.

Rice, M. E. (1997). Violent offender research and implications for the criminal justice system. *American Psychologist, 52*, 414–423.

Rice, M. E., & Harris, G. T. (1995). Violent recidivism: Assessing predictive validity. *Journal of Consulting and Clinical Psychology, 63*, 737–748.

Rice, M. E., & Harris, G. T. (1997). Cross-validation and extension of the Violence Risk Appraisal Guide for child molesters and rapists. *Law and Human Behavior, 21*, 231–241.

Rogers, J. L., Bloom, J. D., & Manson, S. M. (1986). Oregon's PSRB: A comprehensive system for managing insanity acquittees. *Annals of the American Academy of Political and Social Sciences, 484*, 86–99.

Rogers, R., & Bagby, R. (1992). Diversion of mentally disordered offenders: A legitimate role for clinicians? *Behavioral Sciences and the Law, 10*, 407–418.

Rogers, R., Gillis, J. R., Dickens, S. E., & Webster, C. D. (1988). Treatment recommendations for mentally disordered offenders: More than roulette? *Behavioral Sciences and the Law, 6*, 487–495.

Salekin, R. T., Rogers, R., & Sewell, K. W. (1996). A review and meta-analysis of the Psychopathy Checklist and Psychopathy Checklist-Revised: Predictive validity of dangerousness. *Clinical Psychology: Science and Practice, 3*, 203–215.

Sandoval, A. R., & Edens, J. F. (1999). Assessment and treatment of violent offenders in criminal justice settings. In L. VandeCreek & T. L. Jackson (Eds.), *Innovations in clinical practice: A source book, Vol. 17* (pp. 355–375). Sarasota, FL: Professional Resource Press.

Schmidt, P., & Witte, A. D. (1988). *Predicting recidivism using survival models.* New York: Springer-Verlag.

Silver, E., Mulvey, E. P., & Monahan, J. (1999). Assessing violence risk among discharged psychiatric patients: Toward an ecological model. *Law and Human Behavior, 23*, 237–257.

Smith, W. R., & Monastersky, C. (1986). Assessing juvenile sex offenders' risk for reoffending. *Criminal Justice and Behavior, 13*, 115–140.

Solomon, P., & Draine, J. (1995). One-year outcomes of a randomized trial of case management with seriously mentally ill clients leaving jail. *Evaluation Review, 19*, 256–273.

Steadman, H. J., Monahan, J., Robbins, P. C., Appelbaum, P., Grisso, T., Klassen, D., Mulvey, E. P., & Roth, L. (1993). From dangerousness to risk assessment: Implications for appropriate research strategies. In S. Hodgins (Ed.), *Mental disorder and crime* (pp. 39–62). Newbury Park, CA: Sage.

Steadman, H. J., Mulvey, E. P., Monahan, J., Robbins, P. C., Appelbaum, P. S., Grisso, T., Roth, L. H., & Silver, E. (1998). Violence by people discharged from acute psychiatric inpatient facilities and by others in the same neighborhoods. *Archives of General Psychiatry, 55*, 393–401.

Stevens, H. B., & Brodsky, S. L. (1995). Perceived consequences to the predictor: A variable in the release of psychiatric patients. *Psychological Reports, 76*, 1371–1378.

Swanson, J., Borum, R., Swartz, M., & Monahan, J. (1996). Psychotic symptoms and disorders and the risk of violent behavior in the community. *Criminal Behaviour and Mental Health, 6*, 309–329.

Tellefsen, C., Cohen, M. I., Silver S. B., & Dougherty, C. (1992). Predicting success on conditional releases for insanity acquittees: Regionalized versus nonregionalized hospital patients. *Bulletin of the American Academy of Psychiatry and Law, 20*, 87–100.

Tonry, M. (1990). Stated and latent functions of ISP. *Crime and Delinquency, 36*, 174–191.

Van Voorhis, P. (1994). *Psychological classification of the adult male prison inmate.* Albany: State University of New York Press.

Veysey, B. M., Steadman, H. J., Morrissey, J. P., & Johnsen, M. (1997). In search of the missing linkages: Continuity of care in U.S. jails. *Behavioral Sciences and the Law, 15*, 383–397.

Walters, G. D., White, T. W., & Denney, D. (1991). The Lifestyle Criminality Screening Form: Preliminary data. *Criminal Justice and Behavior, 18*, 406–418.

Warren, M., & Staff of the Community Treatment Project. (1966). *Interpersonal maturity level classification: Diagnosis and treatment of low, middle, and high maturity delinquents.* Sacramento: California Youth Authority.

Webster, C. D. (1998). Comment on Thomas Mathiesen's selective incapacitation revisited. *Law and Human Behavior, 22*, 471–476.

Webster, C. D., Douglas, K. S., Eaves, D., & Hart, S. D. (1997). *HCR-20 Assessing risk for violence version 2.* Burnaby, BC: Mental Health, Law & Policy Institute, Simon Fraser University.

Webster, C. D., Harris, G. T., Rice, M., Cormier, C., & Quinsey, V. (1994). *The violence prediction scheme.* Toronto: Centre of Criminology, University of Toronto.

Werner, P. D., & Meloy, J. R. (1992). Decision making about dangerousness in releasing patients from long-term psychiatric hospitalization. *Journal of Psychiatry and Law, 20*, 35–47.

Wiebush, R. G., Baird, C., Krisberg, B., & Onek, D. (1995). Risk assessment and classification for serious, violent, and chronic juvenile offenders. In J. C. Howell, B. Krisberg, J. D. Hawkins, & J. J. Wilson (Eds.), *A sourcebook: Serious, violent, and chronic juvenile offenders* (pp. 171–212). Thousand Oaks, CA: Sage.

Wiederanders, M. R. (1992). Recidivism of disordered offenders who were conditionally versus unconditionally released. *Behavioral Sciences and the Law, 10*, 141–148.

Wierson, M., & Forehand, R. (1995). Predicting recidivism in juvenile delinquents: The role of mental health diagnoses and the qualification of conclusions by race. *Behavior Research and Therapy, 33*, 63–67.

Wilson, D., Tien, G., & Eaves, D. (1995). Increasing the community tenure of mentally disordered offenders: An assertive case management program. *International Journal of Law and Psychiatry, 18*, 61–69.

Wintrup, A. (1996). *Assessing risk of violence in mentally disordered offenders with the HCR-20.* Unpublished master's thesis, Simon Fraser University, Burnaby, British Columbia, Canada.

Chapter 14
AFTERCARE AND RECIDIVISM PREVENTION

José B. Ashford, Bruce D. Sales, and Craig Winston LeCroy

Parole supervision can trace its roots to a number of correctional practices: indenture associated with the houses of refuge and youth reformatories of the early 19th century (Ashford, 1997; Clement, 1993; Pisciotta, 1993), tickets-of-leave from Australian and Irish prison systems (Abadinsky, 1997; Cohn, 1994), indeterminate sentences (Dressler, 1959), and the supervisory release activities of prison societies such as the Philadelphia Society for Alleviating the Miseries of Public Prisons (Giardini, 1959; Hussey & Duffee, 1980; Macht & Ashford, 1991). Aftercare in mental health, on the other hand, is rooted in traditional hospital practices (French, 1940). It was a common practice in the 19th-century hospital for staff to monitor the progress of patients on trial visits with families in the community (Haines, 1920), and not release them from hospital custody until they demonstrated proper functioning in the community (Smith, 1912).

Such mental health aftercare is exemplified by the famous colony for the mentally ill in Gheel, Belgium, where patients were boarded out to families in the community who lived in cottages adjacent to the hospital (Smith, 1912). Under this system, hospitals were responsible for providing services to persons in need of restraint and other acute-oriented services, whereas nondisruptive patients were boarded out to the families (Haines, 1920). Although the nondisruptive patients were in the private care of families, they still were under the public control of hospital authorities. As Adolph Meyer (1922) pointed out, most hospitals offered some form of aftercare before the formal establishment of social casework as a special service for assisting patients in returning to the community.

What emerges from the early descriptions is a portrait of similarities and differences in the development of aftercare in corrections and mental health. As for similarities, both are concerned with the released individual not relapsing (e.g., in corrections—the released offender not recidivating; in mental health—the released patient not having an episode that would require rehospitalization). As for differences, correctional aftercare focused more on monitoring behavior than on being available to provide some community-based services to facilitate successful reintegration into the community.

The lines of development for parole for inmates and aftercare for mentally ill patients began to converge with the introduction of rehabilitation as an alternative correctional goal to punishment (Haines, 1920). By 1930, clinical models of rehabilitation were instituted, which changed traditional approaches to parole supervision (Carney, 1980; Hippchen, 1978). Clinical needs and terminology began to usurp the early 19th-century correctional terminology that focused on issues of forced labor, education, and religion. Yet despite this philosophical shift, as we will discuss later, implementing this philosophy never achieved that which was envisioned in its rhetoric (Duffee & Clark, 1985; Studt, 1972; Waller, 1974).

As a result, the term *aftercare* to this day means different things to different people within the correctional field. For example, some define aftercare simply in terms of whatever follows a given form of treatment. Others consider aftercare a key component of the posttreatment recovery process (National Institute of Drug Abuse, 1993). This chapter focuses on the latter meaning and its significance for the recovery and prevention of recidivism of special need juvenile and adult offenders.

We begin by clarifying terminology and concepts that integrate and sometimes confound social control and rehabilitation goals for services when offenders are released from juvenile and adult correctional facilities. As part of this discussion, we consider the ways in which needs are defined in the aftercare process and the ambiguity encountered in specifying appropriate goals (outcomes sought) for aftercare services to special need offenders released from adult and juvenile correctional facilities. We next review the outcome literature on current aftercare services: (a) case-management and intensive supervision; (b) psychosocial rehabilitation (e.g., supported housing and supported employment); and (c) relapse prevention. The chapter concludes with a brief discussion of the critical directions for future programmatic research on aftercare services that is needed to improve correctional outcomes and correctional–mental health interactions.

Terminology and Constructs

In juvenile justice, postrelease care from correctional settings is termed *juvenile aftercare,* which includes traditional surveillance services in combination with services designed to assist the juvenile in making a proper adjustment to the community (Ashford, 1997; Ashford & LeCroy, 1993). Although the meaning of adjustment varies within and across states, the juvenile justice system adopted the concept of aftercare to fit with its fundamental commitment to principles of treatment and rehabilitation.

The adult system adopted a concept of parole as its version of aftercare. Parole reflects the correctional system's desire to reinforce its fundamental commitment to notions of accountability, responsibility, and societal protection. Indeed the word *parole* is derived from the French word that means taking a person on their word —in this case, their word to no longer engage in criminal activity. Over time, parole as a service emerged to monitor the offender's compliance with the conditions of parole and to assist the offender in readjusting to the community to the extent that such services purportedly would make the offender less likely to recidivate.

Despite this seeming clarity in goals for aftercare in both the juvenile and adult systems, aftercare research and services are plagued by a lack of clear terminology and constructs guiding the planning and implementing of these services. This confusion has resulted because states, and jurisdictions within states, have applied different goals over time, as the executive, legislative, and judicial branches of government have changed leadership and membership, goals, and views of legal and societal obligations to offenders. For example, should aftercare promote social control in the juvenile justice system or remain true to its historical rehabilitative focus? With the advent of increasing juvenile crime, there is increasing public pressure on states to focus on public safety rather than on rehabilitation when responding to juveniles who come within the purview of the justice system. Even when clinical services are provided to offenders, jurisdictions often show confusion about why the services are provided. Mental health professionals may be focusing on amelioration of pathology, whereas correctional administrators are concerned with reducing recidivism.

The Role of Needs and Goals in the Aftercare Process for Offenders With Special Needs

The question arises about how we should determine appropriate offender needs, correctional goals (i.e., desired outcomes), and aftercare services to achieve those goals. The answer to this question depends on whether rehabilitation is still considered an appropriate goal for the criminal justice process. When the adult and juvenile justice systems adopted the rehabilitation ideal, aftercare (parole) services were designed to meet the psychological, physical, and the social needs of offenders that placed them at risk for engaging in future criminal behavior (Allen, 1977). This approach to the rehabilitation of offenders dominated correctional practices up until the mid-1970s, when a number of studies (Hudson, 1973; Romig, 1978; Wheeler, 1978) indicated that persons placed on aftercare fared no better than persons without aftercare services following release from correctional institutions. The results of these studies and other shifts in criminal justice ideology (American Friends Services Committee, 1971; Martinson, 1974; Pitch, 1995) led to the eventual repudiation of rehabilitation as an appropriate goal for aftercare services.

Today aftercare is not intended to rehabilitate the ordinary offender. Most jurisdictions have shifted the focus of aftercare services from a focus on rehabilitation to a focus on control and surveillance functions (e.g., monitoring offender levels of compliance with the conditions of release) with varying degrees of emphasis on providing services to help offenders in making an appropriate readjustment to the community (Duffee & Clark, 1985). However, there are certain classes of offenders that are presumably in need of specialized rehabilitation services on release from correctional facilities: substance abusers, sexual offenders, mentally impaired offenders (severely and persistently mentally ill and mentally retarded offenders) and violent offenders (Blackburn, 1996; Clear, Byrne, Dvoskin, 1993; Henderson & Bell, 1995; Home Office, 1987). These categories of offenders require specialized aftercare services because it is assumed that they have distinct need configurations that influence their relapse potential and likelihood of making a positive adjustment to the community. The first chapter in this book explores different conceptions of offender needs in the criminal justice process; for this reason, it is not necessary to review the controversies plaguing the establishment of clear boundaries between the special and the ordinary needs of offenders. It is enough to say that part of the problem in creating specialized aftercare services for offenders with special needs is the lack of a universally agreed on definition of offender needs (Andrews & Bonta, 1998; Clements, 1996; Duffee & Clark, 1985; Duffee & Duffee, 1981).

In addition to defining offender needs and special needs to develop appropriate programming for special need offenders released from correctional facilities, these definitions need to match appropriate clinical and correctional goals–outcomes. To this end, Heilbrun et al. (1988) argued that mental health professionals must treat separately both clinical and criminal targets in designing effective interventions for mentally disordered offenders. Even though their views are consistent with traditional models of rehabilitation, newer developments in mental health services research stress the integration of services over the use of disease-specific or problem-specific models of intervention. That is, newer models of rehabilitation (Anderson, 1997; Liberman, 1988; Minkoff, 1991; Ragins, 1997) assert that the cure of a clinical pathology and recovery of a noncriminal lifestyle must be pursued concurrently.

This philosophical approach differs substantially from the older models of rehabilitation that stress (a) pursuing a cure of the clinical conditions beforehand, and (b) developing recovery strategies (Ragins, 1997). It operates on the assumption that relapse often has less to do with the illness process than factors relating to the patient's quality of life. In other words, current technology in the field of aftercare is adhering to conceptions of recovery that have expanded the targets for intervention to include other factors besides monitoring symptom and side-effect profiles. Outcomes relevant to recidivism and other psychosocial variables are now assigned a more prominent role in relapse prevention than was previously true of earlier approaches to psychiatric rehabilitation.

In the remaining sections of the chapter, we examine aftercare services with some demonstrated effectiveness in preventing relapse and recidivism in populations of offenders with special needs. These services target the clinical and psychosocial needs of offenders with known significance for preventing relapse in clinical populations and recidivism in offenders with special needs.

Aftercare for Special Need Offenders

Aftercare technology in corrections has not always responded to the diverse needs of offenders in the justice system. Persons with ordinary and special needs often receive similar aftercare regimens. In the next section, we begin our examination of aftercare services by analyzing alternative models of supervision for offenders with serious and persistent mental disorders. Persons diagnosed with serious mental disorders have additional outcomes that cannot be ignored in selecting appropriate kinds of supervision in the community.

Supervising Offenders With Serious and Persistent Mental Impairments (SPMI)

Relapse of released persons with mental disorders has been the bane of mental health professionals (Bachrach, 1978; Solomon, Gordon, & Davis, 1984) since the initial recommendations of the Joint Commission on Mental Illness and Health (1961) on aftercare and rehabilitation of mental patients. Most mental health professionals see behavioral and mental state relapse requiring a hospital or correctional facility readmission as an aftercare failure. To avoid such relapse for seriously mentally ill offenders, community-based treatment must be part of aftercare. Yet part of the difficulty in implementing such treatment is the limits placed by managed care on public sector mental health care (Stroup & Dorwart, 1997) in general. This dilemma is exacerbated in correctional aftercare because existing systems of public sector care are obligated to address the complex needs of persons with serious and persistent mental illness (SPMI) who also present with criminogenic needs.

The seriousness of the relapse problem in noncorrectional mental health care has been documented. Numerous studies have shown that one third of hospital admissions of psychiatric patients are in fact readmissions (Glasscote, Cumming, Rutman, Sussex, & Glassman, 1971; Solomon et al., 1984). Many patients cycle in and out of hospitals because of problems with aftercare resources in the community (Klinkenberg & Calsyn, 1996). This information is relevant to our discussion because many of these patients also have criminal and substance abuse histories that contribute to their adjustment difficulties.

To cope with the needs of persons with SPMI, and in an attempt to address the relapse problem, case management strategies have been instituted to assist patients released from hospitals (Bachrach, 1986; Hawthorne & Hough, 1997; Stein & Santos, 1998; Stein & Test, 1980). Moreover, case management and psychosocial rehabilitation are viewed as key foundations for the development of an effective community support system (CSS) for persons with serious mental health impairments (Anthony & Blanch, 1989; Hawthorne & Hough, 1997; Stroul, 1989).

Case Management Services

Case management is designed to assist persons with SPMI in gaining access to existing community services, rather than relying on emergency services and psychiatric hospitals as most mentally ill persons discharged from hospitals in large cities tend to do (Bond, McDonel, Miller, & Pensec, 1991; Stein & Santos, 1998). Therefore the primary goal of case management is to increase the probability that patients receive the appropriate services when they need them (Reinhardt & Shepherd, 1994). "In particular, the case manager assumes the responsibility for identifying and recommending for the patient those services which he or she believes will most effectively and efficiently return the patient to the expected level of functioning" (Reinhardt & Shepherd, 1994, p. 79).

Case management is not a new concept. It has been viewed as a useful process for the coordination of services for more than a century (Weil, Karls, & Associates, 1985; Moxley, 1997; Zander, 1995). Since the 1960s, case management witnessed increased popularity in human services because of (a) financial pressures to increase the use of particular services for specific populations with specific needs, for limited periods of time, which contributed to the formation of large networks of complex, fragmented, and uncoordinated services for highly specialized groups; and (b) the deinstitutionalization movement (Intagliata, 1982). Within this rapidly changing services environment, networks of services lacked the kinds of coordination needed to ensure quality of care. Fragmented systems of care were particularly burdensome for persons with serious mental impairments previously treated in institutional settings (Intagliata, 1982; President's Panel on Mental Retardation, 1962). In response to this situation, case management emerged as a fundamental strategy for improving the continuity of care for persons discharged from mental health and mental retardation facilities, even though case management "can simultaneously be described as a system, a role, a technology, a process and a service" (Bower, 1992, p. 2–7). The continuity of care objective is achieved by a process that involves five basic functions: (a) assessment of client need; (b) development of a services or treatment plan; (c) arrangement and linkage of persons to existing, available services; (d) monitoring of service delivery; and (e) evaluation/follow-up to determine whether the services are achieving the intended goals (Intagliata, 1982; Moxley, 1997; Rose & Moore, 1995). Some case management models include other functions, such as advocacy for client needs (Henderson & Bell, 1995). Advocacy can be implemented in different ways depending on the model of case management under consideration. For example, consumer-oriented approaches to case management handle advocacy differently from systems-oriented approaches (Rose & Moore, 1995). That is, "these functions may be implemented in different ways, depending on the mission of the case management program, so that, for example, programs with administrative missions implement assessment in a gatekeeping fashion while consumer-driven programs engage in assessment through the identification of client wants and strengths" (Moxley, 1997, p. 55).

It is not surprising therefore that the case management process contains a number of inherent tensions and ambiguities surrounding the responsibilities of case managers. "Is the primary responsibility of the case manager to the client, or to the system? Should the case manager be primarily concerned with the efficient use of resources or with the creation of a high quality, individually tailored service?" (Shepherd, 1993, p. 168). These dilemmas increase when case managers are also dealing with issues of public safety and criminal recidivism.

In corrections, there has been a number of approaches to case management, including the formation of Community Resource Management Teams (CRMTs). In this, as well as in other approaches to correctional case management, the case manager or team is considered a broker of services and not a provider of direct services (Henderson & Bell, 1995; Spica, 1993). In fact, this is often necessitated because some states do not require field officers, who constitute these teams, to be mental health professionals. Thus very few correctional agencies see field officers as having the necessary expertise for actually treating offenders with special needs. Even where field officers have social work training, in many jurisdictions today they are no longer expected to use one-to-one principles of casework in responding to offender needs (Henderson & Bell, 1995). This points out an important tension in the case management literature surrounding the roles of case managers. "Are they simply there to link clients to services in a rather bureaucratic, administrative way, as a kind of broker, or, should they use their relationship with the client as a special kind of therapeutic support" (Shepherd, 1990, p. 169).

Although the debate can be decided politically or by financial exigencies, the choice of which aftercare model to use should be informed by the research literature in aftercare services. For example, brokerage of service approaches to case management have also played a significant role in treating patients with serious mental illness, and has been studied in those contexts. The results have been high rates of recidivism among discharged mental patients, which in turn have stimulated a number of experiments in offering alternatives to traditional brokerage of service models. The most widely researched of these approaches is the Assertive Community Treatment (ACT) or the Assertive Case Management (ACM) model (Stein & Santos, 1998).

ACT differs from traditional broker of services models in that it actively tries to help the client (a) obtain material resources to survive in the community; (b) develop coping skills for dealing with the day-to-day requirements of community life; (c) develop a system of support to motivate him or her to remain involved in community life; (d) free him- or herself from relationships that promoted pathological forms of dependency; and (e) learn to appropriately relate to relevant community individuals including family, landlords, and police (Stein & Test, 1980). Thus ACT provides intensive case support services and is not considered just a human link between the client and a system of services, with case management functions being implemented by a team of professionals who share caseloads and who are on call 24 hours a day (Bond et al., 1991; Stein & Santos, 1998). Members of the team have a comprehensive level of responsibility for the individualized treatment of clients in their homes, neighborhoods, and work settings (Intagliata, 1982; Morse et al., 1997). This obligation even entails members of the team assisting clients in daily living activities "such as laundry upkeep, shopping, cooking, restaurant use, grooming, budgeting, and use of transportation" (Stein & Test, 1980, p. 393).

Thus an important aim of ACT is to improve the quality of a client's life by teaching practical living skills in the natural environment (Duffy & Wong, 1996). When clients do not show up for work or encounter other problems in their daily life, staff are expected to be assertive in responding to these situations. As Stein and Test (1980, p. 293) pointed out,

> the program must be assertive, involve patients in their treatment, and be prepared to go to the [client] . . . to prevent drop out. It must also actively insure continuity of care among treatment agencies rather than assume that a [client] . . . will successfully negotiate the often difficult pathways from one agency to another on his own.

ACT also includes the careful monitoring of client symptoms and medical status, and relies heavily on the use of low staff–client ratios. This allows team members to help the client find a job or a sheltered work environment and to intervene in a client's job-related problems (Stein & Test, 1980). The case management team also aids the client in learning to appropriately use leisure time and develop social skills. Because the team is assertive in each of a client's life domains, ACT clients are exposed to a more intensive system of support and treatment than is presumed likely in traditional broker-of-services models of case management.

There are similar movements in the field of community corrections involving increases in the intensity of supervision of persons on conditional release from correctional facilities [e.g., intensive parole supervision (IPS) and intensive aftercare programs (IAPs)]. Both of these movements in intensive case management are confronting, however, an important empirical question. Are intensive case management models effective in achieving complex clinical and behavioral treatment objectives, and how do their outcomes compare with those achieved with traditional models of case management?

One source of information to answer this question comes from the sizeable body of research that has demonstrated the utility of intensive case management in "facilitating continuity, reducing fragmentation, making appropriate services available, and providing a trusting, consistent relationship for the client with SPMI" (Hawthorne & Hough, 1997, p. 207). This includes several experimental studies that demonstrated that ACT, compared to traditional aftercare, significantly reduces psychiatric inpatient usage (Bond, Miller, Krumwied, & Ward, 1988; Borland, McRae & Lycan, 1989; Lipton, Nutt, & Sabitini, 1988; Stein & Test, 1980). When ACT clients were compared to a sample of clients receiving services at drop-in centers, ACT clients had fewer state hospital admissions (Bond et al., 1990). When ACT patients were admitted to a hospital, they also required fewer days per admission than participants who received only drop-in center services. Bond and colleagues (1990) also uncovered other benefits. ACT clients reported fewer contacts with police, increased overall program participation, and greater satisfaction with their program than participants receiving the services provided by the drop-in center. Bond et al. (1990) also found that ACT saved more than $1500 per client. In spite of the fact that findings are mixed regarding cost savings (Curtis, Millman, Streuning, & O'Ercole, 1992; Franklin, Solovitz, Mason, Clemons, & Miller, 1987; Rosenheck, Neale, Leaf, Milstein, & Frishman, 1995; Rossler, Loffler, Fatkenheuer, & Reicher-Rossler, 1992), most research has consistently documented that ACT programs do reduce use of inpatient psychiatric facilities (Olfson, 1990; Rosenheck, Neale, Leaf, Milstein, & Frisman, 1995).

The use of ACT with homeless subpopulations of persons also reveals some promising results. Morse and colleagues (1997) examined three types of case management to determine their relative effectiveness in treating persons with serious mental illness who were homeless or at risk of homelessness. Their study randomly assigned individuals recruited from a psychiatric emergency room to three treatment conditions:

> broker case management, in which the client's needs were assessed, services were purchased from multiple providers, and the client was monitored; assertive community treatment only, in which comprehensive services were provided for an unlimited period; and assertive community treatment augmented by support from community workers, who assisted in activities of daily living and were available for leisure activities. (Morse et al. 1997, p. 497)

The results of this study indicated that ACT is more effective than brokered case management in providing patients with better program outcomes.

Morse and his colleagues (1997) also found that, compared to brokered case management, patients in ACT achieved more days in stable housing and demonstrated superior outcomes in the area of psychiatric symptoms. However, Morse and his colleagues (1997) did not find that ACT influenced clients' income and abuse of substances. Overall, ACT was more successful than brokered case management in ensuring that clients received intensive levels of services but not necessarily in increasing clients' functioning in all relevant domains of life functioning.

Case management researchers have also examined the relative effectiveness of team and individual caseload approaches to reducing hospital use. Bond and his colleagues (1991) studied the relative efficacy of the individual and team approaches to intensive case management in reducing use of hospitals by patients with a history of frequent use. The results indicated that team approaches proved more effective over time in reducing hospital use than individual approaches.

ACT has also been evaluated in treating young adults suffering from serious mental illness and substance abuse problems. Bond, McDonnel et al. (1991) examined outcomes for mentally ill substance abusers (MISA) who were assigned to two different experimental groups (ACT or Reference Groups (RGs)) and a control group. The reference groups were composed of clients who received four substance abuse group sessions per week led by an RG worker for a specified period of time. The control group received traditional community mental health services. The results indicated that treatment engagement was greater for reference group clients and ACT clients than control clients. However, RG clients were significantly lower in the number of hospitalizations than either ACT or control individuals, although ACT patients had significantly lower numbers of hospital days than RG and controls. Finally, unlike other studies, this study found that ACT and RG clients had higher ratings on measures of quality of life than controls, although no significant differences among groups was evident on measures of employment, time in jail, residential status, and residential moves.

Although results of research on ACT with various subgroups in the SPMI population are demonstrating significant promise (e.g., in reducing hospital use), "long-term outcome data documenting improved quality-of-life and functioning are scarce" (Hawthorne & Hough, 1997, p. 207). "Doubts have also been voiced about the generalizability of previous studies in support of ACT programs because they were well-funded research/demonstration projects executed by ideologically committed leaders in the field" (Rosenheck et al., 1995, p. 129).

Intensive case management (like ACT) with offenders with serious mental impairments has been subjected, however, to less empirical scrutiny. One noteworthy exception is the randomized trial of case management approaches applied to SPMI clients leaving jails (Solomon & Draine, 1995). Persons leaving jails present a number of special problems for community mental health systems. Their living situations are often more tenuous than other groups of SPMI patients and they typically are at increased risk for homelessness and reincarceration (Solomon & Draine, 1995). Solomon and Draine randomly assigned 200 inmates from a large urban city jail to one of three conditions: the ACT Team, forensic specialist case managers located in community mental health agencies, and the usual referral to a community mental health center. The researchers predicted that offenders receiving case management services would have better psychosocial and clinical outcomes than offenders receiving traditional mental health services. However, they did not find any significant differences on these three conditions. Solomon and Draine (1995) pointed out that we should be cautious in interpreting these results, however, because of the serious lack of fidelity to all aspects of the ACT model noted in how the team implemented the ACT case management process. Nonetheless, this study uncovered an important finding that requires closer scrutiny by research and policy scholars. More offenders under case management supervision returned to jail during the follow-up period. If case management increases the use of jails to control treatment noncompliance, is this a positive outcome in the treatment of persons with chronic disturbances and long histories of treatment resistance?

Part of the problem may lie with the behaviors of the mentally disordered offenders other than treatment noncompliance. Feder (1991b) found in a study of the postrelease adjustment of mentally disordered offenders that nonmentally disordered offenders were more likely than mentally disordered offenders to have had their parole revoked; however, mentally disordered offenders were more likely than nonmentally disordered offenders to have committed technical violations. This and other findings (Heilbrun & Griffin, 1993) suggest that mentally disordered offenders encounter significant difficulties in complying with many of the conditions of parole and other forms of postrelease supervision (Jacoby & Kozie-Peak, 1997). Yet some studies do indicate that appropriate supports can reduce the jail time of mentally ill offenders following release from correctional settings (Wilson, Tien, & Eaves, 1995). However, there are no studies in the literature that have used appropriate comparison groups or adequate sample sizes that would allow for reasonable conclusions about the effectiveness of using specialized support services with mentally disordered offenders on measures involving positive social adjustment, improvements in quality of life, and recidivism.

Supervising the Other Categories of Special Need Offenders

Intensive supervision programs (ISPs) have increased in the fields of probation and parole "to manage some special needs of offenders, particularly sex offenders, violent offenders and substance abusers" (Henderson & Bell, 1995). A few of these programs incorporate principles of case management derived from the ACT model of care for the SPMI (Martin & Inciardi, 1997). These programs are founded on the assumption that there is a strong correlation between participation in various forms of treatment and levels of recidivism (Fulton & Stone, 1993; Palmer, 1996). That is, if treatment and services are increased for offenders with special needs, then it will reduce recidivism while increasing rehabilitation (Turner, Petersilia, & Deschenes, 1992). Other models of ISPs attempt to increase the monitoring of substance abusers, violent offenders, and sex offenders in all areas of their environment by increasing levels of offender surveillance (Cullen, Wright, & Applegate, 1996; Greer, 1991). "The close monitoring that is part of ISPs provides the control needed for offenders prone to violence" (Henderson & Bell, 1995). In other words, intensive supervision programs also assume that many offenders with special needs require increased monitoring because of the relationship between their mental impairments or disabilities and lowered inhibitions.

Offenders with substance abuse problems are overwhelming the criminal justice system. Langan and Cunniff (1992) estimated that more than 3 million persons on probation and parole have some form of drug abuse problem. In response to this situation, there is a growing body of literature (Anglin & Hser, 1990; Falkin, Lipton, & Wexler, 1992; Prendergast, Anglin, & Wellisch, 1995) that indicates that treatment of drug-abusing offenders can reduce recidivism whether treatment is voluntary or under some form of coercion. Because the problems of substance-abusing offenders are never completely cured, they require various levels of support and supervision in the community for extended periods of time. Although the importance of this form of aftercare is well-recognized in the substance abuse treatment literature, aftercare services continue to be inadequate in many service systems (Prendergast et al., 1995).

Aftercare is also considered an important component of any ISP for monitoring serious juvenile offenders (Goodstein & Sontheimer, 1997). The field of juvenile aftercare or parole has witnessed a marked increase in experiments in intensive aftercare supervision (IAS; Ashford, 1997). A number of these experiments were funded by the Violent Juvenile Offender Research and Development Program (VJO) of the Office of Juvenile Justice and Delinquency Prevention. Unlike many of the early experiments with adult ISPs, the juvenile programs had a much stronger emphasis on treatment and rehabilitation because of the juvenile justice system's primary orientation to principles of rehabilitation (Goodstein & Sontheimer, 1997).

The VJO's approach to aftercare for juveniles has stressed the following themes: social networking, social learning, provision of opportunities, and goal oriented interventions (Armstrong, 1991; Palmer, 1991). The program has relied on notions of continuous case management, diagnostic assessment, job training skills, placement in work settings, and individual and family counseling to transform the program's pivotal conceptual themes into practice (Ashford, 1997). Palmer (1991, p. 103) has provided a succinct summary of this project:

> In each of the four test sites that met the minimum participation standards—Boston, Memphis, Newark, and Detroit—program clients . . . were first placed for an average of six months in "small secure facilities." After that, they were "reintegrated to the community through transitional facilities via a community based residence." This stage was followed by intensive supervision, e.g., frequent contacts in small caseloads, "upon return to neighborhoods."

Each field officer or aftercare worker maintains a case load of between six to eight youths in the identified VJO programs.

The Paint Creek Youth program in Ohio is another experiment for serious delinquent offenders implemented by a private facility. Youths are placed in either their parental homes, an independent living setting, or a group home after they are released from the facility. Regardless of their housing arrangement, the youths are placed on house arrest "for the first two weeks but are allowed free movement to attend school, participate in treatment, or go to work" (Ashford, 1997, p. 41). Before youths can be discharged, they must have attended either school or work on a regular basis. The field officers maintain two face-to-face contacts with youths on aftercare status. Other programs with similar case load and surveillance features are being implemented in other jurisdictions across the United States (Armstrong, 1991). Many of them have structures, however, that focus primarily on achieving community protection and not rehabilitation.

The trend toward ISPs in adult and juvenile community corrections grew dramatically during the 1980s (Cullen et al., 1996). Much of this work was stimulated by early reports of success with experiments with intensive supervision for adults in Georgia and in New Jersey. These programs placed significant emphasis on the use of punitive approaches to the design of offender supervision (Pearson, 1988). The ISPs in Georgia and in New Jersey were also prison-diversion or prison-reduction programs. The aim was to use the ISP as a community alternative for persons eligible for incarceration in prison. The initial evaluation of the Georgia program reported that ISP participants had a reincarceration rate of 16% (Erwin, 1986). However, this initial evaluation of the Georgia program was challenged on a number of methodological grounds by Byrne, Lurigo, and Band (1989). In particular, they noted stark differences in the levels of comparability between the ISP and control groups.

Initial evaluations of the New Jersey program also pointed to the effectiveness of ISP programs in reducing recidivism (Pearson, 1988). However, the New Jersey study also was criticized for lacking comparable groups in its evaluation design. For this reason, the National Institute of Justice funded the RAND Corporation in Santa Monica to use an improved experimental design to study 14 ISPs in nine different states (Cullen et al., 1996). In this study, offenders were randomly assigned to either ISP, probation, parole, or prison. The results indicated that most ISPs were effective in increasing their surveillance and control functions. That is, ISPs have delivered on their promise of increased officer contact with offenders. However, the RAND results about the potential of ISPs to reduce recidivism were not as promising. Offenders assigned to ISP programs had higher arrests (37%) than controls (33%). But recidivism outcomes were improved when increased attention was devoted to pro-

viding "higher quality and quantity of treatment, as opposed to emphasizing surveillance and control" (Palmer, 1996, p. 145). That is, "the RAND researchers did
detect significant reductions in rearrest for those who participated in treatment programs" (Cullen et al., 1996, p. 87). In fact, ISP participants in treatment in California
and Texas had a 10 to 20% decrease in recidivism (Petersilia & Turner, 1993). These
findings suggest that by giving attention to other aspects of rehabilitation technology,
besides recent developments in areas of control and surveillance, we can significantly
reduce the levels of recidivism of offenders in need of other forms of treatment.
Morever, although Byrne and Pattavian (1992) concluded from a review of the literature that most evaluations of ISP programs do not "support the notion that intensive supervision significantly reduces the risk of offender recidivism" (p. 296), this
may only be true of programs that place minimal attention on providing services
that are responsive to significant offender needs.

Alschuler and Armstrong (1990) reviewed intensive aftercare programs for serious juvenile offenders. They found that the literature lacked a significant body of
studies that would allow for reliable conclusions about the effectiveness of intensive
aftercare supervision programs. Findings from studies by Barton and Butts (1990)
and Fagan, Forst, and Vivoan (1988), which adhered to appropriate methodological
requirements, support the conclusion that intensive aftercare supervision programs
are at least as effective as standard approaches (Palmer, 1996). However, "recent
experiments in juvenile intensive aftercare and probation have directed equal attention to the close monitoring of severely delinquent juvenile offenders and the provision of specialized services to them" (Alschuler & Armstrong, 1994, p. 3). Such
intensive aftercare programs are demonstrating increased success when social control
is combined with increased attention to service and rehabilitation (Alschuler & Armstrong, 1994).

Unfortunately, however, the research is not consistent in its findings. Greenwood, Deschenes, & Adams (1993) evaluated a program of intensive aftercare supervision for high-risk delinquents in Detroit and Pittsburgh. "Youths assigned to
the experimental programs were supposed to be released from their residential placement two months early and to receive the intensive aftercare supervision for the next
six months" (Greenwood et al., 1993, p. IX). Participation in this program did not
significantly affect key behavioral outcomes. That is, researchers did not find significant differences between experimental and control groups in the proportion of
youths arrested, in the proportion of self-reported offenses, or in the proportion of
drug use. In addition, participation in the experimental group was not found to have
any effect on the involvement of youths in work or school. It is hard to be convinced
by this study because it did not provide a key causal factor for success in such
programs—a clearly conceptualized model for psychosocial rehabilitation.

Psychosocial Rehabilitation Services

Persons with SPMI in the criminal justice system experience serious functional in-
capacities and role performance difficulties that require a broad range of rehabilitation services. The term rehabilitation, initially borrowed from the field of physical
medicine, originally incorporated the use of a two-stage process: "(1) treating the
symptoms of someone who has become physically disabled, such as by drugs and

physiotherapy; and (2) then helping the person to make a relatively permanent adaptation to their environment, such as by providing ramps or a wheelchair" (Ekdawi & Conning, 1994, p. 16). In psychiatric rehabilitation, the interaction of the person with his or her environment is also important, but the primary focus is on the social rather than the physical environment (Watts & Bennett, 1983). According to Wing (1990), professionals are more likely to be on common ground in the field of rehabilitation if their aims are geared to preventing "social disablement by dealing with its major components—disease, disability, disadvantage and demoralization or distress" (Wing, 1990, p. 93). Wing's (1990) view is consistent with newer models of psychiatric and psychosocial rehabilitation (Ekdawi & Conning, 1994; Liberman, 1988; Sperry, Brill, Howard, & Grissom, 1996).

The new generation of models for psychosocial rehabilitation for persons with SPMI adopted the principles of the World Health Organization (WHO; Anthony, 1993, p. 12). These models provide an orientation to rehabilitation that assumes that mental disorders cause other negative consequences besides mental impairments or symptoms (e.g., dysfunctions, disabilities, and handicaps) and that these consequences can benefit from rehabilitation services (Anthony, 1993; Liberman, 1988).

When a person has a disorder that impairs the ability to perform a specific task, it is referred to as a *dysfunction* in the rehabilitation literature (Anthony, 1993). A dysfunction includes any restrictions or deficits in a person's ability to perform any activity or task. Examples of dysfunctions commonly seen in persons with SPMI include deficits in self-care skills, such as cooking, cleaning, grooming, and other significant daily life activities (Liberman, 1988). Disability refers to all barriers to a person's ability to perform various social roles. According to Gruenberg (1967), who initially formulated the concept of the social breakdown syndrome, disability was only partly influenced by intrinsic impairments. The extrinsic environment includes many factors that contribute to the formation of barriers that place individuals at a relative position of disadvantage to others in society in performing social roles (Bennett, 1983). Today this is referred to in the rehabilitation literature as a *handicap*. Handicaps are the last in a series of consequences of mental disorders that the current rehabilitation model is designed to change (Liberman, 1988).

Most psychosocial rehabilitation approaches to ameliorating dysfunctions, disabilities, and handicaps include a modified conceptualization of recovery, which defines recovery differently from traditional medical models that stress cure as the targeted outcome (Ekdawi & Conning, 1994). The newer psychosocial rehabilitation approaches "conceptualize recovery more in terms of function than pathology" (Ragins, 1997, p. 2). That is, it is not accurate to assume that persons with mental disorders will be restored to their premorbid state. Although disabilities might remain, it is presumed that the dysfunctions and handicaps can be changed. Recovery involves, therefore, "a deeply personal, unique process of changing one's attitudes, values, feelings, goals, skills and/or roles." (Anthony, 1993, p. 15). In other words, it includes many other forms of change beyond recovery from the illness:

> People with mental illness may have to recover from stigma they have incorporated into their very being; from the iatrogenic effects of treatment settings; from lack of recent opportunities for self-determination; from the negative side effects of unemployment; and from crushed dreams. Recovery is often a complex, time-consuming process. (Anthony, 1993, p. 15)

The need for these forms of change also confront offenders who must adjust to the negative consequences of their incarceration regardless of whether they have additional special needs (Waller, 1974).

Helping people gain or regain skills and resources needed to live an effective life in the community, which is the focus of current rehabilitation technology, is a complex goal because mental disorders affect many domains of life relevant to a person's functioning in the community. These include, "activities of daily living, social skills, ability to manage money, social supports, work skills, life satisfaction, family relationships, burden to family members, use of leisure time, physical health care and personal safety" (Dickerson, 1997, p. 898). Skills training is used to remedy dysfunctions in the social, family, and vocational domains. When skills training is limited by the effects of a disorder, the goals of rehabilitation shift to assisting released patients in compensating for their deficits by locating supportive living and work environments (Liberman, 1988). Supportive living and work environments need to be integrated with other rehabilitation technology for preventing relapse of persons with SPMI, substance abuse, violence, sexual deviations, and other special needs.

Supported Housing

There is scarce information in the research literature on the community adjustment of offenders who had required psychiatric hospitalization while in prison (Feder, 1991a), although there is some information on other categories of mentally disordered offenders (Bogenberger, Pasewark, Gudeman, & Bieber, 1987; Pacht & Cowden, 1974; Rogers & Wettsetin, 1985; Sturgeon & Taylor, 1980). Yet in general it is known that good housing is an essential component for community rehabilitation because it is highly correlated with a number of measures of successful community adjustment (Ogilvie, 1997). Unfortunately, offenders with mental disorders often lack viable housing alternatives that can promote their adjustment in the community following release from correctional facilities. Regardless of which category of MDO is studied, available research indicates that they are provided minimal support from family or friends when they are released back to the community (Feder, 1991a, 1991b; Jacoby & Kozie-Peak, 1997). Because they also typically have had extensive histories of marginal social existence before their contacts with the criminal justice system, these offenders generally require some form of assistance with housing on release from correctional settings.

A position statement of the National Association of State Mental Health Program Directors (NASMHPD) asserts that people with serious psychiatric disabilities should have "the option of living in decent stable, affordable, safe housing, fully integrated in the community that maximizes their independence, where they have made the choice and that is coordinated by all key stakeholders" (Ogilvie, 1997, p. 20). Typically, this requires supported housing, which is any form of coordinated housing that complies with these key characteristics identified in the NASMHPD position statement.

Supported housing is considered an important alternative to the traditional forms of residential aftercare described by Budson (1988): transitional halfway houses, long-term group residences, cooperative apartments, lodge programs, work camps, foster care (family care), and board and care homes. These traditional residential services provide consumers a place to live that is not per se "a home in the context of a supportive community" (Telles, 1992, p. 53). That is, in addition to housing and mental health services, supportive housing offers consumers options for sharing a house or an apartment in a supportive social network (consisting primarily of consumers and staff) that will eventually become their permanent system of social support. This social network is also flexible in that the level of social interaction among community participants is determined by the consumers and not the residential program (Telles, 1992).

Another distinctive characteristic of supported housing is that tenants have the right "to refuse a reasonable number of prospective roommates before financial and other considerations take precedence over their wishes" (Telles, 1992, p. 61). The emphasis is to be placed in the philosophy of supported housing on increasing the choices available to consumers in selecting roommates and other levels of social support in the community, which is what distinguishes this form of housing from other traditional residential aftercare programming (Carling, 1990; Telles, 1992).

The research on supported housing consistently documents that persons living in the worst residential environments are the least likely to have their services met and typically experience increased rates of hospitalization (Ogilvie, 1997). In fact, many studies indicate lower rates of hospitalization for persons receiving supported housing (McCarthy & Nelson, 1991; Rimmerman, Finn, Schnee, & Klein, 1991). Other studies (e.g., Srebnik, Livingston, Gordon, & King, 1995) have documented that consumer choice in housing is positively associated with measures of client satisfaction and personal happiness. In addition, supported housing appears to be associated with having a positive effect on the social networks of patients (Goering et al., 1992) and tends to increase patient levels of independent functioning (Nelson, Hall, & Walsh-Bower, 1995). As might be expected, the influence of the housing program diminishes as support and supervision are reduced, which opens the door for community influences to take over.

Supported Employment

Work has been recognized as an essential prescription for happiness and recovery from mental illness throughout human history (WICHE, 1997). It was a key component of the moral treatment developed by Philippe Pinel in the early 1800s. In addition, "Noted authorities such as Rush, Freud and Kraepelin provided support for the role of work in treatment and rehabilitation." (Jacobs, 1988, p. 247). There also has been a longstanding connection between crime and the lack of a regular means for earning a living. Currie (1985) observed a consistent trend that documents this point in the criminological literature from the 1800s up until the present. Most of the studies that he reviewed indicated that large percentages of individuals incarcerated in prisons and jails were either without an established occupation or were not working full-time in the months before their arrest. In his view, because work is one of the most important ways for individuals to achieve integration in the wider society, "It isn't surprising that those excluded from the world of work will be held less tightly by the bonds that keep a society together" (Currie, 1985, p. 105). Exclusion from work is also highly correlated with "an increase in the incidence of physical and mental illness, asocial behavior, marital problems, and other distress following job loss" (Jacobs, 1988, p. 246).

Although work is included at some level in most measures of quality of life, individuals with serious mental impairments have significant difficulties with obtaining and maintaining employment (Watts, 1983; Jacobs, 1988). In the 1970s, when interest in work rehabilitation regained the attention of the professional community, less than 30% of discharged patients were able to obtain a job (Anthony, Buell, Sharratt, & Althoff, 1972; Watts, 1983). This triggered a number of studies that investigated factors that can predict post hospitalization employment. Many of these studies found that the best predictor was prehospital work history (Jacobs, 1988; Watts, 1983). These and other findings called into question the effectiveness of hospital-based vocational rehabilitation, which was the dominant approach to work restoration at that time.

On the other hand, vocational programs in well-known community rehabilitation centers such as Fountain House of New York (Beard, Malmud, & Rossman, 1978) showed high success rates. The Fountain House program used employment as a central approach to helping discharged mental patients adjust to the community (Jacobs, 1988). The results of research in these rehabilitation centers renewed interest in supported employment as a rehabilitation tool. Supported employment clients work for pay in competitive contexts.[1] "Clients work for pay, preferably the prevailing wage rate, as regular employees in integrated settings, and in regular contact with nonhandicapped workers, and receive ongoing support" (Bond, Drake, Museser, & Becker, 1997). Before the supported employment movement in psychiatric and vocational rehabilitation, most individuals with SPMI worked in nonintegrated or noncompetitive work settings because of myths about schizophrenia (Harding & Zahiner, 1995). For instance, it was widely believed in psychiatric rehabilitation that persons with schizophrenia could only work in low-level positions for short intervals of time. Moreover, it was believed that only about 15% or fewer were able to work in competitive environments (Bond et al., 1997; Harding & Zahniser, 1995). Views about competitive employment for the SPMI changed dramatically in the 1980s.

In the 1980s, supported employment was formally defined in the Rehabilitation Act of 1986 (revised in 1992). This act attempted to provide increased flexibility in developing alternatives to traditional vocational rehabilitation (Bond et al., 1997). It was initially pilot tested with persons with developmental disabilities as an alternative to the use of sheltered workshops. These pilot tests adhered to a novel approach to vocational rehabilitation that stressed placement before training (Wehman, 1981). Persons were successfully placed in positions with job coaches at the work site. The coaches provided intensive training for the clients to accomplish their job roles. Today, the job coach model is a dominant component of most supported employment programs. Other common components include "a goal of competitive employment, minimal screening for employability, avoidance of prevocational training, individualized placement instead of placement in enclaves or mobile work crews, time unlimited support, and consideration for client preferences" (Bond et al., 1997, p. 336).

As to supported employment, Bond and his colleagues (1997) identified six

---

[1]Supported employment differs from sheltered employment. The latter involves an individual working in a setting that affords them an opportunity to earn a living in a noncompetitive context. That is, sheltered employment provides disabled persons with opportunities for work who are not ready for the competitive marketplace. Although sheltered employment is recognized as a component in the traditional continuum of vocational rehabilitation services, we do not discuss it in this chapter because it is not typically related to offenders on aftercare status.

experimental studies, six descriptive studies, three surveys, and one study that used a quasi-experimental design. All of these studies identified significant gains in obtaining employment by patients who were participants in supported employment programs. That is, these programs are capable of helping ex-patients obtain employment in a competitive marketplace. For the available experimental studies, 58% of the supported employment clients were able to achieve competitive employment compared with 21% of the control clients. The results of these experiments also support the conclusion that clients in supported employment spend a longer time in employment and experience increased earnings compared to control individuals. These results suggest that supportive employment programs are a promising approach to the rehabilitation of psychiatric patients.[2] However, the results of these studies provided minimal support for the conclusion that supported employment can achieve the secondary effect of reducing patient symptoms (Bond et al., 1997). Other interventions, however, such as relapse prevention, are demonstrating significant promise in managing patient symptoms.

Relapse Prevention

Treatment in correctional institutions and hospitals bring about many qualitative and quantitative changes in the behavior of offenders with special needs, but maintaining these changes requires other forms of intervention in the aftercare process. Relapse prevention is an approach to treatment that was developed in the addictions literature that has shown significant promise in preventing relapse in psychiatric (Moller & Murphy, 1997) and in offender populations (Pithers, 1991). It relies heavily on self-help and psychoeducational principles in helping offenders address problems associated with maintaining desired behavioral outcomes achieved from completing the formal phase of a treatment program in a prison, hospital, or community setting (Gendreau, 1996; McMurran, 1996). Before developing relapse prevention, interventions focused primarily on treatment. Accordingly, we knew far more about inducing the cessation of symptoms and problem behaviors than about preventing relapse (George & Marlatt, 1989).

The relapse prevention model is guided by two conceptual principles:

> The first focuses on explaining the processes that operate in situations to promote the occurrence of a lapse and to facilitate escalation from a lapse to a relapse. The second component focuses on explaining the operation of more subtle processes that can gradually move the recovered addict toward a set of circumstances capable of inciting a lapse. (George & Marlatt, 1989, p. 7)

That is, offenders are taught in the relapse prevention model to identify psychological

[2]Some experts contend that the transitional employment program implemented at Foundation House differs minimally from current notions of supported employment in the psychosocial rehabilitation literature (Bond et al., 1997). Fountain House pioneered the use of a clubhouse model to make work activities available for all members of the club, regardless of their previous work experience. This model included assignments in transitional employment settings that were identified by staff through negotiations with community employers. Two early outcome studies of this program indicated "that ex-hospitalized patients who participate in the Fountain House program do better in terms of staying out of the hospital and working than nonparticipants" (Glasscote et al., 1971, p. 61).

and situational variables that place them at risk of relapse or reoffending. Lapses are anticipated and offenders are assisted in developing strategies to cope with these "slight slips" (George & Marlatt, 1989). The aim is to prevent the lapse or the behavioral slip from turning into a complete relapse. Treatment personnel are also expected to help offenders understand the connections between "seemingly unimportant decisions" that lead them closer to experiencing a relapse (Laws, 1989) and to help significant others in monitoring signs of relapse and in providing reenforcement for prosocial behavior (Gendreau, 1996). "In some cases exposure to a particular situation [e.g., social pressure] may trigger the sequence of events leading to an offence; in others, it may be a negative emotional state or a specific life event [e.g., interpersonal conflict], such as being reprimanded at work for poor performance" (Epps, 1996, p. 171; see also Cummings, Gordon, & Marlatt, 1980).

However, the sequence of factors that influence a relapse differ from offender to offender (Epps, 1996). The psychological and situational factors are always a concern to treatment professionals, but will have different implications for different kinds of behavioral outcomes. That is, a person experiencing a psychiatric relapse needs to focus on different kinds of high-risk situations from that of a person with addiction problems. For instance, Moller and Murphy (1997) have developed a program to aid persons with SPMI in distinguishing between three states of wellness: unstable, stable, and actualized. In these authors' opinion, relapse occurs when psychiatric symptoms reoccur for more than 24 hours and management strategies are not successful. Their goal is to sensitize patients to taking appropriate steps to prevent relapse when they are in the state of stable wellness. In stable wellness, the psychiatric symptoms are present, but the individual is able to maintain daily activities. In sum, although the high-risk situations might differ among treatment groups, it is assumed that the process of relapse prevention for addicts, sexual offenders, and mentally disordered offenders should follow similar pathways to recovery (National Institute of Drug Abuse [hereinafter NIDA], 1993).

Relapse prevention is a movement in rehabilitation that has triggered interesting research into how to best promote transitions to new crime-free and disorder-free lifestyles. Addiction and crime involve life choices and life styles within distinct subcultures that are incompatible with relapse prevention. A cross-cultural project funded by NIDA (1993) for developing effective aftercare for recovering addicts likened the experiences of this recovery process to that of an immigrant. The authors of this project wrote:

> Recovery is not just the cessation and deactivation of drug use: usually, it also demands adjustment to a new way of life within the culture of the larger community. . . . But—proceeding with the analogy—to make a truly new way of life and not just relocate the old one, people need much more than grit. People must have guidance, acquire new skills, and make new contacts so that they can cease being immigrants. (NIDA, 1993 p. 9)

This NIDA-sponsored project developed a model of relapse prevention and lifestyle change that included a randomized experimental design of the efficacy of this approach with opiate addicts that was evaluated in both America and Hong Kong. The results showed that during the study's follow-up period, aftercare group members, who received relapse prevention training and other aftercare services, abstained significantly more from the use of illicit opiates when compared to the controls (32 to 18%). The experimental intervention was also very effective in helping unemployed participants find jobs compared to controls. The substance abuse literature is replete with other outcome studies (Allsop & Saunders, 1989; Marlatt & Gordon, 1980) demonstrating the effectiveness of relapse prevention as an effective aftercare strategy, including dealing with criminal offenders with substance abuse problems (Gorski, Kelly, Havens, & Peters, 1993).

This technology has also been studied with sex offenders. In the early 1980s, California repealed its legislation that allowed mentally disordered sex offenders to be commited to state hospitals. However, a state hospital program was to be established for the voluntary transfer of selected sex offenders to the state hospital during the last two years of their prison terms. The Department of Mental Health in California established an evaluation design that compared the postrelease activities of three matched groups of research participants: a treatment group consisting of 77 sex offenders who volunteered for treatment and were randomly selected into the study, a volunteer control group consisting of sex offenders who volunteered for treatment but were not randomly selected for treatment, and a nonvolunteer control group consisting of prisoners who qualified for treatment but did not volunteer to participate. In other words, the design controlled for voluntarism as a factor that might bias the interpretation of the study's results.

Although 77 prisoners were selected into the treatment program, the follow-up study was conducted on 36 offenders who completed the treatment program, had a mean length of stay in the treatment program of 20.8 months, and a mean time at risk in the community of 6.5 months when the final data was collected. This group was compared to a matched sample of volunteer controls ($n = 32$) with a mean time at risk of 4.5 months and a matched sample of nonvolunteer controls ($n = 18$) with an at-risk mean time of 6.9 months. The treatment group and volunteer control group both received extensive relapse prevention training in the treatment program and underwent a specialized aftercare phase of the program. Comparisons of treatment group versus volunteer control groups did not differ in terms of criminal history variables, but the volunteer control group had higher rates of offenders with homosexual and bisexual child molester tendencies. The outcome results of this study indicated that one of the participants in the treatment group was returned to prison for a violation of parole. However, none of the participants in the treatment group was arrested for sex crimes. Aftercare providers also did not suspect any reoffenses for the treatment group. There were also no arrests for sex crimes in the other two comparison groups. Each of the other groups had persons returned to prison for parole violations: two in the volunteer control group and three in the control group. The results of this study are inconclusive primarily because individuals were only in the community for approximately 6.5 months (Marques, Day, Nelson, & Miner, 1989).

Another study of relapse prevention with sex offenders was conducted by Pithers and Cumming (1989) using the Vermont treatment program for sexual aggressors. It demonstrated that relapse prevention holds significant promise for prevention of relapse with this population. The Vermont program involves the collaborative efforts of mental health, probation, and parole professionals. Participants in the program experience special conditions of probation and parole that prohibit the offender from engaging in specific high-risk situations. Of the 167 offenders who received the treatment services in the Vermont project, six relapsed and a seventh was awaiting trial at the time of the evaluation. After six years, 4% of the 167 offenders relapsed, which was significantly less than data previously reported for sex offender populations (Pithers & Cumming, 1989). Further descriptions of the Pithers (1990) approach to the prevention of relapse is widely regarded in the literature as an effective approach to treating sex offenders (Andrews & Bonta, 1994; Blackburn, 1993; Epps, 1996).

Moreover, although relapse prevention is a useful approach in treating persons with SPMI (Birchwood, 1992; Moller & Murphy, 1997), there are no available outcome studies that document its utility in working with mentally disordered offenders. Among other factors, such research will have to incorporate support-system variables (e.g., monitoring of SPMI) that are likely to affect potential for relapse. For example, as noted previously monitoring of these persons is essential to identify personal and situational factors associated with relapse. Outcome studies that ignore the critical elements of the *system's* approach to improving relapse prevention are doomed to yield meaningless information.

Where Do We Go From Here

The research on aftercare services suggests that a variety of integrated approaches for handling various categories of offenders with special needs are likely to be effective. Despite this, the data is still relatively silent on integrating specific correctional strategies with proven mental health and psychosocial interventions. In other words, the field lacks data supporting specific models of how to structure the integration of clinical services in mental health with control-oriented services from the field of correctional supervision to achieve desired outcomes. This point is clinically important because control strategies widely used in ISPs can have negative or unforeseen consequences for persons with serious mental impairments.

The picture painted in this chapter of aftercare also illustrates that intensive interventions with teams of professionals providing supportive services is more effective than brokered case management with SPMI persons. However, we still know very little about how to select and how to prescribe the points at which these services should be provided, and we know very little of the relative effectiveness of programs that attempt to improve system linkages between programs in the criminal justice and the mental health system.

Finally, current literature on aftercare services does not include a clearly defined theory of need that can provide clear goals for actions for the dually diagnosed and the multiple problem offender (Wing, 1990). Our conceptions of need should have closer ties to our prescribed actions or systems of interventions in the field of criminal justice. The kinds of services deemed appropriate for a specific need still appear to be highly discretionary (Wing, 1990). Moreover, we have not empirically mapped all the relevant configurations of needs that are associated with proven service responses and differential clinical and criminal justice outcomes. For instance, what is the connection between quality of life needs of persons with SPMI and offender recidivism? Quality of life needs are factors that are highly correlated with forms of symptom and illness relapse. We know very little, however, about their connection with recidivism outcomes in various categories of mentally disordered offenders. In sum, aftercare is a critical topic in offender rehabilitation that still requires substantial programmatic research to clarify how to connect assessments of criminogenic, psychosocial, and clinical needs with prescriptive actions that have known effects on desired outcomes.

References

Abadinsky, H. (1997). *Probation and parole: Theory and practice* (6th ed.). Upper Saddle River, NJ: Prentice Hall.

Allen, F. A. (1977). Legal values and the rehabilitative ideal. In S. L. Radzinowicz & M. E. Wolfgang (Eds.), *Crime and justice: Volume II, The criminal in the arms of the law* (pp. 10–19). New York: Basic Books.

Allsop, B., & Saunders, S. (1989). Relapse and alcohol problems. In M. Gossop (Ed.), *Relapse and addictive behaviour* (pp. 11–40). London: Tavistock/Routledge.

Altschuler, D. M., & Armstrong, T. L. (1990). *Intensive aftercare for high-risk juveniles: An assessment.* Report presented to U.S. Department of Justice, Office of Juvenile Justice and Delinquency Prevention.

Altschuler, D. M., & Armstrong, T. L. (1994, September). *Intensive aftercare for high-risk juveniles: A community care model.* Washington, DC: U.S. Department of Justice, Office of Juvenile Justice and Delinquency Prevention, Office of Justice Programs.

American Friends Services Committee. (1971). *Struggle for justice.* New York: Hill & Wang.

Anderson, A. J. (1997). Comparative impact evaluation of two therapeutic programs for mentally ill chemical abusers. *The International Journal of Psychosocial Rehabilitation, 1(4),* http://www.psychosocial.com/compare.htm.

Andrews, D. A., & Bonta, J. (1994). *The psychology of criminal conduct.* Cincinnati, OH: Anderson.

Andrews, D. A., & Bonta, J. (1998). *The psychology of criminal conduct* (2nd ed.). Cincinnati, OH: Anderson.

Anglin, M. D., & Hser, I. (1990). Legal coercion and drug abuse treatment: Research findings and social policy implications. In J. A. Inciardi (Ed.), *Handbook of drug control in the United States* (pp. 151–176). Westport, CT: Greenwood.

Anthony, W. A. (1993). Recovery from mental illness: The guiding vision of the mental health service system in the 1990s. *Psychosocial Rehabilitation Journal, 16,* 11–23.

Anthony, W. A., & Blanch, A. (1989). Research on community support services: What have we learned. *Psychosocial Rehabilitation Journal, 12,* 55–73.

Anthony, W. W., Buell, G. J., Sharratt, S., & Althoff, M. (1972). Efficacy of psychiatry rehabilitation. *Psychological Bulletin, 78,* 447–456.

Armstrong, T. L. (1991). Introduction. In T. L. Armstrong (Ed.), *Intensive interventions with high-risk youths: Promising approaches in juvenile probation and parole* (pp. 1–26). Monsey, NY: Criminal Justice Press.

Ashford, J. B. (1997). Aftercare: The neglected phase of the juvenile justice process. In C. A. McNeece & A. R. Roberts (Eds.), *Policy & Practice in the Justice System* (pp. 29–47). Chicago: Nelson Hall.

Ashford, J. B., & LeCroy, C. W. (1993). Juvenile parole policy in the United States: Determinate versus indeterminate models. *Justice Quarterly, 10,* 179–195.

Bachrach, L. (1978). A conceptual approach to deinstitutionalization. *Hospital and Community Psychiatry, 29,* 573–578.

Bachrach, L. (1986). Dimensions of disability in the chronic mentally ill. *Hospital and Community Psychiatry, 37,* 981–982.

Barton, W. H., & Butts, J. A. (1990). Viable options: Intensive supervision programs for juvenile delinquents. *Crime & Delinquency, 36,* 238–256.

Beard, J. H., Malmud, T. J., & Rossman, E. (1978). Psychiatric rehabilitation and long-term rehospitalization rates: The findings of two research studies. *Schizophrenia Bulletin, 4*, 622–635.

Bennett, D. (1983). The historical development of rehabilitation services. In F. N. Watts and D. H. Bennett (Eds.), *Theory and practice of psychiatric rehabilitation* (pp. 15–42). Chichester, England: Wiley.

Birchwood, M. (1992). Early intervention in schizophrenia: Theoretical background and clinical strategies. *British Journal of Clinical Psychology, 31*, 257–278.

Blackburn, R. (1993). *The psychology of criminal conduct: Theory, research and practice.* Chichester, England: Wiley.

Blackburn, R. (1996). Mentally disordered offenders. In C. Hollin (Ed.), *Working with offenders: Psychological practice in offender rehabilitation* (pp. 119–149). Chichester, England: Wiley.

Bogenberger, R. P., Pasewark, R. A., Gudeman, H., & Bieber, S. L. (1987). Follow-up of insanity acquittees in Hawaii. *International Journal of Law and Psychiatry, 10*, 283–295.

Bond, G. R., Drake, R. E., Museser, K. T., & Becker, D. R. (1997). An update on supported employment for people with severe mental illness. *Psychiatric Services, 48*, 335–346.

Bond, G. R., McDonel, E. C., Miller, L. D., & Pensec, M. (1991). Assertive community treatment and reference groups: An evaluation of their effectiveness for young adults with serious mental illness and substance abuse problems. *Psychosocial Rehabilitation Journal, 15*, 31–43.

Bond, G., Miller, L., Krumwied, R., & Ward R. (1988). Assertive case management in three CMHCs: A controlled study. *Hospital and Community Psychiatry, 39*, 411–418.

Bond, G. R., Witheridge, T. F., Fincin, J., Wasmer, D., Webb, J., & Degraaf-kaser, R. (1990). Assertive community treatment for frequent users of psychiatric hospitals in a large city: A controlled study. *American Journal of Community Psychology, 18*, 865–891.

Borland, A., McRae, J., & Lycan, C. (1989). Outcomes of five years of continuous intensive case management. *Hospital and Community Psychiatry, 40*, 369–376.

Bower, K. (1992). *Case management by nurses.* Washington, DC: American Nurses Association.

Budson, R. D. (1988). Following hospitalization: Residential aftercare. In J. R. Lion, W. N. Adler, & W. L. Webb, Jr. (Eds.), *Modern hospital psychiatry* (pp. 384–402). New York: W. W. Norton.

Byrne, J., Lurigo, A. J., & Baird, C. (1989). The effectiveness of the new intensive supervision programs. *Research in Corrections, 2*, 1–48.

Byrne, J., & Pattavian, A. (1992). The effectiveness issues: Assessing what works in the adult community corrections system. In J. Byrne, A. Lurigio, & J. Petersilia (Eds.), *Smart sentencing: The emergence of intermediate sanctions* (pp. 281–303). Newbury Park, CA: Sage.

Carling, P. J. (1990). Major mental illness, housing supports. The promise of community integration. *American Psychologist, 45*, 969–975.

Carney, L. P. (1980). *Corrections: Treatment and philosophy.* Englewood Cliffs, NJ: Prentice-Hall.

Clear, T. R., Byrne, J. M., & Dvoskin, J. (1993). The transition from being an inmate: Discharge planning, parole and community-based services for mentally ill offenders. In H. J. Steadman & J. J. Cocozza (Eds.), *Mental illness in America's prisons* (pp. 131–157). Seattle, WA: National Coalition for the Mentally Ill in the Criminal Justice System.

Clement, P. F. (1993). The incorrigible child: Juvenile delinquency in the United States from the 17th through the 19th centuries. In A. G. Hess & P. F. Clement (Eds.), *History of juvenile delinquency* (pp. 453–490). Aalen, Germany: Scientia Verlag.

Clements, C. R. (1996). Offender classification: Two decades of progress. *Criminal Justice and Behavior, 23*, 121–143.

Cohn, A. (1994). History of probation and parole. In American Correctional Association (Eds.), *Field officer resource guide* (pp. 1–11). Baltimore: United Book.

Cullen, F. T., Wright, J. P. & Applegate B. K. (1996). Control in the community: The limits of reform. In A. T. Harland (Ed.), *Choosing correctional options that work: Defining the demand and evaluating the supply* (pp. 69–116). Thousand Oaks, CA: Sage.

Cummings, C., Gordon, J. R., & Marlatt, G. A. (1980). Relapse: Strategies of prevention and prediction. In W. R. Miller (Ed.), *The addictive behaviors* (pp. 291–321). Oxford: Pergamon Press.

Currie, E. (1985). *Confronting crime: An American challenge.* New York: Pantheon Books.

Curtis, J. L., Millman, E. J., Struening, E., & D'Ercole, A. (1992). Effect of care management on rehospitalization and utilization of ambulatory care services. *Hospital and Community Psychiatry, 43*, 895–899.

Dickerson, F. B. (1997). Assessing clinical outcomes: The community functioning of persons with serious mental illness. *Psychiatric Services, 48*, 897–902.

Dressler, D. (1959). *Practice and theory of probation and parole.* New York: Columbia University.

Duffee, D. E., & Clark, D. (1985). The frequency and classification of the needs of offenders in community settings. *Journal of Criminal Justice, 13*, 243–268.

Duffee, D. E., & Dufee, B. W. (1981). Studying the needs of offenders in prerelease centers. *Journal of Research in Crime and Delinquency, 18*, 251–253.

Duffy, K. G., & Wong, F. Y. (1996). *Community psychology.* Boston: Allyn & Bacon.

Ekdawi, M. Y., & Conning, A. M. (1994). *Psychiatric rehabilitation.* London: Chapman & Hall.

Epps, K. (1996). Sex offenders. In C. R. Hollins (Ed.), *Working with offenders: Psychological practice in offender rehabilitation* (pp. 150–187). Chichester, England: Wiley.

Erwin, B. S. (1986). Turning up the heat on probationers in Georgia. *Federal Probation, 50*, 17–24.

Fagan, J., Forst, M., & Vivoan, T. (1988). *Treatment and reintegration of violent juvenile offenders.* San Francisco: URSA Institute.

Falkin, G. P., Lipton, D. S., & Wexler, H. K. (1992). Drug treatment in state prisons. In D. R. Gerstein & H. J. Harwood (Eds.), *Treating drug problems: Volume 2* (pp. 89–131). Washington, DC: National Academy Press.

Feder, L. (1991a). A profile of mentally ill offenders and their adjustment in the community. *Journal of Psychiatry and Law, 19*, 79–98.

Feder, L. (1991b). A comparison of the community adjustment of mentally ill offenders with those from the general prison population: An 18-month follow-up. *Law and Human Behavior, 15*, 477–493.

Franklin, J., Solovitz, B., Mason, M., Clemons, J. R., & Miller, G. E. (1987). An evaluation of case management. *American Journal of Public Health, 77*, 674–678.

French, L. M. (1940). *Psychiatric social work.* London: Oxford University.

Fulton, B., & Stone, S. (1993). The promise of new ISP. *Perspectives* (Winter), 43–45.

Gendreau, P. (1996). The principles of effective interventions with offenders. In A. T. Harland (Ed.), *Choosing correctional options that work: Defining the demand and evaluating the supply* (pp. 117–130). Thousand Oaks, CA: Sage.

George, W. H., & Marlatt, G. A. (1989). Introduction. In D. R. Laws (Ed.), *Relapse prevention with sex offenders* (pp. 1–31). New York: Guilford Press.

Giardini, G. I. (1959). *The parole process.* Springfield, IL: Charles C. Thomas.

Glasscote, R. M., Cumming, E., Rutman, I. D., Sussex, J. N., & Glassman, S. M. (1971). *Rehabilitating the mentally ill in the community: A study of psychosocial rehabilitation centers.* Washington, DC: American Psychiatric Association.

Goering, P., Durbin, J., Foster, R., Boyles, S., Babiak, T., & Lancee, B. (1992). Social networks of residents in supportive housing. *Community Mental Health Journal, 28,* 199–214.

Goodstein, L., & Sontheimer, H. (1997). The implementation of an intensive aftercare program for serious juvenile offenders: A case study. *Criminal Justice and Behavior, 24,* 332–359.

Gorski, T. T., Kelley, J. M., Havens, L., & Peters, R. H. (1993). *Relapse prevention and the substance abusing criminal offender.* Rockville, MD: Center for Substance Abuse Treatment.

Greenwood, P. W., Deschenes, E. P., & Adams, J. (1993). *Chronic juvenile offenders: Final results from the Skillman aftercare experiment.* Santa Monica, CA: RAND.

Greer, W. C. (1991). Aftercare: Community integration following institutional treatment. In G. D. Ryan & S. L. Lane (Eds.), *Juvenile sexual offending* (pp. 377–390). Lexington, MA: D.C. Heath.

Gruenberg, E. M. (1967). Social breakdown syndrome—some origins. *American Journal of Psychiatry, 123,* 1481–1489.

Haines, T. H. (1920). Lessons from the principles governing the parole procedure in hospitals for the insane. In *Conference on Social Work* (pp. 159–166). Chicago: University of Chicago.

Harding, C. M., & Zahniser, J. (1995). Empirical correction of seven myths about schizophrenia. *Acta Psychiatrica Scandinavica, 90,* 140–146.

Hawthorne, W., & Hough, R. (1997). Integrated services for long-term care. In L. Minkoff & D. Pollack (Eds.), *Managed mental healthcare in the public sector: A survival manual* (pp. 205–216). Amsterdam: Harwood Academic.

Heilbrun, K., Bennett, W. S., Evans, J. H., Offutt, R. A., Reiff, H. J., & White, A. J. (1988). Assessing treatability in mentally disordered offenders: A conceptual and methodological note. *Behavioral Sciences & the Law, 6,* 479–486.

Heilbrun, K., & Griffin, P. A. (1993). Community-based forensic treatment of insanity acquittees. *International Journal of Law and Psychiatry, 16,* 133–150.

Henderson, A. Z., & Bell, D. K. (1995). Special needs offenders on probation and parole. In American Correctional Association (Ed.), *Field officer resource guide* (pp. 68–81). Baltimore: United Books.

Hippchen, L. J. (1978). Trends in classification philosophy and practice. In Committee on Classification and Treatment, American Correctional Association (Ed.), *Handbook of correctional classification: Programming for treatment and reintegration* (pp. 1–11). Cincinnati, OH: Anderson.

Home Office. (1987). *Mental Health Act 1983: Supervision and after-care of conditionally discharged restricted patients. Notes for the guidance of social supervisors.* London: Home Office Department of Health and Social Security.

Hudson, C. H. (1973). *Summary report: An experimental study of the different effects of parole supervision on a group of adolescent boys and girls.* Minneapolis: Minnesota Department of Corrections.

Hussey, F. A., & Duffee, D. E. (1980). *Probation, parole, and community field services.* New York: Harper & Row.

Intagliata, J. (1982). Improving the quality of community care for the chronically mentally disabled: The role of case management. *Schizophrenia Bulletin, 8,* 655–674.

Jacobs, H. E. (1988). Vocational rehabilitation. In R. P. Liberman (Ed.), *Psychiatric rehabilitation of chronic mental patients* (pp. 245–284). Washington DC: American Psychiatric Press.

Jacoby, J. E., & Kozie-Peak, B. (1997). The benefits of social support for mentally ill offenders: Prison-to-community transitions. *Behavioral Sciences and the Law, 15,* 483–501.

Joint Commission on Mental Illness and Health. (1961). *Action for mental health*. New York: Basic Books.

Klinkenberg, W. D., & Calsyn, R. J., (1996). Predictors of receipt of aftercare and recidivism among persons with severe mental illness: A review. *Psychiatric Services, 47*, 487–496.

Langan, P. A., & Cunniff, M. A. (1992). *Recidivism of felons on probation: 1986–89*. Washington, DC: National Institute of Justice.

Laws, D. R. (Ed.). (1989). *Relapse prevention with sex offenders*. New York: Guilford Press.

Liberman, R. P. (Ed.). (1988). *Psychiatric rehabilitation of chronic patients*. Washington, DC: American Psychiatric Press.

Lipton, F., Nutt, S., & Sabitini, A. (1988). Housing the homeless mentally ill: A longitudinal study of a treatment approach. *Hospital and Community Psychiatry, 39*, 40–45.

Macht, M. W., & Ashford, J. B. (1991). *Introduction to social work and social welfare* (2nd ed.). New York: Macmillan.

Marlatt, G. A., & Gordon, J. R. (1980). Determinants of relapse: Implications for the maintenance of behavior change. In P. O. Davidson & S. M. Davidson (Eds.), *Behavioral medicine: Changing health lifestyles* (pp. 410–452). New York: Brunner/Mazel.

Marques, J. K., Day, D. M., Nelson, C., & Miner, M. H. (1989). The sex offender treatment and evaluation project: California's relapse prevention program. In D. R. Laws (Ed.), *Relapse prevention with sex offenders* (pp. 247–267). New York: Guilford Press.

Martin, S. S., & Inciardi, J. A. (1997). Case management outcomes for drug-involved offenders. *Prison Journal, 77*, 168–183.

Martinson, R. (1974). What works? Questions and answers about prison reform. *The Public Interest, 35*, 22–54.

McCarthy, J., & Nelson, G. (1991). An evaluation of supportive housing for current and former psychiatric patients. *Hospital and Community Psychiatry. 42*, 1254–1256.

McMurran, M. (1996). Alcohol, drugs, and criminal behaviour. In C. R. Hollin (Ed.), *Working with offenders* (pp. 211–242). Chichester, England: John Wiley & Sons.

Meyer, A. (1922). Historical sketch and outlook of psychiatric social work. *Hospital Social Service, 5*, 22.

Minkoff, K. (1991). Program components of a comprehensive integrated care system for seriously mentally ill patients with substance disorders. In K. Minkoff & R. E. Drake (Eds.), *Dual Diagnosis of major mental illness and substance disorder* (pp. 13–27). San Francisco: Jossey-Bass.

Moller, M. D., & Murphy, M. F. (1997). The three r's rehabilitation program: A prevention approach for the management of relapse symptoms associated with psychiatric diagnosis. *Psychiatric Rehabilitation, 20*, 42–48.

Monahan, J., & Steadman, H. J. (1983). Crime and mental disorder: An epidemiological approach. In N. Morris & M. Tonry (Eds.), *Crime and justice: An annual review of research. Volume 3* (pp. 145–189). Chicago: University of Chicago.

Morse, G. A., Calsyn, R. J., Klinkenberg, W. D., Gerber, F., Smith, R., Tempelhoff, B., & Laeeq, A. (1997). An experimental comparison of three types of case management for homeless mentally ill persons. *Psychiatric Services, 48*, 497–503.

Moxley, D. P. (1997). *Case management by design: Reflections on principles and practices*. Chicago: Nelson-Hall.

National Institute of Drug Abuse. (1993). *Recovery training and self-help: Relapse prevention and aftercare for drug addicts*. Rockville, MD: National Institute of Drug Abuse.

Nelson, G., Hall, G. B., & Walsh-Bower, R. (1998). The relationship between housing characteristics, emotional well-being and the personal empowerment of psychiatric consumers/survivors. *Community Mental Health Journal, 34*, 57–69.

Ogilvie, R. J. (1997). The state of supported housing for mental health consumers: A literature review. *Psychiatric Rehabilitation Journal, 21*, 122–131.

Olfson, M. (1990). Assertive community treatment: An evaluation of the experimental evidence. *Hospital and Community Psychiatry, 41,* 634–641.

Pacht, A., & Cowden, J. (1974). An exploratory study of five hundred sex offenders. *Criminal Justice and Behavior, 1,* 13–20.

Palmer, T. B. (1991). Interventions with juvenile offenders: Recent and long term changes. In T. L. Armstrong (Ed.), *Intensive interventions with high risk youths: Promising approaches in juvenile probation and parole* (pp. 85–120). Monsey, NY: Criminal Justice Press.

Palmer, T. (1996). Programmatic and nonprogrammatic aspects of successful intervention. In A. T. Harland (Ed.), *Choosing correctional options that work: Defining the demand and evaluating the supply* (pp. 131–182). Thousand Oaks, CA: Sage.

Pearson, F. S. (1988). Evaluation of New Jersey's intensive supervision program. *Crime & Delinquency, 34,* 437–448.

Petersilia, J., & Turner, S. (1993). Evaluating intensive supervision probation/parole: Results of a nationwide experiment. In *Research in brief.* Washington, DC: National Institute of Justice.

Pisciotta, A. W. (1993). Child saving or child brokerage? The theory and practice of indenture and parole at the New York House of Refuge, 1825–1935. In A. G. Hess & P. F. Clement (Eds.), *History of juvenile delinquency* (pp. 533–555). Aalen, Germany: Scientia Verlag.

Pitch, T. (1995). *Limited responsibilities: Social movements and criminal justice.* London: Routledge.

Pithers, W. D. (1990). Relapse prevention with sexual aggressors: A method for maintaining therapeutic gain and enhancing external supervision. In W. W. Marshall, D. R. Laws, & H. E. Barbara (Eds.), *Handbook of Sexual Assault: Issues, theories, and treatment of offenders* (pp. 343–361). New York: Plenum Press.

Pithers, W. D. (1991). Relapse with sexual aggressors. *Forum on Corrections Research, 3,* 20–24.

Pithers, W. D., & Cumming, G. F. (1989). Can relapses be prevented? Initial outcome data from the Vermont Treatment program for sexual aggressors. In. D. R. Laws (Ed.), *Relapse prevention with sex offenders* (pp. 313–325). New York: Guilford Press.

Prendergast, M. L., Anglin, M. D., & Wellisch, J. (1995). Treatment for drug-abusing offenders under community supervision. *Federal Probation, 59,* 66–75.

President's Panel on Mental Retardation. (1962). *A proposed program for national action to combat mental retardation.* Washington, DC: U.S. Government Printing Office.

Ragins, M. (1997). Recovery: Changing from a medical model to a psychosocial rehabilitation mode. *The Journal 5*(3), 1–7. Also available online at: http://www.mhsource.com.

Reinhardt, B., & Shepherd, G. L. (1994). Behavioral health case review: Utilization review or case management? One company's view. In S. Shueman, W. G. Troy, & S. L. Mayhugh (Eds.), *Managed behavioral health care* (pp. 76–91). Springfield, IL: Charles C. Thomas.

Rimmerman, A., Finn, H., Schnee, J., & Klein, I. (1991). Token reinforcement in the psychosocial rehabilitation of individuals with chronic mental illness is it effective over time? *Journal of Rehabilitation Research, 14,* 123–130.

Rogers, R., & Wettstein, R. (1984). Relapse of NGRI outpatients: An empirical study. *International Journal of Offender Therapy and Comparative Criminology, 28,* 227–235.

Romig, D. A. (1978). *Justice for children: An examination of juvenile delinquent rehabilitation programs.* New York: Human Sciences Press.

Rose, S. M., & Moore, V. L. (1995). Case management. In R. I. Edwards & J. G. Hopps (Eds.), *Encyclopedia of social work* (19th ed.) (pp. 335–340). Washington, DC: National Association of Social Workers Press.

Rosenheck, R., Neale, M., Leaf, P., Milstein, R., & Frishman, L. (1995). Multisite experimental cost study of intensive psychiatric community care. *Schizophrenia Bulletin, 21,* 129–140.

Rossler, W., Loffler, W., Fatkenheuer, B., & Reicher-Rossler, A. (1992). Does case management reduce the rehospitalization rate? *Acta Psychiatrica Scandinavica, 86*, 445–449.

Sechrest, L., White, S. O., & Brown, E. (Eds.). (1979). *The rehabilitation of criminal offenders: Problems and prospects.* Washington, DC: National Academy of Sciences.

Shepherd, G. (1990). Case management. In W. Watson & A. Grounds (Eds.), *The mentally disordered offender in an era of community care: New directions in provision* (pp. 166–176). Cambridge: Cambridge University Press.

Smith, S. G. (1912). *Social pathology.* New York: Macmillian.

Solomon, P., & Draine, J. (1995). One-year outcomes of a randomized trial of case management with seriously mentally ill clients leaving jail. *Evaluation Review, 19*, 256–273.

Solomon, P. L., Gordon, B. H., & Davis, J. M. (1984). *Community services to discharged psychiatric patients.* Springfield, IL: Charles Thomas.

Sperry, L., Brill, P. L., Howard, K. I., & Grissom, G. R. (1996). *Treatment outcomes in psychotherapy and psychiatric interventions.* New York: Brunner/Mazel.

Spica, R. (1993). What is between human services and offender adjustment? *Perspectives* (Winter) 24–26.

Srebnik, D., Livingston, J., Gordon, J., & King, D. (1995). Housing choice and community success for individuals with serious and persistent mental illness. *Community Mental Health Journal, 31*, 139–152.

Stein, L. I., & Santos, A. B. (1998). *Assertive community treatment of persons with severe mental illness.* New York: W. W. Norton.

Stein, L. I., & Test, M. A. (1980). An alternative to hospital treatment: Conceptual model, treatment program and clinical evaluation. *Archives of General Psychiatry, 37*, 302–397.

Stroul, B. (1989). Community support systems for persons with long-term mental illness: A conceptual framework. *Psychosocial Rehabilitation Journal, 12*, 9–26.

Stroup, T. S., & Dorwart, R. (1997). Overview of public sector managed mental health care. In K. Minkoff & D. Pollack (Eds.), *Managed mental health care in the public sector: A survival manual.* (pp. 1–12). Amsterdam: Harwood Academic Press.

Studt, E. (1972). *Surveillance and service in parole: Report of the parole action study MR-166.* Los Angeles: Institute of Government and Public Affairs, University of California.

Sturgeon, V., & Taylor, J. (1980). Report of a five-year follow up study of mentally disordered sex offenders released from Atascadero State Hospital in 1973. *Criminal Justice Journal, 4*, 31–63.

Telles, L. (1992). The clustered apartment project: A conceptually coherent supported housing model. In L. I. Stein (Ed.), *Innovative community mental health programs* (pp. 53–64). San Francisco: Jossey-Bass.

Turner, S., Petersilia, J., Deschenes, E. P. (1992). Evaluating intensive supervision probation/parole (ISP) for drug offenders. *Crime & Delinquency, 38*, 539–556.

Waller, I. (1974). *Men released from prison.* Toronto: University of Toronto Press.

Watts, F. (1983). Employment. In F. N. Watts & D. H. Bennett (Eds.), *Theory and practice of psychiatric rehabilitation* (pp. 215–240). New York: John Wiley & Sons.

Watts, F., & Bennett, D. (1983). Introduction: The concept of rehabilitation. In F. N. Watts & D. H. Bennett (Eds.), *Theory and practice of psychiatric rehabilitation* (pp. 3–14). New York: John Wiley & Sons.

Wehman, P. (1981). *Competitive employment: New horizons for severely disabled individuals.* Baltimore, MD: Brooks.

Weil, M., Karls, J. M., & Associates. (1985). *Case management in human service practice.* San Francisco: Jossey-Bass.

Western Interstate Commission for Higher Education. (1997). The role of work in recovery from mental illness. *West Link, 18*(2). http://www.wiche.edu/mental health/June97.

Wheeler, G. R. (1978). *Counter-deterrence.* Chicago: Nelson Hall.

Wilson, D., Tien, G., & Eaves, D. (1995). Increasing the community tenure of mentally disordered offenders: An assertive case management program. *International Journal of Law and Psychiatry*, *18*, 61–69.

Wing, J. K. (1990). Defining need and evaluating services. In W. Watson & A. Grounds (Eds.), *The mentally disordered offenders in an era of community care: New directions in provision* (pp. 90–101). Cambridge: Cambridge University Press.

Zander, K. (1995). Collaborative care: Two effective strategies for positive outcomes. In K. Zander (Ed.), *Managing outcomes through collaborative care: The application of care-mapping and case management* (pp. 1–37). Chicago: American Hospital Association.

Part VI

Systems and Settings

Chapter 15
SYSTEMS CONSIDERATIONS IN TREATING JUVENILE OFFENDERS WITH MENTAL DISORDERS

Craig Winston LeCroy, Phillip Stevenson, and Gordon MacNeil

Beginning with the establishment of the juvenile court in Chicago at the outset of the 20th century, there have been two criminal justice systems in place: one for adult offenders and one for juvenile offenders. The first juvenile court systemized an idea that has been around for several thousand years—that youthful offenders should be treated differently than adult offenders. Fundamental differences in the criminal justice system's response to the juvenile and adult offenders suggest that they are not "cut from the same cloth."

The original juvenile court was founded on an image of the juvenile offender as a neglected, abandoned, or poorly socialized child in need of guidance. It is this image of the juvenile offender that drives the juvenile justice system's philosophy of *parens patriae*—the notion that the court has the responsibility to act in place of the parent of the young offender. This portrait of the youthful offender is not of a criminal in training or a "born" criminal but instead of a misguided and poorly socialized child who is in need of supervision and care for the condition(s) that resulted in his or her involvement with the juvenile justice system. Consistent with this image of the young offender, the juvenile justice system originally emphasized treatment strategies over punitive strategies. One might assume, then, that the system would be well-prepared to treat a wide variety of afflictions, including mental disorders, thought to be contributing factors or correlates of youthful offending. Unfortunately, when it comes to mental disorders that is not the case.

Although mental health service provision has always been an integral part of rehabilitation strategies (Aber & Reppucci 1987), the juvenile justice system has been ill-prepared to treat youthful offenders with mental disorders (Bederow & Reamer 1981). Problems that have plagued the development of programs for juvenile offenders with mental disorders include difficulty in determining which agency or agencies are responsible for treatment, the sporadic and nonsystematic criteria used to identify the mentally disordered, the high cost of specialized mental health interventions, and more recently, the call for more punitive and less treatment-oriented responses to the juvenile offender. These problems have impeded the juvenile court's attempts at rehabilitating the juvenile offender.

In this chapter, we address systems considerations in the provision of services to juvenile offenders with mental disorders. No discussion of the U.S. justice system's response to juvenile crime can ignore the theoretical and philosophical issues that surround crime and the criminal. As such, we begin with a discussion of how criminological theory and the policies derived from contrasting images of the juvenile offender have informed official responses to youthful offending. We argue that the juvenile offender is neither a cold and calculating rational actor insensitive to the costs of punishment nor a mindless individual acting on motivations beyond his or her control. As a result, crime control strategies derived from either one of these erroneous images of the juvenile offender will yield unsatisfactory results. A complex image of the juvenile offender must be kept in mind when determining official responses to delinquency.

We then move to a discussion on the issues that affect the juvenile justice system's response to juvenile offenders with mental disorders. Some of the questions we seek answers to are (a) How do we decide who is in need of treatment? (b) Who gets treatment? (c) Who is responsible for treatment? and (d) Who pays for treatment? We conclude this chapter with a discussion of the policy goals of a juvenile justice system dealing with mentally disordered juvenile offenders.

A Complex Image of the Juvenile Offender

Punitive versus treatment-oriented responses to criminal offending are derived from contrasting images of the offender. Punitive responses to youthful offending contradict the juvenile court's image of the youthful offender as an afflicted youth in need of treatment. Instead of care and treatment, proponents of increasingly punitive responses to delinquency argue that the youthful offender is a "criminal in training" who must be severely punished for his or her criminal ways. Driving the call for an increase in punitive responses to juvenile offending is an image of the youthful offender as a hedonistic youth pursuing pleasure in behaviors that are in violation of our legal codes. This image represents a return to classical criminology and its core assumption that offenders are rational individuals who weigh the costs and benefits of behavior.

Much of the work in criminological theory and practice has polarized around these contrasting images of the juvenile offender. Theoretical positivists assume a naturally social actor who, without some force that drives the individual to delinquency, would never think of offending on his or her own (for example, the theories of Cloward & Ohlin, 1960; Cohen, 1955; Merton, 1938; Sutherland & Cressey, 1978). Official response to delinquency derived from this perspective would seek a "cure" for the cause of the youthful offender's affliction, whether it be poverty, lack of success in school, involvement in deviant subcultures, or mental disorders. The war on poverty, school-based interventions (e.g., Headstart), and the use of gang interdiction units in police departments are just a few examples of delinquency-reduction strategies consistent with the positivist perspective.

In contrast, theoretical classicists assume a rational, hedonistic individual (for example the theories of Beccaria 1764/1963 and Bentham 1789/1970). Derived from the logic of the classical perspective, the response of the juvenile justice system would be to increase the costs of delinquent behavior, resulting in correspondingly severe penalties for delinquent acts. This strategy has received public and political support of late.

Given the durability of both theoretical camps and the empirical support for theories within these camps, one must conclude that an image integrating components from both perspectives is most useful for the criminal justice practitioner.[1] The most accurate image of the youthful offender falls somewhere between the extreme images

---

[1]This is a conclusion that is reflected in the growth of theories of crime that fall into a "neo-classical" classification. Neoclassical theories combine assumptions from both the positivist and classical perspectives.

of the misguided, poorly socialized, and afflicted youth and the cold and calculating young criminal. Effective criminal justice policy cannot rely on official responses derived from just one perspective. Both perspectives have merit, and responses to delinquency that are suggested by the logic of the two perspectives must be provided. An effective juvenile justice system must view the youthful offender with a great deal of sensitivity to the wide variety of "causes" of delinquency. Operating with the understanding that the typical juvenile delinquent has been affected by multiple factors that have led to his or her offending, the juvenile justice system's response to delinquency can not be solely punitive. Harsh punishment of the youthful offender, who because of circumstances beyond his or her total control is led to delinquency, is ineffective at best and counterproductive and cruel at worst. This is not to say that the youthful offender is absolved of all responsibility for his or her actions. Instead, we argue that the youthful offender is often times beset with problems, such as mental disorders, that retributive responses alone will not address. The juvenile justice system cannot rely solely on harsh punishments that are ineffective at deterring those who are "driven" to crime. Nor can the system focus exclusively on treatment of those who are unlikely to respond positively to such efforts. Instead, the juvenile justice system must be prepared to provide both punishment and treatment for complex youthful offenders.

More specific to this chapter, the complex image of the juvenile offender underscores the complexity of the problem that plagues the juvenile justice system's responses to juvenile offenders with mental disorders. Both punitive and rehabilitative responses to the juvenile offender must be provided (as well as reparative and reintegrative responses that will be discussed later). What follows is our perspective on some of the more significant issues that face the juvenile justice system when dealing with juvenile offenders with mental disorders.

Organizational and Financial Considerations

Critical aspects in treating juvenile offenders with mental disorders include organizational and financial factors. Major considerations include, Who is in need of treatment? Who gets treatment? Who is responsible for treatment? And who pays for treatment?

How Do We Decide Who Is in Need of Treatment?

There are specific behaviors or acts that juvenile court judges generally respond to by ordering mental health evaluations. Indications of bizarre behavior or heinous crimes almost automatically trigger mental health evaluations (Barnum & Keilitz, 1992; Fagan, 1991). Other offenses, including sexually-oriented illegal acts, homicidal acts, or self-injurious behavior also commonly elicit evaluations. Barnum and Keilitz (1992) stated that "clinical evaluation is done on the basis of risk factors such as seriousness of offense, self-destructive, aggressive, or bizarre behavior, and possibly serious family discord factors such as a history of child abuse" (p. 55). Thus obvious or dramatic aspects of mental disorder are flags to the courts that mental health services are warranted.

Judges have two basic purposes in mind when ordering a mental health evaluation for a juvenile offender (Barnum & Keilitz, 1992). The first purpose is to address specific legal issues that may arise, such as assessing the dangerousness of the individual, determining the individual's competence to stand trial, and his or her ability to consent to treatment. In this sense, the institution is trying to meet its legal requirement to protect the individual and others from harm (O'Leary, 1989). The second purpose is to determine the individual's clinical needs—in other words, to determine if the juvenile is amenable to treatment. In some instances these two purposes overlap, as in the case of juvenile transfers or waivers to criminal courts (Sacks & Reader, 1992). Mental health evaluations for dispositional purposes may address issues of incapacitation, deterrence, retribution, and rehabilitation, or they may only address concern for public safety (Applebaum, 1991). Evaluations for amenability to treatment go beyond assessing specific diagnosis. These evaluations examine features of the individual's situation that may contribute to his or her ability to respond to treatment, as well as logistical concerns about which resources are available to the youthful offender (Barnum & Keilitz, 1992). As Barnum and Keilitz stated,

> To be useful, an amenability to treatment evaluation needs to avoid limiting itself to general treatment prognostication. It needs to offer explicit treatment recommendations that are consistent with the goals of the institutions for which they are performed, and grounded in the real capacities of those institutions to provide the sort of care and treatment which is being recommended. (p. 64)

More subtle problems such as anxiety problems or depression are not as readily identified. The general intent is to identify those most seriously mentally disordered, but offenders suffering from internally-oriented disorders (e.g., depression, anxiety, and obsessions) may not get the same response as those whose disorder disrupts others. This oversight is inconsistent with the fundamental goal of our juvenile system: Treatment for the affliction that led to juvenile offending. It is plausible that these internally oriented disorders lead to juvenile offending just as surely as more overtly directed disorders. Depression can lead to drug use and abuse, for example, and obsessions can lead to the stalking of the object of the obsession. The seemingly benign nature of a mental disorder does not necessarily result in a benign behavior.

In addition to the problem of less dramatic or overt disorders being overlooked in the selection of offenders for treatment, broader problems of classification hamper the juvenile justice system's ability to select appropriate candidates for mental health treatment. There are three broad categories that encompass the range of childhood and adolescent disorders: (a) emotional disorders, (b) behavioral disorders, and (c) mental disorders. Emotional disorders are characterized by their effect on an individual's emotional state. Examples of emotional disorders include separation anxiety, depression, and bipolar disorder. Behavioral disorders are characterized by disruptive behavior, typically in the home or school. Examples of behavioral disorders include conduct disorders, attention-deficit hyperactivity disorder, and oppositional-defiant disorder. Finally, personality disintegration and loss of contact with the environment characterize mental disorders. One example is schizophrenia.

Unfortunately, a significant problem in defining mental health problems is that the terms *emotional, behavioral,* and *mental disorders* are used interchangeably in the literature. For example, the National Institute of Mental Health has identified mental, behavioral, and developmental disorders as focuses of concern in its discussion of seriously emotionally disturbed children and adolescents (NIMH, 1990). It is imperative that we are consistent in our approaches to diagnosing mental disorders. Without this consistency, there is little hope for aggregating empirical work that will lead to accurate and specific assessment of mental disorders.

Merely identifying signs and symptoms and determining a diagnostic label, however, does not resolve the issue of who should receive treatment. Social conditions and environmental stressors and norms partially determine individual behavior. Social interactions with family, peers, and authority figures also contribute to specific behaviors. For example, consider a juvenile with a serious history of child abuse who displays violent behavior when drunk. Consideration must be given to the impact of family socialization, the failure of schools, and society's inability to provide needed support. Thus the extent to which we focus on the behavior, cognition, or emotion eliciting the identification of "mental health problem" becomes a "fundamental social and moral judgment, not only an empirical epidemiological question" (Barnum & Keilitz, 1992, p. 56).

Finally, a juvenile offender's emotional, cognitive, and physical development must be considered when making determinations about consequences for behaviors. For example, we do not expect juveniles at age 12 to demonstrate the same maturity as those at 17 years of age. It is not surprising that juveniles coming in contact with the juvenile justice system typically demonstrate developmental delays, in part because (if their offense is based on an act that has been repeated often) peers who demonstrate appropriate behaviors often ostracize them. Furthermore, most researchers agree that the earlier a juvenile interacts with the justice system particularly for index crimes (criminal acts whether committed by juveniles or adults such as robbery, assault, rape, or homicide), the greater his or her problems are likely to be (Dryfoos, 1990).

Determining Who Gets Treatment

The simple answer to the question of how youth are selected for treatment is that juvenile court judges request evaluations and act on the input of mental health professionals. In some states, all adjudicated youth receiving dispositions of incarceration are first sent to diagnostic facilities where they are educationally, psychologically, and medically evaluated before being placed in the most appropriate setting (Hodge & Andrews, 1996). Where diagnostic facilities are not used, mental health personnel visiting the offender in a detention facility generally perform court-ordered psychiatric evaluations.

But the question of how judges select youth for assessment and treatment is difficult to answer. This issue has both process and content aspects; how do we go about identifying those juveniles in need of mental health services, and what criteria are acceptable for the classification of "mental disorder" sufficient to receive those services (Barnum & Keilitz, 1992)? Although there are limiting factors, some mental disorders are generally acknowledged to be severe enough to warrant treatment in nearly all cases. Florid psychosis with an inability to distinguish internal and external stimuli and depression when the symptoms include active suicidal ideation are two of these conditions (Barnum & Keilitz, 1992). There is also general consensus that problems such as aggressiveness, impulsivity, and noncompliance are more likely to endure than problems of anxieties and fears (Quay & Perry, 1987), and as a result are more likely to result in treatment. But beyond this, there is no consistent agreement that any specific disorder requires mental health intervention by the juvenile justice system.

The heterogeneity of diagnostic labels such as "conduct disorder" require that determinations be made on a case-by-case basis (Dryfoos, 1990). In addition, having arrived at a clinical determination about the specific disorder does not always identify the degree to which the individual is functionally impaired. Although the *DSM* (American Psychiatric Association, 1994) typically states that there must be functional impairment to receive a *DSM* diagnosis, most mental health reports do not include the Axis IV and V codes describing the extent of these impairments.

Whereas the offender's anticipated ability to respond to treatment was once the driving force in determining who received mental health services, more recent determinations are based on judges' impressions that a juvenile is at high risk and needs intensive services (Barnum & Keilitz, 1992). This shift suggests that the courts are moving from a prescriptive position based on resource management to a descriptive position based on the idea that all those in need of services should receive them. Those who find merit in the original motivations of the juvenile court—the treatment and rehabilitation of youth in need—welcome this philosophical change in the juvenile courts.

Finally, specifically addressing the issue of which criteria will be used and how youth will be assessed for treatment, Wiebush, Baird, Krisberg, and Onek (1995) suggest that any system including differential interventions should have

1. Clearly specified criteria for the various programs and levels of intervention;
2. Adequate methods for assessing the degree to which youth meet those criteria; and
3. A selection process that ensures that youth targeted for intervention at each level of the system are in fact youth who are served at that level.

Determining which youth require mental health services should incorporate these components. Wiebush et al. commented that potential problems stemming from offender–intervention mismatches include increased risk to public safety if settings are not sufficiently restrictive, ineffective use of resources where overly-restrictive settings are used for youth who do not require them, and the contamination of program evaluations when intended target populations are not actually being served.

One problem relative to the selection process and definition of which juvenile offenders should get mental health services deserves special comment. Minority youth are overrepresented in the American juvenile justice system, and those same youth are underserved by the mental health system (Briscoe, 1996; Howell, Krisberg, & Jones, 1995; Lewis, Shanok, Cohen, Klingfeld, & Frisone, 1980). Black youths are less likely to be referred to mental health facilities in lieu of incarceration than are White youths, more likely to be sent to public rather than private correctional facilities, and more likely to be detained in the most secure facilities (Snyder & Sickmund, 1995). Lewis et al. (1980) also noted that Black youth are less likely than White youth to have psychopathology identified. Recent efforts have been made to address this discrepancy, including attempts to increase the cultural sensitivity of those conducting assessments (Briscoe, 1996). These efforts warrant continuation.

Determining Who Is Responsible for Treatment

Troubled children typically come to the attention of the state through three systems: child welfare, mental health, and juvenile justice (Maloy, 1995). Children in these systems have similar needs and place similar demands on the systems in which they are involved (National Council of State Legislatures Health and Mental Health Program, 1989; National Council of Juvenile and Family Court Judges, 1984; Shanok & Lewis, 1977). Often it is the job of the judge of the juvenile court, by virtue of his or her jurisdictional authority to provide permanency planning and services necessary to ensure stable and therapeutically sound environments for youth. It is, therefore, the judge's responsibility to determine which system will bear the primary responsibility for meeting the needs of the child (Hardin, 1992; Maloy, 1995). As a consequence, there is an increasing awareness of the gatekeeping role of the court and the need to coordinate services and funding between the three major systems (Maloy, 1995).

The overall goal is placing the offender in an appropriate setting. Although most incarcerated juvenile offenders will be appropriately placed in detention settings in which they will benefit from the structure and consistency provided by that setting (e.g., correctional facilities, training schools, or group homes), those with serious mental disorders will usually respond best in facilities focusing on mental health needs, such as hospitals or residential treatment centers (Kalogerakis, 1992).

But not all jurisdictions base placement decisions on the individual's needs. Some states (e.g., Colorado and Arizona) have taken the position that adjudicated youth are the responsibility of the juvenile justice system and that the correctional system has the responsibility to provide adequate staff and programs (Briscoe, 1996). Other states, such as Oregon and Massachusetts, have placed the responsibility for providing mental health treatment on the state's mental health department or even private providers under the authority of the mental health department. In Texas, youths found to have a mental illness are returned to the committing court for further action (Briscoe, 1996). Texas youth under the juvenile justice system's care, who are not suitable for mental health treatment outside the justice system, have services provided by the justice system.

A general principle of psychological treatment, the least restrictive environment, should have an effect on placement decisions. This principle holds that an offender should be placed in the least restrictive environment that adequately meets the needs of both the individual and society (Wiebush, Baird, Krisbert, & Onek, 1995). Ashford and LeCroy (1988, p. 48) noted that decision making for juvenile offenders is "predicated on the assumption that at the crux of any placement of supervision decision is an issue of restrictiveness." Risk assessments have historically focused on treatment needs (Baird, 1984), but increasingly they are focusing on custody decisions regarding the risks of disruptive behavior, assaultive potential, and potential for victimization (Wiebush et al., 1995).

To date there is little empirical information about how juvenile courts deal with various types of youth and what effect these differences have on disposition decisions and ultimate outcomes for these juveniles and their families. Without a doubt, research that studies the relationship between mental disorders in juvenile offenders and their subsequent placement, as well as the effect that placement decisions have on the juvenile's future behavior, is warranted.

Determining Who Pays for Treatment

A major issue in interactions among agencies is funding for services—who will pay for specialized services necessary for youth whose problems extend beyond the services normally provided by the agency? Traditionally, a categorical approach to multiagency funding has been used—funding flows from multiple funding streams that are separately regulated by federal or state agencies (Meyers, 1994). And funding is often not made available until a crisis occurs and then limited resources are provided (Cole, 1997). Because it is the norm for local and state agencies to consider themselves underfunded to begin with, they are judicious in accepting responsibility for new clients. An additional problem is that the categorical funds that are made available are often limited to expensive inpatient treatment prohibiting the development of alternative treatments that emphasize community reintegration. Making treatment money service-specific creates barriers to developing effective alternative treatments (Cole, 1997).

Stroul and Friedman (1986) have suggested a "system of care" that highlights the need for wrap-around services that focus on the needs of the client rather than focusing on which agency funds those services. Also by "wrapping" services around clients they can often be treated with less restrictive and less expensive alternatives (Stroul, 1993). For example, funds may be used to hire a behavioral technician to train a teacher in behavior management, allowing a child to remain in a school setting rather than be placed in a more secure and costly residential setting, or a youth will be detained for only one or two days during a crisis period and then receive intensive services rather than be placed in a hospital.

A new funding strategy is becoming more prevalent in many states, often referred to as flexible funding and flexible services (Kutash & Rivera, 1996; Rog, 1995). This model is based on the state setting aside a pool of money that is designated for the provision of *services* to a defined population in need (for example, multiple-needs children). Assessment panels representing various agencies (child welfare, mental health, juvenile justice, and so on) review cases brought before them to determine eligibility. Usually the criteria concern multiple problems in the family or individual, potential for out-of-home placement, and so forth. Clients meeting specified criteria are eligible for money from this pool. Agencies coordinate their provision of services to meet all of the identified needs of the client. This funding approach is similar to a basic managed care model in which costs are controlled and efforts are focused by using review techniques specified by the agency (Cole, 1997).

The important distinction is that the money follows the client; it does not flow directly to the agencies providing the services. This is both a technical and political difference because it requires agencies to consider their funding as a consequence of providing services to clients rather than vice versa (Meyers, 1994). Although flexible services and flexible funding options are becoming increasingly common for clients in community settings (Meyers, 1994), these possibilities are more limited when youth are placed in locked facilities. Indeed, managed behavioral health plans are just now being developed for "intensive care" products that provide integrated case management (Cole, 1997). Nonetheless, flexible funding strategies are important for incarcerated youth when we consider their release and return to the community.

Managed care can facilitate the shift to home and community care settings if properly directed by the purchasers of the services (Cole, 1997).

Federal health care financing regulations play an important role in determining funding for youth in juvenile justice, even though Health Care Financing Administration regulations stipulate that no individual in a correctional institution is eligible for Medicaid. Most states have found ways to obtain Medicaid-funded mental health services for offenders based on exceptions to these regulations (Barnum & Keilitz, 1992). Often, youth placed in licensed residential child care institutions or primarily medical facilities continue to be eligible for Medicaid funding reimbursement. In addition, some states (such as Massachusetts) have decided to offer Medicaid-funded mental health services to incarcerated youth even when the federal government does not reimburse them. These states have found that they can contract for services at Medicaid rates that are better than they can negotiate otherwise (Shostak, 1991, as cited in Barnum & Keilitz, 1992). For decades, health insurance has facilitated the process of "transinstitutionalization"—diverting youth to residential treatment centers, private psychiatric hospitals, and chemical dependency programs rather than allowing them to be incarcerated (Maloy, 1995). It is too early to assess the effects a more managed care approach will have on the funding of mental health services for adjudicated youth—even in locked facilities.

Finally, the single largest financial barrier to treatment remains an insufficient amount of resources to meet needs. Although treatment has become much less of a priority of late, most states recognize a statutory right to treatment (Alexander, 1989). Legal cases have established that minimal care for psychiatric and mental health concerns reflect indifference to urgent medical problems. Psychiatric care is included in the right to medical care. In particular, *H.C. by Hewett v. Jarrard 1986* (Alexander, 1989) established that juvenile detainees have the same rights to medical care as convicted offenders and that a delay of three days in treating the juvenile constituted deliberate indifference.

Juvenile Justice System Policy Goals for Mentally Disordered Juvenile Offenders

The complex image of the juvenile offender as a youth who must be held accountable for his or her actions, as well as a child in need of treatment for mental disorders, underscores the difficult task of determining the appropriate justice system response. In the current political climate where advocates of a "get tough on crime" philosophy seek severe and swift retribution for the actions of youthful offenders, harsh punishment is presumed. But the high incidence of mental disorders found in juvenile offenders indicates that treatment must be made available to youthful offenders whenever it is deemed appropriate and potentially effective (Melton & Pagliocca, 1992).

Balancing the Needs of All Involved

Making juvenile justice determinations more complex, the efforts of victim advocacy organizations have provided the victims of crime and delinquency a much deserved position of influence over official responses to juvenile offending. The result is that in juvenile courts, a restitution agreement arrived at during a mediation session between victim and offender often becomes part of the disposition of the youthful offender and in some cases an alternative to formal juvenile court processing.

Finally, with the development of restorative juvenile justice strategies (Bazemore, 1995), community involvement in the juvenile justice process now includes efforts to reintegrate the juvenile offender into the community. Given the needs of the key stakeholders in the process (i.e., the offender, the victim, and the community), the following question arises. Given the complex image of the juvenile offender and the multiple needs of all parties involved, how can the juvenile justice system accommodate the call for retribution, rehabilitation, restitution, and reintegration?

As the rates of homicide and nonnegligent manslaughter by juveniles have reached their highest levels in decades (Bartol & Bartol, 1998), the demand for swift and severe punishment by the public and juvenile justice professionals has also increased. Implicit in the call for punitive responses to youthful offenders is the belief that swift and severe punishment will deter other juveniles, as well as the disposed juvenile, from engaging in similar behaviors by raising the costs of the delinquent act. But the image of the juvenile offender as a rational thinking youth weighing the rewards and punishments of his or her actions is incomplete and at times wholly inaccurate. Pure deterrence strategies have failed time and time again, yet the call for punitive responses remain. This discussion is not a call to abolish punitive justice strategies; rather, it is an acknowledgment that punitive strategies alone have little impact on crime rates, and sole reliance on these types of responses to delinquency is short sighted.

Treatment strategies are not necessarily inconsistent with the public's demand for punitive responses to the youthful offender. Treatment of the disorders that many youthful offenders suffer from does not have to replace punitive responses. Within the secure facility, the public's need for retribution can be met while the juvenile offender receives the necessary treatment for his or her disorder. Being held in a secure residential facility, where one's actions are almost continuously monitored and individual freedom is extremely restricted, *is* punitive. And treatment strategies administered within secure facilities address the dual needs of the youthful offender who is often beset with mental disorders but must still be held accountable for his or her actions.

Victim restitution by the youthful offender can also be made consistent with both the rehabilitative and punitive responses of the juvenile justice system. Requiring the youthful offender to "make right" the harm that he or she has done does no disservice to either punitive or treatment strategies. In fact, it is possible that requiring the youthful offender to replace, repair, or at a minimum acknowledge the harm caused by his or her actions can be incorporated into both rehabilitative and retributive strategies (e.g., Bazemore & Maloney, 1994). Asking the youthful offender to acknowledge and repair harm to the victim caused by his or her actions is a necessary step toward both effective punishment and treatment, because the offender is required to connect his or her actions to his or her current situation (i.e., integration into the juvenile justice system). This makes explicit the connection between the action that the offender took and the response of the juvenile justice system. In today's juvenile justice system, it is not unusual for weeks and sometimes months to pass before a case reaches disposition. At that pace, the response of the court and the act that resulted in the juvenile coming into contact with the court can become disjointed. By connecting action and response, victim restitution forces the juvenile offender to recognize that inappropriate behaviors do not always go unpunished.

Reintegration of the youthful offender into the community is the final step necessary if our juvenile justice responses are to have a positive impact. Reintegration is not simply returning the juvenile to the community. Instead, it involves the acceptance and forgiveness of the juvenile offender by members of the community. As a result, reintegrative strategies require, among other things, the extension of juvenile court services to the youthful ex-offender after he or she has returned to the community. It is imperative to acknowledge that the disorders contributing to the youthful offender's behavior cannot be successfully treated only while the youth is in custody but must be treated after release as well.

The complex image of the youthful offender requires that all individuals and organizations involved (e.g., parents or legal guardians of the juvenile, residential treatment facilities for youth, child protective services, mediation organizations, juvenile courts, juvenile probation, neighborhood associations, and so on) work together toward more effective solutions. A philosophical and organizational restructuring of the juvenile justice system may also be in order. No longer can the juvenile justice system be solely concerned with punishment or treatment of the youthful offender. As we develop and expand our understanding of the juvenile offender and the intended and unintended effects of his or her actions, the range of appropriate and necessary responses to the actions of the offender must expand as well.

Addressing Critical Issues: Priorities for the Future

The need to appropriately respond to the needs of youth who have mental health disorders is recognized in the Juvenile Justice and Delinquency Prevention Act of 1993. The National Coalition for Mental and Substance Abuse Health Care in the Justice System (NCMSAHC) has created a set of principles to promote the socially responsible development of public policy in the juvenile justice field (Rotenberg, 1997). In their publication, *Responding to the Mental Health Needs of Youth in the Juvenile Justice System*, 11 priorities for the provision of mental health services for children in the juvenile justice system were identified. The following comments are based on these priorities.

The call for research aimed at designing screening and assessment tools that determine appropriate mental health intervention needs of youth entering the juvenile justice system is a necessary first step toward increasing the likelihood of successful rehabilitation of the youthful offender. Special emphasis should be placed on the assessment of amenability to treatment. Court decisions should no longer be based on whether a child can fit the limited, existing treatment models. Instead, the focus should be on whether the mental disorder is treatable and in what setting the chances of successful treatment are enhanced. Although the call for public protection and demands for increasing punitive responses must be acknowledged, the juvenile court should place youth in the least restrictive, clinically appropriate setting. Continued development of effective diversion programs may aid in this process. Research on effective assessment tools would help juvenile justice personnel determine these clinically appropriate settings for youthful offenders. Finally, given the prevalence of mental disorders among juvenile offenders, assessment tools should be used at the intake stage of juvenile court processing for every juvenile that comes through the system.

Interagency collaboration would provide a greater range of available services to mentally disordered youth. Again, mentally disordered youth should not be asked to "fit" their affliction into an existing treatment program. Interagency collaboration would help prevent this ineffective, force-fitting strategy. This collaboration would also encourage the development of innovative funding mechanisms.

Focus on the child and not on bureaucratic issues that often result in the breakdown of services to our youth is at the heart of interagency collaboration. A child-focused approach is also central to the issue of funding mechanisms. Successful funding models have been achieved when funding is adapted to the needs of youthful offenders and their families rather than to the rigid, categorical nature of federal, state, and local funding (Friedman, 1994; Meyers, 1994).

Neighborhood-driven programs are necessary not only to play a catalytic role with public agencies but also to provide effective reintegration of youth into the community. John Braithwaite (1989) provided the theoretical foundation on which restorative justice strategies emerged. Crucial to the effectiveness of these strategies is the admonishment and subsequent forgiveness and acceptance of the youthful offender back into the community. This process used the community as a tool of rehabilitation and reintegration and can also reduce the stigma often felt by children with mental disorders.

Education in culturally competent evaluation and treatment strategies for juvenile justice and mental health personnel will go a long way toward eliminating the racial bias that exists in the juvenile justice system. Strict attention should be paid to recent efforts at addressing this bias, such as that found in the work of Briscoe (1996). Related to the subject of cultural competence is the need for treatment specificity. Evaluation and treatment strategies should not only be sensitive to racial and cultural concerns, for example, but also to the varying needs of urban, suburban, and rural youth.

The dissemination of information acquired by juvenile justice and mental health professionals must be improved. Evaluations of continuing and innovative programs developed to attend to the needs of juvenile offenders with mental disorders must continue and the results must be shared with other service providers. We can learn more effective strategies by knowing what has worked, as well as knowing what has failed.

Finally, the participation of youth and their families in the treatment process must be emphasized. Young people and their families may be helpful to service providers in the assessment of service needs. Youth and family involvement may also be incorporated in the restitution process. Such involvement in the restitution process will not only satisfy the need for reparation but may also enhance the participant's treatment.

Implicit in this discussion is a call for expansion of the responsibilities and efforts of the juvenile justice system (and social service agencies affiliated with them) when treating the youthful offender with a mental disorder. Along with this expanded responsibility comes the potential for an attendant multitude of organizational and financial difficulties, some of which have been discussed in this chapter. These difficulties are surmountable. Furthermore, it is imperative that any systemic barriers to treatment for juvenile offenders with mental disorders be overcome by focusing on the multiple needs of these youth. Acceptance of the complex image of the juvenile offender is a necessary first step in this process. Administering both "punishment" and "treatment," as well as using restorative and reintegrative strategies for youthful offenders, provides a greater chance of achieving positive outcomes for all parties involved.

References

Aber, M. S., & Reppucci, N. (1987). The limits of mental health expertise in juvenile and family law. *International Journal of Law and Psychiatry, 10,* 167–184.

Alexander, R., Jr. (1989). The right to treatment in mental and correctional institutions. *Social Work, 34,* 109–112.

American Psychiatric Association. (1994). *Diagnostic and statistical manual of mental disorders* (4th ed.). Washington, DC: Author.

Applebaum, K. L. (1991, June 20). *Dispositional evaluation.* Paper presented at the Annual Conference of the Massachusetts Division of Forensic Mental Health, Auburn, MA.

Ashford, J. B., & LeCroy, C. W. (1988). Decision making for juvenile offenders in aftercare. *Juvenile and Family Court Journal, 39,* 47–53.

Baird, S. C. (1984). *Classification of juveniles in corrections: A model systems approach.* Washington, DC: Author D. Little.

Barnum, R., & Keilitz, I. (1992). Issues in systems interactions affecting mentally disordered juvenile offenders. In J. J. Cocozza (Ed.), *Responding to youth with mental disorders in the juvenile justice system* (pp. 49–87). Lexington, MA: Lexington Books.

Bartol, C. R., & Bartol, A. M. (1998). *Delinquency and justice* (2nd ed.). Upper Saddle River, NJ: Prentice-Hall.

Bazemore, G. (1995). Rethinking the sanctioning function in juvenile court: Retributive or restorative responses to youth crime. *Crime & Delinquency, 41,* 296–316.

Bazemore, G., & Maloney, D. (1994). Rehabilitating community service: Toward restorative service sanctions in a balanced justice system. *Federal Probation, 58,* 24–35.

Beccaria, C. (1963). *On Crimes and Punishments.* Indianapolis: Bobbs-Merrill. (Original work published 1764)

Bederow, L. S., & Reamer, F. G. (1981). *Treating the severely disturbed juvenile offender: A review of issues and programs.* Chicago: National Center for the Assessment of Alternatives to Juvenile Justice Processing.

Bentham, J. (1970). *An introduction to the principles of moral and legislation.* London: Athlone Press. (Original work published 1789)

Braithwaite, J. (1989). *Crime, shame and reintegration.* Cambridge: Cambridge University Press.

Briscoe, J. (1996). A collaborative effort: examining juvenile offenders with mental impairments. *Corrections Today, 58,* 106–109.

Cloward, R., & Ohlin, L. (1960). *Delinquency and opportunity.* New York: Free Press.

Cocozza, J. J. (1992). *Responding to the mental health needs of youth in the juvenile justice system.*

Cohen, Albert K. (1955). *Delinquent boys: The culture of the gang.* New York: Free Press.

Cole, R. F. (1997). Services for children and families. In K. Minkoff & D. Pollack (Eds.), *Managed mental health care in the public sector: A survival manual.* St. Leonards, Australia: Harwood Academic.

Dryfoos, J. (1990). *Adolescents at risk: Prevalence and prevention.* New York: Oxford University Press.

Fagan, J. (1991). Community-based treatment for mentally disordered juvenile offenders. *Journal of Clinical Child Psychology, 20,* 42–50.

Friedman, R. M. (1994). Restructuring of systems to emphasize prevention and family support. *Journal of Clinical Child Psychology, 23,* 48–54.

Hardin, M. (1992). *Establishing a core of services for families subject to state intervention: A blueprint for statutory and regulatory action.* Washington, DC: American Bar Association, Center on Children and the Law.

Hodge, R. D., & Andrews, D. A. (1996). *Assessing the youthful offender.* New York: Plenum Press.

Howell, J. C., Krisberg, B., & Jones, M. (1995). Trends in juvenile crime and youth violence. In J. C. Howell, B. F. Krisberg, J. D. Hawkins, & J. J. Wilson (Eds.), *A source book: Serious, violent, and chronic juvenile offenders* (1–35). Thousand Oaks, CA: Sage.

Kalogerakis, M. G. (1992). *Handbook of psychiatric practice in the juvenile court.* Washington, DC: American Psychiatric Association.

Kutash, K., & Rivera, V. R. (1996). *What work's in children's mental health services?* Baltimore: Paul Brooks Publishing.

Lewis, D. O., Shanok, S. S., Cohen, R. J., Klingfeld, M., & Frisone, G. (1980). Race bias in the diagnosis and disposition of violent adolescents. *American Journal of Psychiatry, 137,* 1211–1216.

Maloy, K. A. (1995). Juvenile justice: Once and future gatekeeper for a system of care. In L. Bickman & D. J. Rog (Eds.), *Children's mental health services: Research, policy and evaluation* (pp. 145–168). Thousand Oaks, CA: Sage.

Melton, G. B., & Pagliocca, P. M. (1992). Treatment in the juvenile justice system: Directions for policy and practice. In J. J. Cocozza (Ed.), *Responding to youth with mental disorders in the juvenile justice system* (pp. 107–139). Lexington, MA: Lexington Books.

Merton, R. K. (1938). Social structure and "anomie." *American Sociological Review, 3,* 672–682.

Meyers, J. C. (1994). Financing strategies to support innovation in service delivery to children. *Journal of Clinical Child Psychology, 23,* 48–54.

National Council of Juvenile and Family Court Judges. (1984). The juvenile court and serious offenders. *Juvenile and Family Court Journal, 35,* 11–19.

National Council of State Legislatures Health and Mental Health Program. (1989). *Coordinating juvenile justice, mental health and child welfare systems* (Office for Treatment Improvement. ADAMHA contract No. 89MF65929901D). Denver, CO: Author.

National Institute of Mental Health. (1990). *A national plan for research on child and adolescent mental disorders* (DHHS Publication No. ADM 90–1683). Rockville, MD: Author.

O'Leary, W. (1989). Issues in custodial suicide. *Psychiatric Quarterly, 60,* 31–71.

Quay, H. C., & Perry, J. S. (1987). *Psychopathological disorders of childhood* (3rd ed.). New York: Wiley.

Rog, D. (1995). The status of children's mental health services: An overview. In L. Bickman & D. Rog (Eds.), *Children's mental health services: Research, policy, and evaluation* (pp. 3–18). Thousand Oaks, CA: Sage.

Rotenberg, S. (1997). Responding to the mental health needs of youth in the juvenile justice system: The inner workings of delinquent youth. *Focal Point, 11,* 2–5.

Sacks, H., & Reader, W. D. (1992). Procedures in the juvenile court. In M. G. Kalogerakis (Ed.), *Handbook of psychiatric practice in the juvenile court.* Washington, DC: American Psychiatric Association.

Shanok, S., & Lewis, D. (1977). Juvenile court versus child guidance referral: Psychosocial and parental factors. *American Journal of Psychiatry, 134,* 1130–1133.

Snyder, H. N., & Sickmund, M. (1995). *Juvenile offenders and victims: A focus on violence.* Pittsburgh, PA: National Center for Juvenile Justice.

Stroul, B. (1993). *Systems of care for children and adolescents with severe emotional disturbances: What are the results?* Washington, DC: Georgetown University, CASSP Technical Assistance Center.

Stroul, B., & Friedman, R. M. (1986). *A system of care for severely emotionally disturbed children and youth.* Washington, DC: Georgetown University, Child and Adolescent Service System Program Technical Assistance Center.

Sutherland, E., & Cressey, D. (1978). *Principles of criminology.* (10th ed.). Philadelphia, PA: Lippincott.

Wiebush, R. G., Baird, C., Krisberg, B., & Onek, D. (1995). Risk assessment and classification for serious, violent, and chronic juvenile offenders. In J. C. Howell, B. F. Krisberg, J. D. Hawkins, & J. J. Wilson (Eds.), *A sourcebook: Serious, violent, and chronic juvenile offenders* (pp. 171–212). Thousand Oaks, CA: Sage.

Chapter 16
ADMINISTRATIVE CONCERNS ASSOCIATED WITH THE TREATMENT OF OFFENDERS WITH MENTAL ILLNESS

Thomas L. Hafemeister, Susan R. Hall, and Joel A. Dvoskin

Offenders[1] with mental health problems[2] present correctional mental health administrators and treatment providers with difficult operational challenges. Many of these administrative considerations are necessitated by the correctional setting itself, which can have profound effects on the delivery of treatment. These operational challenges may vary with the nature and type of correctional setting. For example, the primary difference between jails and prisons is that jails tend to house inmates for relatively shorter periods of time. Because of these generally shorter lengths of stay, jail mental health programs will often place little emphasis on skill building, treatment, and rehabilitation but spend a greater proportional amount of time on screening at intake and aggressive efforts to control active symptoms of mental illness through crisis intervention (Steadman, 1990). Prisons, on the other hand, often place greater emphasis on helping inmates to adapt to their incarceration and on preparing them for their eventual return to society (Dvoskin, 1989b). Nevertheless, jails and prisons are alike in many ways. Both can be very stressful environments because of their emphasis on maintaining order and control, the structured, often para-military manner in which the settings are managed, forced associations, threats of violence, segregation by gender, extremes of noise and temperature, limited opportunities for individuality and self-expression, and absence of personal space (Dvoskin, 1989b; Lindquist & Lindquist, 1997). Administrators responsible for the mental health needs of offenders must recognize that correctional settings are likely to have a direct effect on an inmate's mental illness, as well as the correctional system's necessary and appropriate response to it. Thus a series of unique administrative, managerial, and systemic concerns are associated with providing mental health treatment in correctional settings.[3]

Portions of the material appearing in this chapter appeared previously in "Administration of Treatment Programs for Offenders with Mental Disorders" by Joel A. Dvoskin and Raymond F. Patterson in *Treatment of Offenders With Mental Disorders*, by R. M. Wettstein, ed., and published by Guilford Press in 1998. This use is made with permission.

[1]Throughout this chapter, the terms *offender, inmate,* and *detainee* will be used relatively interchangeably to include those persons sentenced to jails and prisons, as well as those being detained for trial.

[2]Specific estimates vary, but a consensus has developed that a significant proportion of offenders within jails and prisons suffer from serious mental illness (Lamb & Weinberger, 1998). Although some offenders have preexisting histories of mental illness, the correctional environment can bring about psychiatric crises in people who were mentally stable in the community (Gibbs, 1987; McCarthy, 1985). There are a number of different paths by which people can come to experience mental illness and incarceration simultaneously. Once they are incarcerated, however, people with mental illness become the responsibility of correctional mental health administrators.

[3]For a discussion of legal issues related to the treatment of offenders with a mental disorder, see Hafemeister (1998) and Hafemeister and Petrila (1994).

Yet little is available in the literature to guide decisions about the structure and administration of mental health treatment programs in secure adult facilities. This chapter discusses the problems confronting correctional administrators who are involved in designing and managing programs of care and treatment for adult offenders with mental illness, as well as some proposed solutions.

Administrative Challenges

Incarceration is a difficult experience for anyone. For inmates with mental illness, and for correctional administrators responsible for their care and treatment, it can be particularly difficult.

Prison Safety

Correctional administrators are charged with preventing injury to staff and inmates. One threat to institutional safety is posed by those inmates with mental illness whose behavior becomes uncontrolled and violent. Mental illness, especially if inadequately treated, may result in aberrant or disruptive behavior. Inmates with mental illness may be terrified by hallucinations and may stay up all night screaming and keeping other inmates awake (Dvoskin, 1989b). Because of the close proximity in which prisoners live, disruptive or aberrant behavior can be very upsetting and may cause other inmates to become angry or even violent in response. Also, both inmates and staff become highly dependent on orderly and predictable behavior, which inmates with mental illness tend to disrupt. Furthermore, as in the outside world, persons with mental illness may be perceived as strange and bizarre, with their mere presence unsettling and in some cases provoking to other inmates and staff. Inmates with mental illness can be difficult to manage (Haddad, 1991), and when inadequately treated are more likely to be involved in serious disciplinary infractions, including assaults on staff and other inmates (Baskin, Sommers, & Steadman, 1991).

Therefore, mental illness should be treated within the correctional setting to protect staff and inmates and to minimize disruptions and tensions that exacerbate the general likelihood of injury. Programs that teach and assist inmates with mental illness to safely adapt to correctional environments contribute to the safety of staff and inmates alike.

Harm to Inmates With Mental Illness

Inmates experiencing mental illness or psychiatric crisis may engage in self-injurious or suicidal behavior (Stone, 1997). Suicides occur in all levels of correctional settings, but are a particular danger within jails. Furthermore, in part because of their disruptive or bizarre behavior, inmates with mental illness may be in danger of being the victims of serious violence at the hands of other inmates, particularly more predatory inmates (Ogloff, Roesch, & Hart, 1994).

Thus correctional administrators and staff need to protect inmates with mental illness from engaging in self-injurious behavior and from violent, abusive, or predatory acts by other inmates or staff. They should also work to diminish the likelihood that these inmates' mental health will deteriorate as a result of their incarceration. This will require a variety of responses, including skill building, separation, and special housing of some inmates with mental illness, and greater observation of inmates in crisis. In addition, officers can be provided with specialized training on how, without inappropriate force, to best manage inmates with mental illness who act out (Henry, Senese, & Ingley, 1994).

The treatment of inmates with mental illness is often seen as contributing to prison security by decreasing (or at least segregating) unpredictable and violent actions by such inmates. Treatment, however, must not be limited to those inmates who are disruptive. Other inmates with mental illness, who are neither violent nor disruptive, also deserve treatment. The extension of treatment to depressed or "quietly psychotic" inmates to reduce unnecessary human suffering caused by mental illness should be a goal of mental health treatment in correctional facilities as well as in the general community.

Staff Morale

Offenders with mental illness often require a disproportionate amount of attention from correctional staff, preventing staff from attending to and completing other assigned duties. As already noted, such inmates also tend to disrupt the normal routines of correctional institutions, routines on which both staff and inmates become highly dependent, making it more difficult for correctional staff to do their jobs. The presence of inmates with psychiatric symptoms can worsen tensions in general within the correctional setting, both because of the disruptive behavior that may accompany these symptoms (e.g., screaming, violent behavior, throwing of feces) and because of the perceived potential for violence associated with their presence. All of these factors tend to contribute to making the job of correctional staff more difficult and to reduce staff morale. Finally, despite the unflattering stereotype of "guards" in correctional settings as being tough and unfeeling, a completed suicide is often very disturbing to staff, who feel responsible for keeping inmates safe.

Working with inmates whose mental illness is untreated or undertreated places great stress on correctional officers. Prison administrators and security staff should support mental health service improvements because such services are likely to improve the working environment and thereby reduce staff stress, burnout, cynicism, and absenteeism. In addition, correctional staff should receive high-quality training in how to recognize and understand the symptoms of mental illness to increase their feelings of competence in dealing with challenging behaviors.

Danger to the Community

Correctional administrators are under increased pressure to design programs that will diminish the recidivism of inmates after discharge or release. The extent to which correctional rehabilitative and psychiatric programs can contribute to reductions in criminal recidivism has been debated.[4] The absence of such programs, however, minimizes opportunities for the inmate to learn the skills necessary to carry out personal decisions to change his or her lifestyle (Dvoskin & Steadman, 1989). Inmates with mental illness cannot benefit from general correctional programs (e.g., literacy, vocational skill building) and mental health treatment programs if they cannot gain access to and participate in them.

There is also a need to reduce the disabling effects of serious mental illness to maximize each inmate's ability to participate in activities and rehabilitative programs provided within the prison. Treatment that allows inmates with mental illness to more fully participate in correctional programs improves the likelihood that they will take advantage of these programs and thus improves their chances of a successful return to the community. Furthermore, even absent a salutary effect on recidivism, increased program participation can have a positive effect on the overall functioning and safety of the facility.

Because correctional facilities serve mainly to protect the public from individuals that are perceived as dangerous, foreign, or frightening (Mohelsky, 1982), the most important function of jails and prisons in the eyes of the public is to provide secure housing to offenders in general and to inmates with mental illness in particular (Dvoskin & Patterson, 1998). When it is time for offenders with mental illness to be released, the public may also demand that they receive increased scrutiny and supervision in the community (Dvoskin & Patterson, 1998). Thus in addition to devising programming that may diminish the recidivism of inmates in general on discharge or release, administrators should also consider providing programs that incorporate community support systems for inmates with mental illness (e.g., Lanier, 1991; Walsh & Bricout, 1996), including case management programs (Dvoskin & Horn, 1994; Dvoskin & Steadman, 1994).

Special Housing–Management Issues

The placement of offenders with mental illness within the correctional setting, and related housing decisions, is a critical component in developing a program that delivers the services needed by these offenders.

Housing Assignments

Housing assignments within a correctional setting should take into account the needs of inmates both with and without mental illness. Special housing arrangements are required for two reasons. Each facility has an overriding obligation to protect inmates from foreseeable and preventable harm. Second, these facilities may also have a duty

---

[4]Correctional rehabilitative services are therapeutic interventions designed to address the causes of criminal behavior in an attempt to reduce criminal propensities, whereas mental health services are provided to treat serious mental illness within the correctional setting (Adams, 1985). For discussions of the impact of correctional rehabilitation programs on criminal recidivism, see Andrews, Bonta, and Hoge (1990); Brooks (1992); Gendreau and Ross (1987); Genevie, Margolies, and Muhlin (1986); McGuire (1995); MacKain and Streveler (1990); Nolan (1998). For a discussion of correctional psychiatric programs, see Quinsey, Harris, Rice, and Cormier (1998); Wettstein (1998).

to provide medical or psychiatric treatment. Although the two considerations often overlap, the most important aspect of housing arrangements in a correctional setting should be to ensure the safety of everyone who lives and works there. A frequent reason for a request for special housing is the likelihood of disruptive or violent behavior by an inmate with mental illness, either toward self or others (Dvoskin, 1989b). Administrators should call on mental health staff to help make a judgment about the type of housing and level of supervision required to keep the inmate and others safe.

Special management precautions for inmates with mental illness or those experiencing psychiatric distress may be as simple as moving an inmate to a different cell location, such as a safer or less disruptive location or away from an instigating element (such as another inmate). Alternatively, an inmate may be moved to a cell nearer an observation post maintained by staff, allowing for easier and more frequent observation by nursing or other services. In addition, inmates deemed to be at high risk of suicide may be assigned to areas where special watches, such as constant observation or one-to-one staff supervision, can be easily accomplished.

Disciplinary Segregation

Inmates who are not receiving adequate treatment for their serious mental illness may experience a number of unpleasant or harmful consequences. In addition to suicide attempts or gestures, these also include serious or accumulated disciplinary infractions that can lead to disciplinary segregation (Condelli, Dvoskin & Holanchock, 1994; Dvoskin & Steadman, 1989; McShane, 1989; Toch & Adams, 1986). One of the most difficult decisions in managing mentally ill prisoners is when to punish disciplinary violations that do not appear to be related to the inmate's mental illness (Cohen & Dvoskin, 1992). There is no harder dilemma in a correctional setting than deciding what to do with inmates with mental illness who perhaps out of greed or anger (and not because of their mental illness) assault staff or other inmates. Clear and public consequences for such acts are required to keep the correctional facility safe, and a lack of consequences may damage staff and inmate morale. A lack of consequences may also be countertherapeutic if inmates deduce that having mental illness excuses any and all violence or disciplinary violations.

On the other hand, disciplinary segregation can be so unpleasant and anxiety-provoking that some inmates with mental illness will go to extreme lengths, including threatened or completed suicide, to force the system to move them out of segregation (Cohen & Dvoskin, 1992). Further, segregation may truly and severely exacerbate their preexisting mental illness. There is considerable disagreement about the extent to which segregation is psychologically harmful generally (Luise, 1989; Suedfeld, Ramirez, Deaton, & Baker-Brown, 1982). However, there is no disagreement that at least *some* inmates, especially those with current psychosis or suicidal depression, experience segregation as extraordinarily stressful and psychologically harmful.

Although there is no easy answer to this dilemma, at the very least a sensible step is for administrators to ensure that mental health staff maintain a regular presence on every segregation unit, with on-site and regular mental health coverage. This allows for the early identification of inmates likely to experience psychological problems during segregation, with ongoing assessment and support provided for inmates who legitimately have trouble tolerating "hole" time. Although treatment may in some cases be delivered to inmates within the segregation setting, at other times their psychiatric needs will require temporary or even permanent transfers out of segregation and into mental health treatment settings.

Residential Treatment Units (RTUs)

Many correctional facilities now provide for inmates with mental illness or for those experiencing psychological distress special housing such as multibed dormitories with specially focused treatment programs (see, e.g., Haddad, 1991; Steelman, 1987). Such housing has proven effective for responding to inmates' mental health needs within a correctional environment.

These RTUs are used for various reasons. Inmates with severe mental illness often have difficulty dealing with the stresses of prison, are especially vulnerable to the more predatory inmates in the general prison population, and may require an environment that is physically and psychologically safer. Company can help alleviate depression, and inmates who are ambivalent about their own suicidality may watch each other as diligently as do staff (Dvoskin, 1989b).

In other cases, this special housing is intended to concentrate supervision and treatment services by placing inmates who require such services in one location. It is easier for staff to watch a group of people in one room than in individual rooms or cells.

Like community residences in the free world, RTUs have been shown to dramatically improve the quality of life for inmates with mental illnesses, while adding to the safety of the prison environment. A New York study demonstrated that, at least for some inmates with serious mental illnesses, intermediate care programs (i.e., RTUs) reduce psychiatric crises, disciplinary violations, suicide attempts, and hospital transfers by creating a psychologically (and perhaps physically) safer environment (Condelli, Bradigan, & Holanchock, 1997; Condelli et al., 1994).

In addition to providing safer environments, such housing should have some form of significant therapeutic programming, including psychoeducational and behavior modification components (Cohen & Dvoskin, 1992). Inmates should be provided information about their illness, the medications they may need to function, and "how to do time" more successfully.

Three groups of inmates tend to find their way into these longer-term residential programs (Cohen & Dvoskin, 1992). First, there is the "halfway in" inmate who uses this setting to avoid inpatient commitment by being removed for a time from the stresses of the general population. Second, there is the "halfway out" inmate who, after an inpatient stay, uses this setting to readjust to prison life before returning to the general population. For these two groups, the program is transitional and should have a widely varied length of stay. Third, there is the inmate who needs the long-term support and programs provided here and whose placement may represent the highest level of functioning likely to be achieved in a correctional setting. For such inmates, their stay may continue throughout the course of incarceration.[5]

---

[5]Inmates should not be sent to these programs for disciplinary reasons because such inmates may be inappropriate for this setting and their presence may undercut the ability to provide therapeutic programs in general.

These three groups of inmates should not be treated separately (Cohen & Dvoskin, 1992). First, attempting to determine a priori who will and who will not be able to make the transition back to the general population is often impossible. Second, it is important to try moving inmates to less intensive treatment settings or to less secure settings several times before concluding they can never leave the program. Third, a mix of clients with a variety of skills and different levels of strength and impairment can enrich the treatment milieu.

Inmates should be encouraged to participate in as many therapeutic activities as staff deems appropriate, and there should be daily community meetings (Cohen & Dvoskin, 1992). Staff can "progressively" return some RTU inmates to the general population by assigning these inmates to programs within the general population during the day and returning them to the RTU at night, or vice versa. By providing a heavy level of programming, the program will be less attractive to inmates looking merely to escape responsibilities by feigning mental illness. Finally, having mental health staff on site or at nearby units can facilitate adherence to medication schedules and prevent crisis situations from arising or escalating.

Notwithstanding the value of these programs, RTUs can pose some difficult problems for administrators. For one, they typically require a richer staffing level with a need for a greater range of programs. Finding monetary, training, and staff resources may be a significant challenge for an administrator. These special housing areas sometimes receive a full complement of inmates to serve with little or no additional staff or training to enable staff to treat clients effectively. As a result, inmates with mental illness may live in forced association only with other seriously disturbed inmates without adequate security, observation, or mental health care.

An alternative problem may arise because correctional staffing levels are often set on an institution-wide basis. Placing more staff in an RTU may necessitate lowering staff levels in another portion of the correctional facility, with the negative implications that it may have for coverage, safety, and morale in these other areas.

To the extent that working in the RTU is perceived as an easy assignment, it may cause jealousies among officers seeking such assignments. In other instances, however, the behavior sometimes exhibited by the population typically housed in an RTU may be such that this may be considered a relatively undesirable assignment, and the administrator may find it difficult to obtain staff who are willing to work in this area. Furthermore, the nature of this population and the problems they face generally require certain skills of the officers staffing this area. Attitudes and approaches well-suited for the general population may be inappropriate for this group of inmates.

In general, a number of distinct provisions are needed to ensure that special mental health housing will function appropriately. They include

- Regular rounds by qualified mental health personnel (as a supplement to the supervision provided by correctional staff);
- Record keeping that promotes and enhances communication between correctional and mental health staff;
- Special training for correctional staff assigned to this housing to enable them to recognize and address inmates' mental health problems when mental health staff are not immediately available; and
- Prompt and regular evaluations of the mental health of all inmates placed in

this housing, including assessment of the appropriateness of removal to another location for more or less intensive psychological treatment.

Responsibility for Mental Health Services

Various services need to be available to inmates, but they do not necessarily have to be provided by or within the correctional facility itself. Different organizational models for the delivery of mental health services have been noted (see Maier & Miller, 1989; Wardlaw, 1983; Weinberger & Sreenivasan, 1994). Possible providers can include departments of corrections, departments of mental health, local mental health agencies, private contractors, universities and medical schools, or any other competent service provider (Dvoskin & Powitsky, 1984). It is not especially important who provides these services or whether the services are brought to the inmates or the inmates are brought to the services. Rather, a responsive continuity-of-care system should be implemented in which resources are used in the most efficient manner and each inmate is provided timely access to the essential services needed (American Psychiatric Association, 1989).

Departments of Mental Health or Corrections as Service Providers

Observers are divided about whether departments of mental health or corrections are better able to deliver mental health services to inmates (Metzner, Fryer, & Usery, 1990). In making such a decision, administrators should address the following questions.

First, which agency is better able to generate the necessary fiscal resources? The answer to this question will vary from state to state and over time. Without adequate resources, no agency will be able to succeed in meeting the mental health needs of inmates.

Equally important is each agency's organizational commitment to the mental health needs of offenders (see, e.g., Ringel & Segal, 1986). A mental health department that does not care about inmates is just as bad as a prison system that does not care about mental illness.

In many states maximum-security psychiatric hospitals are operated by the mental health system, with outpatient and residential mental health services provided by the correctional system. Other models place responsibility for all mental health services within either the department of corrections or the department of mental health. Though much is made of the formal division of authority, far more important for judging the adequacy of a prison mental health system are the resources made available and how they are used. The key aspect is not each detail of the arrangement but that each agency clearly understands its respective rights and responsibilities within the arrangement (see, e.g., Dvoskin, 1989a; Policy Research Associates, n.d.).

Ducking Responsibility

Typically, multiple agencies are involved in providing services to offenders with mental disorders in a correctional system. Administrators should ensure that their programs are coordinated and interdependent to address the various associated mental health, correctional, housing, welfare, education, and other needs (Greene, 1989; Wardlaw, 1983; Webster, Hucker, & Grossman, 1993).

Often, the agency with primary responsibility for the inmate will be required to provide the inmate with housing (Dvoskin & Patterson, 1998). In addition to its expense, housing may create a perception of responsibility for any subsequent incidents involving the inmate, including liability for any harm that results. Furthermore, certain inmates are frequent sources of disruption, difficult to manage, at high risk of violence, or necessitate special attention or services, adding to the expense and burden of housing these inmates.

Offenders with mental disorders are often considered the most difficult and least desirable group to serve within a correctional population. As a result, agencies often seek to shift responsibility for such inmates to another agency, often by transferring such inmates to a program or facility operated by the other agency. Such shuttling of inmates between correctional and mental health facilities and programs has been referred to as "bus therapy" (McShane, 1989; Toch, 1982; Webster et al., 1993). An inmate who is the subject of frequent transfers may receive diminished care and treatment and become the focus of resentment by agencies that feel that inmates have been "dumped" on them by an irresponsible and manipulative fellow agency.[6]

Unwanted transfers are a chronic source of bad feeling in many states (Dixon, 1990; Dvoskin & Patterson, 1998). When a fight ensues over every tough case, morale suffers in both agencies as someone always feels they got "stuck" with these inmates. However, the agency willing to provide treatment of hard-to-manage offenders with mental illness can actually find rewards associated with accepting such inmates. Receiving a "dumped" client is discouraging. Choosing to take on a "tough case," however, may be very different. Staff may boast about handling inmates that other agencies could not and find that a reputation as an effective and valuable agency is useful when funding requests are submitted.

Another option for resolving conflicts over such transfers is to give control over admissions to one agency but to also set limits over admissions by establishing the total number of beds available in the receiving agency (Dvoskin & Patterson, 1998). When this number is reached, the "back door" must open and the agency initiating the transfers must accept someone back. As a result, the receiving agency maintains control over its census, and the transferring agency feels that it has an additional alternative available for inmates with mental illness who have become difficult to manage, albeit at the "cost" of receiving in return inmates who may have previously been viewed as such. The problem of limited resources remains, but now both agencies have a sense of control over the housing of these inmates.

A frequent intersystem conflict occurs when agency personnel argue over whether an inmate is mentally ill or "merely" a management problem (Dvoskin &

---

[6]Disputes over transfers occur in both prisons and jails (Dvoskin & Patterson, 1998). In prisons, the disputes frequently involve the department of corrections, which is primarily responsible for the housing of inmates, and the department of mental health, which may be responsible for treating the mental illness of inmates. Privatization of correctional or mental health services will change the nature of the disputants accordingly. A more complex scenario may be faced by jail administrators. Because community mental health services are typically assumed by a number of different agencies, staff from many different service providers may become involved in disputes over the appropriate housing and care of offenders assigned to a jail.

Patterson, 1998). The characterization chosen is often viewed as resolving the question of responsibility for housing the inmate, and a rejection of this characterization may be seen as challenging the integrity or competency of the person or agency making the determination. Rather than attacking the "label," personnel asked to provide assistance are well-advised to respond in a more positive fashion, offering to see the inmate and to judge firsthand what services are needed. A willingness to help is thereby extended without incurring an obligation to help.

No interagency relationship will be free of problems, and there will probably always be conflicts between the people responsible for inmates, even when these people work for the same organization. Rather than acting as if these conflicts do not exist, it is better to anticipate them in the service delivery system, thereby diminishing personalized and recurring conflicts.

Use of Private Contractors

In the last decade, many correctional systems have attempted to contract out many traditional correctional services. Contractual arrangements have often involved health care and related services, including mental health services. Attempts to privatize these services have been largely driven by fiscal concerns, as proponents have cited potential cost savings that may occur as a result of privatization, as well as a belief that this can shift the administrative burden to individuals who are better prepared to assume this responsibility.

The private contractor who assumes responsibility for providing mental health services will of course have administrative concerns of its own. Many of these concerns parallel the issues that are discussed throughout this chapter and thus will not be further addressed. But there are some unique issues worth noting. For example, the private contractor who has won this contract by submitting a competitive bid may be under considerable pressure to limit the salaries and benefits of the personnel it hires. This may limit the contractor's ability to attract highly qualified staff. In addition, lower compensation may result in considerable turnover among staff with a resulting disruption in continuity of services. Although supervisory staff can help address deficiencies in direct service staff, budgetary constraints resulting from the contractual arrangement may similarly affect the availability and qualifications of supervisory staff.

Also, correctional staff may harbor animosity toward personnel hired by the private contractor because these individuals and the contractor may be viewed as usurpers of their positions. If private contractors are successful, correctional staff may fear that their positions will ultimately be privatized as well. Even if this does not result in direct sabotage of the efforts of the contractual employees, it may result in a lack of cooperation and communication that is often vital for the successful provision of mental health services in a correctional setting.

Privatization does not necessarily relieve the administrator of a correctional system or facility of legal and programmatic responsibility if the private contractor fails to meet established standards for minimal care and treatment of inmates with a psychiatric disorder. These may be nondelegable responsibilities in general, but particularly so if the administrator retains at least supervisory responsibility for the actions of the private contractor.

Further, contractual arrangements with private contractors in general raise a series of relatively unique administrative concerns. State or local law may impose a host of requirements associated with obtaining and selecting among bids to provide such services. The administrator may have to decide what minimal services a successful bid must contain. The different combinations of services contained within these bids must be weighed in determining what are the most appropriate services for a given correctional setting. The administrator must also ascertain in advance which contractors can best be relied on to effectively and efficiently provide promised services (see Travis, Latessa, & Vito, 1985). The financial and operational capability of the contractor to provide the services promised must also be evaluated.

To address these issues, administrators should carefully consider the private contractors who are offering these services. Their experience in providing these types of services should be carefully scrutinized, as well as their financial stability. The contract that is used to establish the provision of services should be carefully constructed to ensure that adequate and necessary services are provided. At a minimum, the contract should contain a mechanism for resolving disputes that may arise between an administrator of a correctional facility and the individuals responsible for implementing the contract for services.

Finally, an administrator must directly address the concerns of staff that resent or fear the presence of private employees. At the very least, the administrator must ensure that appropriate communication occurs between these different groups. For example, where select services or off-hour services are provided by the employees of a private contractor, it is imperative that crises that occur and the responses taken be documented and communicated between these different groups.

Enhancing the Availability and Deployment of Service Providers

Private or public, mental health professionals are primary care providers in jails and prisons and important members of the correctional community. Administrators, however, may find it enormously difficult to recruit highly qualified mental health staff because correctional facilities have traditionally been viewed as an undesirable location in which to practice as a mental health professional (Metzner, 1992).

Correctional facilities may be placed far from urban centers. Salaries in the public sector may not be competitive. Correctional facilities may be old and poorly maintained. Mental health professionals may find a correctional setting with its emphases on security and order to be unpleasant, unsettling, and antithetical to what they consider necessary for a therapeutic milieu. Professionals may be frightened or otherwise unwilling to interact with criminals in general or find this setting to lack prestige or opportunity for advancement.

Nevertheless, the effectiveness of a mental health program in a correctional setting depends largely on the extent to which administrators have found ways to recruit and retain highly skilled staff. Despite the obstacles, many systems have succeeded in attracting qualified and talented clinicians. Providing the following can enhance recruitment (see Dvoskin & Patterson, 1998).

Salary Increases

Many states have documented their inability to recruit staff for specific locations and have been able to secure geographical cost of living increases, higher initial salaries and salary caps, exceptions to civil service hiring requirements, bonuses for mental health staff, and earlier retirement eligibility. Alternatively, the program may be turned over to private contractors, which as a nongovernmental entity may be able to offer higher clinical salaries than would otherwise be available.

Academic Affiliations

Mental health professionals value academic appointments and participation in collaborative programs (Metzner, 1992). Also, the availability of students, interns, and Fellows is generally stimulating to staff professionals and can bring new information into facilities. Such affiliations may enhance the opportunity for staff to interact with colleagues and to earn additional money from teaching, and provide respect and credibility. These affiliations may also provide a means to expose students, who may be subsequently recruited as staff, to the rewards of working in this environment. Internships and similar training programs can also be an excellent means of recruiting prospective staff to long-term positions.

Recruitment at Professional Conferences

National and regional professional conferences can be very effective and cost-efficient means for recruiting professional staff.[7] These conferences frequently attract professionals who are seeking positions and provide means for bringing candidates and employers together. However, recruiters should not rely exclusively on "job fairs" at these meetings. Many viable candidates can be found at scholarly presentations, including individuals who were not actively seeking a position at the time. It is very flattering to be selected from the many people at a conference as the focus of attention of a prospective employer. In general, administrators should actively solicit applications and not passively wait for applications to arrive.

Opportunities Associated With Employment

Providing a reasonable amount of agency-sponsored travel to professional conferences can overcome fears of professional isolation among staff. Another recruitment tool involves providing a varied forensic experience and opportunities to work in programs that compliment correctional facility responsibilities. For example, opportunities to also work in nearby community programs, to provide consultation and liaison to courts and attorneys, and to assist with program development can be effective recruitment inducements. Enhancing the work environment will also make such positions far more attractive. Supplying private office space, rehabilitating work

---

[7]Virtually all professions have national conferences, typically held on an annual basis. Such professional conferences include those held by the American Psychological Association, the American Psychiatric Association, the American Public Health Association, the National Association of Social Workers, and the American Nurses Association. Many of these professions also host regional or state conferences, which permit more geographically focused recruitment efforts. Meeting dates for conferences can generally be obtained by accessing the home page of the national associations at their Websites.

areas, and ensuring adequate cleaning and maintenance for these areas can promote recruitment and retention of staff.

Line Staff

There is frequently a perception that only mental health professionals can help inmates with mental illness (Ellis, 1993). This is an unfortunate perception because it fails to appreciate the valuable contributions that can be made by line staff. Line staff are important therapeutic agents in the correctional environment. In addition, line staff tend to be far more readily available than mental health professionals, and inmate contact and interaction is the core component of their job.

Roles of line staff. Line staff are the people who generally staff around-the-clock posts, including nurses, psychiatric technicians, and therapy aids, but also correctional officers in general. Prospective candidates for these jobs may believe that correctional facilities are intended merely to provide custody, control, and housing. In fact, there are valuable services beyond this to be provided inmates, services that are both vital to the present well-being of inmates and to inmates' ability to make the transition when they ultimately return to the community. To effectively provide such services demands considerable expertise and commitment to providing quality care.

In many systems, these roles are played by correctional officers who are assigned to mental health settings, preferably with the same level of specialized training and experience as direct care workers in psychiatric hospitals. Because of the challenges associated with this service delivery, mental health line staff in correctional facilities would ideally have even more experience, education, or training than their counterparts in civil hospitals and receive higher salaries.[8] It is important to recognize the therapeutic potential of correctional officers and other line staff. Without adequate training and support for this function, their effect on inmate mental health can be less than helpful or even deleterious. On the other hand, experience has shown that when officers are trained, supervised, and rewarded for supportive and therapeutically appropriate behavior toward inmates with mental illness, they can be a tremendous asset to a program (see, e.g., Ellis, 1993).

An important and often overlooked aspect of responding to the needs of inmates with mental illness is to simply talk and listen to them. Individual psychotherapy and even group sessions may be a rare commodity within a correctional setting. Well-trained and experienced officers can frequently supplement or even replace the need for formal psychotherapy with good results. Line staff simply talking to troubled inmates can have a dramatically beneficial impact. They can resolve a crisis by saying things that will help the inmate to calm down or provide instruction on ways to avoid similar crises in the future. For inmates who are confused and anxious, frequent and surprisingly brief visits by staff can provide reassurance that the inmate has not been psychologically abandoned. Often, simply providing accurate information about the criminal justice process or correctional system can relieve a tremendous amount of anxiety; the information need not be supplied by mental health

---

[8]Earlier retirement eligibility has facilitated the recruitment and retention of staff in many such settings, and in addition can reduce the likelihood that young, physically fit, and violent inmates may injure aging personnel.

professionals. During periods of extreme psychological stress, an important part of therapy is to provide a nonthreatening source of company—it can be comforting simply to have someone who will listen to you.

There are a number of other basic elements of mental health treatment within a correctional facility that can be provided by line staff. These include observing and recording behavior, fielding and relaying requests for assistance, consulting with professional staff, implementing behavioral treatment programs,[9] and monitoring inmates as they are given medicine to determine if they are taking their prescribed medication and experiencing any adverse reactions. Line staff can fill all of these roles. Most inmates with mental illness spend the bulk of their time in the general population of the correctional facility, and line staff, including correctional officers, can perform many of the supportive and treatment activities needed in this setting (Coleman, 1988). Indeed, the ongoing interactions of line staff with inmates and the associated opportunity to observe their day-to-day behavior may provide them insights that mental health professionals never have the opportunity to obtain.[10] For example, correctional officers frequently can provide information on the day-to-day realities of prison life that can drastically affect an inmate's mental health.

These interventions by line staff, however, can constitute a double-edged sword. There is a potential for both positive and negative outcomes. If, for example, an officer's first words to an acutely psychotic and panic stricken inmate are threats of physical harm, the result may be an increase in panic, an exacerbation of psychosis, and an increase in the chances of injury to both the officer and the inmate. At the same time, line staff need to make it clear that the inmate is not allowed to do anything that he or she wants. Correctional officers should understand that a firm but gentle approach is the best response to a crisis. The inmate should understand that the inmate does not need to fear the officer, and indeed can rely on officers to provide protection from real or imagined threats and even self-harm (Ben-David & Silfen, 1994). Well-trained and experienced officers usually respond to such crises with patience, care, and common sense. Indeed, creativity born of experience with many inmates can lead to innovative and effective interventions.

It is also critical that line staff work in conjunction with mental health professionals. Careless, disparaging comments by correctional staff can quickly undercut the work of mental health professionals. In prison, an ideal situation is created when a psychologist, for example, talks to a line staff member about how to better deal

---

[9]In housing units specifically designed for inmates with mental illness, behavioral treatment systems or token economies (Rice, Harris, Quinsey, & Cyr, 1990) are often used where inmates earn or lose certain privileges. Such programs have been shown to be effective clinical devices (Paul & Lentz, 1977; Webster et al., 1993). Line staff, who are constantly present, play a vital role in implementing such programs. Such staff may be particularly well-suited to identify reinforcers, develop schedules, and assess progress. Furthermore, to the extent they are actively engaged in these programs, staff are more likely to support and promote its goals (Menditto, 1990).

[10]Mental health professionals typically have limited opportunity to observe the behavior of inmates with mental illness and to obtain information relevant to assessing symptoms and medication responses. What are primarily available to them are the reports of observations by correctional officers who supervise these inmates and the nurses who dispense the medication. The skillful prison clinician will maximize this source of information by asking good questions, teaching staff specific behaviors for which they should look, and, most important, listening to them. In many cases, reports by line staff may be based on years of observed responses of different inmates, including their reactions to different prescriptions.

with a particular inmate. The goal is not only to resolve the immediate problem but to leave the staff member with new skills or knowledge that will be useful in preventing or resolving similar situations in the future. This type of consultation is an extremely valuable means of maximizing the value of line staff as therapeutic agents. Similarly, clinicians should seek the counsel of experienced officers, who have often learned effective and positive means of communicating with inmates.

A key component of any mental health program within a correctional setting is to enhance communication between correctional and mental health staff. The necessity of being able to obtain assistance from mental health staff during a psychiatric crisis is perhaps obvious. But correctional staff should also be encouraged to call on mental health staff for suggestions on how to manage or proceed with inmates with mental illness in general or for advice about particularly stressful practices and changes in the facility's routine that might improve morale or reduce stress on vulnerable inmates. A simple decision to separate two inmates can often prevent a dangerous assault or a psychiatric crisis, and correctional staff who learn to trust their clinical staff come to value advice in such decisions.

Finally, in addition to positively affecting the mental health of the inmates, mental health professionals can also reduce job-related stress among correctional line staff (Dembo, Williams, & Stafford, 1986–1987). Some of the same stressors of correctional institutions that are often psychologically destructive and demoralizing to inmates who live there have also been shown to affect correctional officers who work in the same environment.

Information provided by line staff, however, does not always find its way to the mental health professional. Too often there is no reason for the line staff to assume that their opinions or observations are welcomed or valued. Far too many mental health professionals do not regard the correctional officer as having an area of expertise and tend to treat inmates in isolation. Even after years of working closely with line staff in a mutually respectful professional relationship, every mental health professional in a correctional facility needs to be reminded that correctional officers can provide a valuable source of information.

Enhancing the role of line staff as therapeutic agents.   To enhance the role of line staff as therapeutic agents, program administrators can use a variety of strategies. The first way to acknowledge and foster this role in line staff is by *consulting* with them. Administrators should talk to them and, more important, *listen* to them. Just as any other behavior can be extinguished, when administrators do not listen to line staff, line staff eventually stop talking to administrators. By actively interacting with staff who are willing to share their observations, administrators can reinforce those who are especially helpful and demonstrate a healthy respect for line staff in general. In return, they may share years of experience in corrections and hours of supervision of individual inmates.

A second method of improving relationships between line staff and mental health professionals is the creation of *treatment teams* within the prison that consist of different types of staff, always including correctional officers. Often called unit team management, this tool has been used successfully by the Federal Bureau of Prisons and a number of state correctional training centers. Treatment teams can contribute to a feeling of cooperative effort. By allowing the correctional officer to make "treatment" decisions and the "treatment staff" to contribute to security decisions, decision making can benefit from both the nurturing and the limit-setting parts of the inmates' world. Perhaps even more important are the changes in the officers, who may move from cynicism to finding fresh meaning in their work. In turn, satisfaction with perceived work conditions and an opportunity to influence institutional policy decisions have been found related to decreased staff turnover (Jurik & Winn, 1987).

A third method of improving the relationship between line staff and mental health professionals is perhaps the most obvious: *training*. It is imperative that mental health professionals take part in training academies for new staff (Miller, Maier, & Kaye, 1988), as well as in-service training programs for veteran staff. This provides an opportunity to create positive attitudes toward treatment services early, before biases have developed, and to break down some of those biases that already exist. Further, it allows mental health professionals to demonstrate sensitivity to security concerns and provides a forum for demonstrating that treatment is a necessity for good security rather than an impediment to it. In addition, brief videotapes can also be shown in the daily briefings that occur before each shift to provide in-service training at very low expense.

Regardless of the setting, training should include learning how to recognize the early signs and symptoms of serious mental illness and suicide; the nature and effects of various psychotropic medications; and how to access mental health services at the prison. Inmates' mental health depends in large part on the ability of correctional officers to identify inmates in psychiatric distress and to make appropriate referrals. It is therefore important to provide officers with basic training in some of the signs of emotional disturbances and how to inform clinicians in a behaviorally specific manner of what led the officer to suspect mental illness.

This training is not intended to make correctional officers into diagnosticians. However, correctional officers can supplement the efforts of clinicians by learning to recognize incipient problems and to help inmates to cope with the everyday stresses of incarceration (Lombardo, 1985). Finally, as discussed elsewhere in this volume, any educational program should include basic suicide prevention training (American Jail Association, 1989; National Center on Institutions and Alternatives and the National Institute of Corrections, U.S. Department of Justice, 1998).

Of course, training is a two-way street. If mental health professionals are to be trusted, they must not only be willing to train but to be trained. By taking part in basic training activities as a trainee, the mental health professional can learn a great deal about the realities of daily prison life and the special stresses that affect officers and inmates alike. This will facilitate an honest respect for the skills of experienced uniformed staff and a humility about the roles of mental health professionals in correctional facilities that has been conspicuously absent. By becoming part of the correctional environment, mental health professionals can enhance their impact on the facility and the individuals who must live and work within it.

A fourth method of enhancing the role of line staff as therapeutic agents is ensuring that *referrals* (i.e., requests for mental health services) are promptly communicated to mental health staff. Referrals can come from a number of sources, including the inmate, other inmates who have noticed aberrant or disturbing behavior by the inmate, family members, or correctional staff. There should be a low threshold for referrals—that is, such requests should be widely encouraged. Furthermore, any request or indication that mental health services may be indicated should warrant at least a brief assessment by a mental health clinician. Prompt processing of referrals can prevent minor problems from becoming major ones and minimize the disruptions posed by these inmates. Prompt responses will also reassure line staff that they can obtain needed assistance in managing such inmates and that their input is heeded and desired.

Administrators may find a number of impediments to these referrals. Some inmates may routinely submit such referrals not as a result of their severe mental illness and need for services, but as referrals may be a means of breaking the boredom of correctional life, of gaining access to mood-altering medication, or of avoiding unpleasant tasks or situations. Correctional staff may become jaundiced to such requests or such requests may become variables in the day-to-day struggles for authority and control that often characterize correctional settings.

Administrators should find means for enhancing the ability of correctional staff to recognize and process appropriate referrals. Any indication of either a history of or current mental illness or psychiatric crisis should serve to facilitate all referrals regarding that inmate to mental health staff and result in evaluation of the inmate's status by mental health staff. Likewise, any unusual or eccentric mannerisms or behaviors observed should be specifically documented and referred for further evaluation.

The fifth method of therapeutically empowering line staff includes a good *record-keeping and record-sharing system* (Severson, 1992). It is imperative that staff document requests for mental health services and the staff's response to these requests. Both legally and programmatically, this documentation must be provided to establish that needed services have been provided. Motivating staff to provide this documentation is often one of the most challenging tasks facing an administrator. Staff routinely perceive their time as being better spent on other tasks, in part because documentation tends to be a relatively uninteresting and unrewarding task. Nevertheless, mental health services must be clearly and legibly documented and available to those responsible for medical care, housing assignments, liaisons to outside agencies and clinics, and various follow-up services. The resulting records must also be maintained in a manner that ensures the privacy and confidentiality of each inmate while still facilitating communication among different mental health and medical providers and correctional staff.

Line staff will be more likely to generate accurate and useful records if they perceive that their efforts directly affect the care of offenders with mental illness. Similarly, if an effective system of record-sharing is in place, line staff will be reassured that they have the information they need to respond appropriately to inmates' needs.

Adequate documentation of crisis responses and communication of this information across shifts is particularly important. Essential aspects of the crisis and responses to it must particularly be communicated to relevant part-time employees, contractors, or those from other agencies. For example, an inmate may loudly threaten suicide over the weekend in response to a letter ending a relationship but be calm and relatively happy by Monday morning. This may indicate the inmate has accepted the loss. It may also mean, however, that the inmate has decided how to execute a suicide attempt and is at considerable risk. Staff cannot make an adequate assessment without full knowledge of the weekend's events.

Special needs presented by the correctional environment, especially those related to security, require certain modifications to the usual principles of psychological and psychiatric confidentiality (Metzner, 1993). For example, administration of psycho-tropic medication in the housing unit and movement to special units for observation or treatment may require the release of information (Metzner, 1993). Correctional officers who are integral members of the treatment team must be allowed access to the inmate's mental health records, but they in turn are bound by the same rules regarding confidentiality as mental health providers. Administrators not only need to be familiar with the relevant laws, rules, and regulations regarding confidentiality but they also need to develop related policies keeping in mind the staff working with inmates. These policies must be explained to the relevant staff and inmates.

A sixth method for optimizing the role of line staff is to make *better use of their time* in conjunction with orders of special observation of prisoners. It is unfair and inappropriate to order line staff coverage when the clinician knows there is inade-quate staff available to perform this watch. Such orders are perceived by correctional staff as an attempt by clinicians to shift responsibility to less well-paid correctional staff. By working together, usually an arrangement can be reached that is both rea-sonable and clinically appropriate. For example, an order for constant observation requires three staff to observe three inmates, even if they are in adjoining cells. An order worded "observe every minute," on the other hand, would allow one officer to walk back and forth, and observe all three inmates at least once per minute.

Finally, the therapeutic use of line staff can be improved by *selecting* staff who are well-suited for this role. In units that are used exclusively or predominately to house inmates with mental illness, correctional staff may be randomly assigned with little attention given to their appropriateness for this setting or their willingness to work with this population. Such assignments may be viewed as undesirable or based on the correctional officer's ability to intimidate or coerce inmates into being man-ageable. As described earlier, line staff can play a critical role in responding to the needs of inmates with mental illness. As a result, administrators should give careful attention to assigning staff also are both suitable for and willing to undertake this assignment.

How Best to Obtain and Use the Resources Needed to Deliver Services

One of the greatest challenges for correctional administrators is balancing the de-mands and needs for appropriate mental health services, knowing their value, with other competing needs in a conservative fiscal environment. Jails and prisons can seem like virtual seas of human service needs, with the resources provided never adequate (Dvoskin, 1989b). In one national survey of prisons and jails operated by the Federal Bureau of Prisons, officials from more than half of the facilities reported insufficient resources (staff, programs, or facilities) as a reason for why some inmates with mental illness go untreated (U.S. General Accounting Office, 1991).

Thus administrators must determine which mental health services are most cost-effective and use resources judiciously. For example, social workers and psychiatric nurses are less expensive than psychiatrists and psychologists, are more available, and are more likely to be more culturally and ethnically similar to the inmates they will serve (Dvoskin, 1989b). For services that do not require specific professions, it may be cost-effective to use a mix of mental health professionals.

Administrators may also have to make difficult decisions on which services to make available to meet the needs of the inmate population. Some program managers have established priority populations within their service parameters. In jails and lockups, for example, screening may be used to distinguish the varying mental health needs of inmates on admission, with resources focused on short-term crisis services designed to protect and treat those inmates who are most vulnerable to suicide, injury, or severe psychological distress. Because of the relatively long-term stay of prison inmates, administrators generally must provide a broad array of "community" mental health services, but they may choose to place greater emphasis on various components.[11] Each setting must focus on the mental health services that best relate to its population and mission (Dvoskin, 1989b).

A critical aspect of an administrator's job is to "sell" budget proposals to regulatory agencies and legislative bodies that provide funding for these programs (Dvoskin & Patterson, 1998). Budgets for mental health services for inmates have traditionally received less support than calls for resources for more sympathetic groups, such as children or elderly individuals. Nevertheless, a strong case can be made for funding services for offenders with mental disorders. A particularly viable strategy is to stress that by addressing the mental health needs of these inmates within the correctional setting, when close attention can be given to these needs, inmates can be better prepared for their transition into the community after release. By stressing the ability to better prepare inmates for their return to the community, police and members of the public who fear that offenders with mental disorders will pose a danger to the community on release can be mobilized in support of fiscal requests for correctional mental health services.

Another way to help obtain resources through the budgetary process is to provide accurate and reliable data that justify such requests. Computerized management information and mental health tracking systems can be used to identify inmates in need of mental health services, justify their need for services, and document the efficient delivery of needed services, housing, and resources (Metzner, 1992).

Correctional leaders can supply a key source of support for administrators seeking resources. No one is surprised when mental health officials seek mental health funds. However, when district attorneys, sheriffs, police chiefs, and correctional staff, including wardens and line staff, lobby for additional funding, particularly when it goes to another agency or entity, this tends to draw considerable attention (Dvoskin & Patterson, 1998). Correctional staff can be persuaded to support these initiatives because better mental health services makes the correctional setting a better place to work and one that is safer for both inmates and staff. Legislative bodies and regulatory agencies may find such sources of support particularly compelling because they appear to have a less vested interest in this outcome. Furthermore, such calls for support can appeal to a broad political spectrum, encompassing both liberals,

---

[11]There are six basic services that should be provided in a correctional setting. They include (a) screening and triage; (b) follow-up evaluations; (c) crisis intervention services (including crisis beds); (d) suicide prevention services; (e) "outpatient" mental health clinic services to the general population (including programs for inmates with special needs, substance abuse problems, and provision of case management); and (f) special housing–management options (including intermediate care programs and longer term residential treatment units). Finally, in addition to these services that are provided within the correctional environment, systems must also have the ability to transfer inmates to inpatient psychiatric hospitals when the inmate's clinical needs cannot be met safely in any other way.

with their traditional support of human services funding, and conservatives, with their support of public safety initiatives.

Special Security Concerns

Frequently within the correctional setting there will be some offenders with mental illness that require an inordinate amount of time and attention from staff and that pose special security concerns.

Disciplinary Proceedings

One of the ongoing challenges for administrators of correctional facilities is to maintain order and discipline. Facility rules and regulations are established to ensure that order and discipline are maintained. When an inmate fails to adhere to these rules and regulations, disciplinary proceedings are instituted against the inmate that may result in the inmate losing privileges (e.g., being deprived of commissary or recreation facility privileges, being confined to his or her cell) or other consequences such as placement in segregated housing and a loss of "good time." Courts have generally recognized the importance of correctional administrators being able to maintain order and discipline, but have also recognized that disciplinary proceedings must contain certain elements of fairness (*Wolff v. McDonald*, 1974).

With regard to inmates with mental illness, the question has arisen whether they should be able to raise their mental health problems as a defense to a charge of a disciplinary violation. Of particular concern to administrators has been the issue of whether an inmate should be able to compel a mental health clinician at the facility to provide testimony regarding the inmate's mental health status at these proceedings. From the administrator's perspective, the danger of this scenario is that it places the mental health professional in a position of being able to exonerate an inmate from a charge initially brought by a correctional officer, potentially creating distrust and tension between these two groups of staff.

One approach that administrators might consider has been applied in New York and upheld by the Second Circuit of the U.S. Court of Appeals (*Powell v. Coughlin*, 1991). This policy bars a prison inmate from using a mental health professional employed in the prison where the prisoner is incarcerated as an expert in a disciplinary hearing. Specifically, the policy allows such employees to testify about facts (e.g., eyewitness accounts of assaults) but prohibits them from testifying about an inmate's mental status while in the presence of the inmate at this hearing. The rationale for this policy is that mental health professionals' direct participation in disciplinary hearings will compromise their role as treatment providers, will give inmates a "model" of how to avoid punishment by claiming mental illness, and divert resources that should be used for treatment (Dvoskin, Petrila, & Stark-Riemer, 1995). Although the Second Circuit did not directly rule on an inmate's right to pursue a formal mental status defense at a disciplinary hearing, by upholding this policy, the decision had the effect of virtually removing formal mental status defenses from these hearings.

Managing "Treatment Failures"

In virtually every correctional setting, there are inmates who, despite repeated and intensive staff efforts, come to be viewed as immutable to treatment interventions. Frequently self-injurious and dangerous to other inmates and staff, there are few "solutions" for the problems posed by these inmates. There are, however, a number of ways in which the destructive potential of such situations can be minimized.

Staff fears of being manipulated by such inmates may exacerbate the difficulties of caring for them. Frustrated staff may respond to behavioral outbursts by such inmates by further limiting their freedoms. Yet when the status quo is intolerable and these inmates feel they have no other means to express their dissatisfaction, they may engage in behaviors that are harmful to themselves or others, further escalating the struggle between themselves and staff who are charged with preventing such behaviors.

For these inmates, the following suggestions might be considered (see Dvoskin & Patterson, 1998).

- Create a specific management plan for each inmate (Rice et al., 1990; Webster et al., 1993). The management plan should address both clinical and custodial interventions. Behavioral programs may teach such inmates how to manage and recognize the impact of their own behavior and alternative means of expressing their frustrations.
- Give staff explicit permission to "do nothing" when in their judgment waiting is the safest response. More coercion does not always increase safety. For some inmates, their fear of staff may be the direct cause of their violent behavior.
- Include staff from all shifts in treatment team meetings addressing these inmates to promote consistency within and across shifts in responding to them. Similarly, hold regular meetings involving representatives from each service provider charged with the care of these inmates to obtain agreement on a consistently applied plan of care.

Of course, one of the most dire consequences of treatment failure occurs when persons with mental illness and criminal histories commit serious and well-publicized acts of criminal violence after their release. The fact that these incidents are rare does nothing to diminish their effect on public perceptions about the dangerousness of people with mental illness, especially those with histories of violent crime. Politicians, courts, and the press have made clear their desire to have individuals with a mental disorder who have committed a crime removed from the community until they no longer pose a threat to the community. But the ability of clinicians to make accurate, long-term predictions about the dangerousness of individuals on release has been repeatedly criticized and is, at best, unproven (Monahan & Steadman, 1994).

At the same time, there is increased acknowledgment of the incapacitating effect of years of institutionalization (Kiesler & Sibulkin, 1987). Long periods of maximum-security care can actually reduce a person's ability to safely return to the community. Thus the best treatment and the best way to ensure an eventual safe return to freedom may require progressive movement to less structured, more independent settings in which a person can learn or relearn the life skills necessary for a safe return to the community.

Role of Research and Program Evaluation

The final important administrative challenge is to incorporate research as an essential component of any correctional mental health system (Ogloff, Roesch, & Hart, 1994). This should include ongoing evaluations of the effectiveness of assessment and treatment programs. Such evaluations can be used by mental health professionals to make recommendations for improving services. Administrators can use the data to guide and inform virtually every important decision, and improve assessment, referral, and treatment phases of a program. Furthermore, such self-assessment efforts can help generate additional budgetary resources (Metzner, 1992).

When correctional mental health systems are involved in litigation, such evaluative data takes on special importance (Metzner & Dubovsky, 1986). They can be used to demonstrate the good faith efforts of administrators to improve conditions and to show that they are exercising professional judgment (*Youngberg v. Romeo*, 1982). However, if the results of studies are ignored, plaintiffs' claims of deliberate indifference may be buttressed.

Conclusion

Correctional mental health administrators are faced with the challenge of providing and managing systems of constitutionally adequate care within environments that are often stark and seemingly unsuited to therapeutic concerns. Further, these services must be provided safely, efficiently, and effectively. Systems hoping to provide care that is clinically sound, cost-effective, and constitutionally sufficient require much of their administrators. Balancing realistic expectations with optimistic standards of excellence is challenging in any setting, but it is especially difficult and yet vital in jails and prisons where the consequences of inadequate treatment are so high for inmates and the systems that house them. Recent experience has demonstrated that it is possible for them to provide inmates with services that in many cases are as good or better than those available in the free community provided administrators are armed with even minimally adequate resources.

References

Adams, K. (1985). Addressing inmate mental health problems: A new direction for prison therapeutic services. *Federal Probation, 49*(4), 27–33.

American Jail Association. (1989). Dealing with inmates at risk for suicide. *Jail Operations Bulletin, 3*(1), 1–6.

American Psychiatric Association. (1989). Position statement on psychiatric services in jails and prisons. *American Journal of Psychiatry, 146*(9), 1244.

Andrews, D. A., Bonta, J., & Hoge, R. D. (1990). Classification for effective rehabilitation: Rediscovering psychology. *Criminal Justice and Behavior, 17*(1), 19–52.

Baskin, D. R., Sommers, I., & Steadman, H. J. (1991). Assessing the impact of psychiatric impairment on prison violence. *Journal of Criminal Justice, 19*, 271–280.

Ben-David, S., & Silfen, P. (1994). In quest of a lost father? Inmates' preferences of staff relation in a psychiatric prison ward. *International Journal of Offender Therapy and Comparative Criminology, 38*(2), 131–139.

Brooks, J. (1992). Addressing recidivism: Legal education in correctional settings. *Rutgers Law Review, 44*, 699–741.

Cohen, F., & Dvoskin, J. (1992). Inmates with mental disorders: A guide to law and practice. *Mental and Physical Disability Law Reporter, 16*(4), 462–470.

Coleman, C. R. (1988). The clinical effectiveness of correctional staff in prison health units. *Psychiatric Annals, 18*(12), 684–691.

Condelli, W. S., Bradigan, B., & Holanchock, H. (1997). Intermediate care programs to reduce risk and better manage inmates with psychiatric disorders. *Behavioral Sciences & the Law, 15*, 460–467.

Condelli, W. S., Dvoskin, J. A., & Holanchock, H. (1994). Intermediate care programs for inmates with psychiatric disorders. *Bulletin of the American Academy of Psychiatry and Law, 22*(1), 63–70.

Dembo, R., Williams, L., & Stafford, B. (1986–1987). The impact of providing mental health and related services at a youth detention center on staff stress. *Journal of Prison and Jail Health, 6*(1), 23–39.

Dixon, L. (1990). Treatment v. security: States address the needs of the mentally ill in prisons. *State Health Reports: Mental Health, Alcoholism & Drug Abuse, 61*, 1–6.

Dvoskin, J. (1989a). The Palm Beach County, Florida, Forensic Program. In H. J. Steadman, D. W. McCarty, & J. P. Morrissey (Eds.), *The mentally ill in jail: Planning for essential services* (pp. 178–197). New York: Guilford Press.

Dvoskin, J. A. (1989b). The structure of correctional mental health services. In R. Rosner & R. B. Harmon (Eds.), *Correctional Psychiatry* (Vol. 6, pp. 380–87). New York: Plenum Press.

Dvoskin, J. A., & Horn, M. F. (1994, July/August). *Parole mental health evaluations.* Community Corrections Report.

Dvoskin, J. A., & Patterson, R. F. (1998). Administration of treatment programs for offenders with mental illness. In R. M. Wettstein (Ed.), *Treatment of offenders with mental disorders* (pp. 1–43). New York: Guilford Press.

Dvoskin, J. A., Petrila, J., & Stark-Riemer, S. (1995). Case note: Powell v. Coughlin and the application of the professional judgment rule to prison mental health. *Mental and Physical Disability Law Reporter, 19*(1), 108–114.

Dvoskin, J. A., & Powitzky, R. (1984). *A paradigm for the delivery of mental health services in prison.* Boulder, CO: National Academy of Corrections.

Dvoskin, J. A., & Steadman, H. J. (1989). Chronically mentally ill inmates: The wrong concept for the right services. *International Journal of Law and Psychiatry, 12*, 203–210.

Dvoskin, J. A., & Steadman, H. J. (1994). Using intensive case management to reduce violence by mentally ill persons in the community. *Hospital and Community Psychiatry, 45*(7), 679–684.

Ellis, J. (1993). Security officer's role in reducing inmate problem behaviors: A program based on contingency management. *Journal of Offender Rehabilitation, 20*(1–2), 61–72.

Gendreau, P., & Ross, R. R. (1987). Revivification of rehabilitation: Evidence from the 1980s. *Justice Quarterly, 4*, 349–407.

Genevie, L., Margolies, E., & Muhlin, G. L. (1986). How effective is correctional intervention? *Social Policy, 16*(3), 52–57.

Gibbs, J. J. (1987). Symptoms of psychopathology among jail prisoners: The effects of exposure to the jail environment. *Criminal Justice and Behavior, 14*(3), 288–310.

Greene, R. T. (1989). A comprehensive mental health care system for prison inmates: Retrospective look at New York's ten year experience. *International Journal of Law and Psychiatry, 11*, 381–389.

Haddad, J. E. (1991). Management of the chronically mentally ill within a correctional environment. *Correct Care, 5*(1), 1–2.

Hafemeister, T. L. (1998). Legal aspects of the treatment of offenders with mental disorders. In R. M. Wettstein (Ed.), *Treatment of offenders with mental disorders* (pp. 44–125). New York: Guilford Press.

Hafemeister, T. L., & Petrila, J. (1994). Treating the mentally disordered offender: Society's uncertain, conflicted, and changing views. *Florida State University Law Review, 21*, 729–871.

Henry, P., Senese, J. D., & Ingley, G. S. (1994). Use of force in America's prisons: An overview of current research. *Corrections Today, July*, 108–114.

Jurik, N. C., & Winn, R. (1987). Describing correctional-security dropouts and rejects: An individual or organizational profile? *Criminal Justice and Behavior, 14*(1), 5–25.

Kiesler, C. A., & Sibulkin, A. E. (1987). *Mental hospitalization: Myths and facts about a national crisis.* Newbury Park, CA: Sage.

Lamb, H. R., & Weinberger, L. E. (1998). Persons with severe mental illness in jails and prisons: A review. *Psychiatric Services, 49*(4), 483–492.

Lanier, C. S., Jr. (1991). Dimensions of father–child interaction in a New York State prison population. *Journal of Offender Rehabilitation, 16*(3–4), 27–42.

Lindquist, C. H., & Lindquist, C. A. (1997). Gender differences in distress: Mental health consequences of environmental stress among jail inmates. *Behavioral Sciences & the Law, 15*, 503–523.

Lombardo, L. X. (1985). Mental health work in prisons and jails: Inmate adjustment and indigenous correctional personnel. *Criminal Justice and Behavior, 12*(1), 17–27.

Luise, M. A. (1989). Note: Solitary Confinement: Legal and psychological considerations. *New England Journal on Criminal and Civil Confinement, 15*, 301–324.

MacKain, S. J., & Streveler, A. (1990). Social and independent living skills for psychiatric patients in a prison setting. *Behavior Modification, 14*(4), 490–518.

Maier, G. J., & Miller, R. D. (1989). Models of mental health delivery to correctional institutions. In R. Rosener & R. B. Harmon (Eds.), *Correctional psychiatry: Critical issues in American psychiatry and the law* (Vol. 6; pp. 231–244). New York: Plenum Press.

McCarthy, B. (1985). *Mentally ill and mentally retarded offenders in corrections. Sourcebook on the mentally disordered offender.* Washington, DC: U.S. Department of Justice, National Institute of Corrections.

McGuire, J. (1995). *What works: Reducing reoffending.* Chichester, England: John Wiley & Sons.

McShane, M. D. (1989). The bus stop revisited: Discipline and psychiatric patients in prison. *The Journal of Psychiatry and Law, 17*, 413–433.

Menditto, A. A. (1990). *Effectiveness of inpatient psychosocial treatment programs as a function of unit-wide patterns of staff-patient interactions.* Doctoral dissertation, University of Houston.

Metzner, J. L. (1992). A survey of university-prison collaboration and computerized tracking services in prisons. *Hospital and Community Psychiatry, 43*(7), 713–715.

Metzner, J. L. (1993). Guidelines for psychiatric services in prisons. *Criminal Behavior and Mental Health, 3*, 252–267.

Metzner, J. L., & Dubovsky, S. L. (1986). The role of the psychiatrist in evaluating a prison mental health system in litigation. *Bulletin of the American Academy of Psychiatry and the Law, 14*(1), 89–95.

Metzner, J. L., Fryer, G. E., & Usery, D. (1990). Prison mental health services: Results of a national survey of standards, resources, administrative structure, and litigation. *Journal of Forensic Sciences, 35*, 433–438.

Miller, R. D., Maier, G. J., & Kaye, M. S. (1988). Orienting the staff of a new maximum security forensic facility. *Hospital and Community Psychiatry, 39*(7), 780–781.

Mohelsky, H. (1982). The mental hospital and its environment. *Canadian Journal of Psychiatry, 27*, 487–481.

Monahan, J., & Steadman, H. J. (Eds.). (1994). *Violence and mental disorder: Developments in risk assessment.* Chicago: University of Chicago Press.

National Center on Institutions and Alternatives and the National Institute of Corrections, U.S. Department of Justice. (1998). *Model suicide prevention programs: Part I. Jail suicide/ mental health update, 7*(3), 1–9.

Nolan, J. L., Jr. (1998). *The therapeutic state: Justifying government at century's end.* New York: New York University Press.

Ogloff, J. R. P., Roesch, R., & Hart, S. D. (1994). Mental health services in jails and prisons: Legal, clinical, and policy issues. *Law and Psychology Review, 18*, 109–135.

Paul, G. L., & Lentz, R. J. (1977). *Psychosocial treatment of chronic mental patients: Milieu versus social-learning programs.* Cambridge, MA: Harvard University Press.

Policy Research Associates. (n.d.). *Blueprint for contracting for mental health services for jail detainees with mental illnesses.* Washington, DC: U.S. Department of Health and Human Services.

Powell v. Coughlin. (1991). 953 F.2d 744 (2d Cir.).

Quinsey, V. L., Harris, G. T., Rice, M. E., & Cormier, C. A. (1998). *Violent offenders: Appraising and managing risk.* Washington, DC: American Psychological Association.

Rice, M. E., Harris, G. T., Quinsey, V. L., & Cyr, M. (1990). Planning treatment programs in secure psychiatric facilities. In D. N. Weisstub (Ed.), *Law and mental health: International perspective* (Vol. 5, pp. 162–230). New York: Pergamon Press.

Ringel, N. B., & Segal, A. C. (1986). A mental health center's influence in a county jail. *Journal of Community Psychology, 14*(2), 171–182.

Severson, M. M. (1992). Redefining the boundaries of mental health services: A holistic approach to inmate mental health. *Federal Probation, 56*(3), 57–63.

Steadman, H. J. (Ed.). (1990). *Jail diversion for the mentally ill: Breaking through the barriers.* Boulder, CO: National Institute of Corrections.

Steelman, D. (1987). *The mentally impaired in New York's prisons: Problems and solutions.* New York: Correctional Association of New York.

Stone, T. H. (1997). Therapeutic implications of incarceration for persons with severe mental disorders: Searching for rational health care policy. *American Journal of Criminal Law, 24*, 283–358.

Suedfeld, P., Ramirez, C., Deaton, J., & Baker-Brown, G. (1982). Reactions and attributes of prisoners in solitary confinement. *Criminal Justice and Behavior, 9*(3), 303–340.

Toch, H. (1982). The disturbed disruptive inmate: Where does the bus stop? *Journal of Psychiatry and Law* (Fall), 327–349.

Toch, H., & Adams, K. (1986). Pathology and disruptiveness among prison inmates. *Research Crime and Delinquency, 23*, 7–21.

Travis, L. F., Latessa, E. J., & Vito, G. F. (1985). Private enterprise and institutional corrections: A call for caution. *Federal Probation, 49*(4), 11–18.

U.S. General Accounting Office. (1991). *Mentally ill inmates: BOP plans to improve screening and care in federal prisons and jails* (GAO/GGD-91-35). Washington, DC: U.S. General Accounting Office.

Walsh, J., & Bricout, J. (1996). Improving jail linkages of detainees with mental health agencies: The role of family contact. *Psychiatric Rehabilitation Journal, 20*(2), 73–76.

Wardlaw, G. (1983). Models for the custody of mentally disordered offenders. *International Journal of Law and Psychiatry, 6*, 159–176.

Webster, C. D., Hucker, S. J., & Grossman, M. G. (1993). Clinical programmes for mentally ill offenders. In K. Howells & C. R. Hollin (Eds.), *Clinical approaches to the mentally disordered offender* (pp. 87–109). Chichester, England: John Wiley & Sons.

Weinberger, L. E., & Sreenivasan, S. (1994). Ethical and professional conflicts in correctional psychology. *Professional Psychology: Research and Practice*, *25*(2), 161–167.

Wettstein, R. M. (1998). *Treatment of offenders with mental disorders*. New York: Guilford Press.

Wolff v. McDonald. (1974). 418 U.S. 539.

Youngberg v. Romeo. (1982). 457 U.S. 307.

Chapter 17
TREATING JUVENILE OFFENDERS IN COMMUNITY SETTINGS

Tamara L. Brown, Charles M. Borduin, and Scott W. Henggeler

Delinquent youth present a considerable problem for the juvenile justice and mental health systems. The juvenile justice system struggles with how to stem the tide of criminal activity among juveniles. Yet rates of serious criminal acts committed by youth continue to increase. The 1994 *Uniform Crime Reports* indicates that 20% of all arrests for violent crimes and 35% of all arrests for property crimes were made on persons under the age of 18 years (FBI, 1994). Arrest data, however, greatly underestimate rates of juvenile criminal behavior because the vast majority of such behavior does not lead to an arrest (Henggeler, 1989).

The mental health system struggles with how to attenuate further criminal activity and produce lasting changes in juvenile offenders, many of whom experience psychosocial and educational problems (Farrington, 1991; Laub & Sampson, 1994). Although a number of structured, skill-oriented treatments (e.g., behavioral parent training, cognitive–behavioral therapy, functional family therapy) have demonstrated efficacy with juvenile offenders in general (Kazdin, 1991; Lipsey, 1992), such treatments have been unsuccessful in treating serious juvenile offenders (see Bank, Marlow, Reid, Patterson, & Weinrott, 1991; Barton, Alexander, Waldron, Turner, & Warburton, 1985; Guerra & Slaby, 1990; Weisz, Walter, Weiss, Fernandez, & Mikow, 1990). Moreover, even favorable outcomes of these treatments with relatively mild forms of antisocial behavior are mitigated by findings that university-based successes seldom extend to community settings (Weiss, Weiss, & Donenberg, 1992). Thus one of the major challenges facing the mental health field is the development and validation of mental health services that are effective with juvenile offenders in community settings.

Despite the bad news that extant interventions for juvenile offenders have been largely unsuccessful, the good news is that some promising community-based treatments have been developed. The purpose of this chapter is to describe community-based treatment approaches that have demonstrated some promise with juvenile offenders at high risk for mental health problems.

Review of Treatments and Treatment Outcomes

In light of the various types of mental health problems that are prevalent among juvenile offenders, treatments should possess the flexibility to address a broad range of such problems. The multicausal nature of serious delinquent behavior (for a review see Henggeler, 1989; Howell, 1997) and of related mental health problems, such as substance abuse (Henggeler, 1997), suggests that effective treatments must consider

Preparation of this chapter was supported by National Institute of Mental Health Grant MH-51852 and National Institute on Drug Abuse Grants R01 DA10079 and DA08029.

variables that reflect major determinants of such behavior (e.g., adolescent cognitions, family relations, peer relations, school performance) and must have the capacity to intervene comprehensively at individual, family, peer, school, and possibly even neighborhood levels. Finally, to optimize the ecological validity of interventions, treatment should be provided in community-based settings that make up the natural environment of youths and their families.

The following review examines several community-based approaches to treating juvenile offenders. Although each of these approaches has wide appeal, few incorporate each of the previously mentioned considerations. So it is not surprising that most of these treatments have had little demonstrated success in treating serious antisocial behavior. Multisystemic therapy, however, which represents a broad-based and multifaceted treatment approach, has demonstrated considerable success in decreasing rates of criminal activity among chronic and violent juvenile offenders.

Adventure-Based Programs

Adventure-based programming, a variant of wilderness therapy (Kelly & Baer, 1971, 1978), has become an increasingly popular approach to treating juvenile offenders (Moote & Wodarski, 1997). This treatment approach uses individual and group counseling and various experiential learning activities (e.g., ropes courses) to help develop participants' interpersonal skills (e.g., communication, problem-solving, cooperation), their capacity to trust, and their self-esteem (Schoenwald, Scherer, & Brondino, 1997). Proponents of adventure-based programs (e.g., Alvarez & Welsh, 1990; Hopkins & Putnam, 1993; Schoel, Prouty, & Radcliffe, 1988) have suggested that their individual (e.g., specific skill training, counseling) and group interventions (e.g., icebreakers, trust/spotting, high and low ropes courses) rely on cognitive (e.g., challenging beliefs) and behavioral (e.g., positive reinforcement) principles to improve youths' emotional responses, enhance their self-esteem, and ultimately, reduce their delinquent behavior. One significant feature of this treatment approach is that it is flexible enough to be adapted to youths of varying ages in a variety of community settings (schools, outpatient treatment facilities).

Fewer than 20 empirical studies have evaluated adventure-based programming (Moote & Wodarski, 1997), and of those, only one included a delinquent sample (Sale, 1992) and one other included a "behaviorally disordered" adolescent sample (Sach & Miller, 1992). In an uncontrolled study with only a pretest–posttest design, Sale (1992) examined the ego and self-concept development of 30 delinquent adolescents. Findings indicated that the adolescents showed significant gains in ego development and self-concept. With no comparison group, however, it is impossible to know whether these short-term changes were a result of participation in the program. Sach and Miller (1992), using a sample of "behaviorally disordered adolescents," compared eight adolescents in an adventure-based program (treatment condition) with eight control group adolescents on social interaction and concluded that the adventure program had a significant short-term impact on participants' cooperative behavior. Small sample sizes and lack of specification of the treatment, however, limit the conclusions that can be drawn from this study. In sum, both studies possess serious methodological problems, thus casting doubt on the validity of the findings.

Although studies of adventure-based programs generally report positive outcomes for participants, more rigorous research is needed beyond these subjective claims. Specifically, the methodological problems in current studies of adventure-based programming need to be addressed in future work in this area. Moreover, the main focus should be to clearly demonstrate effects on delinquent behavior. The issue of how these changes occur is also relevant, but probably less so at this point than showing long-term reductions in delinquency. In addition, available findings suggest that program effects may be short-term and limited to the treatment setting in which they occur, thus calling into question the ecological validity (i.e., generalizability) of this treatment approach. Thus clinical trials are needed to determine whether treatment changes are maintained when the youths and families return to the community (Schoenwald et al., 1997), and whether treatment effects generalize to other settings (e.g., school, home). Finally, the interventions and guidelines of adventure-based programming in the treatment need to be specified in enough detail to permit program replication and evaluation. In the absence of a treatment manual or a detailed description of the treatment procedures, program replication and dissemination are difficult, if not impossible.

Behavioral Parent Training

Behavioral parent training is widely used in mental health, social service, and juvenile justice systems across the United States in treating child antisocial behavior (Serketich & Dumas, 1996). Although the specific components of behavioral parent training programs can vary somewhat, most programs are based on the following assumptions (Bank et al., 1991; Serketich & Dumas, 1996):

- *Youths' problem behaviors are largely a function of contingencies that are provided by parents.* Thus therapists seek to teach parents to identify, monitor, and respond to problem behaviors in new ways. To accomplish these tasks, therapists use didactic instruction, modeling, and role plays with parents.
- *Positive reinforcement is needed to maintain and generalize treatment gains.* Thus therapists not only devote considerable effort to helping parents acquire and implement (e.g., through homework assignments) the skills needed to change their children's problem behaviors but they also provide support for parents' appropriate and consistent implementation of those skills (e.g., by calling parents between sessions to reinforce progress and to answer questions or offer advice).

Behavioral parent training programs have a number of important features. First, they are time-limited. Second, they view parents as the important change agent for adolescent problem behaviors. Third, parent training targets those child behaviors and family interactions that have been empirically demonstrated to cause or contribute to delinquency (e.g., poor parental monitoring, coercive discipline strategies, inconsistent parenting).

Although behavioral parent training has demonstrated success in treating problem behavior of young children (Serketich & Dumas, 1996), results regarding its effectiveness in modifying adolescent behavior have been inconsistent (for a review, see Serketich & Dumas, 1996), and no studies have demonstrated favorable long-term effects with serious juvenile offenders (Serketich & Dumas, 1996). Moreover, the effectiveness of behavioral parent training, even with young children, is seriously limited by parent and family characteristics. Indeed, families characterized by multiple risk factors associated with child/adolescent behavior problems (e.g., marital distress, socioeconomic disadvantage, social isolation, single parenthood, parental depression) tend to show fewer and shorter gains following treatment (for reviews, see Forehand & Kotchick, 1996; Kazdin, 1991; Serketich & Dumas, 1996). It is important to note that these risk factors are relatively common in families of juvenile offenders with mental disorders.

In one of the few controlled clinical trials to evaluate behavioral parent training with families of chronically delinquent youths, Bank et al. (1991) found no differences between parent training treatment and an alternative community treatment in short-term (i.e., during the treatment year) or long-term (i.e. three years following treatment) arrest rates. In addition, the behavioral parent training program was unsuccessful in reducing coercive parent–adolescent relations from pretreatment to posttreatment. The authors reported that their clinical work with the families of the delinquent youths was "extraordinarily difficult" (p. 31) and that they had doubts about the feasibility of using behavioral parent training with these families. More recently, Schoenwald and Henggeler (in press) have questioned whether behavioral parenting training as practiced in treatment studies with well-trained therapists resembles that implemented by community-based practitioners who have more eclectic treatment orientations and who receive no specialized training or adherence monitoring. Thus little evidence supports behavioral parent training as an effective treatment approach for juvenile offenders with mental disorders and their families.

Teaching-Family Model

The teaching-family model is one of the most broadly disseminated community-based group-home treatment approaches for juvenile offenders (Braukmann, et al., 1985; Fixsen & Blase, 1993), and the treatment model has been extended into treatment foster homes and home-based treatment (Fixsen & Blase, 1993). All teaching-family model homes are affiliated with teaching-family association training sites, and these training sites serve as the mechanism by which the teaching-family association remains accountable for ensuring the integrity of the teaching-family model (Fixsen & Blase, 1993).

Each home typically includes about seven chronic juvenile offenders and a trained couple (called "teaching parents") who receive extensive training and supervision in the treatment procedures. Within the home, the teaching-parents administer a behavioral system of points and privileges, with rules regarding behavior and consistent enforcement of contingencies for rule violations. The underlying premise is that youths' behavior will change as a result of residing in structured home environments with parent figures who, through the application of various intervention strategies, provide support and advocacy for youth and teach them about specific skills, self-government, motivation, and relationship development. In addition to providing direct treatment, the teaching-parents also maintain contact with school personnel (youths typically attend the local public school), court and welfare agency personnel, and youths' families (typically youth are allowed live with their families on weekends).

Although approximately 3,000 youths each year receive treatment in the teaching-family model (Fixsen & Blase, 1993), support for the effectiveness of these programs with juvenile offenders is limited. To date, randomized clinical trials have not been used to evaluate program effectiveness. However, in studies that have used a treatment or no-treatment control group, the results have generally indicated that short-term reductions in youths' delinquent behavior or substance use and short-term increases in youths' prosocial behaviors have not been maintained after youths leave the home (Braukmann et al., 1985; Kirigin, Braukman, Atwater, & Wolf, 1982; Mulvey, Arthur, & Reppucci, 1993). Thus although teaching-family homes seem to serve as safe placements for juvenile offenders, they do not seem to produce any lasting improvements for program participants.

The failure of the teaching-family model to produce lasting change in youth antisocial behavior is not surprising for at least two reasons: First, Dishion and Andrews (1995) have shown that increased contact with antisocial peers in treatment settings can exacerbate rather than diminish problem behavior, and, second, treatment is not provided to the youths' families or other key systems (e.g., peers, school, neighborhood) that are known to be related to youths' antisocial behavior and to which the youth return.

Individualized/Wraparound Care

Individualized care or wraparound services is a promising approach to interagency collaboration and commitment to complete flexibility in arranging services for individual youth and their families (Burchard & Clarke, 1990). Wraparound is a process for altering a community's service coordination and service delivery processes in general and on a case by case basis (VanDenBerg & Grealish, 1996). An underlying assumption of wraparound is that children and families with multiple needs require multiple services. Thus youths, parents, and agency representatives collaborate in developing service plans that attempt to "wrap" services around families to meet youth and family short- and long-term needs (Borduin, 1994). Six basic principles serve as the foundation for individualized/wraparound care (Burchard & Clarke, 1990; Melton & Pagliocca, 1992):

- *Unconditional care.* In contrast to treatments that limit services depending on a client's age, legal status, diagnosis, or behavior, individualized care makes a commitment to provide services until they are no longer needed. A case manager is responsible for ensuring that services are provided and that service plans and funding are redesigned to meet families changing needs.
- *Least restrictive care.* Services are provided in as "mainstream" a fashion and setting as possible. Moves to less restrictive settings are based on demonstrated improvements in adjustment rather than on standard time periods, and all decisions regarding placement are made by an interdisciplinary team.
- *Child and family centered care.* This is the core principle of individualized/ wraparound programs. Youths and families are members of the interdisciplinary team and, thus, participate fully in treatment decisions. Moreover, ser-

vice providers are hired because of their ability to meet a specific child's needs rather than on the basis of general professional credentials.

- *Flexible care.* To prevent restrictive placements, the ability to provide immediate interventions that can be increased or decreased as needed, especially in times of crisis, is imperative.
- *Flexible funding.* Funding follows the child. In other words, money is attached to the child for the purchase of services, not to a program for the delivery of services.
- *Interagency care.* An individualized service plan is developed, monitored, and modified by the youth-specific interdisciplinary team. The plan serves to foster collaboration, communication, and accountability in developing and implementing agreed on services.

A notable example of the individualized care or wraparound services model is the Alaska Youth Initiative (AYI; for a description of the program see Burchard, Burchard, Sewell, & VanDenBerg, 1993; Melton & Pagliocca, 1992), a program developed for the purpose of returning youth from out-of-state placements. Consistent with the guiding principles of individualized care, the AYI possesses the flexibility needed to address the multiple factors contributing to youths' problem behaviors; services are individualized, and when appropriate services do not exist they are developed and funded; and treatment is intensive, provided by skilled staff, and implemented in youths' own communities (Borduin, 1994).

Available data indicate that AYI has achieved its initial goals of returning children from out-of-state placements (Melton & Pagliocca, 1992), and has helped to reduce the number of youth placed in residential settings and increased the number of youth served in their own communities (Child Welfare League of America, 1992). Similarly, although no comparison group was used, Yoe, Santarcangelo, Atkins, & Burchard (1996) reported that the Vermont Wraparound Care Initiative successfully moved (and kept) youths in less restrictive living environments during the 12-month study period. Yoe et al. (1996) also reported no change in the youths school placements during treatment, and in spite of reported reductions in the frequency of some externalizing, internalizing, and abuse-related behaviors, program youths evinced increases in public externalizing behaviors such as police contact, truancy, alcohol and substance abuse, and suicide attempts. Clearly, conclusions that wraparound programs are effective are premature and potentially misleading (Rosenblatt, 1996). Thus research to date on wraparound programs must be viewed cautiously.

In sum, approaches used to evaluate wraparound programs are not characterized by the methods needed to demonstrate whether it is an effective service. The absence of controlled evaluations of short- and long-term outcomes (Borduin, 1994; Rosenblatt, 1996), reliance on retrospective case manager reports of behavior and behavior improvements during treatment (Yoe et al., 1996), and lack of statistical power in many of the studies evaluating wraparound programs (Rosenblatt, 1996) make it difficult to draw conclusions about the effectiveness of wraparound initiatives. Moreover, a definition of wraparound/individualized care (Rosenblatt, 1996); operationalization of the wraparound process, which includes the specification of measures of treatment adherence and measures of key success indicators (Clark & Clarke, 1996; Rosenblatt, 1996); and "further elaboration of service-planning decisions and treatment methods will be needed before this flexible, broad-based model of service coordination and delivery can be replicated and evaluated by other investigators" (Borduin, 1994, p. 22).

Family Ties

Family ties is an intensive family preservation program that targets the families of juvenile offenders at imminent risk of out-of-home placement (New York Department of Juvenile Justice, 1990). Based on the home-builders model (Kinney, Haapala, & Booth, 1991), family ties includes individualized ecological interventions that are intensive, flexible, home-based, time-limited, and goal-oriented. Services are provided by a therapist in natural settings (home, school) and include a variety of interventions ranging from individual and family counseling to the provision of concrete needs (child care, employment). Therapists are available 24 hours a day, 7 days a week, and work with families for a minimum of 10 to 15 hours per week over a four- to six-week period.

Since its inception in 1989, the New York Department of Juvenile Justice (1990) estimated that approximately 70% of the youth who participated in family ties programs have avoided institutional placement. However, family ties programs have not been evaluated using controlled (randomized) clinical trials. Moreover, controlled studies comparing the homebuilders model (on which family ties program is based) to traditional community services have failed to support its long-term efficacy (Fraser, Nelson, & Rivard, in press). Thus conclusions about the effectiveness of family ties programs are tentative.

Intensive Supervision Programs

Intensive supervision programs (ISPs) are community-based correctional alternatives to incarceration and regular probation that are designed to both punish and control juvenile offenders in the community. Because ISPs are viewed as a way to "increase the heat on probationers" (Erwin, 1986; Petersilia, 1990), treatment/rehabilitative program components are greatly deemphasized (Gendreau, Paparozzi, Little, & Goddart, 1993). Although some of the interventions used in ISPs are potentially rehabilitative, ISP interventions are not selected based on potential effectiveness for juvenile offenders with mental disorders; rather, ISP interventions are used because they provide negative sanctions (Clear, 1991).

ISPs are appealing because they aim to (a) reduce prison overcrowding by releasing some offenders from prison or by diverting new offenders from incarceration, (b) reduce recidivism as a result of the increased monitoring provided by programs (as compared to that provided by more traditional parole services), (c) enhance regular probation and parole efforts, and (d) reduce costs because it is believed that supervising offenders in the community is less costly than incarceration. The development and spread of ISPs is being driven not only by the continued problem of prison crowding and the lure of possible cost savings from reduced reliance on incarceration (DeJong & Franzeen, 1993), but also by the belief that, whether exercised in prison or in the community, threats of punishment and enhanced surveillance deter criminality (Cullen, Wright, & Applegate, 1996).

Common components of ISPs include frequent contact between offenders and supervisors, confining offenders to their homes, enforcing curfew requirements, random drug testing, work crews, requiring offenders to perform community service and/or pay restitution to victims, electronic monitoring of offenders' whereabouts, and requiring offenders to pay fines and/or pay for the privilege of being supervised. In addition, boot camps (also known as shock incarceration), and other residential/ restrictive placements are often used as adjuncts to ISPs. These components also exist in regular supervision/probation programs. According to Clear (1991), the main (or sometimes only) difference between intensive and regular supervision programs is the intensity/frequency with which program components are applied. Although ISPs vary in the type of offenders they serve (e.g., probationers, parolees, etc.), high-risk offenders (e.g., persons convicted of murder) tend to be excluded from participation.

The review of ISP outcomes is divided into three sections. First, effectiveness of the interventions commonly used in ISPs is reviewed. Second, research on the ability of ISPs to meet their specific aims is discussed. Third, results of the most rigorous empirical evaluation conducted to date of the overall effectiveness of ISPs are summarized.

Interventions

Although a variety of interventions are used with ISPs, the most common are home confinement, electronic monitoring, drug testing, and boot camps.

Home Confinement/Electronic Monitoring

Commonly referred to as "house arrest," the goal of home confinement is to regulate and restrict the freedom of offenders who are released to the community. Although this can be achieved through a variety of means (e.g., visits, telephone calls, etc.), electronic monitoring is commonly used. Evaluations of home confinement programs have yielded discouraging results. In general, research on home confinement/ electronic monitoring (HC/EM) programs has been limited by the low-risk nature of most samples, too few experimental evaluations, and lack of program integrity (Bonta, 1993). Although prison diversion is a primary goal of house confinement, research indicates that most programs are too small in size, and significant threats to program integrity undermine their capacity to reduce prison overcrowding (Cullen et al., 1996). In terms of recidivism, almost all HC/EM programs report low recidivism rates, but this is not surprising given the low-risk nature of the offenders monitored by HC/EM programs (Rogers & Jolin, 1991). Thus the ability of HC/EM programs to reduce recidivism for more serious offenders remains a question (Smith & Akers, 1993). It is also not clear that this intervention reduces technical violations any better than other correctional supervision programs (Cullen et al., 1996).

Electronic Monitoring

Ideally, electronic monitors alert officials whenever offenders leave their place of residence or travel in off-limits areas, and officials are immediately dispatched to the offender's location to handle the situation. It is believed that electronic monitoring deters offenders from engaging in rule violations because of the certainty and immediacy of detection. However, data generally indicate that use of electronic monitoring is costly and does not affect recidivism. Brown and Roy (1995) found that the effectiveness of electronic monitoring varies with the type of offender being monitored in that, as with manual supervision, it is easier to electronically monitor offenders who are unemployed and unmarried. Two of the studies (Austin & Hardyman, 1991; Baumer & Mendelsohn, 1991) reviewed by Cullen et al. (1996) used an experimental design to compare the effects that electronic monitoring versus manual supervision had on rates of recidivism and technical violations. Both evaluations found no significant differences in rearrests or revocation rates after a one-year follow-up, even though the electronic monitoring group had significantly more contacts with officials. About 42% of both the electronically and manually monitored groups had unauthorized absences from the home. Moreover, electronic monitoring is an expensive program to implement because it is labor intensive and requires specialized training, altered organizational structures, and high levels of coordination between the officer in the field and the person or company responsible for notification of an infraction (Baumer & Mendelsohn, 1991). Additional costs include "technology shock, information overload, unanticipated computer programming time, and extra time tracing and verifying negative contacts" (Baumer, Mendelsohn, & Rhine, 1990, p. 35). In sum, the costs associated with establishing electronic monitoring systems seem unnecessary expenditures because electronic monitoring does not appear to be effective, nor does it appear to augment the effectiveness of home confinement programs.

Drug Testing

Drug testing offenders on parole or probation has been used for more than a decade. Programs vary in the frequency (e.g., once per week versus once per month), schedule (e.g., periodic versus scheduled versus random), and methods used (e.g., urine, blood, hair samples) to test for drug activity and in the punishments for positive screens. Research indicates that the ability of drug testing to deter future use and criminal activity is linked with the ability of the program to implement sanctions quickly. For example, in the absence of immediate sanctions (e.g., arrest) which are short but certain, drug testing has little or no effect on criminal behavior (Cullen et al., 1996). Goldkamp and Jones (1992), in an experimental evaluation of whether pretrial drug monitoring would deter defendants from crime and flight, found that drug tested offenders did not have lower rates of rearrest or failure to appear at court hearings. Similarly, Britt, Gottfredson, and Goldkamp (1992) examined the effect of periodic drug testing on rearrest rates and failure to appear for trial and found that monitoring the drug use of offenders had no effect on reducing the level of "pretrial misconduct." These results are even more troubling in light of the annual cost of the drug testing program used in the study, which ranged between $400,000 and $500,000. It appears that part of the explanation for these null findings may be a result of implementation problems. For example, Goldkamp and Jones (1992) reported that sanctions for positive tests were not implemented as designed because sanctioning noncompliant defendants, especially with jail terms, would have required hearings that would have consumed considerable court time and resources and placed a significant demand on jail resources, expenditures that officials were unable to accept. The high cost, poor outcomes, and significant implementation problems associated with drug testing programs make drug testing, in and of itself, a problematic option for communities interested in deterring crime.

Boot Camps

Although specific elements of boot camps (also known as shock incarcerations) vary widely from state to state, they tend to be highly structured residential programs that include military components such as drill and physical training, are designed for nonserious juvenile offenders, and tend to last for three to six months. In general, evaluations of boot camp programs indicate that they do not protect the public (assuming that youths will eventually return to the community), nor do they help the youth so confined. For example, the California Youth Authority (1997) conducted a five-year evaluation of their juvenile boot camp program and found that it did not reduce recidivism. Following the program, boot camp youth did not differ from controls on the number of positive drug tests, criminal activity/rearrests, severity of subsequent offenses, number of days worked, or school attendance. Moreover, cost analyses indicated that the boot camp program was more costly than usual services. Similarly, results of evaluations of New York's shock incarceration program indicate that although program graduates were initially less likely to be reincarcerated than a comparison group of paroled youth who were eligible for the program, these differences disappeared when the groups were followed long-term (Aziz, Korotkin, & MacDonald, 1990). Evaluations of the Louisiana shock incarceration program indicate that program graduates were more likely to be rearrested than dropouts, parolees, or probationers (MacKinsie, 1991), and were more likely to receive revocation for technical violations. A cost-effectiveness summary of juvenile boot camp programs (Washington State Institute for Public Policy, 1998) indicated that they increase criminal justice system costs and crime victim costs, and that this lost revenue is never recovered by the program. This pattern of findings is consistent across almost all boot camp program evaluations (Cullen et al., 1996), and suggests that boot camp programs do not serve a useful treatment function for juvenile offenders.

Specific Aims

There are three specific aims of ISPs: reducing prison overcrowding, reducing recidivism, and reducing costs. In general, and indicated previously, research indicates that ISPs, as currently implemented, do not successfully meet any of their objectives.

Reducing Prison Overcrowding

Some of the interventions used in ISPs to reduce prison overcrowding (e.g., home confinement/electronic monitoring) have been shown to be ineffective in attaining this desired outcome. In fact, ISPs may contribute to the problem of prison overcrowding. Juvenile offenders in ISPs are watched more closely and, as a result, technical violations are more likely to be detected and processed (Gendreau et al., 1993). In addition, ISP offenders typically have more release conditions and may, thus, be a greater risk for rule violations. Moreover, Gendreau et al. (1993) reported that courts may increase prison crowding through ISPs in that some judges have sent potentially eligible probationers to jail on the assumption that they would get into an ISP when, in fact, this sometimes did not happen. In sum, the ability of ISPs to reduce the problem of prison crowding has yet to be demonstrated, and some studies suggest ISPs actually increase prison crowding.

Reducing Recidivism

Another expectation is that ISPs would produce lower recidivism rates than regular probation or parole. According to Gendreau et al., (1993), "Alternative sanctions either as stand-alone programs or incorporated into ISPs inevitably result in about the same or slightly higher recidivism rates than comparable regular probation programs which monitor inmates much less intensively" (p. 33). Moreover, none of the ISP program evaluations we reviewed assessed the quality of the "treatment" services being delivered. To have an effect on recidivism, ISPs will need to pay more attention to overcoming implementation problems and assessing the quality of the treatment services that are delivered, because research (e.g., Pearson, 1987; Petersilia & Turner, 1993a) indicates that the greatest reductions in recidivism occur among high-risk offenders in programs that offer more treatment than regular probation.

Reductions in Cost

ISPs are costly (Washington State Institute for Public Policy, 1998) and some estimates indicate they are about 50% more costly than routine probation supervision (Petersilia & Turner, 1993a). Moreover, as mentioned previously, specific aspects of ISPs, such as drug testing and electronic monitoring, can be very expensive. Given these cost estimates, and the generally negative findings associated with ISPs (and their associated program and adjunct components), it is doubtful that ISPs result in any real cost savings. Instead, it seems likely that ISPs may be more costly because they may inadvertently send offenders to prison who would otherwise be eligible for probation and they cater to low-risk offenders who may not need intense supervision (Gendreau et al., 1993). Moreover, according to Clear and Hardyman (1990), regular probation services, deprived of resources that have been diverted to ISPs, are now forced to monitor higher-risk offenders less closely, thereby jeopardizing public safety.

Overall Evaluation

Because ISPs are used mainly as a means of increasing surveillance but not treatment, evaluations have not shown better recidivism results than regular probation (Howell, 1997). "Every comprehensive review of studies of intensive programs has produced the same general commentary: The success rates of the more intensive programs generally are not better—and often *are even worse*—than those of regular probation" (Clear, 1991, p. 33). The most rigorous evaluation of intensive supervision programs was conducted by the RAND Corporation (Petersilia & Turner, 1993a). The study used an experimental design to evaluate 14 intensive supervision programs in nine states; the findings were consistent across all jurisdictions. The data showed that although the intensive supervision programs succeeded in increasing the surveillance of offenders, surveillance and control had little impact on recidivism rates. Amount of surveillance was not related to recidivism. Furthermore, Petersilia and Turner (1993b) concluded that "at no site did ISP participants experience arrest less often, have a longer time to failure, or experience arrests for less serious offenses" (pp. 310–311). In fact, arrest rates for offenders in the program were higher at the one-year follow-up than for the control group, and when technical violations were considered, the results for program participants were even worse (average violation rate was 65% [range = 50% to 80%] for participants versus an average of 38% for controls). A positive finding was that there was a reduction in rearrests for offenders who participated in treatment programs. The data also showed that the potential of intensive supervision programs to reduce prison crowding by serving as an alternative to incarceration is limited because of obstacles (e.g., resistance from judges) to divert prisoners from prison.

In light of their limited ability to affect offender behavior, use of ISPs as crime control mechanisms, alternatives to incarceration, or solutions to prison overcrowding seems unwarranted. Moreover, the lure of cost savings is unrealized, because ISP are often more costly than regular correctional services yet offer little return on the monetary investment. In addition to addressing the issues raised in this review, if ISPs are to become useful, it will be important to define what constitutes "intensive," and specify the "intervention" that is to be delivered. Currently, ISPs vary extensively in both the amount (e.g., four contacts per month in Ohio versus five contacts per week in Georgia) and duration (e.g., one or more years in Ohio versus only six weeks in Georgia) of surveillance they provide (Cullen et al., 1996), making it difficult to know what *intensive* really is. Also, as currently implemented, it is unlikely that ISPs provide effective treatment for juvenile offenders with mental disorders, because individual differences in youth tend to be ignored in ISPs (Gendreau et al., 1993), and "there have been no ISPs that deliberately matched clients with services" (Gendreau et al., 1993, p. 32). What is promising, however, is the potential for ISPs to serve a rehabilitation function when a viable treatment is added and treatment becomes more of a focus than punishment. Thus developing effective community-based treatments that target juvenile offenders' mental health, behavioral, and family needs seems to be the best bet for making intensive supervision programs feasible.

Multisystemic Therapy

Multisystemic Therapy (MST; Henggeler & Borduin, 1990; Henggeler, Schoenwald, Borduin, Rowland, & Cunningham, 1998) is an intense, time-limited treatment approach that is based on Bronfenbrenner's (1979) social–ecological theory of behavior. Social–ecological theory views the child and family's friends, school, work, neighborhood, and community as interconnected systems with dynamic and reciprocal influences on the behavior of family members. From this perspective, and consistent with the findings of causal modeling studies of delinquency (Henggeler,

1991), adolescent problem behaviors are understood to be multidetermined and linked with key characteristics of the systems in which youths and families are embedded. Thus the scope of MST interventions is not limited to the individual adolescent or family system, but includes transactions between the family and other systems (e.g., between parents and a youth's peers or teachers).

A basic premise of MST is that antisocial behavior is best treated by altering those variables in the natural environment that have been empirically linked with antisocial behavior. Therefore, MST intervenes directly in the systems and processes known to be related to adolescent antisocial behavior, using the strengths of these systems as levers for change. MST includes a range of interventions and techniques shown to be effective in treating each of the varied problems evinced by adolescents and their families.

To promote lasting changes, MST seeks to empower parents and youth to address the developmental, academic, social, and situational challenges that arise throughout adolescence, and treatment is designed in accordance with nine MST principles.

1. The primary purpose of assessment is to understand the "fit" between the identified problems and their broader systemic context.
2. Therapeutic contacts should emphasize the positive and should use systemic strengths as levers for change.
3. Interventions should be designed to promote responsible behavior and decrease irresponsible behavior among family members.
4. Interventions should be present-focused and action-oriented, targeting specific and well-defined problems.
5. Interventions should target sequences of behavior within or between multiple systems that maintain the identified problems.
6. Interventions should be developmentally appropriate and fit the developmental needs of the youth.
7. Interventions should be designed to require daily or weekly effort by family members.
8. Intervention efficacy is evaluated continuously from multiple perspectives, with providers assuming accountability for overcoming barriers to successful outcomes.
9. Interventions should be designed to promote treatment generalization and long-term maintenance of therapeutic change by empowering caregivers to address family members' needs across multiple systemic contexts.

Consistent with a home-based model of service delivery, MST is usually delivered in the family's home (although meetings can sometimes be held in other community settings) at a convenient time, thereby increasing cooperation and enhancing treatment generalization. Problems are identified and targeted conjointly by the family and the therapist. The identified strengths of each system are used to facilitate the identified changes, and considerable emphasis is placed on supporting the parents as primary change agents and on developing a natural social support network to increase the likelihood that changes will be maintained after treatment terminates.

Because of the varying demands of each family, MST therapists must be capable of applying a range of empirically-based therapeutic approaches (e.g., structural family therapy, cognitive–behavioral therapy) and tailoring interventions to the unique needs and strengths of each family. Thus MST therapists are trained as generalists and may intervene directly in one or more systems (e.g., individual, marital, family, peer, school) or at the interface of two systems (e.g., family–school relations). To develop and maintain the focus and treatment adherence needed for favorable outcomes, strong therapist training and support are critical (see Henggeler, Melton, Brondino, Scherer, & Hanley, 1997). To enable therapists to provide such intensive and comprehensive services, the typical MST caseload is four to six families per therapist, and therapists work in teams of three. The treatment team is available to clients 24 hours per day, 7 days per week, and in the initial stages of treatment, contacts are made daily (sometimes several times a day) in most cases. In addition to round-the-clock availability, a unique and central aspect of MST is that therapists are accountable for engaging families in treatment and for outcomes based on concrete evidence of behavior change. Extensive and ongoing training of therapists is an important ingredient to maintaining the integrity of MST, and treatment adherence is strictly monitored.

To date, MST is the only treatment for serious delinquent behavior that has demonstrated both short-term and long-term treatment effects in randomized, controlled clinical trials with violent and chronic juvenile offenders and their families from various cultural and ethnic backgrounds (see Borduin et al., 1995; Henggeler, Melton, Brondino, Scherer, & Hanley, 1997; Henggeler et al., 1992; Henggeler, Melton, Smith, Schoenwald, & Hanley, 1993). In these studies, MST was effective in improving key correlates of juvenile offending (i.e., family and peer relations, individual adjustment) and was able to sustain reductions in violent and other serious criminal behavior for 2.4 (Henggeler et al., 1992, 1993) and 4 years (Borduin et al., 1995) following treatment. In addition, analyses of self-report data from the Henggeler et al. (1992) sample and of arrest data from the Borduin et al. (1995) sample showed that MST was effective in reducing substance use and arrests for substance-related crimes (Henggeler et al., 1991). Henggeler et al. (1997), in a multisite study randomized trial, showed that therapist adherence to the MST principles predicted long-term outcomes regarding rearrest and incarceration. Thus when delivered with integrity, considerable evidence shows that MST can decrease rates of criminal activity and incarceration for serious juvenile offenders.

MST has also been shown to produce cost savings when used with serious juvenile offenders (see Henggeler et al., 1992; Henggeler et al., 1997; Washington State Institute for Public Policy, 1998). For example, in a study of substance abusing and dependent juvenile offenders, Schoenwald, Ward, Henggeler, Pickrel, and Patel (1996) found that the incremental costs of MST (i.e., costs that were above and beyond the usual costs of services for substance abusing/dependent juvenile offenders) were nearly offset by the savings incurred as a result of reductions in days of out-of-home placement during the first year following referral. Such findings point to the potential cost-savings and cost-effectiveness of promising community-based treatment models such as MST—especially when used with youths and families at high risk of out-of-home placement.

Future Directions for Research and Practice

The findings reviewed previously and the conclusions of numerous reviewers (Borduin, 1994; Henggeler, 1989; Howell, 1997; Levesque, 1996; Mulvey, Arthur, &

Reppucci, 1993) suggest that to effectively reduce serious antisocial behavior, treatment models must share at least two broad qualities.

1. Because antisocial behavior is multidetermined from characteristics of the youths and the family, peer, school, and neighborhood systems in which youths are embedded, effective interventions must be capable of addressing problems within and among these systems. Wraparound, Family Ties, and MST attempt to provide comprehensive, yet individualized, services.
2. Services must be provided in the natural ecologies (high ecological validity) of youths and family to enhance the probability of treatment generalization. Again, only Wraparound, Family Ties, and MST provide services that directly attempt to alter behaviors in the natural ecologies of children and families.

Although treatments must have the capacity to address the multiple determinants of antisocial behavior with high ecological validity, several other complex issues must be successfully addressed before such an intervention can be transported or disseminated (Henggeler, Smith, & Schoenwald, 1994), assuming that controlled studies have demonstrated effectiveness.

1. The treatment model must be specified (operationalized) in sufficient detail for a clinician to implement the model with integrity, assuming appropriate training and supervision. Behavioral parent training is an example of a well-specified (though noncomprehensive) treatment model, whereas specification of Wraparound is lacking.
2. Treatment fidelity measures must be developed and validated so that clinicians' adherence to the treatment protocol can be evaluated. Henggeler et al. (1997), for example, showed that MST treatment adherence was predictive of outcomes. Hence evaluations of treatment effectiveness must be capable of verifying that the intended treatment was actually delivered.

Finally, drawing on our experiences in conducting randomized trials of MST and in disseminating MST to private and public provider organizations, considerable efforts toward maintaining quality assurance are needed to promote treatment fidelity. For example, training in MST is extensive and ongoing. Clinicians receive an initial five-day orientation, on-site supervisors trained in MST provide weekly supervision following the MST supervisory protocol, MST experts provide quarterly booster training, and an MST consultant provides weekly consultation to MST treatment teams for the purpose of maintaining treatment fidelity. Hence numerous mechanisms are in place to enhance the performance of MST teams. Moreover, MST programs often have organizational structures with high levels of accountability for family outcomes. Team members who are successful in attaining favorable outcomes reap the benefits of such success, whereas unsuccessful team members receive opportunities for additional training and the support needed to attain outcomes.

In sum, we believe that much of future research and practice with regard to the treatment of serious antisocial behavior in adolescents will focus on the development and validation of ecologically-oriented intervention approaches. The successful versions of these approaches will be complex, comprehensive, delivered with high ecological validity, and include considerable quality assurance mechanisms. Such models of intervention clearly hold the most promise in reducing long-term rates of serious antisocial behavior.

References

Alvarez, A. G., & Welsh, J. J. (1990). Adventure: A model of experiential learning. *Social Work in Education, 13*, 49–57.

Austin, J., & Hardyman, P. (1991). *The use of early parole with electronic monitoring to control prison crowding: Evaluation of the Oklahoma Department of Corrections preparole supervised release with electronic monitoring.* San Francisco: National Council on Crime and Delinquency.

Aziz, D., Korotkin, P., & MacDonald, D. (1990). *Shock incarceration program follow-up study. August 1990.* Albany: New York Department of Correctional Services.

Bank, L., Marlow, J. H., Reid, J. B., Patterson, G. R., & Weinrott, M. R. (1991). A comparative evaluation of parent-training interventions for families of chronic delinquents. *Journal of Abnormal Child Psychology, 19*, 15–33.

Barton, C., Alexander, J. F., Waldron, H., Turner, C. W., & Warburton, J. (1985). Generalizing treatment effects of functional family therapy: Three replications. *American Journal of Family Therapy, 13*, 16–26.

Baumer, T., & Mendelsohn, R. (1991, November). *Comparing methods of monitoring home detention: The results of a field experiment.* Paper presented at the meeting of the American Society of Criminology, San Francisco.

Baumer, T., Mendelsohn, R., & Rhine, C. (1990). *Executive summary—The electronic monitoring of non-violent convicted felons: An experiment in home detention.* Washington, DC: National Institute of Justice.

Bonta, J. (1993). *Everything you wanted to know about electronic monitoring and never bothered to ask.* Ottawa: Ministry Secretariat, Solicitor General Canada.

Borduin, C. M. (1994). Innovative models of treatment and service delivery in the juvenile justice system. *Journal of Clinical Child Psychology, 23*(Suppl.), 19–25.

Borduin, C. M., Mann, B. J., Cone, L. T., Henggeler, S. W., Fucci, B. R., Blaske, D. M., & Williams, R. A. (1995). Multisystemic treatment of serious juvenile offenders: Long-term prevention of criminality and violence. *Journal of Consulting and Clinical Psychology, 63*, 569–578.

Braukmann, C. J., Bedlington, M. M., Belden, B. D., Braukmann, P. D., Husted, J. J., Ramp, K. K., & Wolk, M. M. (1985). Effects of community-based group-home treatment programs on male juvenile offenders' use and abuse of drugs and alcohol. *American Journal of Drug and Alcohol Abuse, 11*, 249–278.

Britt, C. L., Gottfredson, M. R., & Goldkamp, J. S. (1992). Drug testing and pretrial misconduct: An experiment on the specific deterrent effects of drug monitoring defendants on pretrial release. *Journal of Research in Crime and Delinquency, 29*, 62–78.

Bronfenbrenner, U. (1979). *The ecology of human development: Experiments by nature and design.* Cambridge, MA: Harvard University Press.

Brown, M., & Roy, S. (1995). Manual and electronic house arrest: An evaluation of factors related to failure. In J. Smykla & W. Selke (Eds.), *Intermediate sanctions: Sentencing in the '90s* (pp. 37–53). Cincinnati, OH: Anderson.

Burchard, J., Burchard, S., Sewell, R., & VanDenBerg, J. (1993). *One kid at a time—The Alaska Youth Initiative: A demonstration of individualized services*. Washington, DC: Georgetown University Press.

Burchard, J., & Clarke, R. (1990). The role of individualized care in a service delivery system for children and adolescents with severely maladjusted behavior. *Journal of Mental Health Administration, 17*, 48–60.

California Youth Authority. (1997). *LEAD: A boot camp and intensive parole program. Final impact evaluation*. Sacramento: State of California, Department of the Youth Authority.

Child Welfare League of America. (1992). *Sharing innovations: The program exchange compendium*. Washington, DC: Author.

Clark, H. B., & Clarke, R. T. (1996). Research on the wraparound process and individualized services for children with multi-system needs. *Journal of Child and Family Studies, 5*, 1–5.

Clear, T. R. (1991). Juvenile intensive probation supervision: Theory and rationale. In T. L. Armstrong (Ed.), *Intensive interventions with high-risk youths: Promising approaches in juvenile probation and parole* (pp. 29–44). Monsey, NJ: Willow Tree Press.

Clear, T., & Hardyman, P. L. (1990). The new intensive supervision movement. *Crime and Delinquency, 36*, 42–60.

Cullen, F. T., Wright, J. P., & Applegate, B. K. (1996). Control in the community: The limits of reform? In A. T. Harland (Ed.), *Choosing correctional options that work: Defining the demand and evaluating the supply* (pp. 69–116). Thousand Oaks, CA: Sage.

DeJong, W., & Franzeen, S. (1993). On the role of intermediate sanctions in corrections reform: The views of criminal justice professionals. *Journal of Crime and Justice, 16*, 47–73.

Dishion, T. J., & Andrews, D. W. (1995). Preventing escalation in problem behaviors with high-risk young adolescents: Immediate and 1-year outcomes. *Journal of Consulting and Clinical Psychology, 63*, 538–548.

Farrington, D. P. (1991). Childhood aggression and adult violence: Early precursors and later-life outcomes. In D. J. Pepler & K. H. Rubin (Eds.), *The development and treatment of childhood aggression* (pp. 5–29). Hillsdale, NJ: Erlbaum.

Federal Bureau of Investigation, U.S. Department of Justice. (1994). *Uniform crime reports*. Washington, DC: Author.

Fixsen, D. L., & Blase, K. A. (1993). Creating new realities: Program development and dissemination. *Journal of Applied Behavior Analysis, 26*, 597–615

Forehand, R., & Kotchick, B. A. (1996). Cultural diversity: A wake-up call for parent training. *Behavior Therapy, 27*, 187–206.

Fraser, M. W., Nelson, K. E., & Rivard, J. C. (in press). The effectiveness of family preservation services. *Social Work Research*.

Gendreau, P., Paparozzi, M., Little, T., & Goddard, M. (1993). Does "punishing smarter" work?: An assessment of the new generation of alternative sanctions in probation. *Forum on Corrections Research, 5*, 31–34.

Goldkamp, J., & Jones, P. (1992). Pretrial drug-testing experiments in Milwaukee and Prince George's County: The context of implementation. *Journal of Research in Crime and Delinquency, 29*, 430–465.

Guerra, N. G., & Slaby, R. G. (1990). Cognitive mediators of aggression in adolescent offenders: 2. Intervention. *Developmental Psychology, 26*, 269–277.

Henggeler, S. W. (1989). *Delinquency in adolescence*. Newbury Park, CA: Sage.

Henggeler, S. W. (1991). Multidimensional causal models of delinquent behavior. In R. Cohen & A. Siegel (Eds.), *Context and development* (pp. 211–231). Hillsdale, NJ: Erlbaum.

Henggeler, S. W. (1997). The development of effective drug abuse services for youth. In J. A. Egertson, D. M. Fox, & A. I. Leshner (Eds.), *Treating drug abusers effectively* (pp. 253–279). New York: Blackwell.

Henggeler, S. W., & Borduin, C. M. (1990). *Family therapy and beyond: A multisystemic approach to treating the behavior problems of children and adolescents.* Pacific Grove, CA: Brooks/Cole.

Henggeler, S. W., Borduin, C. M., Melton, G. B., Mann, B. J., Smith, L. A., Hall, J. A., Cone, L., & Fucci, B. R. (1991). Effects of multisystemic therapy on drug use and abuse in serious juvenile offenders: A progress report from two outcome studies. *Family Dynamics of Addiction Quarterly, 1,* 40–51.

Henggeler, S. W., Melton, G. B., Brondino, M. J., Scherer, D. G., & Hanley, J. H. (1997). Multisystemic therapy with violent and chronic juvenile offenders and their families: The role of treatment fidelity in successful dissemination. *Journal of Consulting and Clinical Psychology, 65,* 821–833.

Henggeler, S. W., Melton, G. B., & Smith, L. A. (1992). Family preservation using multisystemic therapy: An effective alternative to incarcerating serious juvenile offenders. *Journal of Consulting and Clinical Psychology, 60,* 953–961.

Henggeler, S. W., Melton, G. B., Smith, L. A., Schoenwald, S. K., & Hanley, J. (1993). Family preservation using multisystemic therapy: Long-term follow-up to a clinical trial with serious juvenile offenders. *Journal of Child and Family Studies, 2,* 283–293.

Henggeler, S. W., Schoenwald, S. K., Borduin, C. M., Rowland, M. D., & Cunningham, P. B. (1998). *Multisystemic treatment of antisocial behavior in children and adolescents.* New York: Guilford Press.

Henggeler, S. W., Smith, B. H., & Schoenwald, S. K. (1994). Key theoretical and methodological issues in conducting treatment research in the juvenile justice system. *Journal of Clinical Child Psychology, 23,* 143–150.

Hopkins, D., & Putnam, R. (1993). *Personal growth through adventure.* Great Britain: David Fulton.

Howell, J. C. (1997). *Juvenile justice and youth violence.* Thousand Oaks, CA: Sage.

Kazdin, A. E. (1991). Effectiveness of psychotherapy with children and adolescents. *Journal of Consulting and Clinical Psychology, 59,* 785–798.

Kelly, F., & Baer, D. (1971). Physical challenge as treatment for delinquency. *Crime and Delinquency, 17,* 433–445.

Kelly, F., & Baer, D. (1978). *Outward Bound: An alternative to institutionalization for adolescent delinquent boys.* New York: Fandel Press.

Kinney, J., Haapala, D., & Booth C. (1991). *Keeping families together: The Homebuilders model.* Hawthorne, NY: Aldine de Gruyter.

Kirigin, K. A., Braukman, C. J., Atwater, J. D., & Wolf, M. M. (1982). An evaluation of teaching-family (Achievement Place) group homes for juvenile offenders. *Journal of Applied Behavior Analysis, 15,* 1–16.

Laub, J. H., & Sampson, R. J. (1994). Unemployment, marital discord, and deviant behavior: The long-term correlates of child misbehavior. In T. Hirschi & M. R. Gottfredson (Eds.), *The generality of deviance* (pp. 235–252). New Brunswick, NJ: Transaction.

Levesque, R. J. R. (1996). Is there still a place for violent youth in juvenile justice? *Aggression and Violent Behavior, 1,* 69–79.

Lipsey, M. W. (1992, November). *The effects of treatment on juvenile delinquents: Results from meta-analysis.* Paper presented at the NIMH Meeting for Research to Prevent Youth Violence, Bethesda, MD.

MacKinsie, D. (1991). The parole performance of offenders released from shock incarceration (boot camp prisons): A survival time analysis. *Journal of Quantitative Criminology, 7,* 213–236.

Melton, G. B., & Pagliocca, P. M. (1992). Treatment in the juvenile justice system: Directions for policy and practice. In J. J. Cocozza (Ed.), *Responding to the mental health needs of youth in the juvenile justice system* (pp. 107–139). Seattle, WA: National Coalition for the Mentally Ill in the Criminal Justice System.

Moote, G. T., & Wodarski, J. S. (1997). The acquisition of life skills through adventure-based activities and programs: A review of the literature. *Adolescence, 32*, 143–167.

Mulvey, E. P., Arthur, M. W., & Reppucci, N. D. (1993). The prevention and treatment of juvenile delinquency: A review of the research. *Clinical Psychology Review, 13*, 133–167.

New York Department of Juvenile Justice. (1990). *Family ties.* New York: Author.

Pearson, F. S. (1987). Evaluation of New Jersey's intensive supervision program. *Crime and Delinquency, 34*, 437–448.

Petersilia, J. (1990). When probation becomes more dreaded than prison. *Federal Probation, 54*, 23–27.

Petersilia, J., & Turner, S. (1993a). Evaluating intensive supervision probation and parole. *Overcrowded Times, 4*, 6–10, 16.

Petersilia, J., & Turner, S. (1993b). Intensive probation and parole. In M. Tonry (Ed.), *Crime and justice: A review of research* (Vol. 17, pp. 281–335). Chicago: University of Chicago Press.

Rogers, R., & Jolin, A. (1991). Electronically monitored house arrest: Development and critique. *Indian Journal of Criminology, 19*, 2–8.

Rosenblatt, A. (1996). Bows and ribbons, tape and twine: Wrapping the wraparound process for children with multi-system needs. *Journal of Child and Family Studies, 5*, 101–117.

Sach, J. J., & Miller, S. R. (1992). The impact of a wilderness experience on the social interactions and social expectations of behaviorally disordered adolescents. *Behavioral Disorders, 17*, 89–98.

Sale, P. L. (1992). *Ego and self-concept development among juvenile delinquent participants in adventure-based programs* (Doctoral dissertation Peabody College for Teachers of Vanderbilt University). *Dissertation Abstracts International, 53*, 2253A.

Schoel, J., Prouty, D., & Radcliffe, P. (1988). *Islands of healing: A guide to adventure-based counseling.* Hamilton, MA: Project Adventure.

Schoenwald, S. K., & Henggeler, S. W. (in press). Treatment of oppositional defiant disorder and conduct disorder in home and community settings. In H. C. Quay & A. C. Hogan (Eds.), *Handbook of disruptive behavior disorders.* New York: Plenum Press.

Schoenwald, S. K., Scherer, D. G., & Brondino, M. J. (1997). Effective community-based treatments for serious juvenile offenders. In S. W. Henggeler & A. B. Santos (Eds.), *Innovative approaches for difficult-to-treat populations* (pp. 65–82). Washington, DC: American Psychiatric Press.

Schoenwald, S. K., Ward, D. M., Henggeler, S. W., Pickrel, S. G., & Patel, H. (1996). Multisystemic therapy treatment of substance abusing or dependent adolescent offenders: Costs of reducing incarceration, inpatient, and residential placement. *Journal of Child and Family Studies, 5*, 431–444.

Serketich, W. J., & Dumas, J. E. (1996). The effectiveness of behavioral parent training to modify antisocial behavior in children: A meta-analysis. *Behavior Therapy, 27*, 171–186.

Smith, L., & Akers, R. (1993). A comparison of recidivism of Florida's community control and prison: A five-year survival analysis. *Journal of Research in Crime and Delinquency, 30*, 267–292.

VanDenBerg, J. E., & Grealish, E. M. (1996). Individualized services and supports through the wraparound process: Philosophy and procedures. *Journal of Child and Family Studies, 5*, 7–21.

Washington State Institute for Public Policy. (1998). *Watching the bottom line: Cost-effective interventions for reducing crime in Washington.* Olympia: Washington State Institute for Public Policy.

Weisz, J. R., Walter, B. R., Weiss, B., Fernandez, G. A., & Mikow, V. A. (1990). Arrests among emotionally disturbed violent and assaultive individuals following minimal versus lengthy intervention in North Carolina's Willie M Program. *Journal of Consulting and Clinical Psychology, 58*, 720–728.

Weisz, J. R., Weiss, B., & Donenberg, G. R. (1992). The lab versus the clinic: Effects of child and adolescent psychotherapy. *American Psychologist, 47*, 1578–1585.

Yoe, J. T., Santarcangelo, S., Atkins, M., & Burchard, J. D. (1996). Wraparound care in Vermont: Program development, implementation, and evaluation of a statewide system of individualized services. *Journal of Child and Family Studies, 5*, 23–39.

Chapter 18
ADULT OFFENDERS AND COMMUNITY SETTINGS:
Some Case Examples

H. Richard Lamb and Linda E. Weinberger

Community treatment of mentally disordered offenders is conducted under a variety of circumstances. This chapter focuses on those offenders who remain under the jurisdiction of the criminal justice system, such as individuals who are given probation by the court with one of the conditions being mandatory outpatient treatment. Another instance is individuals who are referred for treatment by their parole officer with the understanding that failure to comply may result in a return to prison. Still another example is when the court uses mental health treatment to divert offenders from the criminal justice system to the mental health system. That is, such individuals may have the prosecution of their criminal case postponed by the judge until they successfully complete a specified treatment program, at which time their criminal charges are dismissed. Though it varies from state to state, there are still other cases, such as the mandatory outpatient treatment of not guilty by reason of insanity acquittees, persons found incompetent to stand trial, persons who fall under the authority of mentally ill dangerous offender laws, and various other forms of mandatory outpatient treatment under the jurisdiction of the criminal justice system.

The Challenge of Treating Mentally Disordered
Offenders in the Community

Mentally ill individuals who have committed criminal offenses represent a challenge to treating clinicians when they present for outpatient treatment. The problem lies not only in working with individuals who may be resistant to treatment but in ensuring safety to the community as well (Wasyliw, Cavanaugh, & Grossman, 1988).

A large proportion of mentally ill persons who commit criminal offenses have a history of being highly resistant to psychiatric treatment (Borzecki & Wormith, 1985; Laberge & Morin, 1995; Lamb, 1987). They may have refused referral, may not have kept appointments, may not have been compliant with psychoactive medications, and may have refused appropriate housing placements. These problems may continue even when the person is under the jurisdiction of the criminal justice system. Moreover, the nature and extent of these individuals' mental illness may place them at risk to the community, particularly if they are resistant to treatment, a fact that the treating professional always has to keep in mind. In recent years, there has been much evidence that supports a relationship between mental illness and violence, especially in persons who are currently psychotic, do not take their medications, and/or are substance abusers (Fulwiler, Grossman, Forbes, & Ruthazer, 1997; Hodgins, Mednick, Brennan, Schulsinger, & Engberg, 1996; Lamb & Weinberger, 1998; Marzuk, 1996; Monahan, 1992; Mulvey, 1994; Steadman, 1997; Swanson et al., 1997; Torrey, 1994).

How do some mentally ill persons become involved initially with the criminal justice system? Many are unable or unwilling to admit that they have a mental illness and to seek treatment. For some others who were involved in treatment, earlier attempts at community interventions often proved unsuccessful. For instance, as Whitmer (1980) observed, previous outpatient treatment in mainstream clinics with such persons "takes on the aspect of a contest that a woefully unprepared therapist must sooner or later forfeit" (p. 67). Hence Whitmer used the term "forfeited patients" to emphasize that these persons were not just passively lost to treatment but that mental health professionals struggled actively to treat them and had to acknowledge defeat. As a consequence, many of these persons were left untreated and unmedicated. Patient characteristics may have thwarted treatment efforts—that is, there may be patients who forget their appointments, are easily overwhelmed and discouraged, are angry and paranoid, or refuse to follow treatment interventions. Moreover, mental health professionals may well have been working in mental health treatment facilities lacking structure, adequate provision for safety of staff, and without the authority and leverage of the criminal justice system.

The mental health system, then, finds many of these resistant mentally ill persons extremely difficult to treat and is reluctant to serve them (Draine, Solomon, & Meyerson, 1994; Jemelka, Trupin, & Chiles, 1989). Without sufficient support from the mental health system, the criminal justice system is forced to intervene when these individuals decompensate and engage in criminal acts (Lamb & Weinberger, 1998). This reluctance by mental health professionals becomes even greater after these persons have committed offenses, become involved in the criminal justice system, and are then referred to community agencies. The disinclination to serve these persons extends to virtually all areas of community-based care, including therapeutic housing, social and vocational rehabilitation, and general social services (Jemelka, Wiegand, Walker, & Trupin, 1992). Moreover, many of these mentally ill offenders are intimidating because of previous violent, fear-inspiring behavior. Treating this group is very different from helping passive, formerly institutionalized patients adapt quietly to life in the community (Bachrach, Talbott, & Meyerson, 1987). Thus community mental health professionals are not only reluctant but may also be afraid to treat mentally disordered offenders (Lamb & Weinberger, 1998).

Identifying a Treatment Philosophy

To work effectively with this extremely difficult group of patients, it is necessary to identify and articulate a treatment philosophy in relation to both theory and practice. This treatment philosophy should strike a balance between individual rights and public safety and use treatment services to address both (Heilbrun & Griffin, 1993). The philosophy described is empirically based and stems from the clinical literature and the authors experience. In this chapter, we stress the components needed to successfully treat mentally ill offenders in the community. We emphasize the need for a clearly articulated, reality-based treatment philosophy that includes: treatment goals, with attention paid to those expressed by the patient; a close liaison with the court or other criminal justice agency monitoring the patient; access to both the criminal justice and mental health systems for developing a comprehensive database on each patient; an emphasis on structure and supervision, with treatment staff who are comfortable with using authority and setting limits; a recognition of the importance of psychoactive medication; a focus on the problems of daily living; an incorporation of the principles of case management; and a recognition of the importance of ensuring the safety of treatment staff and the community.

It is important to identify those features that are related to the patient's inappropriate acting-out behavior—namely, those aspects that contribute to the individual's dangerousness. A patient's risk of dangerous behavior is of paramount concern when treating mentally ill offenders; other aspects of the individual's illness are secondary. At minimum, the interventions should focus on maintaining as high a level of safety to the community with as low a risk of harm to others as possible.

It is also important to emphasize the legal and ethical aspects of treating persons under the jurisdiction of the criminal justice system. Mentally disordered offenders who are being considered for outpatient treatment should be apprised of all the conditions and limitations that will be imposed on them, why they were imposed, and what will happen to them if they do not comply before consenting to treatment (Wack, 1993). This includes limits to confidentiality, with respect to both past and present treatment and criminal history; supervision and monitoring by various authority figures, such as probation–parole officers, judges, therapists, and case managers; mandatory compliance with treatment and other imposed conditions; residence in an appropriate living situation; and knowledge of the possibility that noncompliance with the terms and conditions may result in revocation of their outpatient status. It is also imperative that the treatment staff understand fully the patient's legal status and conditions for community placement and agree to monitor and uphold them.

Treatment Goals of Therapists and Patients

Miraglia and Giglio (1993) stated that community treatment of offenders should focus on stabilizing the illness, enhancing independent functioning, and maintaining internal and external controls that prevent the patient from reoffending and acting violently. These goals, it is hoped, will be shared by the patient. At the very least, patients should have the goal of avoiding further involvement with the criminal justice system (Wasyliw, Cavanaugh, & Grossman, 1988). Important goals in this discussion are that the patient understand which behaviors and symptoms are of concern, why they are of concern, what is expected of the patient by both the clinician and the supervising criminal justice agency, and how the treatment can help the patient to meet these expectations.

Brelje (1985) wrote that to achieve the goals of treatment, the therapist and patient–offender should strive for awareness or insight with the following elements: (a) the patient's awareness of his or her vulnerability to or presence of mental disorder; (b) realistic understanding of the nature of the mental illness; (c) motivation to change or prevent recurrence of symptoms; (d) acceptance of treatment goals and strategies; (e) realistic personal goals; and (f) awareness of one's legal status and its meaning.

Liaison Between Treatment Staff and the Criminal Justice System

Close liaison between treatment staff and the criminal justice system, including the court, the district attorney's office, the departments of probation–parole, and the patient's counsel is an essential aspect of treatment (Bloom, Bradford, & Kofoed, 1988). The core of this liaison is a complete and relevant database, which is fundamental in understanding the extent of the patient's problems, in determining whether the patient is appropriate for outpatient treatment, and in developing a treatment plan. The database should include arrest reports, "rap sheets," court-appointed psychiatric evaluations, results of psychological testing, probation reports, and records from prior hospitalizations, outpatient treatment, and incarcerations. Ongoing and frequent communication between mental health and criminal justice system personnel is another crucial aspect of this liaison. Establishing liaisons between these two systems can be facilitated when criminal justice agencies are informed by mental health clinics that they offer mental health services to mentally disordered offenders.

The Need for Structure

Patients referred for mandatory outpatient treatment in general lack internal controls; they need external controls and structure to organize themselves to cope with life's demands (Buckley & Bigelow, 1992; Lamb, 1997). One basic element of structure for this population is that treatment be mandatory and under the jurisdiction of the criminal justice system, with which the treatment staff should maintain frequent communication. Such ongoing liaison ensures that patients actually receive treatment, or that if patients fail to comply with treatment their cases will be reviewed promptly with the possibility that outpatient status will be revoked. Revocation may result in hospitalization or incarceration.

The possibility of revoking the individual's outpatient status gives the treatment staff powerful leverage. This leverage enhances the various elements of structure that community treatment may provide, such as prescribing and monitoring compliance with psychoactive medications; monitoring for the use of alcohol and illegal drugs; having the person live in supervised and supportive residential settings; requiring regular attendance at individual and group therapy and at social and vocational rehabilitation programs; and improving money management through discussions in treatment and, when necessary, appointing a payee for Supplemental Security Income and other disability checks.

It is important that therapy focus on high-priority reality issues such as the need for the patient to control impulses and inappropriate expressions of anger. In addition, staff should insist that patients' days be structured through meaningful, therapeutic activities such as work, day treatment, and various forms of social therapy.

The importance of psychoactive medications for most members of this mentally disordered population, most of whom have problems centering on control, cannot be overemphasized. Though a full discussion of the pharmacotherapy is beyond the scope of this chapter, effective medications for selected patients include antipsychotics, mood stabilizers, antidepressants, and antianxiety agents (Buckley et al.,

1997; Citrome & Volavka, 1997). In many cases, if compliance is to be ensured, the patient should live in a community facility in which each dose is dispensed by staff.

Integrating Treatment and Case Management

The integration of modern concepts of case management (Bloom et al., 1986; California Department of Mental Health, 1985; Dvoskin & Steadman, 1994) with clinical treatment is another important component if outpatient treatment for mentally ill offenders is to succeed. Almost all of these patients need the basic elements of case management, which starts with the premise that each patient has a designated professional with overall responsibility for his or her care.

The case manager formulates an individualized treatment and rehabilitation plan with the patient's participation. As care progresses, the case manager monitors the patient to determine if he or she is receiving treatment, has an appropriate living situation, has adequate funds, and has access to work on vocational rehabilitation. The case manager also makes sure the patient is not drifting away from his or her supports. In addition, the case manager provides outreach services to the patient wherever he or she is living, and in general gives the patient the help he or she needs to receive appropriate services.

Outreach services may take the form of assertive case management, which deals with patients on a frequent and long-term basis. There is a hands-on approach that may necessitate meeting with patients on their own turf or even seeing patients daily (Wilson, Tien, & Eaves, 1995). This form of contact and familiarity with the patient assists in anticipating and preventing significant decompensation.

It has been recommended that for programs to be effective, case managers of potentially violent mentally ill persons have low caseloads, probably not more than 10, and be available 24 hours a day (Dvoskin & Steadman, 1994). Many violent acts and arrests occur during evenings, nights, and weekends, when traditional treatment programs are closed.

Before accepting case management, some mentally ill offenders first ask themselves, "What's in it for me?" (Dvoskin & Steadman, 1994). Patients who perceive the case manager as someone whose primary intention is to make them "toe the line" will be less likely to form a positive relationship with a case manager. The case manager, therefore, needs to be seen as an advocate for the patient and his or her treatment and rehabilitation, particularly when agencies in the criminal justice system are simultaneously dealing with the patient in more coercive or authoritarian ways.

Living Arrangements

Survival in the community for the great majority of these patients appears to depend on an appropriately supportive and structured living arrangement. This can often be provided by family members. In many cases, however, the kind and degree of structure the patient needs can only be found in a living arrangement outside the family home, where there is a high staff–patient ratio, the dispensing of medication by staff, the enforcement of curfews, close monitoring of the patient's movements, and therapeutic activities that structure most of the patient's day. For many patients, testing for alcohol and narcotics, or a locked community facility (Lamb, 1997) may be needed.

Some patients need a great deal of structure and supervision in their housing situation, others need only a minimal amount, and most fall somewhere in between. The determination of just how much structure a patient needs depends on the individual patient, of course. Although the treatment staff member or the case manager assigned to each patient needs to decide whether a particular living arrangement (family home or facility) has too much structure, the appropriate amount, or not enough to meet the needs of that patient, discussion with and approval from the responsible agent in the criminal justice system is necessary before the suggested living arrangement is made.

Using Authority Comfortably

A clear conception of the clinical uses and therapeutic value of authority appears to be a cornerstone of successful community treatment for mentally disordered offenders (Bloom, Bradford, & Kofoed, 1988; Lamb, Weinberger, & Gross, 1988; Wack, 1993). When treatment is effective, the staff is not ambivalent about the use of authority. They are comfortable about monitoring patients' compliance with prescribed neuroleptic medications and monitoring patients to detect the use of alcohol or illegal drugs. They generally have no problems with insisting that patients live in appropriately structured and supportive residential settings as a condition of remaining in the community. They are willing to promptly rehospitalize patients in community facilities at times of crises, and are willing to contact the responsible criminal justice agency with the opinion that community treatment is no longer appropriate for the patient. The criminal justice agency then will determine if the patient has violated his or her conditions of community status to such a degree as to place the community or patient at risk of harm, and if so, revoke their outpatient status.

Encouraging staff to use their authority and resolve their ambivalence regarding this are essential components for effective mandated outpatient treatment. Although there is far more to this modality than simply setting limits and conducting surveillance, mental health professionals who complain that they did not go into the field to "become a cop" may feel ambivalent about enforcing the essential elements of this type of treatment or may have a need to always be the "good guy" with their patients. In some cases, difficulty in setting limits may indicate a lack of real caring for patients, however (Lamb & Goertzel, 1975).

Staff who work in mandatory outpatient treatment programs should accept and endorse the fundamentals of this form of treatment—give support, set limits, insist consistently and reasonably that the imposed conditions be followed, make use of community resources, and help the patient reexamine his or her lifestyle. Rather than emphasizing highly sophisticated and esoteric treatment modes, staff should pragmatically adhere to the terms and conditions required for patients maintaining community placement and should focus on specific goal planning and on intensive involvement with the patients. If staff are also trained in family dynamics and short-term crisis intervention, they have powerful therapeutic tools to help mentally ill offenders live in the community.

The Therapeutic Use of Conservatorship

Every state has a system of guardianship or conservatorship as a legal mechanism that allows an individual or agency to act on behalf of a gravely disabled mentally ill person to determine what arrangements are necessary to provide adequate food, clothing, shelter, and treatment, including hospitalization when indicated (see, e.g., California Mental Health Services Act, Sacramento, California Health and Welfare Agency, 1974). Granting a conservatorship for some mentally disordered offenders can greatly facilitate effective treatment. Conservatorship can play an important role in clinical management and treatment, particularly if the gravely disabled person does not have close family involvement and support. The benefits of conservatorship can be considerably enhanced by combining it with case management (Lamb & Weinberger, 1993). When family members are appointed as conservators, skilled clinical staff can help them use the leverage of conservatorship therapeutically. By giving up some of their freedom, many conservatees who would ordinarily be hospitalized for long periods are able to retain most of their independence and their outpatient status.

Putting Principles Into Practice

To illustrate the treatment philosophy we have articulated, we will present five case examples of community treatment for mentally ill persons under the jurisdiction of the criminal justice system. Cases with both good and bad outcomes are described. Minor changes have been made in some of the facts of the cases to preserve confidentiality.

Case 1

A 23-year-old single male whose arrest history dates since his early teenage years: Previous arrests include petty theft, grand theft auto, and assault with a deadly weapon. His first psychiatric hospitalization occurred while he was in state prison after a conviction for forcible rape. He was observed to be responding to voices, to have paranoid delusions, and to have disorganization of his thought processes. He was diagnosed as having schizophrenia, paranoid type (*DSM-IV*; American Psychiatric Association, 1994). He was treated with antipsychotic medications and released back to the general prison population. After four years of imprisonment, he was paroled to live with his mother. Among his conditions for parole was treatment in a community mental health clinic. The clinic accepted him with reluctance. At the clinic he was treated with antipsychotic medications and seen in group therapy twice a month. Given his history, there was concern among clinical staff about making too many demands that might provoke him to violence. His attendance at the clinic was sporadic. The parole agent had a large caseload and only required the patient to report to him monthly. With the patient's consent, the parole agent requested a progress report from the treating doctor. However, by the time the doctor had written the letter and mailed it, the patient had been arrested for assault and was in jail.

In retrospect, it can be seen that both this mentally ill offender's supervision in the community and his mental health treatment were inadequate. The parole agent had a very large caseload and was not able to properly monitor the patient and his treatment. For instance, as mentioned earlier when discussing the importance of liaison between the mental health and criminal justice systems, the parole agent in this case should have had more frequent contact with the patient and a closer liaison with clinic staff. In addition, the clinic staff appeared to be intimidated by the patient and did not develop an appropriate treatment program with outreach, monitoring of his living situation, and comfortably using the authority and control of the criminal justice system. When the clinic accepted the parolee as a patient, it should have been with the understanding that the treating staff would communicate with the parole agent about the patient's progress in treatment. With such an agreement among all parties, the patient, the parole agent, and the treating staff, a telephone call by the treating doctor to the parole agent should have been made when the patient first failed to appear for a scheduled appointment. Further, a more comprehensive treatment plan should have been formulated initially by the parole agent and the clinic staff, including case management and other services that would have benefitted the patient, such as vocational rehabilitation. Before accepting persons with this criminal history, a mental health clinic should be sure that it has the resources and expertise to comfortably treat such a population.

Case 2

A 33-year-old divorced woman pled *nolo contendere* (i.e., "chose not to contest") to a charge of assault after hitting a passing stranger on the sidewalk. The patient was living on the streets. At the time of the offense she was expansive, irritable, exhibited pressured speech, and flight of ideas. Before this arrest she experienced similar episodes as well as periods of severe depression. She had had at least six state psychiatric hospitalizations and numerous experiences as an outpatient. She was consistently noncompliant with medications and other outpatient treatment interventions. Her diagnosis was usually bipolar disorder (*DSM-IV*). In addition, she had two previous arrests for assault and was sentenced to jail for both. Before her trial regarding the current offense, she was seen by the jail staff psychiatrist and voluntarily agreed to be placed on Lithium. Before sentencing the defendant, the judge ordered a forensic psychiatric evaluation to assist in a disposition recommendation. The forensic psychiatrist recommended that the defendant continue her medication and if given probation, attend outpatient treatment, but only if there was close monitoring of her medication compliance, placement in a supervised living situation, and frequent progress reports by the clinic to the probation officer.

At sentencing, the judge accepted the forensic psychiatrist's recommendations and placed the defendant on probation for three years with the previously outlined conditions. The defendant accepted these conditions and was referred to a community outpatient clinic. The clinic agreed to treat her under these circumstances, and she gave permission to the clinic to send periodic reports to and communicate with her probation officer and her sister. The clinic assigned her to a case manager, who was given the primary responsibility to not only coordinate her treatment but to collaborate with the probation officer. In outpatient treatment, the emphasis was on monitoring her medications, having her live in a supervised setting (a board-and-care home), having her keep appointments, and work in a sheltered work setting. Her sister was involved in her treatment and named as payee and money manager for her Supplemental Security Income checks, which was extremely helpful in dealing with the patient's problems of many years' standing in managing money. Her medication was dispensed to her at the board-and-care home. She did very well.

This woman had a long history of doing poorly despite many attempts to provide her with treatment. The difference in treatment outcome for this last period appears to have been the close monitoring by her probation officer and his frequent collaboration with her mental health treatment staff through her case manager. Her community treatment was multifaceted, and there was strong family support. All of this provided the structure that she had not had in the past.

Case 3

The patient is a 42-year-old, divorced male who has had multiple psychiatric hospitalizations over the past 16 years. His diagnosis is schizoaffective disorder and alcohol abuse (*DSM-IV*). His history includes an arrest in another state for assault with a deadly weapon. He also has a long history of hitting other patients in board and care homes where he has lived. Poor compliance with medications had been a consistent problem, as is alcohol abuse. In his last episode, he assaulted a customer at a local drugstore, was arrested by the police on a misdemeanor offense, and was placed in jail. While detained there, he was evaluated by the psychiatric staff and transferred to a state hospital under a civil commitment hold. The patient remained delusional and hyperactive at the state hospital. All of his family lived out of state and expressed concern but no inclination to become reinvolved with him. A conservatorship was granted, and the County Public Guardian's Office was named the conservator.

The patient appeared before the criminal trial judge while under a conservatorship. The judge dismissed the charge on the basis of the defendant's conservatorship. He remained at the state hospital for another six months. Despite having a history of doing poorly in board-and-care homes, the patient agreed to live in one and take his medications voluntarily. The hospital treatment staff referred him to a community agency, at which time he was assigned a case manager. The patient did well during the period of his one-year conservatorship; therefore, his conservatorship was not renewed. A few months later, he stopped taking his medications, refused to see his case manager, and became threatening toward the board-and-care staff, who then asked him to leave. He went to live in missions and occasionally on the streets. He was usually too disorganized to make arrangements to receive his SSI checks. Two years after termination of his conservatorship, he was living on the streets, chronically delusional and psychotic, still abusing alcohol, and severely depressed.

Although the criminal trial judge relinquished the authority to exercise social control over the defendant when the charges were dismissed, such social control was maintained during the conservatorship period and would have been ongoing had the conservatorship been renewed. Given his history of assaultive behavior, poor adjustment in the community, psychiatric disorder, and lack of family support, we believe the conservatorship should have been extended to ensure ongoing stability and compliance with an appropriate treatment plan. The patient's conservator could have then continued assertive case management to supervise the conservatee's funding, monitor his medications and treatment, and see that he continued to live in a setting with an appropriate amount of structure. A more extensive period of monitoring could have provided a better assessment of the patient's ability to maintain stability and independent functioning. Unfortunately, this patient's monitoring was terminated prematurely and he was not offered much needed support, management, and assistance, but was left to fend for himself in a world with which he could not cope.

Case 4

A 27-year-old single man was arrested for stealing $50 from his victim, whom he observed walking away from an ATM machine. He had had multiple psychiatric hospitalizations and a previous arrest for a similar crime. He had been diagnosed for the past seven years as having schizophrenia, undifferentiated type and cocaine abuse (*DSM-IV*). He had a pronounced thought disorder and suffered delusions and hallucinations. At the time of this offense, he was living on the streets.

The defendant was evaluated by a clinical psychologist court consultant who recommended that he spend three months in a locked psychiatric facility followed by outpatient treatment, including antipsychotic medications. In addition, her other recommendations included random urine drug screens, attendance in a drug program, and residing in a supervised setting. The judge accepted the recommendations and offered to divert the criminal case and postpone prosecution. These conditions were accepted by the defendant. At the conclusion of his three-month treatment at the residential facility, the staff made arrangements for him to live with his brother and attend outpatient treatment at a local mental health clinic. The judge continued to follow regularly his progress and require that he appear in court every three months while he was residing in the community. At the clinic, because of previous poor compliance with medications, he was given intramuscular fluphenazine decanoate. He was also given random drug testing and referred to Narcotics Anonymous. His brother was highly supportive of the treatment and the treatment staff met with both frequently. At the end of one year, he was doing well and his case was dismissed; although he was not working, he had not been arrested or hospitalized, was living with his brother, and was continuing his treatment.

This case of a diversion plan reflects a successful outcome and highlights the impact of several factors. The court recognized the importance of mental health consultation and followed the recommendations of the clinical psychologist consultant. It also remained involved in the defendant's treatment progress and living situation. Furthermore, the inpatient and outpatient treatment programs accepted the responsibility of providing treatment and good case management, which included drug monitoring and making arrangements for his living situation.

The outpatient treatment staff viewed their major role as providing interventions to add structure to this person's life and to reduce the likelihood of psychiatric decompensation. He continued to exhibit occasional mood swings, but after receiving court-monitored treatment, he was stable in the community. Having a supportive family member who was active in the treatment was another positive factor.

Case 5

This 38-year-old single woman had a history of multiple state hospitalizations and numerous arrests on a variety of charges, including assault, vandalism, and possession of drugs, since age 18. In addition to acute manic episodes, she abused alcohol and a variety of street drugs. Her diagnosis was bipolar disorder and polysubstance dependence (*DSM-IV*). Her parents decided that she could no longer be managed at home and placed her in a board-and-care facility.

The patient was brought to the county jail by the police after she set fire to her room at the facility. While in jail, she refused to take prescribed psychiatric medications. She was eventually found incompetent to stand trial because of her bipolar disorder and was committed to the state forensic hospital. While hospitalized, she took her medications and returned to court after six months as competent to stand trial. She pled not guilty by reason of insanity, but a jury rejected her plea and declared her sane. The judge believed she was mentally ill, and rather than sentence her to prison he granted her probation under the condition that she accept placement in a locked community facility with special programs for psychiatric patients (called Institutes for Mental Disease in California).

After four months, this facility was unable to manage her because of her repeated manic episodes, her hitting other patients, and her resistance to taking medications. The locked community facility called the police, who took her to the county psychiatric hospital. Her symptoms did not remit and a mental health conservatorship was obtained with the probation officer's and the trial court's knowledge.

The Public Guardian's Office was named the conservator. The conservator in collaboration with her probation officer attempted two further community placements, which ended in decompensation. It was concluded that this patient required a long-term, highly structured setting for an indefinite period. Under the powers of her conservatorship, she was returned to the state hospital, where she continues to reside. There are no plans in the near future to place her in a less structured setting. The criminal court closed her case. The patient has been on conservatorship continuously for more than four years.

This case illustrates the difficulty of managing and treating some patients in the community, even with continuous monitoring through the criminal justice and mental health systems, thoughtful management, and close supervision and collaboration. Although attempts were made to place this patient in less restrictive community facilities, she appeared to need a high degree of structure, as is found in a state hospital, on a continuous basis. Even when mental health resources are well-executed, they may not be enough to help a very difficult patient maintain community tenure.

Conclusion

Having a clear and coherent clinical philosophy is fundamental, but it is just as important that the philosophy be understood and practiced by the treatment staff and accepted by the criminal justice agency. An excerpt from a staff report to the court from an outpatient treatment program for judicially committed patients illustrates one facility's understanding of the purposes of mandatory outpatient treatment:

> Our reasons for recommending that this patient's outpatient status be continued are as follows. He denies his illness, does not believe that he is in need of medication, and from most indications would not continue with treatment if he were discharged from this program at this time. The liaison between the treatment staff and the court has been an important component in monitoring his compliance with the treatment plan. The patient's knowledge of the court's involvement has impressed upon him the need to meet the conditions outlined for outpatient status. There certainly is a likelihood that without medication, counseling, the structure imposed in his treatment and the monitoring of his progress, his reality testing and impulse control would diminish; thus, if he were faced with a situation similar to the one he faced at the time of his offense, he could present a danger to the community.

The treatment of mentally disordered offenders in the community requires special understanding of this population and a responsibility to make community safety a high priority. Judicially monitored outpatient treatment for mentally disordered offenders should be seen as preparation for providing further treatment beyond the period of social control over the offender, either on a voluntary basis or through civil procedures, such as conservatorship or guardianship. Given the severity of illness and potential dangerousness of many mentally disordered offenders, as well as the deterioration so frequently observed when conditions for treatment are terminated, the importance of treatment beyond the mandated period cannot be overemphasized.

References

American Psychiatric Association. (1994). *Diagnostic and statistical manual of mental health* (4th ed.). Washington, DC: Author.

Bachrach, L. L., Talbott, J. A., & Meyerson, A. T. (1987). The chronic psychiatric patient as a "difficult" patient: A conceptual analysis. In A. T. Meyerson (Ed.), *Barriers to Treating the Chronic Mentally Ill. New Direction for Mental Health Services, 33*, 35–51.

Bloom, J. D., Bradford, J. M., & Kofoed, L. (1988). An overview of psychiatric treatment approaches to three offender groups. *Hospital and Community Psychiatry, 39*, 151–158.

Bloom, J. D., Williams, M. H., Rogers, J. L., & Barbur, P. (1986). Evaluation and treatment of insanity acquittees in the community. *Bulletin of the American Academy of Psychiatry and Law, 14*, 231–244.

Borzecki, M., & Wormith, J. S. (1985). The criminalization of psychiatrically ill people: a review with a Canadian perspective. *The Psychiatric Journal of the University of Ottawa, 10*, 241–247.

Brelje, T. B. (1985). *Problems of treatment of NGRIs in an inpatient mental health system.* Paper presented at a meeting of the Illinois Association of Community Mental Health Agencies, Chicago.

Buckley, R., & Bigelow, D. A. (1992). The multi-service network: Reaching the unserved multi-problem individual. *Community Mental Health Journal, 28*, 43–50.

Buckley, P. F., Ibrahim, Z. Y., Singer, B., Orr, B., Donenwirth, K., & Brar, P. S. (1997). Aggression and schizophrenia: Efficacy of risperidone. *Journal of the American Academy of Psychiatry and Law, 25,* 173–181.

California Department of Mental Health. (1985). *California Department of Mental Health Conditional Release Program for the Judicially Committed.* Sacramento: Author.

Citrome, L., & Volavka, J. (1997) Psychopharmacology of violence. *Psychiatric Annals, 27,* 691–703.

Draine, J., Solomon, P., & Meyerson, A. (1994). Predictors of reincarceration among patients who received psychiatric services in jail. *Hospital and Community Psychiatry, 45,* 163–167.

Dvoskin, J. A., & Steadman, H. J. (1994). Using intensive case management to reduce violence by mentally ill persons in the community. *Hospital and Community Psychiatry, 45,* 679–684.

Fulwiler, C., Grossman, H., Forbes, C., & Ruthhazer, R. (1997). Early-onset substance abuse and community violence by outpatients with mental illness. *Psychiatric Services, 48,* 1181–1185.

Heilbrun, K., & Griffin, P. A. (1993). Community-based forensic treatment of insanity acquittees. *International Journal of Law and Psychiatry, 16,* 133–150.

Hodgins, S., Mednick, S. A., Brennan, P. A., Schulsinger, F., & Engberg, M. (1996). Mental disorder and crime: Evidence from a Danish birth cohort. *Archives of General Psychiatry, 53,* 489–496.

Jemelka, R., Trupin, E., & Chiles, J. A. (1989). The mentally ill in prisons: A review. *Hospital and Community Psychiatry, 40,* 481–491.

Jemelka, R. P., Wiegand, G., Walker, E., & Trupin, E. W. (1992). Computerized offender assessment: a validation study. *Psychological Assessment, 4,* 138–144.

Laberge, D., & Morin, D. (1995). The overuse of criminal justice dispositions: Failure of diversionary policies in the management of mental health problems. *International Journal of Law and Psychiatry, 18,* 389–414.

Lamb, H. R. (1987). Incompetency to stand trial: Appropriateness and outcome. *Archives of General Psychiatry, 44,* 754–758.

Lamb, H. R. (1997). The new state mental hospitals in the community. *Psychiatric Services, 48,* 1307–1310.

Lamb, H. R., & Goertzel, V. (1975). A community alternative to county jail: The hopes and the realities. *Federal Probation, 39,* 33–39.

Lamb, H. R., & Weinberger, L. E. (1993). Therapeutic use of conservatorship in the treatment of gravely disabled psychiatric patients. *Hospital and Community Psychiatry, 44,* 147–150.

Lamb, H. R., & Weinberger, L. E. (1998). Persons with severe mental illness in jails and prisons: A review. *Psychiatric Services, 49,* 483–492.

Lamb, H. R., Weinberger, L. E., & Gross, B. H. (1988). Court-mandated outpatient treatment for insanity acquittees: Clinical philosophy and implementation. *Hospital and Community Psychiatry, 39,* 1080–1084.

Marzuk, P. M. (1996). Violence, crime and mental illness: How strong a link? *Archives of General Psychiatry, 53,* 481–486.

Miraglia, R. P., & Giglio, C. A. (1993). Refining an aftercare program for New York State's outpatient insanity acquittees. *Psychiatric Quarterly, 64,* 215–234.

Monahan, J. (1992). Mental disorder and violent behavior. *American Psychologist, 47,* 511–521.

Mulvey, E. P. (1994). Assessing the evidence of a link between mental illness and violence. *Hospital and Community Psychiatry, 45,* 663–668.

Steadman, H. J. (1997, May 20). *Risk factors for community violence among acute psychiatric inpatients: The MacArthur risk assessment project.* Paper presented at the Annual Meeting of the American Psychiatric Association, San Diego, CA.

Swanson, J., Estroff, S., Swartz, M., Borum, R., Lachicotte, W., Zimmer, C., & Wagner, R. (1997). Violence and severe mental disorder in clinical and community populations: The effects of psychotic symptoms, comorbidity, and lack of treatment. *Psychiatry, 60*, 1–22.

Torrey, E. F. (1994). Violent behavior by individuals with serious mental illness. *Hospital and Community Psychiatry, 45*, 653–662.

Wack, R. C. (1993). The ongoing risk assessment in the treatment of forensic patients on conditional release status. *Psychiatric Quarterly, 64*, 275–293.

Wasyliw, O. E., Cavanaugh, J. L., & Grossman, L. S. (1988). Clinical considerations in the community treatment of mentally disordered offenders. *International Journal of Law and Psychiatry, 11*, 371–380.

Whitmer, G. E. (1980). From hospitals to jails: The fate of California's deinstitutionalized mentally ill. *American Journal of Orthopsychiatry, 50*, 65–75.

Wilson, D., Tien, G., & Eaves, D. (1995). Increasing the community tenure of mentally disordered offenders: An assertive case management program. *International Journal of Law and Psychiatry, 18*, 61–69.

AUTHOR INDEX

Numbers in italics refer to listings in the reference sections; *n* following a page number indicates listings in a note.

Ganju, V. K., 4, *27*
Ganzer, V. J., 341, *366*
Garb, H. N., 119, *123*, 337, *366*
Gardner, W. I., 8, *23*, 337, *366*
Garfield, S. L., 184, 185, *191*
Garwick, G. B., 207, 208, 209, *219*
Gauthier, R., 299, 300, *309*, 346, *366*
Gautier, J., 211, *218*
Gawinski, B., 145, *164*
Geberth, V. J., 7, *23*
Gebhard, P., 273, *288*
Gedye, A., 212, *218*
Geller, G., 291, 298, *310*
Geller, J., 201, *218*, 319, *328*
Geller, M., 181, *191*
Gemar, M., 179, *195*
Gemignani, M. G., 224, 238, *241*
Gendreau, G. D., 306, *309*
Gendreau, P., 20, *21*, 104, 109, 111, 113,
    121, *123*, 253, 255, *266*, 294, 304,
    306, *308*, 338, 350, 351n, 353n, 357,
    361, *366*, 389, 390, *395*, 422n, *441*,
    451, 454–455, 456, *461*
Genevie, L., 422n, *441*
George, W. H., 32, *46*, 389, 390, *395*
Gerber, C. J., 211, *219*
Gerber, F., 379, 380, *397*
German, J. R., 172, *191*
Gerner, R. H., 178, *191*
Gerry, M., 232, *242*
Gerstein, D. R., 131, 140, 145, 146–147,
    164
Gersten, R., 236, *242*
Gerstley, L., 261, *267*
Getz, M. A., 171, 173, 175, 184, 185, *195*
Giardini, G. I., 373, *395*
Gibbens, T. C. N., 201, 214, *218*, *219*
Gibbons, D. C., 3, *24*
Gibbs, J. C., 104, 105, *125*
Gibbs, J. J., 419n, *441*
Giglio, C. A., 467, *477*
Gilby, R., 201, *218*
Gillis, J. R., 337, *369*
Ginsberg, G. S., 180, *194*
Giulekas, D., 357, *364*
Glaser, B. A., 106, *124*
Glaser, D., 5, *24*, 337, *366*
Glaser, F. B., 138, *167*
Glass, C., 201, 210, *218*
Glass, D. R., *190*

Glasscote, R. M., 389n, *395*
Glasser, W., 106, 113, *123*
Glassman, S. M., 389n, *395*
Gleb, G., 36, *46*
Glick, B., 103, 104, *123*
Goddard, M., 451, 454–455, 456, *461*
Godfrey, C., 39, *45*
Goering, P., 387, *396*
Goertzel, V., 470, *477*
Goggin, C., 338, 350, 351n, 353n, 357, 361,
    366
Gold, M. S., 145–146, *164*
Goldapple, G., 146, *164*
Goldberg, B., 201, *218*
Goldfried, M. R., 118, *122*
Golding, S., 337, *364*
Goldkamp, J., 453–454, *461*
Goldkamp, J. S., 152, 153, *164*, 453, *460*
Goldstein, A., 180, *190*
Goldstein, A. P., 103, 104, *123*, 235, *242*,
    258, 260, *267*
Goodstein, L., 382, *396*
Gordon, A., 300, 302, *311*
Gordon, B. H., 376, 377, *399*
Gordon, J., 109, *126*, 387, *399*
Gordon, J. A., 343, *367*
Gordon, J. R., 390, 391, *395*, *397*
Goretsky, S. R., 153, *168*
Gorski, T. T., 391, *396*
Gostin, L., 34, 35, *46*
Gottfredson, D. M., 337, 343, *366*
Gottfredson, G. D., 305, *309*
Gottfredson, M. R., 3, *24*, 32, *47*, 337, 343,
    366, 453, *460*
Gough, L., 38, 40, *46*
Goulden, K. J., 211, *219*
Grabowski, J., 157, *164*
Graeber, J. L., 8, *23*
Graham, J. R., 353, *364*
Graham, S., 201, 205, *215*, *217*
Grainger, W., 204, *219*
Grant, C. A., 283, *288*
Grant, I., 356, *365*
Grapentine, W. L., 7, 11, *25*
Gray, A. S., 276, 282, *288*
Grealish, E. M., 449, *463*
Green, A., 291, *310*
Green, S., 102, *126*
Green, S. H., 211, *216*
Green, S. M., 102, *128*
Greenberg, L. S., 118, *128*

SUBJECT INDEX

ABOUT THE EDITORS

José B. Ashford, PhD, MSW, is a professor of social work and of social science and the law in the Interdisciplinary Doctoral Program in Justice Studies at Arizona State University, Tempe. His most recent coauthored book is *Human Behavior in the Social Environment: A Multidimensional Perspective* (with LeCroy and Lortie). He is on the editorial boards of *Social Work* and the *Journal of Social Work Education.* He is currently the principal investigator of the Family Drug Court Grant in Pima County (AZ) and of a grant on the discharge of dually diagnosed offenders from the Maricopa County (AZ) jail system. He is widely published in areas involving the assessment, classification, and treatment of offenders with special needs, juvenile aftercare, and forensic social work. Professor Ashford testifies across the country as an expert on the assessment of mitigating factors in capital murder cases. He was a former clinical supervisor and clinic team leader at the Court Diagnostic and Treatment Center of Toledo, Ohio.

Bruce D. Sales, PhD, JD, is director of the Psychology, Public Policy, and Law Program at the University of Arizona, where he is also a professor of psychology, psychiatry, sociology, and law. In 1999, he was awarded an Honorary Doctorate of Science degree from the City University of New York for being the founding father of forensic psychology as an academic discipline. His most recent books are *Family Mediation: Facts, Myths, and Future Prospects* (with Connie J. A. Beck, American Psychological Association [APA], 2001), and *Ethics in Research With Human Participants* (coedited with Susan Folkman, APA, 2000). He has more than 200 other publications to his credit. He is the editor for two APA book series: Law and Mental Health Professionals, and Law and Public Policy: Psychology and the Social Sciences. Dr. Sales is a Fellow of the APA and of the American Psychological Society, a recipient of the APA Award for Distinguished Professional Contributions to Public Service and the Distinguished Contributions Award from the American Psychology–Law Society, and is an elected member of the American Law Institute.

William H. Reid, MD, MPH, is clinical or adjunct professor of psychiatry for the University of Texas Health Science Center, Texas A&M College of Medicine, and Texas Tech Medical Center. He is past president of the American Academy of Psychiatry and the Law and is the former editor-in-chief of the American College of Psychiatrists' Psychiatric Update Series. He is a Fellow of the American Psychiatric Association, the American College of Psychiatrists, the Royal College of Physicians, and the College of Physicians of Philadelphia. He has received many awards, including the National Depressive and Manic Depressive Association's Scientific Advisor Service Award and the *Journal of ECT*'s Investigator's Award for 2000. He has edited, coedited, authored, or coauthored 13 books and written more than 200 clinical and scientific papers, journal articles, monographs, and book chapters in various areas of psychology and psychiatry. His most recent book is *A Clinician's Guide to Legal Issues in Psychotherapy* (1999).